Transforming Business Organisations for Longevity

Challenges and Opportunities

Transforming Business Organisations for Longevity

Challenges and Opportunities

Editors

S.S. Bhakar

Tarika Singh Sikarwar

K.K. Yadav

Aashish Mehra

Narosa Publishing House

New Delhi   Chennai   Mumbai   Kolkata

Editors
S.S. Bhakar
Tarika Singh Sikarwar
K.K. Yadav
Aashish Mehra
Prestige Institute of Management Gwalior
Airport Road, Opp. Deendayal Nagar
Gwalior

Copyright © 2013, Narosa Publishing House Pvt. Ltd.

N A R O S A   P U B L I S H I N G   H O U S E   P V T .   L T D .

22, Delhi Medical Association Road, Daryaganj, New Delhi 110 002
35-36 Greams Road, Thousand Lights, Chennai 600 006
306 Shiv Centre, Sector 17, Vashi, Navi Mumbai 400 703
2F-2G Shivam Chambers, 53 Syed Amir Ali Avenue, Kolkata 700 019

www.narosa.com

ISBN 978-81-8487-225-5

Published by N.K. Mehra for Narosa Publishing House Pvt Ltd.,
22, Delhi Medical Association Road, Daryaganj, New Delhi 110 002

Printed in India

Preface

Business organisations go through different phases in their life cycles. Generally, the total life of an organization is far longer than the life of products or services offered by the organization as portfolio of products and services offered by them undergo changes throughout the life of the organization. The life of organisations depends on the capability of the organisations to keep aligning their product or service portfolio continuously with the changing business environment. Since the life cycle of the products and services offered by business organisations have shrunk considerably in last few decades leading to enormous pressure on the existence of organisations. Business cycles specially the economic slowdown or recession/depression phases of business cycle also put enormous pressure on the existence of organisations.

We are living through a major economic disaster and witnessing the disappearance of major firms, along with the destruction of enormous corporate and individual wealth. If Adam Smith's assumption of self sacrifice and altruism ever applied, business organisations have succumbed to greed and the uncontrollable pursuit of self interest in the 21st century. Enron, Worldcom and Satyam even violated the basic standards of fiduciary, obligation to shareholder's interest. Many other firms appear to have lost their way, especially in the financial sector. Therefore, it is time for many enterprises to consider the way they do business, and to change to more sustainable practices. The changes required are complex and require global solutions.

Capability building is a consistent effort. It is important that capabilities in current competitive environment need to be developed on global standards. Just being best in business, country, and state can't bring best out of the organizational system. World is like a global village. Technological revolutions have connected people up to last mile. We all have to compete globally someday. Unfortunately, many businesses are protected by legal boundaries like anti-dumping etc. Protectionism and licensing may take business to one or two generations. It won't sustain in upcoming unification of the world.

Capabilities can be of many types like people or system. Employees are backbone to any organization. HR has many tools like continuous learning and development. Building them for strong growth is necessary. Organisations or countries can't ignore development of resources and giving them healthy life. Giving them best training is the cost to the organization. Many organisations don't give certificates of completion in fear that employees will fly away. In India, many organisations don't give green belt/black belt certificate to employee as employee will go on higher salary to other organization. Building supply chain capability is core for any FMCG/retail business. Keeping service or quality orientation is must for any customer centric business. Keep innovating and motivating people to development of better future.

Digital tools and technologies have invaded the business environment, triggering significant changes in the way we work, communicate, and sell. Industries and governments alike are undergoing a digital transformation either crisis-induced, as part of a core strategy, or as part of a more controlled business transition. Under all circumstances, leaders need to be well prepared to anticipate the current and future impact of this enduring trend and steer their corporations accordingly at the right speed. This digital wave has not only fuelled a number of fundamental changes in the way organisations produce, sell, and serve, but also changed the way employees work, communicate, and collaborate. It has therefore created a leadership and transformation challenge for most industry participants.

Over the past decades, digital technologies have progressively been embraced by organisations driven by advancement in technology, changing consumer behavior, increasing globalization of the workforce, and a desire to be more productive and innovative. Faced with this transformation challenge and the need to stay relevant in one's industry, leaders have to embrace the implications of this enduring trend on their organisations in order to steer their strategy and drive better operational performance. Unfortunately, recent history is replete with examples of organisations which have not been able to keep pace with this new digital reality. Therefore, at the end of one economic recession and the second recession strongly eminent, it is pertinent to understand how organisations can transform themselves and add to their longevity.

The current book titled **Transforming Organisations for Longevity** discusses various facts of organisational Longevity. The book is based on the selected papers presented during the Third International Conference organised by the Institute during December 28-30, 2011. The book contains 51 research papers organized in five parts based on the contribution of different functional areas of management to the longevity of organisations. The first part of the book **Financial Management** contains 12 chapters covering the discussion on Merger and Acquisitions and Survival of Business, A Revolutionary Model of Investment Decision Making: The Future Beckons, From Community Development to Corporate Social Responsibility – Changing horizons of CSR, Current Economic Recession on Indian Banking Industry: Survival and Recover, Quantitative Scrutiny of Quality of Financial Reporting in Indian Scenario, Direct Tax Code and its Effect, Encouraging and Funding Entrepreneurship: A Pragmatic Strategy for Banks to Counter Recession, Mobile Banking an Innovative Marketing Strategy for Inclusive Growth, Behavioral Finance: An Emerging Trend In Financial Markets, Co-integration Analysis of the Determinants of Inflation in India, Rises The Value of Indian Rupee Against Us Dollar: A Challenge for Indian Economy and Micro Insurance: A Tool for Socio-Economic Transformation.

The second part of the book contains seven chapters on **General Management** covering the discussion on Improving Productivity through Optimum Resource Allocation- A Case Study, Organisational Creativity: The Genesis of a New Era, Role of Values and Human Resources in the Management Process, Supply Chain Management of Perishable Goods in Retail Sector, Organisational Commitment: An Analysis of Impact of HRD Practices in Telecom Sector, Culture of Innovation in Organisations: HRM's Perspective and Transition in Business Negotiation – Cross-Cultural Perspective.

The third part of the book contains nine chapters on **Human Resource Management** covering the discussion on Knowledge Management: Securing Competitive Advantage in the Information Economy, Role of Entrepreneurs in Building an Economy, Resource Management in an Industry, Globalizations: A Boon or Bane, Attrition and Retention in BPO Sector: Key Drivers and Strategies, Biscuits incorporated with Coral jasmine (Medicinal plant): A step towards sustainable development and rural entrepreneurship, The Global Mobility of Talent and its Impact on Global Development, Training and Development and Cross Cultural Transition: Opportunity and Challenges in HRM.

The fourth part of the book contains nine chapters on **Information Technology** covering the discussion on Performance Analysis of Routing Protocols for Application Based Clustered Mobile Ad-hoc Network, Effect of Advertisement on Consumer's Behavior, To Study the Brand Loyalty of Consumers, Job Satisfaction Among Doctors, Data Warehouse Model for University, Cloud Computing – Architecture, Security Issues and Challenges, Performance of ZRP Using Exata Emulator, Security Architecture for Mobile Ad-hoc Networks (Manet), and Study of Broadcasting and its Performance Parameter in VANET

The fourth part of the book contains fourteen chapters on **Marketing Management** covering the discussion on The Strategy of De-Internationalization of Footwear SMEs in the Area Metropolitana De Guadalajara, Effect of T.V. on Purchasing Related Behavior of Different House Hold Equipments, Green Marketing: A Study of Consumer Fondness Towards Green Products, Critical Analysis of Change in Consumer Behavior of Students from U.P. While Selecting A Professional College, CRM in Banking: An Indian Perspective, Effect of Advertising on Children and Their Role, A Study of Rural Marketing in India, A Study on Customer Satisfaction - Private V/S Public Banks, A Study on Customer Satisfaction- Private Vs Public Banks, Brand Salience of the Private Label Brands in Retail, Effect of Advertising on Children and Their Role, Customer Satisfaction Between Public and Private Insurance Sector's, Tourism Industry and its Impact on Indian Economy and Consumers' Preference for the Survival of FMCG Companies in Rural India (A Case Study of Hindustan Unilever Limited).

All the chapters contained in the book are application oriented and therefore will provide useful guidance to the practitioners as much as they will to the researchers.

Contents

GENERAL MANAGEMENT

HUMAN RESOURCE MANAGEMENT

INFORMATION TECHNOLOGY

MARKETING MANAGEMENT

Merger and Acquisitions and Survival of Business: A Case Study of TATA

L.N. Koli[1] and Vartika Verma[2]

[1]Associate Professor, Department of Accountancy and Law, Faculty of Commerce
Dayalbagh Educational Institute (Deemed University), Dayalbagh, Agra
[2]Research Scholar, Dayalbagh, Agra

ABSTRACT

In today's globalised economy, competitiveness and competitive advantage have become the buzzwords for corporate around the world. Mergers and Acquisitions are being increasingly used by companies for entering new markets, to achieve Assets growth, for garnering greater market shares/additional manufacturing capacity and for gaining complementary strengths. One plus one makes three: this equation is the special alchemy of a merger or an acquisition. The key principle behind buying a company is to create shareholder value over and above that of the sum of the two companies. This rationale is particularly alluring to companies when times are tough. Strong companies will act to buy other companies to create a more competitive, cost-efficient company. The companies will come together hoping to gain a greater market share or to achieve greater efficiency. This study deals concept, purpose, benefits, challenges and survival of the merged company. This study deals with the mergers and acquisitions happened in TATA.

Keywords: *Mergers, Acquisitions*

CONCEPT

One plus one makes three: this equation is the special alchemy of a merger or an acquisition. The key principle behind buying a company is to create shareholder value over and above that of the sum of the two companies. This rationale is particularly alluring to companies when times are tough. Strong companies will act to buy other companies to create a more competitive, cost-efficient company. The companies will come together hoping to gain a greater market share or to achieve greater efficiency. Because of these potential benefits, target companies will often agree to be purchased when they know they cannot survive alone.

Mergers and acquisitions are strategic decisions taken for maximization of a company's growth by enhancing its production and marketing operations. They are being used in a wide array of fields such as information technology, telecommunications, and business process outsourcing as well as in traditional businesses in order to gain strength, expand the customer base, cut competition or enter into a new market or product segment.

Acquiring firm shareholders tend to earn zero or negative returns from mergers. Acquiring firm stockholders tend not to do well when their companies engage in acquisitions (Malatesta, 1986). These effects are either statistically insignificant or somewhat negative. Presumably, this reflects that markets are skeptical that the bidder can enjoy synergistic gains, which more than offset the fact that it is paying a premium for the target. The fact that the bidder's stock response is small compared to that of the target is due to the fact that bidders tend to be larger than targets (Jensen and Ruback, 1983).

MERGERS

In a mergers, one of the two existing companies mergers its identity into another existing companies , or one or more of existing companies may form a new company and mergers their identities into the new company. A merger refers to the combination of two companies. This entails that a new organisation structure appears from the two companies combined (Bruner, 2004).

TYPES OF MERGERS

Horizontal merger: Two companies that are in direct competition and share the same product lines and markets.

Vertical merger: A customer and company or a supplier and company. Think of a cone supplier merging with an ice cream maker.

- Market-extension merger   Two companies that sell the same products in different markets.
- Product-extension merger Two companies selling different but related products in the same market.

Conglomeration: Two companies that have no common business areas. There are two types of mergers that are distinguished by how the merger is financed. Each has certain implications for the companies involved and for investors:

Purchase Mergers: this kind of merger occurs when one company purchases another. The purchase is made with cash or through the issue of some kind of debt instrument; the sale is taxable.

Consolidation Mergers: this merger, a brand new company is formed and both companies are bought and combined under the new entity. The tax terms are the same as those of a purchase merger.

Acquisitions

Generally speaking, an acquisition involve acquiring ownership in a properly (tangible a/or intangible}. In the context of business combinations, an acquisition is the purchase by one company, of controlling interest in the share capital of an existing company. An acquisition entails when one company buys another one (Bruner, 2004).

Distinction between Mergers and Acquisitions

The terms merger and acquisition mean slightly different things. When one company takes over another and clearly established itself as the new owner, the purchase is called an acquisition. From a legal point of view, the target company ceases to exist, the buyer "swallows" the business and the buyer's stock continues to be traded.

In the pure sense of the term, a merger happens when two firms, often of about the same size, agree to go forward as a single new company rather than remain separately owned and operated. This kind of action is more precisely referred to as a "merger of equals." Both companies' stocks are surrendered and new company stock is issued in its place. For example, both Daimler-Benz and Chrysler ceased to exist when the two firms merged, and a new company, DaimlerChrysler, was created.

In practice, however, actual mergers of equals don't happen very often. Usually, one company will buy another and, as part of the deal's terms, simply allow the acquired firm to proclaim that the action is a merger of equals, even if it's technically an acquisition. Being bought out often carries negative connotations, therefore, by describing the deal as a merger, deal makers and top managers try to make the takeover more palatable.

A purchase deal will also be called a merger when both CEOs agree that joining together is in the best interest of both of their companies. But when the deal is unfriendly - that is, when the target company does not want to be purchased - it is always regarded as an acquisition.

Whether a purchase is considered a merger or an acquisition really depends on whether the purchase is friendly or hostile and how it is announced. In other words, the real difference lies in how the purchase is communicated to and received by the target company's board of directors, employees and shareholders.

MOTIVES AND BENEFITS OF MERGERS AND ACQUISITIONS

- Maintaining or accelerating a company's growth, particularly when the internal growth is constrained due to paucity of resources.
- Enhancing profitability though cost reduction resulting from economies of scale, operating efficiency and synergy.
- Diversifying the risk of the company, particularly when it acquires those businesses whose income streams are not correlated.
- Reducing tax liability because of the provision of setting- off accumulated losses and unabsorbed depreciation of one company against profits of another.
- Limiting the severity of competition by increasing the company's market power.

Why Indian Companies Look Beyond their Borders?

- The need to capture new Markets.
- The need to expand capabilities and assets.
- The need to expand product or service portfolio.
- The pressures of domestic competition.

REVIEW OF LITERATURE

Jean Dermine (1999), Said that in European countries, mergers have allowed banks to increase efficiency. Mergers do facilitate the coordination of the closing of branches. An alternative way to decrease the excessive size of the distribution network would have been a State-led reduction of capacity as was done in the steel industry. If scale or scope economies do prevail, mergers would be a better way to achieve both efficiency and appropriate scale. But the very large empirical literature on the many potential sources of economies of scale or scope identified in the report raises some doubt as to the significance of these benefits, in particular for banks larger than euro 100 billion. A legitimate question concerns the existence of economies of scale and scope in the future as both new technology and the single currency are transforming rapidly the banking industry. There is clear evidence that size is important to operate on several segments of the capital markets (such as bond and equity underwriting or custodian activities). On the retail markets, it is the author's opinion that size and European coverage will be important to develop a brand and to diversify credit risk. In view of these potential gains to be achieved by mergers, policy makers have to consider the social cost of these mergers.

Objectives of the Study

- To study the concept of merger & acquisition.
- To analyze the merger & acquisition case of TATA and Corus.

Research Methodology

The research methodology is based on the secondary data sourced from various journals and books available on merger & acquisition. Convenient sampling method is used for selecting the sample. The study was centered at identifying the concept, benefits, difficulty faced at the time of merger & acquisition. Based on the information sourced from the books, journals, and websites this paper has been finalized. The emphasis of the study is focused on TATA CORUS merger & acquisition.

Finding of the Research

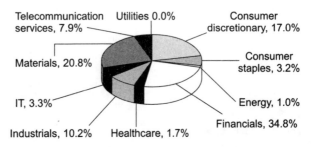

India – M&A deals - Sector wise Break up in FY10

Tata-Corus Merger & Acquisition

Tata acquired Corus, which is four times larger than its size and the largest steel producer in the UK; the deal, created the world's fifth largest steelmaker through India's largest ever foreign takeover.

Tata acquired Corus on the 2nd April 2007 for a price of $ 12 billion. There price share as 608 pence which in 33.6% higher than the first offer which was 455 pence.

Tata Steel Background

- Tata steel a part of the Tata Group, one of the largest diversified business in India.
- Founded in 1907, by Jamshed Ji Nusserwanji Tata.
- In Feb. 2005 acquired Singapore based NatSteel Ltd.
- In Dec 2005 acquired Thailand Millennium steel.

Corus Steel Industry

- Founded on 6th Oct 1999, through merger of 2 companies: British Steel and Koninlljle Hoogorenss.
- Consist of four divisions: strip products, land products, aluminum and distribution building system.
- Operates as an international company.
- Core business in manufacturing, development and allocation of aluminum and steel products and services.
- Wide variety of products and services.
- Largest steel of producer in UK with £ 10,142 million annual revenue and work force of 50,000 employees.

Table showing TATA mergers & acquisitions in last decade

	Tata company	Acquired company	Country	Stake acquired	Value
2010					
January	**Tata Communications**	BT Group's (BT) Mosaic business	UK	100%	£0.5 million
April	TRF	Hewitt Robins International	UK		£3 million
December	Rallis India (through Tata Chemicals)	Metahelix Life Sciences	India	53.5%	Rs 99.5 crore
	Tata Chemicals	British Salt	UK	100% (wholly-owned)	£93 million (approximately ₹650 crore)
	Tata International	Bachi Shoes India	India	76%	
	Tata International	Euro Shoe Components	India	76%	
2009					
January	**Tata Communications**	Neotel	South Africa	30%	
March	**Tata Tea** (now Tata Global Beverages)	Grand	Russia	33.2%	
July	TRF	Dutch Lanka Trailer Manufacturers	Sri Lanka	51%	$8.67 million
October	Tata Motors	Hispano Carrocera SA	Spain	Remaining 79%	
2008					
January	Tata Chemicals	General Chemical Industrial Products (now Tata Chemicals North America)	US	100% stake	
	Tata Projects	Artson Engineering	India		
March	Tata Motors	Jaguar and Land Rover brands	UK		$2.3 billion (approximately)
	Telco Construction Equipment Company (Telcon)	Serviplem SA	Spain	79%	
	Telco Construction Equipment Company (Telcon)	Lebrero SA	Spain	60%	
June	Tata Communications	China Enterprise Communications Limited (CEC)	China	50% equity interest	
August	**Voltas**	Rohini Industrial Electricals	India	51%	₹62 crore
September	Tata Power	Geodynamics	Australia	10%	$37.5 million
October	**Tata Motors European Technical Centre Plc**	Miljøbil Grenland/Innovasjon	Norway	50.3%	Kroner 12 million (₹9.40 crore)
December	TCS	Citigroup Global Services	US	100%	$512 million
2007					
January	Tata Steel	Corus	UK	100%	
March	Tata Steel	Rawmet Industries	India		₹101 crore
April	Indian Hotels	Campton Place Hotel	US		$58 million
	Tata Power	Acquired Coastal Gujarat Power	India		
	Tata Tea through Tetley group (now Tata Global Beverages)	Vitax and Flosana trademarks	Poland		
	Tata Communications	Transtel Telecoms (TT)	South Africa		$33 million (approximately)
June	Tata Power	PT Kaltim Prima Coal and PT Arutmin Indonesia	Indonesia	30% equity stake	

Table Contd...

Table Contd...

October	TRF	York Transport Equipment (Asia)	Singapore	51% stake	
2006					
January	Tata Metaliks	Usha Ispat, Redi Unit	India	100% (wholly-owned)	₹115 crore
	Tata Interactive	Tertia Edusoft Gmbh	Germany	90%	
		Tertia Edusoft AG	Switzerland	90.38%	
February	TCS	Tata Infotech	India		
April	Tata Steel	Millenium Steel	Thailand	67.11%	$167 million (Baht 6.5 billion)
May	**Tata Tea** through Tata Tea (GB) (now Tata Global Beverages)	JEMCA	Czech Republic	Assets: intangible and tangible	GBP11.60 million
June	Tata Coffee (now Tata Global Beverages)	Eight O' Clock Coffee Company	US	100% (wholly-owned)	$220 million (₹1015 crore)
September	**Tata Tea** through Tata Tea (GB) (now Tata Global Beverages)	Joekels Tea Packers	South Africa	33.3%	GBP0.91 million
November	**Indian hotels**	Ritz-Carlton hotel	US		$170 million
2005					
February	Tata Steel	NatSteel Asia Pte	Singapore	100% (wholly-owned)	S$468.10 million
	Tata Motors	Hispano Carrocera	Spain	21%	Euro12 million (₹70 crore)
March	Tata Chemicals	Indo Maroc Phosphore S.A. (IMACID)	Morocco	Equal partner	$38 million (₹166 crore)
April	Tata Motors	Tata Finance	India	Merger	
July	Indian Hotels	The Pierre	US	$9 million	Lease of the property
	Tata Industries	Indigene Pharmaceuticals Inc	US	<30%	
	Tata Communications	Teleglobe International	UK		
August	Tata Technologies	INCAT International	UK		
	Trent	Landmark	India	76%	$24.09 million (₹103.60 crore)
September	Tata AutoComp	Wündsch Weidinger	Germany		Euro7 million
	Tata Communications	Tata Power Broadband	India		
October	**Tata Tea** through Tata Tea (GB)	Good Earth Corporation & F Mali Herb Inc	US	100% (wholly-owned)	$31 million
	TCS	Financial Network Services	Australia		
	TCS	Pearl Group	UK	Structured deal	
November	TCS	Comicrom	Chile		
December	Indian Hotels	Starwood group (W Hotel)	Sydney	100% (wholly-owned)	$29 million
	Tata Chemicals	Brunner Mond (now Tata Chemicals Europe)	UK	63.5% (December 2005) 36.5% (March 2006)	₹508 crore (December 2005) ₹290 crore (March 2006)
2004					
January	TCS	Airline Financial Support Services India (AFS)	India	100 per cent (wholly-owned)	GBP271 million

Table Contd...

Table Contd...

March	Tata Motors	Daewoo Commercial Vehicle Company	Korea	100% (wholly-owned)	KRW120 billion ($102 million/₹465 crore)
	Tata Communications	Dishnet DSL's ISP division	India		
	TCS	Aviation Software Development Consultancy India (ASDC)	India		
June	Tata Chemicals	Hind Lever Chemicals	India	Amalgamation	
July	TCS	Phoenix Global Solutions	India		
November	**Tata Communications**	Tyco Global Network	US		
2003					
July	**Tata Communications**	Gemplex	US		
2002					
February	Tata Sons	Tata Communications (formerly VSNL)	India	100% (wholly-owned)	GBP271 million
September	Indian Hotels	Regent Hotel (renamed Taj Lands End)	India	Effective 100% stake	₹450 crore
December	Tata Teleservices	Hughes Telecom (India)	India	50.83%	₹858.83 crore
2001					
November	Tata Sons (TCS)	Computer Maintenance Corporation (CMC)	India		
2000					
February	**Tata Tea** and Tata Sons (now Tata Global Beverages)	Tetley group	UK	100% (wholly-owned)	GBP271 millionGBP271 million

Objectives of Acquisition

- Tata looking for mature market in Europe for its finished products.
- Corus holds a number of patients and R&D facility
- Cost of acquired lower than setting up a green field planet and marketing and distribution
- Corus wanted to reduce its employees cost and Tata as well known for handling its labors efficiency.
- Higher profitability
- Global no. 5 company
- By 2012, expected production of 40 million tons giving it the position of global no.2
- To gain access to global steel market and expand production capacity to keep pace with growing demand for steel.

The Deal

- Officially announced on April 2nd 2007.
- Tata motive is to capture the market value.
- Total value of this acquisition was $ 12 billion (608 pence per share except 603 per share)

- Corus gained profitable opportunity to exit and a buyer for time.

Finding

With Corus its fold, Tata steel can confidently target becoming one of the top-3 steel maker globally by 2015. The company would have an aggregate capacity of enclose to 56 millions ton per annum, we can say that if the acquisition well planned, execute and than necessary precaution taken for the deal of a company can achieve its strategic objectives and thus ensure its growth and survival through acquisition.

CONCLUSION

It is believed that Mergers & Acquisitions are the strategic tools leading to the maximization of a company's growth by enhancing its production and marketing operations. Mergers and acquisitions result in accelerated growth, enhanced profitability, increased operating efficiency and synergy, reduced severity of competition, and increased market power of the company.

In Current scenario if we analyzed the financial performance indicators of TATA STEEL we find that after Merger Company's performance increased.

References

- Rober f. Bruner (2004), *Applied Mergers and Acquisitions,* Wiley Finance: New York.
- Paul H. Malatesta, "The Wealth Effect of Merger Activity and the Objective Functions of Merging Firms," Journal of Financial Economics 11 (1–4), (April 1983): 155–182; Nikhil P. Varaiya, "An Empirical Investigation of the Bidding Firm's Gains from Corporate Takeovers," *Research in Finance 6* (1986): 149–178.
- Michael Jensen and Richard Ruback, "The Market for Corporate Control: The Scientific Evidence", *Journal of Financial Economics 11* (1–4) (April 1983): 5–50.

A Revolutionary Model of Investment Decision Making: The Future Beckons

Naela Kamil[1] and Bimal Jaiswal[2]
[1]Faculty Member, IILM Academy of Higher, Learning, Viraj Khand, Gomtinagar, Lucknow
[2]Director, IMS, Lucknow University, New Campus, Lucknow

ABSTRACT

The classical economic man model propounds that rational human beings make identical, outcome-maximizing decisions, based on careful evaluation of facts, evidences and alternatives. However, it is now well-researched that individuals have distinctive personalities and make unique decisions based on their demographic and psychographic characteristics.

This research paper attempts to investigate the association between investment behavior of individuals and their gender (selected demographic variable), Extraversion, Agreeableness, Emotional Stability and Openness to Experience (selected psychographic variables).

The analysis of data indicates that male extraverts are more likely to embrace risk than females, however females low on extraversion are more risk averse than female extraverts. Another finding is that females high on agreeableness scale are more likely to consult family and friends for investment decisions as compared to their male counterparts. With regard to openness to experience, male and female investors are similar in their investment approach. The study also reveals other results which bring out the complex interplay of demographic and psychographic traits on investment decision making.

This study has tremendous revolutionary implications for the investment advisory sector, paving way for the construction of customized portfolios based on demographic and psychographic characteristics which will optimize returns for the investors while preserving their psychological well-being.

Keywords: *Extraversion, Agreeableness, Emotional Stability, Openness to Experience, investment decision making*

INTRODUCTION

The classical economic man model propounds that rational human beings make identical, outcome-maximizing decisions, based on careful evaluation of facts, evidences and alternatives. However, it is now well-researched that individuals have distinctive personalities and make unique decisions based on their demographic and psychographic characteristics.

This research paper attempts to investigate the association between investment behavior of individuals and their gender (selected demographic variable), Extraversion, Agreeableness, Emotional Stability and Openness to Experience (selected psychographic variables).

LITERATURE REVIEW

The "economic man model" and other economic theories advocating the "rationality" of humans propounded and advanced by great economists such as Smith, Keynes, Bernoulli, Von Neuman, Jevon et al, became the foundation for the development of numerous financial and investment models like Efficient Market Hypothesis, Markowitz Efficient Frontier, Sharpe's Single Index Model, Capital Asset Pricing Model, Arbitrage Pricing Theory et al. The simplicity of these models lay in the assumption that the most volatile and unpredictable variable in the study, that is the human, was pre-supposed as "rational" and mechanistic and not prone to any behavioral aberration. Rationality is understood to be the ability to make outcome-maximizing decisions after careful analysis of alternative solutions framed using complete information, which leaves no room for ambiguity or mistake on the part of the human investor.

However, after many decades of supremacy, the assumption of human rationality was challenged by a new generation of researchers headed by Daniel Kahneman and Amos Tversky, who in their first research publication on the subject in 1974 discussed "Judgment under Uncertainty: Heuristics and Biases". Further in 1979, Kahneman and Tversky brought to public attention their new "Prospect Theory" in the journal Econometrica, which further challenged the rationality argument and entirely changed the way in which investment decision making was looked upon. Prospect Theory discovered behavior patterns that had never been recognized by the proponents of rational decision making. One of the most striking and useful findings in the Prospect theory of the Israeli psychologist duo Kahneman and Tversky was the asymmetry between the way humans make decisions involving gains and decisions involving losses. Kahneman and Tversky proposed and proved through multiple experiments that the same individual who is a risk averter for a decision involving gains becomes a risk seeker for a loss-avoiding decision.

Spurred by the path breaking Prospect Theory, a series of researches were successfully conducted by a group of academic economists led by Richard Thaler, David Bell, Meir Statman, Hersh Shefrin, Robert Shiller, et al resulting into a new field of study known as Behavioral Finance. Peter Bernstein, the founder editor of The Journal of Portfolio Management, in his incredible landmark book "Against the Gods – The Remarkable Story of Risk", published in 1996 writes –

"Behavioral Finance analyses how investors struggle to find their way through the give and take between risk and return, one moment engaging in cool calculation and the next yielding to emotional impulses. The result of this mixture between the rational and not-so-rational is a capital market that itself fails to perform consistently in the way theoretical models predict that it will perform"

The proponents of Behavioral Finance have stacked up many interesting experimentally verified theories to prove the quasi-rational behavior of humans. According to Richard Thaler (1985), "quasi-rationality is neither fatal nor immediately self-defeating".

In a 1995 paper on "Aspects of Investor Psychology", Kahneman and Mark W Riepe bring forth the beliefs, preferences and biases that humans have which influence their investment decision making. The authors put forward a series of well-researched recommendations for investment advisors to deal with such behavioral issues.

From the psychology perspective, a review of research reveals Investor Psychology is a relatively new development in the ancient science of psychology. However, being application based, it has attracted considerable attention from psychologists and finance (investment) professionals alike. The research in investor behavior can be said to be broadly of two kinds, one that involves individual investors and hence a study of individual psychology and the other a study of group psychology or a study of the market and its movements as a whole.

In this paper we will focus on individual psychology. At present, most research on individual psychology occurs within the context of the Trait Approach. "Personality Traits" are stable dimensions of personality along which people vary, from very low to very high. Three significant works are most commonly cited in context of Trait Theories. The first and earliest effort was of Gordon Allport (1965) who classified traits into secondary, central and cardinal traits. The second, more sophisticated effort, on the subject of personality traits was by Raymond Cattell et al (1977), who conducted extensive research on thousands of individuals to measure individual differences on hundreds of traits. Then using factor analysis Cattell et al identified sixteen source traits which are dimensions of personality that underlie differences in many other, less important, surface traits.

The third is the Big Five Taxonomy of Personality given by Zuckerman, Costa & McCrae (1994) which proposes that there are only five key dimensions of personality, that is, extraversion, agreeableness, conscientiousness, emotional stability and openness to experience, along which all human beings vary from very high to very low.

A significant number of studies have been conducted to demonstrate the inter-linkage and dependence of investment behavior on individual psychology. On the basis of a questionnaire based study of 140 small investors and 175 professional investors/traders, Ira Epstein, a stockbroker and David Garfield, a psychologist, published a book in 1992, entitled "The Psychology of Smart Investing". In this book they presented the analysis of their survey, in which they identified six clusters or 'types' of investors which they named as overly cautious/paranoid investors, conflicted investors, masked investors, revenging/consumed investors, fussy investors and depressed investors. Interestingly, these investor 'types' closely resemble the mental disorder categories described by American Psychiatric Association. (Bernstein, 1996)

In a 2005 research paper, published in The Journal of Behavioral Finance, entitled "Risk Aversion and Personality Types", Greg Filbeck, Patricia Hatfield and Philip Horvath have explored the relationship between the personality type dimensions of the Myers Briggs Type Indicator (MBTI) and the moments approach to individual investor risk tolerance, inherent in expected utility theory.

In the words of Jonathan Myers, author of "Profits without Panics: Investment Psychology for Personal Wealth" and founder of investment website psychonomics. com, "the way to improved financial returns is to match investments with investor's personality and needs". Myers has classified investors into cautious, emotional, technical, busy, casual and informed categories. He has also constructed various questionnaires and tools to determine the investor's personality.

Another interesting element found in related researches is about the role of gender in investment behavior. Are men and women different when it comes to financial decisions? The answer, as found out by many researchers is a resounding affirmative. Myers found that while men tend to be focused on results, goal directed and single minded with higher risk tolerance levels as well as high over-confidence levels, women, on the other hand, are multi-focused, process driven, less tolerant of risk and less prone to over confidence.

Brad Barber and Terrance Odean in their 2001 research paper in the Quarterly Journal of Economics, entitled "Boys will be Boys: Gender, Overconfidence and Common Stock Investment" have also concluded similar results about gender specific financial behaviors. In a 2007 paper in Decision, the journal of IIM, Calcutta, entitled "Investment Decision Making: An exploration of the Role of Gender", Yesh Pal Davar and Suveera Gill have concluded after an intensive statistical enquiry that females have lower levels of awareness, lower confidence levels and lower risk tolerance capacities and hence are more cautious vis-à-vis males with regard to prospective investment in equity (risky) securities, especially if fund availability is low.

RESEARCH PROBLEM

It is evident from the above review of related literature that till the very recent past, finance and psychology were two distinct disciplines with no common area of operation. However, over the past couple of decades, the amalgamation of the two sciences has resulted in a rich collection of research work.

It was noticed by the researchers that although significant work has been done in the area of investor psychology internationally, very little has been done in India. Additionally, in spite of the growing academic literature on the subject, almost no effort has been made to apply the proven knowledge to the investment management practice. This research is an effort by the researchers to construct a psychological-cum-demographic model of investment such that customized portfolios can be constructed for individuals who are known to have a given set of psychological traits and demographic characteristics.

CONCEPTUAL FRAMEWORK

The Big Five Personality Taxonomy

Personality researchers have proposed five basic dimensions of personality which are known as the big five personality factors. The Big Five Personality taxonomy is considered to be one of the most comprehensive, empirical, data-driven research findings in the history of personality psychology. Identifying the traits and structure of human personality has been one of the most fundamental goals in all of psychology. These five broad factors were discovered and defined by several independent sets of researchers who began by studying all known personality traits and then factor-analyzed hundreds of measures of these traits and thereby found these basic, underlying factors of personality.

A brief description of the big five personality categories has been given here:

Extraversion is characterized by positive emotions, surgency, and the tendency to seek out stimulation and the company of others. The trait is marked by pronounced engagement with the external world. Extraverts enjoy being with people, and are often perceived as full of energy. They tend to be enthusiastic, action-oriented individuals who are likely to say "Yes!" or "Let's go!" to opportunities for excitement. In groups they like to talk, assert themselves, and draw attention to themselves.

Agreeableness Agreeableness is a tendency to be compassionate and cooperative rather than suspicious and antagonistic towards others. The trait reflects individual differences in concern for social harmony. Agreeable individuals' value getting along with others. They are generally considerate, friendly, generous, helpful, and willing to compromise their interests with others. Agreeable people also have an optimistic view of human nature. They believe people are basically honest, decent, and trustworthy.

Conscientiousness is a tendency to show self-discipline, act dutifully, and aim for achievement. The trait shows a preference for planned rather than spontaneous behavior. Conscientious individuals avoid trouble and achieve high levels of success through purposeful planning and persistence. They are also positively regarded by others as intelligent and reliable. On the negative side, they can be compulsive perfectionists and workaholics.

Emotional Stability is the tendency to be calm, emotionally stable, and free from persistent negative feelings. The reverse of Emotional Stability is called Neuroticism. Those who score high in neuroticism are emotionally reactive, vulnerable to stress, and are more likely to interpret ordinary situations as threatening, and minor frustrations as hopelessly difficult. Individuals who score high in emotional stability are less easily upset and less emotionally reactive. They tend to be calm, emotionally stable, and free from persistent negative feelings. Freedom from negative feelings does not mean that low scorers experience a lot of positive feelings. Frequency of positive emotions is a component of the Extraversion domain.

Openness to Experience is a general appreciation for art, emotion, adventure, unusual ideas, imagination, curiosity, and variety of experience. The trait distinguishes imaginative people from down-to-earth, conventional people. People who are open to experience are intellectually curious, appreciative of art, and sensitive to beauty. They tend to be, compared to closed people, more creative and more aware of their feelings. They are more likely to hold unconventional beliefs.

Measurement of the Big Five Dimensions Several structured scaling instruments have been developed by various researchers. The significant ones are Oliver John's Big Five Inventory (BFI), Paul Costa and Jeff McCrae's NEO PI-R and NEO Five Factor Inventory (NEO-FFI), Lew Goldberg's set of 100 trait-descriptive adjectives (TDA), Gerard Saucier's Big Five Mini-Markers, Sam Gosling, Jason Rentfrow, and Bill Swann's Ten Item Personality Inventory (TIPI), et al. The NEO PI-R is a 240-item inventory developed by Paul Costa and Jeff McCrae, who also created the NEO-FFI, a 60-item truncated version. The Big Five Inventory (BFI), which has been used in this research, is a 44-item self-report inventory designed to measure the Big Five dimensions. Table 1 presents a very brief (sample) list

of items which are included in personality inventories to measure individuals along the big five dimensions.

Table 1 Big Five Personality Traits and Sample items in scaled testing instruments

Personality Trait	Sample items in scaled instruments
Extraversion	I don't mind being the center of attention. I feel comfortable around people. I start conversations. I talk to a lot of different people at parties.
Agreeableness	I am interested in people. I make people feel at ease. I sympathize with others' feelings. I take time out for others.
Conscientiousness	I am always prepared. I follow a schedule. I get chores done right away. I pay attention to details.
Emotional Stability	I am relaxed most of the time. I seldom feel blue. I am not easily disturbed. I don't worry about things.
Openness to Experience	I have a rich vocabulary. I have a vivid imagination. I have excellent ideas. I spend time reflecting on things.

Risk Appetite

The most significant parameter in any investment decision is the risk appetite of the individual. The economic man model suggests that if a rational human has two investment alternatives, he will select the one with lower risk, given the same level of expected returns and the one with higher returns, given the same level of risk. However, the true situation is quite different. Risk taking ability is an inherent trait. An aggressive risk taker will be ready to bear higher risk for a very small potential gain, whereas a risk-averse individual will take a small quantity of additional risk only in the expectation of huge returns.

Another significant point is that risk does not have a single universal definition. The researchers have viewed risk from many facets in this study. For instance, a prima facie preference for equity market investing exhibits one kind of risk-taking behaviour. Another way to visualize the risk capacity of an individual may be through his behaviour when faced with immediate returns. Another element of risk is the willingness of the individual to use leverage (borrowed funds) for investment. The various constructs, using the above conceptual framework have been defined in Table 2.

Table 2 Investment Constructs and their Definitions

Construct	Definition
Direct Investment in Equity (DIE)	Direct Investment in Equity measures the risk taking behavior of individuals with reference to direct investment in equity markets.
Investment Advice from Parents (IAP)	Investment Advice from Parents measures the extent to which the investor seeks advice from his parents before making the investment decision.
Investment Advice from Friends/ Colleagues (IAF)	Investment Advice from Friends/ Colleagues measures the extent to which the investor seeks advice from his friends and colleagues before making the investment decision.
Investment Advice from Spouse (IAS)	Investment Advice from Spouse measures the extent to which the investor seeks advice from his/her spouse before making the investment decision.
Investment Advice from Financial Advisors (IAFA)	Investment Advice from Financial Advisors measures the extent to which the investor seeks advice from independent financial advisors before making the investment decision.
Loan for Long-term Investment (LFLI)	Loan for Investment is a construct that measures the risk taking behavior of individuals with reference to using leverage (loan) for funding their long term investments.
Loan for Short-term Investment (LFSI)	Loan for Investment is a construct that measures the risk taking behavior of individuals with reference to using leverage (loan) for funding their short-term investments.
Risk for Immediate Returns (RIR)	Risk for Immediate Returns is a construct that measures the amount of risk an individual is prepared to take when offered immediate gratification, like in a game show.
Adherence to Systematic Investment Process (ASIP)	Adherence to Systematic Investment Process is a construct which measures the extent to which individuals follow the systematic investment process, including reviewing investment goals, assessing risk tolerance level, determining return objectives, considering variety of options, consulting experts,

Table Contd...

Table Contd...

	assessing marketability, tax implications and convenience, before making investment decisions.
Tendency towards Active Portfolio Management (TAPM)	Tendency towards Active Portfolio Management describes the inclination of the individual to actively manage his portfolio according to changes in enviroment, due to portfolio non-performance, etc.
Attitude towards Financial Advisors (AFA)	Attitude towards Financial Advisors is a construct which denotes the overall positive or negative attitude of investors towards financial advisors.

OBJECTIVES OF THE STUDY

- To measure and categorize individuals along the identified big five personality dimensions using a structured psychometric scale.
- To study and analyze the behavior of investors with reference to identified investment behavior constructs.
- To test the association between one demographic variable, gender and the investment behavior constructs.
- To test the association between the big five personality dimensions and the investment behavior constructs.

Hypotheses of the Study

$H_{0.1}$: There is no difference between individuals with high extraversion and individuals with low extraversion with reference to investment behavior constructs.

$H_{0.2}$: There is no difference between individuals with high agreeableness and individuals with low agreeableness with reference to investment behavior constructs.

$H_{0.3}$: There is no difference between individuals with high emotional stability and individuals with low emotional stability with reference to investment behavior constructs.

$H_{0.4}$: There is no difference between individuals with high openness to experience and individuals with low openness to experience with reference to investment behavior constructs.

$H_{0.5}$: There is no difference between individuals with high conscientiousness and individuals with low conscientiousness with reference to investment behavior constructs.

H$_{0.6}$: There is no difference between male and female investors with reference to investment behavior constructs.

LIMITATION OF THE STUDY

The measurement of psychological phenomena is a difficult science. The researcher has used a standardized psychometric test (BFI) which has proven reliability and validity. However, the Big Five Inventory (BFI) is a comparatively short scale, 44 item self rating scale and is not as accurate as elaborate scales like NEO PI-R, etc. Another problem that the researchers encountered was due to the direct nature of few questions in the BFI Scale, which may have resulted in deliberately misleading responses from few respondents.

RESEARCH METHODOLOGY

The research study has employed both secondary and primary data. The primary data was collected from salaried investors employed in the public and the private sector (the respondents) with the help of a structured questionnaire. The study employed non-probabilistic sampling method, with a judicious mix of convenience and judgmental sampling. The questionnaires were initially served to 110 individuals, but after adjusting for incomplete and invalid questionnaires, the final sample size came to 87. The analysis of data has been done using SPSS software. The sample was collected during June 2011, from the city of Lucknow, India. The demographic profile of the respondents is elucidated in Table 3.

DATA TABULATION

The data collected through structured questionnaires has been tabulated with regard to the demographic profile (Table 3) and the psychological profile of the respondents (Table 4). The values of the Big Five personality dimensions were calculated using the BFI Scale Scoring Key. Thereafter, the psychological profile data was processed for calculation of measures of central tendency and dispersion, the summary statistics of which are presented in Table 5. Thereafter the frequency distribution of the entire sample along the identified eleven investment behavior constructs has been tabulated with absolute and percentage values in Table 6.

Table 3   Demographic Profile of Respondents

Parametrs	Category	Absolute Values (N = 87)	Percentage Values
Gender	Male	52	59.8
	Female	35	40.2
		Total = 87	Total = 100%
Age	Less than 30 years	21	24.1
	31-40 years	21	24.1
	41-50 years	26	29.9
	More than 50 years	19	21.8
		Total = 87	Total = 100%
Education	Graduate	7	8
	Post graduate	62	71.3
	Doctorate	18	20.7
		Total = 87	Total = 100%
Employ-ment	Govt./Semi Govt./PSU	28	32.2
	Private Sector	59	67.8
		Total = 87	Total = 100%
Monthly Income	Less than ₹25,000/-	10	11.5
	25,001–50,000/-	18	20.7
	50,001 – 75,000/-	39	44.8
	75,001 – 1,00,000/-	12	13.8
	More than 1,00,000/-	8	9.2
		Total = 87	Total = 100%

Table 4   Psychological Profile of Respondents

Parameters	Intensity	Absolute Values (N = 87)	Percentage Values
Extraversion	Very Low	4	4.6
	Low	21	24.1
	Neutral	12	13.8
	High	32	36.8
	Very High	18	20.7
		Total = 87	Total = 100%
Agreeableness	Very Low	9	10.3
	Low	9	10.3
	Neutral	25	28.7
	High	37	42.5
	Very High	7	8
		Total = 87	Total = 100%
Conscien-tiousness	Very Low	2	2.3
	Low	12	13.8
	Neutral	16	18.4
	High	47	54.0
	Very High	10	11.5
		Total = 87	Total = 100%

Table Contd...

Table Contd...

Emotional	Very Low	3	3.4
Stability	Low	17	19.5
	Neutral	17	19.5
	High	42	48.3
	Very High	8	9.2
		Total = 87	Total = 100%
Openness to	Very Low	3	3.4
Experience	Low	15	17.2
	Neutral	30	34.5
	High	29	33.3
	Very High	10	11.5
		Total = 87	Total = 100%

Table 5 Measures of Central Tendency and Dispersion

Trait	Mean	Median	Mode	Standard Deviation (σ)
Extraversion	3.45	4	4	1.198
Agreeableness	3.28	4	4	1.096
Conscientiousness	3.59	4	4	0.947
Emotional Stability	3.40	4	4	1.017
Openness to Experience	3.32	3	3	1.006

TEST OF ASSOCIATION BETWEEN GENDER, PERSONALITY TRAITS AND INVESTMENT BEHAVIOR

The major objective of this research was to find whether there exists any significant association between the big five personality traits, gender and investment behavior. The null hypotheses (detailed above) assume that there is no significant association between each big five personality trait, gender and the identified investment behavior constructs. The chi-square (χ^2), Mann Whitney U Test and Kruskal Wallis Test have been used at 95% level of confidence to test the hypotheses. The results have been tabulated in Tables 7, 8 and 9 and each Chi Square, Mann Whitney U Test or Kruskal Wallis Test value which denotes significant association (that is where the null hypothesis has been rejected) has been marked with asterisk (*).

Table 6 Frequency Distribution of sample w.r.t Investment Behavior constructs

Construct	Options	Absolute Values (N=87)	Percentage Values
Direct Investment in Equity (DIE)	Invest in Equity	38	43.7
	Do not invest in Equity	49	56.3
		Total = 87	Total = 100%
Investment Advice from Parents (IAP)	Never	0	0
	Seldom	5	5.7
	Sometimes	28	32.2
	Often	19	21.8
	Very Often	35	40.2
		Total = 87	Total = 100%
Investment Advice from) Friends/Colleagues (IAF)	Never	0	0
	Seldom	14	16.1
	Sometimes	14	16.1
	Often	30	34.5
	Very Often	29	33.3
		Total = 87	Total = 100%
Investment Advice from Spouse (IAS)	Never	0	0
	Seldom	25	28.7
	Sometimes	13	14.9
	Often	36	41.4
	Very Often	13	14.9
		Total = 87	Total = 100%
Investment Advice from Financial Advisors (IAFA)	Never	0	0
	Seldom	11	12.6
	Sometimes	39	44.8
	Often	30	34.5
	Very Often	7	8.0
		Total = 87	Total = 100%
Loan for Long-term Investment (LFLI)	Not Willing	25	28.7
	Maybe	50	57.5
	Willing	12	13.8
		Total = 87	Total = 100%

Table Contd

Table Contd...

Loan for Short-term Investment (LFSI)	Not Willing	55	63.2
	Maybe	31	35.6
	Willing	1	1.1
		Total = 87	Total = 100%
Risk for Immediate Returns (RIR)	Low Risk	63	72.4
	Moderate Risk	23	26.4
	High Risk	1	1.1
		Total = 87	Total = 100%
Adherence to Systematic Investment Process (ASIP)	Very Low Adherence	7	8.0
	Low Adherence	8	9.2
	Neutral	16	18.4
	High Adherence	45	51.7
	Very High Adherence	11	12.6
		Total = 87	Total = 100%
Tendency towards Active Portfolio Management (TAPM)	Very Low	18	20.7
	Low	31	35.6
	Neutral	19	21.8
	High	11	12.6
	Very High	8	9.2
		Total = 87	Total = 100%
Attitude towards Financial Advisors (AFA)	Very Positive	0	0
	Positive	22	25.3
	Neutral	29	33.3
	Negative	29	33.3
	Very Negative	7	8.0
		Total = 87	Total = 100%

Table 7 Association between Gender, Personality Traits and Investment Behavior Constructs (Pearson's Chi-Square Test)

Constructs	Extraversion		Agreeableness		Conscientiousness		Emotional Stability		Openness to Experience		Gender	
	Value	Sig. (2-sided)	Value	Sig. (2-sided)	Value	Sig (2-sided)	Value	Sig. (2-sided)	Value	Sig. (2-sided)	Value	Sig. (2-sided)
DIE	20.813	.000*	5.894	.207	5.451	.244	15.214	.004*	13.662	.008*	13.35	.000*
IAP	25.504	.013*	18.20	.110	12.796	.384	26.634	.009*	20.452	.059	41.88	.000*
IAF	28.753	.004*	17.84	.021*	9.120	.693	25.978	.061	18.439	.103	28.26	.000*
IAS	21.098	.049*	16.01	.191	9.503	.659	10.119	.605	24.089	.060	50.11	.000*
IAFA	40.744	.000*	19.94	.068	32.588	.001*	15.085	.237	22.258	.035*	46.55	.000*
LFLI	62.041	.000*	24.65	.002*	5.000	.758	18.085	.021*	13.683	.090	16.98	.000*
LFSI	44.179	.000*	27.71	.001*	9.279	.319	20.659	.008*	21.612	.006*	33.01	.000*
RIR	31.402	.000*	22.09	.005*	7.870	.446	27.373	.001*	11.346	.183	21.91	.000*
ASIP	35.449	.003*	11.97	.746	45.235	.000*	14.558	.557	18.425	.300	27.83	.000*
TAPM	44.550	.000*	22.99	.114	16.764	.401	32.902	.008*	28.276	.029*	55.07	.000*
AFA	34.023	.061	12.65	.395	6.782	.872	27.305	.007*	7.080	.852	13.84	.003*

*denotes significant association at 95% level of confidence, that is the null hypothesis is rejected.

Table 8 Association between Gender & Investment Behavior (Mann Whitney U Test)

	DIE	IAP	IAF	IAS	IAFA	LFLI	LFSI	RIR	ASIP	TAPM	AFA
Asymptotic Significance	.000*	.000*	0.960	.000*	.000*	.000*	.000*	.000*	.000*	.000*	.842

*denotes significant association at 95% level of confidence, that is the null hypothesis is rejected.

Table 9 Association between Personality Traits & Investment Behavior (Kruskal Wallis)

	Extraversion	Agreeableness	Conscientiousness	Emotional Stability	Openness to Experience
Constructs			Asymptotic Significance		
DIE	.000*	.213	.250	.005*	.009*
IAP	.021*	.034*	.245	.142	.002*
IAF	.001*	.016*	.993	.051	.133
IAS	.113	.101	.663	.846	.053
IAFA	.002*	.034*	.040*	.234	.008*
LFLI	.000*	.000*	.803	.005*	.022*
LFSI	.000*	.002*	.540	.001*	.001*
RIR	.000*	.015*	.764	.000*	.054
ASIP	.018*	.685	.003*	.636	.308
TAPM	.000*	.052	.166	.031*	.002*
AFA	.054	.410	.580	.599	.664

*denotes significant association at 95% level of confidence, that is the null hypothesis is rejected.

RESULTS AND DISCUSSION

The Chi-Square Test, Mann Whitney U Test and the Kruskal Wallis Test shows that a significant association exists at 95% level of confidence for gender as well as few personality traits with reference to investment behavior constructs. A summary of the results obtained through statistical analysis of data are presented in Table 10.

It is apparent from the data that Gender is the most significant independent variable which influences investment behavior closely followed by Extraversion, as almost every investment dimension considered in this research is significantly affected by both the variables.

With regard to the various dimensions of risk capacity which have been tested, such as investing in equity markets, using leverage for investments and taking advantage of immediate opportunities, it is observed that Male Extraverts are the most intense Risk Takers, followed by Female Extraverts and Male Introverts. Female Introverts are the most Risk Averse. The other dimensions closely related to risk capacity are Emotional Stability, Agreeableness and Openness to Experience. It is clear from the data that Emotionally Stable individuals, more Agreeable individuals and more Open individuals have a higher propensity for bearing risk as opposed to their counterparts.

There is no significant difference between individuals with high Conscientiousness vis-a-vis low Conscientiousness with regard to most aspects of investment behavior. However, Conscientious individuals are more likely to seek advice from Financial Advisors and use the systematic investment process, as compared to their counterparts.

Table 10 Summary of Results

Investment Behavior Construct	Significantly affected by
Equity Market Investing	Gender, Extraversion, and Emotional Stability
Willingness to use leverage for Long-term Investment opportunities	Gender, Extraversion, Agreeableness and Emotional Stability
Willingness to use leverage for Short-term Investment opportunities	Gender, Extraversion, Agreeableness, Openness to Experience and Emotional Stability
Tendency to take risk in Gambling/Game Shows Tendency to seek Investment Advice from Parents	Gender, Extraversion, Agreeableness and Emotional Stability Gender and Extraversion
Tendency to seek Investment Advice from Friends and Colleagues	Gender, Extraversion and Agreeableness
Tendency to seek Investment Advice from Spouse	Gender
Tendency to seek Investment Advice from Financial Advisors	Gender, Extraversion and Conscientiousness
Adherence to Systematic Investment Process	Gender, Extraversion and Conscientiousness
Tendency towards Active Portfolio Management	Gender, Extraversion, Emotional Stability and Openness to Experience
Attitude towards Financial Advisors	Gender

A critical analysis of the results reveals the following key findings:

- Individuals behave in unique ways as influenced by their demographic and psychological characteristics.
- Majority of investors are risk averse, regardless of their unique characteristics, however the degree of averseness is influenced by their respective demographics and psychographics.
- Gender is the single most important parameter with regard to the unique investment behavior of each individual. Females tend to be more risk averse, with reference to equity market investing, with regard to using leverage for investment and even in game shows promising immediate gratification. Males are proportionately less risk averse in each of these dimensions.
- Among the psychographic variables, Extraversion, Emotional Stability and Openness to Experience make individuals less Risk Averse. However, Conscientiousness has no impact on risk capacity.
- Females, Highly Extravert and Agreeable individuals are more likely to seek advice from Parents, Friends and Colleagues for their investment decisions.
- Males generally do not prefer to consult their spouses for the investment decision whereas for females it is a prerequisite for investment.
- As regard the Systematic Investment Process is concerned, generally individuals are not very particular about following each step of the process, but male investors and Conscientious individuals are more likely to be systematic in their approach.
- The individuals in our sample were mostly passive investors, who do not prefer to actively churn their portfolios for better returns, however amongst them, male investors and the ones with higher extraversion and openness to experience were found to be less passive than their counterparts.
- Investors in general do not have a positive attitude towards Financial Advisors.
- The trait of Conscientiousness is not very significant with reference to the investment decision.

CONCLUSION AND IMPLICATIONS

The present study is unique in the sense that it seeks to investigate the association between gender, psychological traits and investment behavior, particularly in context of Indian investors. The results of the study make a strong case for psychological investment decision making.

The study has far reaching implications for the personal finance and investment arena, specially in India and other developing countries, where the concept of investment psychology is still in a very nascent stage and money managers and investors both still use primitive rules-of-thumb when giving financial advice and/or making financial decisions, which results in sub-optimum portfolio performance and low investor satisfaction.

The researchers believe that when this study is replicated at a macro level, a demographic-cum-personality-based investment model may emerge, wherein the personality sketch of an individual can be used as a vital input for construction of customized investment portfolios aimed at optimizing the financial as well as psychological well being of the investor.

References

- Anastasi Anne And Urbina Susana, Psychological Testing, *Prentice Hall-India, Seventh Edition, 2003.*
- Baron Robert A, Psychology, *Pearson Education, Fifth Edition, 2008.*
- Bernstein Peter L., *Against the Gods – The Remarkable Story of Risk, John Wiley & Sons Inc, 1996.*
- Epstein Ira and Garfield David, *the Psychology of Smart Investing, 1992.*
- Feldman, Robert S., Understanding Psychology, *Mcgraw Hill Book Company, 1987.*
- Filbeck, Greg, Hatfield Patricia and Horvath Philip, Risk Aversion and Personality Types, *Journal of Behavioral Finance,* 2005
- Garble, John E., Financial Risk Tolerance and Additional Factors that Affect Risk Taking in Everyday Money Matters, *Journal of Business and Psychology, 14, 4, 2000, 625–630.*
- John, O. P. and Srivastava, S., The Big Five Trait Taxonomy: History, Measurement and Theoretical Perspectives, *Handbook of Personality Theory and Research, 2, 102–138.*
- Kahneman, D. and Riepe Mark W., Aspects of Investor Psychology, *Journal of Portfolio Management, 24, 4.*
- Kahneman, D. and Tversky, Amos, Prospect Theory: An Analysis of Decision under Risk, *Econometrica, 47, 2, 1979, 263–291.*

- Kitces Michael, The Promise of a Good Night's Sleep, *Wealth And Retirement Planner, November-December, 2004, 34–35.*

- Mayfield, Cliff, Perdue et al., Investment Management and Personality Type, Financial Services Review, fall 2008, retrieved August 25, 2009 From Http://Www.Uoregon.Edu/~Sanjay/Bigfive.Html.

- Riley Neil F., and Russon Manuel G., Individual Asset Allocation and Indicators of Perceived Client Risk Tolerance, *Journal of Financial and Strategic Decisions, 8, Number 1, Spring 2005, 65 – 70.*

- Schmitt David P et al., Why Can't a Man be More Like a Woman : Sex Differences in Big 5 Personality Traits Across 55 Cultures, *Journal of Personality & Social Psychology, 94, 1, January 2008.*

- Srivastava, S, (2009), Measuring The Big Five Personality Factors.

- Statman Meir and Shefrin Hersh, Explaining Investor Preference for Cash Dividends, *Journal of Financial Economics, 1984.*

- Tvede Lars, the Psychology of Finance– Understanding the Behavioral Dynamics of Markets, *Wiley Trading, Revised Ed 2002.*

- Venter Gerhard Van De and Michayluk David, a *Longitudinal Study of Financial Risk Tolerance,* January 2009.

From Community Development to Corporate Social Responsibility: Changing Horizons of CSR and Challenges in India

Nikhil Atale[1], Anant Deshmukh[2] and Vinod Gavande[3]

[1]Faculty, Datta Meghe Institute of Management
[2]Associate Professor, Department of Business Management, RTM, Nagpur University
[3]Principal, RBT College, Mauda, District Nagpur

ABSTRACT

The concept of Corporate Social Responsibility has gained prominence from all avenues. Organisations have realized that government alone will not be able to get the success in its endeavor to uplift the downtrodden of society. With rapid changing corporate environment, more functional autonomy for public sector enterprises, CSR is gaining its importance from both the government and the private sector. This paper is based on analysis of secondary data covering the issues of community development to the critical issues of CSR in current context. Given the increasing gap between rural and urban India, a need is felt to adopt a suitable CSR framework by both the private and public sector to meet the changing needs.

Keywords: *Community Development, Corporate Social Responsibility*

INTRODUCTION

Corporate Social Responsibility (CSR), can be described as, the continuous commitment by corporations towards the economic and social development of communities in which they operate. The concept of corporate social responsibility of large industrial groups has occupied a prominent place in the greater national discourse on economic issues since the pre-independence era in India. Gandhi described large business as 'trusts' of the 'wealth of the people' and thus emphasized on the larger social purpose that industrial wealth should serve in independent India. In the early days of the post-independence period, the Indian state under the heavy influence of Nehruvian socialism encouraged private industries to play an active role in the economic and social development of the backward sections of the society, while at the same time setup a mammoth public sector for serving larger societal interests. As Nehru's gentle socialism gave way to the more radical policies of nationalization and extensive state regulation of the Indira Gandhi era, industrial groups desperate to avoid the draconian state policies and regulations in economic affairs resorted to large scale corporate welfare programs to demonstrate that private wealth also played a important role in poverty alleviation and the socio-economic development of the nation and was not anti-people.

DEFINITION OF CSR

Although there is no pre defined definition of CSR, according to Dr. Antony Miller[1], there are possible 350 definitions of CSR. Some of the definitions of CSR are as: "Corporate governance should be recognized as set of standards, which aims to improve a company's image, efficiency, effectiveness and social responsibility- Nigel Kendall. The European Commission's definition of CSR is: "A concept whereby companies integrate social and environmental concerns in their business operations and in their interaction with their stakeholders on a voluntary basis."

In Indian context, CSR is a new terminology, but it's hardly a new concept. As in third century BC, Kautilya's has dealt with the management of people and power commerce and taxations, standardization of weights and measures, and more peace.

ROLE OF GOVERNMENT IN COMMUNITY DEVELOPMENT IN POST INDEPENDENCE INDIA

Given the population landscape of India in 1950s, where over 70% of population was based in rural India, Government felt an urgent need of addressing the issues related to the poor people in rural India. Gandhian notion of Community Development Program (CDP) included key areas such as:

- Rural upliftment and reconstruction
- 19 Point program – Khadi & Village, Industries, Sanitation, Health care, Economic equity, Communal Harmony, Education, Women Empowerment

CDP assumed high propriety after Independence. In 1952 GOI launched 55 CDP projects each covering 300 villages. In 1953 National Extension Service project with similar objectives but to cover larger areas began as a comprehensive development effort to rebuild rural life and livelihood. CD blocks treated as an administrative unit for planning and development with separate budget.

By first 5yr plan (1952-57) – 1114 blocks covering 163,000 villages were operation. By the sixties CDP covered the entire country achieving the economic progress was core objective. CDP was the main program until the 3rd 5yr plan it was very comprehensive in content and it was focused to create conditions for high living standards and upliftment of rural poor especially in the areas of Agriculture, Animal husbandry, Roads, Health, Education, Housing, and Employment. In 1957 Balwant Rai Mehta Committee appointed to suggest measures to remove obstacles from CDP by introducing three tier system of local Government–

- Gram Panchayat (Village level),
- Panchayat Samiti (Block level),
- Zilla Parishad (District level)

The three-tier system aimed to link Government and elected representative. It also led to the emphasis on decentralized decision making and thereby shifting decision making closer to people and encourage their participation as well as placing Bureaucracy under people's control.

Today central government runs number of schemes in coordination with state and village level to address the issues of social development. According to recent statistics millions of rupees are allocated under the five year plan to continue such programs. A strong need is there to evaluate the impact assessment of these development programs.

SOCIAL OBLIGATIONS OF PUBLIC SECTOR ENTERPRISES: DUAL ROLE BY CENTRAL GOVERNMENT

PSEs serve the interest of society by taking responsibility for the impact of their activities on customers, employees, shareholders, communities and the environment in all aspects of their operations.

The Government has issued the guidelines on Corporate Social Responsibility for Central Public Sector Enterprises (CPSEs) following the Committee on Public Undertakings (1993-94) recommended a number of measures in its 24th Report on 'Social Responsibilities and Public Accountability of Public Undertakings'.

Although the Government believes in making PSEs growth oriented and technically dynamic, its policy is to give greater powers to the boards so that PSEs could function professionally. While the focus is on generating surpluses for self-sustaining growth, the PSEs generally undertake certain amount of non-commercial responsibilities, in furtherance of their commercial objectives. All PSEs cannot be treated on an equal footing for undertaking various types of social activities. It is for the individual PSE to identify and implement social responsibilities keeping in view its financial ability to sustain such activities, operating environment and provisions in its MOA/Statute.

It is likely that some social responsibilities may be assigned to PSEs through the issuance of Presidential Directives/guidelines by the concerned administrative Ministries/Departments. While implementation of Presidential Directives is mandatory; the guidelines are also generally to be followed except when the boards of directors of PSEs decide not to adopt them for reasons to be recorded in writing. It is desirable that boards of PSEs have full flexibility in identification and implementation of social responsibilities because as per the Articles of Association they enjoy full autonomy in this regard. PSEs are free to avail the help of State Governments, District Administration and peoples' representatives, wherever necessary.

India has well developed public sector with several huge corporations. PSE companies are operating in various sectors like petroleum, heavy industries, aviation, mining, steel, equipment manufacturing and shipping. The era of liberalization has led to the privatization of several public sector units and others being forced to make switch from being monopolies to being free market players with intense private competition. These dynamic processes have raised several key questions related to the corporate social responsibility of the public sector:

- What should be the social involvement levels of a company or corporation once it is fully or partially privatized?
- Should public sector units continue to play the same social role as they did in the pre-independence era or is there a need to scale back their social responsibility initiatives?
- Given the global nature of some of PSE's what CSR model should they adopt locally and in global markets?

These are questions that are central to the post-liberalization debate and need further analysis and research. Meanwhile many in India sill feel that PSE's should continue to play their traditional role of social development even in the current economic scenario. This is a debatable question. However, under the PSE reform, central government has made it clear that PSE's of strategic nature shall be held by government others include the Indian Railways.

It raises the question that should government continue to undertake CSR activities through panchayati raj initiatives and also through the PSE. This could need further research and analysis as current scope of this paper does not permit to debate this vital issue.

PRIVATE SECTOR PARTICIPATION IN COMMUNITY DEVELOPMENT

Loosely defined as the CSR then, under the Bombay Plan 1944-45, private sector entities such as Birla, Tata & Bajaj initiated community development programs through FICCI. Individual companies took initiatives to "give back" something to the society. Initial focus was on building public hospitals, schools and temples.

The conceptualization of corporate social responsibility up till the 1990's was purely in terms of philanthropy or charity. Welfare programs or initiatives were introduced not as a duty or a responsibility but as a form of charity that was supposed to indicate the virtues of the company or the organisation. Many industrial

groups like the Tata's or Birla's setup charitable trusts that provided financial grants for various worthy causes. Although there were some cases where the corporation took up a more active role like the establishment of the Birla Institute of Technology, Pillani by the Birla's or setting up of primary schools by several major industrial groups for their workers's children but even in these cases the approach was philanthropical. The problem with the philanthropy–based model has several issues including corporations considering these acts as one time or periodical grants basis. Secondly, considered as a charity, a company involved community to a very limited extent thus affecting the transparency, efficiency and effectiveness leading to the poor implementation and not serving the purpose on the wider scale.

However, in the current landscape contemporary issues such as capacity building including skill development, training, environment protection, women's empowerment, etc are largely being followed by major private sector companies in India. As per United Nations and the European Commission, Corporate Social Responsibility (CSR) leads to triple bottom-line: profits, protection of environment and fight for social justice. It is expected that Civil society, activist groups, Government and corporate sectors should work together to create appropriate means and avenues for the marginalized and bring them to the mainstream. The success of CSR lies in practicing it as a core part of a company's development strategy. It is important for the corporate sector to identify, promote and implement successful policies and practices that achieve triple bottom-line results[1]. There are more than 1,000,000 registered companies in India out of which less than 1percent companies are traded on the Indian Stock Exchange. A new Trend has started in Corporate is the establishment of special committees within the board of directors to oversee CSR activities. Groups of corporate are being encouraged to come together to promote CSR. In 2006, Europe created the European Alliance for CSR. It currently consists of 70 multinational corporate houses and 25 national partner organisations and has become a unique resource for building capability in CSR[2].

The change is evident in the statements about corporate social responsibility being made by India's leading industrial groups like the Tata's, "*over the years, the nature of the company's involvement with the community has undergone a change. It has moved away from charity and dependence to empowerment*

---

[1]Suri, Sehgal, Indian Institute of Research and Development

[2]Leo Burke, Norte Dame University

and partnership"[3] and the consistent transformation in their corporate social responsibility practices in the last decade. In the stakeholder model the community in which the corporation is present in is seen as a stakeholder in the company and therefore, the company has certain obligation and duties towards it like it has towards its other stakeholders (customers, employees, shareholders). It is a recognition of the fact that companies perform in non-financial arenas such as human rights, business ethics, environmental policies, corporate contributions, community development, corporate governance, and workplace issues and company should be held accountable for its 'triple bottom-line' that includes social, environmental, and financial performance and not just the financial aspect[4].

Others like S. Sailaja have attributed the shift in conceptualization to a simpler 'benefit' argument that basically implies that the stakeholder model has been adapted as it makes CSR programs more effective and efficient, the need for which is recognized by corporation who see multiple benefits like increased sales and customer loyalty, enhanced brand value and reputation, increased ability to attract and retain quality employees, investors & business partners, better productivity of workforce, cooperation with local communities, efficient operations resulting in improved financial performance, increased stock value, reduced litigation & environmental costs, better and faster governmental approvals, rewards, tax benefits that come from good CSR practices[5].

While both these arguments are pertinent, we would venture to supplement them by drawing attention to two other important reasons for the basic shift in the corporate social responsibility model. Firstly, the post-liberalization phase saw the increased presence of large transnational corporations like IBM in India which have highly developed corporate social responsibility initiatives based on the stakeholder participation model that were introduced in India by them. The success and effectiveness of these programs had a 'rub-off' effect on Indian enterprises, which were also operating in the same market, in their approach to corporate social responsibility initiatives. Secondly as Indian industry started competing in the developed markets of Europe, America and the Far East it had to comply with entry level norms like certification for responsible corporate practices like ISO 14000, SA 8000, AA 100 as well as compliance codes formulated by OECD and UN Global

Compact which meant that they had to adapt new corporate social responsibility standards.

Whatever be the reason, this change in the conceptualization of corporate social responsibility to stakeholder participation model has led to drastic change in the planning, management and implementation of corporate social responsibility initiatives as we illustrate in our new section.

GLOBALIZATION THRUST ON PRIVATE SECTOR: IMPLICATIONS FOR CSR

In post liberalization India, many private sector firms in India including those of Tata's and Birla's have gone multinational. Sectors such as Pharmaceutical, Engineering, Information Technology, Natural Resourses have seen increasing thrust on going global. In context of globalization, it is imperative that these firms adheres to the code of sustainable social development and consider implementing CSR activities across their value chain in both domestic and international markets. Recent incidents including that of British Petroleum and few other resources companies around the world have highlighted need of stricter environmental norms as a part of their CSR activities. In developed countries companies are putting more emphasis on issues such child labor, human rights, equal opportunities, equitable treatment as a part of their CSR programs. Few companies have implemented their CSR activities across the value chain of their businesses and are enforcing same CSR practices to their business partners in the value chain. This is much beyond the traditional concept of "stakeholders". A separate research can be undertaken on evolving trends of CSR in developed countries for that matter. Indian companies exposed to global business environment shall be forced to adopt these models at some point in time sooner than later.

ISSUES & CHALLENGES CSR IN INDIA

Notion of CSR in public sector being made mandatory is still in primitive stages of implementation mainly due to lack of clear strategies and comfort in carrying out the routine social development work. On the contrary in private sector many companies think that corporate social responsibility is a peripheral issue for their business and customer satisfaction more important for them. The concept of successful CSR for building their

---

[3] www.tatasteel.com

[4] www.timesfoundation.org

[5] www.iitk.ac.in

brand and customer loyalty is beyond the understanding of majority of Indian corporate.

Some of the issues pushing Indian companies CSR policies are:

THE ROLE OF GOVERNMENT

The role of government has changed in past six decades. Today, though it may not directly involved in CSR activities, but does play a vital role through PSE's and rural development via panchayati raj institutions for social development. By setting up mandatory CSR norms for PSE, government is setting up examples to the private sector to join the bandwagon.

IMPACT OF GLOBALIZATION

As both PSE's and private sector companies go global, governments, customer and suppliers in global environment are demanding more CSR role from these companies in both local and overseas markets.

USING SUCCESSFUL CSR AS A MARKETING TOOL

Companies like Tata Steel, Hindustan Unilever and ITC have set up well defined CSR strategies and are running businesses with CSR as one the center stage. These companies have realized the importance of successful CSR strategies in building their brands which are more appealing to the consumers than before.

CHANGING LABOR FORCE

Employees are increasingly looking beyond paychecks and benefits, and seeking out employers whose philosophies and operating practices match their own principles. In order to hire and retain skilled employees, companies are being forced to improve working conditions.

CSR ENVIRONMENT PERSPECTIVE IN INDIA

In India, some public sector companies can spend up to 5% of their profits on CSR activities. Pressure groups have been quite successful in inducing companies to fund CSR schemes. Forms of CSR differ according to the country or region. In Europe, for example, notions of CSR probably developed out of the Church

and a sense of ethics. In India, CSR has evolved to encompass employees, customers, stakeholders and notions of sustainable development or corporate citizenship. In transnational companies, the approach to CSR typically emerges from one of three elements including a decentralized strategy (which might examine human rights), a centralized strategy (which would be company-wide) or a globally integrated strategy (which would include Coca Cola or oil companies - where local actions can impinge globally).[6]

The survey conducted by Times of India group on CSR used a sample size of 250 companies involved in CSR activities through a method of online administration of questionnaire. The questionnaire was evolved after due diligence including focus group meetings, consultations with key stakeholders and a pilot in four metros. Finally 82 organisations responded to the questionnaire. These comprised 11 public sector undertakings (PSUs), 39 private national agencies and 32 private multinational organisations. The respondent organisations form a satisfactory percentage of 33 per cent of the sample size, given the fact that only those companies that had direct or indirect involvement in CSR activities were chosen to be approached for the survey. The survey elicited responses from participating organisations about various challenges facing CSR initiatives in different parts of the country. Responses obtained from the participating organisations have been collated and broadly categorized by the research team. These challenges are listed below:

Lack of Community Participation in CSR Activities

There is a lack of interest of the local community in participating and contributing to CSR activities of companies. This is largely attributable to the fact that there exists little or no knowledge about CSR within the local communities as no serious efforts have been made to spread awareness about CSR and instill confidence in the local communities about such initiatives. The situation is further aggravated by a lack of communication between the company and the community at the grassroots.

Need to Build Local Capacities

There is a need for capacity building of the local non-governmental organisations as there is serious dearth of trained and efficient organisations that can effectively contribute to the ongoing CSR activities initiated by companies. This seriously compromises scaling up of

CSR initiatives and subsequently limits the scope of such activities.

Issues of Transparency

Lack of transparency is one of the key issues brought forth by the survey. There is an expression by the companies that there exists lack of transparency on the part of the local implementing agencies as they do not make adequate efforts to disclose information on their programs, audit issues, impact assessment and utilization of funds. This reported lack of transparency negatively impacts the process of trust building between companies and local communities, which is a key to the success of any CSR initiative at the local level.

Non-availability of Well Organized Non-governmental Organisations

It is also reported that there is non-availability of well organized nongovernmental organisations in remote and rural areas that can assess and identify real needs of the community and work along with companies to ensure successful implementation of CSR activities. This also builds the case for investing in local communities by way of building their capacities to undertake development projects at local levels.

Visibility Factor

The role of media in highlighting good cases of successful CSR initiatives is welcomed as it spreads good stories and sensitizes the local population about various ongoing CSR initiatives of companies. This apparent influence of gaining visibility and branding exercise often leads many nongovernmental organisations to involve themselves in event-based programs; in the process, they often miss out on meaningful grassroots interventions.

Narrow Perception towards CSR Initiatives

Non-governmental organisations and Government agencies usually possess a narrow outlook towards the CSR initiatives of companies, often defining CSR initiatives more donor-driven than local in approach. As a result, they find it hard to decide whether they should participate in such activities at all in medium and long run.

Non-availability of Clear CSR Guidelines

There are no clear cut statutory guidelines or policy directives to give a definitive direction to CSR initiatives of companies. It is found that the scale of CSR initiatives of companies should depend upon their business size and profile. In other words, the bigger the company, the bigger is its CSR program.

Lack of Consensus on Implementing CSR Issues

There is a lack of consensus amongst local agencies regarding CSR projects. This lack of consensus often results in duplication of activities by corporate houses in areas of their intervention. This results in a competitive spirit between local implementing agencies rather than building collaborative approaches on issues. This factor limits company's abilities to undertake impact assessment of their initiatives from time to time.

RECOMMENDATIONS FROM SURVEY PARTICIPANTS

From the future perspective of CSR in India the recommendations of the survey are firm indications of the existing state of affairs in the CSR domain; they correspondingly call for necessary and appropriate steps to be initiated to put CSR on firmer ground. Keeping in view the broad results of the survey, the following recommendations are listed for serious consideration by all concerned stakeholders for their effective operationalization to deepen CSR in the company's core business and to build collaborative relationships and effective networks with all involved.

- Need for creation of awareness about CSR amongst the general public to make CSR initiatives more effective. By making effective use of the media, main stream participation from the general public will be encouraging. In addition, other companies will be motivated from such media exercise. Once CSR becomes a corporate movement, it shall change the lively hood of millions in a positive way thus, the social justice agenda of the day would be fulfilled more meaningfully.

- Partnerships between all stakeholders including the private sector, employees, local communities, the Government and society in general are either not effective or not effectively operational at the grassroots level in the CSR domain. This scenario often creates barriers in implementing CSR initiatives. It is recommended that appropriate steps be undertaken to address the issue of building effective bridges amongst all important stakeholders for the successful implementation of CSR initiatives. As a result, a long term and sustainable perspective on CSR activities should be built into the existing and future strategies of all stakeholders involved in CSR initiatives.

- It is noteworthy to underline that the Government's policy documents have adequate levers to ensure 'public cooperation' in planning process. The 1951 Plan Documents and other subsequent policy pronouncements amply demonstrate the intent of the Government in this regard, underscoring the value of participatory approach in the context of larger governance mechanics. The 'public cooperation' element has further been ensured by the involvement of various interest groups in drafting of the 'National Policy on Voluntary Sector 2007', under the aegis of the Planning Commission, Government of India. The National Policy was subsequently cleared by the Cabinet in 2007 and is one of the finest blueprints available on partnerships between the Government, the voluntary sector and the private sector.

- Partnership between the Government and other interest groups have been well defined in policy documents at all levels and as a result have come to stay; the only effort needed now is to develop common strategies to translate policy pronouncements into demonstrable action agendas. This will be of prime importance in ensuring a 'bottom-up' approach for various development initiatives in the country.

- The role and efforts of the private sector in taking development agenda forward with focus on education, health, environment, livelihood, women empowerment, disaster management to mention a few have been visible and effective. Some innovative models are also available of private sector interventions in these areas. In order to push the development agenda in a mission mode, it is recommended that realistic and operational models of engagement between all three important stakeholders – the Government, the non-governmental organisations and the private sector – are jointly explored and addressed.

- Only medium and large corporate houses are involved in CSR activities, that too in selected geographical areas. To address the issue of reaching out to wider geographical areas, the involvement of small and medium enterprises (SMEs) in the CSR domain will be essential.

It is recommended that a campaign should be launched to both spread awareness on CSR issues amongst the general public as well as to involve SMEs to participate more actively in CSR initiatives.

- Corporate houses and non-governmental organisations should actively consider pooling their resources and building synergies to implement best CSR practices to scale up projects and innovate new ones to reach out to more beneficiaries. This will increase the impact of their initiatives on the lives of the common people. After all, both corporate houses and non-governmental organisations stand to serve the people through their respective projects and initiatives.

- Surprisingly many CSR initiatives and programs are taken up in urban areas and localities. As a result, the impact of such projects does not reach the needy and the poor in the rural areas. This does not mean that there are no poor and needy in urban India; they too equally suffer from want of basic facilities and services. While focusing on urban areas, it is recommended that companies should also actively consider their interventions in rural areas on education, health, girl child and child labor as this will directly benefit rural people. After all, more than 70% people still reside in rural India.

- Government should consider rewarding and recognizing corporate houses and their partner non-governmental organisations implementing projects that effectively cover the poor and the underprivileged. Incentives to be offered to the private sector to strengthen their good work must include a formal partnership with local administration, easy grant of 12A, 80G and other fiscal incentives including matching project grants and tax breaks for social and development projects. This will be instrumental in encouraging enhanced voluntary participation of greater number of corporate houses in CSR activities.

- CSR as a subject or discipline should be made compulsory at business schools and in colleges and universities to sensitize students about social and development issues and the role of CSR in helping corporate houses strike a judicious balance between their business and societal concerns. Such an approach will encourage and motivate young minds, prepare them face future development challenges and help them work towards finding more innovative solutions to the concerns of the needy and the poor. It is recommended that involvement of professionals from the corporate sector, nongovernmental organisations and business schools would be key in ensuring youth participation in civic issues.

- There are approximately 250 corporate houses in the country that are directly involved in various CSR initiatives. These companies continue to decide their own projects depending on a number of parameters. These efforts are driven purely by the company's operational perspectives and ease of implementation of their CSR projects. As there are a number of companies involved in CSR activities, it is recommended that an accreditation mechanism should be put in place for companies through an independent agency for mainstreaming and institutionalizing CSR in the main business framework of the companies.

- Companies involved in CSR implement projects in the areas of health, education, environment, livelihood, disaster management and women empowerment, to mention a few. In many such contexts, it's noticed that companies end up duplicating each others' efforts on similar projects in the same geographical locations. This creates problems and induces a competitive spirit amongst companies. Considering the diverse issues and different contexts that exist currently in the CSR domain, it is recommended that companies involved in CSR activities urgently consider pooling their efforts into building a national alliance for corporate social responsibility. This alliance, representing various industry interests, should take up broad development agenda and provide high value services to the poor and the underprivileged. Over the years, the alliance would grow into a special purpose vehicle (SPV) and work closely with stakeholders to raise the level and quality of CSR interventions. There are already such models available in different industry segments both within the country and overseas; all that is needed is to identify and leverage these models to set up a national platform for effective thought alignment between companies and other stakeholders, in order to redefine CSR practices in India.

CONCLUSION

Past two decades of Indian economic era was a major catalyst for the radical transformation in the corporate social responsibility related practices in the country. The change was twofold: transformation of the conceptual understanding of corporate social responsibility and innovations at the implementation level. At the conceptual level, there was a fundamental transformation from the charity-oriented approach to the stakeholder-oriented approach where the target group was seen as stakeholder in the community whose well-being was integral to the long term success of the company. However, the real revolution occurred at the implementation stages where companies have started committing manpower, expertise in addition to financial resources in order to provide a host of services, programs and schemes that are flexible enough to accommodate the needs of the target community. The CSR initiatives have also see greater people participation at all stages and tighter accountability standards. The issue of norms for corporate social responsibility seems to have been adequately dealt with by industry practices like benchmarking, CSR ratings and certification by different agencies. The concept of corporate social responsibility is now firmly rooted on the global business agenda. But in order to move from theory to concrete action, many obstacles need to be overcome. A key challenge facing business is the need for more reliable indicators of progress in the field of CSR, along with the dissemination of CSR strategies. Transparency and dialogue can help to make a business appear more trustworthy, and push up the standards of other organisations at the same time.

While the situation in the private sector seems satisfactory, the progress made by PSE's in enforcing CSR agenda is certainly welcome In addition the dual role of central government one through PSE's and second through budgetary support to panchayeti raj institutions through give year plan needs to be coordinated. We strongly feel that there is a need for extensive research especially in form of empirical studies to address the questions and benefits related to this issue.

References

- Singla, Ashwani and Sagar Prema "Trust and Corporate Social Responsibility: Lessons From India", *Chief Executive Officer, Founder & Principal, Genesis Public Relations Pvt. Ltd.*
- *Eurasia Bulletin 10 11&12 Nov-December 2006.*

- Burke Leo, Associate Dean and Director, Executive Education, Notre Dame University, USA.
- Ministry Of Rural Development, "Panchayeti Raj", 1-3
- Nilesh R. Berad, "Corporate Social Responsibility: Issues and Challenges in India", *MET Institute of Management, Nasik.*
- P. Cappelli, H. Singh, J. Singh, and M. Useem, "The India Way", *Academy of Management Perspectives, 24, 2, May 2010, 6-24.*
- Retrieved from www.chillibreeze.com/articles_Various/CSR-In-India.asp.
- Retrieved from www.ibef.org.
- Retrieved from www.iisd.org/business/issues
- Retrieved from www.iitk.ac.in
- Retrieved from www.tatasteel.com
- Retrieved from www.timesfoundation.org
- *Sehgal Suri, Chairman & Founder Institute Of Rural Research & Development (IRRAD) Gurgaon.*
- Sudip Mahapatra And Kumar Visalaksh, "Emerging Trends in Corporate Social Responsibility: Perspectives and Experiences from Post Liberalized India" *National Academy of Legal Studies and Research, University Of Law, Hydrabad.*
- Times Foundation, "Corporate Social Responsibility Practices In India", *Times Foundation, Corporate Social Responsibility Wing of the Bennett, Coleman & Co. Ltd.*
- Wall Street Journal, "CSR in India: Some Theory and Practice", *April 23, 2009.*
- World Bank. (2003). World Development Report 2004: Making Services Work for Poor People. *Washington D.C.*

Current Economic Recession on Indian Banking Industry Survival amd Recovery: A Comparative Study of PNB and HDFC Bank Ltd.

P.D. Saini[1] and Arun Kumar Singh[2]
[1]Associate Professor, Department of Accountancy and Law, Faculty of Commerce
Dayalbagh Educational Institute (Deemed University)
[2]Research Scholar, Department of Accountancy and Law, Dayalbagh, Agra

ABSTRACT

Current Economic Recession has an impact on each and every sector viz. Banking, Real Estate, Tourism, Investment etc. only the degree of impact varies. The recession which came in Dec. 2007 hit globally and there are still some countries which are having influence of it. In the study an empirical impact of recession on banking industry by selecting a public sector bank Panjab National Bank and a private sector bank HDFC Bank ltd. This study deals with; what is recession? How it has affected the Indian banking industry? What is the impact of recession on selected companies and suggestion?

Keywords: *Recession, Banking*

INTRODUCTION

Recession Concept

National Bureau of Economic Research (NBER) is generally seen as the authority for dating US recessions. The NBER defines an economic recession as: "a significant decline in economic activity spread across the economy, lasting more than a few months, normally visible in real GDP, real income, employment, industrial production, and wholesale-retail sales."

In economics, **a recession is a** business cycle **contraction**, a general slowdown in economic activity. During recessions, many macroeconomic indicators vary in a similar way. Production, as measured by gross domestic product (GDP), employment, investment spending, capacity utilization, household incomes, business profits, and inflation all fall, while bankruptcies and the unemployment rate rise.

Recessions generally occur when there is a widespread drop in spending, often following an adverse supply shock or the bursting of an economic bubble. Governments usually respond to recessions by adopting expansionary macroeconomic policies, such as increasing money supply, increasing government spending and decreasing taxation.

IMPACT OF RECESSION

Savings

In a recession, private sector savings tend to rise. This is because people become more nervous to spend. The spectre of unemployment encourages people to save more and spend less. However, the rise in private sector saving may be offset by a fall in public sector saving (i.e. government borrowing increases to try and stimulate the economy).

Consumption

Consumption will tend to fall because people are worse off.

Investment

Investment will fall. Usually investment is highly cyclical. Therefore, a recession causes a bigger % fall in investment than consumption. Confidence is very important to investment so in a recession, investment tends to dry up.

Government Spending

Automatic fiscal stabilizers will cause government spending to rise. e.g. in recession, government have to spend more on unemployment benefits. Also the government may pursue expansionary fiscal policy to try and increase aggregate demand e.g. spending on infrastructure projects.

Aggregate demand is falling in a recession.

Indian Banking Industry

The Indian Banking industry, which is governed by the Banking Regulation Act of India, 1949 can be broadly classified into two major categories, non-scheduled banks and scheduled banks. Scheduled banks comprise commercial banks and the co-operative banks. In terms of ownership, commercial banks can be further grouped into nationalized banks, the State Bank of India and its group banks, regional rural banks and private sector banks (the old/ new domestic and foreign). These banks have over 67,000 branches spread across the country.

The first phase of financial reforms resulted in the nationalization of 14 major banks in 1969 and resulted in a shift from Class banking to Mass banking. This in turn resulted in a significant growth in the geographical coverage of banks. Every bank had to earmark a minimum percentage of their loan portfolio to sectors identified as "priority sectors". The manufacturing sector also grew during the 1970s in protected environs and the banking sector was a critical source. The next wave of reforms saw the nationalization of 6 more commercial banks in 1980. Since then the number of scheduled commercial banks increased four-fold and the number of branches increased eight-fold.

After the second phase of financial sector reforms and liberalization of the sector in the early nineties, the Public Sector Banks (PSB) s found it extremely difficult to compete with the new private sector banks and the foreign banks. The new private sector banks first made their appearance after the guidelines permitting them were issued in January 1993. Eight new private sector banks are presently in operation. These banks due to their late start have access to state-of-the-art technology, which in turn helps them to save on manpower costs and provide better services. During the year 2000, the State Bank Of India (SBI) and its 7 associates accounted for a 25% share in deposits and 28.1% share in credit. The 20 nationalized banks accounted for 53.2% of the deposits and 47.5% of credit during the same period. The share of foreign banks (numbering 42), regional rural banks and other scheduled commercial banks accounted for 5.7%, 3.9% and 12.2% respectively in deposits and 8.41 percent, 3.14% and 12.85% respectively in credit during the year 2000.

BRIEF PROFILE OF PUNJAB NATIONAL BANK

Punjab National Bank (PNB) is one of India's largest nationalized banks, with some 5,000 locations. The financial institution offers services in personal and corporate banking, including industrial, agricultural, and export finance, as well as international banking. Its personal lending services include loans for housing, autos, and education. PNB's diverse client list includes Indian conglomerates, small and midsized businesses, non-resident Indians, and multinational companies. The bank was established in Lahore in 1895 -- more than 50 years before the country was partitioned into India and Pakistan in 1947.

BRIEF PROFILE OF HDFC BANK LIMITED

HDFC Bank Limited (the Bank) is a banking company. The Bank is engaged in providing a range of banking and financial services. The Bank operates in four segments: treasury, retail banking, wholesale banking and other banking business. The treasury segment primarily consists of net interest earnings from the Bank's investments portfolio, money market borrowing and lending, gains or losses on investment operations and on account of trading in foreign exchange and derivative contracts. The retail banking segment raises deposits from customers and makes loans and provides other services. The wholesale banking segment provides loans, non-fund facilities and transaction services to large corporates, emerging corporates, public sector units, government bodies, financial institutions and medium scale enterprises. The other banking business segment includes income from para banking activities, such as credit cards, debit cards and third party product distribution, primary dealership business.

LITERATURE REVIEW

A period of general economic decline; typically defined as a decline in GDP for two or more consecutive quarters. A recession is typically accompanied by a drop in the stock market, an increase in unemployment, and a decline in the housing market. A recession is generally considered less severe than a depression, and if a recession continues long enough it is often then classified as a depression. (Frederick M. Richardson[1], Gregory D. Kane 2003) said that recessionary business cycles can contribute to corporate failure. Specifically, they test for a relationship between failure and (1) knowledge that failure occurred during a recession and (2) knowledge that the predictor variables were measured during a recession. They are able to show that accounting-based logistic regression models used to predict corporate failure are sensitive to the occurrence of a recession. Furthermore, their results indicate that such models are sensitive to knowledge that the predictor variables were generated during a recession and to knowledge that failure ultimately occurred during a recession.

Vidyakala, Madhumanti, Poornima (2009) said that prudential norms adopted by the Indian banking system and the better regulatory framework in the country have helped the banking system remain stronger even during the global slowdown. There is an apprehension among the customers and the people in the country about the strength of the banking system. The banking system today has ₹36 lakh corer of deposits and ₹26 lakh crore of advances. The money of the people is safe in Indian banks, unlike the western banks. The Indian banking system has the rule of *dharma*, which has taught the sector not to have greed. In the end, the banking industry is likely to be just fine. While some individual banks went down, and continue to struggle, the financial sector as a whole is doing okay, and is likely to recover from this recession without too much trouble. Hopefully, these profits mean that the banks will be more willing to help other companies that need access to credit.

OBJECTIVES OF THE STUDY

1. To study the concept of recession.
2. To analyze the impact of recession on the selected companies.

Hypothesis

Ho: There is no significant impact of recession on selected companies.

Ha: There is a significant impact of recession on selected companies.

Research Methodology

In this study it measures the impact of recession on selected public sector bank Punjab National Bank and private sector bank HDFC Bank ltd. convenient sampling technique is used to select the sample and duration of the study is Dec 2007 onwards. For the purpose of analysis both primary and secondary data were used. Secondary data were collected through websites, magazines, newspaper, journals. Primary data were collected on survey method based on a structured questionnaire. The questionnaires were circulated among 100 top level employees of the selected banks. Statistical tools like weighted average, tables etc. were used and for testing of hypothesis t-test is used.

Finding of the Research

Table 1 showing the responses given by the fifty respondents of Punjab National Bank on the parameters provided by the researcher they are profitability, liquidity, credibility, interest rate, investment, market share, customer base, number of new customers, employment and goodwill. The table is also showing the Likert scale taken into consideration. Weighted average of each parameter is calculated which shows that which parameter is having higher impact or moderate impact or low impact or no impact. The result shows that profitability with 2.36 and credibility with 2.16 and investment with 2.94 and no of new customers with 2.18 are having higher impact of recession according to the responses provided by the respondents of PNB. Table 1.1 shows calculated sd which is 1.22.

Table 2 showing the responses given by the fifty respondents of HDFC Bank Ltd. on the parameters provided by the researcher they are profitability, liquidity, credibility, interest rate, investment, market share, customer base, number of new customers, employment and goodwill. The table is also showing the Likert scale taken into consideration. Weighted average of each parameter is calculated which shows that which parameter is having higher impact or moderate impact or low impact or no impact. The result shows that profitability with 3.74 and liquidity with 3.48 and credibility with 2.16 and investment with 3.62 and

Table 1 Finding from PNB

Weights	5	4	3	2	1		
Parameters	Very high	High	Moderate	Low	No Affect	Total	Mean
Profitability	10	5	3	7	25	50	2.36
Liquidity	2	4	5	4	35	50	1.68
Credibility	3	7	5	15	20	50	2.16
Interest rate	1	2	1	1	45	50	1.26
Investment	3	10	20	15	2	50	2.94
Market share	2	3	5	5	35	50	1.64
Customer base	1	1	2	6	40	50	1.34
No. of new customers	4	6	5	15	20	50	2.18
Employment	1	1	6	20	22	50	1.78
Goodwill	1	1	2	6	40	50	1.34
Total	28	40	54	94	284	500	1.87

Table 1.1 cal. of standard deviation

x	f	fx	x*x	f*x*x
5	28	140	25	700
4	40	160	16	640
3	54	162	9	486
2	94	188	4	376
1	284	284	1	284
15	500	934	55	2486

Standard deviation is 1.22

no. of new customer with 2.28 and employment with 4.12 are having higher impact of recession according to the responses provided by the respondents of HDFC Bank ltd. Table 2.1 shows calculated sd which is 1.66.

The mean of PNB is 1.87 and sd is 1.22 and the mean of HDFC Bank ltd is 2.55 and sd is 1.66. The difference in mean is –0.68 and standard error is 0.284549. The t-value is –2.39678 which represents that the H_{01} is rejected which shows that there is an impact of recession on the selected companies.

Table 2 Finding from HDFC Bank Ltd

Weights	5	4	3	2	1		
Parameters	Very High	High	Moderate	Low	No Affect	Total	Mean
Profitability	23	10	3	9	5	50	3.74
Liquidity	17	4	21	2	6	50	3.48
Credibility	3	5	7	17	18	50	2.16
Interest rate	6	2	1	1	40	50	1.66
Investment	25	5	3	10	7	50	3.62
Market share	2	3	5	5	35	50	1.64
Customer base	1	1	2	6	40	50	1.34
New customers	4	6	5	20	15	50	2.28
Employment	20	21	6	1	2	50	4.12
Goodwill	3	1	2	6	38	50	1.5
Total	104	58	55	77	206	500	2.55

Table 2.1 cal. of standard deviation

x	f	fx	x*x	f*x*x
5	104	520	25	2600
4	58	232	16	928
3	55	165	9	495
2	77	154	4	308
1	206	206	1	206
15	500	1277	55	4537

Standard deviation is 1.66

CONCLUSION

Based on the results of the study it can be concluded that there is slightly more impact of recession on the private sector bank HDFC Bank Ltd. compared with the public sector bank PNB. Further the findings imply that there are certain parameters which are profitability, investment, employment which are having higher impact of recession in private sector bank when compared with b public sector bank. In this way it can be concluded

Table 3 Cal. of t-value

MEAN	SD	MEAN	SD	DIFF.IN MEAN	STANDARD ERROR	t-value	Ho
1.87	1.22	2.55	1.6	− 0.68	0.284549	− 2.39678	reject

that more or less recession has an impact on Indian banking sector.

References

- www.google.com
- Wikipedia
- www.ssrn.com
- Annual reports of PNB and HDFC
- The Hindustan times
- Times of India
- Accounting journals

Quantitative Scrutiny of Quality of Financial Reporting in Indian Scenario

Pramod Kumar[1] and Hina Agarwal[2]

[1]Head, Department of Accountancy and Law, Faculty of Commerce, Dayalbagh Educational
Institute (Deemed University), Dayalbagh, Agra
[2]Research Scholar, Department of Accountancy and Law, Faculty of Commerce, Agra

ABSTRACT

Financial reporting is the process of preparing and distributing financial information to users of such information in various forms. The most common format of formal financial reporting is financial statements. Financial statements are prepared in accordance with rigorously applied standards defined by professional accounting bodies developed according to the legal and professional framework of a specific locale. Also, in an era of increasingly stringent financial reporting requirements, timely and accurate financial information must be deliverable to anyone, anywhere, at anytime.

In view of the above considerations, in the present paper an attempt has been made to judge the quality of financial reporting. Analytical models used in this paper to consider the disclosed public information in related annual reports and other e-sources as the measures of the quality. The most influencing variables of quality such as net profit, net worth, Employees Stock Option Scheme (Sweat Capital), market capitalization; monthly returns etc. are selected for Indian corporate from various sectors. The analysis covered the data series of ten financial years from 2001-02 to 2009-10. The gathered data is analyzed by using different generalized linear regression models. The paper ends with a outcome on the quality of financial reporting and highlighting the limitations of the study.

Keywords: *Financial reporting, Quantitative analysis, generalized linear models, India, Dummy variables, Reliability analysis, Cronbach's alpha*

INTRODUCTION

At the core of the corporate reporting, the financial reporting exists, consisting GAAP-compliant financial statements and accompanying notes (price water house coopers). Financial reporting may be defined as communication of financial information of a business enterprise to external world (i.e., third parties including shareholders, creditors, customers, governmental authorities & the public). It is the reporting of the accounting information of an entity (individual firm, company, government enterprise) to a user or group of users. Financial reporting information is to facilitate the efficient allocation of capital in the economy. It is an indicator of how well or poor a company has performed in a particular financial year. The main expected role of the financial reporting is to meet the external users'

varying needs. Users of financial reports in general and particularly investors require useful information for their decision-making. Financial Reporting gives reader a summary of what happened in a company based purely on the records. These records tell the condition and performance of a business historically, currently and prospectively.

An understanding of the conceptual bases of the corporate financial reporting system and of the preparation of financial statements is essential prerequisites to be a good accountant or a financial analyst. In this way, the primary objective of financial reporting is to provide high-quality financial reporting information concerning economic entities, primarily financial in nature, useful for economic decision making. Providing high quality financial reporting information is important because it will positively influence capital providers and other stakeholders in making investment, credit, and similar resource allocation decisions enhancing overall market efficiency (Ferdy Van Beest, Geert Braam, Suzanne Boelens, 2009).

The very basic premise of financial reporting is to provide a fair, complete and well-informed view of the financial performance of a business, based on a well-defined set of standards, which are used consistently across a whole range of companies (Tanya Branwhite). Financial reporting is done by every business and organisation to assess its financial performance. Currently, while internal financial reporting incorporates both financial and managerial accounting information, external financial reporting is comprised primarily of financial accounting information; hence, very little information in external financial reports relates to the decision-making (planning) function of management (Stanley C. W. Salvary, Canisius College, 1998). Companies report their financial and narrative/contextual information using a wide range of external communication channels, including presentations to analysts and corporate websites.

Preparers of financial information should clearly indicate how changes in accounting have impacted their accounts, so users of financial reports have the opportunity to strip those changes back out (Tanya Branwhite). It is important to report financial information in a timely fashion. The longer a company waits to release its annual report and accompanying financial statements, the more stale the information is and the less useful it is.

Financial reporting affects the public interest in numerous ways. This results a widespread adoption of financial reporting, will produce a more efficient capital market, a more productive economy and a more prosperous society. (Paul B.W. Miller, April 2002)

Corporate financial report communicates economic impact of transactions and other events on the economic resources and the capital structure of the company. The aim is to provide information that is relevant for economic decision-making by investors and creditors. The information is also used to evaluate management in its stewardship function. It is expected that the information in financial report should be presented in such a manner that it is easy to comprehend and analyze (Asish K. Bhattacharyya, 2009).

Corporate financial reporting gives an overall view of the business performance in accordance with the business objectives. To achieve these objectives, financial data and related information is to be summarized into useful reports of the company so that primary and secondary users can use them in efficient manner. Relevant information will be those that have affected a company's development, performance and position during the financial year – as well as those likely to affect its future development, performance and position. There are no hard and fast rules dictating what forward-looking information a company must provide. Companies must decide which information to include – and which to leave out – on the basis of their own unique business dynamics and those of the industry sectors in which they operate.

REVIEW OF LITERATURE

Considerable literature has emerged in the last eighteen years that examines the corporate financial reporting. This section provides a review of both aspects i.e., conceptual framework of corporate financial reporting and its quality determinants.

Conceptual Framework of Corporate Financial Reporting

Stanley C. W. Salvary, Canisius College (1998) examine various theoretical issues in accounting in a historical setting and provides some insight on the manner in which the accounting profession has responded to problems and suggested that the inclusion of managerial accounting information in financial reports would reduce the current level of uncertainty and should lead to increased efficiency in the setting of proper prices in the capital markets. Birgül Caramanolis-Çötelli, Lucien Gardiol, Rajna Gibson-Asner and Nils S. Tuchschmid (2000) investigate the role of the quality of a firm's disclosure policy and of the information channeling process by financial analysts on the stock price reaction around the publication of the annual reports.

McDaniel, Linda; Martin, Roger D.; Maines, Laureen A. (2002) investigate the extent to which financial experts make judgments about financial reporting quality that differ from those of financial literates and suggested that financial experts' frameworks for evaluating overall financial reporting quality for a set of financial statements differ from those of financial literates. They also indicate that experts and literates bring differing viewpoints to the identification and evaluation of specific financial reporting concerns. Stephen H. Penman (2003) questions the quality of financial reporting against the backdrop of the stock market bubble in 1990's. A number of quality features of accounting are identified. Inevitable imperfections due to measurement difficulties are recognized, as a quality warning to analysts and investors. A number of failures of GAAP and financial disclosures are identified that, if not recognized, can promote momentum investing and stock market bubbles.

Feng Li and Nemit O. Shroff (2009) examine the relation between financial reporting quality and economic growth. They developed the hypothesis and apply regression analysis. Their results show that there is no robust relation between the quality of financial reporting in a given country and its economic growth. Feng Chen, Ole-Kristian Hope, Qingyuan Li, Xin Wang (2010) examine the role of FRQ in private firms from emerging markets. They shows that financial reporting quality (FRQ) is positively related to investment efficiency for large U.S. publicly traded companies.

Determinants of Corporate Financial Reporting

P.L. Joshi, Dr. Jasim Abdulla, (1993) make a critical examination of the present accounting standard setting process and current issues and practices of corporate financial reporting (CFR) in an Indian context by referring to 95 annual reports of large sized companies. It is found that Indian accounting standards have many alternative accounting choices which make financial statements of companies less comparable. A review of CFR shows a strong tendency for companies to follow strict legal requirements in the disclosure and preparation of financial statements, there is much diversity in voluntary reporting practice particularly with respect to value added accounting, reporting by segments, inflation accounting, human resource accounting, and corporate social performance reporting, and there has been a tendency towards minimum disclosure. Peter B. Oyelere, Fawzi Laswad and Richard Fisher (2000) examine the extent of IFR by New Zealand companies and the determinants of their WWW presence and IFR practices. They identify the following determinants: (1) size (2) performance (3) liquidity (4) internationalization (5) ownership spread and (6) industry. The results of the study indicate that firm size, efficiency and the spread of ownership motivates the provision of IFR.

Carol Ann Frost, Elizabeth A. Gordon and Grace Pownall (2005) examine associations between financial reporting and disclosure quality, and access to capital in global equity markets by 342 emerging market companies. They examine five proxies for financial reporting and disclosure quality: (1) the financial transparency and information disclosure component of Standard and Poor's Transparency and Disclosure (S&P T&D) index, (2) accounting principles used in the annual report to

shareholders (home GAAP, International Accounting Standards [IAS], reconciliation to U.S. GAAP, and U.S. GAAP), (3) auditor (global versus domestic), (4) whether the annual report to shareholders is available in an English language version, and (5) a categorical variable representing the extent to which the company provides freely available financial and other investor-oriented information on its website. Researchers find strong support for the hypothesis that financial reporting and disclosure quality is positively associated with emerging market companies' global capital market access, after controlling for factors expected to influence emerging market companies' ability to raise capital globally.

Rodrigo S. Verdi (2006) studies the relation between financial reporting quality and investment efficiency on a sample of 49,543 firm-year observations between 1980 and 2003. Researcher considered payout, age, size and rating constraints as determinants and concluded the relation between financial reporting quality and investment efficiency is stronger for firms with low quality information environments. Ferdy van Beest, Geert Braam and Suzanne Boelens (2009) constructed a 21- item index in order to comprehensively measure the quality of financial reporting in terms of the underlying fundamental and enhancing qualitative characteristics i.e. relevance and faithful representation, understandability, comparability, verifiability and timeliness and contributes to improving the quality assessment of financial reporting information, fulfilling a request from both the FASB and the IASB (2008) to make the qualitative characteristics operationally measurable. Qingliang Tang (2008) proposes a system to measure financial reporting quality at country level. He develops quality indicators of five dimensions of financial reporting system: loss avoidance ratio, profit decline avoidance ratio, accruals ratio, qualified audit opinion ratio and non-Big 4 auditor ratio. The study calculates a financial reporting quality score based on these indicators.

RESEARCH METHODOLOGY

In order to determine the quality of financial reporting in India, it was necessary to locate the annual reports of Indian companies, and then find the dimensions of corporate financial reporting. Companies whose annual reports of ten consecutive financial years from 2001-02 to 2009-10 available on their websites and also registered on SEBI, were randomly selected. Five Indian companies named by (1) Bharat Heavy Electricals Limited (BHEL) (the largest engineering and manufacturing enterprise of India in the energy & infrastructure related sectors.); (2)

Grasim Industries Limited (business in viscose staple fibre (VSF), cement, chemicals and textiles. Its core businesses are VSF and cement); (3) Hindalco (the leading producer of aluminium and copper); (4) Infosys Limited (the second largest information technology company in India); (5) Steel Authority of India Limited (SAIL) (the leading steel-making company in India) were selected.

Researchers have scratched many of the variables from the company's financial reports to know the status of the corporate financial reporting in Indian scenario as explained above. And, then, draw descriptive statistics of selected variables to find their range, minimum and maximum value, mean and standard deviation. As the variables are dummy coded, there is no need to calculate skewness or kurtosis. Are all these variables reliable to measure the quality of corporate financial reporting in India? To measure it, Cronbach Coefficient Alpha of Reliability and Item Analysis may be used to identify reliable measurement, to improve existing one, and to evaluate the reliability of variables already in use.

Researchers, then apply Generalized Linear Models on the reliable variables which have identified after Reliability and Item Analysis to know the variation in actual quality of corporate financial reporting in Indian scenario during the FY 2001-02 to 2009-10.

VARIABLES CODING

Researchers have identified some of the determinants (financial and non-financial) that focus on the corporate financial reporting, with consideration of the related literature and also from their own opinion as a way of emphasizing the quality of corporate financial reporting in Indian competitive environment. These determinants are coded as 0 and 1. The dummy coding of the variables are as follows:

Net Profit:	If computation of net profit in accordance with section 349 or 198 or 309 (5) of the Companies Act, 1956 = 1; otherwise = 0
Return On Average Net Worth	If provided = 1; otherwise = 0
Employees Stock Option Scheme (Sweat Capital)	If employees allotted shares under ESOP scheme = 1; otherwise = 0
Market Capitalization	If market capitalization is included in the computation of The Bse-30 Sensitive Index (Sensex), The BSE Dollex, S&P CNX Nifty Index And NASDAQ-100 Index = 1; otherwise = 0

Table Contd...

Table Contd...

Monthly Returns	If provided = 1; otherwise = 0
Contents	If provided = 1; otherwise = 0
Timeliness	If reports are provided on the time = 1; otherwise = 0
Value Added Statement	If provided = 1; otherwise = 0
Corporate Social Responsibility	If provided = 1; otherwise = 0
Corporate Governance	If provided = 1; otherwise = 0
Risk Management Report	If provided = 1; otherwise = 0
Consolidated Financial Statements	If provided = 1; otherwise = 0
Human Resource Accounting	If provided = 1; otherwise = 0
Environment Management	If provided = 1; otherwise = 0
Related Party Disclosures	If provided = 1; otherwise = 0
Segment Reporting	If provided = 1; otherwise = 0

ANALYSIS AND RESULTS

Descriptive Statistics

The above table presented the descriptive statistics for sixteen dummy predictor variables. All the predictor variables for five companies are concerned of ten financial years from FY 2001-02 to FY 2009-10. The N column indicates that all the variables have complete data. The valid N (listwise) is 50, which also indicates that all the predictor variables had data for each company for every year. The range column shows that variables are coded as 0 or 1. The minimum column showing "0" for a minimum and the maximum column showing "1" for a maximum are good because they agree with the codebook. There are four exceptional variables (monthly returns, timeliness, corporate governance and related party disclosures) which do not follow the required values and hence not showing the any deviation. All the remaining variables show some deviation i.e., more or less, so it is clear that these variables response to quality of financial reporting.

Reliability Analysis

From the above description of variables, it is felt that there is a requirement to check the reliability of the selected variables. So, researcher has devised a sixteen-variables statement with which they hope to measure how quality of corporate financial reporting shift in this competitive edge in Indian complex. In order to understand whether the variables in this statement all

Variables	N Statistic	Range Statistic	Minimum Statistic	Maximum Statistic	Mean Statistic	Std. Dev Statistic
Net Profit	50	1	0	1	.58	.499
Net Worth And Its Returns	50	1	0	1	.44	.501
Employees Stock Option Scheme (Sweat Capital)	50	1	0	1	.18	.388
Market Capitalization	50	1	0	1	.10	.303
Monthly Returns	50	0	0	0	.00	.000
Contents	50	1	0	1	.98	.141
Timeliness	50	0	1	1	1.00	.000
Value Added Statement	50	1	0	1	.26	.443
Corporate Social Responsibility	50	1	0	1	.44	.501
Corporate Governance	50	0	1	1	1.00	.000
Consolidated Financial Statement	50	1	0	1	.84	.370
Human Resource Accounting	50	1	0	1	.02	.141
Environmental Disclosures	50	1	0	1	.68	.471
Related Party Disclosures	50	0	1	1	1.00	.000
Segment Reporting	50	1	0	1	.80	.404
Risk Management Report	50	1	0	1	.44	.501
Valid N (listwise)	50					

reliably measure the same latent variable i.e., quality, a Cronbach's coefficient alpha was carry on.

There are five companies who respond to variables for ten financial years, and then compute the variance for each item, and the variance for the sum scale. We can estimate the proportion of 1 score variance that is captured by the variables by comparing the sum of variable variances with the variance of the sum quality of corporate financial reporting. Specifically, we can compute Cronbach's coefficient *alpha* (α):

Cronbach Alpha Test for Quality of Corporate Financial Reporting				
Statistics for	Mean	Variance	Std. Dev	N of Variables
Scale: Quality of Corporate Financial Reporting	5.76	4.676	2.162	12
	Scale mean if item deleted	Scale variance if item deleted	Corrected Item-Total Correlation	Cronbach's Alpha if Item Deleted
Net Profit	5.18	3.702	.378	.578
Net Worth and Its Returns	5.32	3.814	.312	.594
Employees Stock Option Scheme (Sweat Capital)	5.58	4.412	.070	.638
Market Capitalization	5.66	4.147	.354	.593
Contents	4.78	4.461	.327	.611
Value Added Statement	5.50	4.010	.265	.604
Corporate Social Responsibility	5.32	3.732	.357	.583
Consolidated Financial Statement	4.92	3.749	.551	.552
Human Resource Accounting	5.74	4.604	.085	.626
Environmental Disclosures	5.08	4.851	-.191	.696
Segment Reporting	4.96	3.794	.456	.566
Risk Management Report	5.32	3.487	.500	.547
Reliability Coefficients for variables 12	α = .623		Standardized Item Alpha = .635	

Revised Cronbach Alpha Test for Quality of Corporate Financial Reporting				
Statistics for	*Mean*	*Variance*	*Std. Dev*	*No of Variables*
Scale: Quality of Corporate Financial Reporting	5.08	4.851	2.202	11
	Scale mean if item deleted	Scale variance if item deleted	Corrected Item-Total Correlation	Cronbach's Alpha if Item Deleted
Net Profit	4.50	3.847	.386	.668
Net Worth and its Return	4.64	3.827	.394	.667
Employees Stock Option Scheme (Sweat Capital)	4.90	4.663	.022	.722
Market Capitalization	4.98	4.183	.464	.662
Contents	4.10	4.663	.274	.691
Value Added Statement	4.82	3.987	.377	.669
Corporate Social Responsibility	4.64	3.786	.417	.662
Consolidated Financial Statement	4.24	4.104	.406	.666
Human Resource Accounting	5.06	4.751	.128	.699
Segment Reporting	4.28	4.083	.370	.671
Risk Management Report	4.64	3.541	.561	.631
Reliability Coefficients for variables 11	$\alpha = .696$		Standardized Item Alpha = .688	

$$\alpha = (k/(k-1)) * [1 - \Sigma (S_i^2)/S_{sum}^2]$$

Internal reliability of sixteen variables was assessed using the Cronbach's Alpha technique. Variables such as monthly returns, timeliness, corporate governance and related party disclosures have zero variance and removed from the determinants of quality of corporate financial reporting scale. Now the reliability test considers only twelve variables. The scale produced an alpha of .623. Inspection of the table suggested that variable named Environmental Disclosures should be eliminated because of its low and negative correlation with the test as a whole and the indication that its removal would increase internal reliability. A repeat Cronbach's Alpha test minus variable named Environmental Disclosures then produced an alpha of .696, which is more acceptable for quality of corporate financial reporting scale.

Generalized Linear Models

Generalized Linear Models is a generalization of the general linear model. These Models specify the relationship between a dependent (or response) variable Y, and a set of predictor variables. These models can be fitted for binary outcomes, ordinal outcomes, and models for other distributions in the exponential family (e.g., Poisson, negative binomial, gamma). We are using Poisson Distribution for 10 financial years data from selected companies of India.

Using the above selected reliable variables, our Generalized Linear Model on the basis of Poisson distribution will be as follows:

$Y_i = \beta_0 + \beta_1$ *Net Profit* $+ \beta_2$ *Net Worth and its Return* $+ \beta_3$ *Issued Capital* $+ \beta_4$ *Market Capitalization* $+ \beta_5$ *Contents* $+ \beta_6$ *Value Added Statement* $+ \beta_7$ *Corporate Social Responsibility* $+ \beta_8$ *Consolidated Financial Statement* $+ \beta_9$ *Human Resource Accounting* $+ \beta_{10}$ *Segment Reporting* $+ \beta_{11}$ *Risk Management Report* $+ \varepsilon_1$.

Where ε_i represents the residual variable which quantifies the influence of other factors which can determine the quality of corporate financial reporting. This variable is normally distributed with zero mean ($N (0, \sigma 2)$). Using the registered values for the past variables will be estimated the Generalized Linear Model on the basis of Poisson distribution and will result the following model:

$Y_i = \beta_0 + \beta_1$ *Net Profit* $+ \beta_2$ *Net Worth and its Return* $+ \beta_3$ *Issued Capital*
$+ \beta_4$ *Market Capitaliza* $+ \beta_5$ *Contents*
$+ \beta_6$ *Value Added Statment* $+ \beta_7$ *Corporate Social Responsibility*
$+ \beta_8$ *Consolidated Financial Statement*
$+ \beta_9$ *Human Resource Accounting* $+ \beta_{10}$ *Segment Reporting*
$+ \beta_{11}$ *Risk Management Report*.

Variables	β		Std. Error	Estimated marginal mean		Wald Chi-Square	Sig.
	For code "0"	For code "1"		For code "0"	For code "1"		
Net Profit	−.106	.894	.0365	7.15	7.95	8.420	.004
Net Worth and its Return	−.158	.842	.0536	6.97	8.16	8.637	.003
Employees Stock Option Scheme (Sweat Capital)	−.127	.873	.0236	7.07	8.03	29.158	.000
Market Capitalization	−.014	.986	.0320	7.49	7.59	.183	.669
Contents	−.419	.581	.1057	6.11	9.30	15.735	.000
Value Added Statement	−.060	.94	.0337	7.32	7.77	3.198	.074
Corporate Social Responsibility	−.070	.93	.0546	7.28	7.81	1.629	.202
Consolidated Financial Statement	−.403	.597	.0510	6.16	9.22	62.474	.000
Human Resource Accounting	−.350	.650	.0809	6.33	8.98	18.709	.000
Segment Reporting	−.047	.953	.0475	7.36	7.47	.987	.321
Risk Management Report	−.090	.91	.0247	7.21	7.88	13.176	.000
Constant	2.942	2.942	.0848			949.86	.000
Likelihood Ratio Chi-Square = 944.458 (.000)							

Researchers specify the relationship between a dependent variable (quality of financial reporting) *Y*, and a set of predictor variables using Generalized Linear Models. Full log likelihood function is used in computing information and adjusted log likelihood is used in the model fitting omnibus test. Model shows the highly significant relationship at 944.458 (p < .005) between response variable *Y* and a set of predictor variables. The estimated marginal means for code "1" is more than code "0" in case of every predictor variable which shows the enhancement in quality of financial reporting over the years. Wald chi-square showing a very good association between quality of financial reporting and its predictor variables. But Market Capitalization, Corporate Social Responsibility and Segment Reporting are not highly associated with quality of financial reporting as p > .005. Now, the Generalized Linear Models:

(i) For code "0"

$Y_i = 2.942 + (−.106)$ *Net Profit* $+ (−.158)$ *Net Worth and its Return*

$+ (−.127)$ *Issued Capital* $+ (−.014)$ *Market Capitalization*

$+ (−.419)$ *Contents* $+ (−.060)$ *Value Added Statement*

$+ (−.070)$ *Corporate Social Responsibility*

$+ (−.403)$ *Consolidated Financial Statement*

$+ (−.350)$ *Human Resource Statement*

$+ (−.047)$ *Segment Reporting*

$+ (−.090)$ *Risk Management Report.*

(ii) For code "1"

$Y_i = 2.942 + .894$ *Net Profit* $+ .842$ *Net Worth and its Return*

$+ .873$ *Issued Capital* $+ .986$ *Market Capitalization*

$+ .581$ *Contents* $+ .94$ *Value Added Statement*

$+ .93$ *Corporate Social Responsibility*

$+ .597$ *Consolidated Financial Statement*

$+ .650$ *Human Resource Accounting* $+ .953$ *Segment Reporting*

$+ .91$ *Risk Management Report.*

CONCLUSION

To provide greater clarity and granularity on critical elements of the financial reporting, researchers have focused on some of the key areas such as net profit, net worth and its returns, employees stock option scheme (sweat capital), market capitalization, monthly returns, contents, timeliness, value added statement, corporate social responsibility, corporate governance, consolidated financial statement, human resource accounting, environmental disclosures, related party disclosures, segment reporting and risk management report that have an effect on the corporate financial reporting in a direct or indirect way.

From the entire analysis, researchers have concluded that all the variables are good indicators of corporate financial reporting except monthly returns, timeliness, corporate governance, related party disclosures and environmental disclosures. Finally the study is based on lingering eleven indicators which show instant relation with quality of corporate financial reporting. It was also noticed that drastic improvements have taken place in the quality of corporate financial reporting from the

FY 2005-06 in India because many of the companies have started to involve the new reporting aspects like value added statement, corporate social responsibility, human resource accounting etc in their annual reports. In present scenario, companies give an overall view of their business performance in accordance with their business objectives. It helps companies to well run on the basis of comprehensive and accurate information about all aspects of their operations and nothing to fear from providing forward-looking information. Even now they have an opportunity to secure significant competitive edge.

References

- Admin (2009, January 10). Elements and Components of a Complete Set of Financial Statements. Retrieved http://businessaccent.com

- Bhattacharyya Asish, K. Complexity in Corporate Financial Reporting. Business Standard,

- Beest, Ferdy Van, Braam, Geert & Boelens, Suzanne (2009). Quality Of Financial Reporting: Measuring Qualitative Characteristics. Nijmegen Center For Economics (Nice), Institute For Management Research, Radboud University Nijmegen, *Nice Working Paper 09-108,* Retrieved From Http://Www.Ru.Nl/Nice/Workingpapers

- Caramanolis-Çötelli, Birgül, Gardiol, Lucien, Gibson-Asner, Rajna & Tuchschmid, Nils S. (2000). Are Investors Sensitive to the Quality and the Disclosure of Financial Statements? *European Finance Review* 3, 131–159

- Chen, Feng, Hope, Ole-Kristian, Li, Qingyuan & Wang, Xin (2010). Financial Reporting Quality and Investment Efficiency of Private Firms in Emerging Markets.

- Corporate Reporting, Retrieved http://www.pwc.com/corporatereporting

- Frost, Carol Ann, Gordon, Elizabeth A. & Pownall, Grace (2005). Financial Reporting Quality, Disclosure And Emerging Market Companies' Access to Capital in Global Equity Markets, *Working Paper, School of Accountancy, Singapore Management University*

- Frost, Carol Ann, Gordon, Elizabeth A. & Pownall, Grace (2008). Financial Reporting and Disclosure Quality, and Emerging Market Companies' Access to Capital in Global Markets. *Working Paper Series,* Retrieved From http://ssrn.com/abstract=802824

- Joshi, P.L. & Abdulla, Dr. Jasim (1993). Accounting Standards and Corporate Financial Reporting In India. *Asian Review of Accounting,* 3(2), 105 – 124.

- Li, Feng & Shroff, Nemit O. (2009). Financial Reporting Quality and Economic Growth. Retrieved From http://www.isb.edu/accountingresearchconference/file/financialreporting.

- Mcdaniel, Linda; Martin, Roger D.; Maines, Laureen A. (2002). Evaluating Financial Reporting Quality: The Effects of Financial Expertise V/S. Financial Literacy. *Accounting Review*

- Miller, Paul B.W. (2002). Quality Financial Reporting. *Journal Of Accountancy*

- Oyelere, Peter B., Laswad, Fawzi & Fisher, Richard (2000). Corporate Financial Reporting: Firm Characteristics and the Use of the Internet as a Medium of Communication, *Lincoln University, Commerce Division, Discussion 81.*

- Retrieved http://business.rediff.com

- Retrieved http://www.nd.edu/~carecob/workshops/10-11workshops/hopepaper091010.pdf

- Salvary, Stanley C. W. (1998). Accounting and Financial Reporting In a Changing Environment: Historical and Theoretical Perspectives. *Essays In Economic And Business History,* XVI 1998:307-329

- *Statsoft Electronic Statistics Toolbox.* Retrieved www.corporatereporting.com

- Tang, Qingliang (2008). Financial Reporting Quality In Developed And Emerging Markets Tenth. *Annual International Conference On Accounting And Business 2008,* Shanghai, June 6-8

Direct Tax Code and its Effect

Sandeep Shrivastava[1], Saurabh Goyal[2] and Neeraj Dubey[3]
[1]Lecturer, Management Department, Aditya College, Gwalior
[2]Assistant Professor and Head, Department of Management Studies
Shri Ram Institute of Information Technology, Banmore, Near Gwalior
[3]Senior Lecturer, Department of Management Studies,
Shri Ram Institute of Information Technology, Banmore, Near Gwalior

ABSTRACT

Direct Tax Code Bill, 2009, was brought on 12th of August 2009 for making Indian taxation system easy. The Direct Tax Law is trying to make several changes in the country. This Direct Tax Code is expected to be implemented from the financial year 2012 onwards. This tax system as expected to make many important changes. Many individual or corporate persons think it will be definitely change the taxation system of India and will be beneficial to both corporate and individual. In my paper I am trying to analyze the expected impacts of DTC on both individual and corporate.

Keywords: *Tax Code, Accounting*

INTRODUCTION

Direct Tax Code bill, 2009, was announced on 12th August 2009 that sought to revamp and simplify the Direct Tax Law and its administration in the country through several radical changes. The Tax Code which the government had planned to enact and implement from the Financial Year 2012 onwards with suitable changes, if required, envisaged meaningful reduction in the tax rates while simultaneously being revenue neutral for the government. It has aimed to achieve this by increasing the tax base and rationalizing the tax incentives prevalent under the current law. It has sought to bring all Direct Taxes under one Code for providing a single Tax Reporting System. It has also been stated that the new Code is drafted by taking into account the internationally accepted principles of Public Finance and best practices to make it at par with the international practices and not merely to replace the existing Income Tax Act, 1961.

LITERATURE REVIEW

Direct Tax Code Bill 2012, Volume: DTX/18/2010 dated August 31, 2010 focus on Foreign Institution Investor. The Code is silent on the applicability of MAT to foreign companies. Based on judicial precedents, MAT should not be applicable to foreign companies having no presence in India and earning capital gains and income from other sources in India. Direct Taxes Code Bill – Highlights K. Ravi, BA, LLB, FCA, Chairman, Central Taxes Committee, FKCCI, commented Tax on interest on overseas borrowing is a negative factor and it may discourage Leveraging and reduce investment. MAT at 2% of gross assets is a very high rate. The issue of MAT on financial companies has also come under criticism because While MAT in the code for the Banking sector is set at 0.25% it is at 2% for the NBFCs (Non-Banking Finance Companies).

An article on www.business-standard.com says The Direct Taxes Code (DTC) Bill that was introduced in Parliament today proposes some relief to individuals and companies. But a closer read suggests that women taxpayers, developers of special economic zones and units in these areas, as well as those investing in unit-linked insurance plans, are in for harder times.

Direct Tax Code Bill 2010 – Impact on Infrastructure sector by KPMG in India says Introduction of GAAR and CFC signals a tough tax regime for the corporate sector. All in all, DTC seems to be a mixed bag of goodies.

World Vision India on direct tax code which was published on October 22, 2009 says that if this proposed tax comes into existence, Non Profit Organisations will face a number of hurdles that will invariably affect development work - Organisations will be pushed into spending grants or other designated funds received for multi-year projects.

Debmitra (2009) says in paper on direct tax code an impact on individual and corporate says, that this new code may be told that there exists a both good and bad thing. The most benefit for the individual tax payers is that the tax slab is just 10% for the income group (income ranging between ₹1,60,000 to ₹10,00,000). This will be certainly beneficial to the middle class section of the population because the tax which will be charged is just 10%.

The Wikipedia.com has also elaborated the following view about direct tax like DTC removes most of the categories of exempted income. Equity Mutual Funds (ELSS), Term Deposits, NSC (National Savings certificates), Unit Linked Insurance Plans (ULIPs), Long term infrastructures bonds, house loan principal repayment, stamp duty and registration fees on purchase of house property will lose tax benefits.

- Only half of Short-term capital gains will be taxed.
- Surcharge and Education Cess are abolished.
- For incomes arising of House Property: Deductions for Rent and Maintenance would be reduced from 30% to 20% of the Gross Rent. Also all interest paid on house loan for a rented house is deductible from rent.

In summary, the provisions of the DTC are expected to provide fillip to the growth of the Indian infrastructure sector which is very crucial for the overall growth of Indian economy.

In this paper we are trying to show the expected effect of DTC on individual and corporate. We can analyze this thing by following points.

1. The maximum limit of investment under section 80C is proposed to be enhanced and also the effective tax rates have been proposed to be reduced. The DTC has proposed to enhance the limit of investment eligible for deduction under section 80C from ₹1,00,000 to ₹3,00,000.

2. DTC has also proposed a significant increase in the tax slabs for personal income tax. In this paper an attempt has been made to analyze the provisions of the DTC with respect to salaried persons, retired people, and investors separately.

In this exercise, it is necessary to compare the relevant provisions of the Income Tax Act, 1961, with those of the DTC to bring out the consequences of the new provisions.

3. In present, the income up to ₹1,60,000 is the basic income level which is not taxable for all individuals and Hindu Undivided Families who are not resident women and senior citizens. As far as the resident women are concerned, the basic exemption level is ₹1,90,000 and for the senor citizens it is ₹2,40,000. The DTC retains the same level of basic exemption for those categories of tax payers but the tax slabs for all of them have been raised as follows

Total Income	Tax Rate (%)
Up to ₹1,60,000*	Nil
₹1,60,000 to ₹10,00,000	10
₹10,00,000 to ₹25,00,000	20
Above ₹25,00,000	30

Source: Direct Taxes Code Bill, 2009

Note: * ₹1,90,000 for woman and ₹2,40,000 for senior citizen

Even though it may be the fact that every one may be happy with the above reduction of the tax rates, it is also quite evident that the tax rates as suggested by the DTC will help saving in taxes only for the higher income group and not for lower and middle income groups. The very cannons of taxation will, thus, not be adhered to a very large extent. One of the vital objectives of imposing direct taxes is to bring equality and that very objective may be defeated after the implementation of the DTC. The persons with income ranging from ₹5,00,000 to ₹10,00,000 can avoid more than 50% of its present tax burden while persons with income of less than ₹3,00,000 will be practically able to save nothing due to the proposed tax rates. Moreover, they will be facing increased burden of taxes because of the proposed withdrawal of many deductions allowed to them from salary income like perquisites, leave travel concessions, medical reimbursements, etc. So, it can be observed in general that the tax rates proposed by the DTC will favour the rich more than the low and middle income groups.

4. The DTC has proposed imposition of tax on the maturing value of life insurance policies, Public Provident Fund (PPF) and General Provident Fund (GPF). It has proposed to impose tax on

savings in various instruments, including those mentioned above, which at present do not attract any sort of tax. Certainly, this will affect the savings mentality of the middle class people. The tax incentives on interest paid on home loans have also been proposed to be withdrawn as a result of which a larger section of middle and lower middle people is expected to be de-motivated in taking the house building loan. Moreover, it has been specifically suggested that gratuity will also come under the purview of taxation, if the amount is not invested in a specified scheme. And, this specified scheme may have same linkage with the stock market as a result of which the retrial benefits received by an employee after a prolonged service may be jeopardized to a very great extent.

5. Introduction of long term capital gains tax and abolition of the Securities Transaction Tax have been proposed by the DTC. It has proposed to do away with the distinction between long-term and short-term capital gains. It can be stated here that the Indian middle class people, in recent times, have become interested to invest a part of their savings in the stock market and this has helped to some extent to boost up the Indian capital market in general. The proposal of imposing tax on long-term capital gain will discourage the Indian investors in general and middle class people in particular to participate in the Indian capital market. However, the proposal to abolish the Securities Transaction Tax (STT) may help to attract the Indian investors to some extent.

6. The DTC has proposed to include all types perquisites, e.g., interest free loan, free lunch, etc., while computing the total income and those will be taxed accordingly.

ANALYSIS OF IMPACT OF DIRECT TAX CODE

1. The DTC has proposed to reduce the corporate tax rate from 33% (including surcharge) to 25%. This will benefit companies in all sectors but it will benefit specially the FMCG sector and the Banking sector where the effective tax rate is around 33%. This reduction in tax rate will lower the generation of government revenue as a result of which it will become difficult for the government to initiate and/ or continue effectively many developmental programs for the benefit of the common people.

The DTC has proposed to provide for some investment-based activities. In respect of revenue and capital expenditure on scientific research and development, deduction to the extent of 150% of the expenditure has been proposed to be allowed to all companies. It has proposed that tax liability will accrue in various specified infrastructure sectors only after 100% of the capital expenditure is recovered, allowing these companies to postpone the tax liability. The sectors to be covered are generation, transmission and distribution of power, specified infrastructure projects, food processing, packaging, cold storage, agricultural warehouse, Oil and Gas, SEZ, etc. This proposal will, no doubt, help promote the growth of basic infrastructural facilities in India regarding which India is still far behind the developed countries. But constant vigil should be there to ensure that no company is taking the advantage of abovementioned tax benefit by fraudulent manipulation.

(a) The DTC has proposed a drastic change in the provisions of Minimum Alternate Tax (MAT). Under the DTC, MAT will be paid at a specified percentage of gross assets of a company, which broadly equates to capital employed, though it is not clear whether net or gross current assets will be considered for the purpose of computation. The specified percentage is 0.25% for banking companies and 2% for all other companies. Though it is intended to widen the tax base by reducing tax evasion, the proposal of a new MAT appears onerous on several counts mentioned below.

(i) Companies suffering from genuine losses due to initial gestation period or cyclical down turn would also have to pay MAT @ 2% of its gross assets. This may be highly detrimental to the very survival of the company itself.

(ii) Moreover, the credit of MAT will not be available, making the provisions more onerous.

CONCLUSIONS

It may be observed that there exist both good and bad things in the DTC. The biggest advantage for the individual tax payers is that the tax slab is just 10% for the income group (income ranging between ₹1,60,000 to ₹10,00,000). This will be certainly beneficial to the middle class section of the population because the tax which will be charged is just 10%. The taxable salary will go up because of some changes but real tax liability will actually reduce. Though, at the last, it may not get reduced too much but surely it will be a reason to cheer.

But it is obvious that the tax rates as proposed by the DTC will help in tax savings only for higher income group and not for lower middle income group. It actually defeats all the cannons of taxation which always advocate that the main aim of direct taxation is to reduce the economic disparity in the society. With this new rate of taxation, the individuals, with income ranging from ₹5,00,000 to ₹10,00,000, will be able to save more than 50% of their present tax burden, while the persons, with income of less than ₹3,00,000 will be able to save nothing due to the proposed tax rates. Not only this, this section of people will be facing increased burden of taxes because of withdrawal of many deductions allowed to them from salary income like perquisites, leave travel concessions, medical reimbursements, etc. Even persons with income upto ₹50,00,000 can save nearly 20% on taxes. So, it can be observed that the tax rates and the other provisions proposed in the DTC are more in favour of the rich people than the people who belong to middle and lower income groups. According to the paper writer, the basic exemption should, at least, be raised to ₹3,00,000 which is the present ceiling for the 10% slab. If it is accepted and incorporated accordingly in the DTC, everyone will be benefitted. Further this basic exemption should be linked to the cost of living index. So, it can be increased every year based on inflation levels. Most of the time, the increase in salary is linked to inflation and it is also essential that such increase should be protected from the tax burden. Here, the paper writer does not deny the fact that the rich are getting more benefits from tax savings but it has to be ensured that the low and middle income groups are also benefited by the DTC.

First, the tax rate for companies (both domestic and foreign) has been proposed to be reduced to 25% from its existing rate 33%. So, for the industries, which fall in the full tax bracket (33% tax), the proposal of reducing tax rate is positive. But this drastic reduction is likely to bring adverse effect on the government exchequer as a result of which the pro-people activities of the government may be substantially affected. Under the DTC, the basis of computing MAT has been changed from "book profits" to "gross assets". MAT will be charged at 2% of gross assets and that will be the final tax and will not be available as tax credit in the subsequent years. Discontinuance of the provision to carry forward MAT is a negative proposal for the companies availing MAT. Under the DTC, rates of depreciation on plant and machinery is proposed to be reduced to 15% which may result in some sort of negative impact for those companies availing of the benefits of high rates of depreciation. In the DTC, there is a proposal to eliminate export-based incentive available under section 10 of the present Act, which may have negative impact on those companies engaged in export activities.

Based this discussion, it may be concluded that the proposed "Direct Tax Code Bill" will bring certain definite advantages and disadvantages for both individual and corporate tax payers. The provisions of DTC must be thoroughly debated throughout the country so that, before giving final shape to it, the loopholes should be minimized. And, if that is done, it will be best for everybody.

References

- Dr Mitra Direct Taxes Code : "Its probable effect on Individuals & Corporate.
- "Shetty, S.L. (2010), Mare Tax Concessions for More Inequality, *Economic & Political Weekly*, 2010 XLV (11), March 13.
- Retrieved from http://www.saraltaxoffice.com/articles/direct-tax-code-highlights.php
- Retrieved from http://www.saraltaxoffice.com/articles/direct-tax-code-highlights.php
- Retrieved from http://www.want2rich.com/2011/07/personal-finance/direct-tax-code-and-its-implications-on-investments/
- Retrieved from http://www.kpmg.com/IN/en/WhatWeDo/Tax/Documents/KPMG_Flash_News_DTC_impact_Infrastructure_sector.pdf
- Rao, M., Rao, G. and Rao, K. R. (2009), Direct Taxes Code: Need for Greater Reflection, *Economic & Political Weekly*, XLIV(37), September

Encouraging and Funding Entrepreneurship: A Pragmatic Strategy for Banks to Counter Recession

S.N. Ghosal

Retd. Banker and faculty member of reputed Management Institute, Kolkata

ABSTRACT

The present financial turmoil has shaken the confidence of both depositors and lenders all over the world. In fact lenders are more disturbed as all of a sudden they found that their most sophisticated instruments like derivatives that were yielding huge profit in the recent past now proving highly risky and almost leading them to bankruptcy. This fatal blow has shaken their confidence and despite induction of capital by the state and regulators to restore confidence and help them to come out from the turmoil almost unscathed; it is surprising to find them still groping in dark to come out of the tunnel which unfortunately self created by them out of sheer greed. An attempt has therefore been made in this paper to conceive a strategy that would help these institutions to come out of this grove and once again become vibrant and healthy institution to restore confidence of people and the market.

It is obvious that under economic recession almost all business barons and institutions adopt caution and wait and see policy initiatives of government and regulatory authorities; and banks are no exception to it. It is therefore not surprising that despite constant cajoling and even offering lollypops to banks by central banks and governments of both developing and developed countries of the world, banks are in general avoiding lending and lowering lending rates. In fact most of them including state owned banks could not be persuaded or even cajoled to liberalize interest rate and credit disbursement to big and medium sized corporate and in fact most of them rather preferred to hold their liquid assets in cash even at a cost instead of opening their doors to borrowers both corporate and individuals. This phenomenon is not happening only in INDIA but could be seen globally. In fact the present global recession has shaken the confidence of all financial institutions and despite heavy doses of bailout offered by central banks and governments of countries, all over the world; these institutions are yet to restore their confidence to lend money in a big way and hence the story of depression and gloom still prevails in the financial markets all over the world.

Keywords: *Entrepreneurship, Recession*

PAY DUE ATTENTION TO SIGNALS FROM PASSIVE PART OF BRAIN

It is however interesting to note that all these is happening as because we are foxed and overawed with the present financial tsunami and looking around with our eyes only and listening also only through our ears and ignoring signals from brains. In fact we are doing nothing today to change our thought process to break the traditional beliefs attitudes and even patterns of thinking to break away from the grooves and allow our brains to change dramatically our perception and thinking which would create creativity and capacity to change and come out from the present depressing mindset and environment. In fact it has been proved that our brains are structured to enhance our intelligence, creativity and also to implement the same in real life. This change of mindset and taking important but highly risky decision is made by our brain by a process known as reticular activating trend (RAT). It is therefore a story of RAT that executives of banks have to listen to so that they may come out with innovative strategies and services that would help them to come out successfully from the present financial recession unscathed.

DEVELOP CONVICTION AND CLARITY IN GOAL SETTING

It is not just motivation as it is fleeting. It is conviction and clarity of goal setting by the executives of banks that would help them achieve what may otherwise appear to be impossible to achieve. In fact there is an irresistible force within us that helps us to achieve what otherwise appears to be unachievable. In this regard it is worth quoting JOHN ASSARAF and MURRAY SMITH who in their recent book THE ANSWER has rightly said " the UNITED STATES today is buried under a staggering mountain of debt—trillions of dollars' worth. How this country ever is able to get out from under? There is one and only one way that will ever happen: through the efforts of creative and passionate people building the business of their dreams."

PAY DUE ATTENTION TO ECOLOGY AND ENVIRONMENT

Further it has been rightly observed in the above study that 'the planet's ecology is also facing some serious threats right now. How will we ever be able to solve our worldwide energy needs without ruining the planet in the process? There is one only one way: through the ingenuity and passion of entrepreneurs. This is exactly what is happening. China has shown the way by developing most economic energy source from sunshine. India is also going ahead in developing energy source from wind as well as sunshine. These all are evidences that if like to change and rewrite the strategy for the good of institution and society they can do it. It has been rightly observed that in 21st century it is the 'individual man and woman passionately in pursuit of their business dreams will have a positive, transformative impact on everyone's lives.

SUBJECT VISION TO FIVE TESTS

In fact creating a clear business vision would be the first critical strategy to transform and overcome recession. It is easier said than done. The key to this could be to subject your vision to following five tests:

1. Does it stir your soul?
2. Could you excel in performing the same?
3. Could you recondition your mind to think that it is achievable?
4. Could you perceive that it would generate money?
5. Could you regularly act on it without any immediate gain?

ACTIVATE INACTIVE BRAIN

It is therefore obvious that to create and adopt a new vision is not very simple and easy task. It requires activation of that part of brain which all of us think lying inactive. However it is interesting to note that this part of the brain when activated leads to many innovations. For example, THOMAS EDISON would deliberately put himself to sleep to solve some of the intractable problems that he encountered from time to time while working for his invention. This elaboration itself indicates the power of supposedly idle brains and its power of creating infinite possibility that could be available to every individual when the same is put to use. Furthermore this has happened with many other inventors in the past.

STRATEGY OF RETAIL BANKING DURING ASIAN CRISIS

One wonders why this could not be put into practice by bank executives to encounter the challenge of recession. In fact during Asian crisis when banks were facing similar challenges some of them rose to the occasion and completely changed their strategy from corporate banking to retail banking. One of the illustrious and a successful example was the initiative taken by Siamese Bank in Bangkok. In fact this bank totally changed the culture by bringing some non banker (retail head of UNILEVER at Bangkok) to transform and adopt the culture of retail banking.

DEVELOPING AND FUNDING ENTREPRENEURS

In today's' scenario it would be helpful if banks could once again change their strategy from retail banking to entrepreneurial development banking to sustain the economic growth through innovations; and sharing initial risks like venture capital institutions, of new enterprises developed in rural, semi-urban as well as in urban areas by unemployed youths. It is true that Indians are in general risk averse and look for employment opportunities rather than engaging in business and industry. However in recent years some change is visible particularly in urban and metropolitan areas. It may also be mentioned that some sections of Indian people have earned name and fame globally as entrepreneur of small retail business houses particularly in provisions, clothes, and gold and silver ornaments businesses. It is interesting to note that such entrepreneurs could be traced in most of the counties of the world as since time immemorial these people have migrated from India to set up their trading businesses in various parts of the world. It would be further interesting to note that most of these people migrated from their villages and towns and stayed over there for generation. In fact even in agriculture like sugarcane etc Indian farmers have enriched many backward countries through their entrepreneurial skill. However it is equally true that India lagged in Schumpeterian model of entrepreneurship for quite some time and of late only this could be seen emerging in metropolitan and also in some developed parts of urban areas.

GLUED TO FARMING

Most of the Indian villagers remained glued to farming only partly because the traditional farming was seasonal and provide enough time to laze away. It also needed no formal education. Moreover but for monsoon failure, the risk in farming was almost negligible and hence remained attractive for generations. However with the emergence of risks beside monsoon viz. seeds, attack of pesticide and volatility of prices of agricultural products farmers over the years developed a mindset of fatalist and cursed their fates for any calamities and sought doles, waiver and charity from governments and charitable institutions. It would not be wrong to say that successive governments and politicians even after independence followed a policy to keep farmers and artisans under their thumbs by making them dependent on their doles, grants and subsidies etc. as that helped them to build their vote banks. However it would be wrong to assume that villagers could not be transformed as entrepreneurs as they have been found developing many innovations even with primitive traditional knowledge for survival. It would be possible to develop an appropriate entrepreneurship model if rural youths are empowered with marketable skills.

FORTUNE AT THE BOTTOM OF PYRAMID

Dr. K. Prahlad of Wharton in his famous book 'The Fortune at the bottom of Pyramid' has brought out how poor people in rural India could become employable by adopting new growth models suitable for generation of new employment opportunities and economic growth.

In this regard he stressed that the role of multinational companies has to be re-defined. He emphasized that the present trend of MNCs to cater for mature markets need to be changed and to extend the same even to poorly developed markets in villages and semi-urban areas by introducing some strategic changes like packaging and pricing. It would not be difficult as the recently developed supply chain management techniques empowers industries to reach easily and in cost-effective way to the remotest area of any place. Some initiative of this nature has already been taken by some consumer goods industries and no doubt these efforts have helped these industries to capture more space and also have helped villagers not only to earn and spend but also to produce and consume these along with people residing in urban and metropolitan towns. However these efforts have led to growth of market for MNCs but have not helped villagers to develop their latent potentiality of becoming full fledged entrepreneur as manufacturer of goods. It is true some of the villagers could develop some supply chain management and retail business in the process.

NEED CHANGE IN MINDSET IN FRAMING POLICY

It appears there is need for some paradigm change in our policy thinking as well as our mindset particularly of our politicians. In this regard our ex- President Kalam's vision of providing urban facilities in rural areas (PURA) is worth mentioning as this is possibly one such step that would help transforming agri-business potential through knowledge, institution and technology platform. It would therefore need to be multiplied to help spreading knowledge and technology to rural youth. It has to be borne in mind that technological innovations could also emerge in the laboratories of life as rightly pointed out by Dr. Mashelkar. Accordingly this has to be stressed in all efforts to rejuvenate rural youth and transform them as entrepreneurs.

FOCUS ON DISPARITY IN INVESTMENT IN RURAL AREAS

In fact investments made in rural areas though undertaken extensively and at times even massive amounts have been earmarked for various rural projects but all these generally have proven ineffective as most of these are in the form of subsidies, doles and waiver of loans instead of investment in infrastructure development in rural areas. These also failed to generate effective delivery institutions and virtually generated highly corrupt institutions manned and fanned by politicians and rural elites. In fact the highly noticeable disparity in between rural and urban infrastructure like roads, transports, power and communication have created the hiatus in economic growth of rural and urban areas. Lack of infrastructure in rural areas have made private sector also hesitant to develop industries over there. It is true the scene is changing and some new industries are growing in villages or its outskirts. But essentially villages have remained agrarian with low and disguised unemployment. It is therefore high time for policy makers not to introduce employment opportunity plan like ROJGAR YOJNA (NREG) where unemployed rural youths are either given work of mud lifting or paid even when no work could be allotted to them. This would obviously make them lazy and some of them even come out to refuse digging mud and to carry the same for dumping at some allotted place. It is difficult to fathom out the type of mindset of politicians who actively advertise such projects and feel complacent and happy as if they have been doing great work for poor villagers. In fact it would not be wrong to state that 'the program seemed well designed for bureaucrats and politicians to siphon off money'.

NEED TO CHANGE MINDSET OF POLICY MAKERS AND BANKERS

However if something has to be done for rural poor it would be necessary to change the mindset of policy makers and bureaucrats. In fact rural areas should not be considered as agricultural belts and rural youth should not be taken for granted as farmers and artisans only. In fact rural youth like all other youth should be considered as human resource and could be shaped like all other youths as entrepreneurs, innovators, professionals and managers. In fact many rural youth after getting some education have migrated to urban areas and have developed many new business and even industries. It is therefore natural question that would arise in the mind of any rational man what for these migrations should continue and why not such thing could not be done in rural areas. The answer is not very far to seek. It is the lack of infrastructure that has led to such migration of youth. It would therefore be necessary for government, enlightened institutions including banks and individuals to come forward with projects both for modernizing agriculture and other sectors including service and manufacturing to provide opportunities to rural youths to work in these village projects and enterprises.

MODEL RECOMMENDED

In this regard it is worthwhile to keep in mind that there would be some lag in developing village entrepreneurs as there would be dearth of capital to develop village projects and enterprises but this could be dealt with by developing institutional entrepreneurship as is done to meet the capital needs of urban entrepreneurs by creating development banks. However in this strategy also there could be some difficulty as overall supply of individual entrepreneurs and mangers with necessary education and aptitude might not be readily available. It would therefore be imperative that institutions under public private partnership model should be developed by banks to fund and organize ventures to provide services and to manufacture product. Such organisations should conceive projects for compact lands for farming and for clusters of artisans for manufacturing, trade and commerce. States in developing countries have assumed the role entrepreneurs. In some of the developing countries including India some efforts have been made to institutionalize development activities even in rural areas but these have not been specifically assigned the much needed role to act as catalyst for growth of individual entrepreneurs. In fact villagers could have been as good as city dwellers but for lack of infrastructure including education. It would therefore be necessary to hold the hands of villagers for some period and enable them to grow as entrepreneurs and managers without getting the shocks of market and monsoon or such other natural risks for some time as these have created fear psychosis in villagers for generations and obviously they need some time to get over such psychology and become an entrepreneur rather than remain as fatalist and dependent on doles alms and such other charities.

APPLICATION OF RECOMMENDED MODEL

In recent years some efforts have been made to hold hands of farmers and artisans by some micro financing institutions particularly in south. Pragati Bandhus in Karnataka is one such model as these groups of marginal farmers named as Pragati Bandhus not only provided hassle free loans to farmers but also physically stayed with them to help them to prepare crop planning along with marketing and technology support. This obviously a better model than usual pattern followed by micro financing institutions to act as lender to farmers, however to achieve real success it is imperative that these institutions should shoulder the risk of farms and firms in rural areas run by rural farmers and artisans. The ultimate need is to enable them to get enough confidence and managerial and financial strength to become entrepreneurs on their own. Only with such transformation of rural people particularly youth who outnumber others could make India a developed country and decouple her from the present global meltdown.

CONCLUSION

Banks in India should take this cue and adopt a strategy to not only funding entrepreneurs but also to groom unemployed youth to become entrepreneurs and employable. It is true most of rural youth prefer to go and work in cities as they find life in rural areas not conducive for growth as these places lack most of the essential infrastructure like roads, electricity etc. it would be an opportunity for banks and government to join hands with local youth in villages to build up institutions to create necessary infrastructure and groom and fund them to run any enterprise that could be developed over there. In recent years some banks have developed rural agriculture institutes but the need is to develop rural polytechnic schools and groom rural youth to become entrepreneurs either on their own or joining hands with others including banks and government. However special care should be taken to keep them away from political and bureaucrats.

A LIVE CASE STUDY OF CANADA-A SUCCESS STORY*

*(adapted from www.tbs-sct.gc.c; www.rural.gc.c; www.google.co)

Business Development and Entrepreneurs

Small businesses are the source of nearly 80 per cent of new jobs in Western Canada. These are the employment engine of the region. In recognition of the importance of community-based delivery of services and support to Small- and Medium-sized Enterprises (SME) development, western economic development (WD) program provided funding to third-party organisations including industry associations and those making up the Western Canada Business Service Network (WCBSN), which in turn deliver business services and support to entrepreneurs. This has obviously led to improved access to business information, training, business advisory services and capital for all western Canadians, including women and francophone entrepreneurs, and people located in rural communities.

Improve Business Productivity

It provided operating and loan funding to a number of other organisations that in turn delivered targeted loan programs, business advisory services and training for entrepreneurs. It improved business productivity by addressing the needs of SMEs and entrepreneurs through a number of service delivery mechanisms and partnerships including more than 100 offices. It engaged Community volunteers, who knew local issues and could identify business opportunities, mainly helped in achieving success in grooming entrepreneurs and their business enterprises in 2005-2006; this organisation was stabilized through new, multi-year agreements providing operating support for member

Community Futures Development Corporations (CFDCs)

Furthermore CFDCs were floated as a national community economic development program implementation organisation that would help people in rural communities respond to local needs. It has provided operating funding to the CFDCs since 1995 to enable them to provide local strategic economic planning services, business counseling and loans to small businesses in rural communities.

Women's Enterprise Initiatives (WEIs)

WEIs work to provide customized services to help women entrepreneurs face challenges and succeed. Operating from head offices located in Kelowna, Calgary, Saskatoon and Winnipeg, the WEIs improve access to financing, education and training, business advice, loan aftercare, information, networking and mentoring for women entrepreneurs.

Francophone Economic Development Organisations (FEDOs)

FEDOs enhance the vitality of Official Language Minority Communities (OLMCs) in Western Canada and strengthen economic opportunities for francophone business. With head offices in Winnipeg, Regina, Edmonton and Vancouver, FEDOs provide enhanced services to francophone entrepreneurs, including training, business and community economic development, access to capital, information services, marketing advice, and networking.

Canada Business Services Centers (CBSCs)

The CBSCs provide a single, seamless gateway to information for businesses and maintain an extensive database of business and trade information from federal, provincial, municipal and non-government sources. Western Canada CBSCs are located in Vancouver, Edmonton, Saskatoon and Winnipeg and services are also available through a network of regional CBSC and Aboriginal service sites.

In addition to support through the WCBSN, WD has undertaken a number of initiatives to encourage SMEs and R&D organisations to be innovative in improving their productivity and competitiveness. These include lean manufacturing practices (identification of new trends, the development of innovative strategies and the implementation of new processes), technology and management training and academic and industry internships and exchanges.

Sub-Activity: Access to Capital

A 2004 Statistics Canada Survey on Financing of Small- and Medium-sized Enterprises found that 20 per cent of SMEs cited obtaining financing as an obstacle to business growth. Those more likely to experience difficulties in obtaining financing included innovative businesses (40 per cent), young enterprises - defined as those that started operation in 2002 (34 per cent), exporters (29 per cent) and manufacturers (27 per cent).

Through work with financial institutions, members of the WCBSN and other organisations, WD has contributed to increased investment in targeted western Canadian firms. In particular, WD has responded with the development of two types of SME loan programs;

Evaluation

1. **WD Loan and Investment Program (previously the Loan Investment Fund Program)** at: http://www.wd.gc.ca/rpts/audit/lifp/ic-eng.asp.-source

   The evaluation found that:

   Only 16 per cent of Loan and Investment Program loan clients could have obtained financing from other sources;

   82 per cent of the small business financing experts surveyed indicated that there are gaps in loan financing available to small-and medium-sized enterprises; and 64 per cent indicated that the Government of Canada should influence private sector financial institutions to do lending to eliminate the gaps; and

   The Loan and Investment Program does not significantly duplicate other loan programs and services.

   Loan loss agreements have been negotiated to leverage additional loan capital from credit

unions for rural business lending by CFDCs in British Columbia. The urban micro-loan, Advice and Business Loans to Entrepreneurs with Disabilities loan (ABLED) and francophone (FEDO) agreements provide loans averaging $14,000 to very small and start-up businesses...

2. **Developmental loans delivered by the Western Canada Business Service Network and Entrepreneurs with Disabilities Program (EDP) urban delivery agents**

   WD has provided WCBSN network members with funds to support repayable loans to SMEs in rural areas, and SMEs operated by women, francophone, young entrepreneurs or those with disabilities. WD's network members also provide SMEs with path finding services and referrals to alternative sources of financing.

Results for 2005-2006

An evaluation of the Entrepreneurs with Disabilities Program (EDP) and the Urban Entrepreneurs with Disabilities Initiative Fund (UEDI) undertaken in 2005 is available on WD's website at: http://www.wd.gc.ca/rpts/audit/edp-uedi/default-eng.asp. In the evaluation, Ference Weiker & Company estimated that "the average EDP and UEDI loan client generates 260,000 in revenues and 6 person years of employment over the first five-year period after they receive assistance that is attributable to the assistance that they received."

In 2005-2006, total external financing leveraged by FEDOs was estimated at $2.3 million. The results for CFDCs in rural areas and WEIs serving women entrepreneurs are summarized below:

CFDC/WEI Results for 2005-2006

Total statistics above include: 68 loans to entrepreneurs with disabilities, totaling $1.4 million and projected to create or maintain 156 jobs; 113 loans to youth, totaling $2.3 million; and, 236 loans to Aboriginal clients, totaling $7.18 million.

Program Activity: Innovation

A innovation process that translates knowledge into new products and services is an important driver of long-term economic competitiveness and prosperity. WD investments in innovation are an important building block for creating a diversified economy in Western Canada. These investments support the emergence and growth of technology clusters in key sectors - such as environmental technologies, life sciences, information and communications technology (ICT) and value added resources and contribute to the development and commercialization of new technologies and technology based services and products in Western Canada.

According to the cluster life-cycle model, most of the western technology clusters are in their earliest formative stages. Recognizing this, the majority of WD investments have been made in knowledge infrastructure and technology adoption and commercialization, which help set the foundation for clusters and future growth. As the clusters mature, investments will address gaps and opportunities and will be connected to markets and collaborative research opportunities with the United States through the ERI.

By strengthening the innovation system and enhancing technology clusters, resources such as highly qualified personnel (HQP), large anchor companies, venture capital, investments in R&D and knowledge infrastructure are drawn to and developed in the region. Firms in clusters are often active in export markets and international supply chains, and contribute to economic growth and diversification by reinvesting in new R&D activities and creating or retaining highly skilled jobs.

In 2005-2006, WD approved almost $52.7 million to support the growth and development of technology clusters and the innovation system as a whole. The following graph illustrates this distribution:

WD Innovation Approvals by Sector
Total $52.7 M

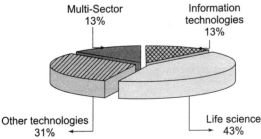

Multi-Sector 13%
Information technologies 13%
Other technologies 31%
Life science 43%

Source: Info Quest Database, May 26, 2006

WD works with many partners when developing and funding innovation projects. On average, the department contributes 33 per cent of the costs of an innovation project. For innovation projects approved in 2005-2006, WD support will leverage funding of $146.4 million from other sources.

WD Innovation Approvals By Activity 2005-2206
Total $52.7 M

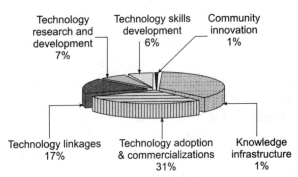

Technology research and development 7%
Technology skills development 6%
Community innovation 1%
Technology linkages 17%
Technology adoption & commercializations 31%
Knowledge infrastructure 1%

Source: Info Quest Database, May 26, 2006

Sub-Activity: Technology Adoption and Commercialization Technology commercialization ultimately occurs in industry. WD supports all phases along the technology commercialization continuum from support to organisations such as university technology transfer offices that identify, protect and license technologies to support that encourages technology adoption and adaptation.

Increasing investment and support for the commercialization of new technologies in Western Canada is a priority for WD. The department's work in this area has led to broad results including an increase in the number of technologies developed in research institutions that have commercialization potential, as demonstrated by intellectual property (IP) protection, licensed to an external user, or form the basis for a new company. The ultimate goal is to bring new products and services to the marketplace. In addition, WD's efforts have led to increased technologies adopted by existing firms.

Sub-Activity: Technology Linkages Through its work in innovation, WD has increased connections and synergies among innovation system members through new partnerships/networks, collaboration, and conferences to exchange information and increase awareness.

Sub-Activity: Technology Research and Development To support technology R&D, WD has invested in applied R&D leading to a new product or process that will have a near or mid-term commercial potential. This has resulted not only in applied R&D leading to technologies with commercialization potential, but also support for the operating or increased capacity of R&D canters and increased availability of skilled personnel.

Sub-Activity: Community Innovation Innovation at the community level can identify new opportunities and enhance the viability of traditional sectors. WD's support for community innovation in 2005-2006 resulted in planning studies used by communities as a tool for economic development, increased capacity in communities based on the generation of new knowledge, and community businesses adopting new technologies.

Sub-Activity: Technology Skills Development Under this sub-activity, WD supports projects that increase training, education and skill building in the new economy sectors. WD has contributed to several initiatives that increase the number of qualified individuals in the field and build linkages with industry.

Sub-Activity: Knowledge Infrastructure Investments in knowledge Infrastructure provides the foundation for technology clusters. WD's investments in this area have resulted in increased physical assets for R&D and/or training and new investments to the field.

CONCLUSION

It is obvious therefore that the present lag in entrepreneurial development in rural areas in India could be overcome if institutional entrepreneurs under public private partnerships are formed. This would not only help in risk minimizing but also in risk sharing and that would help risk averse rural youth to undertake business and farming with more gusto and less fear. It would make them also real entrepreneurs after they start tasting success in their enterprises jointly managed with state partnership. In the process they would also be groomed as better managers under the enlightened and better educated executives drawn and recruited by the state.

References

- The Answer by John Assaraf and Murray Smith.
- Entrepreneurship: Playing to Win by Baty, Gordon B.
- Entrepreneurship and Venture Management by Baumbach, Clifford M, Mancuso, Joseph R.

Mobile Banking an Innovative Marketing Strategy for Inclusive Growth

S.N. Ghosal

Retd. Banker and faculty member of reputed Management Institute, Kolkata

ABSTRACT

Inclusive growth has become prima-Dona of all public institutions including banks. In fact it has now largely proven fact that bottom of the pyramid provides permanent sustainability to all financial institutions and banks are no exception. Since banks are intermediary to outreach resource to rich and poor it has become imperative to develop a suitable model to outreach poor as rich are generally focused by banks for obvious reasons. In fact not only there is growth of rural economy but there is also growth of technology both to outreach and asseses poor and uplift the bottom of pyramid.

Keywords: *Mobile Banking, Marketing Strategies*

INTRODUCTION

There is no doubt that the most popular mandate in developing countries is to outreach poor by creating employment opportunities and providing financial support to the poor through state interventions. Obviously such intermediation often fail to reach the poor as these intermediaries floated by the state are loaded with bureaucrats and politicians who are more prone to exploit the poor and ignorant rather than to outreach the bottom of the pyramid and or to hold their hands in running their farms or firms and to provide succor to overcome calamities they often encounter. Indeed it is widely held view that rural micro- entrepreneurs are not capable to organize themselves to conceive, run and bear risk of any sustainable economic enterprises and therefore they need support and hand holding by the state government and or economic institutions promoted and run by the state and people (PPP). No wonder that state policies and programs for alleviation of poverty are all routed through state political and economic institutions.

Failed Intermediation

It is an irony that in practice it has been observed that such intermediation has failed to outreach bottom of the pyramid as because these institutions are found in practice keener to fill their pockets rather than provide succor and support to the poor. Saibal and Parhasib and Benjamin and Piperek in their research studies (1990 & 1997) have brought out very vividly that the traditional approach of funding the bottom of the pyramid only through state intervention as has been generally practiced due to perhaps the influence of Keynes's theory of state intervention to prop up the economy need not only revisiting but also rewriting. In fact doles and subsidies provided by the state not only fail to reach through such intermediation by the state but on the other hand weakens the self confidence and initiative of the poor and make them more and more dependent on the state as if state is next to god to ameliorate their misery and poverty. This obviously over the years have made them laggards and fatalistic.

Encourage Disintermediation to Reach The Poor

It is therefore imperative to conceive tools and technologies to outreach poor with least intermediation and creating direct accessibility to finance and other support services. In fact the revolution in information technology has created an opportunity to reach directly to the customers irrespective of time and place. It has become possible outreach people residing in far flung rural areas and has access to finance and services at any time i.e. 24 hours. This has created new paradigm for financial institutions particularly banks as has been portrayed below.

New Paradigm

- Growth of Rural Economy;
- Risk Assessment and Hedging Opportunities;
- Emergence of New Technology to Outreach Poor;
- Growth of Innovating Institutions like MFIS etc.

Emerging Opportunities

It is obvious therefore that the new paradigm has provided greater opportunity to banks and financial institutions to outreach rural and far flung areas to cater financial services and products to people of those areas. In fact in the last decade banks and other financial institutions have developed the delivery technology dynamically in terms of client outreach and enlarging the space. These institutions particularly banks have acquired technology support like ATM , biometric security and internet banking along with core banking and electronic money transfer hardware and software. This has obviously led them to consider the possibility and feasibility to introduce mobile banking. In fact some banks have already availed this facility in a limited way to facilitate money transfer and payment system. However the most asked for facility that mobile banking is expected to provide is reach out villagers to enable them to avail financial facilities with ease and least cost. In fact RBI is also keen to introduce mobile banking facilities by banks. In this regard it has already circulated guidelines and has set up a working group under the CHAIRPERSON of a deputy Governor Mrs. Thorat to find out suitable strategy to help banks to introduce this facility.

Emergence of MFIs

It is true that in recent years a paradigm shift has occurred due to emergence of micro financing institutions. However it is facing some challenges of which following may be particularly mentioned as these have blurred the impact and raised eyebrows of social reformers as to the efficacy and transparency of these institutions in their efforts to alleviate poverty. These challenges could be summed up as follows:

- How can the micro-finance approach could be harmonized with other basic needs such as political, cultural , economic sustainability along with the primary objective i.e. social;

- How such an approach be made to balance the multiple demands and the relationship among the various operators nay actors of the system; and
- How such an institution can be sustainable and risk free without asking for some heavy price for its operation.

Since micro finance is a community based approach and practice it has to be operated keeping in view community norms, traditions, values and practices and therefore its operation should not only be transparent but also cost effective. But these are obviously appearing to be insurmountable but that should not mean that one should raise hand and ignore these. In fact recent technologies have empowered these institutions including banks to overcome some of these challenges with ease and efficiency.

Challenges to Be Encountered

However there are some difficulties in adopting such facilities; of these major one is the non availability of reliable data with regard to the financial health and transactions of rural people. The volume of data the mobile network operators (MNO) usually collect on the basis user's transaction records are not adequate to assess risk and provide comprehensive banking services though transactions like bill payment could reflect through its regularity, frequency and volume some idea with regard to financial capability and avidity of users of such facilities. In fact that need to be collected should reveal not only the credit worthiness of the customer but also their capability and capacity to take risk and proneness to save and spend within their means.

In a recent study made by the Political and Economics Research Council (PERC) of the Brookings Institution has brought out that value of non conventional data based on bill payment history etc. if put to use could be of some value as follows:

1. it would enhance the reliability of measuring credit risk by only 10%;
2. It would also help enhancement of measuring credit score by 22.4% only.

Help Building Comprehensive Database

It is obvious therefore mobile banking transactions that are presently practiced could help to a very limited extent to measure and evaluate risks of all types banking transactions. The most important challenge therefore is to make it feasible to use data made available through MNO, M banking, and M payment system should be comprehensive and dependable information for credit and other financial risk assessment. To develop the same obviously the first step would be to asses the present gap that could not be filled by the data made available though MNO and Mobile payment facilities that are now available through mobile phones. That would also be necessary to examine the level of interest of all stakeholders to build comprehensive database for their use. This would obviously not just one time exercise as the interest of stakeholders would vary with the growth of volume and customers and also technology to enhance reachable and reduce cost.

NEED TO DEVELOP COLLABORATIVE MODEL

However as has been pointed out by K.C. Chakravarty Dy. Governor of R.B.I. that indeed it is a great opportunity for banks to outreach the bottom of the pyramid but there is need to develop an effective collaboration between mobile service provider and banks. He also emphasized that it would be necessary to open accounts with the bank before bank could provide banking services and products to him. In fact he has rightly raised some limitations of banks to fast forward this scheme. These are as follows:

1. Banking technology is of recent origin and therefore there is need for scaling up the same and that would obviously take some time and investment;

2. Payment facilities are only one area where banks could be active and for that also there is need to develop appropriate delivery model; and

3. The recent initiative taken by RBI to permit banks to appoint correspondents need to be trained to the latest gadgets of mobile telephony and internet banking.

In fact he was frank enough to opine that banks are laggards and therefore to expedite the introduction of the system one has to look for alternative non-bank models.

Open Up Opportunities to MFIs

Even if one may not hold such a pessimistic view, it cannot be overlooked that there exist considerable gap in the technology and database that hinders the development of a suitable model for banks to reach the poor to provide comprehensive banking services to the rural poor. In fact mobile banking is a subset of electronic banking. It may be defined as a method to deliver financial services using mobile communication technologies such as GSM and CDMA including mobile devices such as cellular phones and personal digital assistance. In fact under M banking customer can carry out basic financial transactions like remittances and payments.

Recent Models Evolved For Collaboration

Presently there are four types of M. banking model viz. wap, sms, and pda and sim toolk it.

WAP (wireless application model) is based on micro website and the model is similar to internet banking.

SMS banking is based on GSM standard service to exchange text messages that a customer could send to obtain information or to provide an information and or instruction to the banker.

PDA model is designed with a mobile phone to provide more access and to store data to enable customer to operate on individual software. It therefore helps processing loan applications also.

Similarly mobile phone with SIM toolkits also enhances the capacity of users and banks to deliver more services.

Collaboration of Internet, Mobile and Banks

However to make mobile banking a real tool for disintermediation which is perhaps the prime need in India to avoid corruption and high cost it would be necessary to avail the latest development in mobiles that provide storage and internet facilities. In this regard Google has advanced considerably and one would expect as the present trend indicates the prices of these handsets would come down and become affordable. Further it would also be helpful to strengthen the organisations like Financial information network (FINO) to build necessary financial portals to help banks to draw upon these as and when considered necessary.

In fact it would be imperative to develop biometric ATMs along with mobile phones in the initial stage as that would help educating the rural youths to become familiar with these technologies and would not hesitate to contact directly the banks for seeking their services and products. In this regard it is really encouraging news that banks have started exploring the ways to leverage the Unique Identification Number project. In fact it is interesting news that after meeting the officials of UIN 14 banks and telecom companies as well as officials of RBI had a meeting to identify a model to integrate these innovations for inclusive growth.

Behavioral Finance: An Emerging Trend in Financial Markets

Supriya Nagvani
Career Counselor at SR Group of Institutions, Jhansi

ABSTRACT

Today, research on Behavioral Finance is gaining importance in the minds of Indian audience. The field involves concepts of finance, economics and psychology to understand the human behavior in the financial markets. It explains how and why markets might be inefficient. It is generally seen that people seem to overestimate the probability of unlikely events occurring and underestimate the probability of moderately likely events occurring. Popularity of lotteries best explains the statement. Thus, Cognitive Psychology is gaining importance.

Behavioral Finance is relevant in many ways. It educates investors about how to avoid biases, designing long and short term strategies to exploit biases; and being aware that decision-makers in financial markets are human beings with biases. More research on Behavioral Finance should take place in areas like Asset Pricing, Project Appraisal and Investment decisions and other areas of corporate finance, so that managers can avoid the decision traps.

Keywords: *Cognitive Psychology, Asset Pricing*

INTRODUCTION

If only I had acted differently, if only, if only, if only. This is one question that investors have asked themselves over the past two years.

Here's the problem: We know that we made investment mistakes, and vow not to repeat them, most people realize *why* they made them. Why did we think and feel and behave as we did? Why did we act in a way that today it seems so obviously stupid? Only by understanding the answer to these questions can we begin to improve our financial future.

This is where behavioral finance comes in. Most investors are intelligent people, neither irrational nor insane. But behavioral finance tells us we are also normal, with brains that are often full and emotions that are often overflowing. And that means we are normal smart at times, and normal stupid at others. The trick, therefore, is to learn to increase our ratio of smart behavior to stupid. And since we cannot (thank goodness) turn ourselves into computer-like people, we need to find tools to help us act smart even when our thinking and feelings tempt us to be stupid.

Basically behavioral finance has two building blocks: cognitive psychology and the limits to arbitrage. Cognitive refers to how people think and Limits to arbitrage refers to predicting in what circumstances arbitrage forces will be effective, and when they won't be. Thus we can say that Behavioral Finance is the study of how people in general and investors in particular make common errors in their financial decision making due to their emotions. It is the study of psychology and finance. This is the common sense approach to investing!

LITERATURE SURVEY

Earlier economics was closely attached to psychology, which was amply displayed in the book "The Crowd: A study of the popular Mind" published in 1896 by Gustave le Ban. The book was one of the greatest and most influential books of social psychology ever written. But with the development of Neo-classical economics, it has been taught to us that:

1. People have rational preferences among outcomes that can be identified and associated with a value

2. Individuals maximize utility and times maximize profits and

3. People act independently on the basis of full and relevant information.

At that time, expected-utility and discounted-utility models began to gain wide acceptance generating testable hypotheses about decision making under uncertainty and inter-temporal consumption respectively. By this time psychology had largely disappeared from economic and finance discussions.

A revolutionary paper in the development of the behavioral finance and economics was published in 1979. Two famous psychologists Kahneman and Iversky published their paper "Prospect theory - An Analysis of Decision under Risk" and where cognitive psychological techniques were used to explain a number of documented divergences of economic decision making from neo-classical theory.

In 1985, Wenner F.M. De Bondt and Richard Thaler published, "Does the Stock Market Over-react?" This is another milestone in linking psychology with Financial-Market and form the start of Behavioral Finance. They discovered that people systematically over-react to unexpected and dramatic news events, results in substantial weak form inefficiencies in the stock market, which was both surprising and profound.

Gradually a number of psychological effects and factors have been incorporated into behavioral finance only to strengthen the subject.

BEHAVIORAL FINANCE: KEY CONCEPTS

1. *Prospect Theory:* This theory contends that people value gains and losses differently, and, as such, will base decisions on perceived gains rather than perceived losses. Thus, if a person were given two equal choices, one expressed in terms of possible gains and the other in possible losses, people would choose the former - even when they achieve the same economic end result.

   According to prospect theory, losses have more emotional impact than an equivalent amount of gains. For example, in a traditional way of thinking, the amount of utility gained from receiving $50 should be equal to a situation in which you gained $100 and then lost $50. In both situations, the end result is a net gain of $50. However, despite the fact that you still end up with a $50 gain in either case, most people

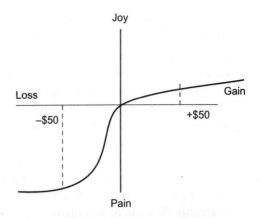

view a single gain of $50 more favorably than gaining $100 and then losing $50.

It is key to note that not everyone would have a value function that looks exactly like this; this is the general trend. The most evident feature is how a loss creates a greater feeling of pain compared to the joy created by an equivalent gain. For example, the absolute joy felt in finding $50 is a lot less than the absolute pain caused by losing $50. ˙

2. *Overreaction and Availability Bias:* One consequence of having emotion in the stock market is the overreaction toward new information. According to market efficiency, new information should more or less be reflected instantly in a security's price. For example, good news should raise a business' share price accordingly, and that gain in share price should not decline if no new information has been released since.

   Reality, however, tends to contradict this theory. Oftentimes, participants in the stock market predictably overreact to new information, creating a larger-than-appropriate effect on a security's price. Furthermore, it also appears that this price surge is not a permanent trend - although the price change is usually sudden and sizable, the surge erodes over time.

   According to the availability bias, people tend to heavily weight their decisions toward more recent information, making any new opinion biased toward that latest news. This happens in real life all the time. For example, suppose you see a car accident along a stretch of road that you regularly drive to work. Chances are, you'll begin driving extra cautiously for the next week or so. Although the road might be no more dangerous than it has ever been, seeing the accident causes you to overreact, but you'll be back to your old driving habits by the following week.

3. *Overconfidence*: Overconfidence (i.e., overestimating or exaggerating one's ability to successfully perform a particular task) is not a trait that applies only to fund managers. Consider the number of times that you've participated in a competition or contest with the attitude that you have what it takes to win - regardless of the number of competitors or the fact that there can only be one winner. In terms of investing, overconfidence can be detrimental to your stock-picking ability in the long run

4. *Herd Behavior:* This is the tendency for individuals to mimic the actions (rational or irrational) of a larger group. Individually, however, most people would not necessarily make the same choice. There are a couple of reasons why herd behavior happens. The first is the social pressure of conformity. You probably know from experience that this can be a powerful force. This is because most people are very sociable and have a natural desire to be accepted by a group, rather than be branded as an outcast. Therefore, following the group is an ideal way of becoming a member. The second reason is the common rationale that it's unlikely that such a large group could be wrong. After all, even if you are convinced that a particular idea or course or action is irrational or incorrect, you might still follow the herd, believing they know something that you don't. This is especially prevalent in situations in which an individual has very little experience.

Herd behavior, as the dotcom bubble illustrates, is usually not a very profitable investment strategy. Investors that employ a herd-mentality investment strategy constantly buy and sell their investment assets in pursuit of the newest and hottest investment trends. For example, if a herd investor hears that internet stocks are the best investments right now, he will free up his investment capital and then dump it on internet stocks. If biotech stocks are all the rage six months later, he'll probably move his money again, perhaps before he has even experienced significant appreciation in his internet investments.

While it's tempting to follow the newest investment trends, an investor is generally better off steering clear of the herd. Just because everyone is jumping on a certain investment doesn't necessarily mean the strategy is correct. Therefore, the soundest advice is to always do your homework before following any trend.

5. *Anchoring:* Similar to how a house should be built upon a good, solid foundation, our ideas and opinions should also be based on relevant and correct facts in order to be considered valid. However, this is not always so. The concept draws on the tendency to attach or "anchor" our thoughts to a reference point - even though it may have no logical relevance to the decision at hand. Although it may seem an unlikely phenomenon, anchoring is fairly prevalent in situations where people are dealing with concepts that are new and novel.

Anchoring can also be a source of frustration in the financial world, as investors base their decisions on irrelevant figures and statistics. For example, some investors invest in the stocks of companies that have fallen considerably in a very short amount of time. In this case, the investor is anchoring on a recent "high" that the stock has achieved and consequently believes that the drop in price provides an opportunity to buy the stock at a discount.

When it comes to avoiding anchoring, there's no substitute for rigorous critical thinking.

CONCLUSION

Whether it's mental accounting, irrelevant anchoring or just following the herd, chances are we've all been guilty of at least some of the biases and irrational behavior highlighted in this tutorial. Now that you can identify some of the biases, it's time to apply that knowledge to your own investing and if need be take corrective action. Hopefully, your future financial decisions will be a bit more rational and lot more lucrative as well. Here are some tips of applying Behavioral finance:-

Don't anchor on historical information/perceptions/stock prices

- Keep an open mind
- Update your initial estimate of intrinsic value
- Erase historical prices from your mind; don't fall into the "I missed it" trap
- Think in terms of enterprise value not stock price

– Set buy and sell targets

- Admit and learn from mistakes–but learn the right lessons and don't obsess
  - Put the initial investment thesis in writing so you can refer back to it
  - Sell your mistakes and move on; you don't have to make it back the same way you lost it
  - But be careful of panicking and selling at the bottom
- Don't get fooled by randomness.

So, psychological research teaches as about the true form of preferences, allowing us to make finance more realistic within the rational choice framework. This is the reason today Behavioral finance is a rapidly growing area that deals with the influence of psychology on the behavior of financial practitioners. The above-mentioned arguments are provided for why movements towards greater psychological realism in finance will improve mainstream finance. Apart from these things this particular area also collectively predict some outcomes where the traditional models failed along with reaches, the same current predictions as the traditional models.

Co-integration Analysis of the Determinants of Inflation in India

Swami P. Saxena[1] and Sonam Bhadauriya[2]

[1]Associate Professor (Finance), [2]Department of Applied Business Economics
Dayalbagh Educational Institute (Deened University), Dayalbagh, Agra

ABSTRACT

Inflation refers to a general rise in prices measured against a standard level of purchasing power. The most well known measures of Inflation are the CPI which measures consumer prices, and the GDP deflator, which measures inflation in the whole of the domestic economy. In India, the average inflation rate from 1969 to 2010 is measured at 7.99% with historical high of 34.68% in September of 1974 and a record low of −11.31% in May of 1976. The inflation rate in India was reported at 8.43% in July 2011. Economists generally agree that high rates of inflation are caused by an excessive growth of money supply, but there are many factors (real or monetary) which have influence on inflation indices.

This paper seeks to shed some light on the determinants of inflation in India during April 2001-March 2011 (ten years' data) using econometric analysis. The analysis includes Gross domestic product, Money supply, Prime lending rate, Nominal exchange rate, Index of wages, Index of industrial production and International crude oil prices as explanatory variables; and consumer price indices as explained variable. The study, with a view to estimate a more specific relationship between inflation and its determinants employs econometric technique of Johansen co-integration and Vector error correction modeling (VECM).

Keywords: *Inflation, Vector error correction, Co-integration*

INTRODUCTION

Inflation is a rise in the general level of prices of goods and services in an economy during a period of time. When the general price level rises, each unit of currency buys fewer goods and services. Consequently, inflation also reflects erosion in the purchasing power of money – a loss of real value in the internal medium of exchange and unit of account in the economy. On one hand, inflation's effects on an economy are positive as they ensure central banks to adjust nominal interest rates and encourages investment in non-monetary capital projects, on the other, the effects may be negative as they include a decrease in the real value of money and other monetary items over time. Uncertainty over future inflation may discourage investment and savings, and high inflation may lead to shortage of goods if consumers begin hoarding out of concern that prices will increase in the future.

The inflation rate in India is recorded highest in September, 1974 (34.68%) and lowest in May, 1976 (−11.31%) for the period of last three decades. Average inflation rate for that period was 7.99%. The last recorded inflation rate in India was 8.43% in July, 2011. Economists generally agree that the high rates of are caused by an excessive growth of the money supply. Low or moderate inflation may be attributed to fluctuations in real demand for goods and services as well as to growth in the money supply. However, long sustained period of inflation is caused by money supply growing faster than the rate of economic growth. Dlamini, Dlamini & Nxumalo (2001) revealed that inflation rate in the economy is significantly related to the other macroeconomic determinants of the country; mainly the gross domestic product and index of industrial production. Increases in nominal wages are also another factor expected to have contributed positively to the rise in the price level in India. Relationship between the inflation rate and the nominal prime-lending rate is supposed to be positive on the basis theoretical expectation. Changes in the international prices as oil prices and changes in the exchange rates have also an impact on the inflation in domestic market.

There are various measures of inflation which depend on the specific circumstance. A chief measure of price inflation is the inflation rate, the annualized percentage change in a general price index over time, known as the Consumer Price Index (CPI). In this paper, researchers focus on the CPI as the measure of inflation because changes in CPI are used to assess price changes associated with the cost of living. CPI is one of the most frequently used statistics for identifying state of inflation or deflation.

The present study seeks to investigate the possible relationship (both the long run equilibrium and short run dynamics) between the monthly consumer price index and its selected determinants. This paper is organized in five sections. Section one includes basic framework of the research problem. Selected studies on inflation in India and abroad are reviewed in section two. Third section contains the data and the methodology. Detailed analysis of the problem using econometric techniques is presented in section four. The paper ends with the conclusion in section five.

LITERATURE REVIEW

Numerous studies have been conducted on the inflationary process in both developing and developed countries. This section briefly reviews some of these studies to identify the possible determinants of inflation in India.

Canetti and Greene (1991) used Granger and Pierce causality tests for investigating the role of domestic money supply in inflation changes for six African countries and found that growth in money supply and the nominal exchange rate had a significant casual influence on inflation. Bank of Botswana (1998) in a paper titled "Inflation in Southern Africa" published in its Research Bulletin considered changes in the cost of labour a major cause of inflation variations in developed countries, but not in developing countries. It further mentioned that in an open and import dependent economy, where domestic inflation is largely determined by foreign prices and nominal exchange rate depreciation, the initial improvement of export competitiveness resulting from depreciation may eventually be offset by the consequent increase in prices.

Altissimo, Benigno and Palenzuala (2005) analyzed the long-run determinants of inflation differentials in a monetary union. The study aimed at establishing some stylized facts relating the regional dispersion in headline inflation rates in the euro area as well as in the main components of the consumer price index. The researchers found that a relatively large proportion of inflation occurs in the Service category of the EU's harmonized consumer price index. Andersson, Masuch and Schiffbauer (2009) also analyzed the determinants of inflation differentials and price levels in the euro countries. Using dynamical panel analysis the researchers concluded that inflation differentials are primarily determined by cyclical positions and the inflation persistence. Akbari and Rankaduwa (2005) in their paper titled "Determinants of Inflation and Feasibility of Inflation Targeting in a Small Emerging Market Economy: The Case of Pakistan", using econometric analysis tried to identify key determinants of inflation in Pakistan. The evidence presented in the study suggested that political stability and better functioning of markets are essential pre-requisites for achieving the desired effects of any macroeconomic policy.

Saryal (2007) applied GARCH to estimate conditional stock market volatility using monthly data series in Turkey and Canada and found rate of inflation has high predictive power for stock market volatility in Turkey, whereas it is weaker, but still significant for Canada. The study suggested that higher rates of inflation are coincident with greater stock market risk. Kandil and Morsy (2009) studied determinants of inflation in Gulf Cooperation Council (GCC) since 2003 using an empirical model that includes domestic and external factors. The authors concluded that Inflation in major trading partners of GCC appears to be the most relevant foreign factor. In addition, oil revenues through growth of credit and aggregate spending have reinforced inflationary pressures.

Kandil and Morsy (2009) studied determinants of inflation in Gulf Cooperation Council since 2003 using an empirical model that includes domestic and external factors and find that inflation in major trading partners appears the most relevant to domestic inflation in GCC among the foreign factors and also find that in Kuwait, Oman, and the United Arab Emirates, higher public investment is the main inflationary pressure in the long run and in United Arab Emirates public investment reducing the inflation in long run.

Bhattacharya and Mukherjee (2003), applying the techniques of unitroot tests, co-integration and the longrun Granger noncausality test investigated the nature of the causal relationship between stock prices and macroeconomic aggregates in the foreign sector in India. They suggested that there is no causal linkage between stock prices, and the three variables under consideration. Kishor (2009) studied the role of real money gap and the deviation of real money balance from its long-run equilibrium level for predicting inflation in India. He concluded that the real money gap is a significant predictor of inflation in India. The empirical results of the study conducted by Patra and Ray (2010) indicated that Inflation expectations play a significant role in setting and conducting monetary policy in modern India, and it is believed that imperfect information regarding central bank's intentions has been one of the source of inertia in the formation of inflation expectations.

DATA AND METHODOLOGY

Data Description

The analysis includes Gross domestic product, Money supply, Prime lending rate, Nominal exchange rate, Index of wages, Index of industrial production and International crude oil prices as explanatory variables; and Consumer price indices as explained variable. Monthly observations of all the data series are taken into consideration for analysis purpose spanning from April 2001 to March 2011 (ten financial years). The sources of data compilation are presented in the Table 1.

RESEARCH METHODOLOGY

The following econometric tools (available in STATA IC 10 software) have been applied for empirical investigation.

Unit Root Test Before using the time series data for further investigation, it must be tested for unit root and stationary. To test the stationary, Augmented Dickey Fuller (ADF) test for unit root, a 't' test for checking the favor of stationary, has been applied. The model form of ADF test is:

$$\Delta y_t = \alpha + \beta y_{t-1} + \delta t +_1 \Delta y_{t-1} +_2 \Delta y_{t-2} + \ldots +_k \Delta y_{t-k} + \in_t$$

Where, k is the number of lag, y_t is the time series data under consideration. The test is based on the null hypothesis that the variable contains a unit root, and alternative hypothesis is that the variables are generated by a stationary process.

Johansen Co-integration In econometrics, before estimating the parameters of VECM, investigator has to choose the number of co-integrating equations. Co-integration means the long-run equilibrium relationship among the variables, which interprets that if the time series data are co-integrated, then those series in long run will come into an equilibrium point. The present study employs Johansen's method to estimate the co-integrating rank of a VECM. Johansen proposes two different likelihood ratio tests of significance, named Trace Statistic Test and Maximum Eigen Value Test. The researchers, in this paper have applied Trace Statistic because it is quite simple than Maximum Eigen Value Test and it starts testing at $r = 0$. Johansen model for Trace Statistic is expressed as:

$$Q_{\text{trace}} = -T \sum_{i=r+1}^{k} \ln(1 - \lambda_i)$$

Where, T is the number of observations and λ_i is the ith largest Eigen value. This tests the null hypothesis of r co-integrating vectors against the null hypothesis of k co-integrating vectors.

Vector Error Correction Model VECMs are used to model the stationary relationships between multiple time series that contain unit roots. VECM implements Johansen approach for estimating parameters. If x_t and y_t are co-integrated, there is a long run equilibrium relationship between them. Furthermore, the short run dynamics can be described by the error correction model. This is known as Granger representation theorem.

Table 1 List of Variables

Variable Name	Symbol	Data Source
Explained Variable		
Consumer Price Index Monthly Average (Base : 2000-01) CPI	www.rbi.org	
Explanatory Variables		
Gross Domestic Product (Thousand Crore ₹)	GDP	www.rbi.org
Index of Industrial Production (Base : 1993-94)	IIP	www.rbi.org
Money Supply: M3 (Thousand Crore ₹)	MOS	www.rbi.org
Interest Rate (Prime Lending Rate)	PLR	www.rbi.org
Index of Wage Rate (Base: 1963-65)	IWR	labour.nic.in
Foreign Exchange Rate (₹ per unit of US $)	EXR	www.rbi.org
Crude Oil Spot Price (WTI Dollars per Barrel)	CRO	www.eia.org

If $x_t \sim I(1)$, $y_t \sim I(1)$, and $z_t = y_t - \beta x_t$ is $I(0)$, then x and y are said to be co-integrated. The Granger representation theorem says that in this case x_t and y_t may be considered to be generated by VECMs as-

$$\Delta x_t = \rho_1 z_{t-1} + \text{lagged}(\Delta x_t, \Delta y_t) + \varepsilon_{1t}$$

$$\Delta y_t = \rho_2 z_{t-1} + \text{lagged}(\Delta x_t, \Delta y_t) + \varepsilon_{2t}$$

Where, at least one of ρ_1 and ρ_2 is non-zero and z_{1t} and z_{2t} are the white noise errors.

ANALYSIS AND EMPIRICAL RESULTS

Summary Statistics Some relevant information about the selected explained and explanatory variables is summarized in the Table 2. Number of observations for all the variables is one hundred twenty as the study covers the monthly observations for ten years. Results of descriptive statistics show that over the period from 2001-02 to 2010-11 CPI fluctuated between 95 and 188 points. The relative range for the values of other variables is highest in case of CRO and lowest for EXR.

The values of mean and standard deviation shown in the table indicate clearly that relatively EXR and PLR are the most consistent variables, but MOS, CRO, and GDP are the most inconsistent variables as they have maximum coefficient of variation. Table also shows positive skewness for all the distributions excepting PLR and EXR, indicating that the large tail of the distribution lies towards the higher values of the variable. Kurtosis, the degree of peakedness in a curve of the frequency distribution is for highest PLR and lowest for CRO. For tracing the closeness between the volatility in CPI and its determinants, monthly exponential growth of all the variables is depicted in Fig. 1.

Table 2   Results of Summary Statistics

Var.	Obs.	Min.	Max.	Mean	S.D.	Variance	Skewness (S.E.)	Kurtosis (S.E.)
CPI	120	95.00	188.00	124.79	27.84	775.15	0.788 (.221)	−0.627 (.438)
GDP	120	433.00	1535.00	838.83	307.34	94460	0.581 (.221)	−0.794 (.438)
IIP	120	154.90	350.40	221.59	49.38	2439	0.440 (.221)	−0.871 (.438)
MOS	120	1348.0	6496.00	3159.10	1505.51	2267000	0.644 (.221)	−0.867 (.438)
PLR	120	7.50	13.62	11.22	1.23	1.53	−0.858 (.221)	1.829 (.438)
IWR	120	3438.7	5112.40	4198.00	529.46	280300	0.343 (.221)	−1.147 (.438)
EXR	120	39.32	51.20	45.55	2.55	6.53	−0.661 (.221)	0.179 (.438)
CRO	120	19.38	133.88	57.66	26.36	695.10	0.615 (.221)	0.007 (.438)

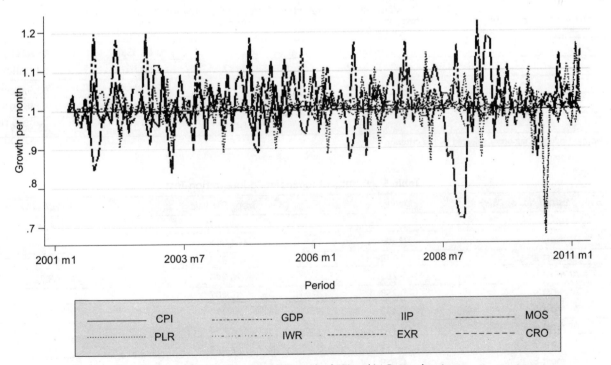

Fig. 1   *Monthly Exponential Growth of CPI and its Determinants*

Lag Order Selection To identify the proper lag order for conducting the co-integration analysis and vector error correction modeling, the researchers applied several minimum value based criterions. The results of Likelihood Ratio (LR) test are contained in Table 3.

Based on the results LR test, a model with four lags order is selected. The Final Prediction Error (FPE) and Akaike Information Criterion (AIC) also suggest lags order of four for the model. However, Schwarz Information Criterion (SIC) and Hannan-Quinn Information Criterion (HQIC) chosen a model with three lags and one lag respectively.

Augmented Dickey Fuller Unit Root Test Before applying co-integration analysis on the selected variables, a formal test is required to confirm time series properties. For this purpose Augmented Dickey Fuller (ADF) test of unit root is applied. The lag length is four based on the FPE and AIC. In this test, the null hypothesis is that a variable contains a unit root, and alternative hypothesis is that the variables are generated by a stationary process. The test results clearly indicate that the p value of all the variables is less than critical value. Hence, the null hypothesis is accepted, and it can be said that all the variables are generated by a non stationary process.

Johansen Co-integration Test Johansen co-integration test is applied to investigate the long run relationship between the variables under study if the data set is

Table 4 Results of Augmented Dickey Fuller Test

Variables	Z(t)	P-Value
CPI	2.184	0.998
GDP	0.690	0.989
IIP	0.618	0.988
MOS	4.909	1.000
PLR	−1.537	0.515
IWR	0.095	0.965
EXR	−2.317	0.166
CRO	1.533	0.517

Note: 1%, 5% and 10% critical values are −3.505, −2.889 and −2.579 respectively.

non-stationary. In case the variables are generated by a stationary process, we apply vector auto-regression.

Since the variables under study are generated by a non stationary process, the researchers have applied Johansen Co-integration test with a view to find out the long run relationship between CPI and the selected explanatory variables. In this test our null hypothesis is that there is no co-integrating equation among the selected variables. The empirical results contained in Table 5 show that the value of trace statistic 39.407 is less than critical value 47.21 for at the most four co-integrating equations at 5% level of significance. Hence, there are four long-run equilibrium relationships between CPI and its selected determinants.

Table 3 VEC Lag Order Selection Criteria (Monthly Analysis)

Lag	LR	FPE	AIC	SC	HQ
0	---	6.2e+19	68.2814	68.3585	68.4713
1	2084.6	3.0e+12	51.4137	52.1075	53.1228*
2	204.3	1.5e+12	50.7548	52.0654	53.9832
3	199.98	8.7e+11	50.1343	52.0616*	54.8819
4	185.03	5.7e+11*	49.6427*	52.1867	55.9095

Notes: *indicates lag order selected by the criterion

Table 5 Results of Johansen Co-integration Test

Hypothesized No. of CE(s)	Eigen value	Trace Statistic	5% Critical Value
None	---	269.295	156.00
At most 1	0.596	164.096	124.24
At most 2	0.378	108.873	94.15
At most 3	0.283	70.245	68.52
At most 4	0.233	39.407*	47.21
At most 5	0.151	20.373	29.68
At most 6	0.104	7.630	15.41
At most 7	0.045	2.229	3.76
At most 8	0.019	---	---

Note: *Denotes rejection of null hypothesis at 5% significance level.

Vector Error Correction Model To investigate short run dynamics between inflation and its determinants, the researchers made an attempt to apply Vector Error Correction Model VECM. The results of multivariate vector error correction model with four lags and four co-integrating equations are presented in Table 6. The table contains values of adjustment coefficient (short run parameters) of the model developed for CPI and its determinants. It shows that the highest adjustment coefficients of GDP (3.662) for CPI at its second lag difference. Thus, when the monthly growth in GDP is too high, the CPI quickly adjusts toward the GDP.

After GDP, CPI follows the changes in Index of Wage Rate (IWR) and Money Supply (MOS) as their coefficients are 1.948 and 0.758 respectively at their second lag difference. CPI quickly adjusts itself towards the fluctuations in industrial production (adjustment coefficient of IIP being 0.163 at second lag difference), followed by variations in Crude Oil Spot Prices (CRO) and Foreign Exchange Rate (EXR) as their adjustment coefficients are 0.131 and 0.018 at second and first difference. Role of Interest Rates (PLR) is lowest in the short run dynamics of CPI. Thus, CPI follows the changes in domestic macroeconomic indicators before changes in the international indicators.

The above description is about the short run adjustments of CPI for its determinants. But the results of short run adjustment of the determinants of CPI towards it are adverse as PLR is found to be adjusting itself quickly with the changes CPI level. Among other selected variables GDP is the second last and IWR is the last followers of change in CPI.

CONCLUSION

In this paper, researchers have made a modest attempt to investigate the long run equilibrium and short run dynamic relationship between inflation and its determinants in India. The results of Johansen co-integration test indicated four long run equilibrium relationships for inflation with its determinants. Comparing inflation rate against the growth rate of GDP, one would expect a adverse relationship, but, the results of VECM indicated positive relationship between GDP and the CPI. Economic theory suggests a high degree of interdependence between money supply and inflation,

Table 6 Vector Error Correction Model in a Multivariate Framework

	CPI_{LD}	CPI_{L2D}	CPI_{L3D}	GDP_{LD}	GDP_{L2D}	GDP_{L3D}
D_CPI				0.000	−0.009	−0.012
D_GDP	3.239	3.662	1.883			
	CPI_{LD}	CPI_{L2D}	CPI_{L3D}	IIP_{LD}	IIP_{L2D}	IIP_{L3D}
D_CPI				−0.084	−0.101	−0.012
D_IIP	0.139	0.163	−0.136			
	CPI_{LD}	CPI_{L2D}	CPI_{L3D}	MOS_{LD}	MOS_{L2D}	MOS_{L3D}
D_CPI				−0.018	−0.018	−0.012
D_MOS	0.536	0.758	0.693			
	CPI_{LD}	CPI_{L2D}	CPI_{L3D}	PLR_{LD}	PLR_{L2D}	PLR_{L3D}
D_CPI				−2.087	−0.303	0.219
D_PLR	0.000	0.011	0.010			
	CPI_{LD}	CPI_{L2D}	CPI_{L3D}	IWR_{LD}	IWR_{L2D}	IWR_{L3D}
D_CPI				0.005	−0.009	−0.003
D_IWR	0.717	1.948	−0.151			
	CPI_{LD}	CPI_{L2D}	CPI_{L3D}	EXR_{LD}	EXR_{L2D}	EXR_{L3D}
D_CPI				−0.630	0.075	−0.625
D_EXR	0.018	0.005	−0.016			
	CPI_{LD}	CPI_{L2D}	CPI_{L3D}	CRO_{LD}	CRO_{L2D}	CRO_{L3D}
D_CPI				−0.092	0.014	0.088
D_CRO	0.119	0.131	0.036			

Notes: LD, L2D and L3D refer the value of adjustment coefficient for first lag difference, second lag difference and third lag difference respectively.

and it is supported by our study too. Changes in international prices of crude oil also are found to have a notable impact on the inflation in India. The evidence of analysis in this paper supports the conclusions drawn in previous studied conducted on inflationary process by Dlamini (2001), Kandil (2009), Kishor (2009) & Patra (2010). The limitation of the study is that researchers could study only a single country with a limited number of variables. Hence, there is scope of further research using more number of variables and the economies.

References

- Akbari, H.A. & Rankaduwa, W. (2005), Determinants of Inflation and Feasibility of Inflation Targeting in a Small Emerging Market Economy: The Case of Pakistan, *SBP Bulletin,* 2(1), 169-190.

- Altissimo, F., Benigno, P. & Palenzuela, D.R. (2005), *Long-Run Determinants of Inflation Differentials in a Monetary Union*, NBE. 11473.

- Andersson, M., Masuch, K. & Schiffbauer, M. (2009), *Determinants of Inflation and Price Level Differentials Across the Euro Area Countries*, European central bank 1129

- Bank of Botswana (1998), Inflation in Southern Africa, *The Research Bulletin*, 16(1).

- Bhattacharya, B. & Mukherjee, J. (2003), Causal Relationship between Stock Market and Exchange Rate, Foreign Exchange Reserves and Value of Trade Balance: A Case Study for India, *Fifth Annual Conference on Money and Finance in the Indian Economy*, January.

- Canetti, E. and Greene, J. (1991), *Monetary Growth and Exchange Rate Depreciations as Causes of Inflation in African Countries: An Empirical Analysis*, Mimeo, IMF, Washington.

- Dlamini, A, Dlamini, A. & Nxumalo, T. (2001), A Co-integration analysis of the Determinants of Inflation in Swaziland, *Central Bank of Swaziland Publications,* 1-37.

- Johansen, S. (1991), Estimation and Hypothesis Testing of Co-integrating Vectors in Gaussian Vector Autoregressive Models, *Econometrica*, 59.

- Kandil, M. & Morsy, H. (2009), *Determinants of Inflation in GCC*, IMF Working Paper, WP/09/82.

- Kishor N Kundan (2009), *Modeling Inflation in India: The Role of Money*, MPRA Paper No. 16098.

- Patra, M.D. & Ray, P. (2010), *Inflation Expectations and Monetary Policy in India: An Empirical Exploration*, WP/10/84.

- Saryal, S. Fatma (2007), Does Inflation Have An Impact On Conditional Stock Market Volatility? Evidence from Turkey and Canada, *International Research Journal of Finance and Economics*, 11, 123-133.

Rises the Value of Indian Rupee against US Dollar: A Challenge for Indian Economy

Tarun K. Tayal and Renu Sharma

Agra (U.P.)

ABSTRACT

Foreign exchange rates play a very vital role in the international trade scenario. The rises of Indian Rupee against US dollar are the trend that is noticed in the Indian Economy since 2003. This trend is of much concern for Indian Industry as a big share of International trade is with US and apart from it US dollar carries a global reputation as an important worldwide acceptable currency. This paper aims to study the effects of this phenomenon on the Indian Industry and Economy. The paper further attempts to come up with certain Business policy solution for the Indian Industries in this present situation.

Keywords: *International Trade, Exchange Rate*

INTRODUCTION

Foreign exchange rate is the price of unit of foreign currency in term of the domestic currency. In Floating exchange rate mechanism followed in India and USA, foreign exchange rate is determined in same way as price of any commodity in a free market economy. The foreign exchange rate is a price which is determined by the demand and supply of foreign exchange. The equilibrium in the foreign exchange market gets disturbed if some changes take place in the factors that influence the demand and supply of foreign exchange. Foreign exchange rate play a vital role in determining the financial health and future of an economy. The foreign exchange rate influences the prices of tradable and non tradable goods and services, and thereby induces shifts in consumption and production patterns and also the profitability of the export industry.

So the exchange rate adjustment in concurrence with other macro economic policies is a necessary part of the balance of payments strategy of the less developed countries as it directly or indirectly affects the economy of a country. Further exchange rate, through linking the currencies of different countries determine the flow of international trade in term of volume and composition. There are various factors which influence exchange rate like rate and also demand and supply of foreign exchange thus are responsible for variations in rate of exchange. The appreciation and depreciation of the domestic currency depend up on the supply, policy of central bank, differences in the interest rate and inflation rate between the concerned economies.

TRECENT TRENDS IN INDIAN ECONOMY

The knotty aspect of the exchange rate till year 2002 was the declining value of Indian rupee against major currencies of the world. The trends show that US dollar appreciated continuously against Indian rupee with marginal variation till 2002. A trend in the monthly average exchange rate of the Indian rupee US dollar in the year 2002-03 and 2003-04 indicates that the rupee dropped to low of ₹48.50 against the US dollar in may 2002. The reason for it was the border tension of the country. The rupee has almost consistently gained against the US dollar since May 2002. In May 2002 the rupee started with a bearish trend and slowly breached ₹49 per dollar, which was very much in the value. It was expected that level should be reached by November 2002. Then came the reverse trend as the rupee started reached strength and gained steadily to touch a height of ₹47.97 per dollar in the month of December and closed the year 2002 at ₹47.92. The sharpest month over one month rises in value of Rupee vis-à-vis US dollar was observed in the months of July and October 2003. The Rupee rose by almost 6.7% in 2003. It began strengthening thereafter to reach a monthly average of ₹45.02 against US dollar in March 2004. Between 2 July 2002 and April 2004, the Rupee rose by 10.7% against the US dollar, with the steepest increase occurring during 23-31 March of 2004, when the currency moved from ₹45.09 to ₹42.35 per US Dollar. In the first quarter of 2004 it rose by 4.7%. Most of the increase was in the month of March 2004 Vis-à-vis the US dollar, the Indian rupee, which started transformation from June 2002 onwards. On a annual basis, against the US dollar, the Rupee rose by 5.3% in 2003-04 and further by 2.1% in April-January 2004-05. During early 2004-05, the Rupee ended a continuous twenty four months run of appreciation against the US dollar and started weakening from May 2004 onward. The new phase however turned out to be comparatively short lived as the rupee started to gain against the US dollar from September 2004. The last three month of 2004 (October – December) saw a sharp rise for the Rupee against US dollar with the nominal monthly appreciation a high of 2.6% in December 2004. The Rupee rose by around 2.2% against the US dollar in 2004-05 and recorded an annual average value of ₹44.95.

At the end of first three quarters of 2005-06, i.e. from 2005 April-January 2006 the Rupee rose by around 2.1% against the US dollar compared to the corresponding period of the previous year. Such rise maintained the progressively strengthening trend displayed by the rupee against US dollar in recent years. Month wise analysis reveals that after July 2005, the rupee had depreciated against the US dollar in all months up to November 2005, during this period, the sharpest monthly depreciation about more than 2% were observed in October and November 2005. Since December 2005 the Rupee began strengthening again. The Rupee further fluctuated in year 2006 with appreciation against US dollar 2% approximate in the month of October.

CONCERN FOR INDIAN ECONOMY

This recent observed circumstances of Rupee appreciation against US dollar is much concerned with Indian Economy as the direction of India's foreign trade pointed out that the major share of USA in India's total export and imports. This study has a larger significance in present scenario since the liberalization of the Indian economy has increased continuously since the launching of economic reforms in 1991.

Under the economic reforms in India, not only we have opened up the economy but have also liberalized the industrial sector, made our currency convertible and allowed exchange rate to adjust freely. Further as India has adopted flexible exchange rate creates a situation of instability and uncertainty. It is additionally argued that to frequent fluctuation in exchange rate under it creates uncertainty about the amount of receipts and payments in foreign exchange transactions. This instability strangles foreign trade and capital movement between the countries. Along with trimming in tariff, India has also reduced non tariff restrictions. Even the new WTO regime has helped in reducing the international trade barriers between the countries. In India importers have also galloped because of increasing requirement of capital goods, defense equipments, petroleum products and raw materials. Exports have remained comparatively sluggish owing to lack of exportable surplus, competition in the international market, inflation at home and increasing protective policies of the developed countries. In the light of such recent foreign trading phenomenon against dollar becomes more important as international trade is largely influenced by this recent phenomenon and in the process it has affected the profit margins of corporate sector.

Effects of appreciating Rupee against US Dollars

A rise in Rupee does affect the economy of a country. We will analyze such effects in perspective of Indian economy. Let us first look at the benefits that follow a rising Rupee:

Benefits for Importers

A rise in Rupee helps importers to buy goods and services at a cheaper rate than earlier. It is essential for a developing economy that relieves heavily on imports. So those who import from dollar linked countries and foreigners who invest dollars in India will be the beneficiaries of the rises. Also during last few years a tendency among Indian corporate to expand their industrial capacities has been noticed. Thus, with this phenomenon persisting in future a significant proportion of new plant and machinery will be imported and that too at low cost. If, say 40% of the capital cost of a new project is spent on imports from countries transacting in dollars, a 10% rise in the rupee will mean an effective discount on capital costs of 4%. This is beneficial for developing country as India which needs infrastructure and new investments for stepping up its economic status.

With the country's imports being higher than its exports, it may prove to be a blessing in disguise. Moreover, a stronger Rupee may also induce higher foreign direct investments in the country. Import intensive sectors, particularly infrastructure in which a lot of capital investment are, or will be, taking place, will clearly benefit from Rupee appreciation. The quantum of benefit depends, how long the scenario persists.

IMPORT-INTENSIVE SECTORS

Any rise in rupee against the dollar would be beneficial for the import-intensive sectors. A number of sectors depend on overseas markets for their energy needs, capital goods and raw materials. India is a major importer of oil and gas, engineering and capital goods, edible oils and fertilizers. Those using these products would benefit if the dollar depreciates. Being the largest importer of oil and gas sector may be a beneficiary due to the lower cost of crude oil purchases. The benefit is, however neutralized as the selling price and the raw material price are both linked to international prices. As the product selling price and the raw material price are both linked to international prices, depreciation in US Dollar will result in decline in sales remittance as well as purchase costs. Analysis reveals that infrastructure and other capital intensive sectors may prove to be the beneficiaries. Power sector would benefit because of reduction in project costs leading to better tariff setting, while the telecom industry gain from reduced cost of equipment in rupee terms as most of it is imports.

EXPORTER'S DISADVANTAGE

The exporters are at a disadvantage due to currency appreciation making their produce expensive in the international market compared to other competing countries, whose currency have not appreciated in a same proportion. This take away a part of the advantage from Indian companies, enjoyed due to their cost competitiveness. However, it should be noted that despite the sharp currency appreciation for last quarters, Indian exports have continued to grow.

The rises in raw material and energy prices have resulted in slower growth in revenues for corporate India. Sharp upswing in exports from sectors like technology, steel, cement, automobiles and ancillaries, pharmaceuticals and textiles has helped India post a higher growth in turnover. Pharmaceutical companies have a significant dependence on exports. Dollar depreciation may have a constraining impact, although limited, on the overall sales value and profits of companies. However, the extent of impact may vary from sector to sector depending upon the amount of exports which US dollar is denominated. In case of textiles, the impact of dollar depreciation may not be helpful for the sector especially in light of the fact that the Yuan (Chinese currency) is relatively fixed vis-à-vis dollar. In case of automobile and cement companies where the domestic market is large and exports have picked up recently, the impact of dollar depreciation would not be significant.

Dollar Denominated Earnings Hurt

The strengthening Rupee has an adverse impact on various companies/sectors, which derive a substantial portion of their revenue from the US markets (or in dollar denominate economies). To fighting this, Indian companies need to hedge their dollar earnings, which involve a cost. Further, their earnings tend to face pressure because of the fact that while a major part of their revenue is in US dollar terms, as exports form a major source of their revenues, the costs incurred are in rupee terms. Other sectors hit by this phenomenon include the domestic gems and jewelry, pharmaceuticals and textiles industries, which have a similar revenue model and largest export sector of Indian economy.

A small case which was recently observed in Indian market will help us to understand this. A record rise in the Indian rupee at the foreign exchange market by 3.8% affected the operating margins of Infosys technologies Ltd by two percent during the third quarter of the financial year 2007. Despite of taking forward cover and hedging $373 million during the third quarter of 2007, the rupee appreciated to ₹44.53 from ₹46.29 and affected the operating margins of Infosys by 2% which led to a re nue loss of ₹1.45 billion. Further this Rupee rises phe .enon influenced the stock market. Infosys Technolog stock fell on funds due to the rise in the rupee against the US dollars hurting earning, dragging the IT sector index by over 138 points.

Other Disadvantages

Appreciation of Indian rupee against US dollar is harmful for Indian global competitiveness against countries like China. China who has kept their currency pegged to the US dollar has been able to prevent any movement against the dollar. Indian products will have to face greater competition from Chinese goods, both at home and abroad. If rupee appreciates our imports will be affected very much by Chinese competition as the markets for current and prospective Chinese imports in India are price-sensitive. We must see ir future, our consumer markets flooded with Chinese products for last one decade. Government adopted different measures to check this phenomenon of rupee rise against US dollar. In this process government sucked the excess of dollars from the market which did push the excess of money supply in the economy resulted in high inflation in the country. Often government absorbs back this excess supply of money though tighten monetary policy, in term of hike in PLR, repo rate, reverse repo rate and selling bonds in the market but any delay or reluctance in doing this will certainly push up the inflation rate in the economy.

ADVERSE EFFECT OF FOREIGN PORTFOLIO INVESTMENT

India has noticed a huge influx of capital inflow mainly in the Foreign Portfolio Investment (FPI) which has resulted in the rise of Indian rupee against US dollars. This type of investment is not preferred by most countries and economies. Generally FDI is preferred to FPI as it is linked to the performance of the real economy and secondly it is less inconstant then FPI. FDI directly helps in stimulating investment activity in the economy. The FDI can have the effect of not only bringing in additional resources, but also leading to progressing absorption of domestic savings. The most important disadvantage of FPI flows is that it tends to be pro cyclical, in the sense that it comes to be strong and the interest rate structure in the country are favorable and goes out when the BOP position is expected to weaken and when the interest rates are unfavorable. In case of countries like India, where the foreign exchange markets are very thin as compared to the international market, a free FPI regime carries the danger and speculative movements, which may lead to serious punctuate in the economy as noticed among the countries that went through East-Asian crisis.

RUPEE APPRECIATION AND ITS DEGREE OF IMPACT OVER FOREIGN TRADE

It is difficult to quantify the impact of a rising rupee on individual sector. However the impact will certainly differ due to different individual price elasticizes of imports and exports. Moreover, the impact will also depend on the import intensity of exports of different goods. The export of goods with low import content will suffer the most and vice versa as due to rupee appreciation the cost of imports will fall. The import component in diamond exports is about 75% thus it will be benefited in the

international trade market. Oil is important as an input for all industrial sectors of economy. Its imports meet more than 80% of the energy needs of the economy.

On the other side products like naphtha, diesel oil, fuel oil and ATF (aviation turbine fuel) are emerging as important export items. The increase in the price of oil in the global market, partly neutralized by the rise of the rupee may not be worth from the point of view of imports but it is good from the side of exports. Future is uncertain but for the present, Indian companies seem to suffer heavily from rupee rise, as import intensity of exports has steadily declined in recent years. The import intensity of exports measured as number of times imports as percentage of sales over exports as percentage of sales, has declined from 2.3 in 1995-96 to 1.61 in 2002-2003.

BUSINESS STRATEGIES

Indian companies have to face this phenomenon of rise in Indian rupee against US dollar but they can adopt few business strategies to minimize the consequences and offset the risk of this phenomenon and to maximize the benefits coming out of it.

To safeguard against themselves from the adverse effect of rupee rise against US dollar, Indian companies can take the benefits of forward exchange transaction facilities or hedging of currencies by foreign exchange market. The forward transaction is an agreement between two parties, requiring the delivery reports at some specified future date of a specified amount of foreign currency by one of the parties, against payment in domestic currency by the other party, at the price agreed upon in the contract. The rate of exchange applicable to the forward contract is called the forward exchange rate and the market for the forward transaction is known as forward market. So business firms may enter into forward transaction contract to protect themselves against the risk of present and future exchange rate changes. This transaction is known as "Hedging".

Further Indian exporters can shift the export invoices to other strong currency like Euro. With the Rupee rise expected to continue, billing in Euro is a much better step to diversify their currency risk. This trend is presently noticed in Indian economy. According to the Federation of Indian Export Organisation (FIEO) in mid of this decade the Euro accounts has increased to about 30% of the trading volumes in the domestic foreign exchange markets or about $300 millions per day. So it seems better that Indian companies should fix the prices of their export products in Europe rather than in dollar, if the Rupee continues to depreciate against the Europe. But appreciate against the dollar; Indian exporters will gain in dollars.

Even companies can shift their factories or open subsidiary units, to countries like China if they can better exchange rate from there.

China has kept his currency pegged to the US dollar and not allowing the currency to appreciate. So by virtue of their fixed currency peg they have been able to prevent movements against the dollar.

The effect will certainly differ from product to product due to their different individual price elasticity's of imports and exports.

Further the impact will also depend on the import intensity of exports of different goods. As exports of goods with low import content will suffer the most due to the Rupee rise, vis-à-vis the cost of imports will decreased. Indian companies should focus more on producing and exporting goods with higher import content, or processed goods.

Additionally, some short term actions which the Indian companies may follow to minimize the impact of a strong Rupee rely on cost cutting in selling/ marketing and general/administrative expenses etc.

Indian company should rely on such steps but a question still raises how long this Rupee raise will continue and how it will affect Indian economy. Despite of fact that government is taking measures to prevent its adverse effects but the question is still remains that how long these measures will be effective keeping off the bad effects and offset the risk of it on Indian economy, inflation the foremost of them.

CONCLUSION

Whether Indian Rupee will continue to appreciate in future is a big dilemma. The future movements of the Rupee against the dollar would depend on many imponderable factors such as timing of US recovery, the interest rate policy of Fed, timing of recovery in European Union and future investment climate in Europe, Japan and China related to the US, the inflation rate in India vis-à-vis the US, the exchange rate policy of China, the political and economic developments in the gulf countries. Take for example - if OPEC countries take a decision to fix oil prices in Europe instead of US dollar, it may signal a shift to global economic power centre from US to Europe with far- reaching implications for the exchange rate of US dollar against currencies, including the Indian Rupee according

to various statements given by the OPEC president time to time. There are various advantages as well as disadvantages of a rising Rupee, one need to understand whether the rise in the Rupee is sustainable to drive any reasonable conclusion at this stage. The weakness of the US dollar is largely due to relative unattractiveness of US assets. This is imparting due to a very low or zero interest role regime prevalent in the US currently. Already there are indications that, lower interest rate may not be sustainable for long period. This means that US rates may go up and likely to strengthen the US dollar, but it is important to note that favorable interest rate structure in India as compared to US is not the sole cause of Rupee appreciation. Though it is believed that the rise of Rupee may not be sustainable for a long while but for the time being Indian government and companies have to adopt suitable policies to reduce the adverse affects and maximize the profits arising out of the Rupee appreciation.

References

- Economic Survey (2003-04), *Government Of India, Ministry Of Finance, Economic Division, New Delhi.*
- Economic Survey (2004-05), *Government Of India, Ministry Of Finance, Economic Division, New Delhi*
- Economic Survey (2005-06), *Government Of India, Ministry Of Finance, Economic Division, New Delhi.*
- Prakash Kandari (2008), Appreciation Of Indian Rupee Against US Dollar, *Journal Of Management, 6 : Issue 1, 72-77*
- India: A Decade Of Economic Reforms 1991-2001, (2003), M.M. Sury, *New Century Publications, New Delhi-110002*
- Cherunilam Francis, (2001), International Economics, *Tata McGraw-Hill Publishing Company Limited, New Delhi*
- James, C., Ingram, (1986), International Economics, Second Edition, *JOHN Wiley & Sons, United States Of America.*
- Macroeconomics (2004), *Ahuja, H.L., Chand, S. & Company Ltd., Ramanagar, New Delhi-110055*
- The Indian Economy: Problems And Prospects, (2003), *Bimal Jalan Various Articles Published In Financial Express In Year 2004.*
- Retrieved From http://www.indiadaily.com
- Retrieved From http://www.commerce.nic.in

Micro Insurance: A Tool for Socio-Economic Transformation

Vijay Kumar Gangal and Kirti Singh

Director, Ashoka Centre for Business and Computer Studies, Nashik

ABSTRACT

With a population of 1.2 bn, India is the second-most populated country in the world. Though, in recent years, strong GDP growth has been experienced, yet percentage of persons living below poverty remains is too high, especially among the 70% of the population that resides in rural areas. In decade of 50, Government of India nationalized insurance industry and liberalized in 1999 to allow private insurers. Since then insurance premiums have grown rapidly. India is unique in that the government plays a proactive role in providing insurance to the very poor (those below the $1/per day threshold) through various social security programmers and subsidized insurance schemes. Therefore the micro insurance market in India should largely be regarded as the low-income population living on less than $1/day.

The paper discusses the issues and concludes that 'broad' social- economic transformation in Indian low-income market which creates enormous scope and need for micro insurance which has an important role in interrupting risk and vulnerability among the chronic poor.

Keyword: *Micro insurance, Low income, Need, socio-economic, transformation*

Micro-insurance is the tool of financial inclusion developed to alleviate poverty and low-income people from specific perils. Micro insurance includes all principles of insurance in general, but products and services are designed to view the requirements of financially and socially backward people who are situated at the bottom of the pyramid.

Micro insurance is featured by low coverage limit, low premium and typical risk pooling. The marketing of micro insurance products are designed to reach low income group effectively.

"Micro insurance is the protection for the low -income population against specific dangers in exchange for regular payments of proportional premiums to the probability and costs of the involved risks."

Micro-insurance is therefore designed with the objective of protecting poor people and also designed with the environment that surrounds them, their needs, and possibilities. It is necessary that the product is developed for people ignored by traditional insurance markets.

By helping low-income households manage risks, micro-insurance can assist them to maintain a sense of financial confidence even in the face of significant vulnerability. If governments, donors, development agencies and others working for the welfare of the poorer community are serious about combating poverty, insurance has to be one of the weapons in their arsenal.

The chief players involved in micro-insurance in Indian market are:

- Insurance Companies; (e.g., LIC, TATA AIG Insurance, SBI Insurance, & Bajaj Allianz etc.)
- Micro-Finance Institutions; (e.g., Asmitha microfinance Ltd., SKS microfinance Pvt. Ltd., Grameen Kota, Sadhana microfinance society, Microcredit foundation of India, & Micro Save, etc).
- Non-Governmental Organizations (NGOs);
- Banking Institutions
- Central/State Governments;
- Cooperative Societies;

- Village councils (Panchayat samitis);
- Employers' Organizations;
- Health Providers & various other third parties related to health insurance

MICRO-INSURANCE HISTORICAL BACKGROUND

"Government of India and certain NGOs started the micro-insurance scheme in India. Although the reach of these insurance schemes is limited only to the 10 million individuals but there is a huge potential seen in the near future. The overall market is estimated to reach Rs. 250 billion by 2008 (ILO 2004)".

"For micro-insurance facilities to be available to the poor, the IRDA has divided the poor block of people under the two broad categories which are:

(a) RURAL SECTOR,

(b) SOCIAL SECTOR".

And there are the obligations set by the IRDA to be fulfilled in both of these sectors. These obligations are:

- The rural obligations are in terms of certain minimum percentage of total policies written by life insurance companies and, for general insurance companies, these obligations are in terms of percentage of total gross premium collected.

- The social obligations are in terms of number of individuals to be covered by both life and non-life insurers in certain identified sections of the society.

In order to fulfill all these requirements of "IRDA all the insurance companies have designed products especially for the poorer sections, rural sections and also for the low income group. These insurance companies in collaboration with the nodal agencies have been able to cater to the low-income segment of the economy". These nodal agencies which organize the poor, impart training, and work for the welfare of the low-income people play an important role both in generating both the demand for insurance as well as the supply of cost-effective insurance.

DIFFERENCE AMONG MICRO INSURANCE AND TRADITIONAL INSURANCE

NEED OF THE STUDY

Micro-insurance is a key element in the financial services package for people at the bottom of the pyramid. The poor face more risks than the well-off, but more importantly they are more vulnerable to the same risk. Usually, the poor face two types of risks – idiosyncratic (specific to the household) and covariate (common, e.g., drought, epidemic, etc.). To combat these risks, the poor do pro-active risk management – grain storage, savings,

Table 1

Basis	Traditional Insurance	Micro Insurance
Target Market	High and medium income individuals Market is largely aware of insurance benefits	Low income individuals Extremely limited Insurance awareness/knowledge
Product Design	Multiple coverage and features Risk-based pricing driven by multiple parameters; good data quality	Simple product design with easy-to-understand features Community or group pricing; limited actuarial data
Marketing and Distribution	Employ conventional channels including agents, banks, internet	Insurance sold by licensed intermediaries Innovative distribution with multiple tie-ups Usually sold as combined product through micro finance institutions
Underwriting	Comprehensive underwriting; large sum assured Complex language with multiple exclusions and terms and conditions	Simple underwriting practices; Small sum assured Simple policy language with minimal or no exclusion
Administration	Regular payment paid by cheque, direct bank debit, credit card	Irregular premium payments, by cash or bundled with other products
Claims Handling	Comprehensive process; detailed documentation	Simple and quick claim turnovers process; limited documentation
Asset Management	As per regulatory norms or investment rules of the risk- carriers.	As per regulatory norms or investment rules of the risk- carriers.

(*Source:* Sigma report 2010:- micro insurance-Risk Protection for 4 billion people)

asset accumulation (especially bullocks), loans from friends and relatives, etc. However, the prevalent forms of risk management (in kind savings, self-insurance, mutual insurance) which were appropriate earlier are no longer adequate.

Thus, in this paper an attempt has been made to know the importance of micro insurance that how it is helpful in socio-economic transformation of low income people.

Table 2 Micro Insurance Products Currently Available To the Companies

Financial Year	Name of Insurer	Name of the Product	Inoperation From (Opening Date)	Remarks
2007-08	Bajaj Allianz Life Insurance Co. Ltd.	Bajaj Allianz Jana Vikas Yojana	4/Apr/07	Single Premium Life Insurance
2007-08	Bajaj Allianz Life Insurance Co. Ltd.	Bajaj Allianz Saral Suraksha Yojana	4/Apr/07	Term Assurance
2007-08	Bajaj Allianz Life Insurance Co. Ltd.	Bajaj Allianz Alp Nivesh Yojana	4/Apr/07	Endowment Plan
2007-08	AVIVA Life Ins. Co. India Pvt.Ltd.	Grameen Suraksha	16/Mar/07	Term Assurance
2007-08	Birla Sun Life Insurance Co. Ltd.	Birla Sun Life Insurance Bima Suraksha Super	13/Aug/07	Life Insurance
2007-08	Birla Sun Life Insurance Co. Ltd.	Birla Sun Life Insurance Bima Dhan Sanchay	13/Aug/07	Endowment + LI
2008-09	ICICI Prudential Life Insurance Co. Ltd	ICICI PruSarv Jana Suraksha	2/Jun/08	Term Assurance
2007-08	ING Vysya Life Insurance Co. Ltd.	ING Vysya Saral Suraksha	3/Sep/07	Life Insurance
2006-07	Life Insurance Corporation of India	LIC's Jeevan Madhur	14/Sep/06	Endowment + LI
2009-10	Life Insurance Corporation of India	LIC's Jeevan Mangal	4/May/09	Term Assurance
2008-09	Met Life India	Met Vishwas	2/Jun/08	Single Premium Term Assurance
2007-08	SBI Life Insurance Co. Ltd.	SBI Life Grameen Shakti	6/Sep/07	Group Micro Insurance
2007-08	SBI Life Insurance Co. Ltd.	SBI Life Grameen Super Suraksha	6/Sep/07	Group Term Assurance
2006-07	TATA AIG Life Insurance Co. Ltd.	AyushmanYojana	30/May/0	Single Premium LI
2006-07	TATA AIG Life Insurance Co. Ltd.	Navkalyan Yojana	30/May/0	Term Plan
2006-07	TATA AIG Life Insurance Co. Ltd.	Sampoorn Bima Yojana	2/Jun/06	Endowment + LI
2008-09	TATA AIG Life Insurance Co. Ltd.	Tata AIG Sumangal Bima Yojana	3/Jun/08	Limited Payment Money Back
2007-08	Shriram Life Insurance Co. Ltd.	Shri Sahay	7/Feb/07	Li
2007-08	Shriram Life Insurance Co. Ltd.	Sri Sahay (AP)	24/Apr/07	Li
2008-09	IDBI Fortis Life Insurance Co.Ltd.	IDBI Fortis Group Micro-insurance Plan	5/Nov/08	Group Micro Insurance
2008-09	DLF Pramerica Life InsuranceCo. Ltd	DLF PramericaSarvSuraksha	16/Mar/09	Group Term MicroInsurance
2008-09	Star Union Dai-ichi Life Insurance Co Ltd.	SUD Life Paraspar Suraksha Plan	17/Mar/09	Group Micro Insurance

(*Source:* IRDA website)

GOVERNMENT AND PRIVATE COMPANIES INITIATIVES

A complete list of Micro-insurance products currently available in the market is provided below in Table 2:

OBJECTIVES OF THE STUDY

1. To find the awareness of micro insurance among the people living at the bottom of the pyramid.
2. To find the customer need and preference of various products of micro insurance.
3. To estimate the minimum amount of premium which poorest group of society agrees to pay.

RESEARCH METHODOLOGY

This paper is based on both primary and secondary data. A questionnaire/schedule has been prepared to know the awareness, need of Micro insurance among poor people and find out the minimum amount of premium they are ready to pay. Primary data have been collected from weaker section of the society of Agra City through structured questionnaires/ schedule conducted among 500 respondents. Out of 500, 135 did not give any response. 58 questionnaires were incomplete and not included in study. For analysis 163 who were not aware about micro insurance have been left out.

Secondary data have been collected from various official sites i.e., www.irda.org.in, www. adl.com/ micro-insurance, www.microsave.org and http://www. ilo.org etc. The study has been carried out from June to August 2011.

ANALYSIS OF DATA

Table 3 is showing the respondents profile all of the respondents are daily earners, chosen randomly, with age more than 25 years. Maximum respondents are shoe workers and Petha workers, some of them are college, Hostel and banks gate keepers. Major portion of respondents belongs to income group 15000-30000; only 11% respondent's family income is more than 45000 thousands as there is more than one earner in their family.

Table 3 also shows, most of the respondents are married having one or two children. 32% of respondent shave family of size 5, 27% and 26% of respondents live in a family of 4 and six respectively.

Table 3

Profile of Respondent	
Occupation	Percentage of respondent
Shoe Workers	38%
Petha Workers	24%
Gate Keepers	16%
Auto & Riksha Pullers	22%
Annual Family Income	
Income (₹)	Percentage of respondent
Less than 15000	12%
15000-30000	46%
30000-45000	31%
Above 45000- Below 60000	11%
Size of Family	
No. of Family members	Percentage of respondent
2	4%
3	5%
4	27%
5	32%
6	26%
More than 6	6%

(*Source:* Survey Analysis)

Table 4 Respondent Awareness About Micro Insurance

Awareness	Percentage of respondent
Yes	47%
No	53%
Investment in Any Insurance Policy	
Have Policy	Percentage of respondent
Yes	43%
No	57%

(*Source:* Survey Analysis)

From Table 4 is clear that majority of respondent are unaware about micro insurance (53%) and till now not invested in any insurance policy (57%). Only 47% respondents are aware and 43% have insurance policy.

Table 5 Reason for Taking/Will Take Micro Insurance

Reasons	Percentage of respondent
To fulfill the basic needs	31.04%
Deal with emergencies like illness, flood, death etc.	43.28%
Improve standard of living	25.64%

(*Source:* Survey Analysis)

Table 5 displaying that maximum percentage of respondent taking micro insurance so that they can easily deal with emergencies like death, illness i.e., 43.28% where as to fulfill the basic needs is the second most reason for taking micro insurance by low income people.

The Table 6 is showing the two things together the most reliable source of taking micro insurance and the most preferable insurance company by respondents.

Table 6

Most Reliable Sources of Taking Micro Insurance	
Sources	*Percentage of respondent*
Public Insurance companies	34.67%
Private Insurance Companies	21.86%
Self Help Groups	8%
Co-operative Societies	10.13%
Post Office	12.34%
Others	13%
Most Preferable Insurance Company By Respondents	
Companies	*Percentage of respondent*
LIC	32.12%
TATA AIG	14.23%
BAJAJ	12.32%
SBI	12.3%
ICICI	9%
HDFC	14.03%
Other	6%

(*Source:* Survey Analysis)

Most of the respondents rely on public insurance company followed by private insurance companies contributing about 56.53% as there reliable source of taking micro insurance and then post office i.e., 22% whereas co-operative societies and others contributes about 23.13% for total respondents whereas self-help group have just 8% showing that self-help should be formed in Agra as we know that self- help group have played a very significant role in the south India for helping low income people.

From Table 6 it is also clear LIC of India is the utmost preferable company by customers because it's a public sector company and low income people generally trust government. Therefore they mostly go for public sector Company instead of private.

It is inferred from the Table 7 that 44% of total respondents are agrees to pay micro insurance premium up to 85 per annum whereas 32% respondents are willing to pay premium 90 per annum belong to low income group. On an average people are ready to pay ₹85 per annum as premium.

Table 7 Amount of Premium Respondent Willing to Pay Towards Micro Insurance

Amount of Premium Per annum	Number of respondents	Percentage of respondent
75	14	4%
80	68	20%
85	148	44%
90	107	32%
Mean = 85 & Stander Deviation = 4.14		

(*Source:* Survey Analysis)

Table 8 Micro Insurance a Tool to Eradicate Poverty

Options	Percentage of respondent
Yes	59%
No	23%
Can't say	18%

(*Source:* Survey Analysis)

Most of the respondents feels that micro insurance will help to eradicate poverty i.e. 59% of the respondents as it have helped them to earn their livelihood where as 23% says no and rest were not able to make their judgment on this issue.

Table 9 Anticipated Future of Micro Insurance

Prosperous	Scale	1	2	3	4	5	Non-
	Number of respondent	98	78	73	53	35	pros-perous

(Source: Survey Analysis)

The Table 9 and figure 1 displays that the future of micro insurance in Agra is going to be prosperous as most of the respondents are between the scaling rates of 1 to 2 i.e. about 176 out of 500 respondents.

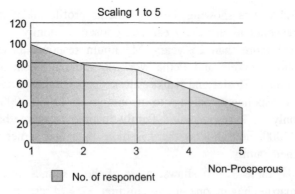

Scaling 1 to 5

No. of respondent   Non-Prosperous

Fig. 1

(*Source:* Survey Analysis)

FINDING

- Maximum of respondents were daily earners their income varies from season to season, in their peak seasons they earns 200-300 per day but in off season their earning decreases significantly, those respondents who were salaried people get monthly salary ranging from 3000-5000 per months.

- Most of respondents are married having one or two children. 34% of respondents have family of size 5, 27% and 28% of respondents live in a family of 4 and six respectively. Those families which have five or more than five members; they generally live in combined family and these families have income level more than five thousand per month.

- Most of the respondents have heard about insurance but they are totally unaware of Micro insurance, they believe depositing their money in bank or post-office is more profitable than putting money in insurance; also ease of withdrawing money from bank and post-office makes their investment more liquid.

- Only 43% respondents have invested in insurance policy, all of them belongs to income level of more than ₹45000 Per annum out of which 2 have invested their money only for one and 3 years only and they stopped giving premium for their insurance due to some problems and all of them invested in LIC's policy.

- After explaining those about need and benefits of insurance respondents want to invest in insurance policy to deal with emergencies, to fulfill basic necessities of life but lack of knowledge and awareness about micro insurance stop them for investing. Many of them told that they don't need insurance as there is very low chance miss happening to them. In spite of they are more vulnerable to risks; negligence and ignorance of risk for their health or life also prevent them for investing in insurance.

- Maximum of respondents choose government companies rather than private insurance firms as they think they are cheaper, reliable and ease in claiming insurance money.

- Most of the respondents have taken micro insurance from LIC i.e. about 32.12% followed by TATA AIG which is about 14.26% whereas ICICI, Bajaj and SBI insurance are not being regarded as better source for taking micro insurance in Agra.

- Majority of the individuals have the capacity to pay premiums towards insurance. On an average they have capacity to pay ₹85 per annum per head. This indicates that there is enormous scope for the insurance companies to innovate micro insurance products which should be affordable by the poor.

- An appropriate premium has to be devised which suit the pocket of the poor. This will be done by offering micro insurance products to this sector of society.

- About 59% of the total respondents say that, it will help to remove the poverty so it can be seen as tool to remove poverty from Agra.

SUGGESTIONS

- People should be made aware about Self-Help Groups and various steps should be taken by various Private and Public banks to form Self Help Groups among masses.

- Various NGO's should come forward to help poor people by helping them to provide micro insurance at low premium rates so that they can deal with risks and shocks.

- People's reliability over Local-money-lenders should be tried to decrease as they exploit poor and making them fool.

- There should be MFI's such as SSK working in South India, which is not only working successful but also main reason for the success of micro insurance in South India and also there is a need to establish a council of micro insurance representatives, regulator and government. This body should meet on a regular basis to discuss the issues and strategies to develop the sector. This body can also help to develop regulations. It could help facilitate the sharing of information between insurers.

- Most MFIs and insurance companies are willing to start life insurance schemes since it is easy to design and operate and its fund generation prospect is good; but actual need in the market is for quality health care, agriculture & assets etc therefore they should also focus on this.

- Low income people have fluctuations in income patterns and flow. Premium collection should consider these fluctuations, and should coincide with maximum flow and minimum variations. Also it could be integrated with saving or loans so that it eases out the pressure for money at the people's side.

CONCLUSION

This field of micro insurance is just emerging and through it has number of issues at all the three levels-people, Insurance companies and MFI's, this sector has big potential. More innovation in product design, processes and practices is bound to happen as the sector evolves and expend. The survey confirmed results of qualitative research that needs for micro-insurance among poor and vulnerable households in Agra are very high. These needs are much more accentuated among lower income group. Given that micro-insurance is an unknown service for majority of Agra people, the effective demand declared by survey households is substantial. The market development projections show that the market for all three micro-insurance products (health, life, property) is prospective in short-term.

References

1. Craig Churchill, Protecting the poor-Amicro insurance compendium, Munich Re Foundation from Knowledge to Action; by international labor organization.

2. http://www.microinsurancenetwork.org/history. php

3. Dr. Debabrata Mitra & Amlan Ghosh, Rural Life Insurance in Post Reform Era in India: Growth and Opportunities; International Journal of Rural Development and Management Studies Volume 3, Number 2, December 2009.

4. James Roth, Craig Churchill, Gabriele Ramm and Namerta, Micro-insurance and Microfinance Institutions-Evidence from India; CGAP Working Group on Micro-insurance, Good and Bad Practices, Case Study No. 15, September 2005.

- Micro insurance-risk protection for 4 billion people; Sigma report, November 2010
- http://www.irda.gov.in
- http://en.wikipedia.org/wiki/Micro_insurance
- www.adl.com/microinsurance

A Comparative Study of Timeliness of Private Sector and Public Sector Banks

Shanul Gawshinde[1] and Amitabh Joshi[2]
[1]Student, Prestige Institute of Management Dewas
[2]Faculty, Prestige Institute of Management Dewas

ABSTRACT

Timeliness of financial reporting is an attribute of good corporate governance. Shareholders and other stakeholders need information, while it is still fresh and the more time passes between year-end and disclosure, the more stale the information becomes and the less value it has. Policymakers are concerned about the timeliness of financial accounting disclosures. Disclosure of timeliness is of concern because a report's usefulness may be inversely related to the reporting delay. An attempt has been made to identify total time lag, auditors time lag and reporting time lag of information disclosure in annual reports of 30 banks out of which 15 are public sector and 15 are private sector banks.

Keywords: *Corporate Governance, Disclosures, Banking Sector*

INTRODUCTION

Timeliness of financial reporting is an attribute of good corporate governance. Shareholders and other stakeholders need information, while it is still fresh and the more time passes between year-end and disclosure, the more stale the information becomes and the less value it has. Policymakers are concerned about the timeliness of financial accounting disclosures. Disclosure of timeliness is of concern because a report's usefulness may be inversely related to the reporting delay. As the delay increases, it is likely that decisions will have to be made without benefit of the information. Furthermore, longer lags increase the likelihood that some of the information contained in the earnings disclosure may be preempted by other, more timely sources such as relevant intra-industry announcements (Foster (1981)), costly private search for pre disclosure information, or management forecasts (Foster (1973); Patell (1976); Penman (1980)). While reporting delays may reduce the usefulness of many types of disclosures to various groups of users. It has been pointed out by Bibuti Pradhan that "Timeliness of annual reports is an important determinant of their usefulness. Value of information depends upon a particular's person's need

of desire to use. However, economic and financial decisions by users of the annual reports are greatly influenced by the time value of information. In general, the value of the information diminishes with increase of time lag in publication of annual report of a concern. The need for timeliness in corporate reporting has been recognized by company law, accounting profession, stock exchanges and other relevant acts of incorporation of corporate bodies".

The timing of an annual report announcement is a disclosure decision that manager must make. The user recognizes timeliness as important characteristics of usefulness of accounting information. Many studies concluded that the timeliness of annual reports announcements is affected by good-bad news (measured by profitability), size (measured by total assets), financial risk and other firm characteristics.

REVIEW OF LITERATURE

Wang & Jun Gu (2009) investigated the influence of management disclosure to the timeliness of earnings announcement based on the Scheduled Disclosure Policy in China as well as the requirements on Earnings Predict and Express. Our finding suggests that the traditional timing patterns still remain in China market, but differs from most other countries that the timing patterns follow the random walk process, the timing pattern in China is based on the scheduled disclosure date.

McGee & Tarangelo (2005) said transparency is one of those terms that have many facets. It is used in different ways. It can refer to the openness of governmental functions. It can refer to a country's economy. Or it can refer to various aspects of corporate governance and financial reporting. According to their view, transparency includes the following eight concepts: accuracy, consistency, appropriateness, completeness, clarity, timeliness, convenience, and governance and enforcement. This paper focuses on just one aspect of transparency-timeliness.

Owusu-Ansah (2000) reported on the results of an empirical investigation of the timeliness of annual reporting by 47 non-financial companies listed on the Zimbabwe Stock Exchange. It also reports on the factors that affect timely reporting by these companies. The results of a descriptive analysis indicate that 98% of the companies in the sample reported promptly to the public (i.e., submitted their audited annual reports to the Zimbabwe Stock Exchange by the regulatory deadline).

Atlase et al. (1987) study employed a multivariate approach, which controls for firm size, in investigating the relationship between the timeliness of annual earnings disclosure and the associated security price reaction. The study's results support the hypothesis that after controlling for firm size, the length of the reporting delay is inversely related to the magnitude of report period price revaluations. That is, longer delays are associated with smaller market reactions, when firm size is held constant. There is some evidence that this relation may be stronger for earnings announcements which convey "bad news."

Keller (1986) research was prompted by the recent proliferation of interest in the information content of the subject to audit qualification. In particular, the necessity for more exact specification of announcement dates in qualified opinion research is pertinent and is extensively addressed in Dodd, et al., (1984). Such announcement dates have been variously defined in past research; but Davis (1982), Keller and Davidson (1983), and Dodd, et al., (1984) all provide arguments that the day of release of a company's annual report (or form 10-K, if earlier) is the appropriate event-day for qualified opinion research.

Zeghal (1984) evidence presented in this study supports the view that timeliness is a relevant characteristic of the usefulness of accounting information. According to the results, accounting reports with shorter delay have a higher informational content than those with longer delay. At the time of release to the capital market, the effect of delay on the information content seems to be more significant in the case of the interim rather than the annual reports. This may be explained by the major characteristics which differentiate the information contained in the interim reports from that contained in the annual reports, and the differences in their role in the investor's decision process.

Chambers et al., (1984) provided descriptive evidence on the relationship between timeliness of earnings reports and stock price behavior surrounding their release. Timeliness is defined in two ways. In the first phase of the paper, we define it as the reporting lag from the end of the fiscal period covered by the report to the date of the report, and compare the variability of stock returns (price changes) associated with the release of reports published relatively promptly after fiscal close with that associated with less timely reports.

Givoly & Palmon (1982) examined several aspects of the timeliness of earnings announcements which have implications for regulatory actions as well as for research design. The results show a considerable shortening of the reporting lag over the years. This implies that the assumption conveniently made in many "event studies" that the announcement week or month is fixed over the years is inappropriate and tends to weaken the power of the tests.

Whittered(1980) study over the period since their data terminated to the most recent financial year for which complete data are available, that is, the six-year period 1972-77 inclusive. The primary purpose in doing this is to assess the effect on time lags (if any) of a new listing requirement adopted by the Australian Associated Stock Exchanges in 1972. That requirement stated that "The interval between the close of the financial year of the company and the issue of accounts relating to it shall not exceed four months".

RATIONALE OF THE STUDY

Timely reporting contributes to the prompt and efficient performance of stock markets in their pricing and evaluation functions. Timely reporting helps to mitigate (or reduce the level of) insider trading, leaks and rumors in the market. As a result, most stock exchanges in the world, demand from their listed companies prompt release of audited financial reports to the markets.

Timely reporting is a function of audit-related and company-specific factors. Audit-related factors are those that are likely to impede (or help) the auditor in carrying out the audit assignment and issuing the audit report promptly. In contrast, company-specific factors are those that either enable management to produce a more timely annual report or reduce costs associated with undue delay in reporting.

The timeliness of an annual report release is a function of the reporting company's size. Usually, large companies are timely reporters for several reasons. For example, they have more resources, more accounting staff and sophisticated accounting information systems that result in more timely annual reports.

This study is based on the relationship between independent variables (like experience, size and activity) and dependent variable i.e. auditor's time lag, reporting time lag and total time lag. This study will help to analyze the timeliness of public and private banks.

OBJECTIVES OF THE STUDY

1. To analyse whether any difference is there in observed timeliness and mandatory timeliness.
2. To analyse whether any variation in timeliness exist in between companies of different experiences.
3. To analyse whether any variation in timeliness exist in between companies of different size group.
4. To analyse whether any variation in timeliness exist in between companies of different activity group.

METHODOLOGY

The Sample

A attempt has been made to identify total time lag of information of 15 public and 15 private banks for the year 2010-2011 and then the aggregate position of the some.

Experience: It is assumed that as the firm grows older as its experience and expertise would increase. Therefore, the accounting would be smooth and it would result timely finalization of accounts, auditing etc. Viewed from different angle, the older firm would

have to deal with accounting problems relating to earlier periods. With the increase in age accounting becomes more complex. Hence delay in compilation of accounts, completion of audit etc.

Size: It is expected that big enterprises in terms of capital employed, possessing large financial and physical resources, would be in a position to have expert staff and mechanical accounting system. Viewed from different angle, big enterprise would have complex activities, various products and big plans. For this structure, they have to maintain complex accounting structure. This may lead to delay in finalization of accounts and other matters.

Activity: It is said that an enterprise earning higher rate of return would like to put its achievement on record at earliest possible movement, and therefore, such enterprise expedite the finalization of account and other matters. It would also like to conduct its AGM at earliest date. On the other hand, the enterprise, which is earning below expectation may defer announcement and may not be interested in early compilation of accounts, audit and AGM.

In all 4 hypotheses were tested. The details are as follows:

◇ **$H_01.0$: There is no significant difference in timeliness in companies with respect to experience**

- $H_01.1$: There is no significant difference in auditor's timeliness with respect to experience
- $H_01.2$: There is no significant difference in reporting timeliness with respect to experience
- $H_01.3$: There is no significant difference in total timeliness with respect to experience

◇ **$H_02.0$: There is no significant difference in timeliness in companies with respect to experience**

- $H_02.1$: There is no significant difference in auditor's timeliness with respect to size
- $H_02.2$: There is no significant difference in reporting timeliness with respect to size
- $H_02.3$: There is no significant difference in total timeliness with respect to size

◇ **$H_03.0$: There is no significant difference in timeliness in companies with respect to experience**

- $H_03.1$: There is no significant difference in auditor's timeliness with respect to activity.
- $H_03.2$: There is no significant difference in reporting timeliness with respect to activity.
- $H_03.3$: There is no significant difference in total timeliness with respect to activity.

TOOLS & TECHNIQUES

Data Collection: Sample consists of secondary data collected from the annual reports of 30 Banks which consist of 15 Public Bank and 15 Private Bank.

Data Analysis: A causal study has been undertaken to study the correlation between various company characteristics and different type of timeliness in reporting. The contributory factors to total time lag has been identified Total Time Lag (The total time lag of corporate reporting is identified as difference between the last day of the accounting year and the day of annual general meeting for finalization and display of final accounts), Auditor time lag (The auditor time lag is the difference between the date of auditors signature and the date of last day of accounting year) and Reporting time period (The reporting time lag is the time lag which is equal to the difference between the date of annual general meeting and date of auditors report). Calculation of various reporting time lag has been calculated as mentioned. T test has been used for the purpose of data analysis.

RESULTS & DISCUSSIONS

- **$H_0$1.1: There is no significant difference in auditor's timeliness with respect to experience. Hypothesis accepted**. It can be observed from Annexure that calculated value of 't' is 0. 0.951 < 2.145 at 5% level of significance and at 14 degree of freedom. The value of t is more than tabulated value. It can be said that there is no variation in the two age groups of the sample because mandatory audit procedure is same for all the banks.

- **$H_0$1.2: There is no significant difference in reporting timeliness with respect to experience. Hypothesis accepted**. It can be observed from Annexure that calculated value of 't' is 0.0402 < 2.145 at 5% level of significance and at 14 degree of freedom respectively. The value of t is less than tabulated value. It can be said that there is no variation in the two age groups of the sample.

- **$H_0$1.3: There is no significant difference in total timeliness with respect to experience. Hypothesis accepted**. It can be observed from Annexure that calculated value of 't' is 0.0563 < 2.145 at 1% level of significance and at 14 degree of freedom respectively. The value of t is less than tabulated value. It can be said that

there is no variation in the two age groups of the sample.

- **$H_0$2.1: There is no significant difference in auditor's timeliness with respect to size: Hypothesis accepted**. It can be observed from Annexure that calculated value of 't' is 0.4703 < 2.145 at 5% level of significance and at 14 degree of freedom respectively. The value of t is less than tabulated value. It can be said that there is no variation in the two size groups of the sample.

- **$H_0$2.2: There is no significant difference in reporting timeliness with respect to size. Hypothesis accepted**. It can be observed from Annexure that calculated value of 't' is 0.1772 < 2.576 at 5% level of significance and at 14 degree of freedom respectively. The value of t is less than tabulated value. It can be said that there is no variation in the two size groups of the sample.

- **$H_0$2.3: There is no significant difference in total timeliness with respect to size: Hypothesis accepted**. It can be observed from Annexure that calculated value of 't' is 0.1926 < 2.145 at 5% level of significance and at 14 degree of freedom respectively. The value of t is less than tabulated value. . It can be said that there is no variation in the two size groups of the sample.

- **$H_0$3.1: There is no significant difference in auditor's timeliness with respect to activity: Hypothesis accepted**. It can be observed from Annexure that calculated value of 't' is 0.6632 < 2.145 at 5% level of significance and at 14 degree of freedom respectively. The value of t is less than tabulated value. It can be said that there is no variation in the two activity groups of the sample.

- **$H_0$3.2: There is no significant difference in reporting timeliness with respect to activity: Hypothesis accepted**. It can be observed from Annexure that calculated value of 't' is 0.1153 < 2.145 at 5% level of significance and at 14 degree of freedom respectively. The value of t is less than tabulated value. It can be said that there is no variation in the two activity groups of the sample.

- **$H_0$3.3: There is no significant difference in total timeliness with respect to activity: Hypothesis accepted**. It can be observed from Annexure that calculated value of 't' is 0.1124 < 2.145 at 5% level of significance and at

14 degree of freedom respectively. The value of t is less than tabulated value. It can be said that there is no variation in the two activity groups of the sample.

SUGGESTIONS

Financial reporting can be seen simply as an "add-on" to an organization's activities and management. The general view in most countries is that the type of information published in the past (on government business enterprises) will not be adequate for users' current requirements. External reports have generally concentrated on financial results rather than overall performance. More information is being demanded on how funds are spent, how better use can be made of resources, what is being achieved and how accountability mechanisms can be improved. Reporting practices should be left to market forces and government should not interfere in the reporting practices of the companies. Pressure from analysts and from investors will force the companies to prepare and present their reports within time.

CONCLUSION

The analysis shows that the hypothesis related to size, experience and activity of the firm are accepted so they does not affect Auditors time lag, Reporting time lag and Total time lag. So the banks disclose their reports well on time. As timeliness of reporting is an essential element of adequate disclosure.

References

- Atlase et al., (1987), Timeliness of financial reporting, the firm
- Chambers et al., (1984), Timeliness of Reporting and the Stock Price Reaction to Earnings Announcements, Journal of Accounting Research, Vol. 22 No. 1.
- Givoly & Palmon (1982), Timeliness of Annual Earnings Announcements: Some Empirical Evidence, The Accounting Review, Vol LVIL, No 3.
- Keller (1986), Reporting Timeliness In The Presence of Suject To The Audit Qualifications, Journal of Business Finance & Accounting, 13(1), Spring 1986, 0306 686X.
- McGee & Tarangelo (2005), Corporate Governance, The Timeliness of Financial Reporting and The Russian Banking System: An Empirical Study, Working paper.
- Owusu-Ansah (2000), Timeliness of Corporate Financial Reporting in Emerging Capital Markets: Empirical Evidence From Zimbabwe Stock Exchange, Forthcoming in Accounting & Business Research, Vol. 30, No. 3.
- size effect, and stock price reactions to annual earnings announcements, Contemporary Accounting Research Vol. 5 No. 2 pp. 526-552.
- Wang & Jun Gu (2009), Management Disclosure and Timeliness of Earnings Announcement: An Empirical Study, Submission to APJAE.
- Whittered(1980), The Timeliness of the Australian Annual Report: 1972-1977, journal of Accounting research Vol. 18 No. 2.
- Zeghal (1984), Timeliness Of Accounting Reports and Their Informational Content on The Capital Market, Journal of Business Finance & Accounting, 11(3), Autumn 1984, 0306 686X.

Improving Productivity through Optimum Resource Allocation: A Case Study

Ankur Pareek

Associate Professor, Department of Mechanical Engineering, Government Engineering College, Ajmer, Rajasthan

ABSTRACT

Health of any organisation can be judged by its productivity level. Higher productivity is an indicator of good performance and therefore profit. It is a measure of how efficiently the available resources are utilized to yield maximum profit. This paper aims to analyze the productivity level of an organisation and develop strategies to improve the same. Using various statistical tools like multiple regression analysis and optimization techniques involving both linear and non-linear expressions, a relation between the output and all the key input factors has been developed, so that each of these may be optimized. In other words, the total resources can be allocated in a way which results in maximum gains for the company. Alternately, the inputs may be planned for any desired output. Four strategies have been developed to maximize the productivity levels of the organisation, and any one of these may be applied depending on the prevailing conditions.

Keywords: *Optimisation, productivity, regression, strategy*

INTRODUCTION

Productivity is the ratio of tangible output to tangible input, and is a good indicator of the performance of any organisation. In fact, it indicates the efficiency at which the inputs are converted into outputs. Productivity and not profitability, is the true measure of a company's performance. A company may make profits for some time despite low level of productivity due to lack of quality competition. But as soon as competition comes in, the profits are sure to fade away. On the other hand, if efforts are made to maximize productivity, profits automatically come in. Thus, in today's world of cut throat competition, it is very important for companies to run their plants efficiently—to maximize the output and minimize the costs, i.e. optimize their productivity level. By comparing the productivity level of a company with that of an ideal one, standards could be set. Then, steps can be taken to improve productivity to approach these standards. These include going for latest technology, automation, business process reengineering etc.

While it is necessary to update the technology, it is more essential and perhaps less costly to utilize the available resources in an efficient manner. Using statistical tools, a relationship can be obtained between output and various key input factors. This equation can be used to analyze the contribution of each input parameter and to predict output for a set of input values. The relation can also be translated into the productivity equation. Various strategies may be developed to increase productivity. For each strategy, productivity can be optimized using linear or non-linear programming techniques, after identifying all constraints of the manufacturing system. The plant must operate at the optimum value of each input parameter on which the final output and hence the profit depends.

LITERATURE REVIEW

The concept of productivity is often vaguely defined and poorly understood, although it is a widely discussed topic. Different meanings, definitions, interpretations and concepts have emerged as experts working in various areas of operations have looked at it from their own perspectives. Often the terms 'performance' and 'productivity' are used incorrectly. People who claim to be discussing productivity are actually looking at the more general issue of performance. Productivity is a fairly specific concept while performance includes many more attributes (Thomas & Baron, 1994).

The strictest interpretation of productivity is outputs divided by inputs (O/I). A number of people use this interpretation because it is easily defined, calculated, and implemented (Sumanth, 1984). Performance is a broader term than productivity. It includes factors that are not easily quantified, such as quality, customer satisfaction, and worker morale. The inclusion of these fuzzy terms into the mix reduces the crispness of the measure and makes the calculation more difficult. However, these terms more fully describe what actually occurs in production. These and several other non-economic performance measures consume the input resources and as such should get fully projected in a model to measure productivity (Sardana and Vrat, 1987). The difficulty in applying productivity measures frequently can be attributed to an overlapping of these two subjects.

Bridges (1992) states, "The keystone to implementing productivity improvements is putting everything in measurable terms." Frazelle (1992) says "productivity must be understood before it is effectively measured." Productivity improvement is tied to productivity measurement, which is tied to the measurement of the work. The beginning step is measuring work.

Productivity measurement should have three objectives: (1) to identify potential improvements; (2) to decide how to reallocate resources; and (3) to determine how well previously established goals have been met (Sardana and Vrat, 1987).

Productivity measurement refers to the way in which productivity is indexed. In the strictest sense, a measurement is a numerical index. Consequently, the same inputs should produce the same outputs, i.e., the same index number, each time the output is calculated. The advantage of this is that the index does not depend on who collects the data or when it is collected (Chowdary *et al.*, 1998). Evaluation allows the use of measurements that are not strictly quantitative. Rather than being restricted to measures that are quantifiable, one may use qualitative measures such as "good," "bad," "poor," "superior," "fast," etc. This makes manipulation of the measures difficult, but allows previously unmeasured aspects of work to be measured (Galperin, 2004). The application of fuzzy mathematics to such terms has made them more useful (Chen *et al.*, 1996).

Productivity improvement refers to the change sought, noted, or measured in productivity. Productivity improvement can refer to the designed change in an operation to produce a positive change in the measured productivity of that operation. The term can also refer to the change in productivity that results from such a design change (Gunasekaran *et al.*, 1994).

Numerous techniques for handling linear scheduling problems have been developed in recent decades. Several studies have adopted mathematical programming, such as linear programming and integer programming. Huang and Halpin (1999) propose a graphical-based approach called POLO System to assist in the linear programming (LP) modelling of linear scheduling problems. Mattila (1998) presented an integer programming model for allocating the resources into various activities. Furthermore, some significant studies have been conducted using dynamic programming. Selinger (1980) employed dynamic programming approach to minimize project duration. Moreover, Russell and Caselton (1998) extended the work of Selinger in developing a two-state variable, N-stage dynamic programming formulation that minimizes the cycle time. Additional research has utilized dynamic programming in minimizing total cost by integrating cost, time categories, or heuristic rules (El-Rayes & Moselhi, 2001; Moselhi & Hassanein, 2003). Given the rapid development of computer-based techniques, researchers have used artificial intelligence techniques, such as genetic algorithms, to solve the increasing complexity of optimizing resource allocation. For example, Kang *et al.* (2001) developed a scheduling model using a conceptual approach for improving the efficiency of various resources for a multiple repetitive process. Leu and Hwang (2001) addressed a GA-based resource-constrained linear optimization model. Hyari and El-Rayes (2006) constructed a multi-objective optimization model that includes genetic algorithms for planning and scheduling repetitive activities, and helps planners in evaluating optimum plans by minimizing cycle time and maximizing work continuity simultaneously. Liu & Wang (2007) developed a flexible model for resolving linear scheduling problems involving different objectives and resource assignment tasks.

METHODOLOGY

The work was carried out for a manufacturing company and the details are being presented as a case study. The selected organisation is engaged in manufacture and export of automobile lighting equipments. The company is having a wide range of products manufactured at different plants. One such unit produces a range of automotive head lamps and halogen bulbs, which are supplied to leading automobile manufacturers (OEM's) as well as sold in replacement market. The annual turnover of this unit was reported to be forty eight million US dollars in the year ending 2010-2011. A systemic methodology was adopted for data collection, result computation and analysis. The methodology is described below.

1. Understanding the process and recognizing the key inputs.
2. Collection of data pertaining to output and all key inputs.
3. Performing multiple regression by SPSS software and analyzing the results.
4. Obtaining a mathematical relation, expressing output as a function of various key inputs.
5. Obtaining an expression of input as an equation of key input factors.
6. Identifying the existing levels of output, input and productivity.
7. Identifying all types of constraints including the upper and lower limits of the variables.
8. Developing Strategies to improve productivity, and optimizing them by linear programming techniques.

MODEL FORMULATION

Data Collection

Data has been collected from the various departments like shop-floor, planning, personnel, MIS, accounting, finance, etc. after spending enough time to study the conversion process. It has been recorded on a monthly basis for a period of twenty months. Data has been collected under various headings, such as, output, raw material, labour, energy consumption, working capital and overheads which cover everything not covered in any of the above headings, such as general and administrative expenses, salary of non-production staff, touring, advertising and marketing expenses, etc. Human input has been recorded in man-hours per month, energy in units (Kwhr) consumed per month, and the rest in terms of their monetary values (million Indian rupees) converted to base period values by suitable deflators, to eliminate the effect of inflation.

Output

A multiple linear regression was performed using SPSS software, with output as the dependent variable and the various inputs as independent or predictor variables. Two variables raw material and energy showed co-linearity. One of these had to be dropped from the equation. Energy with lower value of beta coefficient was dropped. Regression was performed again, with output as the dependent variable, and labour (u_1), raw material (u_2), working capital (u_3) and overheads (u_4) as independent variables. The results were checked for linearity. The value of R square was quite high and all the residuals were random and normally distributed and did not exhibit any non-linear trend. Thus, the results were acceptable.

The output equation obtained from regression by SPSS software is:

$$\text{Output} = 164.19u_1 + 2.27u_2 + 0.17u_3 - 0.34u_4 - 51.93 \quad \text{(i)}$$

Input

The input can be expressed as summation of the cost of these input variables.

$$\text{Input} = \sum_{i=1}^{4} b_i \cdot u_i,$$

where b_i is the coefficient of the cost of each input element in the base period. Thus,

$$\text{Input} = 11.48u_1 + 1.00u_2 + 0.017u_3 + 1.00u_4 \quad \text{(ii)}$$

Constraints

Various constraints as well as upper and lower bounds of variables have been gathered from the plant records. Where limits were not available, the highest and the lowest values of that particular variable from the data have been selected as the upper and lower limits respectively.

Capacity of the plant = 594.00

Last month:

output = 145.60	(from data)
input = 95.58	(from data)
productivity = 1.52	(output/input)

(1) Output constraints:

(a) Output should be greater than output in last month.

$$164.19u_1 + 2.27u_2 + 0.17u_3 - 0.34u_4 - 51.93 \geq 145.60$$

Re-arranging,

$$164.19u_1 + 2.27u_2 + 0.17u_3 - 0.34u_4 \geq 197.53$$

(iii)

(b) Output should be constant at last month's value.

$$164.19u_1 + 2.27u_2 + 0.17u_3 - 0.34u_4 = 197.53$$

(iv)

(c) Output should be less than output in last month.

$$164.19u_1 + 2.27u_2 + 0.17u_3 - 0.34u_4 \leq 197.53$$

(v)

(2) Input constraints:

(a) Input should be more than input in last month.

$$11.48u_1 + 1.00u_2 + 0.017u_3 + 1.00u_4 \geq 95.58$$

(vi)

(b) Input should be constant at last month's value.

$$11.48u_1 + 1.00u_2 + 0.017u_3 + 1.00u_4 = 95.58$$

(vii)

(c) Input should be less than input in last month.

$$11.48u_1 + 1.00u_2 + 0.017u_3 + 1.00u_4 \leq 95.58$$

(viii)

(3) Capacity constraint: output cannot exceed capacity of the plant.

$$164.19u_1 + 2.27u_2 + 0.17u_3 - 0.34u_4 \geq 645.93 \quad (ix)$$

(4) Productivity constraint: productivity must be more than the productivity in last month.

$$\text{Productivity} = \text{output/input} \geq 1.52$$

$$= [164.19u_1 + 2.27u_2 + 0.17u_3 - 0.34u_4 - 51.93]/$$
$$[11.48u_1 + 1.00u_2 + 0.017u_3 + 1.00u_4] \geq 1.52$$

Solving,

$$146.74u_1 + 0.75u_2 + 0.144u_3 - 1.86u_4 \geq 51.93 \quad (x)$$

(5) Upper and lower bounds of the variables

$$u_1 \geq 0.31 \quad \text{(xi)}$$
$$u_1 \leq 0.35 \quad \text{(xii)}$$
$$u_2 \geq 38.075 \quad \text{(xiii)}$$
$$u_2 \leq 85.44 \quad \text{(xiv)}$$
$$u_3 \geq 26.25 \quad \text{(xv)}$$
$$u_3 \leq 102.003 \quad \text{(xvi)}$$
$$u_4 \geq 16.50 \quad \text{(xvii)}$$
$$u_4 \leq 44.00 \quad \text{(xviii)}$$

Strategies for Improving Productivity

Productivity = output/input

There are four ways of increasing it ---------

Strategy 1: Minimizing input, keeping output constant.

Strategy 2: Maximizing output, keeping input constant.

Strategy 3: Increasing both, but increasing output relatively more.

Strategy 4: Decreasing both, but decreasing input relatively more.

The objective function and constraints for each strategy are shown in Table 1.

Table 1 Formulation of Linear Programming Optimization Model

Strategy	Objective function	Constraionts [Eq. (no.)]
Strategy 1	minimize input	Output constraint [Eq. (iv)], upper and lower bounds [Eqs (xi–xviii)]
Strategy 2	maximize output	Input constraint [Eq. (vii)], capacity constraint constraint [Eq. (ix), upper and lower bounds [Eqs. (xi–xviii)]
Strategy 3	maximize productivity	Output constraint [Eq. input constraint [Eq. (vi)], capacity constraint [Eq. (ix)], productivity constraint [Eq. (10)], upper and lower bounds [Eqs. (xi-xviii)]
Strategy 4	maximize productivity	Output constraint [Eq. (v)], input constraint [Eq. (viii)], productivity constraint [Eq. (x)], upper and lower bounds [Eqs. (xi-xviii)]

Table 2 Results and Resource Allocation

Strategy	Objective function	Labour (u_1)	Raw material (u_2)	Working capital (u_3)	Overheads (u_4)	output	input	productivity
1	78.7864	0.3500	56.5344	102.0030	16.5000	145.6	78.7864	1.8480
2	183.72	0.3500	73.3279	102.0030	16.5000	183.72	95.5800	1.9220
3	1.9535	0.3440	85.3010	101.8387	16.4731	209.9095	107.4554	1.9535
4	1.8412	0.3464	56.4960	101.9212	16.4882	144.9170	78.7060	1.8412

RESULTS

Linear programming techniques can be used to optimize the productivity level for the first two strategies; while for the last two strategies, fractional linear programming problem can be converted into an equivalent linear programming problem using Charmer and Cooker technique and then solved.

These optimizing problems have been solved by using the software TORA and the results are shown in Table 2.

DISCUSSION AND CONCLUSION

It may be observed that productivity level under all four strategies is more than the productivity in the last month (1.52). It is maximum under strategy 3 when both output and inputs are increased and minimum when both are decreased (strategy 4). Thus productivity enhances as the output is increased, and increases even further if more resources are pumped in, to be transformed into products, and ultimately profits. Opposite effect is noticed on restricting production or squeezing the resources.

The regression equation can be used to plan the output for a known set of input parameters, as well as help in decision making regarding resource allocation for any particular demand. This helps in increasing flexibility in the system. The productivity level may be used as a measure of performance and help in planning various manufacturing strategies. Any of the above four strategies may be adopted by the organisation depending on various factors such as fluctuation in demand, resources available, etc. or to meet out any sudden internal or external situations that are quite common in any manufacturing environment.

References

1. Aubauer, H.P. (2006), A Just and Efficient Reduction of Resource Throughput to Optimum, *Ecological Economics*, 58(3), 637-649.

2. Bridges & Bernisha M.(1992), To Measure or not to Measure, that is the Question, *Institute of Industrial Engineers*, 92(1), 412-419.

3. Chen, L.-H., Kao, C., Kuo, S., Wang, T.-Y., & Jang, Y.-C. (1996), Productivity Diagnosis via Fuzzy Clustering and Classification: an Application to Machinery Industry, *Omega*, 24(3), 309-319.

4. Chowdary, B.V., Rao, K.S.P., & Kanda, A. (1998), Integrated Manufacturing Performance Measure for Advanced Manufacturing Systems - A Case Study, *I.E. Journal*, 27(1), 16-22.

5. Coccia, M. (2009), What is the Optimal Rate of R&D Investment to Maximize Productivity Growth?, *Technological Forecasting and Social Change*, 76(3), 433-446.

6. Fariñas, J.C., & Ruano, S.(2005), Firm Productivity, Heterogeneity, Sunk Costs and Market Selection, *International Journal of Industrial Organisation*, 23(7-8), 505-534.

7. Frazelle & Sandra J.(1992), "A Process for Process Improvement in a White Collar Environment," *Productivity and Quality Improvement in Government*, 92(2), 347-350.

8. Galperin, E.A. (2004), Balance Set and Pareto Solutions in Linear Space with Application to Ongoing Optimal Resource Allocation, Investment Planning, Production, and Control Problems with Multiple Objectives, *Mathematical and Computer Modelling*, 40(1-2), 137-149.

9. Gunasekaran, A., Korukonda, A.R., Virtanen, I., & Yli-Olli, P. (1994), Improving Productivity and Quality in Manufacturing Organisations, *International Journal of Production Economics*, 36(2), 169-183.

10. Hannula, M. (2002), Total Productivity Measurement Based on Partial Productivity Ratios, *International Journal of Production Economics*, 78(1), 57-67.

11. Huang, R.-Y. & Halpin, D.W. (1999), Graphically based LP modelling for linear scheduling analysis – the POLO system, *Engineering Construction and Architectural Management*, 17 (1), 41–51.

12. Hyari, K. & El-Rayes, K. (2006), Optimal planning and scheduling for repetitive construction projects, *Journal of Management in Engineering*, 22 (1), 11–19.

13. Jenrich, R.I. (1995), *An Introduction to Computational Statistics- Regression Analysis*, New Jersey: Prentice Hall.

14. Kang, L.S., Park, I.C. & Lee, B.H. (2001), Optimal schedule planning for multiple, repetitive construction process, *Journal of Construction Engineering and Management*, 127 (5), 382–390.

15. Kauhanen, A. & Roponen S. (2010), Productivity Dispersion: a Case Study, *Research in Economics*, 64(2), 97-100.

16. Lee, B.L., Prasada Rao, D.S., & Shepherd, W. (2007), Comparisons of Real Output and Productivity of Chinese and Indian Manufacturing, 1980–2002, *Journal of Development Economics*, 84(1), 378-416.

17. Leu, S.S. & Hwang, S.T. (2001), Optimal repetitive scheduling model with shareable resource constraint, *Journal of Construction Engineering and Management*, 127(4), 270–280.

18. Liu, S.-S. & Wang, C.-J. (2007), Optimization model for resource assignment problems of linear construction projects, *Automation in Construction*, 16, 460 – 473.

19. Mattila, K.G. & D.M. Abraham, D.M. (1998), Resource levelling of linear schedules using integer linear programming, *Journal of Construction Engineering and Management*, 124 (3), 232–244.

20. Moselhi, O. & El-Rayes, K. (1993), Scheduling of repetitive projects with cost optimization, *Journal of Construction Engineering and Management*, 119(4), 681–697.

21. Moselhi, O. & Hassanein, A. (2003), Optimized scheduling of linear projects, *Journal of Construction Engineering and Management*, 129 (6), 664–673.

22. Norusis, M.J.(1993), *SPSS for Windows – Base System User's Guide Release 6.0*, USA: SPSS Inc.

23. Patriksson, M. (2008), A Survey on the Continuous Nonlinear Resource Allocation Problem, *European Journal of Operational Research*, 185(1), 1-46.

24. Rangkakulnuwat, P. & Holly Wang, H. (2011), Productivity Growth Decomposition with FE-IV Approach: Rethinking Thai Commercial Banks After the Financial Crisis, *Economic Modelling*, 28(6), 2579-2588.

25. Ravi Kumar, K., Hadjinicola,G.C. (1996), Resource Allocation to Defensive Marketing and Manufacturing Strategies, *European Journal of Operational Research*, 94(3), 453-466.

26. Sardana, G.D. & Vrat, P. (1987), A Model for Productivity Measurement in a Multi-Product Organisation Using Programming and Multi-Attribute Utility Theory, *Productivity Management Frontiers I*, 35-48.

27. Selinger, S. (1980), Construction planning for linear projects, *Journal of the Construction Division*, 106 (2), 195–205.

28. Son, Y.K. (1991), A Cost Estimation Model for Advanced Manufacturing Systems, *International Journal of Production Research*, 29(3), 441-452.

29. Sumanth, D.J. (1984), *Productivity Engineering and Management*, New York: McGraw Hill.

30. Thomas, B.E. & Baron, J.P. (1994), Evaluating Knowledge Worker Productivity: Literature Review, *USACERL Interim Report*, 94(27).

31. Tomaszewski, P. & Lundberg, L. (2006), The Increase of Productivity over Time—an Industrial Case Study, *Information and Software Technology*, 48(9), 915-927.

32. Weber, W.L. & Domazlicky, B.R. (1999), Total Factor Productivity Growth in Manufacturing: a Regional Approach Using Linear Programming, *Regional Science and Urban Economics*, 29(1), 105-122.

Supply Chain Management of Perishable Goods in Retail Sector

G.P. Dinesh

Dean Management Studies, Ballari Institute of Technology and Management

ABSTRACT

In India, about 60% of food quality is lost in the supply chain from the farm to the final consumer. Consumers actually end up paying approximately about 35 % more than what they could be paying if the supply chain was improved, because of wastage as well as multiple margins in the current supply structure.

Effective management must take into account coordinating all the different pieces of this chain as quickly as possible without losing any of the quality or customer satisfaction, while still keeping costs down. Key to the success of a supply chain is the speed in which these activities can be accomplished and the realization that customer needs and customer satisfaction are the very reasons for the network. Reduced inventories, lower operating costs, product availability and customer satisfaction are all benefits which grow out of effective supply chain management.

Keywords: *Retailing, Supply Chain Management, and Perishable goods.*

1. INTRODUCTION

Retailing is the interface between the producer and the individual consumer buying for personal consumption. This excludes direct interface between the manufacturer and institutional buyers such as the government and other bulk customers. A retailer is one who stocks the producer's goods and is involved in the act of selling it to the individual consumer, at a margin of profit. As such, retailing is the last link that connects the individual consumer with the manufacturing and distribution chain. Retailing is emerging as a sunrise industry in India and is presently the largest employer after agriculture. In the year 2004, the size of Indian organized retail industry was ₹28,000 Crore, which was only 3% of the total retailing market. Retailing in its present form started in the latter half of 20th Century in USA and Europe and today constitutes 20% of US GDP. It is the 3rd largest employer segment in USA. Organized retailing in India is projected to grow at the rate of 25% 30% PA and is estimated to reach an astounding ₹1,00,000 Crore by 2010. The contribution of organized retail is expected to rise from 3% to 9% by the end of the decade. The entry of foreign and Indian retail giants like Wal-Mart, Metro,

Reliance, Birla, Tata etc. made Indian market more competitive which is at cut throat level. So how retailers can reach to their end customers, to win the mind share and increase the basket size of each shopping trip.

India retail industry is the largest industry in India, with an employment of around 8% and contributing to over 10% of the country's GDP. Retail industry in India is expected to rise 25% yearly being driven by strong income growth, changing lifestyles, and favorable demographics.

In India, about 60% of food quality is lost in the supply chain from the farm to the final consumer. Consumers actually end up paying approximately about 35% more than what they could be paying if the supply chain was improved, because of wastage as well as multiple margins in the current supply structure.

Retail is the fastest growing sector in Indian economy. Retail Organisations intended to bring quality fresh food to the customers at an affordable price. Organisations started its retail operations of Fresh stores with following supply chain model. Procuring directly from the farmers and operating with moderate margin but mass selling was key to these organisations operation for first few months. Company had to strengthen its links with farmers; the company is setting up Integrated Agri-Retail Business Centre's, which include three processing and distribution centers. Many companies, looking at the retail boom in food and grocery, are setting up ventures to help retailers source these goods.

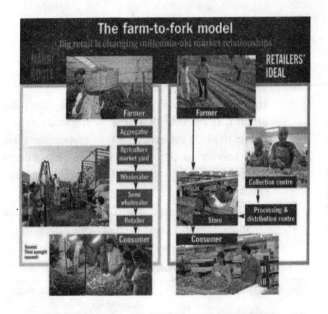

The problem under study is "Supply Chain Management of Perishable Goods" Here we are analyzing the movement of the perishable goods and all about the inventory level.

The following are the obstacles faced by the companies:

- Increasing Variety of Products
- Decreasing product Life Cycle
- Increase in Demanding Customer
- Fragmentation of supply chain ownership
- Difficulty in Executing New Strategies

The main objective of this study is to identify the areas of strength and weaknesses of Supply Chain network and inventory management of perishable goods and suggest an action plan for improvement in those areas, which have key impact in the effectiveness of the Supply chain Integration.

Following are the specific objectives of the study:

- To Study the basic of supply chain system
- To study the effectiveness of the current supply chain system.
- To analyze the strategic plan regarding supply chain integration.
- To focus the general problem creating areas in the supply chain network.
- To recommend new ways for better supply chain integration to gain more competitive advantage and for better customer response

Research Methodology

The researcher has used combination of exploratory and descriptive research design to collect the data from 30 stores across the city of Bangalore by using Interview and discussion techniques'. The collected data is analyzed by using simple statistical tools to arrive at a solution.

Data Analysis

1. **Managing companies supply chain:**

Table 1

Managing supply chain	No of respondents	Percentage
Successful	30	100%
Not Successful	0	0%

Interpretation: From the above table and graph it is inferred that 100% respondents believe that company is managing successful supply chain system, which helps in proper documentation of different business process.

2. **Major benefits of going for a supply chain management system in your company:** Interpretation: From the above table and graph it inferred that 100% respondents believe that all the above listed benefits are

Table 2

Major benefit	No of respondents	Percentage
Provides linkage between food production stage, suppliers and consumers - [A]	0	0%
Assures timely and efficient distribution of food to meet the consumers demand - [B]	0	0%
Maintains quality and safety of food until purchased by consumers - [C]	0	0%
All the above - [D]	30	100%

needed to manage the supply chain of the company.

3. Types of systems currently in use in your company to support Supply Chain Management:

Table 3

Types of systems	No of respondents	Percentage
Material requirement planning	3	10%
Enterprise resource planning	17	56%
Supplier relationship management	2	7%
Warehouse management system	3	10%
Just in time	0	0%
Customer relationship management	5	17%

Interpretation: From the above table and graph it is inferred that 10% of the respondents said that the company's supply chain is supported either by material requirement planning or warehouse management system, 56% respondents said it is majorly supported by enterprise resource planning, 17% supported by customer relationship management, 7% by supplier relationship management for smooth working of the entire organisation.

- Thus it can be inferred that 56% of respondents said supply chain of the company is majorly supported by enterprise resource planning.

4. Number of complaints (department-wise):

Table 4

Department	No of Complaints	Percentage
Logistics	25	83%
Dealers	5	17%

Interpretation: From the above table and graph it is inferred that 83% of the respondents believe that supply chain of the company has most of the complaints are from logistics department and 17% of complaints are from dealers department.

- Thus it is inferred that 83% respondents believe that major complaints are from logistics department.

5. Order placements:

Table 5

Order placement	Number of respondents	Percentage
Phone 6	2	0%
Web service	2	6%
Forecast system	20	7%
Personal	2	7%

Interpretation: From above table and the graph it is inferred that 20% of respondents use phone to place the orders, 6% of respondents use web service to place orders, 67% respondents use forecasting system and 6% placing personal order.

- Thus it is inferred that 67% of the orders are placed on the basis of forecasting.

6. Tracking of goods:

Table 6

Tracking by	No of respondents	Percentage
Communication channel	6	20%
Web enabled system	2	7%
GPRS	22	73%

Interpretation: From the above table and graph that it is inferred that 20% of the respondents said that orders are tracked by communication channel, 73% of the respondents said that majorly orders are tracked by GPRS, 7% by web enabled system.

- Thus it is inferred that 73% of the respondents use GPRS for tracking the goods

7. Order processing time:

Table 7

Order processing Time	No of Respondents	Percentage
Make to order	5	17%
Make to stock	25	83%

Interpretation: From the above table and graph that it is inferred that 17% of the respondents said that order processing is done by make to order, 83% of them said it is make to order.

- Thus it is inferred that 83% of respondents said majorly order processing is done by make to order.

8. Is SAP package is reducing the lead-time and Cycle time:

Table 8

SAP reduce L.T and C.T	No of respondents	Percentage
Agree	30	100%
Disagree	0	0%

Interpretation: From the above table and graph it inferred that 100% of the respondents agree that SAP package is reducing lead time and cycle time.

9. Quality control in business process:

Table 9

Quality Control	No of respondents	Percentage
Agree	28	93%
Disagree	2	7%

Interpretation: From the above table and graph it is inferred 93% of the respondents agree that company is following quality control measures in different business processes, 17% of the respondents disagree.

10. Company have its own logistics:

Table 10

Company has own logistics	No of respondents	Percentage
YES	30	100%
NO	0	0%

Interpretation: From the above table and graph it is inferred that 100% of respondents said that the company has its own distribution logistic support system.

11. Distribution Network Option:

Table 11

Distribution network	No of respondents	Percentage
Airways	0	0%
Road Ways	0	0%
Water Ways	0	0%
All the above	30	100%

Interpretation: From above table and graph it is inferred that 100% of the respondents know that the company is using road ways, water ways and air ways as a transportation mode in the distribution process for its operation.

12. Maintaining the Reverse Logistics Process:

Table 12

Reverse Logistic Process	No of respondents	Percentage
Yes	30	100%
No	0	0%

Interpretation: From the above table and graph inferred that 100% of the respondents said the company is using the reverse logistics process to bring all the stock keeping unit back to the delivery center (DC). Hence it will increase the space in various stores.

13. On what criteria do you judge the effectiveness of supply chain in your company:

Table 13

Criteria for effectiveness of supply chain	Timely deliver	Quality and cost	Availability of stock	Less damage of goods	All the above
No of respondents	4	0	5	0	21
Percentage	13%	0%	17%	0	70%

Interpretation: From the above table and graph it is inferred that 13% of the respondents believe that timey delivery is the important criteria to judge the effectiveness of the supply chain, 17% believe it is due to availability of stock, 0% believes that it is due either by quality of cost or less damage of goods and 70% believe that all the above factors are the criteria. Thus it is inferred that 70% of respondents said that the effectiveness of the supply chain can be judged by all the above listed criteria.

14. Effectiveness in managing its companies supply chain:

Table 14

Effectiveness in managing supply chain	Not successful at all	Not successful	Somewhat successful	Successful	Very successful
No of respondents	0	3	22	5	0
Percentage	0%	10%	73%	17%	0%

Interpretation: From the above table and graph shows that it is inferred that 10% of the respondents believe that the company is not managing the supply chain effectively, 73% of respondents believe that the company is somewhat managing its supply chain, 17% of respondents said successfully managing supply chain

Thus it is inferred that 73% of the respondents believe that the company more or less successful in managing the supply chain.

15. Managing supply chain:

Table 15

Manage your supply chain	No of respondents	Percentage
Close partnerships with suppliers	0	0%

Contd...

Contd...

E-procurement	0	0%
JIT-supply	0	0%
Outsourcing	5	16%
Sub-contracting	12	40%
Plan-strategically	13	43%

Interpretation: From the above table and graph it is inferred that 16% of the respondents believe that company manages the supply chain by outsourcing, 40% believe that supply chain is managed by sub contracting and 43% by planning strategically.

Thus it is inferred that 43% respondents believe that company manages supply chain by planning strategically.

Table 16

Working strategies of supply chain	Outstanding	Excellent	Good	Average
No of respondents	0	6	24	0
Percentage	0%	20%	80%	0%

16. Rate the working strategies of supply chain management department on the basis of the current programs:

Interpretation: From the above table and graph it is inferred that 20% of respondents rate that working strategies of supply chain as

excellent, 80% rate the working strategies as good for effective and successfully implementation of supply chain.

- Thus it is inferred that 80% of the respondents rate the working strategies of the supply chain as good.

Table 17

Supply chain problems	During storage	Packaging	Testing of packaging	Evaluation of defective material
No of respondents	18	6	2	4
Percentage	60%	20%	7%	13%

17. Supply chain department is facing problem:

Interpretation: From the above table and graph it is inferred that 60% of respondents believe that supply chain department is facing problems during storage, 20% during packaging,

17% during evaluation of defective material and 7% during testing.

- Thus it is inferred that 60% of the respondents believe the supply chain department is facing problem majorly during storage.

Table 18

Inventory bought from	Producers/farmers	Wholesalers	Brokers/agents	others
No of respondents	21	9	0	0
Percentage	70%	30%	0%	0%

Table 19

Factors to select members of supply chain	Price	Availability of stock	Quality	All the above
No of respondents	0	0	0	30
Percentage	0%	0%	0%	100%

18. **Inventory is brought:**

    Interpretation: From the above table and graph it is inferred that 70% of respondents said that company gets its inventory mostly from producers/farmers and 30% from wholesalers.

19. **On which factor do you select the member of a supply chain:**

    Interpretation: From the above table and graph it is inferred that 100% of respondents said that selection of the members of supply chain is based on price, quality and availability of stock.

20. Which technology is used to secure supply chain in your company from competitors?

    According to the response to the above question, the company uses SAP material management mode in order to secure the companies details from its competitors

21. Recommend improvements/new ways for better supply chain integration?

    According to the response to the above question, it appears that every member in the supply chain should look at centralizing company's supply chain management both at dry and wet DC so as to bring about effective cost management methods.

SUMMARY OF FINDING

1. The basic supply chain of the retailers operating efficiently which helps in proper documentation of different business process.
   - 100% respondents believe that company is managing successful supply chain system,
   - Order placement is done by forecasting as it is based on real time data with help of SAP. Hence it helps to build a good reputation with the customer.
   - GPRS system is used for tracking of the goods. It can be suggested that web enabled tracking system also can be used which will helps saving time and cost incurred in tracking of goods, and it is important for the

individual customers to have a login ID for effective tracking system.
   - The current stock-processing system practiced by the company is make-to-stock as it ensures cost reduction in the warehouse as well as quick response.
   - Order placement is done by forecasting as it is based on real time data with help of SAP. Hence it helps to build a good reputation with the customer.
   - Cycle time and the lead time are reduced by the use of SAP, which is good sign for the company to make good benefits out of SAP.

2. The effectiveness of the supply chain is judged based on Timely deliver, quality and cost, availability of stock & less damage of goods and effectiveness is also maintained by the quality control processes.
   - 73% of the respondents believe that the company more or less successful in managing the supply chain.
   - 70% of respondents said that the effectiveness of the supply chain can be judged by Timely deliver, quality and cost, availability of stock & less damage of goods.

3. The strategies that are followed to manage the supply chain of the company are quite effective and successfully implemented in order to have smooth working.
   - 80% of the respondents rate the working strategies of the supply chain as good.
   - 43% respondents believe that company manages supply chain by planning strategically.

4. The general problem creating areas in Supply chain department is during storage of perishable goods and the maximum number of complaints is receiving from logistics department i.e. mainly due to in efficient timely delivery of inventory.
   - Inventory to reliance stores is brought from farmers. Reliance is providing a guaranteed market for the farmers' produce, reducing transaction costs and training the farmers in

better and sustainable farming practices. And also get inventory from wholesalers.

5. New ways for better supply chain integration is by

  • The company uses SAP material mode management to secure its information from competitors.

  • Big retailers are maintaining the Reverse Logistics Process as it brings the entire stock keeping unit back to the delivery center (DC). Hence it will increase the space in various stores.

  • Big Retailers have their own logistics function called as Re-Logistics. It adds an extra responsibility on the company, as it has to see that there is for proper & timely delivery of goods and it also reduces cost.

  • Company uses most of the SAP modules like ERP, customer relationship management which is reducing lead time and cycle time.

SUGGESTIONS

1. Requirement of Improved transportation practices in fresh from DC to the reliance fresh store.

2. Believe less shrink and maintain freshness during transportation, in warehouse and retail shop until it reaches to customers

3. Improve inventory control methods

4. Retailers should look at centralizing supply chain modules both at dry and wet DC so as to bring about effective cost management methods.

CONCLUSION

The concept of supply Chain Management is still in infancy in India and the advanced Information Technology has yet to touch many untapped areas. The nature of competition is rapidly changing, and with this change comes the need to redefine and reappraise the modes of management prevailing, so as to equip us with more appropriate ways to manage in the 21st century. The whole study reveals that the reference company is on the right track to integrate its supply chain operations with the incorporation of information Technology through SAP system. This has blessed them to reduce cost in many functional areas like procurement of raw materials vendor selection, and production planning and scheduling, distribution etc. But still there are some areas where father improvement can be done for more comprehensive approach in the total supply chain network.

To leverage what company can derive best out of its current supply chain operation an integrated approach is required with focus to give maximum value to its customer, that optimize the entire supply chain operation, thereby reducing operational cost. Keeping this in mind, this study has been conducted that address the supply chain management of Perishable Goods in Retail Sector.

References

• Chopra, Sunil and Meindle, Peter Supply Chain Management-Strategy, Planning and Operation, PHI, 3rd edition, 2007.

• Donald, J. Bowersox & David, J. Closs, M. Bixby Coluper, Supply Chain Logistic Management, TMH, Second Edition, 2008.

• Kothari, C. R. Research Methodology, Vishwa Prakashan, 2002.

• Richard tr. Levin & David, S. Rubin, Statistics for Management, Pearson, 7th edition.

• Kotler, Philip Marketing Management, PHI, Millennium Edition.

Transition in Business Negotiation: Cross-Cultural Perspective

Jitka Odehnalová

Faculty of International Relations, University of Economics, PragueWinston Churchill Sq. 4, 130 67 Prague, Czech Republic

ABSTRACT

To succeed dynamic changes within business environment in the 21st century business organisations need to deal with interconnectedness of business relations and perform a fast transformation of business strategies, methods and techniques which enables them to survive. This paper focuses on the key business stage any business organisation must go through – Business Negotiation while focusing on the inputs influencing the successful negotiation outputs. Cross-cultural issues come up as an exclamation mark as a result of the enormously increasing international cooperation which inevitably requires sensitivity to existing cultural differences.

The paper aims to point out the need of transition in Business Negotiation strategies and tactics, challenges and opportunities business organisations face to avoid the risk that insufficient cross-cultural competences would lead to business failures. As a result of the worldwide economic development, Chinese counterparts create one of the most powerful "group", business organisations deal with. Therefore the author decided to focuses on the Chinese Business culture needed to be reflected in business communication and negotiation preparation.

Keywords: *Business Negotiation Culture, Cross-Cultural Business Negotiation, Cross-Cultural Competence, Transition in Business Negotiation, Chinese Philosophies, Good and Bad human Nature, Hierarchy*

INTRODUCTION

Being active in Business in the 21st century places the companies and their representatives into a very unstable and demanding position. As a result of the fast developing environment the business activities are becoming global while the technical opportunities make the distances in the world become closer which on one hand supports the business activities as such on the other hand competition is stronger and the traditional aspects of success in business are changing while a "good product" is not anymore the only sufficient asset. The question to be asked sounds: "Why companies with good products or services, good entry studies and proper market research often fail while creating or maintaining business connections?"

The answer lies within the term: cross-cultural competence – being able to deal with members of various cultures while avoiding cross-cultural miss-understandings and conflicts. The dynamic development and global interconnectedness moved the "good product" to one of the basic necessary aspects of business success. What makes the difference are the strong relations with business partners that make the "good" product have the opportunity to be placed on the market which requires the focus on the business negotiation culture.

Since China happened to become one of the key economic players in the World, this paper explores the Chinese business negotiation behaviour.

The output of a business negotiation depends on many factors. Aside the technical aspects of the object of business negotiation, the human factor on the side of the negotiators plays an important role. No wonder that recent research points out that one of the aspects influencing people´s behaviour is their culture including the history, philosophies, teachings and religions. Therefore this paper aims to present particular thoughts and teachings which have been followed by Chinese and further developed through a long time and ended up in influencing tremendously the Chinese behaviour reflected in the Chinese Business Behaviour. Such can be the causes of possible cross-cultural misunderstandings or even conflicts while negotiating across members of different cultures. Since one paper cannot subscribe such a complex area completely, the author chose to focus on three important aspects determining people´s behaviour connected tight and reflected in the negotiation behaviour and so the origin and development of the perspective of good and bad human nature and authority.

The philosophies and thoughts to be mentioned show what values and norms were established and promoted and the base of judging good and bad humans – analogically appropriate or inappropriate business partners and so on. They shape the negotiator´s expectations and perception of success, formulating goals and defining the right way to reach the goals. It shows the meaning of the team members´ roles, appropriate behaviour and rules.

All these aspects do foreigners have to face and take into account while working with Chinese business counterparts.

Good and Bad Human Nature and Authority

During 250 years after the dead of Confucius the Chinese world succumbed to immense changes. Power was increasingly executed by feudal rather than united under the rule of one dynasty.

Good Human Nature

Mencius (Mengzi, 77, 385? - 312? BC) was the only pioneer of the view on human nature that spread not only all over China, but also among the rest of the eastern Confucian Asia - in the minds of intellectuals and social elite as well as in the system of values of the whole culture.

Mencius was given the name Ke which means disappointment for he was born in the middle of difficult times. Despite the adversity of those times and the poverty his family was going through his mother did everything she could to provide him with education which she found very important. The story called "Mencius' Mother Moving Three Times" is familiar to many Chinese. Thanks to the environment provided by his mother Mencius had the opportunity to get acquainted with Confucius' teachings. Once he said: "The world hasn't known a greater man than Confucius throughout the life of the mankind." and became a Confucian master. While Confucius proclaimed love, duty, decency and wisdom to be the greatest values, Mencius filled the theoretical gap of these thoughts by trying to find out why it is so. The answer he came to

was that people are born good and with good intentions. He was able to keep this conviction although he lived in the times of horrifying war violence and poverty leading to cannibalism in its most terrible form. He was an example for others of how to remain honest and good regardless of the disappointment and sorrow that life can bring. He proclaimed the importance of life and even more the importance of faith and spirit which make our lives meaningful. He was a defender of the ideal of a "good human" who can be corrupted neither by money nor by power, whose courage overcomes poverty and all the troubles and who can't be silenced by any tyrant or oppressor. "If heaven decides to put a great responsibility on one's shoulders it firstly frustrates his spirit, exhausts his muscles and bones, exposes him to hardship and poverty, showers him with misfortune and failure only to motivate his spirit, strengthen his health and extend his abilities in the end." This Mencius' thought has had an enormous influence on Chinese civilization and many people follow this example in their lives.

His work "Mencius" is a record of talks between Mencius himself, the rulers of enemy feudal states and the supporters and opponents of his philosophy. It also includes proclamations concerning various topics as for example the human nature or governing techniques. Mencius referred to Confucius and broadened his idea of "ren" (humanity). He also presented an additional principal "yi" that represented justice (correctness) as a complex idea of what was right in particular situations and under specific conditions. Probably under the influence of his opponents (Mohists and Legalists), he was strongly aware of people's basic needs – food, clothes, shelter and education – that have to be satisfied in order to enable human beings to exist. He presented four origins – natural tendencies –that according to him can develop in humanity (ren), justice (yi), decency and wisdom. Feelings of regret and empathy are an origin of humanity, justice originates in feelings of shame and resistance, feelings of modesty and agreement are basics for decency and the sense of good and bad is the origin of wisdom. Everyone possesses these four origins as everyone possesses four extremities. "There is no man without the tendency to be good as there is no water without the tendency to flow downwards" (Bloom and de Bary, 1999, p. 147). What he meant by the idea is that "an individual is enabled to do good and if he acts wrong it is not a problem of his possibilities." (Bloom and de Bary, 1999, p. 149)Things of the same kind have common characteristics as people have the same perception of good, bad, pleasant, unpleasant.

Mencius, also known as the kindly saint of ages, fearlessly proclaimed his theories of organisation of the state and rule: "The most important element of the state is its common people, then come the goods of soil and crops and the ruler himself has the least importance." Undoubtedly, this is the first formulation of democracy in China. His answer to the question whether he wasn't scared to state such anti-ruler thoughts was: "I long both for a fish and for a bear paw. If I can't have them both I'll do without the fish and go for the bear paw. I long for life and at the same time I long for justice. If I can't have both I'll do without life and go for justice." (Bloom and de Bary, 1999, p. 151) "There are things we long for more than for life and things we detest more than death. Not only exemplary individuals think this way but all living beings do. The difference is that exemplary individuals are able to prevent the loss of this thinking that is all." (Bloom and de Bary, 1999, p. 152) On the topic of how to convince he stated: "If violence is applied to make people submit, they won't submit from their hearts but only because of lack of their own power. If it's honesty that is applied to make people submit they are satisfied from the deep of their hearts and they submit sincerely." (Bloom and de Bary, 1999, p. 128) If the ruler is able to bring welfare to his people even the peoples from surrounding states will think of him as a father. Therefore, as no one has ever made anybody kill their parents, such a ruler will have no enemies. Who has no enemies is a delegate of Heaven and such a person can't fail as a king. "Those who use wisdom in their work can lead; those who use power are meant to be led." (Bloom and de Bary, 1999, p. 132).

Mencius claims that if someone only cares for his own interests he can't avoid conflict which can only lead to chaos in the county. On the contrary if the ruler is benevolent and just he gains the support of his people which is the most important precondition of a constructive development of a state. It is possible to achieve a standardized law, strong economy and well educated ambitious people in a benevolent state.

Among other Mencius' statements we can mention: "To share ones possessions is goodness. To teach others to be good is devotion. "(Bloom and de Bary, 1999, p. 133) "There is a feeling between parents and children, justice between a ruler and his minister, separate functions between a man and a woman, a proper order between the older and the younger brother and there is fidelity between friends." (Bloom and de Bary, 1999, p. 133) „Diversity of things is their nature. Some are more precious... an effort to unify them would only bring chaos to the world.

If big shoes cost the same as small ones who would produce them?" (Bloom and de Bary, 1999, p. 134) "Goodness itself isn't a sufficient element of governing; laws can't implement themselves." (Bloom and de Bary, 1999, p. 137) "Whenever one's activity doesn't lead to success he should turn on himself and see what is happening inside him."(Bloom and de Bary, 1999, p. 138) "Which is the greatest of services? It is the service to one's parents. Which is the greatest of wariness? It is the wariness towards oneself." (Bloom and de Bary, 1999, str. 139) "If the ruler views his ministers as his arms and legs, the ministers will view their ruler as their stomach and heart. If the ruler views his ministers as dogs and horses, the ministers will view their ruler only as another person. If the ruler views his ministers as dirt and grass, the ministers will view him as an exploiter and enemy. If the ruler is humane, everyone will be humane. If the ruler does good, everyone will do good. If the ruler is correct, everyone will be correct. Once the ruler follows the right direction, the state will be well organized." (Bloom and de Bary, 1999, p. 140) "A ceremony that is not a proper ceremony, correctness that is not properly correct – a noble individual does not exercises those. Noble is who does not lose the mind of a child." (Bloom and de Bary, 1999, p. 141).

While it is Confucius who is widely known in western countries and hardly anyone knows Mencius, they both are much respected in China.

Bad Human Nature

Who could be able to unite "all under the Heaven" and how? Xunzi (Xun Kuang, Xun Qing) also known as Master Xun (310? - 219? BC) occupied himself – like Mencius – with this question. The works of these two authors differ mainly in their form, on the other hand we can find similarities in content – they both reflect on the matter of rule and personal development, which is, after all, typical for all Confucian works.

His view of the world was more negative than Mencius'. His thoughts – mainly those concerning rule, education and the relation between the world of humans and Heaven (natural order) – are further linked to those of Mohists, Taoists and also Legalists (Legalism is to be analyzed further in this text). Unlike his works Debates and Mencius the work called Xunzi is focused on topics concerning Xunzi himself, for example learning, self-education, rule, military affairs, Heaven and Nature, ceremonies, language and human nature. Unlike Mencius he states that human nature is bad! At the same time, people are born with the ability of both recognizing humanity, justice, appropriate rules and honesty and of practicing them. However, goodness is an outcome of a purposeful activity. It is necessary to work on oneself and to love others. The necessity to work on oneself is clearly emphasized: "A noble individual who studies a lot and examines himself every day is to reach the pure mind and perfection in behaviour." (Bloom and de Bary, 1999, p. 161) It is vital to use our abilities of being good. "A noble person is of no difference from others at the moment of birth, but it makes a good use of outer things." (Bloom and de Bary, 1999, p. 162) "A noble person uses things; a minor being is used by things." (Bloom and de Bary, 1999, p. 166) "A person who knows things will handle each thing as a separate part. A person who knows the path – Tao – will consider things a whole." (Bloom and de Bary, 1999, p. 179) "Who walks two paths at the same time will get nowhere. Who serves two masters will satisfy none of them...." (Bloom and de Bary, 1999, p. 163).

While Mencius speaks about the development of an infinite, flowing qi (which he associates to accumulation of justice leading to the connection of an individual with Heaven and Earth) Xunzi explicitly offers recommended ways of regulating qi and developing mind in order to become a balanced and harmonious personality.

Unlike Mencius who refuses to Xunzi isn't afraid to describe particular ways of governing adequate to the individual who understands power – adequate to lord protector, true king. We can – in today's terms – speak about Human Resources Management. "If they do their work without problems, accept them as your subjects. If they don't execute their work easily, fire them. As for those who suffer from one of the deficiencies (dumbness, blindness, deafness, handicap, missing arm or leg or underdevelopment) support them, gather them around, nourish them and give them work according to their abilities. Employ them, clothe them and feed them and make sure no one of them remains omitted. If someone is caught using his talents to behave against good, condemn him to death. This is called the power of Heaven and rule of the king." (Bloom and de Bary, 1999, p. 167) He underlines the necessity of hierarchical organisation of society! "No distinction will exist where all the social classes are equal. No unity will exist where the power is distributed equally. If the masses are all at the same level, it will be impossible to employ them. The existence of Heaven and Earth demonstrates that there is a difference between superior and inferior, but it could only happen after the installation of an enlightened king and the establishment of a state governed by

rules. Rules, ceremonies, established models and limits created by the ruler are necessary for the improvement of human emotional nature, its correction, further education and metamorphosis and they serve as a clue to the establishment of order. Equality can only exist where inequality exists as well." (Bloom and de Bary, 1999, p. 168) The path of Heaven doesn't change as a result of human rule; the key to human welfare is human endeavour. It was Xunzi's statement – that thanks to the recognition of relations between the three levels (Heaven, ruler, Earth) people are able to create a triad along with Heaven and Earth – what became the principal thought of ethical cosmologic Confucian thinking. "Heaven has its phases, Earth has its resources and people have their government." (Bloom and de Bary, 1999, str. 171) "A noble individual follows what is permanent; a petty individual plans his success. Because a noble person cares for what he shall he and doesn't desire what belongs to Heaven, he moves forward day by day. Because a limited person lays aside what he is meant to do and desires what belongs to Heaven he moves back day by day. "When Stars are falling or trees are moaning... It doesn't mean anything, it's just Heaven turning into Earth and yin turning into yang; it happens sometimes... while it is right to marvel at such phenomenon it is wrong to fear them" (Bloom and de Bary, 1999, p. 173).

Hierarchical Self-Regulation

Another work of which the authorship is unsure is "Zuo's Commentary" (or "Commentary of Master Zuo") traditionally considered as the commentary on "Spring and Autumn Annals". It deals with the relation between moral nature of people and the dynamism of their lives and political activity. Basically, it clarifies Confucius' thoughts and intentions. His clearly hierarchical self-regulatory idea of Heaven's influence is apparent from the following comment: "Heaven gave life to people and appointed their rulers so that they supervised and led while at the same time remained human beings who need assistants and advisors... The ruler has his highest advisors who have their ministers and those have indirect relationships with gentlemen who have their friends and companions, common people craftsmen, merchants, servants, shepherds and partners. All of them have their relatives and close acquaintances who support and help them. When an individual does good, they praise him. When he makes mistakes, they correct him. When he is in trouble, they save him. When he is lost, they replace him." (Bloom and de Bary, 1999, p. 185).

Law and Punishment as a Management Tool

Legalism (fajia) comprises ideas and rules linked to the growth of bureaucratic state of China in the course of second and first century BC. Its cornerstone is "fa" representing the possible arrangement and execution of state power through laws and punishments, by means of administrative and military system, strategic planning, diplomacy and personnel management. This trend arose from the need of logical organisation of society and resources and the need of the reinforcement of state's position against its rivals. This movement–diametrically opposite to Confucianism in terms of ideology–advocated outright for war as a means of ruler's power reinforcement, state's expansion and toughening, submissiveness and discipline of people, so that people lived modestly and obediently to the states interest in peace as well as during war. Refusing the traditional ethic values completely, considering a rule based on law rather than on personal example and disdaining traditional ideas Legalists represented the opposite to the Confucian ideas while drawing certain thoughts from Taoists and Mohists. Legatists' objectives reflect mainly Mozi's emphasis on unity and mobilisation of the people in order to reach gains and Laozi's thought of active passivity (Wu Wei) applied on the sovereign who doesn't participate directly on the rule, but presides to sophisticated legal governmental administration as a semi divine puppet. The administration itself then foregoes the need of ruler's involvement of any kind in governing.

CONCLUSION

This paper is bringing a detailed view into chosen particular Chinese thoughts, teachings and philosophies creating and supporting believes of members of Chinese culture. The environment, conditions and situations are changing with the time, while the symbolism, meaning and ways to reach the goal remain. The emperor and his role can always be the analogy to the boss, or team leader. Ways of recommended behaviour, rules of successful handling of power were discussed in detail including individual expressions in order to show how much they are connected to nowadays business negotiation.

While focusing on exploring and understanding those, negotiators from all over the world gain a significant negotiating advantage. When representing their companies they might apply their understanding and avoid misunderstanding and potential conflicts as a result of being able to explain well their Chinese partner´s behaviour and simultaneously adjust their own

behaviour so that their Chinese counterparts understand and react according to their will.

Such shift in perception, explanation and reaction within business negotiation representing the key part of business communication, allows abroad active companies which are facing cultural differences to succeed on the fast growing global market. Knowledge required can be read in books, heard in seminars, while the most efficient way is the personal experience therefore a well designed culture training combining both the gain of knowledge and experience is the right tool.

In the 21st century when country borders are being erased and the economic environment including the business environment has been transformed the negotiation preparation, skills and practices needed to bring success in business are being transformed. To survive and succeed the implementation of cross-cultural trainings info human resource management are highly recommended.

Limitations are brought by the aspect that the human environment, set of values, norms and believes is changing as the living environment is transforming, To have up to date skill in this respect means to explore the development of the cultural aspects of negotiation behaviour continuously. From this point of view the philosophies discussed in this article are the only, inevitable, good and valuable start – first step on the way to further analysis of later thoughts and teachings up to date.

References

- A Survey of the Chinese Civilization, (2007), Chinese travelling publicationagency, Beijing.
- Adair, W., Brett, J., Lempereur, A., Okumura, T., Shikhirev, P., Tinsley, C., Lytle, A.: Culture and Negotiation Strategy: Research Report, (2004), *Negotiation Journal, Blackwell Publishing* , 2004, 87-111,
- Björkman, I. and Kock, S. (1995), "Social relationships and business networks: the case of western companies in China", International Business, 4, 519-35.
- Bloom, I., de Bary, Wm., T.(1999): Sources of Chinese Tradition, Volume 1; From Earliest Times To 1600, New York, Columbia University Press, .
- Bond, M.H. and Hwang, K.K. (1986), "The social psychology of Chinese people", in Bond, M.H. (Ed.), The Psychology of the Chinese People, Oxford University Press, Hong Kong, 213-66

- Cai, A., Wilson, R., Drake, E., Culture in the context of intercultural negotiation.. Individualism-collectivism and paths to integrative agreements, Human Communication Research 26 (4), 591-617, 2000.
- Campbell, N. and Adlington, P. (1988), China Business Strategies, Pergamon, Oxford.
- Chu, C.-N. (1991), The Asian Mind Game, Rawson Associates, New York, NY.
- De Bary, Wm., T., Lufrano, R.: Source of Chinese Tradition, Volume 2; From 1600 Through the Twentieth Century, 2nd Edition, New York, Coumbia University Press, 2000, ISBN 0-231-11271-8
- Drake, L.E. (2001): "The culture-negotiation link. Integrative and distributive bargaining through an intercultural communication lens. Human Communication Research". 27,. 3, 317–349.
- Faure, G.O. (2002): International Negotiation: The Cultural Dimension. In International Negotiation: Analysis, Approaches, Issues, edited by V. A. Kremenyuk. San Francisco: Jossey-Bass/Wiley.
- Faure, G.O. (1995). Nonverbal negotiation in China. *Negotiation Journal* 11 (1): 11-17.
- Gelfand, M. J., Dyer N., A cultural Perspective on Negotiation: Progress, Pitfalls, and Prospects, Applied Psychology, An International Review, 2000, 49 (1), 62-99
- Ghauri, P., N., Fang, T., The chinese business negotiation process: a socio-cultural analysis, research paper, Graduate School/Research Institute, Systems, Organisations and Management (SOM), Retrived from http://som.rug.nl/, 1999.
- Graham, J. L., The Influence of Culture on the process of business negotiations: An Exploratory Study Journal of International Business Studies, Spring 1985, 16,, 81-96
- Hampden-Turner, Ch., Trompenaars, F(1997)., Response to Geert Hofstede, Int. J. Intercultural Rel. Vol. 21. No. 1, 149-159,.
- Hofstede, G. (1980): Cultures consequences: International differences in work related values. Beverly Hills, CA: Sage Publications.
- Hofstede, G., Challenges of Cultural Diversity, Interview by Sarah Powell, Human Resource Management International Digest, Emerald Group Publishing Limited,. 14,(3),
- Jamal A. Al-Khatib, Stacy M. Vollmers, Yusin Liu., The Business to business negotiating in China: the role of morality, Journal of Business & Industrial Marketing.: 2007, 22, 2, 84 (nic)
- Odehnalová, J. (2008b): Specific of Chinese Business Negotation Practices. Revista Amfiteatru Economic. Č. 24, s. 283–296. ISSN 1582-9146.
- Odehnalová, J. (2008c): Specifika obchodního jednání v Číně. Marketing & komunikace. Roč. 18, č. 2, s. 20–22. ISSN 1211-5622.
- Odehnalová, J. (2009): Povaha čínského obchodního jednání – Na válečném poli či mezi gentlemany. Acta Oeconomica Pragensia. Roč. 17, č. 6, s. 52-56. ISSN 0572-3043.
- Pruitt, D.G. (1981): Negotiation Behavior. New York: Academic Press.
- Ruane, A. E. (2006): "Real Men "and Diplomats: Intercultural Diplomatic Negotiation and Masculinities in China and the United States, International Studies Perspectives, Vol. 7, 342-359.
- Sawyer, J.; gutzekow, H. (1965): Bargaining and Negotiation in International Relations, In H. C. Kelman, ed. International Behaviour, A Social-Psychological Analysis. New York: Holt, Rinehart and Winston, pp. 464-520.
- Thomas, A. (2005): Intercultural Training, Conditions-Process-Results Preparation-Implementation-Evaluation. Regensburg: Regensburg University, Institute for Psychology.
- Ting-Toomey, S. (2000): Managing Intercultural Conflict Effectively. In Intercultural Communication A Reader (7th edn), edited by L. A. Samovar and R. E. Porter. Belmont: Wadsworth/International Thomson.
- Xu, Yuanxiang, Confucius - A Philosopher for Ages; Ancient Sages of China, China International Press, 2007, Beijing, ISBN 7-5085-1037-2
- Xu, Yuanxiang, Yin Yongjian Lao Tzu – The Eternal Tao Te Ching, Ancient Sages of China, China International Press, 2007, Beijing, ISBN 7-5085-1038-0
- Xu, Yuanxiang, Zhang, Bing, Mencius - A Benevolent Saint for the Ages; Ancient Sages of China, China International Press, 2007, Beijing, ISBN 7-5085-1039-9

Knowledge Management: Securing Competitive Advantage in the Information Economy

Joshua O. Miluwi

Department of Commerce and Management, Career College and Barkatullah University, Bhopal

ABSTRACT

Today, Executives in small, Medium and large organisations know that they must develop better techniques to manage knowledge, which is increasingly becoming their greatest asset. Organisations currently create and maintain knowledge in isolated systems targeted at specific. Innovative organisations are examining how they can better manage their intellectual capital. This emerging field, called knowledge management, addresses the broad process of locating, organizing, transferring and more efficiently using the information and expertise within an organisation. Knowledge management is not one single discipline. Rather, it an integration of numerous endeavors and fields of study. As the pace of global competition quickens, executives realize that their edge lies in more efficiently transferring knowledge across the organisation. It addresses the broad processes of locating, organizing, transferring and more efficiently using information and expertise within an organisation. New market forces and infrastructure changes have prompted an interest in knowledge management. Market forces include new corporate models that emphasize corporate growth and efficiency, the need for cycle time reduction, knowledge lost from downsizing and the need to share information across the organisation, which often means across the globe. The barriers to sharing information have been dramatically lowered by intranet technologies. Now companies comprehend the extent to which knowledge can be shared across the organisation; however, they also realize how many of their existing knowledge assets are accessible only to a small part of the organisation. To lower these barriers to sharing knowledge, leading executives recognize the need to institute new knowledge-centric practices. This paper provides a framework for characterizing the various tools (methods, practices and technologies) available to knowledge management practitioners. It provides a high-level overview of a number of key terms and concepts, describes the framework, provides examples of how to use it, and explores a variety of potential application areas. Under increasing competitive pressure, many companies are examining how they can better manage their intellectual capital.

Keywords: *Knowledge Management, Organisation, Information Technology, Global Idea, and National Importance*

INTRODUCTION

The emergence of rapidly expanding technologies for distribution and dissemination of information and knowledge has brought to focus the opportunities for development of knowledge-based networks, knowledge dissemination and knowledge management technologies and their potential applications for enhancing productivity of knowledge work. The challenging and complex problems of the future can be best addressed by developing the knowledge management as a new discipline based on an integrative synthesis of hard and soft sciences. A knowledge management professional society can provide a framework for catalyzing the development of proposed synthesis as well serve as a focal point for coordination of professional activities in the strategic areas of education, research and technology development. Preliminary concepts for the development of the knowledge management discipline and the professional society are explored.

Within this context of knowledge management discipline and the professional society, potential opportunities for application of information technologies for more effectively delivering or transferring information and knowledge (i.e., resulting from the NASA's Mission to Planet Earth) for the development of policy options in critical areas of national and global importance (i.e., policy decisions in economic and environmental2 areas) can be explored, particularly those policy areas where a global collaborative knowledge network is likely to be critical to the acceptance of the policies.

"We need systematic work on the quality of knowledge and the productivity of knowledge--neither even defined so far. The performance capacity, if not the survival, of any organisation in the knowledge society will come increasingly to depend on those two factors. But so will the performance capacity, if not the survival, of any individual in the knowledge society."

Peter F. Drucker, The Age of Social Transformation, The Atlantic Monthly, November, 1994.

As we approach the dawn of the 21st century we are humbled by the scale of challenges our world faces at the global scale. The unprecedented development and growth of knowledge during the 20th century notwithstanding, the evolution of a peaceful 21st century will depend on our ability to address three interdependent global challenges of prosperity, security, sustainability. The new world order, though far from being fully defined and agreed to, is beginning to already point at some of the strategic threats and opportunities that would be determining factors in our ability to help shape a new century that we can look back as symbolic of the human spirit and its collective accomplishment at its best and most current stage in the evolution. As it begins to dawn on us that for the first time in human history we may be able to see the impact of human decisions on the evolution of our society in our own lifetime, we become acutely aware of the unprecedented responsibility and the de-facto power we all posses to influence the path of our evolution. Traditional disciplinary knowledge is limited in its ability to support the challenging decisions that lie ahead. Global stability in the future will depend upon our ability as a society to simultaneously address the three fundamental issues of prosperity, security and sustainability.

"The only irreplaceable capital an organisation possesses is the knowledge and ability of its people. The productivity of that capital depends on how effectively people share their competence with those who can use it." Andrew Carnegie

Today, well over three billion people across the globe earn less than two dollars a day. As they move toward achieving prosperity they are likely to emulate our past overemphasis on material wealth, which has enormous consequences for the environment and global sustainability. At the same time, a vast number of citizens of the world remain illiterate, posing an enormous challenge for us in providing the necessary education and training to create global prosperity in the knowledge-based economy. We must find effective ways for capitalizing on emerging information technology to help the citizens of the world to gain access to education and opportunities for adapting and prospering in the next century. We are entering into an era where the future will be essentially determined by our ability to wisely use knowledge, a precious global resource that is the embodiment of human intellectual capital and technology. As we begin to expand our understanding of knowledge as an essential asset we realize that in many ways our future is limited only by our imagination and ability to leverage the human mind. The future of the world lies in front of us unexplored and uncharted, and is full with great opportunities for expanding peace and prosperity in the next millennium through the responsible use of the knowledge. As knowledge increasingly becomes the key strategic resource of the future our need to develop comprehensive understanding of knowledge processes for the creation, transfer and deployment of this unique asset are becoming critical. In the face of a globally expanding and highly competitive knowledge-based economy the traditional organisations are urgently seeking fundamental insights to help them nurture, harvest and manage the immense potential of their knowledge assets for capability to excel at the leading edge of innovation. Schools (K-12), universities, and training organisations (traditional suppliers of knowledge); and businesses and knowledge based organisations in public sector (growing users of knowledge) are in need of an integrative discipline for studying, researching and learning about the knowledge assets–human intellectual capital and technology. This would be similar to the development of Operations Research as an integrative discipline during the Second World War. An international society of knowledge professionals (as proposed in the Appendix I) can provide the necessary focus for fostering collaboration among the best minds and organisations of our time on study, research and learning dedicated to the underlying disciplines and their integrative evolution in to the emergence of Knowledge Management as a new discipline. The task of developing the Knowledge

Management as a new discipline is a challenging endeavor. This new discipline must successfully respond to the Diverse needs of Knowledge based organisations and the knowledge professionals in a timely fashion.

The pioneers of Knowledge Management Must recognize that a great many of the organisations of today are primarily run largely on the basis of insights gained from the successes of the Manufacturing based capital intensive industrial economy of the past. These Organisations have fallen or are rapidly falling out of alignment with the Evolutionary direction of the future as the economy transitions from the Industrial economy to one that is rapidly becoming an intellectual capital and Technology based global knowledge economy. The problems of the future will be open-ended, complex, global and adaptive in nature. As academics we must look for a new synthesis of knowledge, integrating hard and soft sciences, to create the knowledge assets necessary for addressing the challenges in a rapid evolutionary era. The participation of experts from traditional academic disciplines (i.e., information technology, management, cognitive sciences, economics, finance, policy, law, social sciences), and business and government will be essential to the cohesion of an integrative body of knowledge leading to the formation of Knowledge Management discipline and a community of scholars, teachers and professionals associated with this new discipline.

"Sharing knowledge is not about giving people something, or getting something from them. That is only valid for information sharing. Sharing knowledge occurs when people are genuinely interested in helping one another develop new capacities for action; it is about creating learning processes."

Peter Senge

The professional society can serve as a home for enabling the development of the Knowledge Management discipline. However, it must be created as a hybrid, independent and entrepreneuring organisation with strong global participation and ties to leaders in academia, industry and government. In order to fulfill its mission the professional society need to foster three functions: academic education, research and advanced technology program. These three interconnected set of functions need to be pursued in a hybrid way by combining the strengths of the distinct institutional methods of academia, industry and think-tank. The professional society may become an incubator for implementing new 21st century models of operations for each of the three functions: an experiential learning

based academic environment; a collaborative research community dedicated to life-long knowledge based learning; and a multimedia and information technology based knowledge-era tools development program for supporting the performance of the knowledge professionals and organisations.

"Knowledge is an achievement sublime. A learning experience, one day at a time. Knowledge is power...even if we choose not to use it, imperatively. From the day we are born, we are blessed with the right to study our world, to give our minds flight. To hunger for more, to expand our potential. Knowledge is something truly essential. Answers to questions the mind can impart, nurtures the hunger for knowledge, to startb the process of learning, the beginning of growth, a personal quest and a personal oath, to become the very best one can be. Yes, that is the road I have chosen for me! It's all up to us... that desire to learn. An impression within our hearts, it should burn, and daily, the blessings, upon us will shower. Always hold to the truth, that...Knowledge is Power!"

The professional society needs to foster the developments in the three strategic areas through the establishment of founding partnerships with innovative universities, premier research universities/institutes and a group of leading edge industry and government collaborators from the United States and abroad. One of these founding partners needs to step up and become the founding home of the professional society, where the society's activity will be coordinated. Beyond the founding partners, opportunity for participation in the society should be open to all credible academic, government, NGOs and industrial organisations worldwide, including students, research fellows and professionals across a range of disciplines. The first strategic development focus for the professional society needs to be in the area of education. There is need for a comprehensive executive education program in Knowledge Management for leaders, executives, knowledge professionals and policy makers. The program may offer an executive Master of Science degree, and should be designed to include the state-of-the-art topics addressed through scholarly rigor-enabling it to earn support of faculty members at the leading universities as well as accreditation. This degree program, in collaboration with the leading edge developers of multimedia and information technology based knowledge-delivery-tools, can serve as an alpha site for testing and implementing state-of-the-art innovations in global instruction and learning delivered through the distance learning technology (including learning and instruction delivered locally in real life settings at a representative set of host organisations who are the leaders in applying knowledge management). The post graduate educational commitment should be explored as a means for testing and implementing network based tools for delivering just-in-time learning to the graduates of the masters degree programs throughout their professional careers. The knowledge network consisting of student, faculty and graduates across the globe can form the prototype of a knowledge community/university of the future where on-going learning, resident in the network, will be the true competitive advantage. The educational function, by convening annual real/virtual conferences addressing the topics at the frontiers of the Knowledge Management, by serving as a knowledge resource network for sharing the latest research insights, and by providing professional advice and mentoring to instill the career self-management philosophy, can serve as a basis for facilitating the formation of a network based global knowledge management professional society.

HISTORY OF KNOWLEDGE MANAGEMENT

A historical perspective of today's KM, indicates that this is an old quest. Knowledge, including knowing and reasons for knowing, were documented by Western philosophers for millennia, and with little doubt, long before that. Eastern philosophers have an equally long documented tradition of emphasizing knowledge and understanding for conducting spiritual and secular life. Much of these efforts were directed to obtain theoretical and abstract understandings of what knowledge is about. Practical needs to know–or particularly, needs for expertise and operational under-standing–have been important since the battle for survival first started, perhaps be-fore the first human. Managing practical knowledge was implicit and unsystematic at first, and often still is! However, the craft-guilds and apprentice-journeyman-master systems of the 13th century were based on systematic and pragmatic KM considerations. Still, the practical concerns for knowledge and the theoretical and abstract epistemological and religious perspectives were not integrated then, and still are mostly kept separate.

Our present focus on knowledge, particularly for KM, is often explicitly oriented towards commercial effectiveness. However, there are emerging realizations that to achieve the level of effective behavior required for competitive excellence, the whole person must be considered. We must integrate cognition, motivation, personal satisfaction, feeling of security, and many other factors.

The present KM focus is not driven by commercial pressures alone. A practical, often implicit, aspect of KM is that effective people behavior required for success rests on delegating intellectual tasks and authority to knowledgeable and empowered individuals. KM also represents an evolution of the move towards personal and intellectual freedom that started with the age of enlightenment and reason over 200 years ago. One notion was that through proper education, humanity itself could be altered, its nature changed for the better. As other social movements, this has taken a long time to penetrate, particularly into the conservative ranks and practices of management. The emergence of the explicit knowledge focus and the introduction of the term "KM" in the 1980s was no accident and did not happen by chance although it happened gradually and often was met with management uncertainty, it was a natural evolution brought about by the confluence of many factors. The developments that have led to our present perspectives on KM come from many areas. Some are intellectually based, others are pragmatic and rooted in the need to innovate to secure real life performance.

From our present-day perspective, in spite of increasing advances in thinking, there were little change in needs for practical KM until the industrial revolution changed the economic landscape in the 17th century. The introduction of factories and the related systematic specialization be-came more pronounced to support the ability to create and deliver goods in greater quantities and at lower costs. Still, KM was implicit and largely based on the apprentice-journeyman-master model. Schools and universities mostly fulfilled a tacit mission to provide education as required for a leading minority. To some extent, this tacit perspective survives to this day. Education, be it primary, secondary, or higher, is perceived to be "good" and of general value, of-ten with less thought given to which knowledge must be developed for which specific purposes.

"The 'knowledge movement' has now been with us for about two decades, at least if we trace its origins to Ikujiro Nanaka's research on 'organisational information creation' in the 1980's" Charles Savage in Fifth Generation Management writes of the Knowledge Age as the third wave of human socio-economic development (Wikipedia, 2008). "The first wave was the Agricultural Age when wealth was defined as ownership of land. In the second wave, the Industrial Age wealth was based on ownership of capital (i.e., factories). In the Knowledge Age, wealth is based upon the ownership of knowledge and the ability to use that knowledge to create or improve goods and services. Product improvements include cost, durability, suitability, timeliness of delivery, and security. In the Knowledge Age, 2% of the working population will work on the land, 10% will work in Industry and the rest will be Knowledge Workers [a term coined by Peter Drucker in 1959]" (Wikipedia, 2008). According to Peter Drucker, "knowledge has become the key economic resource and the dominant – and perhaps even the only – source of comparative advantage" (Drucker, 1995, as cited in Ruggles, 1998, p.80). (Smoliar, S.W., 2003, p. 337).

Managing knowledge is a notion that began as early as Aristotle. Generally, the public sector has been relatively slow to embrace the concept, with the notable exceptions of health care and education. Large corporations have provided significant leadership in this area and offer several "lessons learned" that may be adaptable (with appropriate modifications) to the public sector. Models of KM began to emerge in the literature in the mid-to late-1980's. "KM as a conscious discipline evolved from the thinking of academics and pioneers such as Peter Drucker in the 1970s, Karl-Erik Sveiby in the late 1980s, Nonaka and Takeuchi in the 1990s" (National Health Service, 2006). For many, the modern development of KM began with the dawn of the Internet in 1969. Drucker who coined the term 'knowledge worker' n2 and, in 1966, said "every knowledge worker in [a] modern organisation is an 'executive' if, by virtue of his position or knowledge, he is responsible for a contribution that materially affects the capacity of the organisation to perform and to obtain results." (Drucker, 1967) Sveiby, whose work is revisited in the Evaluating KM section of this paper, contributed the three elements of the intellectual capital framework (employee competence or human capital; internal structure structural or organisational capital; and external structure-customer or relationship capital to early thinking. As early as 1938, H.G. Wells, though never using the actual term knowledge management, described a 'World Brain' which would represent "a universal organisation and clarification of knowledge and ideas" (Dalkir et al., 2007, p.12). Of course all of this is pre-dated by "the elder, the traditional healer, and the mid-wife in the village who have been the living repositories of distilled experience in the life of the community for time immemorial" (Dalkir et al., 2007, p.12).

By the early 1990s, the private sector, notably large companies such as IBM, Xerox, Hewlett-Packard, and Chevron, n3 had begun to apply their considerable technological capabilities to managing knowledge. Frequently cited as the beginning of KM,

the Association for Information Systems: America's Conference on Information Systems held in Boston in 1993 (http://amcis.aisnet.org/) was specifically devoted to KM. Key themes included attempts, often theoretical, to define KM and differentiate it from data and information. With the exceptions of schools and health care settings, the early adopters of KM beginning in the late1990's, the public sector has been slower to embrace KM. Knowledge management is here to stay. "Knowledge and learning have become the new strategic imperative of organisations. At least one half of US companies and up to 72% of overseas firms, have some kind of KM initiative underway... Chief Knowledge Officers and Chief Learning Offices are popping up everywhere" (Bate & Robert, 2002, p.648). While ubiquitous, KM is recognized to be a slow process. In a study undertaken by Szulanski (Jackson Grayson & O'Dell, 1998), even in the best of firms, in-house best practices took an average of 27 months to wind their way from one part of the organisation to another.

REVIEW OF THE LITERATURE

A very large proportion of the literature on KM and organisational learning is developed by, and aimed at, commercial businesses and firms. Many organisations in the corporate sector look to KM as a solution to the new challenges of the information age. Knowledge and information are becoming crucial core assets for businesses, who have to learn to handle these assets in new ways. Traditional accounting and monitoring systems designed to deal with tangible inputs and outputs are no longer adequate. Instead, organisations now find that they have to share information internally more efficiently and learn to adapt more quickly to external circumstances in order to retain their competitive advantage. In response to this situation, the 'first generation' of KM strategies aimed to improve knowledge sharing within organisations (McElroy, 2000). The first generation of KM was very focused on information technology and systems; technical tools were used to collect and codify existing knowledge in order to make the organisation run more smoothly.

A 'second generation' of KM strategies has now emerged, which focuses more on organisational processes and the creation of new knowledge in order to keep the organisation one step ahead of its competitors. For example, the most successful organisations are shifting from strategies based on prediction to strategies based on anticipation of surprises (Savage, 2000). They are shifting from management based on compliance to management based on self-control and self-organisation. They are also shifting from utilization of already known knowledge to the creation of new knowledge, from pure 'technology' KM applications to also include 'process' applications (Binney, 2001).

When and how these shifts should be undertaken depends on the type of organisation in question. Accenture's (2002) presentation of a typology of work settings distinguishes between four different types of organisations – 'process', 'systems', 'network' and 'competence' – based on the different levels of interdependence and complexity that are required in different work situations. For example, the 'competence' model describes a workplace that is highly reliant on individual expertise (low level of interdependence) in order to carry out evaluation and judgment-oriented work (high level of interpretation). The 'network' model denotes a workplace that depends on fluid deployment of flexible teams (high level of interdependence) in order to improvise and meet new challenges as they arise (high level of interpretation). Different work settings require different ways of handling and processing information to create the necessary knowledge.

Some of the most significant and frequently cited authors on KM and learning are Argyris (1992), Senge (1990), Nonaka (1995), Levitt and March (1988), March (1991) and Schein (1992). They all situate themselves within the second generation of KM strategies and work within the corporate sector. While Argyris (1992) and Senge (1990) base their ideas on experiences as management consultants for big Western companies, Nonaka (1995) draws on his experiences from Japanese businesses. Many of their recommendations are similar, especially as they all focus on the importance of thinking about processes and connections. Senge (1990) in particular concentrates on 'systems thinking'. He argues that organisational learning is only successful when it is based on an understanding of how the whole organisational system is connected, rather than a focus on individual parts. Argyris (1992) further develops the idea of learning by distinguishing between single and double loop learning. The objective of single loop learning is to bring organisational activity back on track. This is no doubt important, but does not foster organisational innovation. On the other hand, double loop learning is the ability of the organisation's members to think critically and creatively about the underlying frameworks. Levitt and March (1988) are less positive about the capacity of organisations to manage knowledge effectively and to learn from past experiences. Their oft-quoted 1988 article, and a later article by March (1991), highlight instead the considerable limitations that impede

organisational learning. These include the complexity of organisational experiences, human habits, hierarchical structures, routines, and differing interpretations by different sub-groups within an organisation. Schein (1992) touches on many of the same issues as Levitt and March, but in a more optimistic manner. He argues that the limitations to learning within an organisation can be overcome through good leadership. By good leadership he means the ability of the leader to guide the organisation through various stages of a change process, to contain anxiety, and influence the organisational culture in a positive way throughout this process.

Malhotra (2001) and Stacey (1995) take a slightly different view on the role of management in relation to learning. They both argue that the most important learning processes within an organisation are precisely those that cannot be managed. They draw on chaos theory to describe 'semi-confusing information systems' (Malhotra, 2001) and 'nonlinear feedback networks' (Stacey, 1995). Innovation often takes place in informal 'shadow' networks of individuals interested in the same issues. In order to support and strengthen this creativity, Malhotra and Stacey argue that organisations should allow staff room to act on incomplete information, trust their own judgment, and feed input from informal fora into formal structures.

DIFFERENT BRANDS OF KNOWLEDGE MANAGEMENT

We must specify what we mean by, and include within broad KM. A few advanced enterprises pursue a central strategic thrust with four tactical foci as indicated in Fig. 1. However, most tailor KM practices to their needs and environments and have narrower perspectives. Of these, some focus on knowledge sharing among individuals or on building elaborate educational and knowledge distribution capabilities. Some emphasize use of technology to capture, manipulate, and locate knowledge and initially, many focus on knowledge-related information management rather than on KM. Others focus on knowledge utilization to improve the enterprise's operational and overall effectiveness. Still others pursue building and exploiting IC to enhance the enterprise's economic value. Some exceptional enterprises have created "knowledge-vigilant" environments to focus constant, widespread attention on ensuring competitive IC to sustain long-term success and vi-ability. The presumption is that competitive IC, properly utilized and exploited, is the central resource behind effective behavior. Broad KM is the systematic and explicit management of knowledge-related activities, practices, programs, and policies within the enterprise. Consequently, the enterprise's viability depends directly on: Our definition of KM is broad and embraces related approaches and activities throughout the organisation. From this view, KM is partly practical, basic, and directly aimed at supporting the enterprise's ultimate objectives. Other parts of KM are quite sophisticated and rely on under-standing of underlying processes to allow targeted KM focused on the organisation's needs and capabilities. Many design systematic and explicit KM practices to create enterprise-wide, adaptive, contextual, comprehensive, and people-centric environments that promote continual personal focus on knowledge-related matters.

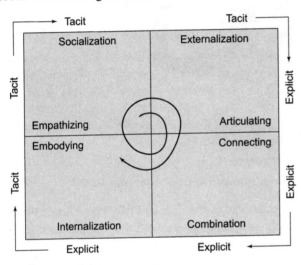

Fig. 1

Source: Benbasat, Izak; Zmud, Robert (1999). "Empirical research in information systems: The practice of relevance"

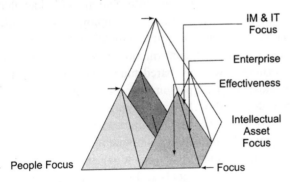

Fig. 2 Comprehensive Knowledge Management Strategy Focus Areas

"The goal of Knowledge Management is to build and exploit intellectual capital effectively and gainfully." This goal is valid for the entire enterprise, for all of the enterprise's activities, and has considerable complexity behind it.

The emergence of KM may be explained by the confluence and natural evolution of several factors. The needs to manage knowledge are strong. For those who now are engaged in KM it is not an alternative or a luxury. It is a necessity driven by the forces of competition, market place demands, new operating and management practices, and the availability of KM approaches and information technology.

Benefits of Knowledge Management

To really understand the benefits of knowledge management it's important to understand exactly what knowledge management is. The term is just over ten years old, and refers to the ability to understand and manage knowledge within an organisation. Knowledge typically refers to individual knowledge and that shared by a group, and knowledge management is how that information is arrived at, shared and analyzed. Distinguishing between general data and what's considered knowledge is important, as well. Data or a collection of data are not necessarily information, but can be just random numbers or ideas. It's taking that data and understanding its purpose and where it can be applied that turns it into information and analysis of that information that allows people to see patterns and where the information is best applied that turn it into real knowledge. The insights gained through information also become part of that knowledge.

Knowledge Management Example

For instance, a company that knows it sold 20 units of a product in a single month has that data available to them. Knowledge management could include the process of taking that data, comparing it to other months to create an average number of units sold, then comparing that to the sales of other products. The demographics for the product, the method of sales and the other items purchase with it could be analyzed to reach some conclusions about the product such as that more of the product is sold during certain times of the year. This can help the company create better advertising during the slow periods and push sales during the times it sells the most to maximize the good periods. All of that took the raw data, turned it into useful knowledge and applied it.

A company faced with data and information needs to have a knowledge management process to make the best use of the information it has in order to achieve the biggest benefits.

Three Categories of Knowledge Management Benefits Once you take a good look at the concept of managing knowledge within an organisation, it's

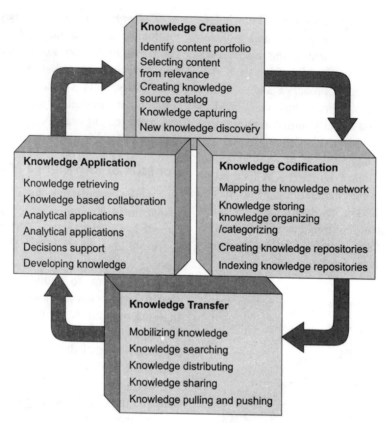

Fig. 3 Knowledge Management Cycle

Source: Alavi, Maryam; Leidner, Dorothy E. (1999). "Knowledge management systems: issues, challenges, and benefits"

easier to imagine some of the benefits versus the lost opportunities if information isn't looked at in this way. There are actually three general categories of benefits that come with a good method of managing information: knowledge, intermediate and organisational. Knowledge benefits are basic and immediate benefits that a company can see, such as better handling of information and a better understanding of how to use knowledge within a company. This category also covers the ability to find information quickly and have an idea of what a particular piece of information is good for. Intermediate benefits cover the advantages a company gains when employee efficiency is improved because of good knowledge sharing and handling. This also covers how effective the sharing of knowledge is. Organisational benefits refer to those benefits a company sees that are end results of good knowledge handling, and the ways in which knowledge management can affect the company's bottom-line goals. Specific Examples of Benefits At the most basic level of benefits, the knowledge benefits, and people within a company will have fast access to shared knowledge and know how to find the information they need. Because the knowledge has been categorized and everyone has been made aware of the important of information, employees understand which information

can help them at the time and they know how to find it. People will better understand their responsibilities and the responsibilities of others.

Some of the benefits that fall into the intermediate category include things like the ability to solve problems faster and to approach problems with new ideas because of the availability of information and knowledge regarding those problems. New employees will be able to become efficient much more quickly because there'll be a clear guide to the information they need. And because information will be shared much better throughout the organisation, each person can benefit from what's already been done without having to reinvent the wheel each time. Benefits on the organisational level include overall heightened productivity and output, better innovation and implementation of new ideas and better customer service. All of the goals and end results can be reached more quickly and more efficiently thanks to the benefits of knowledge management.

More General Benefits of Knowledge Management

When all the people in an organisation understand what they already know, what they need to know and what they don't yet know about something but need to find

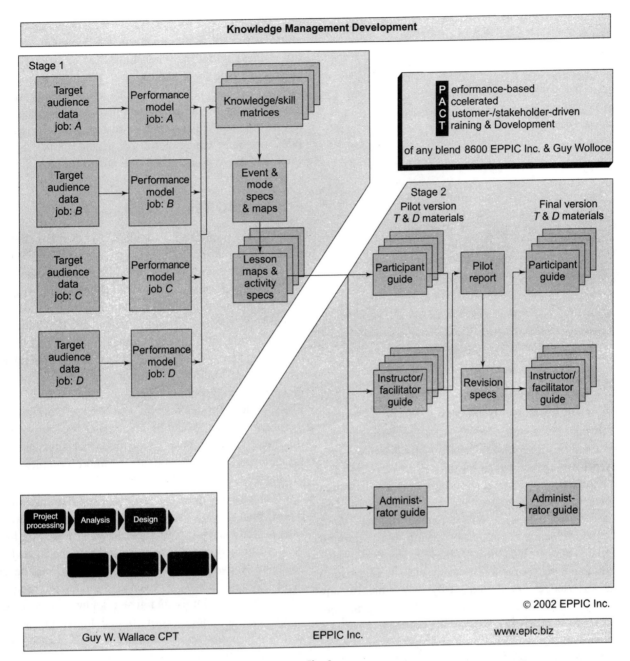

Fig. 4

Source: "Networks, Organisational Learning and Knowledge Management: NHS Cancer Networks"

out, then people can work together better to reach a goal. Individuals will get more accomplished because of the knowledge shared within a group, and groups can collaborate better because they have a common goal and a clear starting point. The benefits of knowledge management can take a company that's struggling with the information processing cycle and productivity and make it a much more efficient and success-oriented workplace. Whenever you decide on investing in a new strategy, program, process, or project, you need to make sure that it is really worth investing and value-adding.

You also need to analyze the cost-benefits of such an investment and the return or value that you get out of that investment. These are some issues that need to be considered before going in for knowledge management initiatives. Today's increasingly difficult economic times pose the need for cost-effective initiatives such as knowledge management programs and practices. Organisation heads always need a clear understanding of the bottom line Knowledge management benefits before they invest in such initiatives. The Knowledge management benefits can be categorized into three which include:

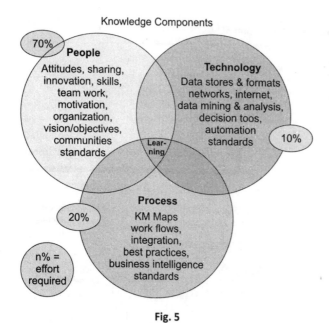

Knowledge Components

Fig. 5

Source: Andriessen, Daniel (2004). "Reconciling the rigor-relevance dilemma in intellectual capital research"

- knowledge benefits
- intermediate benefits
- organisational benefits

A typical example would be of an organisation such as a manufacturing firm or an academic institution or a government agency which has numerous physical files. Categorization and segregation into working databases allows the employees who need specific information to access the databases more efficiently through word or category searches instead of having to sift through so many folders. Updating of these databases will also result in having the most recent and relevant information and knowledge stored and easily accessible by any employee who may need any specific information. These are the benefits which will have an impact on the way an organisation thinks and operates to achieve its objective, for example, to provide quality education, quality products and services, or quality programs to bring about the good of civil society.

In a constantly evolving and competitive environment, organisations are faced with the problem of having to continuously improve in the area of creating innovative products and service that would meet the constantly evolving needs and wants of their customers. Patronage from customers is the only way ahead for the success of any organisation both small and big. Considering the huge number of physical files in an organisation example, as the databases are organized the decision maker has the necessary information and knowledge to substantiate or justify research and development initiatives that leads to more innovations which in turn leads to the creation of

new products and services. These initiatives may seem a bit costlier for the company in the beginning stages. But if these initiatives when looked at on a long-term perspective help the organisation to create products and services and then sell them to a market that needs or wants them. This helps the organisation to actually reap the rewards of satisfied customers translating into increased sales revenues which helps offset the initial capital sunk into the research and development initiatives.

CONCLUSIONS

Knowledge implications applied to the Excellence model are applicable to all types of organisations. Some fundamentals are addressed in the document; some will be inherent in current practices while others will be new. Simple messages that could be emphasized are that cultural and process issues are critical for KM success. Implementing an Intranet, although important in itself, is not sufficient. Often cries are heard, "My intranet does not get used!" Why? Because it was not developed in the context of business objectives or staff needs. Most likely, it does not address the way people work and/or the processes that should be implemented to support the Intranet. This may be a simplistic conclusion and the reasons for failure is probably far more complex, but the point being.

If a company does not recognize some of the issues raised, then don't be surprised if one day a competitor sails passed carrying your client base. KM is not a fad; we have been doing it for years, but now the focus has changed. Knowledge is a valuable asset and one needs to use to gain that edge. Even if the company does a lot to change cultures and foster knowledge sharing, in the end it comes down to one thing: unless the knowledge is put into action, there is no reward, only pain. Selecting knowledge management technologies is often a daunting and risky task. Without an independent frame of reference, attempts to compare knowledge management technologies can be very confusing and fail to drive needed decisions. By providing a means to differentiate technologies according to their impacts on agents, artifacts and behaviors, the characterization framework described in this paper provides just the kind of neutral reference point organisations often need. The framework also adds value to supporting analytical, design, development and deployment activities by guiding the analysis of knowledge flows and construction of a usefully comprehensive picture. The framework provides a mechanism for developing a balanced, high-level view that can be used to set the stage for deeper analysis, identifying the compelling and critical issues that warrant more careful examination. Once the picture is complete, the framework can be used to identify the specific needs that can be met with off-the-shelf technology, localized customizations or change-management programs. By using the same framework to relate technologies, methods and practices back to targeted knowledge flows and their associated behavioral goals, it becomes easier to balance technical and non-technical approaches. This allows project teams to take a more rational, whole systems approach to development and deployment, improving their ability to develop tools and approaches that target and resolve root problems and not just symptoms, improve organisational performance and lower overall life cycle risks.

Reference

- Peter Drucker (1959). Landmarks of tomorrow
- Druker, P.F. (1995) Managing in a Time of Great Change, Butterworth-Heinemann
- Ruggles, R., (1998). The State of the Notion: Knowledge Management in Practice. *California Management Review*, Vol.40, No. 3, 80–89.
- Smoliar, S.W., 2003, "Interaction management: The next (and necessary) step beyond knowledge management." Business Process Management Journal 9(3): p. 337–353.
- Drucker (1967). *To make my name good: A Reexamination of the Southern Kwakiutl Potlatch*
- Dalkir, K., Wiseman, E., Shulha, M., and McIntyre, S. (2007). An intellectual capital valuation approach to a government organisation. *Management Decision*, 45(9)
- Bate S. P., Robert G. (2002) Knowledge management and communities of practice in the private sector: lessons for modernizing the National Health Service in England and Wales *Public Administration* 80, 4, 643–663.
- O'Dell, C., and Grayson, C. 1998. If Only We Knew What We Know: Identification And Transfer Of Internal Best Practices. California Management Review 40(3): 154–174.
- McElroy, M.W. (2000). Integrating complex theory, knowledge management and organisation learning. *Journal of knowledge management*, 4(3), 195–203.
- Binney, D., (2001). The knowledge management spectrum - understanding the KM landscape, *Journal of Knowledge Management*, 5, 1, 33-42.
- Argyris, C. and D. Schön (1992). Organisational Learning: A Theory of Action Perspective, Reading, M.A., Addison Wesley.
- Senge, Peter. 1990. The Fifth Discipline: the Art and Practice of the Learning Organisation. New York: Doubleday.
- Nonaka, I. & Takeuchi, H. (1995). *The knowledge-creating company.* New York: Oxford University Press
- Levitt, B., & March, J.G. (1988). Organisation learning. Annual Review of Sociology, 14: 319–340
- Schein (1992). 'The Learning Leader as Culture Manager' in *Organisational Culture and*
- *Leadership.* San Francisco: Jossey-Bass Publishers.
- March (1991) 'Exploration and exploitation in organisational learning' *Organisation*
- *Science* 2(1): 71–87.
- Stacey, Ralph (1995) 'The Role of Chaos and Self-Organisation in the Development of Creative
- Organisations', in Alain Albert (ed.) *Chaos and Society.* Amsterdam: IOS Press.
- Malhotra (2001) 'Organisational controls as enablers and constraints in successful
- knowledge management systems implementation' in Yogesh Malhotra (ed.) *Knowledge*
- *Management and Business Model Innovation.* Hershey, PA, USA: Idea Group Publishing.

Role of Entrepreneurs in Building an Economy

Mohammed Naveed U.

Faculty HKBK College of Engineering, Dept. of Management Studies

ABSTRACT

Entrepreneurship is not all about opportunism, the potential start up dreamers need to pick up an important business problem right from the outset. The Millennium Indian Entrepreneur faces a challenge to create a spirit in the form of continuous, careful but rapid experimentation and capturing opportunities that emerge. In an economy as big as India there is always money to encourage an Entrepreneur. Thus the purpose of this paper is to highlight the role of entrepreneurs in the development of an economy.

Keywords: *Entrepreneurship, economy*

The names are ubiquitous and the success stories scripted are legends in their own right and by every right that could exist. Take the undisputable king of calls, Sunil Bharti Mittal, whose company Bharti enterprises boasts of a humongous market capitalization of ₹727 Billion. He was an entrepreneur then and remains now. Take the ingenious examples of Subhas Chandra, Exemplary Kiran Mazumdar Shaw, News channel czars, Pronoy Roy and Raghav Behl to the world icons of software Azim Premji and Narayan Murthy the galaxy of India's Entrepreneurial superstars is as drawn out as it is illustrious. Not surprisingly that this year's Forbes listing of the wealthiest has more billionaires additions from India than any other nation, apart from the U.S. This spoke loudly of the role of entrepreneurs in the economic Development of India. Ten million jobs need to be in order by the year 2020 as estimated by CII and NASSCOM. So, Entrepreneurial contribution towards this cause assumes critical importance. Entrepreneurship was previously considered to be unknown quality of an individual and hence it was believed that entrepreneurs are born and not made. But recent studies have proved that Entrepreneurial activities can be planned and developed in an individual through creation of opportunities, extended Facilities, Allowing Incentives, Developing Competence and group sensitiveness in an individual for all those factors. In the end According to Czarniawska Georges and wolft who chose the language of theoretical performance rather than Economics to distinguish among Management, Leadership and Entrepreneurship offers a very illuminating characterization of entrepreneurship. According to him management is the activity of introducing order by coordinating flows of things and people through collective action, Leadership is symbolic performance, expressing the hope of control over destiny and entrepreneurship is quite simple: "The making of Entire new world". Thus the purpose of this paper is to highlight the role of entrepreneurs in the development of an economy.

LITERATURE REVIEW

The entrepreneur has been a fundamental agent in most production, distribution, and growth theories. The role of entrepreneurship as the driving force of economic growth found its most explicit foundation in Prof. Joseph Schumpeter's theory of long waves.

Prof. Joseph Alois Schumpeter, a famous Austrian-American economist pointed out over one hundred years ago that entrepreneurship is crucial for understanding economic development. Today, despite the global downturn, entrepreneurs are enjoying a renaissance the world over according to a recent survey in the *Economist* magazine (Woolridge, 2009). The dynamics of the process can be vastly different depending on the institutional context and level of development within an economy. Entrepreneurship within any country can be productive, destructive, or unproductive. If one is interested in studying entrepreneurship within or across countries, the broad nexus between entrepreneurship, institutions, and economic development is a critical area of inquiry and one which can determine the eventual impact of that entrepreneurial activity. The interdependence between incentives and institutions, affect other characteristics, such as quality of governance, access to capital and other resources, and the perceptions of what entrepreneurs perceive.

Lynda Applegate, head of Harvard's Entrepreneurial Management Unit, believes smart management is a key to helping small companies position themselves to survive – and thrive – in turbulent times. "Never let a crisis go to waste," she writes quoting a Harvard motto.

"We can't fix our current economic problems by simply spending more money to buy bad debts," she writes in *Building Business in Turbulent Times* (In Harvard Business School Working Knowledge, April 27, 2009). "Rather we need real innovation that creates jobs and drive productive economic growth. Companies that survive the financial crisis by identifying and exploiting innovation will serve as economic growth engines in the future – and will be the industry leaders of tomorrow." Applegate believes that downsizing can be a quick fix but not a permanent solution. "Cutting back and hunkering down may get you through the short-term crisis but will not position you to be a leader in the future," she writes. "That's why you need a mindset that says: 'I'm not just going to survive – I am going to thrive.

Espousing the same general theme Bhaskar Chakravorti, a senior Harvard lecturer and consultant with McKinsey & Company, points out many successful products, services and pivotal ideas have launched during an economic lull, Berger (2009) in his Working Knowledge article (February 23, 2009) entitled *Creative Entrepreneurship in a Downtown.*

"If history is any guide, we can expect some significant industry shapers to emerge from the current crisis," he adds. "During the 1930s alone – the period to which we often compare our situation today -there were entrepreneurial start-ups that went on to become household names: Motorola, Hewlett-Packard, Texas Instruments and many others. He adds that other major players today such as Southwest Airlines and Revlon cosmetics were launched during economic downturns.

INTRODUCTION

Entrepreneurs occupy a central position in a market economy. For it's the entrepreneurs who serve as the spark plug in the economy's engine, activating and stimulating all economic activity. The economic success of nations worldwide is the result of encouraging and rewarding the entrepreneurial instinct.

Entrepreneurs seek disequilibrium--a gap between the wants and needs of customers and the products and services that are currently available. The entrepreneur then brings together the factors of production necessary to produce, offer and sell desired products and services. They invest and risk their money--and other people's money--to produce a product or service that can be sold at a profit.

More than any other member of our society, entrepreneurs are unique because they're capable of bringing together the money, raw materials, manufacturing facilities, skilled labor and land or buildings required to produce a product or service. And they're capable of arranging the marketing, sales and distribution of that product or service.

Entrepreneurs are optimistic and future oriented; they believe that success is possible and are willing to risk their resources in the pursuit of profit. They're fast moving, willing to try many different strategies to achieve their goals of profits. And they're flexible, willing to change quickly when they get new information.

Entrepreneurs are skilled at selling against the competition by creating perceptions of difference and uniqueness in their products and services. They continually seek out customer needs that the competition is not satisfying and find ways to offer their products and services in such a way that what they are offering is more attractive than anything else available.

The emergence of entrepreneurship in this part of the country got localized and spread effect, took its own time. The concept of growth theory seems to be closely related in explaining the theory of entrepreneurship development as well.

After the Second World War entrepreneurship received new meaning for attaining economic development within the shortest possible time. But in the process they were seriously handicapped by the rigid institutional set-up, political instability, marketing imperfection and traditional value system.

The entrepreneurship is usually understood with reference to individual business. Entrepreneurship has rightly been identified with the individual, as success of enterprise depends upon imagination, vision, innovativeness and risk taking. The production is possible due to the cooperation of the various factors of production, popularly known as land, labour, capital, market, management and of course entrepreneurship. The entrepreneurship is a risk-taking factor, which is responsible for the end result in the form of profit or loss.

The economic activity with a profit motive can only be generated by promoting an attitude towards entrepreneurship. The renewed interest in the development of entrepreneurship to take up new venture should emphasize on the integrated approach. The developments of entrepreneurship will optimize the use of the unexploited resources, generate self-employment and a self sufficient economy.

WHO IS AN ENTREPRENUER?

An entrepreneur is a person who comes up with a new idea or invention and brings together a country's resources (land, labor and capital) to take the idea to the marketplace. Entrepreneurs manage and assume the risk of a business enterprise. They improve established products and services, or they create new ones. Entrepreneurs are people who do things, which are not generally done in the ordinary course of a business. It is not surprising that every fortune 500 Enterprise in existence is the result of an entrepreneur's enterprise and perseverance. Entrepreneurs, according to Karl Vasper, are pillars of industrial strength – the movers and shakers who constructively disrupt status quo.

Entrepreneurs are the driving forces behind any economy. They create large corporations out of backyard enterprises. Henry ford, Irving Berlins, Bill Gates, King Gillette and Rose Perot were people who envisioned a dream and took risk to achieve this Dream. They marched to a different beat. They were innovators, inventors, and adventurers. Entrepreneurship is a social phenomenon and it is not inherent within a person, rather it exists in the interaction between people. To be a successful Entrepreneur it requires practicing as a manager by acquiring various skills and efforts in learning to understand a business. Entrepreneurship is the future of the modern society. It reflects a ray of hope for the unemployed to earn a living and maintain a dignified life and also for the economic development of the country. The present paper focuses mainly on the dual aspect of Economic Development and how entrepreneurship can improve the status of women in the Indian Society.

Why is the country that has such a strong knowledge advantage lagging behind others in overall economic development? While Indians the world over are recognized for the central role they are playing in the IT revolution, they themselves do not even have uninterrupted power supply. It seems our economic progress is more driven by it's endorsement by the stock market than by real and distributed value it has created. The lack of entrepreneurial initiatives, the large debt burden and the bureaucratic red tapism can be accorded as obstacles to the growth and development of India. We understand reforms, we all understand liberalization – but what we need here is discipline, considering the licensing and regulatory nightmares faced by potential Indian Entrepreneurs. The challenges faced by an entrepreneur in the 21st century emphasize the need for a spirit of risk taking and Initiative.

"Entrepreneurship is about marrying Passion and Process with good dose of perseverance" By: (Vijay Thadani C.E.O, NIIT Ltd).

Entrepreneurship is not all about opportunism, the potential start up dreamers need to pick up an important business problem right from the outset. The Millennium Indian Entrepreneur faces a challenge to create a spirit in the form of continuous, careful but rapid experimentation and capturing opportunities that emerge.

Media Tycoon Ted Turner's jocular one liner," My son Is an Entrepreneur " That's what you are called when you don't have a job, couldn't ring truer, in contrast, if you take the prevalent Indian business scenario into perspective. consider any domain of business operation creating ripples from airlines to organized retail to telecom to software, I would venture safely to state that the big poppa pop on the block today is none other in most cases but a virtual unknown, someone who would most likely have been pooh poohed before he or she swept the rug of complacence from beneath the traditional players unsuspecting feet. The names are ubiquitous and the success stories scripted are legends in their own right and by every right that could exist. Take the undisputable king of calls, Sunil bharti mittal, whose company Bharti enterprises boasts of a humongous market capitalization of ₹727 Billion. He was an entrepreneur then and remains now. Take the ingenious examples of Subhas Chandra, Exemplary kiran Mazumdar Shaw, News channel czars, Pronoy Roy and Raghav Behl to the world icons of software Azim Premji and Narayan Murthy the galaxy of India's Entrepreneurial superstars is as drawn out as it is illustrious. Entrepreneurship was previously considered to be unknown quality of an individual and hence it was believed that entrepreneurs are born and not made. But recent studies have proved that Entrepreneurial activities can be planned and developed in an individual through creation of opportunities, extended Facilities, Allowing Incentives, Developing Competence and group sensitiveness in an individual for all those factors.

In the end According to Czarniawska Georges and wolft who chose the language of theoretical performance rather than Economics to distinguish among Management, Leadership and Entrepreneurship offers a very illuminating characterization of entrepreneurship. According to him management is the activity of introducing order by coordinating flows of things and people through collective action, Leadership is symbolic performance, expressing the hope of control over destiny and entrepreneurship is quite simple: "The making of Entire new world".

THE ENTREPRENEURIAL PROCESS

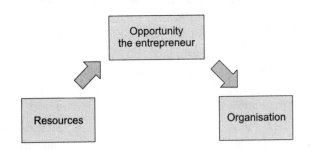

An Entrepreneur is the key figure in the process of economic growth. He is an economic person who tries to maximize his profits by innovation and thus aggressively contributing towards economic development. He is an organizer and speculator who is doing new things or doing things that are already being done in a new way. Entrepreneur is the individual who lies at the heart of Entrepreneurial process that is the Manager who drives the whole process forward.

Entrepreneurial Process

Opportunity: It's the potential to serve customers better than they are being served at present. An entrepreneur is held responsible for scanning the business landscape for unexploited opportunities. The improved way of doing is the innovation that the entrepreneur presents to the market.

Resources: Resources include the money invested in the venture; the people include their efforts, Knowledge and skills to it etc. It also includes the intangible assets such as brand name, reputation of the company and the goodwill of the company.

Organisation: Every organisation consists of number of factors such as their size, their rate of growth, the industry they operate in and the type of products they deliver.

Entrepreneurship and India

Indian entrepreneurship is second to none and activity levels are at an all time high. According to the Global Entrepreneurship Monitor 2006, one in every ten Indians is engaged in some entrepreneurial activity or the other. Of this, opportunity based entrepreneurship (70%) is significantly higher than necessity based.

A lot of entrepreneurship activity is centered on the IT and BPO industry; but, there are a few outstanding examples in other fields. These companies have successfully exploited a product, service, or business model to create a step change in the market structure.

This new breed of entrepreneurs made their own rules and revolutionized the way business was done. They used a winning combination of customer insight, industry knowledge, and out of the box thinking to create winning innovations. While Ambani's Reliance Communications made mobile telephony affordable to the common man, Captain Gopinath's Air Deccan made air travel as commonplace as travel by train and Biyani's Big Bazaar changed the face of retail in India. Tata Motors with their $2,000 car promise to do the same to the auto sector. Entrepreneurs are driving the growth of the Indian economy. For the first time in 200 years, India is getting back its position as an economic power. With GDP growing at 8+%, experts are expecting the Indian economy to overtake developed countries in the decades to come.

The Indian entrepreneur is thinking big and aiming high. The recent spate of global acquisitions by Indian industry leaders has forced the business community the world over to sit up and take notice of Indian economic power. The Tata-Corus deal set the tone for the year and was followed by Birla's acquisition of Novelis. With the Indian rupee up against the dollar and the global economy as playing field, we can expect to see more such deals in the future. There is enough reason to be optimistic about India's entrepreneurial energy. However, we need to create an ecosystem that will foster and support early stage entrepreneurs. This will enable a scalable and sustainable model for creating a new breed of entrepreneurs in the years to come. Access to seed capital is one of the key areas of potential investment. Venture Funds have entered the Indian market, but these funds are more focused on 'growth capital' rather than 'seed capital'. While associations such as TiE are seeking to bridge the gap, there is an urgent need to build a network of angels willing to support a young business.

Our educational system rewards 'remembering' as opposed to 'learning' with limited scope for creativity. Engineering schools focus on imparting fantastic technical skills while business schools focus on pure management techniques. This ensures a strong ability to replicate ideas and reverse engineering and reinforces our dependence on a cost based competitive advantage. Schools in the West have a greater focus on leadership and entrepreneurship. Our educational system needs a revamp to be able to create more leaders and entrepreneurs. The focus of entrepreneurship needs to move to innovation, including process innovation, product innovation, management innovation, and business model innovation to win in the global market. The rapid pace of globalization and growth of the Indian economy offers tremendous opportunities for entrepreneurs. We have heard stories of people who succeeded 'in spite' of the system. It is now time to build an ecosystem which will enable Indians to succeed 'because' of the system. This ecosystem will form the bedrock for the evolution of India Inc into an undisputed leader of the global economy.

The characteristics of a unique entrepreneur are:

- He is a person who develops and owns his own enterprise
- He is a moderate risk taker and works under uncertainty for achieving the goal
- He is innovative
- He peruses the deviant pursuits
- Reflects strong urge to be independent
- Persistently tries to do something better
- Dissatisfied with routine activities
- Prepared to withstand the hard life
- Determined but patient
- Exhibits sense of leadership
- Also exhibits sense of competitiveness
- Takes personal responsibility
- Oriented towards the future
- Tends to persist in the face to adversity
- Convert a situation into opportunity.

Factors for Entrepreneurial growth

Entrepreneurship does not emerge and develop automatically and spontaneously, its emergence and development largely depend on various supportive conditions.

These supportive depend on various supportive conditions. These supportive conditions or factors are popularly known as economic and non-economic factors for entrepreneurial growth.

So entrepreneurial growth is not spontaneous and as such it is dependent on economic, social, political and psychological factors. Various factors affect5ing entrepreneurial growth may be stated in the following diagram.

Economic environment influences the entrepreneurship to a great extent. It refers to all those economic factors which affect the functioning of a business enterprise. Dependence of business on economic environment is total i.e. for input and also to sell the finished goods.

Economic environment has reference to the economic system which the entrepreneur has to operate. The present day economic environment of business is a complex one. The business sector has economic relations with the government, capital market, household sector and with global sector.

These sectors together influence the trends and structure of economic system is conditioned by socio-political arrangements.

The survival and success of a business enterprise is finally decided by the economic environment and various market conditions. The important external factors that affect the economic environment of a business.

The major roles played by an entrepreneur in the economic development of an economy are discussed in a systematic and orderly manner as follows:

Promotes Capital Formation

Entrepreneurs promote capital formation by mobilising the idle savings of public. They employ their own as well as borrowed resources for setting up their enterprises. Such type of entrepreneurial activities leads to value addition and creation of wealth, which is very essential for the industrial and economic development of the country.

Creates Large-Scale Employment Opportunities

Entrepreneurs provide immediate large-scale employment to the unemployed which is a chronic problem of underdeveloped nations. With the setting up of more and more units by entrepreneurs, both on small and large-scale numerous job opportunities are created for others. As time passes, these enterprises grow, providing direct and indirect employment opportunities to many more. In this way, entrepreneurs play an effective role in reducing the problem of unemployment in the country which in turn clears the path towards economic development of the nation.

Promotes Balanced Regional Development

Entrepreneurs help to remove regional disparities through setting up of industries in less developed and backward areas. The growth of industries and business in these areas lead to a large number of public benefits like road transport, health, education, entertainment, etc. Setting up of more industries leads to more development of backward regions and thereby promotes balance.

National Income

National Income consists of the goods and services produced in the country and imported. The goods and services produced are for consumption within the country as well as to meet the demand of exports. The domestic demand increases with increase in population and increase in standard of living. The export demand also increases to meet the needs of growing imports due to various reasons. An increasing number of entrepreneurs are required to meet this increasing demand for goods and services.

Reduces Concentration of Economic Power

Economic power is the natural outcome of industrial and business activity. Industrial development normally leads to concentration of economic power in the hands of a few individuals which results in the growth of monopolies. In order to redress this problem a large number of entrepreneurs need to be developed, which will help reduce the concentration of economic power amongst the population.

Wealth Creation and Distribution

It stimulates equitable redistribution of wealth and income in the interest of the country to more people and geographic areas, thus giving benefit to larger sections of the society. Entrepreneurial activities also generate more activities and give a multiplier effect in the economy.

Increasing Gross National Product and Per Capita Income

Entrepreneurs are always on the lookout for opportunities. They explore and exploit opportunities, encourage effective resource mobilisation of capital and skill, bring in new products and services and develops markets for growth of the economy. In this way, they help increasing gross national product as well as per capita income of the people in a country. Increase in gross national product and per capita income of the people in a country, is a sign of economic growth.

Improvement in the Standard of Living

Increase in the standard of living of the people is a characteristic feature of economic development of the country. Entrepreneurs play a key role in increasing the standard of living of the people by adopting latest innovations in the production of wide variety of goods and services in large scale that too at a lower cost. This enables the people to avail better quality goods at lower prices which results in the improvement of their standard of living.

Promotes Country's Export Trade

Entrepreneurs help in promoting a country's export-trade, which is an important ingredient of economic development. They produce goods and services in large scale for the purpose earning huge amount of foreign exchange from export in order to combat the import dues requirement. Hence import substitution and export promotion ensure economic independence and development.

Induces Backward and Forward Linkages

Entrepreneurs like to work in an environment of change and try to maximise profits by innovation. When an enterprise is established in accordance with the changing technology, it induces backward and forward linkages which stimulate the process of economic development in the country.

Facilitates Overall Development

Entrepreneurs act as catalytic agent for change which results in chain reaction. Once an enterprise is established, the process of industrialisation is set in motion. This unit will generate demand for various types of units required by it and there will be so many other units which require the output of this unit. This leads to overall development of an area due to increase in demand and setting up of more and more units. In this way, the entrepreneurs multiply their entrepreneurial activities, thus creating an environment of enthusiasm and conveying an impetus for overall development of the area.

SUCCESSFUL ENTREPRENEURS LIST

Muhammad Yunus

Founded a banking system 30 years ago to lend small amounts of money to the rural poor in Bangladeshi villages. In 2006 he won Nobel Peace Prize.

Mary Kay

The women behind many gorgeous faces and the founder of Mary Kay Cosmetics, Inc. Mary Kay Ash wrote a book to help women in business. The book later became the plan of action for starting the company with a mere investment of $5000.

Alvin Ailey

Alvin Ailey, the revolutionary, the dancer and the choreographer, saw the bigger picture while he grew up in the times of violent racial segregation. His signature work has its roots in the great sense of pride in the black race.

Bill Gates

This successful entrepreneur and philanthropist began programming at the age of 13, which later became his dream. **Bill Gates** built his dream with Microsoft Corporation, a company boasting a workforce of 93,000 employees in over 100 countries.

Ben & Jerry

For Ben Cohen and Jerry Greenfield, the sweet taste of success came in many flavors. The duo started the Ben & Jerry's in a gas station after a lot of toil and turmoil and failed attempts at alternative ways of earning money!

Walt Disney, the film producer, director, screenwriter, voice actor, animator, entrepreneur, entertainer, international icon, philanthropist and above all the creator of Mickey Mouse.

Donald Trump

The real man behind the real-estate development, **Donald Trump** is an American business magnate, socialite, celebrity and a television personality. The anchor of 'The Apprentice' has been an ardent student of life himself, which has gained him laurels after laurels.

Other Most Successful Entrepreneurs

- P.T. Barnum - Entertainment (Barnum & Bailey)
- Jeff Bezos - Internet (Amazon)
- Andrew Carnegie - Steel (US Steel)
- Michael Dell - Computers (Dell Computer)
- Larry Ellison - Software (Oracle)
- Joyce Hall - Greeting Cards (Hallmark)
- Milton Hershey - Chocolate
- J. W. Marriott - Hospitality
- Louis B. Mayer - Entertainment (MGM)
- Rupert Murdoch - Media

- David Packard - Electronics (Hewlett-Packard)
- John D. Rockefeller - Oil (Standard Oil)
- Sam Walton - Discount Retail (Wal-Mart)
- Oprah Winfrey - Entertainment
- Steve Case - Internet (America Online)
- Debbi Fields - Cookies (Mrs. Fields)
- A. P. Giannini - Banking (Bank of America)

CONCLUSION

A society is prosperous only to the degree to which it rewards and encourages entrepreneurial activity because it is the entrepreneurs and their activities that are the critical determinant of the level of success, prosperity, growth and opportunity in any economy. The most dynamic societies in the world are the ones that have the most entrepreneurs, plus the economic and legal structure to encourage and motivate entrepreneurs to greater activities.

References

- Barbara Czarniawska. *Dramas of Institutional Identity*. The University Of Chicago Press Books Retrieved, From Http://Www.Press.Uchicago.Edu/Ucp/Books/Book/Chicago/N/Bo3644345.Html

- Chakravorti, Bhaskar, *Senior Lecturer,* Harvard Business School *Co-Leader, Mckinsey & Company's Innovation Practice*; Retrieved, Http://Legatum.Mit.Edu/Bhaskarchakravorti

- James T. Berger (2009). *Two Harvard Experts Provide Perspective on Building Entrepreneurial Businesses in Troubled Economic Times*; Retrieved, Http://Www.Wiglafjournal.Com/Corporate/2009/05/Two-Harvard-Experts-Provide-Perspective-On-Building-Entrepreneurial-Businesses-In-Troubled-Economic-Times/

- Jeffrey M. Wooldridge (2009) - Michigan State University, *Introductory Econometrics: A Modern Approach, 4th Edition,* Cengage Learning, ISBN-10: 0324581629 ISBN-13: 9780324581621 896 Pages CB ©2009. Retrieved, Http://Websites.Swlearning.Com/Search/Productoverview.

- Applegate Lynda M, *Sarofim-Rock Professor Of Business Administration Unit Head,* Entrepreneurial Management Chair, Opm,

- Bosman Neils, Hardin Rebecca. *Global Entrepreneurship Monitor 2006;*

- Retrieved, from Http://Drfd.Hbs.Edu/Fit/Public/Facultyinfo.Do?Facinfo=Res&Facid=6411
- Retrieved, Http://Www.Brainyquote.Com/Quotes/Authors/T/Ted_Turner.Html
- Retrieved, Http://Www.Gemconsortium.Org/Download/1318067263215/GEM_2006_Global_Results_Summary_V2.Pdf
- Robert Ronstadt, Rein Peterson and Karl Vasper (Jul 1986). *Frontiers Of Entrepreneurship* om/S?Ie=UTF8&Rh=N%3A283155%2Cp_2 7%3akarl%20Vasper&Field-Author=Karl%20 Vasper&Page=1

Globalisation: A Boon or Bane

Prakash Vir Khatri[1] and Suman Yadav[2]
[1]Senior Faculty Member of the University of Delhi
[2]Assistant Professor in Swami Shraddhanand College
University of Delhi

ABSTRACT

Now-a-days the term "GLOBALISATION" enjoys immense popularity. This word is dominant, not only in theoretical and political discourse but also in every day language. It is at the centre of diverse intellectual and political agendas, raising crucial questions about what is widely considered to be the fundamental dynamic of our time- an apoch-defining set of changes that is radically transforming social and economic relations and institutions in the 21st century. Globalisation is the movement towards the expansion of economic, social and cultural ties between countries through the spread of corporate institutions and the capitalist philosophy that leads to the shrinking of the world in various terms.

Keywords: *Globalisation, Transformation*

INTRODUCTION

However the critiques of "Globalisation" consider it as the political project of a transnational capitalist class which is formed on the basis of an institutional structure set up to serve and advance the interests of this class. According to them it is a systematic ploy to divide the society into classes in the long run. They view globalisation as a class project rather than as an inevitable process tends to see the changes associated with it differently. Those who view globalisation as a class project rather than as an inevitable process tend to see the changes associated with it differently. In the first place, "globalisation" is regarded as not a particularly useful term for describing the dynamics of the project. It is seen, rather, as we do-as an ideological tool used for prescription rather than accurate description. In this context it can be counter posed with a term that has considerably greater descriptive value and explanatory power: imperialism. Using this concept, the network of institutions that define the structure of the new global economic system is viewed not in structural terms, but as intentional and contingent, subject to the control of individuals who represent and seek to advance the interests of a new international capitalist class. Globalisation is neither inevitable nor necessary.

No system is perfect in itself. It is to be seen whether globalisation will serve the objectives of the various economies in equitable and just growth and development of the subjects of nations.

Globalisation is the new buzzword that has come to dominate the world since the nineties of the last century with the end of the cold war and the break-up of the former Soviet Union and the global trend towards the rolling ball. The frontiers of the state with increased reliance on the market economy and renewed faith in the private capital and resources, a process of structural adjustment spurred by the studies and influences of the World Bank and other International organisations have started in many of the developing countries. Also Globalisation has brought in new opportunities to developing countries. Greater access to developed country markets and technology transfer hold out promise improved productivity and higher living standard.

But globalisation has also thrown up new challenges like growing inequality across and within nations, volatility in financial market and environmental deteriorations. Another negative aspect of globalisation is that a great majority of developing countries remain removed from the process. Till the nineties the process of globalisation of the Indian economy was constrained by the barriers to trade and investment liberalisation of trade, investment and financial flows initiated in the nineties has progressively lowered the barriers to competition and hastened the pace of globalisation.

Now-a-days the term "GLOBALISATION" enjoys immense popularity. This word is dominant, not only in theoretical and political discourse but also in everyday language. It is at the centre of diverse intellectual and political agendas, raising crucial questions about what is widely considered to be the fundamental dynamic of our time- an apoch-defining set of changes that is radically transforming social and economic relations and institutions in the 21st century. Globalisation is the movement towards the expansion of economic, social and cultural ties between countries through the spread of corporate institutions and the capitalist philosophy that leads to the shrinking of the world in various terms.

The term Globalisation can be used as:

- An economic phenomenon.
- A social phenomenon.
- A cultural phenomenon.

As an economic phenomenon it refers to the process of increasing economic integration and growing economic interdependence between nations. It means integration of different economies of the world into one global economy thereby reducing the economic gap between different countries. This is achieved through the process of privatisation and liberalisation by removing all restrictions on the movement of goods, services, capital, labour and technology between nations. Globalisation leads to an increased level of interaction and interdependence among different countries. There is free flow of goods, services, technology, management practices and culture across national boundaries. From a country's viewpoint, globalisation is the process of integration of the domestic economy with the world economy.

According to the International Monetary Fund, Globalisation means "the growing economic interdependence of countries world wide through increasing volume and variety of cross-border transactions in good and services and of international capital flows and also through the more rapid and widespread diffusion of technology".

Globalisation implies being able to manufacture in the most cost-effective way possible anywhere in the world, being able to procure raw materials and management resources from the cheapest source anywhere in the world, and having the entire world as one market. The global corporations of today conduct their operations worldwide as if the entire world were a single entity. It also implies emergence of a world where innovation can arise anywhere in the world.

The Process of globalisation requires among the countries of the world:

- free trade
- capital market liberalisation
- flexible exchange rates
- market–determined interest rates
- the deregulation of markets
- the transfer of assets from the public to the private sector
- the tight focus of public expenditure on well–directed social targets
- balanced budgets
- tax reform
- secure property rights
- the protection of intellectual property rights.

The term "globalisation" has been used in a multiplicity of senses. Concepts like "the global interdependence of nations," "the growth of a world system," "accumulation on a world scale," "the global village" and many others are rooted in the more general notion that the accumulation of capital, trade and investment is no longer confined to the nation-state. In its most general sense, "globalisation" refers to cross national flows of goods, investment, production and technology.

Globalisation can be viewed and studied from different angles shown by the above picture:

Integration of Economies

- The increasing reliance of economies on each other
- The opportunities to be able to buy and sell in any country in the world
- The opportunities for labour and capital to locate anywhere in the world
- The growth of global markets in finance

Integration of Economies is made possible by:

- Technology
- Communication networks
- Internet access
- Growth of economic cooperation – trading blocs (EU, NAFTA, SAARC, G-20, ASEAN. etc.)
- Collapse of 'communism'
- Movement to free trade

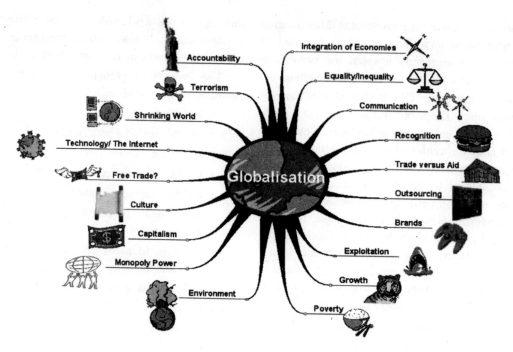

Trade Vs. Aid

- Benefits of Trade:
  - Increased choice
  - Greater potential for growth
  - Increase international economies of scale
  - Greater employment opportunities
  - More competition among traders leads to enhanced quality of good and services
  - Consumer's sovereignty.
- Disadvantages of trade:
  - Increase in gap between the rich and the poor
  - Dominance of global trade by the rich, northern hemisphere countries
  - Lack of opportunities for the poor to be able to have access to markets
  - Exploitation of workers and growers.
    Corporate Expansion:
- Multi-national or trans-national corporations (MNCs or TNCs) – businesses with a headquarters in one country but with business operations in a number of others countries.

Characteristics:

  - Expanding revenue
  - Lowering costs
  - Sourcing raw materials
  - Controlling key supplies
  - Control of processing
  - Global economies of scale

Globalisation is both a description and a prescription. As a description, "Globalisation" refers to the widening and deepening of the international flows of trade, capital, technology and information within a single integrated global market. Like terms such as "the global village," it identifies a complex of changes produced by the dynamics of capitalist development as well as the diffusion of values and cultural practices associated with this development. As a prescription, "globalisation" involves the liberalisation of national and global markets in the belief that free flows of trade, capital and information will produce the best outcome for growth and human welfare. Globalisation is a set of interrelated processes inscribed within the structures of the operating system based on capitalist modes of global production. It is also considered as the outcome of a consciously pursued strategy. According to Keith Griffin (1995), a well known proponent of "human development" and a declared advocate of radical changes or social transformation, globalisation is inevitable. From this inevitability – of-globalisation perspective, the issue is how a particular country, or group of countries, can adjust to changes in the world economy and insert themselves into the globalisation process under the most favourable conditions.

Globalization—An unstoppable force?

There was a time when Coca Cola was the hallmark of a global company, selling its soft drink virtually in every country, in virtually every languages. But now the world is used to MacDonald's selling hamburgers in Moscow, Beijing and Karachi, while Toyota pick-up trucks roam the African Sahel, and Sony televisions occupy a central location in homes worldwide.

This is the golden age for business, commerce and trade. Never before in the history of the world there has been such an opportunity to sell as many goods to as many people as there is right now.

It's not just big companies that are in on the explosion—although they may dominate. Instant information and communications have allowed indigenous people in Guyana to market handmade hammocks through the Internet, and even the fifty or so people living on remote Pitcairn Island can sell their handicrafts anywhere.

With instant information and communication, virtually everything is available to anyone, anywhere. Markets are now global and many corporations are often richer and more powerful than many countries.

There has always been trade between countries and societies, but never on a scale close to today's levels. A combination of reduced trade barriers, financial liberalisation and a 112 technological revolutions have completely changed the nature of business in virtually all of the industrialized countries.

- The countries of the world are exporting ten times the amount they did in 1950, and more money—more than $1.5 trillion a day—now moves across borders. In 1973, that figure was only $15 billion.
- More people are travelling than ever before, with 590 million going abroad in 1996, compared to about 260 million in 1980.
- More people are making international telephone calls than ever before, and are paying less. A three minute phone call from New York to London cost $245 in 1930—in 1990 it cost just $3.

Globalization does not stop there. With the Internet and state-of-the-art telecommunications, sales and technical representatives based in India can answer customer questions in the United States. Back-office insurance jobs can be located thousands of miles from company headquarters, in different parts of the country, in different countries, and on different continents.

More trade, more markets, more business, more information, more jobs, more opportunities.

This is the promise of a globalized world. The tide of globalization has already brought considerable wealth to areas of the world long accustomed to only poverty, and even more wealth to areas that were doing quite well already. In East and South-East Asia, countries have turned to export-based economies to propel themselves up the development ladder. In the coastal regions of China, global market-oriented businesses have helped raise living standards for millions of people.

This whirlwind of economic activity has brought many benefits, and wealth, to many people.

There has been faster economic growth, higher living standards, accelerated innovation, and new opportunities for both individuals and countries. Accompanied by a revolution in information and technology, the world is very much a smaller and more integrated planet than ever before.

However the critiques of "Globalisation" consider it as the political project of a transnational capitalist class which is formed on the basis of an institutional structure set up to serve and advance the interests of this class. According to them it is a systematic ploy to divide the society into classes in the long run. They view globalisation as a class project rather than as an inevitable process tends to see the changes associated with it differently. Those who view globalisation as a class project rather than as an inevitable process tend to see the changes associated with it differently. In the first place, "globalisation" is regarded as not a particularly useful term for describing the dynamics of the project. It is seen, rather, as we do-as an ideological tool used for prescription rather than accurate description. In this context it can be counter posed with a term that has considerably greater descriptive value and explanatory power: imperialism.

Using this concept, the network of institutions that define the structure of the new global economic system is viewed not in structural terms, but as intentional and contingent, subject to the control of individuals who represent and seek to advance the interests of a new international capitalist class. Globalisation is neither inevitable nor necessary.

Clearly, not everyone is happy about globalization. Many people don't like globalization because, it allows rich and powerful outside business interests to intrude into a local culture, overrides local traditions, and threatens a way of life. There were many who cheered for a French farmer who vandalized a McDonald's. Starbucks coffee shops have been favourite targets for people protesting globalization.

In more traditional societies, globalization threatens the cultural and religious underpinnings of society. In both industrialized and developing countries, many people feel threatened—and are threatened—by the globalization process. A globalized economy presents a myriad of challenges, from protecting local cultures to protecting the environment to protecting local jobs.

The backlash is very real. During the failed World Trade Organisation talks in Seattle that were intended to further expand trading opportunities last December, thousands of demonstrators who agree on little else aside from a common dislike for globalization, caused major disruptions.

Labour Unions protested, fearing that a new trade agreement would provide an incentive for companies to move their jobs abroad. Environmentalists protested, fearing that global trade agreements would undercut domestic environmental safeguards. And there were nationalists, who feared that further globalization would diminish national sovereignty, and possibly lead to a loss of freedom, liberty or rights.

Whether it is viewed as an ominous juggernaut that crushes everything in its path, or whether it holds the promise of a better future, globalization is a phenomenon that is with us. Like the weather, it is, and will be, a source for endless discussion, but little can be done about it. But also like the weather, it is a force to which people can adapt.

DEVELOPING COUNTRIES WARY

Developing countries, however, are nervous about the imposition of conditions. They already must meet a plethora of conditions to receive loans from the International Monetary Fund or the World Bank—and some of these conditions have been more damaging than helpful.

Consequently, they are leery of the push for greater corporate responsibility. While they support labour standards, environmental protection, and human rights, many of these countries are wary that they are just a smokescreen for greater protectionism in the richer countries. They fear that without resources, they will be hopelessly unable to enforce these principles, and will then be the target of sanctions. Their fears are not unfounded, as United States President Bill Clinton raised the spectrum of sanctions in Seattle during the WTO talks.

Developing countries have also been slow to support the Global Compact initiative, as many believe that the principles selected contain a northern bias. Of greater concern to developing countries are the behaviour of monopolies, the need for foreign corporations to contribute to the tax base, and a sharing of technology.

NEW CHALLENGES

There is no world government to regulate all the facets of globalization, and very few people want one. Yet to manage globalization to ensure that all enjoy its benefits, there is a need for more comprehensive global governance—a system of international law based on the principle of multilateralism that will spell out the ground rules for all participants in the global economy.

Many areas of interdependence need global attention. The benefits of a globalized economy must be accompanied by greater global cooperation to prevent and contain the spread of "global bads," such as the spread of economic crises, epidemics, environmental degradation, crime and drugs. Cooperation is to address macroeconomic policies, and on trade, aid and the need for a fair and equitable system to protect intellectual property.

At present, there are organisations to address many of these issues, but by and large, their work is uncoordinated, and poorly supported by the international community. To achieve a more integrated degree of policy coherence, gaps must be filled and existing structures improved. Not to dominate national governments and overpower cultures and societies, the essential role for global governance is to define objectives, set standards, and to monitor compliance.

The United Nations, a treaty organisation made up of 189 countries, is part of the answer. But to address the needs of people, it needs the support not only of governments, but also of civil society, the private sector, parliamentarians, local authorities, the scientific community, and many others.

As a result of globalization, the world's commitment to the poor is being recognized not only as a moral imperative but also as a common interest. Each country must still take primary responsibility for its own programmes of economic growth and poverty reduction.

To this end, it may be proposed for concrete actions, urging the developed countries in particular to:

- Grant free access to their markets for good produced in poor countries.
- Implement debt relief programme, including cancellation of all official debts of the heavily indebted poor countries, in return for those countries making demonstrable commitments to poverty reduction.
- Grant more generous development assistance.
- Work with pharmaceutical countries and other partners to develop an effective and affordable vaccine against HIV.
- Make special provision for the needs of the most under developed nations.

Key Issues:

- Damage to the environment?
- Exploitation of labour
- Monopoly power
- Economic degradation
- Non-renewable resources
- Damage to cultures

Other Issues:

- Accountability of Global businesses?
- Increased gap between rich and poor fuels potential terrorist reaction
- Ethical responsibility of business?
- Efforts to remove trade barriers.
- Of the world's six billion people, 1.2 billion live in extreme poverty, or on an income of roughly US $1 a day or less. Just fewer than 3 billion people live on $2 a day or less.
- Industrialized countries, with 19 % of the world's population, account for 71% of global trade in goods and services, 58% of foreign direct investment, and 91% of all Internet users.
- More than US$1.5 billion is now exchanged on the world's currency markets each day.
- Foreign investment topped US$400 billion in 1997, seven times the level, in real terms, of the 1970s.
- Between 1983 and 1993, cross-border sales of US Treasury bonds increased from $30 billion to $500 billion per year.
- International bank lending grew from $265 billion in 1975 to $4.2 trillion in 1994.
- The world's 200 richest people more than doubled their net worth in the four years before 1998, to more than $1 trillion. The assets of the top three billionaires total more than the combined GNP of all the least developed countries with their 600 million people.

BUT IF GLOBALIZATION CAN GENERATE WEALTH, IT CAN ALSO TAKE IT AWAY:

- The billions of investment dollars that washed up on Asian shores in the mid-1990's abruptly reversed direction in 1997, sending millions of people back into poverty in what has become known as the Asian financial crises, although its impact was so widespread it affected countries on virtually every continent. Hardly a fluke economic condition, the Asian crisis marked the fifth serious international monetary and financial crisis in the last two decades, all which have left a trail of financial devastation and ruin from Russia to Latin America.

- The benefits of globalization have largely bypassed over half of the world's population, or close to 3 billion people who make do on less than US$2 a day. These are people who have not shared in the new wealth, are not connected to the Internet, and for the most part, lack the necessary skills that are needed to participate in this brave new economic world.

- In Central Asia and Eastern Europe, where many countries have not adapted to the global economy, more people today are living in poverty than ten years ago. Now the time will only tell whether globalisation will meet the challenges of various economies. It will serve the mankind or it will result in concentration of wealth and economic power in the hands of a few to the detriments of rest of all.

"The greatest challenge we face today is to ensure that globalization becomes a positive force for the entire world's people, instead of leaving billions of them behind in squalor. Inclusive globalization must be built on the great enabling force of the market, but market forces alone will not achieve it. It requires a broader effort to create a shared future, based upon our common humanity in all its diversity".

From the Millennium Report

References

- Bhagwati, Jagdish (2004). *In Defense of Globalization*. Oxford, New York: Oxford University Press.
- Sheila. L. Croucher. *Globalization and Belonging: The Politics of Identity in a Changing World*. Rowman & Littlefield. (2004).
- "Globalization". *Oxford English Dictionary Online*. September 2009. Retrieved November 5 2010.
- Friedman, Thomas L. "The Dell Theory of Conflict Prevention". *Emergin: A Reader*. Ed. Barclay Barrios. Boston: Bedford, St. Martins, 2008.
- Takis Fotopoulos,(2001)"Globalization, the reformist Left and the Anti-Globalization 'Movement'", Democracy & Nature: The International Journal of Inclusive Democracy.

- Convers See, Daniele (2010) 'The limits of cultural globalisation?', *Journal of Critical Globalisation* Studies, 3,
- ^ Andre Gunder Frank, "Reorient: Global economy in the Asian age" U.C. Berkeley Press, 1998.
- "The Columbian Exchange". The University of North Carolina.
- "PBS.org". PBS.org. 1929-10-24. Retrieved 2010-07-31.
- Encyclopædia Britannica's Great Inventions", Encyclopædia Britannica
- "World Exports as Percentage of Gross World Product". Global Policy Forum. Archived from the original on 12 July 2008. Retrieved 11 November 2009.
- Nouriel Roubini (January 15, 2009). "A Global Breakdown Of The Recession In 2009". *Forbes*.
- A Global Retreat As Economies Dry Up. The Washington Post. March 5, 2009.
- Economic Crisis Poses Threat To Global Stability. NPR. February 18, 2009.
- "In Recession, China Solidifies Its Lead in Global Trade". The New York Times. October 13, 2009.
- ^ Axel Dreher, Noel Gaston, Pim Martens, *Measuring Globalisation: Gauging Its Consequences*, Springer, ISBN 978-0-387-74067-6.
- ^ "KOF Index of Globalization". Globalization-index.org. Retrieved 2010-07-31.
- ^ "Globalisation shakes the world". BBC News. January 21, 2007.
- ^ "China and Africa: Stronger Economic Ties Mean More Migration". By Malia Politzer, *Migration Information Source*. August 2008.
- ^ "Africa, China's new frontier". Times Online. February 10, 2008.
- ^ "Globalization[dead link]". Microsoft Encarta Online Encyclopedia 2009. Archived 2009-10-31.
- ^ "World Port Rankings 2005". American Association of Port Authorities. 2005. Retrieved 2009-09-15.
- ^ "World Port Rankings 2006". American Association of Port Authorities. 2006. Retrieved 2009-09-15.
- "World Port Rankings 2007". American Association of Port Authorities. 2007. Retrieved 2009-09-15.[dead link]
- The birth of China's "special economic zones", Spiegel.de
- "4 Indians in Forbes' top 10 billionaires list". The Hindu Business Line. March 6, 2008.
- Scherer, J. (2007). "Globalization, promotional culture and the production/consumption of online games: Engaging Adidas's "Beat Rugby" campaign". *New Media & Society* .
- Pawel Zaleski *Global Non-governmental Administrative System: Geosociology of the Third Sector*, [in:] Gawin, Dariusz & Glinski, Piotr [ed.]: "Civil Society in the Making", IFiS Publishers, Warszawa 2006
- McAlister, Elizabeth. 2005. "Globalization and the Religious Production of Space." Journal for the Scientific Study of Religion, Vol. 44, No 3, September 2005, 249–255.
- Iagin Russia. "Towards The Theory of Alter Globalism Ghost of Alter Globalization". Retrieved 2009-04-09.
- Bhagwati, Jagdish N. *In defense of Globalization*. 2005 New York: Oxford University Press
- Worldbank.org[dead link]
- Longworth, Richard, C. *Caught in the Middle: America's the Age of Globalism*. New York: Bloomsbury, 2007.
- Steger, Manfred.*Globalization*. New York: Sterling Publishing, 2009.
- "Economics focus: Cash machines". 2011-04-16. Retrieved 2011-04-16.
- Noah, Timothy. "The United States of Inequality, Introducing the great Divergence", Slate, Sept 3, 2010.http://www.slate.com/id/2266025/entry/2266026/
- "Brain drain in Africa[dead link]"
- "Students' exodus costs India forex outflow of $10 bn: Assocham". Thaindian News. January 26, 2009.
- ^ "Globalexchange.org". Globalexchange.org. 2007-10-28. Retrieved 2010-07-31.
  "Educatingforjustice.org". Educatingforjustice.org. Retrieved 2010-07-31.
- Kuruvilla; Ranganathan (October 2008). "Economic Development Strategies and Macro- And Micro-Level Human Resource Policies: The Case of India's "Outsourcing"

Industry". *Industrial & Labor Relations Review* **62** (1):

- "Outsourcing to Africa: The world economy calls". 2011-04-16. Retrieved 2011-04-16.
- "China overtakes US as world's biggest CO_2 emitter". Guardian.co.uk. June 19, 2007.
- "Brazil Amazon deforestation soars". BBC News. January 24, 2008.
- "Japan depletes Borneo's rainforests; China remains largest log importer"
- Oil price 'may hit $200 a barrel', BBC News
- "Running Out of Planet to Exploit". The New York Times. April 21, 2008.
- "International Petroleum (Oil) Consumption Data". U.S. Energy Information Administration. Retrieved 2007-12-20.
- "Booming nations 'threaten Earth'". BBC News. January 12, 2006.
- "China is black hole of Asia's deforestation." Asia News. March 24, 2008.
- "Earth's natural wealth: an audit". New Scientist. May 23, 2007.
- "Effects of Over-Consumption and Increasing Populations". September 26 2001. Retrieved on 19 June 2007
- von Braun, "High and Rising Food Prices", 2008.
- "Global food production will have to increase 70% for additional 2.3 billion people by 2050". Finfacts.com. September 24, 2009.
- Tainter, JA 1996. Complexity, Problem Solving, and Sustainable Societies. In Costanza, R, Segura,O & Martinez-Alier, J (eds) Getting Down to Earth: Practical Applications of Ecological Economics. Washington, D.C.: Island Press.
- Pimentel, D & Pimentel, M 2008. Food, Energy, and Society. 3rd edition. Boca Raton, Florida: CRC Press.
- Catton, WR Jr 1980. Overshoot: The Ecological Basis of Revolutionary Change. Urbana: University of Illinois Press.
- Helga Vierich "Before farming and after globalization: the future of hunter- gatherers may be brighter than you think", In Before Farming 2008/4 article 4(1). See also discussion at: Waspress.co.uk
- "'Only 50 years left' for sea fish", BBC News. November 2; 2006.
- Juliet Eilperin (2 November 2006). "Seafood Population Depleted by 2048, Study Finds". The Washington Post.
- Dr Daulaire. *Globalization and Health*. Retrieved October 11, 2006 fromhttp://www.globalhealth.org/assets/html/drmed3.html
- ^ Stéphane Barry and Norbert Gualde, in *L'Histoire* n° 310, June 2006, pp.45–46, say "between one-third and two-thirds"; Robert Gottfried (1983). "Black Death" in *Dictionary of the Middle Ages*, volume 2, pp.257–67, says "between 25 and 45%".
- "The Impact of Globalization on Infectious Disease Emergence and Control: Exploring the Consequences and Opportunities, Workshop Summary – Forum on Microbial Threats". Nap.edu. 2003-06-01. Retrieved on July7, 2007.
- "The virus from Africa reached the U.S. by way of Haiti, a genetic study shows". Los Angelese Times. October 30, 2007.
- "Chagas disease", HealthCentral.com.
- "Trends in Tuberculosis Incidence --- United States, 2006". CDC.gov. March 23, 2007 / 56(11).
- Vogel, Ezra F. (1991). *The Four Little Dragons: The Spread of Industrialization in East Asia*. Cambridge, Massachusetts: Harvard University Press.
- "China trade blamed for 2.4 mln lost US jobs-report". Reuters. March 23, 2010.
- "Factory jobs: 3 million lost since 2000". USATODAY.com. April 20, 2007.
- Hanksworth John and Cookson, Gordon. *The World in 2050, Beyond the BRICs: a broader look at emerging market growth prospects*. PricewaterhouseCoopers LLP. http://www.pwc.com/gx/en/world-2050/pdf/world_2050_brics.pdf
- EM Equity in Two Decades, A Changing Landscape. *Global Economics Paper No: 204*, Goldman Sachs Global Economics, Comodities and Strategy Research
- "Economic Crisis in a Globalized World". Public Broadcasting Service (PBS). November 21, 2008
- "The fruit of hypocrisy". The Guardian. September 16, 2008
- "Banks Taking Same Risks That Led to Crisis: ECB's Noyer". CNBC.com. October 26, 2009.

- "UN.org". UN.org. Retrieved 2010-07-31.
- "Drug Trade". BBC News.
- "Will traditional Chinese medicine mean the end of the wild tiger?". San Francisco Chronicle. November 11, 2007.
- "India says Chinese medicine fuels tiger poaching". Reuters. September 17, 2009.
- "Rhino rescue plan decimates Asian antelopes". New Scientist. February 12, 2003.
- Chapman, Roger. Culture wars: an encyclopedia of issues, viewpoints, and voices, Volume 1. 2009: M.E. Sharp
- Fiss, Peer and Hirsch, Pal: "The Discourse of Globalization: Framing and Sensemaking of an Emerging Concept. American Sociological Review, February 2005.. 70 1 29–52.
- Greg Ip: "The Declining Value Of Your College Degree", *Wall Street Journal*. July 17, 2008.
- Gordon, Philip. 2004. "Globalization: Europe's Wary Embrace". *Yale Global*, 1 November 2004. http://yaleglobal.yale.edu/content/globalization-europes-wary-embrace
- Noah, Timothy. 2010.. "The United States of Inequality, Introducing the great Divergence", Slate, Sept 3,
- Gordon, Philip. 2004. "Globalization: Europe's Wary Embrace". Yale Global, 1 November 2004. http://yaleglobal.yale.edu/content/globalization-europes-wary-embrace
- Takenaka Heizo and Chida Ryokichi. 1998. "Japan," *Domestic Adjustments to Globalization*; (ed, Charles E. Morrison and Hadi Soesastro), Tokyo: Japan center for International Exchange, 1998.
- "Widespread Unease about Economy and Globalization". *BBC World Service Poll*.http://www.worldpublicopinion.org/pipa/pdf/feb08/BBCEcon_Feb08_rpt.pdf
- "Africans and Asians Tend to View Globalization Favorably. Europeans and Americans are More Skeptical". World Public Opinion.org. November 7, 2006.
- "Widesread Unease about Economy and Globalization". *BBC World Service Poll*. http://www.worldpublicopinion.org/pipa/pdf/feb08/BBCEcon_Feb08_rpt.pdf
- Bhagwati, Jagdish N. In defense of Globalization. 2005 New York: Oxford University Press
- Shoa S. Rajgopal. 2002. Reclaiming Democracy, the Anti-globalization Movement in South Asia". Feminist review. 2002. http://visuality.org/globalization/wmst250_readings/the_antiglobalization_mvmnt.pdf.
- Carol Graham "Winners and Losers: Perspectives on Globalization from the Emerging Market Economies" Brookings. Saturday, January 1, 2011 http://www.brookings.edu/articles/2001/fall_globaleconomics_graham.aspx
- John Parker, Burgeoning bourgeoisie, A special report on the new middle classes in emerging markets. The Economist .Feb 12th 2009. http://www.economist.com/node/13063298?story_id=13063298&source=hptextfeature
- "Globalization and the Rural-Urban Divide". IATRC Summer Symposium, June 30 – July 2, 2008.http://aede.osu.edu/programs/anderson/trade/Seoul_Symposium_Report.pdf
- Shoa S. Rajgopal. 2002. Reclaiming Democracy, the Anti-globalization Movement in South Asia". *Feminist review* 2002. http://visuality.org/globalization/wmst250_readings/the_antiglobalization_mvmnt.pdf
- Antoaneta Becker (8 October 2010). "CHINA: Resentment Rises With Widening Wealth Gaps". Global Geopolitics & Political Economy / IPS. Retrieved December 31 2010.
- "Rural unrest in China Worries about poverty and instability in central China". The Economist. Mar 15th 2007
- Kine Phelim. "China's Summer Of Labor Unrest"July, 23, 2010. Forbes.com
- Held, David. McGrew Anthony. "Globalization", in *The Oxford Companion to Politics of the World* by Joel Krieger (Aug 2, 2001) Oxford University Press.
- Fiss, Peer and Hirsch, Pal: "The Discourse of Globalization: Framing and Sensemaking of an Emerging Concept.*American Sociological Review*, February 2005. vol. 70 no 1.
- Sachs, Jeffrey (2005). *The End of Poverty*. New York, New York: The Penguin Press. ISBN 1-59420-045-9.
- "World Bank, Poverty Rates, 1981–2002" (PDF). Retrieved 2007-06-04.
- Marshall McLuhan and Bruce R. Powers (Sep 17, 1992) The Global Village: Transformations in World Life and Media in the 21st Century Oxford University Press: Sep 17, 1992

- Chapman, Roger. *Culture wars: an encyclopedia of issues, viewpoints, and voices, Volume 1*. 2009: M.E.Sharp
- "USACOR.org". USACOR.org. 2009-07-28. Retrieved 2010-07-31.
- .Marable, Manning, "Globalization and Racialization" Synthesis/Regeneration 39 (Winter 2006)http://www.greens.org/s-r/39/39-06.html
- No Logo: No Space, No Choice, No Jobs, Naomi Klein.
- Hirst and Thompson "The Future of Globalisation" Published: Cooperation and Conflict, Vol. 37, No. 3, 247–265 (2002)DOI: 10.1177/0010836702037003671 CAC.sagepub.com
- Morris, Douglas "Globalization and Media Democracy: The Case of Indymedia", *Shaping the Network Society*, MIT Press2003. Courtesy link to(pre-publication version) FIS.utoronto.ca
- Convention.allacademic.com Podobnik, Bruce, *Resistance to Globalization: Cycles and Evolutions in the Globalization Protest Movement*, p. 2.
- Stiglitz, Joseph & Charlton *Fair Trade for All: How Trade Can Promote Development*. 2005 p. 54 n. 23
- "The Happy Planet Index". Neweconomics.org. Retrieved 2010-07-31.[dead link]
- The New Economics Foundation[dead link]
- Capra, Fritjof (2002). *The Hidden Connections*. New York, New York: Random House. ISBN 0-385-49471-8.
- Noam Chomsky Znet 07 May 2002/ The Croatian Feral Tribune April 27 2002 ZMAG.org
- Interview by Sniježana Matejčić, June 2005 en 2.htm[dead link]
- Hurst, E. Charles. Social Inequality: Forms, Causes, and consequences, 6th ed. P.41
- Chossudovsky, Michel. The globalization of poverty and the new world order/by Michel Chossudovsky. Edition 2nd ed. Imprint Shanty Bay, Ont.: Global Outlook, c2003.
- Pavcnik, Nina; Pavcnik, Nina (2005). "Child Labor in the Global Economy". *Journal of Economic Perspectives***19** (1): 199–220. doi: 10.1257/0895330053147895.
- Branko Milanovic (2006-11-02). "Developing Countries Worse Off Than Once Thought – Carnegie Endowment for International Peace". Carnegieendowment.org. Retrieved 2010-07-31.
- "Fórum Social Mundial". Forumsocialmundial.org.br. Retrieved 2010-07-31.
- Wade, Robert Hunter. 'The Rising Inequality of World Income Distribution', Finance & Development, Vol 38, No December 4 2001
- "Xabier Gorostiaga," "World has become a 'champagne glass' globalization will fill it fuller for a wealthy few 'National Catholic Reporter, Jan 27, 1995'". Findarticles.com. 1995. Retrieved 2010-07-31.
- United Nations Development Program. 1992 Human Development Report, 1992 (New York, Oxford University Press)
- Perkins, John (2004). *Confessions of an Economic Hit Man*. San Francisco, California: Berrett-Koehler. ISBN 1-57675-301-8.

Biscuits Incorporated with Coral Jasmine (Medicinal Plant): A Step Towards Sustainable Development and Rural Entrepreneurship

Shailja Jain[1] and Anamika Jain[2]

[1]Department of Home Science (Food and Nutrition), Goverment KRGPG Autonomous College Gwalior

[2]Department of Food Technology, Jiwaji University, Gwalior

ABSTRACT

The agricultural production in India holds the key to rural development, rural economy and most importantly rural health. The problem of migration of rural population to the urban areas especially for search of job is becoming more and more severe day by day. Sustainable development and rural entrepreneurship is a concept that needs to be taken seriously in order to avoid rural migration, to provide bread and butter to the unemployed and to make best and optimum use of the available resources. The people being mostly illiterate are not aware of the available opportunities and prospects. The need of the hour is that people from the government or academics or industries should come forward and educate them about such projects as would be feasible to run in rural areas.

The present study is a step in this direction. A medicinal plant, Coral jasmine, has enormous therapeutic properties. The extract of its leaves can be incorporated in various food products (like biscuits), and then marketed as a functional food. The whole process starting from the cultivation of crops to the final product can be handled by the rural people (men as well as women), and an industry can be set up initially on small scale and later on large scale.

Keywords: *Sustainable development, entrepreneurship, rural/urban areas, coral jasmine, functional food*

INTRODUCTION

According to www2.hawaii.edu, From a nation dependent on food imports to feed its population, India today is not only self-sufficient in grain production but also has a substantial reserve. Agriculture and allied activities constitute the single largest contributor to the Gross Domestic Product, almost 33% of it. Agriculture is the means of livelihood of about two-thirds of the workforce in the country. Today, India ranks second worldwide in farm output. Despite a steady decline of its share in the GDP, agriculture and forestry are still the largest economic sector and play a significant role in the overall socio-economic development of India.

According to web.worldbank.org, Although agriculture contributes only 21% of India's GDP, its importance in the country's economic, social, and political fabric goes well beyond this indicator. The rural areas are still home to some 72% of the India's 1.1 billion people, a large number of whom are poor. Most of the rural poor depend on rain-fed agriculture and fragile forests for their livelihoods. The sharp rise in food grain production during India's Green Revolution of the 1970s enabled the country to achieve self-sufficiency in food grains and stave off the threat of famine. Agricultural intensification in the 1970s to 1980s saw an increased demand for rural labor that raised rural wages and, together with declining food prices, reduced rural poverty.

According to www.oppapers.com, this increase in agricultural production has been brought about by bringing additional area under cultivation, extension of irrigation facilities, the use of improved high-yielding variety of seeds, better techniques evolved through agricultural research, water management, and plant protection through judicious use of fertilizers, pesticides and cropping practices.

ENTREPRENEURSHIP

According to en.wikipedia.org, The acts of entrepreneurship are often associated with true uncertainty, particularly when it involves bringing something really novel to the world, whose market never exists. However, even if a market already exists, there is no guarantee that a market exists for a particular new player in the cola category. Entrepreneurship is the act of being an entrepreneur, which is a French word meaning "one who undertakes innovations, finance and business acumen in an effort to transform innovations into economic goods". This may result in new organisations or may be part of revitalizing mature organisations in response to a perceived opportunity. The most obvious form of entrepreneurship is that of starting new businesses (referred to as Startup Company); however, in recent years, the term has been extended to include social and political forms of entrepreneurial activity. When entrepreneurship is describing activities within a firm or large organisation it is referred to as intrapreneurship and may include corporate venturing, when large entities spin-off organisations.

RURAL ENTREPRENEURSHIP

Rural entrepreneurs should be connected to external markets, regionally, nationally, and internationally so that they are not dependent upon stagnant local markets for their goods and services. Rural entrepreneurship is one of the newest areas of research in the entrepreneurship field. It has become one of the significant supportive factors for rural economic development and agribusiness. After over 5 decades of independence and industrialization in our country, still a very large part of population remains under poverty line. Agriculture continues to be the back bone of rural society. As per a study, 70% of holdings are held by small and marginal farmers resulting in overcrowding on the agricultural land and diminishing farm produce. This also results in migration of farm workers in large numbers to the urban areas. In both the cases the population remains under poverty line.

Agricultural work force has a share of 70% in the total work force of the country. Cultivators who own farmland come to about 68% of this work force while agricultural labor accounts for the remaining 32%. These cultivators are increasing in number over the years but the large increase was among the agricultural labor which went up from 20% of the rural work force to 32%. One also needs to keep in mind that there is a continuous growth of population. Thus, the policy for rural development has to tackle, the problems by providing other occupation options to the rural youths.

The training for development of rural entrepreneurship has to be different from the entrepreneurship development training in urban areas. This is the reason that government initiated the integrated rural development programs. The aim of the present study is to integrate rural entrepreneurship, with the current rural entrepreneurship research into an entrepreneurship typology, and hence analyze data sources and research methods being used and eventually develop the rural economy.

HEALTH DETERMINANTS IN RURAL AREAS

Physical Environment

Several studies report lower water quality and crowding of households as factors affecting disease control in rural and remote locations. As well, insufficient wastewater treatments, lack of paved roads and exposure to agricultural chemicals have been identified as additional environmental concerns for those living in rural locations.

Health Care Services

According to en.wikipedia.org, some would say that there is an "inverse care law" in operation. People in rural communities have poorer health status and greater needs for primary health care, yet they are not as well served and have more difficulty accessing health care services than people in urban centres.

IMPORTANT AND MAIN HEALTH ISSUES

People in rural areas face some different health issues than people who live in towns and cities. Getting health care can be a problem when you live in a remote area.

- Underserviced delivery due to lack or misdistribution of resources, both in terms of money and labor.

• Lack of specialty services: Medical specialists often do not have enough 'critical mass' of patients to allow them to economically serve a low population area. The hardship on patients can be particularly demanding in some illnesses, say cancer, in which treatment requires regular long distance travel.

JOINT PAIN

According to www.joint-pain.com, Joint pain is a resource for osteoarthritis, rheumatoid arthritis and gout sufferers, as well as those with similar chronic pain conditions. Millions of people possess the painful symptoms of arthritis and related diseases, which include inflammation, swelling, redness, pain and stiffness. Although there are literally hundreds of different kinds of arthritis, osteoarthritis, rheumatoid arthritis and gout following three are the most common.

OSTEOARTHRITIS

Osteoarthritis occurs as the protective, cushiony cartilage covering the bones wears away, resulting in bones rubbing together. This friction causes joint pain and swelling, and worsens as the cartilage breaks down further. Osteoarthritis most commonly affects the hands, hips, knees and spine, and worsens with age.

GOUT

This is a painful arthritis-related condition. This most commonly affects the toes, knees and wrists, and is marked by the body's inability to rid itself of uric acid, a naturally forming substance. This buildup causes needle-like crystals in the joints which can be extremely painful.

OSTEOMALACIA

Osteomalacia is the softening of the bones due to defective bone mineralization. Osteomalacia in children is known as rickets, and because of this, use of the term Osteomalacia is often restricted to the milder, adult form of the disease. It may show signs as diffuse body pains, muscle weakness, and fragility of the bones. A common cause of the disease is a deficiency in vitamin D, which is normally obtained from the diet and/or sunlight exposure.

TRADITIONAL AND ANALGESIC DRUG CORAL JASMINE

According to www.aiaer.net, For the past several decades on this planet, man has been dependent on nature for curing various human body diseases. From ancient civilization various parts of different plants were used to free pain, control suffering and counteract diseases. A number of plants are being used for the treatment of several ailments; Coral Jasmine is one of them. It is a common wild herb with a strong potential, which can be used as a medicinal ingredient in functional food.

Coral Jasmine Leaf

CORAL JASMINE LEAF

There are many grounds for using coral jasmine as a therapeutic drug. It contains alkaloids, tannins, flavonoids, cardiac glycosides and sugar.

These have an impact on human physiology and may help explain some of the therapeutic uses of *Nyctanthes arbortristis Linn.*

CORAL JASMINE IN VARIOUS FORMS

Abdominal discomfort: Seeds of coral jasmine are ground together with some quantity of the black pepper and dried ginger to make a paste.

Constipation: Juice from the leaves of coral jasmine is extracted and then taken one teaspoonful orally in empty stomach. (preferably in early morning).

Jaundice: Extract juice from the leaves of coral jasmine is extracted and then taken one teaspoonful of this juice orally with a glass of sugar, candy, water. This process is continued twice a day for five days.

Malaria: Juice from the leaves of *Nyctanthes arbortristis Linn.* is extracted and taken one teaspoonful.

Antiviral activity: Nyctantic acid, friedlin, beta-sitosterol and oleanolic acid isolated from leaves are used for this purpose.

Antibacterial activity: *Nyctanthes arbortristis Linn.* can be used to discover bioactive natural products that may serve for leads for the development of new pharmaceuticals that address hither unmet therapeutic needs.

Anti allergic activity: Extract of coral jasmine leaves is traditionally used in India for anti allergic disorders.

Immunomodulatory effect: *Nyctanthes arbortristis Linn* has even been shown to here immunomodulatory effect.

Digestive aid: Indian people have used coral jasmine to facilitate better digestion. Plant leaf can exert numerous therapeutic actions in the human body.

CNS activity: The water soluble portion of the alcoholic extract of leaves was screened for some CNS activities (viz. hypnotic tranquilizing activities).

Immuno bio activities: There are studies which confirm the strong immunobioactivities in extract of *Nyctanthes arbortristis Linn.*

Anti inflammatory activity: *Nyctanthes arbortristis Linn* leaves extract is used extensively in ayurvedic medicine for the treatment of various diseases such as sciatica, rheumatism and anti inflammatory activity.

Ulcerogenic activity: *Nyctanthes arbortristis Linn.* leaf extract has been observed to have significant analgesic and antipyretic activity

Antioxidant activity: The acetone soluble fraction of its ethyl acetate extract showed impressive antioxidant activity as revealed by several in vitro experiments, e.g. DPPH, hydroxyl and superoxide radicals as well as H_2O_2 scavenging activity.

INCORPORATION IN FOOD PRODUCT

In all the above studies, the extract of leaves has been used as the drug; but its taste and flavor are so pungent that it would be worthwhile if it is incorporated in some common food products, which are usually consumed by rural population. Hence, it is proposed to fortify biscuits (common food product) with acceptable quantity of the leaves extract and then use it as a drug for various ailments. A typical flow chart showing the procedure is as follows:

Fresh leaves of coral jasmine are collected

↓

Washed with running water

↓

Extraction of remedial component from fresh leaves

↓

Incorporation of extract in biscuits

Commercialization of Food Product in Rural Areas

According to linkinghub. elsevier.com, Commercialization of agricultural production is an endogenous process and is accompanied by economic growth, urbanization and withdrawal of labor from the agricultural sector. However, it can be highlighted that appropriate government policies including investment in rural infrastructure and crop improvement research and extension, establishment of secure rights to land and water, and development and liberalization of capital markets, can help alleviate many of the possible adverse transitional consequences. Rural marketing is the much talked about subject for the business establishments. A large number of companies have made a big headway by focusing themselves on rural markets. It proved to be an opportunity rather than a problem for the marketers to concentrate on rural markets and the poor. Many of them who had earlier ignored this segment due to lot of investment requirements and low returns have again started foraying into it and targeted the rural masses. They attempted all the feasible approaches to sell the products to the rural consumers that met their lifestyles and living standards. Several large companies like HLL, ITC, Coca-Cola, LG, Britannia, Philips, Colgate-Palmolive etc., penetrated aggressively into the rural markets and spent heavily in the rural areas. Some of them even invested money to create separate sales and marketing teams exclusively for rural markets. They also appointed specialist agencies who could advise them on rural marketing.

- The growth of rural marketed depends on the following factors:
  - The rise in disposable income of the rural families
  - The economic boom
  - Timely rains
  - Rural population involved themselves in business other than agriculture
  - Increase white-collar jobs in nearby towns

- ° Commercialization of agriculture
- ° Saturation of the urban markets
- ° Media penetration in rural areas (particularly satellite channels)
- ° Globalization
- ° Economic liberalization
- ° Revolution in the Information Technology
- ° Women empowerment
- ° Improving infrastructure

Apart from rural marketing, this study deals with rural entrepreneurship and rural/urban marketing. The food product proposed can be easily manufactured by several people and will find a very good market in rural as well as urban population. The project can be taken up on large scale in collaborate with some established industries or on small scale by rural people themselves.

1. Recipe Formulation in Large Scale/Industrially

Select and weigh ingredients (flour, sugar, fat, coral jasmine leaves extract)

↓

Mix ingredients to form dough

↓

Knead, roll and, if appropriate, layer dough

↓

Cut dough into individual biscuit shapes

↓

Bake dough in commercial ovens

↓

Cool baked product and finish with topping, filling or coating

↓

Quality assurance – check final biscuit

↓

Package

↓

Quality check again

↓

Storage and distribution

2. Recipe Formulation in Small Scale/Rural Areas

Select and weigh ingredients (flour, sugar, fat, coral jasmine leaves extract)

↓

Mix ingredients to form dough

Knead, roll and, if appropriate, layer dough

↓

Cut dough into individual biscuit shapes

↓

Bake dough in solar ovens

↓

Cool baked product and finish with topping, filling or coating

↓

Quality assurance – check final biscuit

↓

Package

↓

Quality check again

↓

Storage and distribution

MARKETING OF FOOD PRODUCT IN RURAL / URBAN AREAS:

Advances in the areas of food technology, food biochemistry and the nutritional sciences (including nutritional genomics) are providing consumers with access to fresh and often supplemented produce with recognizable health benefits that previously were not available. New methods being used by the functional food industry to isolate, characterize, extract and purify nutraceuticals from bacterial, plant and animal sources are resulting in decreased costs to the industry as well as providing new options for use of functional food products.

If the marketer truly understands the needs of the rural/urban consumers, he should strive to provide them with those products and services that would meet their requirements. Companies like Calvin Care who launched their shampoo in sachets, Britannia who conveniently packaged its Tiger brand biscuits with low price tag are the best examples of understanding the rural customer's needs. The companies need to make proper assessment while marketing for the rural/urban India. It is very essential for the rural marketer to understand the psychology of their consumers in terms of their usage habits and shopping behavior along with their emotions and value systems. The integration of both technological and managerial knowledge would help them to develop the various marketing strategies for the rural/urban Indian markets.

CONCEPT OF ENTREPRENEURSHIP

1. Cultivation Coral jasmine leaves are easily cultivated in rural areas/ urban areas. specially in sub Himalayan regions ranges Nepal, Assam, Burma, Bengal and Central India like Rajasthan, Madhya Pradesh and south wards to Godavari and other parts of world like Indonesia and Malaysia. The local plantation can be organized in consultation with agriculture experts.

2. Collection The leaves with definite life (fresh/ few days old/very old) need to be collected for further processing. This can be very well done by rural house ladies, so that they also participate in entrepreneurship.

3. Extraction Extraction of coral jasmine leaves is done by decoction method and extract will be collected in glass containers.

4. Incorporate in food product The coral jasmine leaves extract is incorporated in different types of food product for example biscuit. These types of biscuits will act as functional food and can be used to cure various types of disease especially related to joint pain.

5. Laboratory study Quality parameters of biscuits can be checked by the laboratory in urban areas.

6. Packaging Biscuit are packaged for selling purpose. Some important points to be kept in mind:

- Protect the biscuits against contamination, loss of damage (due to micro organism, exposure to heat, moisture).
- Biscuits are packaged in appropriate packaging material.
- Now-a-days plastic/ paper container are used for packaging of biscuits.
- Poly olefins such as poly propylene and poly ethylene are also used.
- Cartons are used for both retail and whole sale. They are made of combination of food grade paper and wax or plastics.

7. Storage and distribution Biscuits are stored in cool place and distribution is the last and final stage of the market.

References

- Retrieved from envfor.nic.in/divisions/ic/wssd/doc4/consul_book_ch4.pdf
www2.hawaii.edu/.../...
- *Retrieved from* www.oppapers.com › Science › Agriculture Research Papers
*kunkalamarru.net/**agriculture**.html*
- web.worldbank.org › Countries › South Asia › Agriculture › Countries
- *Retrieved from* www.mediavoicemag.com/.../4570-musings-of-the-chief-editor.html
- *Retrieved from* www.radhanathswami.com/projects/venu-madhuri/
- *Retrieved from* www.kashmirstudycircle.ewebsite.com/.../blog--sarfaraz-mohammad-...
- *Retrived from* www.kashmirstudycircle.ewebsite.com
- *Retrived from* www.oppapers.com › Science › Chemistry Research Papers
*en.wikipedia.org/wiki/**Entrepreneurship***
books.google.co.in/books?isbn=9380156685...
- *Retrieved from* www.scribd.com/doc/61261148/Entrepreneurship
*en.wikipedia.org/wiki/**Rural_health***
- *Retrieved from* www.joint-pain.com/
ghcherbal.com/orthoflex. drshakunayurveda.com/solutions.aspx?id=1009*html*
- *Retrieved from* www.aiaer.net conferenceabstractsnov2011/abstract/J.pdf

Job Satisfaction Among Doctors

Deepti Bhargava
Head, Department of Management Studies
Shrinathji Institute of Technology and Engineering, Nathdwara
Rajsamand, Rajasthan

ABSTRACT

Job satisfaction is in regard to one's feelings or state-of-mind regarding the nature of their work. Job satisfaction can be influenced by a variety of factors, eg, the quality of one's relationship with their supervisor, the quality of the physical environment in which they work, degree of fulfillment in their work, etc. Job satisfaction is a complex function of many variables. Job satisfaction may be defined as any combination of psychological, physiological, and environmental circumstances that causes a person to truthfully say "I am satisfied with my job" (Bailey, 1997). Different writers have described job satisfaction in similar ways. Locke (1976) describes job satisfaction as a positive emotional state emanating from an individual's job experience. Similarly, Weiss (2002) regards it as an affective reaction and attitude towards a person's job. A person may be satisfied with one or more aspects of his/her job but at the same time may be unhappy with other things related to the job.

The research has taken two things in mind while doing research, first is that people deserve to be treated fairly and with respect. Job satisfaction is some extent is the reflection of good treatment. Secondly, the job satisfaction can lead to behavior and it increases organizational functioning. It is also the reflection of organizational functioning.

Keywords: *Job Satisfaction, Organisation Functioning*

NEED OF JOB SATISFACTION AMONG MEDICAL PERSONNEL

Medical profession is regarded as one of the noblest professions in the world. It is only natural that professional bodies as well as the general public expect the medical practitioners to demonstrate the highest standards of professionalism (Alam and Haque, 2010). They are also expected to hold to these high standards even in the face of such adversity as unfavorable job environment, poor conditions and low earning levels. Though the doctors have achieved noticeable success in terms of career and finances, they often remain over worked and stressed and somehow not satisfied with the working environment.

Any type of dissatisfaction lead to low morale and doctors cannot do the work with full efficiency. The inefficiency makes hurdles in their growth and development and decrease productivity of the hospitals. Medical professional have difficulties in meeting the patient need if their own need are dissatisfied.

The job of medical personnel requires fulltime and efficiency in the workplace. For doctors working environment build on cordial relationship is very important because generally they spent most of the hours in workplace. According to Herzberg two factor motivation theory, motivation is associated with job satisfaction. Herzberg, Mausner, and Snyderman (1959) named the determinants of satisfaction "motivators" (achievement, recognition, work itself, responsibility, advancement) and the determinants of dissatisfaction "hygienes" (policy and administration, supervision, salary, interpersonal relations, working conditions).So if they satisfied with Hygiene and motivational factor then they are easily motivated and fulfill the personal as well as organizational objective.

REVIEW OF LITERATURE

Job satisfaction is one of the most researched concepts. It is regarded as central to work and organizational psychology. It serves as a mediator for creating relationship between working conditions, on the one hand, and individual/organizational outcome on the other (Dormann and Zapf, 2001).

It is generally believed that doctors are increasingly showing dissatisfaction with their jobs. A cross sectional study carried out in the USA, in 1986 (Medical Outcome Study) and 1997 (Study of Primary Care Performance in Massachusetts), conducted by Murray and colleagues, found a declining trend in the satisfaction level among general internists and family practitioners of Massachusetts (Murray *et al.,* 2001). Though the doctors have achieved noticeable success in terms of career and finances, they often remain over worked and stressed. Consequently, the frustration, anger and restlessness are leading many of them to lose sight of their career goals and personal ambitions. Another study concludes that the workload, unsuitable working hours and lack of incentives are the major contributors to the dissatisfaction of public health.

Dr Jack Mkubwa in his study recommends that focus should be given to working conditions, relations with hospital administration, salary, professional development and promotion. Since physicians are guided by their professional ethos, it is possible to conclude that their job dissatisfaction or lack of job satisfaction may indeed emanate from the failure to fulfill their professional obligations due to lack of an enabling environment.

Khuwaja AK, Qureshi R, Andrades M, Fatmi Z, Khuwaja NK, conducted a study Comparing of job satisfaction and stress among male and female doctors in teaching hospitals of Karachi and found that Majority of doctors working at these teaching hospitals of Karachi had poor satisfaction level for workplace characteristics and higher levels of job stress. This suggests that immediate steps should be taken for their control and management. This study invites further research to explore, implement and evaluate intervention strategies for prevention of stress and improvement in job satisfaction.

A study conducted on 333 doctors in Scotland indicated that higher clinical workloads were related to higher stress (Deary *et al.,* 1996) Responsibility for others and career development were found to be of significant relationship with work stress among doctors (Nusair and Deibageh, 1997).

On the basis of the review of literature we are of the opinion that stress always affects the efficiency and performance of the doctors working in hospitals. Academicians, researchers, administrators and consultants have identified a number of factors responsible for role stress among doctors.

OBJECTIVES OF THE STUDY

- To study the stress levels and Job satisfaction among doctors.
- To identify which factor affect the most in job satisfaction.

RESEARCH METHODOLOGY

Data Collection: Data Sources

(i) Secondary Data through Internet, Magazine, Journals, Books etc.

(ii) Primary Data through Questionnaire

The Study

The study is exploratory in nature and was conducted on the Doctors working in Public and Private Hospitals/ nursing home and clinic. The data was collected from Uttar pradesh, Rajasthan and Punjab.

The Sample

The sample of the study was constituted of 85 respondents. The sample was drawn on random basis.

Tools for Data Collection

A questionnaire was designed with the Factors like working environment, Work stress, opportunity for growth and development, salary & benefits, interpersonal relation and Timings. A Five point rating scale was used to obtain the responses on the satisfaction of employees.

The tool employed for generating responses will questionnaire based survey of doctors to their perception and opinion towards different factors of job satisfaction.

The above diagram shows the different factors which affect the job satisfaction among doctors. The dissatisfaction will also increase the turnover rate among doctors in hospitals. So it is necessary to identify which factor affect the most and how can administrator satisfied the individual.

The motivator-hygiene theory was credited with propelling and advancing research on job satisfaction (Steers & Porter, 1992). The premise of the motivator-hygiene theory (Herzberg, Mausner, & Snyderman, 1959) was that jobs had specific factors which were related to job satisfaction or dissatisfaction. The five factors thought to facilitate job satisfaction were achievement, recognition, work itself, responsibility, and advancement. The five factors identified by Herzberg et al., as determinants of job dissatisfaction, were policy and administration, supervision, salary, interpersonal relations, and working conditions. Subsequent research efforts (Bowen, 1980; Padilla-Velez, 1993) defined the motivator and hygiene factors as hypothesized by Herzberg *et al.*; Following is a description of the motivator-hygiene factors according to Padilla-Velez (1993, pp. 20-21) and Bowen (1980, pp. 13-14).

- Recognition - Acts of notice, praise, or blame supplied by one or more superior, peer, colleague, management person, client, and/or the general public.
- Achievement - Accomplishment of endeavors including instances wherein failures were incurred. Similarly, instances were included wherein neither success nor failures were incurred. Possibility of Growth - Whether a change in status was possible, irrespective of the fact that the change could be upward or downward in status.
- Advancement - Designated an actual change in job status.
- Salary - All sequences of events in which compensation plays a major role.
- Interpersonal Relations - Relationships involving superiors, subordinates, and peers.
- Supervision - The supervisor's willingness or unwillingness to delegate responsibility and/or willingness to teach subordinates.
- Responsibility - Satisfaction derived from being given control of personal work or the work of others and/or new job responsibilities.
- Policy and Administration – Events in which some or all aspects of the organization were related to job satisfaction.

- Working Condition – Physical working conditions, facilities, and quality of work as related to job satisfaction.
- Work Itself - The actual job performance related to job satisfaction.

RELATIONSHIP BETWEEN JOB STRESS AND JOB SATISFACTION

Several studies have tried to determine the link between stress and job satisfaction. Job satisfaction and job stress are the two hot focuses in human resource management researches. According to S amps & Piedmonte (1986) job satisfaction has been found significant relationship with job stress. One study of general practitioners in England identified four job stressors that were predictive of job dissatisfaction (Cooper, *et al.*, 1989). In other study, Vinokur-Kaplan (1991) stated that organization factors such as workload and working condition were negatively related with job satisfaction. Fletcher & Payne (1980) identified that a lack of satisfaction can be a source of stress, while high satisfaction can alleviate the effects of stress. This study reveals that, both of job stress and job satisfaction were found to be interrelated. The study of Landsbergis (1988) and Terry *et al.*, (1993) showed that high levels of work stress are associated with low levels of job satisfaction. Moreover, Cummins (1990) have emphasized that job stressors are predictive of job dissatisfaction and greater propensity to leave the organization. Sheena *et al.*, (2005) studied in UK found that there are some occupations that are reporting worse than average scores on each of the factors such as physical health, psychological well being, and job satisfaction. In this way we can say that there is strong relationship between job stress and job satisfaction.

DATA ANALYSIS AND INTERPRETATION

Table 1   Distribution of Respondents according to type of organisation

Type of Organisation	N	%
Public	50	58.82
Private	35	41.18
Total	85	100.00

The table shows that total respondent is 85 and out of that 50 are working in Public sector and 35 are working in Private sector.

We have designed a detail questionnaire covering all determinants of Job Satisfaction. The result was collected by respondent and then Factor analysis was

Mean Scores

Statement	Mean Score
1. The Nature of My Work Makes me stressed	2.94
2. I get irritated when my wife/children or any family member ask for something upon reaching home	3.04
3. I have lot of work pressure on me at my work	2.87
4. Upon reaching home from work I am mentally exhausted completely	2.95
5. My Work does not allow me to give sufficient time to my family	2.65
6. I do not get sufficient payment from my work.	2.62
7. Economic problems make me worried	2.42
8. The nature of my work does not allow me to give quality time to my family	2.54
9. I do not get sufficient time to pursue my hobbies	2.74
10. The nature of my work does not allow me to enjoy work and life equally with full enthusiasm	2.61
11. I do not get sufficient leaves given by the administration to balance between work and family life	2.33
12. I do not get sufficient time for further study and research	2.76
13. My colleagues and other staff work as a team	3.67
14. I am satisfied with overall working environment.	3.24
15. Relationship between doctors and administration/management are cordial	3.38
16. My colleagues, seniors, juniors and management staff co-operate with me.	3.51
17. Management/Administration at my hospital is co-operative /supportive and listens to my problem if I tell them	3.34
18. I receive sufficient support and encouragement from my administration for further study and research if I want to do	2.98
19. My work environment motivates me to do further studies and research work.	3.33
20. I have sufficient opportunity of growth and development related to my work at my organization.	3.07
21. I receive support and encouragement from my administration for further study and research work.	2.94
22. My hospital/nursing home have advance facilities so that I can update myself	2.84
23. My organization support and sponsor the employee to attend conferences and seminars.	2.89
24. The appraisal system of hospital gives more focus on research and publication.	2.81
25. I find sufficient opportunity for growth and development at my work place.	2.93

*Statement no. 1-12 are reversed scored

done. The mean score was calculated for each statement of questionnaire. On the basis of Mean score following major findings was drawn:

- Respondent has neutral opinion toward stress and work load (2.94,2.87) in the organization. It means Doctors feel stressed due to work at some level.
- Most of respondent exhausted with work and do not spent time with family (2.95,2.65,2.54).
- Most of the respondents have not quality time for family and hobbies (2.74,2.61).
- Most of the respondent agrees that they do not have sufficient time for further study (2.76).
- The score toward agree scale (3.04) shows that they do not irritate on their family members even if they feel some sort of work stress.
- Most of the respondent toward strongly agrees that they have strong interpersonal relationship. They have cordial relation with superior and

colleagues. The administration also encourage to build cordial relationship and work in a team. (3.67, 3.38, 3.51, 3.34).

- Most of the doctors find that they do not have enough support for further study and research. (2.94)
- The working environment is fully satisfied, administration always encourage and motivate for further study and research, growth and development related work (2.98, 3.33, 3.07).
- Most of doctors said that their administration is not implementing the rules regarding salary and benefits. They are not satisfied with salary and benefits and generally feel economic burden.
- There is slightly lower level was found in sponsoring the candidate for attending conference and seminar (2.89), to provide facility by administration (2.89) and appraisal system does not give more importance to research and publication (2.81).

Factors

Factors	Mean	Rank
Interpersonal Relations	3.39	1
Lack of Relaxation Time	2.72	4
Opportunity for Growth and Development	2.85	3
Salary and Benefits	2.70	6
Work Environment	3.11	2
Work Pressure /Stress	2.71	5

The above table shows that doctors of public and private sector give more importance to Interpersonal Relation. Their job itself give mental stress, so that they want that working environment should be cordial and work in team. The second rank they are giving to working environment. The results show that medical practitioners are less satisfied with Timings, opportunity for growth and development, Salary and they feel work stress. It means that they need further growth and development; the environment should be more encouraging and supporting to do research work. There should be opportunity for growth and development.

The analysis shows that for all factors the mean score was found less than 3.00 except two factor ie. Interpersonal Relation and work environment. It means that out of six factors doctors are less satisfied with the timings, salary and benefits, work stress and opportunity for growth and development. The finding also shows that doctors feel stress due to workload, salary and compensation, relaxation time and management policy which lead to dissatisfaction.

Organisational Creativity: The Genesis of a New Era

Anshika Vasandani

Lecturer (MBA), at SR Group of Institutions, Jhansi

ABSTRACT

Creativity is the essence of an individual's life and so is of an organisation. Around the globe, organisations are acknowledging the fact that creativity will be the call of the day. It will not only help in building a high morale but also contribute in improving organisational performance. HR managers will look for creativity as an essential element in a candidate, be it at any level.

A very novel trend is emerging in leadership - **creative leadership** - which says employees will give higher inputs if they work under a creative leader. Corporate giants like IBM, Microsoft and many more are emphasizing on this facet as well. Though, a lot needs to be done to not only to make employees realize about their **creative interest** but make this creativity available for organisational growth. In this paper, the factors affecting organisational creativity, its requirements, various practices, consequences and novel techniques are highlighted.

Keywords: *Creative leadership, creative interest*

INTRODUCTION

Creativity has always been a sought after element, be it Science or Art. It has always provided a winning edge to the party, who possessed it. Creativity is typically defined as the development of ideas that are 1) novel or original, and 2) useful (or potentially so) (Oldham and Cummings, 1996; Amabile *et al.*, 1996b; Paulus, 2000), and creativity is seen as a prerequisite for innovation (e.g., the implementation of useful ideas in the organisation). In the ancient times, a creative war strategy not only saved the life of the one who suggested it but of the entire province. Similarly, Organisational Creativity works as a lifeline for an organisation. It helps to break the status quo and emerge from the cocoon of monotony.

DETERMINANTS OF ORGANISATIONAL CREATIVITY

There are numerous factors that affect the evolution of creativity in an organisation.

Organisational climate, organisational culture, leadership style, resource and skill, and structure and systems are five factors that affect organisational creativity

ORGANISATIONAL CLIMATE AND ORGANISATIONAL CULTURE

Before understanding the impact, it is essential to differentiate between organisational climate and culture. An organisation's culture refers to the values, beliefs, history and traditions reflecting the foundations of the organisation. It is long standing, deeply rooted and changes gradually whereas organisation's climate refers to the recurring patterns of behavior exhibited in the day to day environment of the organisation as experienced by the individuals within that organisation.

Organisational climate penetrates through three levels-individual, team and organisation. The aim of the organisation should be to take creativity from the individual level to the organisational level. It is only then that an overwhelming effect of creativity will be witnessed.

Organisational culture shows the way people think, the things they value and the coherence between their thoughts, priorities and commitment. Culture is good or bad depending on its sync with organisational goals. A positive culture is required to support the emergence of creativity.

LEADERSHIP

As per Peter Cook (1998), a fundamental challenge leaders will face in the 21st century is how to profit from individual potential and then leverage it so that it produces organisational innovation and excellence. Leadership styles conducive to creativity are participative leadership, leader's vision for creativity and ability to develop effective groups. Individuals with strong leadership will consider themselves to have more potential for innovation and will be more likely to practice them when they perceive strong support from work place.

RESOURCE AND SKILL

The availability of appropriate resources and skills enables an organisation to adapt to changes, creativity being a change, in a faster and efficient way. This saves time in accepting as well as applying the changes.

STRUCTURE AND SYSTEMS

The structure and systems are required for creativity include long term employment of employees, a flat structure, fair supportive evaluation of employees and rewarding of creative performance (Amabile, 1979, 1983, 1990)

MODEL OF ORGANISATIONAL CREATIVITY

A Framework Depicting the Various Factors Leading to Organisational Creativity

The figure shows a framework that summarizes the ideas, variables, and relationships. It suggests that individual, group, and organisational characteristics have an impact on the creative process and situation, resulting in the creative product for the organisation. The components of creative persons, creative processes, creative situations, and creative products are essential for a comprehensive understanding of creativity in complex social systems. It provides a way to conceptualize the crucial links among persons, processes, situations, and creative product. The characteristics shown in the Figure do not suggest an exhaustive list.

Conceptual Links Among Creative Persons Processes. Situations and Products

Numerous variables at the individual, group, and organisational levels can be linked with creative behavior. For example, individual characteristics believed important for explaining some aspects of creativity can be grouped into cognitive, personality, motivational orientation, and knowledge categories.

These individual characteristics interact with social influence processes and environmental influence processes at both the group and organisational level. An important aspect of social influence is determined by such group characteristics as norms, enacted roles and task assignments, degree of cohesiveness, and so on.

Important organisational characteristics include cultural influences, resource availability, organisational mission and strategy, reward policies, structure, and technology. This complex mosaic of individual, group, and organisational characteristics creates the context-the creative situation-within which individual and group behaviors are played out. Many of these characteristics can be investigated in terms of their ability to enhance or constrain the creative accomplishment of individuals and groups.

The organisational creative process is composed of both salient behaviors and creative situations.

The creative situation is defined as the sum total of social and environmental (contextual) influences on creative behavior. The creative process in the organisation results in the creative product-novel ideas, products, services, procedures, or processes.

ORGANISATIONS PRACTICING CREATIVITY

IBM

IBM has identified organisational creativity as an essential element of organisations aiming to excel in this era of unpredictable changes. IBM Leadership Study 2011, says that more creativity is needed among leaders. It found that leaders who embrace the dynamic tension between creative disruption and operational efficiency can create new models of extraordinary value. Creative leadership in action enables a wide range of product, process and business model innovations. Organisations will need to act upon three imperatives to accelerate the development of creative capital:

• **Uncover the key capabilities of the creative organisation** Empower the organisation's ability to understand how the world behaves. Expose those

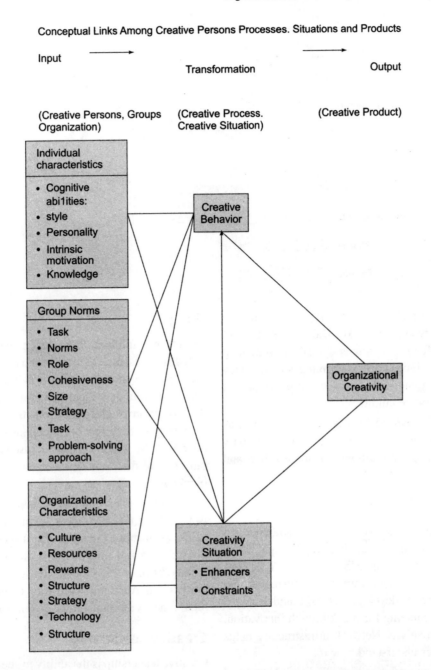

Conceptual Links Among Creative Persons Processes. Situations and Products

individuals who see opportunities where others do not and map out what is found. Connect ideas and people in novel ways. Try many and various ideas. Inspire belief that action is possible. Maintain the discipline to get things done.

• **Unlock and catalyze the creative capabilities of leaders** Create high-impact, experiential learning tied to real business challenges. Develop inspirational role models who demonstrate accomplishment and empowered leadership. Unleash small, diverse teams to pursue bold ideas in response to challenges. Create work structures and incentives aligned with intrinsic motivation. Promote a culture of inspiring vision built on authenticity and powered by trust.

• **Unleash and scale organisational creativity** Share information for collective vision. Tap into global expertise networks. Expand management and communication style repertoires. Build *ad hoc* constituencies of those sharing common goals. Influence collective behavior through real-time analytics.

The Key Findings of the Study are Represented in the Following Graph

Disney

Walt Disney has also conducted various breakout sessions to discuss how various arts agencies can adapt their style to make a difference. It conducts an exhaustive

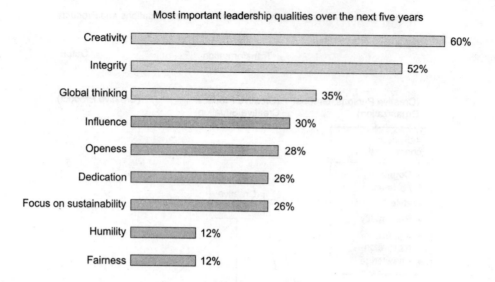

Most important leadership qualities over the next five years

Creativity	60%
Integrity	52%
Global thinking	35%
Influence	30%
Openess	28%
Dedication	26%
Focus on sustainability	26%
Humility	12%
Fairness	12%

two-day session to make the state art agencies realize what their future would look like. Day 1 was spent in developing an effective vision and mission statement which involved a rigorous brainstorming session. Day 2 dealt with discussion on more practical issues of creating a collaborative culture.

Disney Leadership Model states that leaders serve as the centerpiece of the three pieces of the Org. Creativity Model by providing commitment, responsibility and inspiration.

Microsoft

Bill Gates, CEO Microsoft, also acknowledged organisational creativity as an important requisite of a transforming organisation. MS developed The Four Alpha Process for fostering creativity. Organized around a four-part framework developed at MIT and Harvard for leading and organizing for breakthrough innovation, the Four Alpha Creativity Network infrastructure helps the people to better understand how to:

- Spot the opportunities to do their job better and with more productive outcomes
- Take notice of the world around them and look for unmet needs and desires that can provide opportunities for the company's growth
- Discover sources of information on current and new technologies and consumer needs
- Come up with innovative ideas for new products and services and new sources of innovation
- Make timely decisions about implementing their ideas and determining their likelihood of success
- Share insights and opportunities for growth with creative team mates throughout the organisation

Google

Google has initiated "innovation reviews" where each executive presents the most promising ideas from within their own division. CEO Eric Schmidt listens to them and so do founders Page and Brin. The problem lies in the evolution of the idea from the early stage, to the next stage where the development of the prototype is observed. So there's a new consensus at Google that only few of their one-day-a-week ideas are turning into blockbusters.

Another way Google is addressing the problem is to give a few engineers, with extremely promising ideas, even more than one day a week–in some cases, giving them full-time to work on their idea. The new collaboration tool, Google Wave, resulted when two brothers in Australia were told to go all-out on their idea, a new communication system to replace email.

Creative Leadership

Creative leadership is the ability to shed long-held beliefs and come up with original and at times radical concepts and execution. And this requires bold, breakthrough thinking. It isn't about having a lone creative leader at the top but rather about creating a "field" of creative leadership, by igniting the collective creativity of the organisation from the bottom up. In essence, creative leaders excel at creating creative leaders.

The focus should be on developing creative leaders across their organisations, deepening partnerships with employees and customers and achieving operational agility. Creative leaders in these firms are more prepared and willing to make deeper business model changes to realize their strategies. To win, they take more calculated risks and keep innovating in how they lead and communicate. They are ready to alter the status quo even if it is successful and are committed to ongoing experimentation with disruptive business solutions.

Changing the work culture, unlearning and selectively forgetting past success formulas, and co-creating future products and services with employees, customers, and external partners are hallmarks of the creative leaders.

Few Creative Leaders

Steve Jobs, co-founder and CEO of Apple, Inc., immediately comes to mind with market leading innovations including iPod, iMac and soon to be launched iPhone. Larry Page and Sergey Brin, founders of Google, developed the innovative search technology that provides relevant answers which went on to become the world's largest search engine.

Jeff Bezos, founder and CEO of Amazon.com, made the world's largest online bookstore and the most popular online retail site.

Pierre Omidyar, founder and chairman of eBay, changed the face of Internet commerce in 1995 when he launched eBay which went on to become the world's largest marketplace.

A.G. Lafley, CEO of Proctor & Gamble, states: "Great leaders create conditions that get people organized to attack problems. They help others learn how to think, how to exercise judgment and how to take action." (at a Kellogg event)

Michael Dell, founder and chairman of Dell, who always thought big, and made Dell the number one computer company, and is on a mission to connect the next billion people all over the world.

Jim Donald, president and CEO of Starbucks, who is fanatical about communicating using his Treo, replies to every email, returns calls at 6 a.m., and always stays close to the customers.

The Three Keys to Organisational Creativity

Teresa Amabile, Harvard Business School's leading authority on creativity, has identified the three keys to fostering creativity practiced at **Palo Alto Research Center** PARC.

1. **Smart people who think differently** "The first threat to business creativity is our endangered education system, with its downward trends in science and math, and its increasingly narrow focus on basic subjects. The four dozen people working at PARC were really smart, with two important kinds of smarts. First, they had deep expertise — in computer science, optical science, and system dynamics, as well as broad acquaintance with seemingly unrelated fields. Second, the PARC inventors had creative smarts. Rather than getting trapped by what was already inside their heads, they voraciously consumed new information and combined it in ways no one had previously imagined."

2. **Passionate engagement** "My research has shown that people are most creative when they are on a mission, intrinsically motivated by a love for what they are doing. Robert Bauer and his colleagues found immense interest, enjoyment, satisfaction, and challenge in 'dreaming, proving and making things that had never been done before.' Indulging their passion was so exciting, and so much fun, that they worked their tails off."

3. **A creative atmosphere** "Like all great organisational cultures, this one started with a bold vision. PARC's founder, George Pake, was out to create 'the office of the future.' He and Bob Taylor, head of PARC's Computer Science Laboratory, built a near-perfect work environment for creativity: freedom to pursue passions, challenging goals, collaborative norms, sufficient time to really think, and the resources people needed to follow their dreams. Most people who got into PARC never wanted to leave."

CONCLUSION

After a thorough study of organisational creativity and its various facets, it is clear that it is not only a factor contributing to success of an organisation, but also an asset to it. Although the organisations have to handle an extra stress of unending change, the results are worth it. Also, it provides a winning edge to the organisation which keeps high the momentum of efforts.

One more thing to notice is, determinants of organisational creativity also undergo a change like the organisation in which it is applied i.e. no factor can continually assure to contribute toward creativity. MNCs like Microsoft, Google, Disney and specially IBM have also recognized it as a factor that will keep organisations afloat not only now but also in the coming times.

Therefore, the aim of the organisation should be not to create a creative leader in the organisation but to develop a creative leader in every employee. This will help in prospering an atmosphere of sustainable development and will eventually lead to organisational creativity-lifeline of the organisations in the current era.

References

- Patterson Christina, *"Individual and organisational creativity"*, Halifax, Nova Scotia, Canada
- Steiner Gerald, *"Organisational Creativity as a Prerequisite for the Generation of Innovation"*, Institute of Innovation- and Environmental Management, University of Graz, Austria
- Job P A, Sanghamitra Bhattacharyya *"Creativity and Innovation for Competitive Excellence in Organisations"* IIT Madras
- Serrat, Olivier *"Harnessing Creativity and Innovation in the Workplace"*, Regional and Sustainable Development Department, Asian Development Bank
- Morris Wayne, *"A Survey of Organisational Creativity"*
- Retrieved from http:/blogs.hbr.org/cs/2010/05/how_to_ignite_creative_leaders.htm
- Retrieved from http://keithsawyer.wordpress.com/2009/07/09/innovation-at-google/
- Retrieved from http://www.creativity-the-most-important-leadership-quality-for-ceos-study.htm/

Role of Values and Human Resources in the Management Process

Charanjeet Kaur[1] and Poonam Yadav[2]

[1]Assistant Professor, Home Science, [2]Research Scholor Goverment KRGPG Autonomous College, Gwalior

[2]Research Scholar, Govt. K.R.G. Autonomous P.G. College, Gwalior

ABSTRACT

According to www.apexcpe.com, In any organisation, management is a necessary element. Through the management process, certain goals may be achieved in any organisation. The process of using a company's resources in the most efficient way possible. These resources can include tangible resources such as goods and equipment, financial resources and labor resources such as employees. Management of human resources, while is the most important component, helps in achieving the largest. Indian value has emphasized moral and spiritual values as the foundation of human growth. These values elevate personality to the level where one man deals with other with love, affection, equality and concern for their welfare. This character efficiency becomes a spring board for managerial effectiveness resulting in better productivity, better profitability and better and smooth human relationship.

Keywords: *HRM, Values*

INTRODUCTION

Management science is based on psychology. Every country has its own cultural characteristics and values. The Indian Shastras clearly bring out that work is not just for bread, cloths and home but it also provides an opportunity to grow towards infinite perfection and joy. Our Vedas concepts have a lot to contribute in management practice. The root of all skills and knowledge is in Vedas. The ancient scriptures and culture of the particular country or society have a remarkable influence on there life, education, business management and administrative set up. Indian work culture and life is based of its ancient scriptures. Today the private and public companies and organisations realize that the western management theories, values, ideas are not fully applicable in India. Modern management forces a lot of challenges, so there is need to follow the principles and values of Indian ancient scriptures.

VALUES REALLY IMPORTANT FOR MANAGEMENT

According to iris.nyit.edu, Ethics can be defined as a system of moral principles and values. It is generally an indirect governing force behind human conduct, both in case of an individual as well as of an organisation. Ethics directs human behavior and differentiates between proper and improper, between right and wrong, between fair and unfair human action. Vales are contemporary standards of principles that govern the actions and behaviors of an individual within the organisation. They provide a basis for determining what is right or wrong in-terms of given situation. Values motivate the organizer to establish organisational policies and code of professional ethics pertaining to his behavior in his own section in particular and in the whole organisation in general. Thus ethical values established by an individual in his organisational setting would make him go a head successfully in the long-run.

The very concept of human resource is based on value and hence HRM approach on the part of management will facilitate a cordial industrial climate. An organisation or its management views its people as dignified individuals to be drawn on or to be depended upon. HRM views the growth and development of each individual as its first priority, "People are our organisation" approach aims at developing the people first by which the organisation improves its performance, which primarily needs and value approach.

Human resource development and human resource planning are the two sides of the coin, while the letter integrates with its career planning and succession planning. So, that people get to know in advance about their career path and prospects for growth. HRM approach is not only concern with converting the strengths of individuals into achievements, but with enabling the individuals to over come their weaknesses. Human values are the basis ingredients of HRM intervention. Thus it can be stressed that there is a great need for ethical value approach is human resource management. Human value practiced in an organisation may be the strongest source of organisational culture.

According to www.b-u.ac.in, Human values are the values which an organisation cherishes, which focus on valuable norms, views and conditions that take care of human dignity and worth.

Values are guide to behavior. Values may be defined as an enduring belief that a specific mode of conduct is personally or socially preferable to an opposite or converse mode of conduct. Values are the basis of prolonged success in any organisation, the values which influenced the success of a company which are shared first by the top management and then all the members of the organisation.

"If you want to be big, you have to think big.

If you want to become world-level Corporation, you must have world-class technology and human talents."

Values are worked out by each individual on the basis of what seem most valid to him. However an adequate value system must meet certain valid to him. However an adequate value system must meet certain general criteria of ethical, human and moral values which facilitate human life and welfare. Values, which an individual foster, provide self direction to him.

The values are communicated through some delivery mechanisms. The mechanisms such as leadership, communication, motivation rewards and recognition, sanctions and punishments, management style, resourcing training and development systems, policies and procedure, organisation etc. are considered as most important in terms of delivering and message about the values of an organisation. The mode of communication in one organisation and provides the message to the employees are motivated by positive rewards or by negative means, also reflects the values of an organisation and its prevailing culture. Ethical conduct varies from person to person and in the same person even in different situations.

Management style also reflects the values as well as the prevailing organisation culture. The mode of recruitment, selection, promotion, training and development and appraisal etc., of an organisation gives as idea about values of that organisation. Through training and development, organisation delivers corporate philosophies and educate employees. Through policies, procedures and systems, employees learn what is important in their organisation and what the organisation expect from them.

In the organisation many such values motivate the people to from knowledge, skills, creative abilities, aptitudes of an organisation, workforce, attitude, belief of the individuals involved in the affairs of the organisation. These values and work ethics are considerably influence by the work culture and organisation culture. Hence, change in the work culture or organisation culture may influence change in the value system. The human resources are multidimensional in nature. HRM is concern with getting better results with the collaboration of people.

According to www.iaabd.org, A healthy climate with values of openness, enthusiasm, trust, mutuality and collaboration is essential for developing human resources. Employees feel highly motivated if the organisation provides for satisfaction of their basic and higher level needs. Globalization of business, liberalization of policies, modernization of plants and machinery, automation etc., have also resulted in change in the value system. The tremendous change in the value system have even gone to the extent of giving birth to various types of socio-economic problem. In the changing global scenario, the solution to problems in management in India does not lie in copying western styles, but trying to dwell upon culture specific management. India has been as excellent country with excellent people and our culture has been rich with original wisdom. Therefore it is the time when the human resource management should be done with the different value described in Indian ancient scriptures, like Vedas, Upanished and the Bhagwat Gita etc.

At last but not least HRM should be linked with strategic goals, ethics value and objectives in order to improve business performance and develop organisational cultures. All the above goals and objectives should be based on 3 H's of heart, head and hand i.e. feel by heart, think by Head and implement by hand.

References

- Retrieved from www.apexcpe.com/publications/471001.pdf
- Retrieved from pmbook.ce.cmu.edu/02_Organizing_for_Project_**Management**.html
- Retrieved from *iris.nyit.edu/~shartman/mba0101/ethics.htm*
- Retrieved from www.b-u.ac.in/syl_college/ug_ve.pdf
- Retrieved from www.iaabd.org/pdf/2010peer Reviewed.pdf

Organisational Commitment: An Analysis of Impact of HRD Practices in Telecom Sector

Garima Mathur[1], Gaurav Jaiswal[2] and Navita Nathani[3]
[1]Associate Professor, Prestige Institute of Management, Gwalior
[2]Assistant Professor, Prestige Institute of Management, Gwalior
[3]HOD, Management, Prestige Institute of Management, Gwalior

ABSTRACT

Organisational commitment is the employee's psychological attachment to the organisation. An employee having a high degree of organisational commitment attaches himself with the organisational goals and perceives his job as a long term career. It is also proved by many studies that high organisational commitment leads to the high Job satisfaction, high retention and higher productivity, that is why today's organisations recognized its importance and trying to enhance commitment by providing various opportunities and benefits to the employees. To develop a committed employee, organisations need to work upon various things such as training, career planning etc. so that employees can be attracted to retain for long time in the organisation. Present study is an attempt to analyze the impact of different HRD Practices such as Training, Career Development and Employee Participation on the Organisational Commitment. The results were achieved through different analytical techniques like reliability, factor analysis, regression. The measures were validated through item to total correlation, reliability and factor analysis. Through multiple regression Training and employee participation showed clear significant positive relationship with organisational commitment where as for career objectives the relationship was insignificant.

Keywords: *Training, Employee participation, career development and organisational commitment*

INTRODUCTION

From the beginning of industrial revolution to the recent globalization, organisations have experienced many developments. In the early stages of industrial revolution employees were treated as means of production and management were treating them inhumanly but with the growth of industries, the field of behavioral science also grew. Many behavioral scientist, Psychologist and Social thinkers proved through their studies that employees are the most precious assets for any organisation. Employers must develop the attitude to nurture their employees and involve them in the organisational process. Developing organisational commitment among the employees is very important for the organisations because it leads to job satisfaction, high retention and loyalty for it.

The purpose of this research is to gather information about human resource development (HRD) practices that is used in telecom industries and the effect of these practices on employees' feelings of commitment towards the organisation. HRD practices include Comprehensive training, career development and employee participation. This has been done because there are different attitudes towards organisational commitment. The older they are and the longer they stay within an organisation do not imply that they will be committed towards their organisation. The impact of new forms of participation, including high-involvement work systems and partnership, is also considered. This study emphasizes the role of such HRD variables as inculcating and enhancing organisational commitment, and suggests that HRD practitioners and researchers should further develop commitment-oriented organisation policies. Although organisational commitment has been discussed frequently in organisational psychology for almost four decades, few studies have involved software professionals, our research is also an attempt to analyze that these HRD variables influence on organisational commitment of employees in telecom industries. The variables researched in the study can be described as:

Organisational Commitment

Organisational commitment is the employee's psychological attachment to the organisation. It is a kind of employee's attitude towards the organisation which is reflected through the behaviour. Organisational scientists have developed many definitions of organisational commitment, and numerous scales to measure them. Major contribution in this area is the work of (Meyer & Allen, 1991). They proposed three-component model of commitment, prior research indicated that there are three "mind sets" which can characterize an employee's commitment to the organisation:

Affective Commitment: It contains emotional segment of an employee. He or she strongly identifies with the goals of the organisation and desires to remain a part of the organisation. The employee commits to the organisation because he/she "wants to". In developing this concept, Meyer and Allen drew largely on **Mowdey, Porter and Steers's (1982)** concept of commitment.

Continuance Commitment: The individual commits to the organisation because he/she perceives high costs of losing organisational membership (**Becker's 1960** "side bet theory"), including economic losses (such as pension accruals) and social costs (friendship ties with co-workers) that would have to be given up. The employee remains a member of the organisation because he/she "has to".

Normative Commitment: The individual commits to and remains with an organisation because of feelings of obligation. For instance, the organisation may have invested resources in training an employee who then feels an obligation to put forth effort on the job and stay with the organisation to 'repay the debt.' It may also reflect an internalized norm, developed before the person joins the organisation through family or other socialization processes, that one should be loyal to one's organisation. The employee stays with the organisation because he/she "ought to".

Training

Many researchers tried to explain the concept of training. According to Kenny *et al.,* (1979), "Training an individual means helping him to learn how to carry out his present job satisfactorily. Development can be defined as preparing the individual for a future job". Training may be viewed as combination of planned programs undertaken to improve technical and behavioural skills of an employee so as to improve the performance in the organisation. It is a short process but not limited to technical staff only but range from lower, middle and senior level. Few more authors defined training as the ability of an organisation to develop skills and knowledge to do present and future job (Guest, 1997; Guest, Michie, Conway & Sheehan, 2003).

Career Development

Career development is basically providing chances or environment by management to the employees so that they can take up higher positions in an organisation and on the other hand the employees to put in their all efforts to utilize the opportunities provided by the organisation.

A person's career is made up of choice he or she makes during his/ her life. Career is an on-going process which includes number of work related activities both paid as well as unpaid. Careers are 'constructed' through the series of choices we make throughout our lives. To have a successful career one needs to plan. Career development may be understood as a process of planning work related activities through out one's life. It is a combined effort of everyone mainly employer and employee. It asks for duties from both sides to be fulfilled such as education, training and development activities, learning new skills and self improvements to help in career.

Employee Participation

Employee participation is the process whereby management involves employees in decision making processes, rather than just assigning duties and responsibilities. Employee participation is part of a process of empowerment in the workplace. Employee participation is also referred as employee involvement. According to Farnham (1997) Employee Participation is one of four policy choices for managing the employment relationship. Farnham further states: '... an employee has the right to question and influence organisation decision making' and '.... this may involve representative workplace democracy.' A number of examples of employee's participation can be considered such as delegation of authority, suggestion schemes, consultation exercises, quality circles etc.

REVIEW OF LITERATURE

Koys (1988) looked at the influence of selected human resource management practices on employee's commitment to the organisation. He found that his subjects positively related organisational commitment to their perceptions of their human resource department's motivation for implementing the different practices. Bhatti and Qureshi (2007) developed a significant positive relationship between employee participation, job satisfaction and organisational commitment in a study conducted in Pakistan.

Organisational commitment can be defined as 'the relative strength of an individual's identification with an organisation' (Mowday *et al.*, 1979: 225). Organisation identification is "some degree of belongingness or loyalty" (Lee, 1971). Organisational identification is the degree to which a member defines themselves by the same attributes that they believe define their organisations (Dutton et al., 1994). Most of the researchers described commitment as involving some form of psychological bond between people and organisation. For example, Salancik (1979) identified four determinants that measure the degree of human acts. The determinants included explicitness, or the deniability of the act, revocability of the act, volition, or the motivation behind the act, and publicity, or the linkage of the act in a social context. O'Reilly and Caldwell (1981) measured the relationship between commitment and internal motives such as intrinsic interest in the job, one's feelings about the job, responsibility the job provides, and the opportunity for advancement and external motives for selecting jobs and extrinsic motives which included family concerns, salary, advice of others, and geographical location. They surveyed fresher employees such as MBA graduates immediately after they accepted job offers. Results suggested that the internal and external factors were significantly related to subsequent commitment. Most of the studies were related to job satisfaction. Like wise, Jermier & Berkes (1979) collected data on organisational commitment from over 800 police officers. The researchers were investigating the relationship between job satisfaction and organisational commitment. Findings revealed that employees who were more satisfied with their job had higher levels of organisational commitment.

Wiener & Vardi (1980) looked at the effect that organisational commitment had on commitment to the job and career commitment. The researchers reported positive relationships between organisational commitment and the two other types of commitment. In a separate study Weiner (1982) argued that normative commitment is the result of a combination of internalized experiences resulting from cultural and early organisational socialization experiences.

Batt and Appelbaum (1995) investigated whether different forms of employee participation affect employee attitudes, commitment, and perception of work performance. Loui (1995) examined the relationship between the broad construct of organisational commitment and the outcome measures of supervisory trust, job involvement, and job satisfaction. In all three areas, Loui (1995) reported positive relationships with organisational commitment. More specifically, perceived trust in the supervisor, an ability to be involved with the job, and feelings of job satisfaction were major determinants of organisational commitment. Salanchik (1979) stated that commitment can be increased and harnessed to obtain support for the organisational ends and interests through such things as participation in decision-making.

A hand of literature is available stating the importance of training in attaining employee commitment. Considerably Ayodeji, Oyelerel, Tunde & Gbajumo-Sheriff (2011) found training to be positively related to employee commitment. Ayodeji *et al.*, (2011) reviewed that training according to Brum (2010), Owen (2006) increases employees' commitment, which can further counter the numerous direct and indirect costs associated with employees' turnover. Tsui, Pearce, Porter and Tripoli (1997) suggested that training depicts commitment from the organisation to the employees, which results in employee response as showing affective organisational commitment.

Very few researches have been reported stating the relationship of career development and employee commitment but few studied the impact of career development on career commitment. Though Hall (1971) defines career commitment as the strength of ones motivation to work in a chosen career role which is different from the original concept of this paper employee commitment yet the association can be studied as career development in the same organisation may lead to attain committed workforce.

OBJECTIVES OF THE STUDY

The literature search raised the many objectives. Though the broad objective is to study the effect of HRD practices on organisational commitment, the detail objectives are as follows:

1. To develop and standardize measure for training, career development, employee participation.
2. To standardize measure for organisational commitment.
3. To study and analyze the impact of HRD practices on organisational commitment.

On the basis of these objectives a hypothesis was formulated:

Ho = There is no significant effect of training, employee participation and career development on organisational commitment.

RESEARCH METHODOLOGY

The study was empirical in nature with survey being used as method for completing the study. Population included the employees of telecom companies especially BSNL, IDEA, AIRTEL of central India. The data was collected from 250 respondents. The data was collected through non-probability judgemental sampling technique as most of the employees were not intended to fill the questionnaire. The responses were taken from the individuals who were able to understand English so that they could answer correctly. Self designed questionnaires were used for evaluating all the HRD variables such as training, career development and employee participation and for organisational commitment a standardized measure of Allen & Mayer (1990) was used. Data was collected on a Likert type scale where 1 stands for minimum agreement and 7 stands for maximum agreement. The questionnaires were standardized through various methods such as Item to total correlation, Reliability and Factor analysis. The role of HRD variables in determining commitment of employees was assessed through single and multiple linear Regressions.

RESULTS AND DISCUSSION

Standardization of Measure

For the purpose of this research various measures were standardized.

Consistency, Reliability and Validity: Internal Consistency of all the items in the questionnaires was checked through item to total correlation. Under this correlation of every item with total was measure and the computed value was compared with standard correlation value for 250 samples i.e. 0.177. When the computed value was found less than the standard value then that statement was dropped and termed inconsistent.

Results of Item to total correlation indicate that all the three HRD variables were had consistent item in the questionnaires. Only one item in the organisational commitment questionnaire was dropped as found to be inconsistent. Reliability test was carried out by using SPSS software and the Cronbach's alpha value was found to be as follows:

Table 1 Showing Alpha values

Variable	Alpha Value	Number of Items
Training	0.837	14
Employee Participation	0.744	15
Career Development	0.816	15
Organisational Commitment	0.901	24

Above table shows that all the values of alpha were on higher side. The higher the alpha coefficient, the more reliable is the test. There is no universally agreed cut-off figure, but a Cronbach Alpha of 0.7 and above is usually acceptable (Nunnally & Bernstein, 1994).

Face validity was ensured as questionnaire was checked by panel of experts and found to be suitable for present study. Kalpan and Sucuzzo (1993) state that face validity is the mere appearance that a measure is valid or not. To ensure construct validity factor analysis was applied.

Factor Analysis: Fourteen statements were subjected to principal component analysis using varimax rotation which resulted in five factors for each of the HRD variables (See Table 3, 4, 5) and six factors for organisational commitment (See Table 6).

Regression Analysis

A multiple regression analysis was conducted to identify the predictors of committed workforce. As shown in Table 2, the results demonstrated that two variables significantly contributed to Organisational commitment. Among the significant predictors, the training proved to

Table 2 showing results of regression **Coefficients**[a]

Model		Unstandardized Coefficients		Standardized Coefficients		
		B	Std. Error	Beta	t	Sig
1	(Constant)	.159	2.127		.075	.940
	VAR00001	1.356	.074	.807	18.208	.000
	VAR00002	.296	.071	.184	4.145	.000
	VAR00003	.013	.035	.008	.373	.710

[a.] Dependent Variable: VAR00004

be the best predictor of organisational commitment (b = 0.807, p < 0.000).

Organisational commitment = 0.159 + 0.807 (Training) + 0.184 (Employee Participation) + 0.008 (Career development)

Adjusted R^2 explains 96.6% variance in the organisational commitment by HRD variables (Table 7). In the second step employee participation predicts organisational commitment (b = 0.184, p < 0.000) but career development became insignificant when entered with two other variables.

The results of this study indicate that the organisations which are focusing on the training part of the employee development are much better in obtaining a committed workforce. In this rapidly changing world each employee need to get himself prepared for any kind of changes. Major part of this capability is fulfilled by training in required areas, be it skill requirement or behavioural part. Once the employee is sure of his ability to face any kind of challenge he becomes receptive. This receptivity ultimately makes him feel good about the organisation. The results are consistent with the findings of (Ayodeji, Oyelerel, Tunde and Gbajumo-Sheriff (2011); Tsui, Pearce,, Porter, and Tripoli, A. M. (1997)). Barrett and O' Connell (2001) also support the notion that the organisations which are able to create an environment where training is given due importance by employees and management can achieve greater commitment outcomes such as low employees' turnover.

Though it is not possible to identify areas where actual training is required hence it becomes mandatory to involve employee identification as well as implementation of training. In addition to this employee participation also create sense of belongingness and responsibility in the individual. Bhatti & Qureshi (2007) also reported a significant positive relationship between employee participation and commitment in Pakistan. Though career development is also an important variable but on this population it was not significant predictor of commitment.

CONCLUSION

This research has been concluded that HRD practices showed significant impact on organisational commitment. Under HRD practices three variables are taken training, employee participation and career development. With the help of primary and secondary data we have applied the item to total correlation, factor analysis, regression and multiple regression to identify, which

one is highly effective on organisational commitment. The study's results emphasize the role of such HRD variables as inculcating and enhancing organisational commitment, and suggest that HRD practitioners and researchers should further develop commitment-oriented organisation policies. The conclusion of this is that managers, who are so desirous of enhancing organisational commitment among their subordinates, should pay more attention to training. In this study, the level of participation that employees felt predicted their level of organisational commitment.

References

- Allen, N.J. & Meyer, J.P. (1990), "The measurement and antecedents of affective, continuance and normative commitment to the organisation", Journal of Occupational Psychology, 63(2), 1-18.

- Batt Rosemary and Eileen Appelbaum Polly A. Phipps (Dec 1995). "Employee participation, work reorganisation, and job design - Workplace Management". Monthly Labor Review.

- Barrett, A., and O' Connell, P. (2001). Does Training Generally Work?: The return to In-Company Training. *Industrial and labour Relations Review*, 53 (3), 647-662.Becker, T. E. (1960), "Notes on the concept of commitment", American Journal of Sociology, 66, 32-42.

- Bhatti Komal Khalid and Tahir Masood Qureshi (2007), Impact of Employee Participation On Job Satisfaction, Employee Commitment And Employee Productivity, *International Review of Business Research Papers* Vol.3 No.2, Pp. 54 - 68.

- Brum, S. (2010). *What Impact Does Training have on Employee Commitment and Employee Turnover.* [Online] Retrived January 2011 from http://www.uri.edu/research/lrc/research/papers/Brum-Commitment.pdf.

- Dutton, J.E. Dukerich, J. M. and Harquail, C.V (1994) 'Organisational images and member identification', *Administrative Science Quarterly*, 39 2, 239-263.

- Dutton, Jane E., Janet M. Dukerich, and Celia V. Harquail (1994) Organisational images and member identification'. *Administrative Science Quarterly* 39/2: 239–263.

- Farnham, D. (1993) Employee Relations Exeter: Short Run Press, p.361

- Guest, D. (1997). Human Resource Management and Performance. *International Journal of Human Resource Management*, 8 (3), 263-275.
- Guest, D.E., Michie, J., Conway, N., and Sheehan, M. (2003). Human Resource Management and Corporate Performance in the UK. *British Journal of Industrial Relations,* 41 (2), 291-314.
- Hall, D.T. (1971), A theoretical model of career sub-identity development in organisational settings. *Organisational Behaviour and Human Performance*, 3(1), 50 - 76.
- Jermier, J. & Berkes, L. (1979). Leader behavior in a police command bureaucracy: A closer look at the quasi-military model. Administrative Science Quarterly, 24, 1-23.
- Kaplan, R.M. And Saccuzzo, D.P. (1993), Psychological Testing Principles, Applications and Issues, Brooks/Cole: Belmont.
- Kenny, Laurence, Lung-fei Lee, G. S. Maddala and Robert Trost (1979), Returns to College Education: An Investigation of Self-Selection Bias based on Project Talent Data, International Economic Review, 20, 775-789.
- Koys, D.J. (1991). Fairness, legal compliance, and organisational commitment. Employee Responsibilities and Rights Journal. 4(4). 283-291.
- Lee MM (1971) 'Holistic Learning in new Central Europe' in MM Lee, H Letiche, R Crawshaw and M Thomas (eds) Management Education in the New Europe London: Internal Thompson pp 249-236
- Loui, K. (1995), Understanding Employee Commitment in the Public Organisation: A Study of the Juvenile Detention Center, International Journal of Public Administration, *18*(8), 1269-1295
- Mathieu, J.E. & Zajac, D.M. (1990), A Review and Meta-Analysis the Antecedents, Correlates, and Consequences of Organisational Commitment, Psychological Bulletin, 108(2). 171-194.
- Meyer, J.P., & Allen, N.J., (1991), A three-component conceptualization of Organisational Commitment, Human Resource Management Review, 1(1), 61-89.
- Mowday, R. T., Porter, L. W., & Steers, R. (1982), Organisational Linkages: The Psychology of Commitment, Absenteeism, and Turnover, Academic Press, New York.
- Mowday, R.T, Porter, L.W. and Steers, R.M (1979), 'The measurement of organisational commitment', *Journal of Vocational Behavior*, 14, 224-247.
- Nunnally J. C. & Bernstein I. H. (1994), Psychometric Theory (3rd Ed.), McGraw-Hill, New York.
- O'Reilly, C.A. and Caldwell, D.F. (1981). The commitment and job tenure of new employees: Some evidence of post-decisional justification. Administrative Science Quarterly. 26(4). 597-616.
- Owens, P. L. (2006). One More Reason Not to Cut your Training Tudget: The Relationship between Training and Organisational Outcomes. *Public Personnel Management*, 35(2), 163-171.
- Owoyemi, Oluwakemi Ayodeji, Oyelere, Michael, Elegbede, Tunde & Gbajumo-Sheriff, Mariam (2011), Enhancing Employees' Commitment to Organisation through Training, International Journal of Business and Management, Vol. 6, No. 7, 280-286.
- Salanchik, G.R. (1979). Commitment and the control of organisational behavior and belief. In Motivation and Work Behavior. R.M. Steers and L.W. Porter (Eds.) New York: McGraw-Hill.
- Tsui, A. S., Pearce, J. L., Porter, L. W., & Tripoli, A. M. (1997), Alternative approaches to the employee-organisation relationship, *Academy of Management Journal, 40,* 1089–1121.
- Wiener, Y. & Vardi, Y. (1980). Relationships between job, organisation, and career commitments and work outcomes: An integrative approach. Organisational Behavior and Human Performance, 26, 81-96.
- Wiener, Y. (1982). Commitment in organisations. A normative view. Academy of Management Review. 7(3). 418-428.

ANNEXURE

Table 3 Showing results of Factor Analysis for 'Training'

Factor No.	Eigen values	Factor name	Variables Convergence	% of variance	Loadings
1.	5.055	Availability	2 Sufficient duration	36.104	0.752
			3 Excellent opportunity to learn about the organisation		0.729
			1 Adequate importance		0.699
			4 Management takes interest		0.667
			5 Management spends time with new staff.		0.629
2.	1.989	Motivation	11 Determining the employees participation, they need	14.210	0.848
			10 Employees are sponsored for identified developmental needs.		0.763
3.	1.912	Perceived benefits	7 To acquire technical skills and knowledge	13.659	0.908
			6 New recruits find training very useful		0.781
4.	1.167	Acquiring human skills	8 Developing managerial capabilities	8.333	0.897
			9 Human relations competencies are adequate		0.810
			12 HR department conducts briefing for training		0.494
5.	1.066	Growing Environment	14 Managers provide right climate to implement new ideas and methods	7.612	0.867
			13 Employees are given free time to plan improvements.		0.511

Table 4 Showing results of Factor Analysis for 'Employee Participation'

Factor No.	Eigen values	Factor name	Variables No.	Variables Convergence	% of variance	Loadings
1.	5.159	Flexibility	3	Regularly working at different locations.	34.349	0.862
			2	Flexible working for employees		0.721
			4	Encourages in health promotion.		0.675
			5	Decision making programs		0.662
2.	2.191	Intrinsic motives	11	Provides more career opportunities	14.605	0.843
			10	Help to satisfy their needs		0.754
			13	To increase job satisfaction		0.482
3.	1.927	On-line participation	8	Encourages to take initiatives	12.849	0.865
			9	Helps to reduce the stress		0.827
			12	Helps to reduce resistance to change		0.594
4.	1.379	Job Performance	7	Help to reduce industrial disputes	9.194	0.925
			6	Depends on salary patterns		0.784
5.	1.079	Cohesiveness	15	Encourage through training and development	7.196	0.814
			14	Employees feel independence		0.725
			1	Policies allow employees to job share		0.548

Table 5 Showing results of Factor Analysis for 'Career Development'

Factor No.	Eigen values	Factor name	Variables No.	Variables Convergence	% of variance	Loadings
1.	4.975	Job involvement	13	Able to protect my personal interests	33.166	0.782
			12	Manager takes flexible approach		0.686
			10	Manager encourages career development		0.665
			11	Encourages participation in decisions		0.645
			5	Expert in their field		0.598

Contd...

Contd...

2.	2.291	Job rotation	7	To move geographical area for career development	15.275	0.869
			6	To move work area		0.804
			14	Staff working co-operatively		0.612
3.	1.943	Competency and development	3	Personal growth and development	12.954	0.838
			4	Work at higher level position		0.623
4.	1.288	Recognition	15	Training courses are supported	8.585	0.758
			2	Current career opportunities		0.731
			1	Achieved all want to achieve		0.676
5.	1.139	Appraisal	8	Managers provides performance feedback	7.594	0.878
			9	Managers allow taking initiative in performing the job.		0.824

Table 6   showing results of Factor Analysis for 'Organisational Commitment'

Factor No.	Eigen values	Factor name	Variables No.	Variables Convergence	% of variance	Loadings
1.	8.377	Affective Commitment	19	Loyal towards the organisation	34.905	0.850
			4	Feel guilty if leave the organisation		0.850
			3	Emotionally attached to organisation		0.785
			18	Employee's career development		0.785
			5	Organisation's problem are own		0.574
			20	Easy to find a job in other department		0.574
2.	3.906	Normative Commitment	22	Coordination among the employees help to increase the productivity	16.275	0.887
			7	Not feel like the part of family		0.887
			21	My chances are being promoted		0.859
			6	Long term security as long as job well		0.859
			14	Increment in salary is based on job		0.485
3.	3.236	Continuance commitment	8	Not leave organisation because of obligation of people	13.481	0.919
			23	Enough opportunities		0.919
			9	Life would be disrupted if leave the organisation		0.826
			24	Participate in decision making		0.826
4.	2.050	Loyalty	1	Organisation has great deal of personal meaning	8.543	0.846
			16	See with this organisation five years from now		0.846
			15	Manage the pressure to job well		0.715
5.	1.801	Job Satisfaction	17	Satisfies with total benefit package	7.504	0.839
			2	Few options to consider leaving the organisation		0.839
6.	1.131	Work Culture	11	People mutually respect each other	4.713	0.102
			10	Job requires to use complex		0.280
			13	Rewarded for the job done well		0.833
			12	People mutually trust each other		0.771

Table 7 Showing results of regression

Model	R	R Square	Adjusted R Square	Std. Error of the Estimate
1	.983[a]	.967	.966	3.01546

a. Predictors: (Constant), VAR00003, VAR00002, VAR00001

ANOVA[b]

Model		Sum of Squares	df	Mean Square	F	Sig.
1	Regression	30568.011	3	10189.337	1120.569	.000[a]
	Residual	1054.789	116	9.093		
	Total	31622.800	119			

a. Predictors: (Constant), VAR00003, VAR00002, VAR00001

b. Dependent Variable: VAR00004

Culture of Innovation in Organisations: HRM's Perspective

Geetika Puri[1] and Sakshi Bagga[2]

[1]Assistant Professor, School of Business Administration Lovely Professional University
[2]Lecturer, GAD Goverment College, Tarn Taran

ABSTRACT

Every organisation dreams of being the next Google or Apple but do not want to go the extra mile that these organisations have gone. Google and other innovative organisations have set up these benchmarks by adopting a culture that sustains innovation. This is not an innovation-on-demand culture but represents a more subtle and patient approach to innovation mistakes (whether in the fuzzy front end or end product end). This is a culture that promotes the mistakes and errors so that better products and services can be offered to the customers. The demand for a perfect innovation overnight is illogical and undoable. This paper studies the culture of these innovative organisations that have set the benchmarks and then suggests steps that can help an ordinary organisation set up a culture that sustains innovation.

Keywords: *Culture, Innovation, Human Resource*

Most industries type not withstanding have an understanding of what innovation is and why is it important. Every organisation dreams of being a radical innovator, bringing breakthrough innovations to the market and cementing its place in the industry for years to come. What these organisations miss is that innovation is not an 'on demand process', just because and organisation wants an innovative product or service they are not going to get it overnight. There are a lot of hurdles in the path and the first hurdle that an organisation needs to overcome is that of culture. Organisational culture is defined as 'the way we do things around here.' More specifically ,' it is the pattern of values, norms, beliefs, attitudes and assumptions which might not have been articulated but which shape the ways in which people in organisations behave and get things done.' (Armstrong, 2010) Innovation denotes a new idea that has been put into practice and is used, such as new product or service, on one hand and on the other hand is also used when describing the process through which a novel idea is turned into this new product or service. (Fay, Shipton, 2008) Organisational culture should be such that it promotes innovation and supports innovative employees. Since, anything to do with organisational falls within the realms of HR and OD specialists, this paper tries to throw light on how the HR department can help the organisation by adopting some measures that helps in embedding the innovative culture in the organisation.

MEASURE 1: UNDERSTANDING INNOVATION AND ITS PROCESS

Though innovation is defined above but innovation changes in its focus, orientation, nature, and scope. It may be administered or technical in its focus, product and process in its orientation, radical or incremental in its nature and architectural and component in its scope. Administrative innovations involve new organisational structures and administrative processes such as recruiting personnel, allocating resources etc. technical innovations can be product or process innovations (Gopalkrishan *et al.*, 2010) Product innovations are new products or services introduced to meet a market need while process innovations are new elements introduced into an organisation's production or service operations. Radical innovations are those that go beyond the existing ideas to build something new to the industry and they irrevocably change how things are typically done in a filed or domain. Incremental innovations reflect additive improvements to the ideas that already exist in the business. An innovation is component in nature if it does not change the overall system configuration of the product and architectural in nature if it requires changing the system configuration. (Gopalkrishan *et al.*, 2010)

There is also a need to understand the process of innovation. The process of innovation can be broadly divided into 2 phases: a phase of creativity and a phase of implementation (Fay, Shipton, 2008). Creativity refers to the 'generation of new idea that is regarded as novel and useful while implementation implies transforming the idea into reality'. The idea generation phase is also typically viewed as a fuzzy front end. A lot of ideas from the first stage typically do not proceed to the second stage because of numerous problems cropping up, ranging from feasibility to compatibility with the strategic direction. The implementation phase has 2 stages. In the first stage of the frequently encountered is the structured methodology phase which typically consists of some type of stage gate system. (Ahmed, 1998) The stage gate system consists of some hoops that the idea has to pass from to its feasibility and the compatibility with the organisational objectives. The second stage is that of the commercialization of the idea. It is the phase of actually making the idea commercially feasible.

MEASURE 2: FINDING INNOVATIVE WORKFORCE

Dyer, Gregson and Christensen (2009) in their article in Harvard Business Review studied that innovators are different from other intelligent people and that the organisations need to identify them. They identified 'discovery skills'. These discovery skills are:

- Associating
- Questioning
- Observing
- Experimenting

Associating is the ability to successfully connect seemingly unrelated questions, problems or ideas from different fields. It is seen that the world's most innovative companies prosper by capitalizing on the divergent associations of their founders, executives and employees. Steve Jobs is able to generate new ideas after ideas because he has spent a lifetime exploring new and unrelated things – the art of calligraphy, meditation practices in an Indian ashram and the fine details of a Mercedes Benz.

Innovators constantly ask questions that challenge common wisdom or as Tata Group Chairman Ratan Tata puts it, 'question the unquestionable'. The innovators spent a long time asking the question 'Why does it happen in this way?' They like to think out of the box and question the status quo that exists in this world. Innovators also keep on observing the things that go around them. Discovery driven executives produce uncommon business ideas by scrutinizing common phenomena, especially the behavior of potential customers. People keep on getting ideas from observing plight of people in some kind of trouble. Ratan Tata got inspired to make the world's cheapest car by observing the plight of a family of four seated on a scooter. Experimentation that also engages an innovator a lot. The innovators constantly keep on experimenting to keep transforming their ideas. The innovators are not satisfied because they want to keep on changing their ideas. Devoting time and energy to finding and testing ideas through a network of diverse individuals gives innovators a radically different perspective. To extend their own knowledge domains, innovators mostly go out of their way to meet people that have different kinds of ideas and perspectives.

MEASURE 3: CELEBRATE MISTAKES OF YOUR EMPLOYEES

To set up an innovative culture in your organisation, it is important to celebrate mistakes of your employees. The founders of Google say they love when their employees make mistakes because that means that they can launch the new-improved version of the product. A failed product should not be penalized but treated as a good try. This approach works if managers follow a typical guideline, 'Fail cheap and fast.' (Frangos, 2011)

MEASURE 4: RISK TOLERANCE

Business leaders must have a risk tolerance. For this risk tolerance, leaders must first closely examine their own attitudes towards risk taking and failure and then avoid any behaviors that discourage risk taking (such as punishing people when their ideas don't work out) the organisation has to decide what percentage of failure is acceptable. The percentage will vary from organisation to organisation, based on industry, the type of project and other factors.

MEASURE 5: PROVIDE THE RIGHT COMPENSATION

To encourage the risk taking and innovation, the organisation must reward it. The question is not whether the reward is financial or non financial. Research shows that innovators view recognition from management, colleagues and others than other financial rewards. Moving an idea from imagination to reality entails hard work and people need rewards and incentives to go beyond what is expected from them. Effective rewards can take various forms including public recognition, exposure to influential executives and opportunities to undertake special projects a person feels passionate about.

MEASURE 6: CREATE DISTINCT CAREER PATHS FOR INNOVATORS

Innovators know that they can help launch and establish billion dollar companies but they might never find themselves in those positions in the organisation that may be leadership one. O'Connor, Corbett and Pierantozzi in their article in Harvard Business Review suggested creating three distinct career paths for innovators. Proposing that innovation can be broken up in three phases the HR team of an organisation can make three distinct career paths for innovators. In discovery phase the employees mostly end up doing bench science or technological experiments because they are thinking how their experiment can satisfy a need in the marketplace. The bench scientist of this phase eventually may want to be involved in the policy discussions about emerging technologies and how it may influence the company's future. During incubation, the employee's experiment recurring with technology and market opportunities so as to see the shift the innovation can bring in the market opportunities. The incubator of the organisation may be interested in pursuing a technological path. During the acceleration phase, the established business capabilities such as scaling business processes, imposing discipline and specialization is required. The accelerator of the organisation may want to take a leadership role as the business grows but in a functional specialty or might want to move in the other general management roles in the organisation.

Just assuming that as an innovation grows the innovator also grows from one skill set to another is a wrong assumption. Discover in which three phases of innovation (discovery, incubation and acceleration) is the innovator of the organisation most comfortable in and create a career path accordingly. An innovator with a broad skill set is hard to find. Best would be to help the innovator grow in the organisation in those roles he is most comfortable in.

MEASURE 7: MANAGE CREATIVE AND INNOVATIVE PEOPLE EFFECTIVELY

Uncreative people put a bad impact on creative people. They tend to be creativity killers, killing good ideas and encouraging bad ones and asking for multiple rounds of improvements if they don't like or understand the idea. The leadership of the innovative people should be such that the innovators don't feel threatened by their leaders. Innovative leaders have traits like that they are willing to do things differently and that they are visionary about new products and innovations.

MEASURE 8: INNOVATIVE CULTURE AND CORPORATE CULTURE

Having a clear cut corporate philosophy enables the employees working in the organisation to get proper and precise instructions and to do their tasks in a more coordinated and precise way. Ineffective statements are unable to motivate and encourage people to follow their tasks that take the organisations towards a common goal. An effective corporate philosophy or statements can help in motivating people not only in completing their tasks effectively and efficiently but also in going beyond the call of duty, in achieving their creative goals and caring a bit more about their work.

MEASURE 9: EMPOWERING EMPLOYEES

The responsibility of empowering employees falls on the shoulders of the employers. Empowering people to creative and to innovative is one of the best ways for leader to mobilize the energies of his employees. Empowerment in the presence of strong culture that guide actions and behavior produces both energy and enthusiasm for consistent work towards an innovative goals. (Ahmed, 1998) Empowerment when it occurs in an organisation without a strong value system capable of driving activities in a unified and aligned manner to the super ordinate goals of the organisation. Empowerment alone may be ineffective in providing the employees freedom to innovate. The organisational barriers may become a problem for them and it might inhibit an innovation. Some organisational barriers that may be encountered are:

- Unwarranted assumptions about innovations
- One correct answer thinking
- Failing to challenge the obvious
- Pressure to conform
- Fear of looking foolish

Taking these Measures: Organisations that Rank High on Innovation

Google

With a search engine called 'Backrub' in 1996, two Stanford University graduate students Larry Page and Sergey Brin created something that would become a pioneer in the innovation history. In 1998, they formally formed a company that today we know as 'Google'. The name 'Google' derives itself from the word 'googol' meaning one followed by a hundred zeros. Since, its founding in 1998, the company deals in a lot of diversified products and services that have broadened its product line beyond the core search engine business. Google has launched Google Map (later known as Google Earth) that has high resolution monochrome images of the earth. The company in 2006 acquired YouTube which facilitates the uploading and viewing of videos. Then Gmail is the email service of Google with a never ending storage space claiming that you can now forget the delete button. Gmail has a built in Gtalk platform from which you can chat; do voice calls and video conferencing. The company also launched a browser called 'Chrome' to compete with Microsoft's Internet Explorer. To compete with 'Facebook' in its social networking segment, it has Orkut and newly launched Google You+. Google Wave products help users instantly communicate, collaborate and work together. Google has also entered the smart phone software market with the Android phone operating system. This phone system competes with Apple's iPhone and RIM's Blackberry.

The Ten Principles which govern the company and that also give it its competitive edge are illustrated below:

- Create products that help in users' daily life.
- Launch products often, rather than trying to perfect the idea.
- Streamlining the employees' task so that they don't waste time in tedious operations.
- Daring to innovate new products and services that makes users comfortable and also speeds up their work.
- Do not kill the ideas but morph them into something that is quite useful.
- Let the employees follow their dreams by letting them pursue their own projects too. (Google has a 70-20-10 rule; it means that the company spends 70% of its engineering resources on core products, 20% on emerging areas and 10% on wild and crazy ideas).
- Google believes that to do serious work you don't have to let your employees dress in a suit at all times. Since, your work is all that matters you don't need to be in a suit to show off your talent.
- The company believes that there is new information out there at all times to access and the efforts to access that information needs just a little bit more creativity.
- Data can beat an opinion any time so research the facts properly before going in the deep end.
- Employees at Google are encouraged to look at something great as a starting point and not an end point so that there is always more room for improvement.

A number of factors that have already been identified in the research seem to be present in the culture of Google. Its ability to recruit, retain and manage an innovative workforce, its design of the organisational structure and culture promoting freedom and risk taking has made it one of the most innovative companies on board.

APPLE INC

Apple Computers was established in April, 1976 in Cupertino, California and incorporated on January 3, 1977. The company was known as Apple Computers for the first thirty years of its establishment but it removed the word 'Computer' from its name on January 9, 2007 to reflect the company's ongoing expansion into the consumer electronics market in addition to is traditional focus on personal computers. Apple was established by Steve Jobs and Steve Wozniak. It has a rather turbulent past but as of September 2011, Apple is the largest publicly traded company in the world by market capitalization and the largest technology company in the world. Though the pioneers of personal computers, its rise in personal computer market came from products like Apple II, Macintosh, Power book (which laid out laptops would look in the future) MacOS and Newton that laid the future for the PDA market. The 1994-1997 period saw a rapid downfall for the Apple market. In 1997, Jobs was made the CEO of Apple again and he began restructuring the company. The 'Think Different' culture was reflected in products like the iPod, iPhone, iTV, iPad and MacBook Air.

Some principles of Apple that are integrated in its culture are:

- Empower your employees and help them make a difference in the workplace.
- Do everything that is important internally. At Apple everything important is done internally like industrial design, operating system, hardware design and sales channel.

- Care and cherish the innovators by offering them what they need to be creative and innovative.
- Work is more important than rules in Apple's culture. Employees are expected to put in their 100% but without any strict rules and regulations.
- Keep doing what works for you.
- Don't make people do things, make them better at doing things.

Working at innovative but a secretive cult like culture at Apple's the employee identification with the organisation is high. Though it is difficult to say what exactly ticks Apple but the late founder's Steve Jobs obsessive and zealous need to innovative is certainly reflected in the products and services.

JOHNSON AND JOHNSON'S (J&J)

Johnson and Johnson is a large and well diversified firm that is an innovative leader in health care industry. Started in 1886 in New Jersey by three brothers, Robert Wood Johnson, James Wood Johnson and Edward Mead Johnson the company now operates worldwide in more than 60 countries, employing over a 100,000 employees. It has three divisions that consist of pharmaceuticals, medical devices and diagnostics and the consumer market. The company's pioneering products were First aid kits, Maternity kits and baby powder now deals in pharmaceutical drugs for various ailments like neurological disorders, blood disorders and auto-immune diseases and pain, diagnostic and medical division offers products such as surgical equipment, monitoring equipment, orthopedic products and contact lenses. The consumer cares are baby care, skin care, oral care, first aid and women's health. Among its product innovations there is Band-Aid bandages, Acuvue lenses, Neutrogena skin care products and Tylenol medications.

A part of Johnson's and Johnson's success can be attributed to the fact that it believes in open innovation. Though a few years ago the company has closed innovation systems that were beneficial for the paradigm that existed at that time and made investment in innovation accordingly. But with changing times the company found it better to adopt open innovation systems. Today, J&J seeks knowledge from other firms, universities and research institutes across disciplines and geographic areas.

The Organisational 'Credo', the guiding principles of J&J has also helped in developing a culture that fosters individuality and diversity, helps employees in achieving their personal goals. The organisation has open communication channels that encourage the open exchange of ideas, suggestions and complaints between the employees, their managers and leaders. The organisation also provides equal opportunities for all their employees in development and advancement recognizing that they are different and hence their needs would also be different. Innovation is considered important to maintain competitiveness in the market. The organisation supports innovations through the leadership, alignment, success metrics, communications and rewards and recognition, skill development and tools. The leveraging of innovation is done through six-sigma, innovation framework and lean and design six-sigma.

CONCLUSION

Innovation is not waiting for the 'a-ha' movement occurring in isolation but innovation is the responsibility of all in the organisation who aspire for the organisation to be innovative. This paper though merely focuses on innovation from the point of view of HRM, the list of measures mentioned here can no way be called exhaustive but have been seen in use by the most innovative organisations in the world. These measures can help an organisation gain a innovation competitive edge. Innovation has become an important differentiating factor for the sustainable factor and the managers must look beyond the hype of the information that surrounds them to the fundamentals. Innovation is not just hiring an innovative workforce but providing the workforce an innovative culture. Indeed, this is the central theme of this paper, the understanding of innovation and how the human resource department by taking these small steps can make a difference.

References

- Ahmed, P.K., (1998) Culture and Climate for Innovation. *European Journal of Innovation Management.* 1, 30-43
- Amabile, T.M. (1998). A model of creativity and innovation in organisations. In B.M. Stze and L.L. Cummings (Eds), *Research in organisational behavior*, 10, 123-167. Greenwish, CT: JAI Press.
- Amabile T.M., & Khair, M. (2008). Creativity and the role of the leader. Harvard Business Review, 86 (10), 100
- Apple Inc. (2011) Retrieved September, 2011 from http://www.bnet.com/blog/ceo/10-ways-

to-think-different-inside-apples-cult-like-culture/6899.

- Apple Inc. (2011) Retrieved September, 2011 http://www.apple.com/jobs/us/benefits.

- Armstrong, M. (2010). *Essentials of Human Resource Management*. London: Kogan Page.

- Dyer, J.H., Gregersen, H.B., & Christensen, C.M. (December, 2009). The Innovator's DNA. Harvard Business Review South Asia. 44-50

- Fay, D., Shipton, H. (2008). Innovation and Creativity in Today's Organisation: a Human Resource Management Perspective. In Ashton Centre for Human Resources (Ed.) *Strategic Human Resource Management – Building Research based Practice* (2008) (pp 213-230) Mumbai: Jaico Publications

- Frangos, C. (2011 February). How to Embed Innovation into Your Organisational Culture. *Harvard Business Review*, 13, No. 1

- Frangos, C. (2011 March - April). How to Embed Innovation into Your Organisational Culture, Part 2: Adopting and Sustaining Ideas. *Harvard Business Review*, 13

- Google Inc. (2011) Retrieved September 10, 2011 http://www.google.co.in/about/corporate/company .

- Google Inc. (2011) Retrieved September,2011 http://www.google.co.in/about/corporate/company/culture

- Google Inc. (2011) Retrieved September,2011 http://www.google.co.in/about/corporate/company/tenthings.

- Google Inc., (2011) Retrieved September 10,2011 http://www.google.co.in/about/corporate/company/software_principles.html,

- Gopalkrishan, S., Kessler, E.H. & Scillitoe, J.L., (2010) Navigating the Innovation Landscape: Past Research, Present Practice and Future Trends. *Organisational Management Journal* (262-277)

- Iyer, B. & Daven, T. H., (2008, April). Reverse Engineering Google's Innovation Machine. *Harvard Business Review*, 3, 39-48

- Johnson and Johnson Inc. (2011). Retrieved September15,2011 http://mcneilcanada.com/our-workplace-culture.aspx.

- Johnson and Johnson Inc. (2011). Retrieved September15,2011 http://www.jnj.com/wps/wcm/connect/ .

- O'Connor, G.C., Corbett, A. & Pierantozzi, R. (December, 2009). Create three distinct career paths for innovators. Harvard Business Review South Asia. 62-63.

Resource Management in an Industry

Neha Sharma

MBA Scholar, Prestige Institute of Management, Gwalior

ABSTRACT

Resources are keen important for the health of the business. It helps the industry to grow and to sink, depending upon the usage of the resources. An efficient management is the skill to control and coordinate the values of resources according to the proper fixation with respect to time. In this paper, we studied the resources and management and we made amendments to proper utilize the resources like finance, inventory, manpower and work to enhance the overall the workability of the organisation. This way we find the proper match of personal to engage with work and other factors in the same expression of time.

Keywords: *Resources, management, workability, efficient management*

INTRODUCTION

In the rapidly changing management scenario, Resource Management has an important role to play. Resource Management is a highly productive corporate asset and the overall performance of companies and corporations depends upon the extent to which it is effectively developed and utilized. The four major components of management is —supply, demand, regulation and environment—and the concepts and principles be-hind successful management. Effective Resource Management not only impacts profitability by optimizing utilization and minimizing bench time, but when done well, can generate goodwill and loyalty that translate to competitive advantages in recruiting and retaining the best talent. It can also give you the ability to move beyond tactical project management to strategic portfolio planning. The problem is that with all of the inefficiencies created by the systems we have in place to manage our current resources, most of us have trouble finding the time to improve our Resource Management processes or upgrade our systems. The good news is that achieving more effective Resource Management is possible – if you take it one step at a time. The following steps aren't always easy to achieve, but you'll find they are worth the effort to master. Resource management is the efficient and effective deployment of an organisation's resources when they are needed .such resources: are inventories, human skills, production etc.

IMPROVED RESOURCE UTILIZATION

As manufacturing processes become more sophisticated and as the philosophies of elimination of waste and constraint management achieve broader acceptance, manufacturers place increased emphasis upon planning and controlling capacity. The creation of an accurate, achievable production schedule requires the availability of both material and capacity. It is useless and indeed wasteful to have financial resources tied up in material if the capacity is insufficient or improperly planned waste not only raises cost, it also affects customer service level and customer goodwill.

By the management, they have simulation capabilities that will help the capacity and resource planner to simulate the various capacity and resource utilization scenarios and choose the best option.

RESEARCH METHODOLOGY

The research methodology prompts for the following prospects:

1. **Know Your Projects:** From a traditional supply and demand perspective, your project portfolio represents the demand side of the equation. Simply put, Resource Management understands this demand to effectively allocate your supply. In order to support a service-oriented business model that will meet that

demand, you must have consistent, centralized, proactive Project visibility. The goal is to identify which resources are required, by time period into the future as far as is reasonable, and then to schedule them as effectively as possible to ensure seamless coverage across all project requirements. The challenge is moving beyond reactionary decision making by implementing and tracking the right metrics to create better predictive models and allow you adequate time to make key staffing decisions.

2. **Know Your People:** If Projects represent the demand side of equation, then your people represent the Supply side available to fulfill that demand. But unless you know your resource capabilities, you can't possibly begin to allocate them efface or effectively. That means knowing your employees skill sets and availability. Individual matrix such as efficiency and track record will also help you to assign the right individuals the right t the right time. Examine the leadership issues involved in managing energy from organisational behavior and change management to project management and communication skills. Gain insight into how to develop your own leadership style. Learn how to successfully move your organisation ahead by creating effective strategies for energy management, including you're most important asset—people.

3. **Automate Manual Processes:** Without having adequate visibility into their resource pool, firms are unable to make consistent optimized business decisions. As a result, costly and time-consuming adjustments create ill-among staff; project managers miss deadlines due to personnel short-falls; clients find key resources are unavailable; and ultimately, revenue, margin, and utilization all suffer. Firms must have a consistent, enterprise-level resource management system. Gain perspectives on current trends and technologies and examine the environmental fundamentals—planning, development and implementation. Using home-grown solutions, standalone spreadsheets, telephone conversations, and other no integrated methods to make staffing decisions means that key decisions are often based on inaccurate, untimely information. Often, many critical inputs to staffing decisions are not captors are seriously out of date.

4. **Future Prospects:** you've leveraged technology to eliminate the time and errors associated with manual data aggregation, it's time to begin looking forward, to ensure that you're proactively planning and scheduling resources to map to the project timeline. In order to ensure appropriate coverage, you should constantly be modeling your existing skill sets against pipeline project requirements to identify any gaps, and begin on-boarding and ramping new resources prior to closing key projects. It's also critical to aggregate the metrics you track for individual projects to gain better overall visibility into your project portfolio performance. This will help you to identify any project interdependencies or gaps, and prioritize new project opportunities accordingly.

5. **Updating of Organisation:** minimizing bench time was one of the biggest challenges facing most service providers. Today, however, Economic Growth coupled with a shortage of skilled labor has made Employee Retention a mission critical priority for the Professional Services Organisation. Once you've invested the effort, time, and money to recruit, hire, and train top talent, the last thing you want to do is lose them to a competitor because they feel undervalued, unhappy, or overworked. This relieves the pressure on individual SME's that can lead to burnout, develops loyalty and morale among your employees, and creates resource redundancies that can provide you much better flexibility for future scheduling exercises. Motivated employees create happy customers; so many organisations are now measuring employee satisfaction.

FIVE CHALLENGES IN RESOURCE OPTIMIZATION

Towards more effective resource management: Optimization is not just efficient and effective in an economic sense—it allows businesses to accommodate customer and employee preferences while taking into consideration a much wider set of requirements. Customers wait less and get better service. Employees can easily arrange their schedules around shift and vacation preference without disrupting business operations or service levels People can make highly informed decisions more quickly and more accurately than ever before.

Resource scheduling issues are difficult to resolve manually, and software applications are usually employed to assist in the process. The trouble with such traditional applications, however, is that they are actually quite limited in terms of sophistication and they don't really stand up to challenges found in the real world.

CHALLENGES IN RESOURCE OPTIMIZATION

We know what the goal is: optimizing resources. We have software tools to help achieve this goal. Where's the problem?

The reality is that there isn't one problem: there are at least five. Traditional software solutions cannot effectively address the following five challenges in resource optimization:

1. Turning a large volume of data into meaningful information, and then into effective decisions;
2. Ensuring software accuracy and solution relevance;
3. Increasing the speed of solution generation, together with the power of the solution, while dealing with operational complexity;
4. Providing decision support swiftly and flexibly during operations, with rapid reaction to unplanned events and operational disruptions
5. Flexibly and intelligently interacting with the user (at all levels of the organisation) to leverage their knowledge.

CONCLUSION

There are limited resources .economic resources by the definition, are scarce: therefore the managers are responsible for their allocation. this requires not only that managers be effective in achieving the goal or goals that are established but they be efficient management of human resource is a crucial factor in determining the growth and prosperity of business enterprise. This is particularly true in the case of small industry where owners are forced to have a close and more personal association with their employees. To develop a strategic plan for small scale units and improve the present process, recommendations of activity elimination, activity reduction, and activity sharing are suggested. Further more support from the top executive management to create a special department and appointment for resource management and to allocate resource is needed for the efficient implementation and long term success of the year of business.

References

1. Annual results of the sample companies. Backer, B. and Gerhart, B. (1996) The impact of human resource management on organisational performance-progress and prospects. *Academy of Management Journal.*
2. Backer, B. and Gerhart, B. (1996). The impact of human resource management on Organisational performance-progress and prospects. *Academy of Management Journal*
3. Frank H. Robert, S Ben. Bernake. Principles of economics.
4. [Ames 2002] Ames Research Center,
5. [Port 2001] Otis Port, Virtual Prospecting, Business Week, March 23, 2001

Attrition and Retention in BPO Sector: Key Drivers and Strategies

Rajnish Ratna[1], Navin Shrivastava[2], Saniya Chawla[3] and Uma Yadav[4]

[1]Ph.D. Scholar (IIT Kharagpur) and Assistant Professor, (HR&OB) Amity Business School
Amity University Sector 125, Noida, Uttar Pradesh
[2]Assistant Professor, BIMTECH, Greater Noida
[4]Officer, Bank of Baroda

ABSTRACT

A high rate of employee attrition is a challenge for most companies in the BPO sector. Retention strategies in BPO's are always were a matter of concern to the employers because employees leave the job if they feel the organisation is not paying the right concern and support to them. An insight to which are the most effective retention strategies that can have a long-term impact. Companies now adopt more than one technique to create an internal environment that will retain their employees. The purpose of the study was to identify the key drivers behind attrition and studying the persisting retention strategies to formulate the best employee retention strategy for the organisation. This study is descriptive in nature. Data is collected by 100 employees of different age group of leading companies of BPO in Delhi through questionnaire, designed on 11 important factors responsible for higher attrition in BPO. Mean Score Analysis, Chi square test and Control/Impact matrix with the help of SPSS software, does analysis. It was found that various factors like compensation, delinquent boss, rewards and recognition, communication gap might result into employee attrition. Hence, to retain employees in the process requires formation of effective employee retention strategies on various reasons with which employees are dissatisfied and may leave the company one by can help save company from losses incurred due to employee attrition.

Keywords: *Attrition, Retention Strategies, Outsourcing, Career Growth, and Compensation*

INTRODUCTION

Attrition is gradual reduction in employees without firing, as through retirement or resignation. It is a phenomenon affecting most of the business organisations. The company's most valuable assets are its people, based in all concerns of the company.

Attrition Rate

Attrition rates can be calculated using a simple formula:

Attrition = (No. of employees who left in the year/ average employees in the year) × 100

Thus, if the company had 1,000 employees in April 2004, 2,000 in March 2005, and 300 quit in the year, then the average employee strength is 1,500 and attrition is $100 \times (300/1500) = 20\%$.

There is no standard formula to calculate the attrition rate of a company. This is because of certain factors as:

- The employee base changes each month. So if a company has 1,000 employees in April 2004 and 2,000 in March 2005, then they may take their base as 2,000 or as 1,500 (average for the year). If the number of employees who left is 300, then the attrition figure could be 15 % or 20% depending on what base you take.

- Many firms may not include attrition of fresher that leave because of higher studies or within three months of joining.

Attrition Rate in Different Sectors in India

Table 1 Attrition rate in various sectors in India as of 2009

Vertical Market	Annual Attrition Rate
Outsourcing	54
Services	50
Finance	32
Retail & Distribution	30
Telecoms	23
Public Sector	18
Transport & Travel	15
IT	14
Mean Average	**32**

(Source: High Attrition Rate: A Big Challenge, http://www.bpoindia. org/research/attrition-rate-big-challenge.shtml)

Employee Retention

Employee retention is a process in which the employees are encouraged to remain with the organisation for the maximum period of time or until the completion of the project. Hiring knowledgeable people for the job is a priority for an employer. But retention is even more important than hiring. There is no lack of opportunity for a talented person. If a person is not satisfied by the job he's doing, he may switch over to some other more suitable job. In today's environment it becomes very important for organisations to retain their employees. A strong retention strategy becomes a powerful recruitment tool because high rate of attrition is a major concern for most of the companies and especially for BPO companies. The attrition rate is highest in this sector and this incurs a heavy loss to the company. The cost which organisation incurred in terms of recruitment cost, training and development cost, loss of productivity, Customer dissatisfaction and Ripple effect and company's image is much higher than the cost, which employers pay to retain their talent. Organisation wants the committed people and would like to create the culture where employees feel strongly associated with the organisation.

The retention of quality employee is one of the major challenges, which HR professionals are facing today. Companies have realized the importance of their quality employees and to retain their top talent in one of the top most priorities of employers today. Thus the major challenge, which HR professionals have to face, is that due to the intense competition in the market and globalization, the demand is increasing but the supply of quality employees is less. So organisations need to think out of the way to retain their talent. Retention has emerged as the focus of much time and attention in recent years. Employee retention is more than just keeping employees on the job. It is also about sustaining employees, primarily by enhancing their job satisfaction. Job satisfaction, in turn, can increase productivity and keep employees energized and motivated to give their best. Job satisfaction can equate to employees who stick with their current employer and strive to perform at or above expectations and standards. Employee retention is commonly considered to be the most essential and challenging task to enhance and sustain abilities of performing employees so as to maintain a stable workforce. *Companies that can recruit the best talent and retain them will have an edge in the long run.*

Table 2 Some retention strategies of companies of various sectors

S. No.	Organisations	Retention Strategies
1.	WIPRO (Spectra mind)	• Company's brand as an employer • Early opportunities for growth • High degree of autonomy • Value compatibility • Innovative people program • Tied up with BITS, Pilani and SIBM to provide distance learning programs to employees. • Throws in an incentive for employees- if they perform well at work, Spectra mind may pick up entire tab for the course. • Also has 'Gentlemen's agreement' with seven other BPO from which it does not hire. (Non Poaching Agreement)
2.	ICICI (OneSource)	• Gives scholarship of up to Rs 50, 000 to employees who want to enroll in distance learning programs. • Employees are allowed to apply for jobs at other ICICI group companies such as ICICI bank and ICICI InfoTech. • Hire outstation candidate's (mainly non-metros) and provide them shared company accommodation.
3.	HCL Tech BPO	• Use various psychometric Services tests to get people who can work at night and can handle the monotony. • Also, believes that giving career counseling and planning career paths to its employees helps to control attrition.

Contd...

Contd...

4.	Infosys BPO	• To newcomers, they provide an assured place for permanent stay, community atmosphere, healthy, hygienic and secure living and 24/7 facilities. • Infosys facilities team offers an exclusive women's wing with dedicated female service staff, security and a host of gender specific facilities.
5.	IBM (Daksh)	• Holds open house session every quarter where junior staff is encouraged to discuss problems in work place. • It also involves staff at all levels in brainstorming sessions for fresh ideas.

Table 3 Services offered by Genpact and Wipro

SERVICES		
Finance & Accounting	Collection & Customer Relation	Procurement & Supply
Accounts Payable	Collections	Sourcing &
Order to Cash	Customer Services	Procurement
Treasury & Tax	Originations	Logistics Services
General Accounting	Order Management	Marketing & Sales
Governance Risk		Support
Financial Planning & Analysis		After sales support
Insurance	**Software**	**IT Infrastructure**
Product development	Enterprise Application	End – user Computing
Sales & Marketing	Technology Integration	Enterprise Computing
Policy Administration	Application Maintenance	Network Services
Underwriting	Content Solutions	Security Services
Corporate Functions		

REVIEW OF LITERATURE

Bilginsoy, Cihan, (2003), studied apprenticeship programs in the United States, which provide workers with the broad-based skills required for practicing a trade via on-the-job training, are sponsored either unilaterally by employers or jointly by employers and trade unions. A comparison of the attrition and retention rates in these programs shows that program completion is more likely for apprentices in joint programs than for similar apprentices in unilateral programs. Rates of completion are lower for women than for men, and lower for ethnic and racial minorities than for whites.

Kulshreshtha, Ashutosh Kumar, T. Krishna (2005), develops a theoretical model for employee contribution and compensation and explores the problem of attrition from an economic point of view. Model based on the characteristics of the employee and the organisational environment; Employee value and employee cost to company; Motivation and salary hike.

Bhatnagar, Jyotsna. (2007), Investigates talent management and its relationship to levels of employee engagement using a mixed method research design. In the first phase low factor loadings indicated low engagement scores at the beginning of the career and at completion of 16 months with the organisation. High factor loadings at intermediate stages of employment were indicative of high engagement levels, but the interview data reflected that this may mean high loyalty, but only for a limited time. In the second phase factor loadings indicated three distinct factors of organisational culture, career planning along with incentives and organisational support. The first two were indicative of high attrition.

Niranjan, T. T. Srivastava, Samir, K. (2008), discusses about the Bangalore based Sparsh Call Centre was set up as a subsidiary of the major telecom software company IP-Trinity, with ambitious plans of becoming a significant player in the booming BPO (business process outsourcing) space. Its strategy, in line with that of its parent group, was to focus on telecom related services. People management was, to a great extent, managed by sophisticated workforce management software, supplemented by supervisory actions by managers. This case is useful in highlighting the complexities of managing call centre's and the unique people issues involved. In particular, high employee attrition can cause reduction in service quality as well as reduced capacity. Cost effective innovative retention schemes may be needed to retain call centre staff to achieve this scale up.

Franckeiss, Anton. (2010), demonstrates how to re-engage talented employees after they have left an organisation. The "Green Room" is a facilitated process that moves beyond a simple employee exit survey approach to build rapport that supports not only re-engagement, but also the identification and actioning of critical push and pull factors at play within an organisation. This enables it to develop and strengthen its employee value proposition and its positioning as an employer of choice. Through the provision of confidentiality and skilled third party practitioners, the

Green Room process not only leads to the successful return of a percentage of previously departed key talent, but informs an organisation's talent management, recruitment and retention strategies and practices, and can significantly reduce attrition rates.

RESEARCH METHODOLOGY

Research Objectives

The objective of the paper is

1. To find study about the key drivers of attrition.
2. To Study the persisting retention strategies of the organisation so as to formulate the best employee retention strategy for the organisation.
3. To design a control/impact matrix through analyzing questionnaire and secondary data which shows vital few and trivial many reasons of attrition.

Statistical Tool

1. **Sample Size:** 100 employees are chosen from the total population of Wipro and Genpact consisting of band 4 (Process Associates and Process Developers) and band 5 employees (Management Trainees and Assistant Manager).
2. **Sampling Type:** The sampling used for this study was a 'simple random sampling' method.
3. **Sampling Unit:** The sampling unit is only the employees of the three organisations. Sample unit consists of one employee per questionnaire.
4. **Questionnaire:** The data collected from the questionnaire was expressed in concise and logical form with the help of line graphs, tables and using SPSS (Mean score analysis using tables and graphs and Chi-square test).
5. **Type of Research:** It is a descriptive research.

Data Collection

- **Primary Data:** The questionnaire was filled by directly meeting the employees of the organisations.
- **Secondary Data:** Secondary data were collected from newspapers, magazines journals, online resources etc.

DATA ANALYSIS, INTERPRETATION AND FINDING

Analysis part is divided into three phases i.e. Mean Score Analysis, Chi square test and designing retention framework. Mean Score Analysis and chi-square test have been done with the help of SPSS software. At last Control/Impact matrix is designed on the basis of analysis of questionnaire and unstructured interviews of employees.

Sample Distribution

The number of employees taken from each company is 50. The respondents belong to various positions of band 4 and band 5 employees.

Table 4 Sample distribution of employees with respect to age

Age Group (yrs.)	Job Title	Frequency
22-26	Band 4 and Assistant Managers	56
27-40	Band 5	24
40-55	Band 5 and above	20

Phase 1: Mean Score Analysis

This section represents the analysis of different parameters. The mean score is calculated for each parameter and analysis for that variable is done.

Phase 2: Chi-Square Test

Step 1: Set Hypothesis

H_0: There is no association between impact of age on rate of attrition in IT - BPOs companies.

H_1: There is an association between impacts of age on rate of attrition in IT - BPOs companies.

Step 2: Significance Value; Alpha (α) = 0.05 (5% significance)

Step 3: Calculate Chi-Square

Step 4: Decision Criteria

If, *p* **value > alpha** (α)then; H_0 is accepted & H_1 is rejected

Step 5: Implication

From the above applied Chi-Square test it is conferred that demographic detail like age has an impact over the factors causing attrition in IT-BPOs. It is also drawn that age has no relation with company's policies and procedures which further implies that the policies and procedures are pre planned and designed and they do not change with respect to employee turnover. Company's policies and procedures are the transformational factor and do not get changed easily. Again in the case of employee value addition, age factor does not play any role. Infact, this is based on the employees conscious about whether they want to add value to themselves at workplace or not. The reason could be internal/external

Table 5   Mean Score Analysis of parameters

S. No	Parameters/Factors	Mean Value	Remarks
On a scale of 5 (Likert Scale)			
1	Company's Policies and Procedures	4.15	85% of the employees agree that company's policies and procedures are clear, transparent and create a positive working environment at workplace.
2	Career Planning and Career Opportunity	3.38	It is clear from mean value that career planning of many employees is not done by their managers and they don't foresee adequate career opportunity for them within company. Hence, effective career planning of each employee of the process is very essential in order to retain them in the process.
3	Manager and Employee Relation	3.46	Friendly relationship lacks between manager and band5 employees i.e. there is very much of professionalism and employees don't discuss any issues with manager over and above their professional issues if any.
On a Scale of 2 (Dichotomous Scale)			
4	Education @ Work	1.51	People have an inclination towards education but are not enrolled due to lack of awareness and financial problems but in likely future they wish to join the courses provided by the companies like HRO/AP/AR (A/C Payables, A/C Receivables etc.).
5	Employee Value Addition	1.86	It is clear that with the mean value 1.8 that most of the employees feel that they are adding value to them while working in company and also have a sense of belonging for the same.
6	Compensation	1.55	Employees think they are not fairly compensated for the work they do. For them, Salary is most important because they may leave the company for better pay package in another company.
Multiple Choices Questions**			
7	Rewards & Recognition		For most of the employees (65%) getting 'Awards' (monetary and non-monetary both) for their work performance and achievements is the best reward for them. Also, last time when the work of approximately 70% employees got recognized is more than a month back. Work recognition of the employees is late in the organisation.
8	Front Line Manager (FLM) Effectiveness		72% of the sample population have discussions with their manager after a month or beyond which is very late from an employee's point of view.
9	Performance Goals set by Managers		About 81% of sample population says that performance goals set by their manager are achievable.
10	Employee Motivation Factors		R& R (Rewards & Recognition) acts as a motivational factor to a limited extent only. Appreciation from leadership is the most impacting motivational factor for most of the employees.
11	Employees Anticipation		Employees anticipate career opportunities and night shift as major changes in their life in next 3-6 months. Employees may attrite from company because of these reasons. Also, some of them have problems with manager. If issues not solved now, then could finally lead to attrition of these employees.

**Multiple choice questions don't have any mean score because of subjective nature

Table 6   Showing Case Processing Summary of Chi-Square Test

Cases	Value	Df	p value (Asym sig. 2 sided)	Inference (Null Hypothesis)
Age*Company's Policies and Procedures	10.474	8	.233	Accepted
Age*Career Planning and Opportunity	22.187	6	.001	Rejected
Age*Manager and Employee Relation	40.557	8	.000	Rejected
Age*Education at Work	11.289	2	.004	Rejected
Age*Employee Value Addition	5.423	2	.066	Accepted
Age*Compensation	16.967	2	.010	Rejected

Table 7 Showing implications of cases for results obtained

S. No.	Factors	Inference (Null Hypothesis, H_0)	Implication
1	Company's Policies & Procedures	Accepted 0.233 > 0.05 i.e. (p value > α)	There is no impact of age on company's policies and procedures which is a factor of attrition.
2	Career Planning and Career Opportunity	**Rejected** 0.001 < 0.05 (p value < α)	Age factor does have an impact on attrition and therefore we can see there is an impact of age on career planning and opportunity.
3	Manager and Employee Relation	**Rejected** 0.00 < 0.05	Age factor has an impact on manager and employee relation.
4	Education at Work	**Rejected** 0.004 < 0.05	Age has an impact on education at work which is again a factor of attrition in IT-BPOs.
5	Employee Value Addition	Accepted 0.066 > 0.050	There is no impact of age on employee value addition
6	Compensation	**Rejected** 0.010 < 0.050	There is an impact of age on compensation which is again a factor of attrition in IT-BPOs.

motivation, achieving targets, personal/professional growth etc. The factor is irrespective of the age and hence doesn't show any relation between them.

PHASE 3: CONTROL/IMPACT MATRIX AND EMPLOYEE RETENTION FRAMEWORK

(a) *The Control – Impact matrix* is a visual tool that helps in separating the vital few from the trivial many.

It is a simple prioritization tool that talks about high or low control on one axis and high or low impact on the other axis. We can use it for various purposes, one common use is for short listing Xs (root causes) in Six Sigma project. We can use it to prioritize our Xs (root causes) by classifying them as factors we have high or low control over and whether these Xs will have high or low impact.

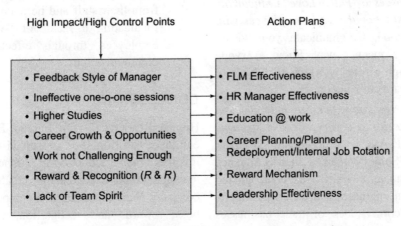

Fig. 1 Showing High causes of attrition and their action plans

(b) *Employee Retention Strategy* (Features)

- Be a Company, people want to work for: Build a culture that encourages, and rewards commitment and creates an employer of choice
- Select the right people in the right place: Define the talent needed. Recruit from the right source, assessing, screening, effective interviews
- Get them off to a good start: Feeling welcomed, valued, prepared and challenged

- Blend employees with the company culture: Make employees feel they are an important asset for the organisation so that they feel committed towards the organisation

- Coach & Reward to sustain commitment: Managers must directly manage performance agreement, recognize results, and facilitate employees 'career growth and advancement

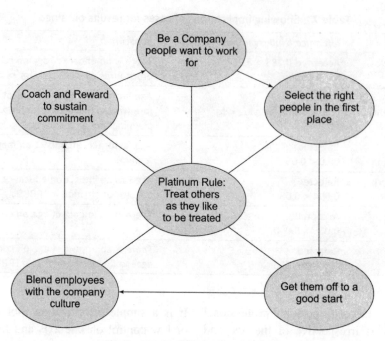

Fig. 2 Employee Retention Strategy

RECOMMENDATIONS

1. *Treat your employees like you treat your most valuable clients.* It is cheaper to keep your good employees than it is to hire and train new ones.

2. *Get your employees to "Fall in Love" i.e inculcate a factor of institutional love in employees with your organisation.* Communicate your vision in an assertive manner way. Show everyone the path through a role by which they have to contribute towards this vision.

3. *Making employee committees to help develop retention strategies is a very effective strategy.* Get their input! Ask, what do people like about working here? Some companies, such as Advance Fibre Communication (AFC), have recognized that the special engineers and technical experts that are the cornerstones of their businesses require special attention.

4. *Remember, the "Fun Factor" is very important to many employees.* Greg Peters, Past President and CEO of Mahi Networks in Petaluma, is one of many executives who reported that retention is often related to interpersonal connections and amount of FUN in work teams.

5. Know the trends in benefit packages. Do your best to offer the ones your employees need.

6. *Recognition, in various forms, is a powerful retention strategy.* It does not have to cost a lot.

US Dept. of Labor - 46% of people leave their jobs because they feel unappreciated.

7. *Leadership must be deeply invested in retention.* Management must be skillfully communicating company's policies in a way that creates "buy-in" from their staff and be open to employee input. Inculcating a factor of "ownership" in your employees through effective and assertive communication.

CONCLUSION

Human Resource is life line of BPO Company and employee attrition is very crucial to the company. It involves gradual reduction in number of employees due to resignation or death and thus results in huge loss to the company. Various factors like compensation, delinquent boss, rewards and recognition, communication gap may result into employee attrition. Hence, to retain employees in the process requires formation of effective employee retention strategies. And formation of effective strategies requires the knowledge of various reasons with which employees are dissatisfied and may leave the company. During the study various reasons causing employee attrition in the process were found out and then strategies for retaining them in the process were formulated. The best way of retaining employees in the process is to increase communication and interaction between manager and band 5 employees. If strategies formulated at leadership, FLM and HR Manager Levels are implemented in the process then it will result in increased employee satisfaction and thus increasing the chance of them continuing their job in the process and thus controlling attrition to a certain extent. Therefore, by taking care of few small things and with the implementation of retention strategies in the process can help save company from losses incurred due to employee attrition.

References

- Bilginsoy, Cihan (2003), The Hazards of Training: Attrition and Retention in Construction Industry Apprenticeship Programs, *Industrial & Labor Relations Review; Oct 2003, 57* (1), 54-67, 14, 4 Charts, 2 Graphs.
- Kulshreshtha, Ashutosh Kumar, T. Krishna (2005), Economic Model for Optimum Attrition Rate, *IIMB Management Review (Indian Institute of Management, Bangalore)*; Jun 2005, 17, 2, 103-108, 6.
- Bhatnagar, Jyotsna (2007), Talent management strategy of employee engagement in Indian ITES employees: key to retention, *Employee Relations; 2007, Vol. 29* 6, 640-663, 24.
- Niranjan, T. T., Srivastava, Samir, K. (2008), Managing Capacity at Sparsh Call Centre, *Asian Case Research Journal; Jun 2008, 12,* 1, 73-103, 31, 2 Diagrams, 2 Charts, 2 Graphs.
- Franckeiss, Anton (2010), Mining the good from the goodbyes, *Strategic HR Review; 2010,* 5, 24-29, 6.

Books
- Varma, Anil. Challenges of Attrition and Retention Strategies, Publisher: ICFAI.
- Parsloe E, Wray M (2007), *Coaching and Mentoring* 1st ed. 78-112
- Dessler, G. (2005). *Human Resource Management*, 9th ed. 271- 280
- Ivancevich, John M. (2003) *Human Resource Management*, 392-412

- McConnell, John H. (2003) How to Identify Your Organisation's Talent: A *Practical Guide to Needs Analysis*, 103-119

Websites
- Employee retention strategies, Retrieved from http://www.employeeretentionstrategies.com/
- Employee Retention: Tips and Tools for Employee Retention, Retrieved from http://humanresources.about.com/od/retention/Retention_of_Employees_Tips_and_Tools_for_Employee_Retention.htm
- High Attrition Rate: A Big Challenge, Retrieved from http://www.bpoindia.org/research/attrition-rate-big-challenge.shtml
- Retrieved from http://businesstoday.digitaltoday.in/carrots-with-strings-177.html
- Retrieved from http://retention.naukrihub.com/attrition-rate.html
- Retrieved from http://retention.naukrihub.com/importance-of-employee-retention.html
- Retrieved from http://retention.naukrihub.com/what-makes-employees-leave.html
- Retrieved from http://retention.naukrihub.com/retention.html
- Retrieved from http://www.orcworldwide.com/sightlines/sl0312.php
- Retrieved from http://www.w3.org/1999/xhtml
- Is the BPO Iceberg Melting Under Attrition Heat?" Economic Times (February 10, 2005b). <economictimes.indiatimes.com/articleshow/1036152.cms?headline=BPO~attriition> (Accessed on October 6, 2009)
- Retention strategies that work, Retrieved from http://www.expresshospitality.com/20100315/hospitalitylife01.shtml
- The Challenge of Retaining Top Talent: The Workforce Attrition Crisis, By B. Lynn Ware and Bruce Fern, Retrieved from http://www.itsinc.net/retention-research.htm

The Global Mobility of Talent and its Impact on Global Development

Sneha Alan

Assistant Professor, SB Patil Institute of Management, Pune

ABSTRACT

Human talent is the key asset and managing these talents is the challenge for all the organisation. Talent has a large economic value and its mobility has increased with globalization, speed of new information technologies, and lower transportation cost. As more skilled or talented people move across borders both temporarily and permanently the economics of fortune of both rich and poor countries are bound in inextricable ways. The global mobility has lot of impact on source nations, receiving nations and on the global economy and society. For sending countries the emigration of talent can reduce their human capital base and in contrast receiving countries will benefit from an inflow of talent that increases their qualified human resource. This paper focuses on the policy issues related to the international mobility of talented individuals and its impact on the sending and receiving countries.

Keywords: *international migration, international mobility, human resources*

INTRODUCTION

Human talent is a key economic resource and a source of creative power in science, technology, business, arts and culture and other activities. Talent has a large economic value and its mobility has increased with globalization, the spread of new information technologies and lower transportation costs. Well educated and/or talented people are often more internationally mobile than unskilled workers and face more favorable immigration policies in receiving countries, typically high per capita income economies short of information technology experts, scientists, medical doctors and other type of talent. Individuals from developing countries are increasingly meeting the global demand for talent. This is the case of medical doctors from the Caribbean, Sub-Saharan African countries or the Philippines, information technology experts from India, Taiwan and China, engineers and mathematicians from the former Soviet Union, indigenous singers from Africa, professionals and writers from Latin America and others.

The economic value of talent stems from its various uses. Talent can be a productive resource for current production (e.g. information technology experts and engineers), or a source of wealth creation (entrepreneurs), a source of knowledge (scientists), provide a social service (nurses, physicians) or cultural work (artists). The sociology of talent is interesting; talents constitute international elite in the economic, financial, or cultural areas. These international elites can be in trans-national corporations, in the bureaucracy of international organisations, or in more independent locations. Talented individuals usually have considerable influence at national and international levels as they are often well connected, shape ideas, values and beliefs. In turn, many of them are decision makers in the private sector or government. The international mobility of talent can have important development effects on the source nations, on the receiving countries and on the global economy and society. In source countries, the emigration of talent can reduce their human capital base. Developing countries that see their entrepreneurs, scientists, technology experts, medical doctors emigrate can experience a retard in their development potential. In contrast, receiving countries will benefit from an inflow of talent that enlarges their qualified human resource base relieving shortages of high skills people. Depending on the type of human capital received, recipient countries can benefit in the science sector, in health and in culture. Return migration and the international circulation of ideas, technology, and expertise can counter-balance, to some extent, a skewed distribution of gains from the mobility of talent toward receiving countries.

Categories of Talent

This section offers a classification (taxonomy) of different types of talent according to occupational characteristics and work relations (e.g. self-employed and employee). Different types of talent can have a differentiated development contribution. Someone contribute directly to wealth creation, others to technological advancement, and others to cultural activities. The classification goes as follows:

(i) Technical talent

(ii) Scientists and academics

(iii) Professionals in the health sector: medical doctors and nurses

(iv) Entrepreneurs and managers

(vi) Cultural talent.

Determinants of The International Mobility of Talent

1. *The rewards structure*

The market rewards to talent is a key determinant of the allocation of talent both at national and international levels. If the earnings of lawyers are higher than the earnings of teachers we can expect that more talented people will study law than education as talent allocation at national level depends on the rewards of alternative occupations. In turn, the international mobility of talent depends on the expected income differential that can be earned abroad with respect to earnings at home in a given activity

Example - International income differentials across countries may be substantial: it is reported that a Filipino nurses can earn between US$75–200 per month in the Philippines compared to US$3,000–4,000 in the United States (Bach 2003).

Rewarding talent engaged in starting new activities and developing new products or techniques—the distinctive role of the entrepreneur according to Schumpeter—in which the demand is difficult to anticipate, presents several problems Thereby, talent needs to be compensated for this fundamental uncertainty.

Valuing talent is also difficult in the 'creative industries' (see Caves 2000) of painters, writers, singers, classic musicians, film-makers, designers and others. In the creative industry there is often uncertainty related to the ways markets will value new paintings, new books,

2. *Linguistic compatibility, networks and socio-cultural affinity*

The standard characterization of immigrants—alien to the culture of industrial countries, without domain of the local language, essentially a socially marginalized individual—certainly does not square with the 'talent super-elite' formed by CEOs of large multinational corporations, well-recognized scientists, international investors, and famous artists and writers. These people often have high education, knowledge of more than one language, understanding of cultural differences among countries, etc. These traits facilitate their international mobility and ease their adjustment to other countries and realities. The international elite of talent have often studied abroad, belong to professional and alumni networks of prestigious universities and have developed a dense net of contacts with well-placed individuals around the world that facilitate their mobility.

3. *Shortage of skilled professionals in industrialized countries*

The shortage of certain skilled professionals such as information technology experts and Computer science specialists, nurses, medical doctors is an important factor behind the increase in demand for talent in the world economy. Countries such as the US, UK, Germany, and others have special visa programs for IT experts, nurses and medical doctors, international scientist and graduate students.

Conceptual Framework

The economic literature evaluating the developmental and global effects of the emigration of human capital has evolved through time. Early analysis based on neoclassical growth models with human capital as a factor of production, assumed perfect competition, perfect information, and full wage flexibility. The conclusion of those analyses was that for small amounts of highly skilled, emigration would leave the economic welfare of the remaining population unaffected (Johnson 1967; Grubel and Scott 1966). In fact, the highly skilled emigrant removed only their personal marginal product, then the remaining population would be unaffected by a reduction in the skilled labour force.

The modifications of the original assumptions of neoclassical models suggested that the emigration of HSIs can generate economic losses for the country sending the emigrants. There can be a loss of welfare for the remaining population because of externalities due to a loss of scarce skills. As the high skills emigrants are individuals with a large endowment of knowledge, they generate positive externalities that may be sector-specific (i.e. the output of academics depend on the availability of a mass of researchers). In other words, knowledge generation is an activity with increasing returns (see Solimano, 2002a). The externality argument rests on the assumption that the social marginal product of a highly skilled emigrant is greater than his private marginal product. Some of these conclusions have received analytical support from "new growth" or "endogenous growth" theories that highlight the cumulative value of human capital in economic development. New growth theories stress that the average level of human capital in a society has positive effects on productivity of an individual worker above and beyond their own personal endowment of human capital (the point just made in the previous paragraph). The greater a country average level of education, the greater its economic growth (Lee and Barro 1993; Barro and Sala-I-Martin 1995)15. Thus, receiving countries in particular benefit from increased knowledge gained from highly skilled immigrants.

Brain Drain, Brain Circulation

Not all departure of qualified human resources has to be considered as a *brain drain* associated with permanent emigration of scientists, professionals, technology experts, and others. In modern times, there is a pattern of *brain circulation*. The human capital that has emigrated may return home after a few years (or decades) bringing along accumulated knowledge, skills, contacts, access to international best practices and possible financial capital, with the ensuing contribution to national development. This return migration certainly benefits the home country.

Scientific Diasporas

In addition, during the period the emigrant stays abroad, he may transfer part of their knowledge and experience to the home country through periodic visits and by participation in "knowledge networks" or *scientific diasporas*16 set-up abroad (Solimano, 2002). The Scientific Diasporas have created knowledge networks of nationals belonging to a certain scientific field that work or study abroad. A main purpose of these networks is to connect professionals and scientists scattered around the globe, and interested in maintaining contact among them. In addition, they are also interested in helping to promote the scientific and economic development of their home countries. These networks may have a link and be supported by national governments or may be fully independent. Examples of these networks are the Chinese Scholars Abroad (CHISA), The Colombian Network of Engineers Abroad (Red Caldas), The Global Korean Network, The Sillycon Valley Indian

Professionals Association (SIPA), scientific Diasporas enable, to some extent, the de-linking of the contribution of scientists from their physical place of residence. This can help the transfer of knowledge to developing countries. In Taiwan the formation and development of Hsinchu Science – based Industrial Park (HSIP) greatly benefited from return Taiwanese entrepreneurial and engineers return immigrants from Silicon Valley (Saxenian and Chuen-Yueh Li, 2003). In fact, several of the successful Indians and Taiwanese in the high tech industry in the US also set up software and hardware companies in their home countries contributing to growth in the source countries.

The objective of the study

- To study how the emigration of human capital has evolved through time
- To study the impact of global mobility on the sending and receiving country.

Research Methodology

Research type: Qualitative Research

Method of Data collection: Secondary method

1. Internet

Findings

Emigration of human capital evolved

1. (Johnson 1967; Grubel and Scott 1966)The conclusion based on neoclassical growth models was that for small amounts of highly skilled, emigration would leave the economic welfare of the remaining population unaffected.

2. According to Solimano report in 2002 there was modifications in the original assumptions of neoclassical models that suggested that the emigration of HSIs can generate economic losses for the country sending the emigrants. There can be a loss of welfare for the remaining population because of externalities due to a loss of scarce skills. As the high skills emigrants are individuals with a large endowment of knowledge, they generate positive externalities that may be sector-specific.

3. This assumptions was supported by,' New growth theories "that stressed that the average level of human capital in a society has positive effects on productivity of an individual worker above and beyond their own personal endowment of human capital. (this was supports by a study of 111 countries from 1960 to 1990 found that one

year increase in the average education of a nation workforce increases the output per worker by 5 and 15% (see ILO 1998; Topel 1998).

4. Andres Solimano and Molly Pollack 2004 report modern studies have shown *brain circulation*. The human capital that has emigrated may return home after a few years (or decades) bringing along accumulated knowledge, skills, contacts, access to international best practices and possible financial capital, with the ensuing contribution to national development. This return migration certainly benefits the home country and *Scientific diasporas* Impact of Global mobility on Receiving and Sending countries.

5. Positive impact on receiving countries, 32% of US Nobel-prize winners in Chemistry between 1985 and 1999 were foreign-born Skilled migrant.

6. It is estimated that a quarter of Silicon Valley firms in 1998 were headed by immigrants from China and India, collectively generating almost USD 17 billion in sales and 52,300 jobs.

7. In 2000 Germany and Israel accounted for 86% of science and technology Russian emigrants (Gokhberg and Nekipelova 2001: 180). In Canada the shortages were estimated at 20,000 in the mid-1990s compared to US-estimated shortages of 190,000 (Zhao *et al.*, 2000: 9). Other countries such as Australia and Singapore also exhibit shortages of IT labour as evidenced by inflows of IT workers from Malaysia, China, and other neighboring countries (Solimano and Pollack 2004: 4). Receiving countries more than make up for their inability to generate talent at home and enhance the quality of the national workforce, as the Russians did for Israel (Solimano 2001: 9).. In early 2001 it was estimated that there were one million Indian born individuals in the US and more than 75% of the working age population had a bachelor's degree or better (Desai et al. 2003: 1). Thirty-eight per cent of India-born US working age residents had post-graduate degrees compared with 9% of US born residents.

8. Negative impact on sending countries - African countries suffer from the emigration of technical professionals and healthcare workers. For example, between 1985 and 1990 Africa lost 60,000 professionals through emigration (Wickramasekara 2002: 5).

9. Positive impact on sending countries with low income - Low-income and small economies tend to benefit the most from remittances as they contribute substantially to national income which could be used for economic development purposes (D'Costa 2004) Female workers from Sri Lanka and Philippines contribute considerably to remittance income (Hugo 2003: 15). A recent World Bank estimate put the total remittance inflows to developing countries at $126 billion in 2004.

SENDING COUNTRIES: POSSIBLE POSITIVE EFFECTS

Development effects

- Increased knowledge flows and collaboration, higher international mobility leads to increased ties with foreign research institutions
- Remittances and venture capital from diasporas networks
- Successful overseas entrepreneurs bring valuable management experience, capital and increased access to global networks.

Sending Countries: Possible Negative Effects

- "Brain drain", lose of productive potential due to (at least temporary) absence of higher skilled workers
- Reduced Growth
- Inequality.

RECEIVING COUNTRIES: POSSIBLE POSITIVE EFFECTS

Development and Technology Effects

- Increased R&D due to enhanced availability of individuals with a higher stock of knowledge
- Knowledge flows and collaboration with sending Countries
- Immigrants can foster diversity and creativity
- Skilled Labor, R&D Boost, Profitability/Efficiency of Firms
- Job Creation through skilled entrepreneurs.

Receiving Countries: Possible Negative Effects

- Decreased incentive of natives to seek higher skills in certain fields.
- Unemployment
- Leakage of Critical Information.

Possible Global Effects

- Increased flows of knowledge across countries, formation of international research/technology clusters (Silicon Valley, CERN).
- Increased efficiency in global labor markets for high skills workers, researchers, information technology experts.
- Increased concentration of global expenditure in science and technology in OECD countries.
- Increase in global real income due to human capital reallocation from lower return countries to higher return.

CONCLUSION

Uncontrolled immigration is neither politically feasible nor socially acceptable in receiving countries. For sending countries the challenge is to retain talent and lure previous emigrants back to further national development. Government should take initiatives to lure professionals back and the rapid development of the home market can contribute to the return flow of talent. Many other professionals, though settled abroad, could 'circulate' between sending and receiving countries In an era of foreign aid fatigue there is greater reason to promote development in labour-abundant countries so that 'brain drain' is transformed to 'brain gain, If there is proper balance between the receiving countries and sending countries then only global mobility can benefit both receiving and sending countries.

References

- Bach, Steven. (2008). "International Mobility of Health Professionals: Brain Drain or Brain Exchange?" In Andres Solimano, ed., *the International Mobility of Talent: Types, Causes and Development Impacts* Oxford University Press.
- D'Costa, Anthony, P. (2008). "The International Mobility of Technical Talent: Trends and Development Implications." In Andres Solimano, ed., *The International Mobility of Talent: Types, Causes and Development Impacts,* Oxford University Press.
- Kapur, D. (2003). *Remittances: The New Development Mantra?* Cambridge, MA: Weather head Center for International Affairs.
- Murphy, K., Shleifer, A. and Vishny R. (1991) 'The Allocation of Talent: Implications for Growth', *Quarterly Journal of Economics,* 106(2): 503-30.
- Saxenian, A.L. (2006). 'International Mobility of Engineers and the Rise of Entrepreneurship in the Periphery', WIDER Research Paper 2006/142, Helsinki: UNU-WIDER
- Saxenian, AnnaLee. (2008). "The International Mobility of Entrepreneurs and Regional Upgrading in India and China."In Andres Solimano, ed., *The International Mobility of Talent: Types, Causes and Development Impacts.* Oxford University Press.
- Silicon. India (2004). Brighter Job Market in U.S. for NRIs: Report,' www.silicon.com. 2004.
- Solimano, A. (2001). *International Migration and the Global Economic Order: An Overview.* Washington, DC: World Bank.
- Solimano, A. (2002). *Globalizing Talent and Human Capital: Implications for Developing Countries.* Macroeconomia del desarrollo. Santiago: ECLAC, Economic Development Division.
- Solimano, A. and Pollack M. (2004). *International Mobility of the Highly Skilled: The Case between Europe and Latin America.* Santiago: ECLAC.
- Sorensen, N.N. (2004). 'The Development Dimension of Migrant Remittances.' Migration Policy Research Working Papers Series, 1 (June).
- World Bank (2008), *Global Economic Prospects2008.* Washington, DC: World Bank.

Training and Development

Syed Yaseen

Aakash Institute of Management Studies, Bangalore, Karnataka

ABSTRACT

Training and development play an important role in the effectiveness of organisations and to the experiences of people in work. Training has implications for productivity, health and safety at work and personal development. All organisations employing people need to train and develop their staff. Most organisations are cognizant of this requirement and invest effort and other resources in training and development. Such investment can take the form of employing specialist training and development staff and paying salaries to staff undergoing training and development. Investment in training and development entails obtaining and maintaining space and equipment. It also means that operational personnel, employed in the organisation's main business functions, such as production, maintenance, sales, marketing and management support, must also direct their attention and effort from time to time towards supporting training development and delivery. This means they are required to give less attention to activities that are obviously more productive in terms of the organisation's main business. However, investment in training and development is generally regarded as good management practice to maintain appropriate expertise now and in the future.

The process of increasing the knowledge and skills of the workforce to enable them to perform their jobs effectively Training is, therefore, a process whereby an individual acquires *job-related skills and knowledge.* Training costs can be significant in any business. However, many employers are prepared to incur these costs because they expect their business to benefit from employees' development and progress.

Keywords: *Training, Development, Effectiveness*

CONCEPT OF TRAINING

The efficiency of organisation depends directly on the capability and talents of its personal and how motivated they are. Capability of person depends on his ability to work and the type of training he receives. While his personal capability is evaluated through proper selection procedure, his training is taken care of by the organisation after he has been employed by the organisation. Since training inputs may vary from on-the job experience to of f the job training, most of the organisation under take some kind of training for their employees. In Indian organisation, training and development activities have assumed high importance in recent years because of their contribution to the achievements of organisational objectives.

TRAINING AND DEVELOPMENT; A COMPARISON

Often some confusion arises in using the terms training and development. Many people see both as synonymous but many people differentiate between the two. The term 'training' is concerned with imparting specific skills for a particular purpose. For example, flippo has defined training as ''the act of increasing the knowledge and skills of an employee for doing a particular job.'' The term development refers broadly to the nature and direction of change induced in employees through the process of training and education. For example, development has been defined as follows:

"Management development is all those activities and programmers when recognized and controlled, have substantial influence in changing the capacity of individual to perform his assignment better and on so doing are likely to increase his potential for future management assignment"

Fundamental Difference between Training and Development

Training	Development
Short term process	Long term process
Knowledge & skill for specific purpose	For over all development
Primary related to technical skill learning	Related to managerial behavioral and attitudinal development.

Considering the current practices in the corporate sector, we may say that the term training being used for all types of development programs, since the development programmers have not remained confined to management development only. Companies are organizing development programmers for not only white-collar employees but also for blue-collar employees like shop-floor operator, clerical and support staff even for unskilled workers.

In addition to technical training with regard to their jobs and machines, developmental programmers are being conducted in attitudinal, behavioral and self-development areas for the white collar employees.

'The aim of training is to develop potential knowledge and skills of the trainees to carry out defined tasks and responsibilities'.

'Training enhances efficiency and develops a systematic way of performing duties and assigned tasks'.

'The aim of training is to infuse scientific thinking and planning and working methodically and efficiently'.

'Training is a process of learning and unlearning- to acquire/enhance skills and knowledge and apply them in practice-to enable the trainee to do his job efficiently'.

ROLE OF TRAINING

The primary concern of an organisation is its viability, and hence its efficiency. There is a continuous environmental pressure of efficiency, and if the organisation does not respond to this pressure, it may find itself rapidly losing whatever market share it has, Training imparts skills and knowledge to employees in order that they contribute to the organisation's efficiency and be able to cope with the pressures of a constantly changing environment. The viability of an organisation depends, to a considerable extent on the skills of different employees, especially that of its managerial cadre, to align the organisation successfully within its environment.

Thus, training can play the following roles in an organisation.

Increase in Efficiency

Training plays an active role in increasing the efficiency of employees in an organisation. Training increases skills for doing a job in a better way by enhancing competencies. Though an employee can learns many things while he is in job, he can do much better if he learns how best to do the job. This becomes more important especially in the context of changing technology because the old method of working may no longer be relevant. In such a case, training is required even to maintain a level of output. For example, working on an automatic machine may require skills very different from those required to handle a manually operated machine.

Increased in Morale of Employees

Morale is a mental condition of an individual or group which determines the willingness to cooperate and voluntarily give his best. Training increases employee morale by upgrading their skills in line with their job requirements.

Better Human Relation

Growing complexity and high degrees of specialization of jobs in large organisations have led to various human problems like alienation, depression, inter-personal and inter-group problems. Many of these problems can be overcome by suitable human relations training. Many techniques have been developed through which people can be trained and developed to tackle many problems of social and psychological nature.

Reduced Supervision

Trained employees require less supervision. They need more autonomy and freedom. Such autonomy and freedom can be given if the employees are trained properly to handle their jobs without the help of supervision, which can save much cost to the organisation and speed up communication and decision making.

Increased Organisational Viability and Resilience

Trained people are necessary to maintain organisational viability and flexibility. Viability relates to an organisations ability to tide over bad days, and resilience relates to its ability to sustain its effectiveness despite the loss of its key personnel and making do for the short term adjustment with its existing personnel. Such adjustment is possible if the organisation has trained people who can smoothly move into the positions vacated by key personnel.

Introduction of New Strategies and Working Methods in the Organisation

In this world of intense competition, an organisation, whether engaged in business activities or in social development is constantly striving to gain a competitive advantage over other contenders. It explores ways and means to increase its productivity, level of proficiency of the staff, or its ability to provide more efficient and cost-effective services to its client groups. For achieving this, the organisation may, at any given point in time, introduce new working methods, procedures or practices.

Advancement in Technology

In view of innovations and changes in technology, related to its methods of production, a business organisation may consider it imperative to update the skills of its staff. New machinery is installed or new plants are commissioned but for producing new products or providing new services, the staff needs to be trained to operate the new equipment.

Organisational Policy

Some organisations have a policy of sending their staff for training on a regular basis. For instance, in India, defense forces and some financial institutions send their staff for training programmers as part of regular update, regardless of whether a training need exists or not. Some major private and public sector organisations also follow a similar practice. In most cases, the objective is to keep its staff abreast with the latest working methods, innovations and management practices. This could either be a response to competition or a strategy to keep the staff in a high state of efficiency and preparedness.

NEED AND IMPORTANCE OF TRAINING

The need for training may be better understood in the light of the following situations, one or several of which may simultaneously impact an organisation and/or its personnel;

Rapid technological innovations impacting the workplace have made it necessary for people to constantly update their knowledge and skills. People have to work in multi-dimensional areas, which are usually far removed from their area of specialization

1. Change in the style of management.
2. Due to non-practical college education.
3. Lack of proper and scientific selection procedure.
4. or career advancement.
5. For higher motivation and productivity.
6. To make the job challenging and interesting.
7. For self development.
8. For employee motivation and retention
9. To improve organisational climate.
10. Prevention of obsolesce
11. To help the organisation to fulfill its future manpower needs.
12. To keep pace with the times.
13. To bridge the gap between skills requirement and skills availability.
14. for the survival and growth of the organisation and the nation.

TYPES OF TRAINING

Training may be broadly categorized into two types;
  (i) On-the-job Training.
  (ii) Off-the-job Training.

On- The-Job Training

The setting for on-the-job training depends on the nature of the responsibilities that the individual is expected to carry out. It can either be within the organisation itself or in the field. Some managers rely considerably on the value of learning through experience on the job. People learn best by actually doing things; the exercise needs to be planned and properly structured.

FOCUS ON INDIVIDUALISED TRAINING

1. In informal training, there is greater focus on the individual. His training and needs are the prime concern of those responsible for organizing the informal training programme.

2. The training activities and the specific tasks given to the trainer may be determined on the basis of his learning styles. The pace of learning can also be set in accordance with the learning ability of the individual. There, is therefore, considerable flexibility in the training programme.

3. Because of its focus on the individual, there is greater commitment and involvement of the trainer in the training process.

4. Individualized training provides opportunities to an individual to be creative and explore his own potentialities in a systematic way.

TRAINING NEEDS ASSESSMENT

WHY TRAINING NEEDS ARISE?

The gap between actual and expected performance behavior and attitude leads to emergence of training needs. But the main purpose of training is to attain that level of performance, behavior and attitude in employees, which leads to fulfillment of the objectives of any organisation. Thus, the training needs arise when there is a condition of requirements to move to a particular level of performance, behavior and attitude.

WHEN TO TRAIN?

- Gap in the level of performance, behavior and attitude
- Need for training arises
- Training needs assessed
- Training imparted as per assessment

WHEN DO TRAINING NEEDS ARISE?

(i) When existing level of performance, behavior and attitude of employees is not contributing to the success of the organisation.

(ii) When the level of motivation and morale is low among the employees in the organisation.

(ii) When employees themselves convey to the organisation through management about the key areas in which they are not much competent.

(iv) When there is need for updating the knowledge of employees as per the industry scenario. This is especially the case in relation to market scenario and legislations.

(v) When the organisation takes special interest in some employee, thereby intending his development, for promotion or succession purposes.

(vi) When business plan or business strategy demands new orientation in knowledge, skills, attitude or behavioral orientation, And when external changes have impact in the organisation.

WHOM TO TRAIN?

Training is imparted to employees for whom the training needs have been recognized. Training needs can arise for employees at all levels.

SOME PARCTICAL EXAMPLES

Training is imparted to a cricket team so that they are brought from the existing level of performance to the desired level of performance.

Training both technical and voice and accent, is imparted to the candidates joining any BPO industry.

Management students go through on-the-job summer training process before starting their careers in management.

Even nursery class teachers receive training before they are expected to develop young kids.

Pilots go through rigorous training before they earn their pilots license and assume the responsibility for the lives of passengers and crew.

Cadets are trained at special defense academies before joining the army. They are hardened to lead a disciplined life because they have to care of nation's security, often under the most arduous and dangers situations.

APPROACHES TO TRAINING NEED ASSESSMENT

What is required before one embarks on an exercise to assess training needs depends on the approach we choose to apply the process. Direct approach, Professional approach, Secret shopper approach, Buying Cooperatives, Public Seminars, Online learning and Consultants.

LEVELS OF TRAINING NEEDS

1. **Individual Level:** Every employee has **unique** needs owing to the particular combination of his job profile, educational and cultural background, experience and personality. Emphasis on individual needs assessment makes it possible to have development programmers that are tailored to individual needs aim at results that are visible and understandable to each individual concerned and for which he can feel responsible.

2. **Group and Team level:** To identify and meet needs, we also have to group employees for the following reasons; while some of their needs are individual and unique, other needs are common,

as mentioned above, employees do not work as isolated individuals, but in groups and teams; this brings out needs that could not be identified in dealing with each individual separately. Also, needs that concern relations and interaction with other employees often have to be treated through collective training and development? Therefore at the second level, we could deal with groups and teams of employees within an organisation.

3. **Organisation Level:** This level is particularly important for relating management development and training and needs to organisation systems, problems, diagnoses, objectives and performance improvement programmed. Typical organisation level management development needs are those related to organisational culture. Organisations that have developed a set of shared values, constituting their specific culture, tend to use management development programmers for strengthen this value system, in particular in training newly recruited and junior managers and staff members.

4. **Sectoral Level:** The definition of sectoral need may be quite meaningful if a sect oral development policy and the plan is being considered ,or if the sect oral body intend to alert the organisation in the sector to their management problem or to imbalance in the managerial manpower supply and demand, and provide service for dealing with these problems.

5. **Country (National) Level:** In similar event, we are often interested in common nationwide characteristics and need of the management pollution, in planning or suggesting country level programmed or in establishing national management Institute, centers, faculties or foundation. Typically, country level needs are examined by national surveys and studies. Often, these surveys are also used as sect oral breakdown differentiate between regions.

CHECK LIST FOR DESIGNING A TRAINING PROGRAMME

1. Who will be the Participants (Target group)?
2. What are the Objectives of the programmed?
3. What would be the content/ Coverage/ structure of programmed?
4. What is the Expected outcome of the programmed?
5. Who will be the faculty (Trainers)?
6. What would be the training Methods?
7. What would be the mechanism to monitor the application of training inputs by the participants?
8. What would be the Venue, Date and Timings of the Programmed?
9. What would be the programmed Scheduled?
10. What would be the sequence of coverage, Methodology of training, time and training aids to be used (Lesson/Session plan)?

CONCLUSION

Training and Development are the most Important tool for an organisation so that the organisation can sharpen the skills of the employee which is one of the most important aspects in today's competitive environment.

References

1. Retrieved from www./su.edu/hrmtraining
2. Retrieved from www.training and development. com
3. Gray Dessler, HRM prentice-Hall of India 187.
4. Hamblin, AC Evaluation &control of Training (New York, McGraw Hill, 1974) 6-7
5. Mitchell, W. Sijr (1984), wanted: professional management training need analysis.

Cross Cultural Transition: Opportunity and Challenges in HRM

Vijay Kulkarni

Director, Aditya Institute of Management, Pune

ABSTRACT

The development and success of an organisation as well as a country largely depends upon the creative skills and abilities of its human resources, in which training plays important role. Effective corporate governance mechanisms and strategies are commonly referred to as the area of management that deals with getting the best performance from employees within the organisation at hand. Whilst the activities involved in the management of people for their optimal performance have been carried out for generations, it is only relatively recently that attempts have been made to identify, describe and refine the practices of effective governance mechanisms and strategies. It explores the the impact of Globalization and liberalization on developing countries. Globalisation has imposed internal pressure and external pressure to bear with Cross Cultural Transition in HRM.

Keywords: *Cross cultural Transition, Performance, Human Resource Management*

INTRODUCTION

The rapid globalization of world markets has encouraged companies of all sizes and national origins to expand internationally. Globalization has been defined by the International Monetary Fund (IMF) as the increasing integration of economies around the world, particularly through trade and financial flows. (IMF, 2000) As economies become integrated issues emerge with regards to the benefits and costs of such integration and which outweighs the other.

Prof. Sklair (2000) state that the combination of the discourse of sustainable development with that of national and international competitiveness provides powerful weapons for the transnational capitalist class. In this context globalization is not a Western term but a "globalizing capitalist ideology," whose discourse and practices are necessary to stop the growing class polarization and ecological crises characteristic of this latest stage in the long history of capitalism.

Over the past 10 or 12 years, the term globalisation has gone from nowhere to be everywhere and now the notion of globalization has become attraction of business world.

India have an extended history of international trade going back centuries ago, their economies were until recently highly protected and controlled to a large extent. However after 1991 the scenario is changed and the Indian doors are opened for the foreign investments. There by the foreign Industries have come to India and automatically the employment opportunities have increased.

It has definitely opened itself to globalization especially as a result of changes in economic policies in the early 90's and will have to face increasing world competition given its commitments at the WTO.

The phenomenon of globalization has however affected given the large populations, big land mass and abundant resource bases, India has relied on indigenous capabilities to a large extent to develop a wide range of goods for their internal markets. Seventy-five percent of executives in multinational firms believed that their companies needed more employees with global leadership abilities; however, less than 8% of the companies had programs to address this shortage [Black, Morrison, & Gregersen, 1999, p.7].

GLOBALIZATION

This contemporary issue has been formulated differently by many academics while the basic notion that some cross-border trade and investment are happening between nations due to interdependency and an increasingly integrated international economic system, should be a starting point in developing any such paradigm. One could then argue about whether the concept is new and if not how does it differ from the old 'globalisation'? The main difference comes from the impact of technological progress and also from the idea of free trade with receding barriers promoting Ricardo's agenda of comparative advantage. The world's national economies are being redefined and interconnected at an unprecedented rate due to an increase in the mobility of capital as a consequence of deregulation, new communications and information technology.

Rosamond (1999) suggests that globalization can be a powerful component of the social construction of external context that, in turn, helps to legitimize certain sorts of policy. He notes that the term "globalization did not enter discourse until the mid to late 1980s. Rosamond (1999) points out that the concept of globalization has spread beyond the academic world and is frequently employed to signify worldwide economic changes of profound significance. Globalization is a term that is loosely defined; it can represent rapid changes in communication, transport and technology, or the integration of markets. Academics debate whether globalization is taking place or has already occurred, what the connection is to prosperity and problems, and the historical significance.

Encounters with Globalization

Some of the major impacts feared by nations due to globalisation are such as giving away of national sovereignty and some new forms of colonialism by MNCs, The decline of the State as a protector of individuals and groups and the rise of virtual states depending on investment and production abroad. This sort of argument is very common in India.

This paper shows the impact of globalisation on the formulation of two different styles of the management and implementation of public policy in relation to issues like privatization of State Owned Enterprises, government approaches to deal with FDI and technology policy and development. WTO rules and regulations, in other words, the State will have to give away some of its sovereignty on economic matters and international trade.

Foreign direct investment is the locomotive of globalisation and India unlike many other third world countries have a sizeable number of highly skilled workers as well as an enormous supply of low unskilled labour, their development are closely linked to similar sectors in which they have comparative advantage and therefore face similar challenges like other countries such as China.

Importance of HRM

Human beings are the most important resource in an organisation. A firm's success depends on the capabilities of its members. Most problems, challenges, opportunities and frustrations in an organisation are people related.

Human Resources Management is one of the toughest duties of a manager since humans differ in terms of attitudes, values, aspirations, motivations, assumptions, psychology, and life goals.

Looking at today's competitive world, managerial level staff will require more conceptual and strategic skills. Thus, managers should for example ensure a suitable, relevant and up-to-date training for specific skills of lower level employees.

Managers have to be proactive, able to anticipate technological developments and prepare their staff for whatever technological changes that might take place.

This will be a successful task only when the HRM itself is fully aware of those changes and has the means to deal with them.

HR managers have a number of roles to fulfill. They are the guardians of the key assets of the organisations. They are also counselor and protector of employees and directly responsible for productivity. The government, including the Ministry of Labor, expects HR managers not only to comply with labor laws, but also to promote harmony at the workplace; this will directly contribute to healthier and more attractive work environment. As a result, both job hunters and seekers will feel compelled to target such organisations in their search for new job opportunities.

The success or failure of HR depends also on the top management recognition of the importance of HRM and secondly on its commitment to assist HR to carry out its functions. Human Resources jobholders need capability, integrity and professionalism in order to succeed in the ever-changing environment. Globalisation has imposed internal pressure and external pressure to bear with Cross Cultural Transition in HRM.

GLOBALIZATION AND STRATEGY

The discussion of globalization and its many facets to a discussion of the costs and benefits to globalization discussion of "Globalization and Strategy" where the options for a multinational firm are introduced. This section begins with a discussion of the various strategies for global corporations. The four basic strategies are a multi-domestic strategy, an international strategy, a global strategy or a transnational strategy. A **multi-domestic strategy** is where a company has operations in more than one country. The goal of a multi domestic strategy is to optimize local competitive advantages, revenues, and profits. A **global strategy** is where a company has integrated operations in more than one country. A global strategy seeks to maximize worldwide performance through sharing and integration. An **international strategy** is where core competencies are centralized and other activities are decentralized. Finally a **transnational strategy** is a typically a global matrix that seeks to be both locally responsive and efficient. This strategy is based on the simultaneous attainment of location and experience curve economies, local responsiveness, and global learning.

In this section a recent article by Bartlett and Ghoshal (2003) is discussed. These authors present four types of managers for the transnational organisation. The four types of managers are the business manager, the country manager, the functional manager, and the corporate manager. This is dicussed in greater detail in the "Globalization and Strateygy" section. The survey goes on to introduce the factors that affect a corporation's strategy to invest abroad. Yip (1989) discusses four industry drivers that affect this decision: market drivers, cost drivers, government drivers and competitive drivers. **Market drivers** include the level of homogeneous needs, global customer base, available global channels, and transferable marketing. **Cost drivers** include economies of scale and scope, learning and experience curves, favorable logistics, differences in country costs and skills, and product development costs. **Governmental drivers** include favorable trade policies, compatible technical standards, and common marketing regulations. Finally, **competitive drivers** include the interdependence of countries and competitors who are global or becoming global. Lovelock and Yip (1996) apply this analysis to the service industry.

As we explore the opportunities of corporate strategies with regards to globalization Rugman (2000), adds a word of caution "a pure globalization strategy" that is typified by *high economic integration* and *low national responsiveness* will not always work in the

21st century. It is along these lines that he emphasizes a regional focus and discusses five lessons that have been learned as corporations go beyond national boundaries. The five lessons are (1) learn to deal with different cultures and be nationally responsive rather than assuming an integrated global market, (2) managers should develop network organisational competencies rather than relying on international divisions or global product divisions, (3) organisations should make alliances and foster cross-cultural awareness in senior managers (4) managers should develop analytical methods for assessing regional drivers of success, and (5) managers should "think regional, act local – and forget global." Rugman (2000) seems to see the benefits of globalization but with cautious optimism, and emphasizes a regional focus rather than a purely global strategy.

In summary, globalization has many facets and the decision to invest abroad is not a straightforward one. In fact, managers must weigh both the benefits and costs of a corporate strategy to determine the appropriate opportunities to exploit. Managers today face a dual challenge—managers need to figure out what the global strategy is and then must successfully implement the strategy. Many authors such as Rugman (2000) and Rugman and Moore (2001) seem to be leaning towards a regional focus rather than a global one. Finally, in determining the appropriate global strategy the existing organisational culture must be taken into consideration.

ORGANISATION CULTURE

Hofstede (1980) defines culture as "the collective programming of the mind which distinguishes the members of one category (i.e. national, regional, gender, age, social class, profession) of people from another. Organisational culture is different from national culture in that it is partial and voluntary where national culture is permanent and involuntary. Hofstede (1980) looks at organisational culture and defines six dimensions: process-oriented versus results-oriented cultures, job-oriented versus employee-oriented cultures, professional versus parochial cultures, open system versus closed system cultures, tightly versus loosely controlled cultures, pragmatic versus normative cultures. Process-oriented cultures are dominated by technical and bureaucratic routines while results-oriented cultures focus on outcomes. Job-oriented cultures only assume responsibility for the employees' job performance while employee-oriented cultures assume responsibility for the employees' well-being. In professional cultures members identify with their profession while in parochial cultures members identify with the organisation for which they work. In an open system outsiders are welcome while it is harder for newcomers to be admitted into closed system cultures. In tightly controlled organisations there is more formality and punctuality while loosely controlled organisations are more flexible. Finally, in pragmatic cultures organisations are more flexible with customers while normative cultures are more rigid.

Once the organisational culture of an organisation is assessed, top management should decide whether to optimize the existing culture or attempt to change it. If the decision is made to change the existing culture, a cost benefit analysis should first be considered. Changing an organisation's culture requires appealing to feelings are well as intellect; gaining support from key management and employees; adapting new functions, departments, locations, and tasks, as well as recruitment, training and promotion.

Hofstede (1980) proposed that structure should follow culture. The purpose of an organisation's structure is to co-ordinate activities. The best structure at any given moment depends on the company's people, resources, and goals. The integration of organisations across national borders requires managers to have insight into organisational structures, leadership styles, motivation patterns, and training and development models as they relate to organisational and national culture.

HR AND GLOBALISED CULTURE

The Human Resource management is globalisation oriented when each employee is able to (and expected to) grasp, and adapt to, conceptual and operational realities at different levels and in different cultures.

1. The new approach of HR is to emphasize new mindsets and new ways of thinking about business instead of sticking to policies and bureaucratic patterns. HR professionals should and must focus on cultural change, and the development of human capital, especially in international organisations. 'Think globally. Act locally".

2. HR should sponsor a model of change, which will help the employees adapt to and be comfortable with changes. Here, a lot of question may arise, such as: How do we decide which The first corner stone to achieve is the development of new initiatives, programs and agendas. Human Resources must move beyond being the "police of policy" and "regulatory guard". Instead, HR must be the pioneers in assisting the organisations achieve results, especially by helping employees to enhance their capabilities to ensure organisational objectives are met.

3. The future of HR depends on its ability to align HR with the changes that are happening in the workplace and the economy. New models of competitiveness are needed so that organisations can better service their customers. Consequently HR must be the champions to help gear employees to provide added value.

4. The practice to be transformed and which should be kept for purpose of continuity? How do we change and learn rapidly? How do we honor the past yet change the future? How do we capture the hearts and minds of employees?

HUMAN RESOURCE MANAGEMENT: THE CHALLENGES

Human resource challenges that face today's managers may be categorized according to their primary focus: the environment, the organisation; or the individual. Firms that deal with these challenges effectively are likely to outperform those that do not.

A. Environmental Challenges

Environmental challenges refer to forces external to the firm that are largely beyond management's control but influence organisational performance. They include: rapid change, the Internet revolution, workforce diversity, globalization, legislation, evolving work and family roles, and skill shortages and the rise of the service sector.

B. Organisational Challenges

Organisational challenges refer to concerns that are internal to the firm. However, they are often a byproduct of environmental forces because no firm operates in a vacuum. These issues include: competitive position (cost, quality, and distinctive capability), decentralization, downsizing, organisational restructuring, self-managed work teams, small businesses, technology, outsourcing, and organisational culture.

Organisational culture is a particularly important element. Culture is the basic assumptions and beliefs shared by members of the organisation that express themselves through the rules, norms, dominant values, philosophy, and climate. Firms that regularly make adjustments to these elements to match environmental changes are likely to outperform those whose culture is rigid and unresponsive to external factors.

C. Individual Challenges

Human resource issues at the individual level address concerns that are most pertinent to decisions involving specific employees. These issues almost always reflect what is happening in the larger organisation. How individuals are treated also is likely to have an effect on organisational issues. For instance, if many key employees leave a firm to join its competitor, it will affect the competitive posture of the firm. The individual issues include matching people and organisation, ethics and social responsibility, productivity, empowerment, brain drain, and job insecurity.

II. PLANNING & IMPLEMENTING STRATEGIC HR POLICIES

To be successful, firms must closely align their HR strategies and programs (tactics) with environmental opportunities, business strategies, and the organisation's unique characteristics and distinctive competence. A firm with a poorly defined HR strategy or a business strategy that does not explicitly incorporate human resources is likely to lose ground to its competitors. Similarly, a firm may have a well-articulated HR strategy yet fail if its HR tactics/policies do not help to implement its HR strategy effectively.

A. The Benefits of Strategic HR Planning

Formulating HR strategies and establishing programs to implement them is strategic human resource planning. Successful HR strategic planning provides many benefits for the company, including (1) encouraging proactive rather than reactive behavior, (2) explicit communication of company goals, (3) stimulation of critical thinking and ongoing examination of assumptions, (4) identification of gaps between current situation and future vision, (5) encouragement of line managers' participation, (6) identification of HR constraints and opportunities, and (7) creation of common bonds.

B. The Challenges of Strategic HR Planning

In developing HR strategy, organisations face several important challenges including (1) maintaining a competitive advantage, (2) reinforcing overall business strategy, (3) avoiding excessive concentration on day-to-day problems, (4) developing HR strategies suited to unique organisational features, (5) coping with the environment, (6) securing management commitment, (7) translating the strategic plan into action, (8) combining intended and emergent strategies, and (9) accommodating change.

C. Strategic HR Choices

Human resource strategies, which are implemented through HR activities and programs, may affect the performance of the business. The options that a firm has available in designing its HR system are its strategic HR choices. Figure 1-5 shows a sampling, rather than an exhaustive list, of strategic HR choices. Firms may fall near the left, right, or middle of such a continuum.

III. SELECTING HR STRATEGIES TO INCREASE FIRM PERFORMANCE

No HR Strategy is "good" or "bad" in and of itself. The success of HR strategies depends on the situation or context in which they are used. In other words, an HR strategy's effect on firm performance is always dependent on how well it fits with some of the factors. *Fit* refers to the consistency or compatibility between HR strategies and other important aspects of the organisation.

A. Fit with Organisational Strategies

Organisational strategies may be examined at two levels: corporate and business.

Corporate strategy refers to the mix of businesses a corporation decides to hold and the flow of resources among those businesses. This involves decisions pertaining to acquisition, divestment, diversification, and growth. At one end of the spectrum is the evolutionary business strategy; at the other end is the steady-state strategy.

Business unit strategies refer to those established by firms or autonomous units of the corporation. Well-known business strategies were formulated by Porter (overall cost leadership strategy, differentiation business strategy, and focus strategy) and Miles and Snow (defender strategy and prospector strategy).

Strategies for Changes

1. The first corner stone to achieve is the development of new initiatives, programs and agendas. Human Resources must move beyond being the "police of policy" and "regulatory guard". Instead, HR must be the pioneers in assisting the organisations achieve results, especially by helping employees to enhance their capabilities to ensure organisational objectives are met.

2. The future of HR depends on its ability to align HR with the changes that are happening in the workplace and the economy. New models of competitiveness are needed so that organisations

can better service their customers. Consequently HR must be the champions to help gear employees to provide added value.

3. The new approach of HR is to emphasize new mindsets and new ways of thinking about business instead of sticking to policies and bureaucratic patterns. HR professionals should and must focus on cultural change, and the development of human capital, especially in international organisations. 'Think globally. Act locally".

4. HR should sponsor a model of change, which will help the employees adapt to and be comfortable with changes. Here, a lot of question may arise, such as: How do we decide which practices to be transformed and which should be kept for purpose of continuity? How do we change and learn rapidly? How do we honor the past yet change the future? How do we capture the hearts and minds of employees?

Reshaping HR

- The changes which affect the HR performance in cross culture are:
- HR should not act as a therapy clinic
- HR must measure their outcomes
- HR should take in to consideration the cross cultural challanges
- HR practices must create value by increasing the organisation's intellectual capital
- HR must attempt to make employees committed to achieving organisational goals, and not merely to make employees happy
- HR practices must be aligned with company strategies
- HR must champion the needs and development of employees and yet become partners in the business
- HR should receive corporate priority. Business firms should be ready to boost their investment in staff development; this is rewarding on the long run if its properly implemented
- HR should focus on the skills to be acquired taking into consideration the understanding of the international dimensions of political, economic, social and cultural development.

- HR should promote the collaboration between public training institutions, the universities and the public sector in terms of planning an effective training program

CONCLUSION

Actually, the nation's capacity to face the challenges of globalization and industrialization of business towards the 21st century depends heavily on the human resources.

Firms have the capital, technology and human resources; but the HR is the one who can help facing the challenges of business globalization. Capital can be generated. So can technology. But the human resources are needed to propel the organisation and the nation through the coming challenges with encouragement and motivation in the competitive era of the globalization. The economic life is hard despite the fact that reforms and globalisation have created various new opportunities and also challenge to cope up with imposed internal pressure and external pressure to bear with Cross Cultural Transition in HRM.

References

Bartlett, Christopher A.; Ghoshal, Sumantra (2003). "What is a Global Manager?" Harvard Business Review, (2003), 81 8, 101.

Black, Stewart. Morrison, Allen, & Gregersen, Hal, (1999). Global Explorers: The Next Generation of Leaders. New York: Routledge.

Hofstede, G. 1980. *Culture's Consequences*. London: Sage.

International Monetary Fund, (2000), Globalization: Threat or Opportunity? corrected January 2002 (Washington)

Leslie, Sklair. (Paperback- Apr 11 2002). Globalisation: Capitalism and its Alternatives

Rugman, Alan and Moore, Karl, (2001) "The Myths of Globalization" Ivey Business Journal 66 (1) September, 64-68.

Yip, George. (1989). "Global strategy in a world of nations?" *Slone Management Review* 30, 29-41.

Performance Analysis of Routing Protocols for Application Based Clustered Mobile Ad-hoc Network

Ashish Saxena and Vishnu Mishra

SRITM College, Jabalpur

ABSTRACT

Mobile ad hoc networks by their nature are highly adaptive systems that can come into existence on an as needed basis. They can grow, reduce in size, fragment, and dismantle as desired. The dynamic and very flexible nature of ad hoc networks can be taken to a further level of sophistication by allowing these networks to retune and adapt themselves according to prevailing network conditions. Mobile wireless ad-hoc networks can be deployed amongst them, allowing these devices to communicate data with each other. Routing protocols of mobile ad-hoc networks differ from the existing internet protocols which are designed for the fixed structure based wireless networks. MANET protocols have to face high challenges due to dynamically changing of topologies, low transmission power and asymmetric links. Due to link instability, node mobility and frequently changing topologies routing becomes one of the core issues in MANETs. Many researchers are still working on the developments of MANET routing protocols. This paper presents both a review of current MANET and a new MANET namely Application based Clustered Mobile Ad-hoc Network (AC-MANET) for the four dominant protocols (namely AODV, DSR, OLSR and TORA). In AC-MANET the network into cluster on the basis of application such as ftp, http, e-mail and remote login .The performance of these four routing protocols has been analyzed using OPNET 14.0.

Keywords: *AC-MANET, MANET, Routing Protocols*

INTRODUCTION

Mobile Ad-hoc Network (MANET) is a collection of independent mobile nodes that can communicate to each other via radio waves. The mobile nodes that are in radio range of each other can directly communicate, whereas others needs the aid of intermediate nodes to route their packets. Ad hoc networks are networks are not (necessarily) connected to any static (i.e. wired) infrastructure. An ad-hoc network is a LAN or other small network, especially one with wireless connections, in which some of the network devices are part of the network only for the duration of a communications session or, in the case of mobile or portable devices, while in some close proximity to the rest of the network.

Mobile ad hoc networks by their nature are highly adaptive systems that can come into existence on an as needed basis. They can grow, reduce in size, fragment, and dismantle as desired. The dynamic and very flexible nature of ad hoc networks can be taken to a further level of sophistication by allowing these networks to retune and adapt themselves according to prevailing network conditions. Ad hoc networks are very much about doing what is needed, when it is needed. In a mobile ad hoc network a node may find itself in a small fast-moving network carrying limited amounts of traffic that suddenly merges with a large network, which results in a huge increase in activity, and hence traffic throughput, at the node.

Ad-hoc nodes need to be able to deal with these types of changing patterns. One way of doing this is to have as much flexibility as possible within an ad hoc node so as to allow the node to reconfigure in line with the prevailing network conditions and demands.

High levels of flexibility can be enabled by treating all parameters associated with the ad hoc node as

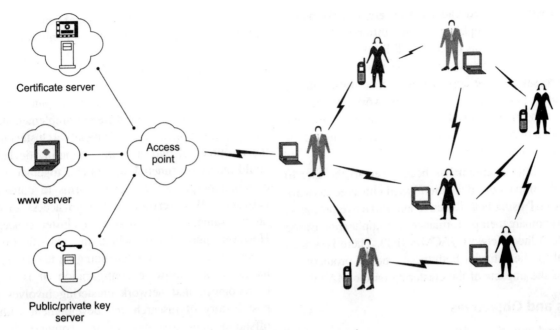

Fig. 1 Ad-Hoc wireless network

variables. So, for example, the routing protocol in use, the medium access control (MAC) scheme in use, as well as the individual parameters of these and any other layers are all treated as variables that can be configured and reconfigured as and when needed. It should be emphasized at this point that this article focuses on very dynamic and mobile ad hoc networks rather than on more spatially immobile and resource-constrained networks such as sensor networks.

MANET stands for Mobile Ad hoc Network. It is a decentralized autonomous wireless system which consists of free nodes. MANET sometimes called mobile mesh network, is a self configurable wireless network. A MANET consists of mobile nodes, a router with multiple hosts and wireless communication devices. The wireless communication devices are transmitters, receivers and smart antennas. These antennas can be of any kind and nodes can be fixed or mobile. The term node referred to as, which are free to move arbitrarily in every direction. These nodes can be a mobile phone, laptop, personal digital assistance, MP3 player and personal computer. These nodes can be located in cars, ships, airplanes or with people having small electronic devices. Nodes can connect each other randomly and forming arbitrary topologies. Nodes communicate to each other and also forward packets to neighbor nodes as a router. The ability of self configuration of these nodes makes them more suitable for urgently required network connection. For example, in disaster hit areas where there is no communication infrastructure. It is greatly desired to have a quick communication infrastructure.

MANET is the quick remedy for any disaster situation. MANET is a spontaneous network. It is useful when dealing with wireless devices in which some of the devices are part of the network only for the duration of a communication session. The MANET working group (WG) within the Internet Engineering Task Force (IETF) works specifically on developing IP routing protocols topologies. To improve mobile routing and interface definition standards for use within the Internet protocol suite. After huge research work on MANET, still it does not have a complete form of Internet based standards. The identification of experimental Request for Comments (RFCs) since 2003 is used. In these RFCs the questions are unanswered concerning of implementation or deployment of these routing protocols. But these proposed algorithms are identified as a trial technology and there are high chances that they will be developed into a standard.

Extensive research work in this area is progress with major studies on different routing protocols such as Dynamic Source Routing (DSR), AODV. Temporarily Ordered Routing Algorithm (TORA) and Optimized Link State Routing (OLSR) . Along with the standardization of routing and interface solutions for mobile networking support through Internet Engineering Task Force (IETF) MANET Working Group WG.

Problem Statement

Previously the works done on performance comparison of protocols and the analysis of cluster based routing protocols. The Cluster Based Routing Protocol (i.e. CBRP) is studied under the different performance parameters and comparing it with different Proactive and Reactive protocols for MANET. Routing in wireless mobile ad-hoc networks should be time efficient and resource saving. The approach to reduce traffic during the routing process is to divide the network into clusters has also been introduced by various authors. But the evaluation of Application based Clustered Mobile Adhoc Network is never done.

Very little attention has been given to the fact to study the impact of application based clustered network in MANET using both Reactive and Proactive protocols and to compare their performances for Application Based Mobile Adhoc Network (ACMANET). There is a need to analyze the behavior both these types of protocols as well as the impacts of the clustering on the MANETs.

Aims and Objectives

Aims and objectives of this paper work are summarized as follow

- The study focus on analysis of protocols in MANET & ACMANET and its effect.
- Simulating the MANET & ACMANET using Proactive and Reactive routing protocols.
- Analyzing the effects of application base clustering in the light of Network load, throughput and End to End delay, Data Dropped, Media Access Delay, Retransmission Attempts in MANET & AC-MANET.
- Comparing the results of both application based network and application based clustered network for Proactive and Reactive protocols to analyze which of these two types of protocols is more efficient.
- Determine best protocol for respective type of network.

Applications of MANETs

The properties of MANET make it so much favorable that would bring so many benefits. There are so many research areas in MANET which is under studies now. The most important area is vehicle to vehicle communication. Where the vehicle would communicate with each other, keeping a safe distance between them as well as collision warnings to the drivers. MANET can be used for automated battlefield and war games. One of the most important areas where MANETs are applied is emergency services such as disaster recovery and relief activities, where traditional wired network is already destroyed. There are so many other application areas such as entertainment, education and commercial where MANETs are playing their role for connecting people.

CLUSTERED NETWORK

The word "cluster" is used broadly in computer networking to refer to a number of different implementations of shared computing resources. Typically, a cluster integrates the resources of two or more computing devices (that could otherwise function separately) together for some common purpose. Web server farms (a collection of networked Web servers, each with access to content on the same site) function as a cluster conceptually. However, purists may debate the classification of a server farm as a cluster, depending on the details of the hardware and software configuration. It is important to recognize that network clustering involves a long past history of research and development with many offshoots and variations. In any complex distributed system of nodes, clustering of nodes into groups results in simplification of addressing and management of the nodes and also yields better performance since details about the remote parts of the distributed system can be handled in an aggregate manner. Thus, imposition of a hierarchical organisation is beneficial for the management of a complex system, and results in scalability of operations. The wired Internet, for example, cannot be managed without hierarchical addressing and management. Essential services like routing are highly scalable owing to this hierarchical organisation.

Clustering methods allow fast connection and also better routing and topology management of MANET (mobile ad hoc networks). A survey on clustering techniques for MANET is presented. Some preliminary concepts that form the basis for the development of clustering algorithms are introduced. These related issues have to do with the network topology, routing schemes, graph partitioning and mobility algorithms. A successful method for dealing with the maintenance of mobile ad hoc networks is by partitioning the network into clusters. In this way the network becomes more manageable. It must be clear though that a clustering technique is not a routing protocol. Clustering is a method which aggregates nodes into groups. These groups are contained by the network and they are known as clusters. A cluster is basically a subset of nodes of the network that satisfies a certain property. Clusters are analogous to cells in a cellular network. However, the cluster organisation of an ad hoc network cannot be achieved offline as in fixed networks. Clustering presents several advantages for the medium access layer and the network layer in MANET.

The implementation of clustering schemes allows a better performance of the protocols for the Medium Access Control (MAC) layer by improving the spatial reuse, throughput, scalability and power consumption. On the other hand, clustering helps improve routing at the network layer by reducing the size of the routing tables and by decreasing transmission overhead due to the update of routing tables after topological changes occur. Clustering helps aggregate topology information since the number of nodes of a cluster is smaller than the number of nodes of the entire network. Therefore, each node only needs to store a fraction of the total network routing information.

AC-MANET (Application based Clustered Mobile Ad-hoc Network)

AC-MANET is type of mobile ad-hoc network which is divided into number of clusters. In this type of network each cluster uses different application. Each application is run by a host which provides service to their respective mobile node. These different clusters combine to form an AC-MANET.

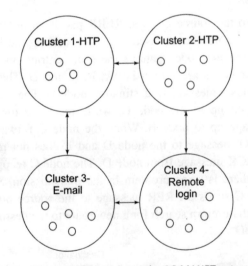

Fig. 2 The above figure shows the AC-MANET network.

In AC-MANET, the node in each cluster can communicate with the node which shares the same application. Two node having different applications can't communicate with each other but in case when two nodes of same application are out of range of each other. These two nodes can communicate which each other through the third node (or nodes) which may or may not be of same cluster or application i.e. the node having different application can only forward data towards destination. So to enable this type of network to communicate a routing protocol is needed.

For example, considering the situation after earthquake various small ad-hoc networks can be deployed easily. Let the ad-hoc networks are using different applications such as FTP, HTTP, Remote Login, E-mail etc. then the nodes which are out of range with each other can communicate through various nodes. These different application clustered network combine to form an ad-hoc network.

DSR (Dynamic Source Routing)

Dynamic Source Routing Protocol is a reactive routing protocol and is called on demand routing protocol. It is a source routing protocol that is why it is a simple and an efficient protocol. It can be used in multi hop wireless ad hoc networks. The DSR network is totally self organizing and self configuring. The protocols is just compose of two mechanisms i.e. route discovery and route maintenance.

The DSR regularly updates its route cache for the sake of new available easy routes. If some new available routes were found the node will directs the packet to that route. The packet has to know about the route direction. So the information about the route was set in the packet to reach its destination from its sender. This information was kept in the packet to avoid periodic findings it has the capability to find out its route by this way.

DSR has two basic mechanisms for its operation i.e. route discovery and route maintenance. In route discovery, it has two messages i.e. route request (RREQ) and route reply (RREP). When a node wishes to send a message to a specific destination, it broadcast the RREQ packet in the network. The neighbor nodes in the broadcast range receive this RREQ message and add their own address and again rebroadcast it in the network. This RREQ message if reached to the destination, so that is the route to the specific destination. In the case if the message did not reached to the destination then the node which received the RREQ packet will look that previously a route used for the specific destination or not. Each node maintains its route cache which is kept in the memory for the discovered route. The node will check its route cache for the desired destination before rebroadcasting the RREQ message. By maintaining the route cache at every node in the network, it reduces the memory overhead which is generated by the route discovery procedure. If a route is found in that node route cache then it will not rebroadcast the RREQ in the whole network. So it will forward the RREQ message to the destination node. The first message reached to the destination has full information about the route. That node will send a RREP packet to the sender having complete route information. This route is considered the shortest path taken by the RREQ packet. The source node now has complete information about the route in its route cache and can starts routing of packets.

Figure 6 shows the route discovery procedure. Here we have four nodes i.e. A, B, C and D such as node A is the source and node D is destination. When node A wish to send a data packet to the node D, It will first check its route cache that whether it has direct route to node D or not. If node A does not have a direct route to node D, then it will broadcast a RREQ message in the network. The neighbor node B will get the RREQ message. First node B will check its route cache that

whether it have a direct route to the destination node D or not, If it finds a route to the destination node D. So it will send a RREP message to the source node A. In the reply of that message the source node A will start sending the data packets (DP) on the discovered route. If it didn't discover the route from node B to node D so it forwards the message RREQ to the next node C and store the route AB in the cache. The process is going on until the RREQ message reached to destination node D. The destination node D caches the routes AB, BC and CD in its memory and sends a RREP message to the source node A.

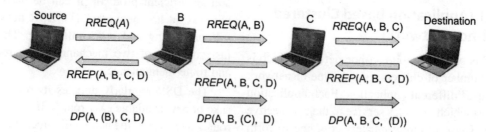

Fig. 3 Route discovery procedure in MANET using DSR

The next mechanism is the route maintenance. The route maintenance uses two kind of messages i.e. route error (RERR) and acknowledgement (ACK). The messages successfully received by the destination nodes send an acknowledgement ACK to the sender. Such as the packets transmitted successfully to the next neighbors nodes gets acknowledgement. If there is some problem in the communication network a route error message denoted by RERR is transmitted to the sender, that there is some problem in the transmission. In other words the source didn't get the ACK packet due to some problem.

So the source gets the RERR packet in order to re initiate a new route discovery. By receiving the RERR message the nodes remove the route entries. In figure 7 four nodes are shown i.e. A, B, C and D. The node A sends a message to destination node D. The message goes on up to the node C, while receiving the ACK message up to node B. When the node C forward the RREQ message to the node D and it does not receive the ACK message from node D. The node C recognizes that there is some problem in the transmission. So the node C sends a RRER message to the source node A. Which in return search for a new route to the destination node D.

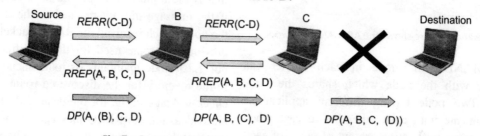

Fig. 7 Route maintenance procedure in MANET using DSR

References

- Hassain M. Amar, Youssef MohamedI., Zahra Mohamed M.(2006), "Evaluation of Ad hoc Routing Protocols in Real Simulation Environments", Electronics and Electrical Communications Department, Faculty of Engineering, Al-ajar University Cairo, Egypt, 288 – 293

- Bertocchi, F, Bergamo P, Mazzini G, Zorzi M, (2003), "Performance Comparison of Routing Protocols for Ad hoc Networks",

DI, University of Ferrara, Italy, 1-5, 2,1033 – 1037, 2

- MANET (Mobile Ad-hoc Network), Retrieved From http://www.ietf.org/rfc/rfc2501.txt
- RahmanMd. Anisur, Islam Md. Shohidul, Talevski, A. (2009), "Performance Measurement of Various Routing Protocols in Adhoc Network". Proceedings of the International Multi-Conference of Engineers and Computer Scientists.
- Usop, Abdullah Azizol, "Performance Evaluation of AODV, DSDV & DSR Routing Protocol in Grid Environment", IJCSNS International Journal of Computer Science and Network Security, 7.
- Opnet Technologies, Inc. "Opnet Simulator," Internet: www.opnet.com,
- Misra, Rajiv and Manda, C. R. (2007), "Performance Comparison of AODV/DSR On-demand Routing Protocols for Ad hoc Networks in Constrained Situation", Indian Institute of Technology, Kharagpur (India).
- Talooki, Vahid Nazari & Ziarati, Koorush (2006), "Performance Comparison of Routing Protocols For Mobile Ad hoc Networks", Dept. of Computer Science and Engineering, School of Engineering, Shiraz University,

Data Warehouse Model for University

Dharmendra Badal[1], Rakesh Kumar Arora[2] and Manoj Kumar Gupta[3]
[1]Faculty and Incharge (Computer Division), Bundelkhand University, Jhansi
[2,3]Research Scholar, Bundelkhand University, Jhansi

ABSTRACT

This paper focuses on various aspects of implementing a data warehouse for a University where large amount of data is being maintained to provide supports to different individuals. The different types information that need to be maintained in any University includes number of courses provided by the University for students, number of students enrolled in different programs, number of employees at different levels, In-house material production, inventory management etc. Data was collected over the years in the form of ledgers, manuscripts, data books and databases from various sources/departments of the University and was used for certain needs through the manual system.

With the advent of technology data warehousing became an important strategy to integrate heterogeneous information sources in organisations and to enable online analytical processing. The Data Warehouse concept evolved from the growing competitive need to quickly analyze the business/institutional information. Data Warehouse (DW) is a repository of integrated institutional data for efficient querying and analysis. It is a copy of transaction data specifically designed to give decision makers instant access to information through the usage of query and reporting tools, enabling knowledge tools such as analysis, forecasting and trending. The aim of this paper is to motivate and propose the concept of a Data Warehouse in University. This paper proposes Data Warehouse model for University along with its architecture, requirements engineering, use of the University's DW, applications which can be thought of, various users and their roles, the security and quality issues.

Keywords: *Data Warehouse, Legacy Systems, Operational Systems, OLAP, Data Mining, Data Security*

INTRODUCTION

According to www.educause.edu, The management of its data is very important issue for any organisation. In India, since two decades, most of the Universities & other Educational Institutions have relied upon Information technology to run or assist the key functions of the University with their legacy systems. There are several legacy systems already in place at various departments of the University like computerized systems for the students registration, evaluation (for continuous evaluation as well as for the semester wise examination), inventory and assets management, finance department, planning department and for its affiliate schools, centers and institutes. The University also provides support to the students through its website. Older technologies and the legacy systems collected the data without analyzing them. The data stored using the legacy systems was limitedly used and there is an untapped value in those large database. Current data warehousing and business intelligence systems are light years ahead of the earlier ones. They provide complex, versatile, multidimensional time series analysis, rather than just data collection and viewing.

WHY DATA WAREHOUSE IS REQUIRED FOR UNIVERSITY?

According to docs.oracle.com, A Data Warehouse is huge data repository, which stores integrated information from various databases, for efficient querying and analysis. A Data Warehouse is a subject-oriented, integrated, time-varying, non-volatile collection of data in support of the management's decision-making process (Arun K. Pujari, 2001). The information is extracted from heterogeneous sources as it is generated or updated. The information is then translated into a common data model and integrated with existing data at the data warehouse. Placing an adhoc query to the data warehouse whose data came from heterogeneous sources can retrieve complex information. Key advantages of Data Warehousing for Universities include:

- Immediate information delivery for the complex queries.
- Since query execution does not involve data translation and communication with remote sources, complex queries can be executed easily and efficiently.
- Data integration across the University.
- End users can use a single data model and query language.
- System design becomes simples. For example, there is no need to perform query optimization over heterogeneous sources, a very difficult problem faced by other approaches.
- Information sources may be unreliable and may purge data. On the other hand, information at the warehouse is under the control of the warehouse users; it can be stored safely and reliably for as long as necessary.
- Future, vision from historical trends.
- End user empowerment.

According to msdn.microsoft.com, unlike the operational systems that are being updated throughout the day, the Data Warehouse is a separate system that stores information by subject category for the sole purpose of efficient data retrieval. It places all the data files into a central repository, creating a multidimensional view of the business based on transactions. Data Warehouses uses a process called demoralization and summarization to build linkages, or relationships, between data to provide a multidimensional view. It more comprehensive view of any transaction by extracting the data from various related data files.

In addition to the Data Warehouse, the OLAP engine is a core technology to a successful system. An on-line analytical processing engine is an optimized query generator that understands how the Data Warehouse is constructed, and thus can retrieve the right information from the warehouse to accommodate. The features of the University's Data Warehouse to be considered are:

- Speed and flexibility
- Availability
- Efficiency
- Interoperability
- Portability
- Robustness
- Scalability
- Expandability
- Respond to change to cope with time dependence and variance
- Query Performance
- Security
- Data Quality

Every University needs a view of its performance across all its operations. Yet vital performance data is usually spread across multiple operational systems running on various IT platforms, in different departments/divisions with different physical data structures and different identification schemes. Many organisations/ institutions use Data Warehouse to store a copy of data drawn from operational systems using Extract, Transform and Load (ETL) technology. Such Data Warehouse present data on demand to the users and analysts via business intelligence.

MODELS TO IMPLEMENT DATA WAREHOUSE

There are basically four different models to implement a University Data Warehouse:

- **Custom-Built Enterprises Data Warehouse**

  This is specifically designed for a given enterprises model and often inflexible to change. Solutions are available from major database like ORACLE, SYBASE, IBM and Netezza [4].

- **ERP Data Warehouse**

  Many ERP vendors now include a packaged Data Warehouse in their product suite, but these are usually focused around operational reporting from the ERP package. They are most often custom-built Data Warehouse designed by the vendor from their ERP package. Solutions are available from ERP packaged Data Warehouse like SAP Business Warehouse, PeopleSoft Enterprises Warehouse and Seibel Analytical and Business Data Warehouse [4].

- **Adaptive Enterprises Data Warehouse**

  These are readily adaptable to changes in the business model, a new breed of Data Warehouse. Solutions are available from Kalido 8 [4].

- **Virtual Data Warehouse**

  A number of approaches have used advanced messaging technologies to link together disparate data sources into a Virtual Data Warehouse. Solutions are available from IBM Federated DB2 etc [4].

REQUIREMENTS FOR IMPLEMENTING DATA WAREHOUSE

The various requirements must be considered before looking into the actual design and the architecture of the University Data Warehouse. The requirements can be broadly categorized into functional, information and Interface [7]. The various types of requirements along with their attributes are being defined below:

- **Functional Requirements**
  - ○ Data Staging (Data Extraction, Data Transformation, Data Cleansing, Data Loading, Data Acquisition and Architecture requirements).
  - ○ Data Management (Administration/ Maintenance. Data Backup and Recovery, Metadata Management)
  - ○ Front End Requirements (Viewing, Data Export, Layout, Searching, Roll Out)
- **Information Requirements**
  - ○ Data Sources (Operational Systems, Other legacy system, data mapping, Other sources)
  - ○ Query/Reporting Requirements (Reporting tools, Data Mining, EIS/MIS Data Visualization, AD hoc Queries)
  - ○ OLAP requirements (Performance indicators, Measures, Analysis Dimensions, Conformed Analysis Dimensions, Time Dimensions, Changing Dimension Strategies, Data Cubes)
- **Interface Requirements**
  - ○ Graphical user interface (GUI)
  - ○ Database Interface
  - ○ External Interface

According to www.gantthead.com, Data from external sources may also be fed into system. After extracting data from multiple operational databases and from external sources the next step is concerned with cleansing, transforming and integrating this data for loading into the Data Warehouse server and of course, with periodically refreshing the Warehouse. The four processes from extraction to loading are often referred to collectively as Data Staging.

Metadata, "Data about Data". It is useful to have a central information repository to tell users and the query tools what's in the Data Warehouse, where to find it,

who is authorized to access it and what summaries have been recalculated.

Query tools

According to www.researchjournals.co.uk, These usually include end-user interface for posing questions to the database, in a process called OLAP. They also include automated tools for uncovering patterns in the data, often referred to as Data Mining Uses of the Data Warehouse.

The Data Warehouse provides information to staff in all major areas of the University. This includes data related to Academic Affairs, Divisions, Finance and Administrative Services, Payroll, Human Resources, Student Registration, Alumni and Development, Internal Audit, Student Support, Evaluation, Library, Assets, Centre's and Institutes within University. In addition to reporting services, the information in the Data Warehouse may be used by several web applications that provide inter-active services to the academic, non-academic staff and students.

Refreshing of the Data in the Data Warehouse

The type of data determines the extract frequency. Financial data may be extracted daily. Payroll data may be extracted biweekly. Student data may be extracted weekly. Certain student variables should be updated daily - admissions, names, addresses and phone numbers. Census data are frozen at appropriate census dates. Evaluation data would be updated daily at the time of declaration of the results otherwise may be though of updating weekly [1][5].

DATA SECURITY

The Data Warehouse contains confidential and sensitive University's data. Therefore necessary efforts like the physical security, access control through some software with password protection, encryption etc. may be thought in order to protect the data. Unauthorized users should be restricting to use the data [6].

Responsibilities and Confidentiality

In order to use the data in the Data Warehouse, the users must have proper authorization. Authorization means that users have the authority to use the data and the responsibility to share stewardship of the data with the other users of the collection. Once authorized, you can access the data that you need to do your job. All authorized users are cautioned, however, that they are entrusted to sue the data they retrieve from Warehouse with care. Confidential data should not be released to others except for those with a "legitimate need to know".

Querying Data with Security Restrictions

Each authorized user may be assigned with privileges depending upon their designations and the usage and as per these assigned privileges they are permitted to access the data.

Remote Access

Remote access may be provided to the authorized users who are sitting in the various departments, via the Internal by establishing a secure connection. Encryption and Decryption should be taken into consideration.

SUCCESS FACTORS

In order to support the data warehousing facility the University should:

- Appoint the technical staff or data administration activities, maintenance and for providing services to the staff for efficient use.
- Some Committee/task force may be appointed in order to look after the coordination activities and enforcing standards.
- The technical team should be able to ensure the data quality, which includes the intrinsic information quality, representational information quality, accessibility information quality, security and the ease of access to the users.

- There should be an availability of the data dictionary with the technical team.
- Understanding of client's needs and a determination to meet those needs should be considered.

References

- Pujari, Arun K., "Data Mining Techniques", University Press 2001.
- Retrieved from www.educause.edu › ... › Volume 28, Number 4, 2005.
- Retrieved from www.anvari.net/23_BI/turban_ bi2e_tif_ch02.doc
- Retrieved from *crpit.com/confpapers/ crpitv68sahama.pdf*
- Retrieved from *en.wikipedia.org/wiki/**Database***
- Retrieved from *msdn.microsoft.com/en-us/library/ aa902672(v=sql.80).aspx*
- Retrieved from www.peterindia.net/ DataWarehousingView.html
- Retrieved from www.gantthead.com › Processes
- Retrieved from *dssresources.com/papers/features/ langseth/langseth02082004.html*
- Retrieved from www.edbt.org/Proceedings/2009-StPetersburg/.../p0001-Dayal.pdf
- Retrieved from www.researchjournals.co.uk/ documents/.../RJEBI_Vol1_Article_09.p...
- Retrived fromsonatech.academia.edu/.../ **DATA_MINING_**CONCEPTS_AND_...

Cloud Computing: Architecture, Security Issues and Challenges

Dharmendra Badal[1], Rakesh Kumar Arora[2] and Manoj Kumar Gupta[3]
[1]Faculty and Incharge (Computer Division), Bundelkhand University, Jhansi
[2,3]Research Scholar, Bundelkhand University, Jhansi

ABSTRACT

According to www.e-technologymanagement.com, Cloud computing technology has been a new buzzword in the IT industry and expecting a new horizon for coming world. It is a style of computing which is having dynamically scalable virtualized resources provided as a service over the Internet. It reduces the time required to procure heavy resources and boot new server instances in minutes, allowing one to quickly scale capacity, both up and down, as ones requirement changes. As per one of the estimates from Gartner, Software as a Service is forecast to have a compound annual growth rate of 17% through 2011 for CRM, ERP and SCM markets in SMB segment.

Cloud computing customers do not generally own the physical infrastructure serving as host to the software platform in question. Instead, they avoid capital expenditure by renting usage from a third-party provider. Many Cloud computing offerings employ the utility computing model, which is analogous to how traditional utility services (such as electricity) are consumed, while others bill on a subscription basis. Sharing "perishable and intangible" computing power among multiple tenants can improve utilization rates, as servers are not unnecessarily left idle (which can reduce costs significantly while increasing the speed of application development).

This paper provides brief details about the cloud computing with an overview of key features to give a glimpse about the new focused technology. Later it will discusses about the architecture of cloud computing and types of services offered by it. Finally, this paper discusses the various security issues and challenges of cloud computing.

Keywords: *Cloud Computing, Cloud Services, IaaS, PaaS, SaaS, Cloud Architecture, Private Cloud, Public Cloud, Hybrid Cloud, Cloud Security, Cloud Privacy, Cloud Data Management, Cloud Security Challenges*

INTRODUCTION

According to www.wikinvest.com, Cloud computing is a technology that uses the internet and central remote servers to maintain data and applications. Cloud computing allows consumers and businesses to use applications without installation and access their personal files at any computer with internet access. This technology allows for much more inefficient computing by centralizing storage, memory, processing and bandwidth.

A simple example of cloud computing is Yahoo email, Gmail, or Hotmail etc. You don't need software or a server to use them. All a consumer would need is just an internet connection and you can start sending emails. The server and email management software is all on the cloud (internet) and is totally managed by the cloud service provider Yeah, Google etc. The consumer gets to use the software alone and enjoy the benefits. The analogy is, 'If you need milk, would you buy a cow?'

According to www.infoworld.com, Cloud computing comes into focus only when you think about what IT always needs: a way to increase capacity or add capabilities on the fly without investing in new infrastructure, training new personnel, or licensing new software [7]. Cloud computing encompasses any subscription-based or pay-per-use service that,

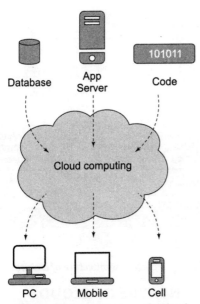

Fig. 1 *Basic architecture of a cloud*

in real time over the Internet, extends IT's existing capabilities.

According to www.saviance.com, Cloud computing is emerging at the convergence of three major trends — service orientation, virtualization and standardization of computing through the Internet. Cloud computing enables users and developers to utilize services without knowledge of, expertise with, nor control over the technology infrastructure that supports them.

According to www.poornima.org, Users avoid capital expenditure (CapEx) on hardware, software, and services when they pay a provider only for what they use. Consumption is billed on a utility (e.g. resources consumed, like electricity) or subscription (e.g. time based, like a newspaper) basis with little or no upfront cost.

32.2 CLOUD AS A SERVICE

Cloud Services can be dived into 3 stacks:

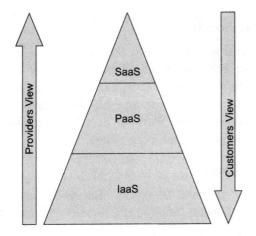

Fig. 2 *Services of cloud computing*

(a) Infrastructure as a Service (IaaS)

(b) Platform as a Service (PaaS)

(c) Software as a Service (SaaS)

Infrastructure as a Service (IaaS)

According to www.techno-pulse.com, This is the base layer of the cloud stack. It serves as a foundation for the other two layers, for their execution. The keyword behind this stack is *Virtualization.* In Amazon EC2 (Elastic Compute Cloud) your application will be executed on a virtual computer (instance). You have the choice of virtual computer, where you can select a configuration of CPU, memory & storage that is optimal for your application. The whole cloud infrastructure viz. servers, routers, hardware based load-balancing, firewalls, storage & other network equipments are provided by the IaaS provider. The customers buy these resources as a service on a need basis. Some IaaS Providers are: Microsoft *SQL Azure, Amazon EC3, Rackspace Cloud, Amazon EC2, Zimory, Elastichosts* [12].

Platform As a Service (PaaS)

According to www.igrandee.com/jsp, Now you don't need to invest millions of $$$ to get that development foundation ready for your developers. The PaaS provider will deliver the platform on the web, and in most of the cases you can consume the platform using your browser, i.e. no need to download any software. It has definitely empowered small & mid-size companies or even an individual developer to launch their own SaaS leveraging the power of these platform providers, without any initial investment.[8][10]. Some PaaS Provider are: *MicroSoft (Windows Azure), Amazon (Amazon Web Services), IBM (Blue Cloud), Google (Gmail, GoogleDocs, Google Labs), Force.com, Salesforce CRM, SAP Business by Design.*

Software as a Service (SaaS)

According to www.techno-pulse.com, This is the Top most layer of the cloud computing stack - directly consumed by end user – i.e. SaaS (Software as a Service). On-Premise applications are quite expensive, affordable only to big enterprises. Because On-Premise applications had a very high upfront CapEx(Capital Expenditure); which results in a high TCO (Total Cost of Ownership). On-Premise apps also require a higher number of skilled developers to maintain the application. In its current avatar SaaS is going to be the best bet for SMEs/SMBs (Small & Mid size businesses). Now, they can afford best software solution for their business without investing anything at all on the infrastructure or development platform or skilled manpower. The only requirement for SaaS is a computer with browser, quite basic. Some Saas Providers are: *Sales Force CRM, Google Apps, ZOHO Support, CloudBerry, ImpelCRM, Wipro w-SaaS.*

CLOUD ARCHITECTURE

According to www.digitalterrain.com, When talking about a cloud computing system, it's helpful to divide it into two sections: the **front end and the back end.** The front end includes the client's computer (or computer network) and the application required to access the cloud computing system. Not all cloud computing systems have the same user interface. Services like Web-based e-mail programs leverage existing Web browsers like Internet Explorer or Firefox. Other systems have unique applications that provide network access to clients like Team Viewer.

On the back end of the system are the various computers, servers and data storage systems that create the "cloud" of computing services. In theory, a cloud computing system could include practically any computer program you can imagine, from data processing to video games. Usually, each application will have its own dedicated server.

Under user application platform layer comes. Platform layer includes services run by application and cloud vendor, queues of services. Platform just work like an operating system "cloud operating system".

Controller administrates the system, monitoring traffic and client demands to ensure everything runs smoothly. It follows a set of rules called **protocols** and uses a special kind of software called **middleware.** Middleware allows networked computers to communicate with each other. Most of the time, servers don't run at full capacity. That means there's unused processing power going to waste. It's possible to fool a physical server into thinking it's actually multiple servers, each running with its own Independent operating system. The Technique is called server virtualization [11].

By maximizing the output of individual servers, server virtualization reduces the need for more physical machines. If a cloud computing company has a lot of clients, there's likely to be a high demand for a lot of storage space. Some companies require hundreds of digital storage devices. A cloud computing system must make a copy of all its clients' information and store it on other devices. The copies enable the central server to access backup machines to retrieve data that otherwise would be unreachable.

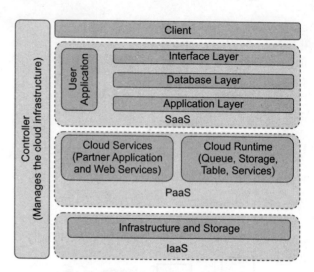

Fig. 3 *Technical architecture of a cloud*

DEPLOYMENT TYPE OF CLOUD

According to onlinearticles.in, Similar to Paas/Iaas/SaaS, clouds may be hosted and employed in different fashions, depending on the use case, respectively the business model of the provider. So far, there has been a tendency of clouds to evolve from private, internal solutions (private clouds) to manage the local infrastructure and the amount of requests e.g. to ensure availability of highly requested data. This is due to the fact that data centers initiating cloud capabilities made use of these features for internal purposes before considering selling the capabilities publicly (public clouds) [5]. Only now that the providers have gained confidence in publication and exposition of cloud features do the first hybrid solutions emerge. This movement from private via public to combined solutions is often considered a "natural" evolution of such systems, though there is no reason for providers to not start up with hybrid solutions, once the necessary technologies have reached a mature enough position. We can hence distinguish between the following deployment types:

Private Clouds

Private clouds are typically owned by the respective enterprise and/or leased. Functionalities are not directly exposed to the customer, though in some cases services with cloud enhanced features may be offered – this is similar to (Cloud) Software as a Service from the customer point of view. E.g.: e-Bay.

Public Clouds

According to cordis.europa.eu, Enterprises may use cloud functionality from others, respectively offer their own services to users outside of the company. Providing the user with the actual capability to exploit the cloud features for his/her own purposes also allows other enterprises to outsource their services to such cloud providers, thus reducing costs and effort to build up their own infrastructure [8]. As noted in the context of cloud *types*, the scope of functionalities thereby may differ. Example: Amazon, Google Apps, Windows Azure.

Hybrid Clouds

According to onlinearticles.in, though public clouds allow enterprises to outsource parts of their infrastructure to cloud providers, they at the same time would lose control over the resources and the distribution / management of code and data. *Hybrid clouds* consist of a mixed employment of *private* and *public cloud* infrastructures so as to achieve a maximum of cost reduction through outsourcing whilst maintaining the desired degree of control over e.g. sensitive data by employing local private clouds [8][9]. There are not many hybrid clouds actually in use today, though initial initiatives such as the one by IBM and Juniper already introduce base technologies for their realization.

CLOUD VENDORS

There are many companies who are into the market offering various ranges of services on Cloud Computing. The major players are Vmware, Apple(iCloud), Sun Microsystems, Rackspace US, IBM, Amazon(AWS), Google, Microsoft(Azure), and Yahoo. Cloud services are also being adopted by individual users through large enterprises including Vmware, General Electric, and Procter & Gamble. The vendor hosts and manages the infrastructure required with the respective technology.

TECHNICAL ASPECTS

The main technological challenges that can be identified and that are commonly associated with cloud systems are:

Virtualization

According to www.scribd.com, Virtualization is an essential technological characteristic of clouds which hides the technical complexity from the user and enables enhanced flexibility (through aggregation, routing and translation). More concretely, virtualization supports the following features:

(a) *Ease of use:* through hiding the complexity of the infrastructure (including management, configuration etc.) virtualization can make it easier for the user to develop new applications, as well as reduces the overhead for controlling the system.

(b) *Infrastructure independency:* in principle, virtualization allows for higher interoperability by making the code platform independent.

(c) *Flexibility and Adaptability:* by exposing a virtual execution environment, the underlying infrastructure can change more flexible according to different conditions and requirements (assigning more resources, etc.).

(d) *Location independence:* services can be accessed independent of the physical location of the user and the resource.

Multi-Tenancy

Multi-tenancy is a highly essential issue in cloud systems, where the location of code and/or data is principally unknown and the same resource may be assigned to multiple users (potentially at the same time). This affects infrastructure resources as well as data/applications/services that are hosted on shared resources but need to be made available in multiple isolated instances. Classically, all information is maintained in separate databases or tables, yet in more complicated cases information may be concurrently altered, even though maintained for isolated tenants [12][13]. Multi-tenancy implies a lot of potential issues, ranging from data protection to legislator issues.

Security, Privacy and Compliance

Security, Privacy and Compliance is obviously essential in all systems dealing with potentially sensitive data and code.

Data Management

Data Management is an essential aspect in particular for storage clouds, where data is flexibly distributed across multiple resources. Implicitly, data consistency needs to be maintained over a wide distribution of *replicated* data sources. At the same time, the system always needs to be aware of the data location (when replicating across data centers) taking latencies and particularly workload into consideration. As size of data may change at any time, data management addresses both horizontal and vertical aspects of scalability. Another crucial aspect of data management is the provided consistency guarantees (eventual vs. strong consistency, transactional isolation vs. no isolation, atomic operations over individual data items vs. multiple data times etc.).

APIs and/or Programming Enhancements

APIs and/or Programming Enhancements are essential to exploit the cloud features: common programming models require that the developer takes care of the scalability and autonomic capabilities himself, whilst a cloud environment provides the features in a fashion that allows the user to leave such management to the system.

Metering

Metering of any kind of resource and service consumption is essential in order to offer elastic pricing, charging and billing. It is therefore a pre-condition for the elasticity of clouds.

Tools

Tools are generally necessary to support development, adaptation and usage of cloud services.

SECURITY & PRIVACY ISSUES

In order to ensure that data is secure (that it cannot be accessed by unauthorized users or simply lost) and that data privacy is maintained, cloud providers attend to the following areas:

Data Protection

To be considered protected, data from one customer must be properly segregated from that of another; it must be stored securely when "at rest" and it must be able to move securely from one location to another. Cloud providers have systems in place to prevent data leaks or access by third parties. Proper separation of duties should ensure that auditing and/or monitoring cannot be defeated, even by privileged users at the cloud provider.

Identity Management

Every enterprise will have its own identity management system to control access to information and computing resources. Cloud providers either integrate the customer's identity management system into their own infrastructure, using federation or SSO technology, or provide an identity management solution of their own.

Physical and Personnel Security

Providers ensure that physical machines are adequately secure and that access to these machines as well as all relevant customer data is not only restricted but that access is documented.

Availability

Cloud providers assure customers that they will have regular and predictable access to their data and applications.

Application Security

Cloud providers ensure that applications available as a service via the cloud are secure by implementing testing and acceptance procedures for outsourced or packaged application code. It also requires application security measures (application-level firewalls) be in place in the production environment.

Privacy

Finally, providers ensure that all critical data (credit card numbers, for example) are masked and that only authorized users have access to data in its entirety [7]. Moreover, digital identities and credentials must be protected as should any data that the provider collects or produces about customer activity in the cloud.

CHALLENGES

As any technology is a boon for an evaluation as the history is evidence, there are disadvantages too which cannot be ignored. Despite a fact cloud computing has so many features which can be awaiting a new horizon there are also key factors which cannot be ignored. Few have been summed up below:

- Lack of connectivity causes 100% downtime, whereas with traditional applications, lack of connectivity allows for some local function to continue until connectivity is restored [11].

- The lack of industry-wide standards means that a usage surge can easily overwhelm capacity without the ability to push that usage to another provider [4].

- Companies providing computing services will over-sell these services similar to how bandwidth is over-sold based on average or "peak" usage, instead of "maximum" usage. ISP's typically operate at multiples of 4 to 1, where they sell 4 times more than they have in capacity, assuming users will not use more than 25% of their allotted resources. This works, until there is a popular YouTube video that everyone wants to see at the same time resulting in outages. Cloud computing is even more vulnerable to the peak-usage problem than internet bandwidth.

- "Denial of service" attacks, currently common, become easier. What's more they become easier to trace, as compromised "cloud resources" can be leveraged to launch the attacks, rather than compromised "individual pc's" [15].
- Cloud computing is vulnerable to massive security exploits. Currently, when a system is broken into, only the resources of that system are compromised. With cloud computing, the damages caused by a security breach are multiplied exponentially.
- By "centralizing" services, cloud computing increases the likelihood that a systems failure becomes "catastrophic", rather than "isolated" [14].
- No political approach has been made till date to control the uncontrolled factors to bring the service under the boundary lines of trust and owner ship, as these services are beyond country lines.

SUGGESTIONS

Few suggestions are made as regarding to challenges:

- Public cloud could use access code mechanism through which a control mechanism could be achieved. That means only authorized user can access information on the cloud [4][6].
- In public cloud as all the data updated concurrently by many users every time, this could be an overhead. This problem can be solved by updating data in SaaS fashion (one time updation) [4].
- The idea of an ad-hoc cloud is to deploy cloud services over an organisation's existing infrastructure, rather than using dedicated machines within data centers. Key to this approach is the ability to manage the use of computational and storage resources on individual machines, by the cloud infrastructure, to the extent that the cloud is sufficiently non-intrusive that individuals will permit its operation on their machines. This project will investigate how this may be achieved [6].
- Since all the data reside on the third party datacenters, there could be chance of data theft and data leakage intentionally or unintentionally. So there should be governing committee for surveillance of cloud provider around the world [11].

- Since cloud computing required 100% connectivity all the time. Network infrastructure should be robust and sustainable [4].
- Use of distributed severs rather than centralized server solve problem of catastrophic failure, cloud hosts could use distributed server as under surveillance of a master server. Servers under master server could work independently, in case of master server failure.

CONCLUSION

The key motive to publish this paper is to give a glimpse of understanding on cloud computing as a technology for a new era. Its potential is considered so vast that it is surely going to give up a new dimension for the generation to come. So, in the long run, most of the companies (large, mid size or small) do not want to have the overhead cost associated with running a large IT department that is solely involved in sustaining existing enterprise application. Large companies do not have the risk tolerance to start using cloud computing immediately. Most CEO's and top IT Executives in large organisations will wait for the technology to mature before putting even the most non-essential applications on someone else's servers. It gives a new aspect to do a business without owing so much. There is a big push for cloud computing services by several big companies. Amazon.com has been at the forefront of the cloud computing movement. Google and Microsoft have also been very publicly working on cloud computing offerings. Some of the other companies to watch for in this field are Yahoo!, IBM, Intel, HP and SAP. Several large universities have also been busy with large scale cloud computing research projects. This year alone the move to the cloud by much business has been phenomenal, so much so that some cloud business have grown by over 200%. Do not be surprised if the cloud bursts with offerings over the next 24 months.

References

1. Retrieved from www.e-technologymanagement. com
2. Retrieved frome-technologymanagement.com
3. Retrieved from www.poornima.org
4. Retrieved from www.wikinvest.com
5. Retrieved from mictunis.micnetwork.org
6. Retrieved from www.allianceprosys.com
7. Retrieved from www.infoworld.com
8. Retrieved from duracloud.org

9. Retrived from www.saviance.com
10. Retrived from www.liquidhub.com
11. Retrived from www.slapos.org
12. Retrived from www.techno-pulse.com
13. Retrived from www.igrandee.com/jsp
14. Retrived from www.techno-pulse.com
15. Retrived from amateurpad.wordpress.com
16. Retrived from www.digitalterrain.com
17. Retrived from cordis.europa.eu
18. Retrived from www.scribd.com

Performance of ZRP using Exata Emulator

Krishan Kant Yadav[1] and Rajesh Shrivastava[2]
[1]Student (M.E.-IV Sem.), Shri Ram Institute of Technology, Jabalpur
[2]Faculty, Shri Ram Institute of Technology, Jabalpur

ABSTRACT

A mobile ad-hoc network is a collection of nodes, which are able to connect on a wireless medium forming an arbitrary and dynamic network. This is established by nodes acting as routers and transferring packets from one to another in ad-hoc networks. Routing in these networks is highly complex due to moving nodes and hence many protocols have been developed. Mobile ad hoc networks are networks without fixed infrastructure. These mobile Ad-hoc networks perform both as a host and a router forwarding packets to other nodes. Due to the special nature of Ad-hoc networks, there are special demands for Ad-hoc routing protocols. Security is also an interesting issue for different protocols.

ZRP is very important protocol in mobile Ad-hoc protocols. Self-configurability and easy deployment feature of the MANET resulted in numerous applications in this modern era. Efficient routing protocols will make MANETs reliable. The purpose of this paper is to introduce various simulator parameters such as first packet received, last packet received, simulation time, throughput of ZRP, average jitter of ZRP etc. using Exata emulator.

Keywords: *Routing Protocol, Zone Routing Protocol (ZRP), Simulator parameters, Jitter time, Throughput*

INTRODUCTION

Mobile Ad-hoc Network (MANET) is a wireless system that comprises mobile users. it is usually referred to a decentralized autonomous system. Mobile nodes engaged in MANET often work as client/servers [9]. Nodes in the network can be either as fixed or mobile. Mobile nodes include laptop, mobile phone, MP3 player home computer or personal digital assistance. Nodes may be located on ships, airlanes or land irrespective of their location as they can participate in communication. Self connectivity and easy development of MANETs makes it apt for emergency, surveillance situations and rescue operations. In MANET, a wireless node can be the source, the destination, or an intermediate node of data transmission [1]. When a wireless node plays the role of intermediate node, it serves as a router that can receive and forward data packets to its neighbor closer to the destination node. Due to the nature of an ad-hoc network, wireless nodes tend to keep moving rather than they still. Therefore the network topology changes from time to time. We consider a routing protocol called the Zone routing protocol that has been proposed for wireless ad-hoc networks with bidirectional links [6]. The ZRP employs a hybrid proactive (table driven) and reactive (on demand) methodology to provide scalable routing in the Ad-hoc network [3].

IDEA OF WORK

We propose extensions to ZRP to support its deployment when unidirectional links are present.ZRP was introduced in 1997 by Haas and Pearlman. it is either a proactive or reactive protocol. It is a hybrid routing protocol. It takes the advantage of proactive discovery within a node's local neighborhoods (Interzone routing Protocol: IERP). The Broadcast Resolution Protocol (BRP) is responsible for the forwarding of a route request [5]. ZRP divides its network in different zones. That's the nodes local neighborhood. Each node may be within multiple overlapping zones and each zone may be a different size. The size of a zone is not determined

Fig. 1　Mobile Ad-hoc network

by geographical measurement. It is given by radius of length, where the number of hopes is the perimeter of the zone. Each node has its own zone.

Ad-hoc networks consist of peer to peer communicating nodes that are highly mobile. As such an ad-hoc network lacks infrastructure and topology of the network changes dynamicity. The task of routing data from a source to a destination in such a network is challenging [8].

MANET has various potential applications. Some typical examples include emergency search rescue operations, meeting events, conferences and battlefield communication between moving vehicles and/or soldiers [5, 8]. With the abilities to meet the new demand of mobile computation, the MANET has a very bright future.

The idea of this paper is to introduce differences between two different ad hoc protocols using different performance metrics. For this one, we have been taken various parameters on the simulators. ZRP is a hybrid protocol. ZRP is an example of reactive and proactive routing protocol based on parameter called routing zone [1, 4]. A routing zone (of radius p) is defined for each node and includes the nodes whose minimum distance in hops from the node in question is at most p hopes. In ZRP each node is assumed to maintain routing information only for those nodes that are within its routing zone. Because the updates are only propagated locally, the amount of update traffic required to maintain a routing zone does not depend on the total number of network nodes.

SIMULATION SETUP

EXata is the only network evaluation tool that can create "software virtual networks" (SVNs) exact digital replicas of physical networks in virtual space that are indistinguishable to applications, devices or users [9].

Unlike traditional modeling and simulation products, SVNs created in Exata can interoperate with all components of physical networks:- devices, applications, network management tools and users.

Table 1　Simulation Setup Parameters

Sr.	Particular	Value
1	Simulation Area	1000m *1000m
2	Mobility Model	Random Waypoint
3	Simulation Time	10 Min
4	Number of Nodes	40
5	Node Speed	1-10 m/second
6	Type of traffic	Constant Bit Rate(voice)
7	Packet size	512 bytes(or~4096 bits)
8	Sending frequency	4 packets/second
9	Traffic destination	Random

RESULT AND ANALYSIS

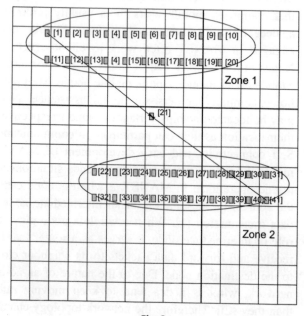

Fig. 2

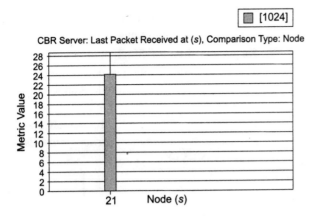

Fig. 3 First packet received (EXata)

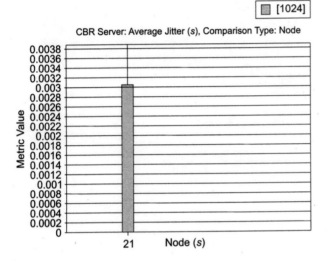

Fig. 4 Last packet received (Exata)

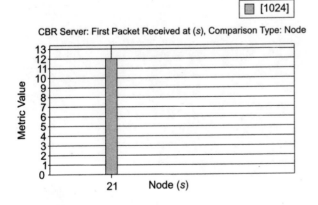

Fig. 5 Throughput of ZRP (Exata)

Secure communication, an important aspect of any networking environment, is an especially significant challenge in ad hoc networks [8, 9]. The MANET

paradigm seeks to enable communication across networks whose topology and membership can change frequently. Its distinctive feature is that network nodes need to collaborate with their peers in supporting the network functionally. in such an environment, malicious or selfish nodes can disrupt or even deny the communication of potentially any node within the ad hoc networking domain [7]. This is so exactly because every node in the network is not only entitled, but is in fact required, to assist in the network establishment, the network maintenance and the network operation.

CONCLUSION

This paper has given the idea about ZRP protocol based on the Exata emulator. The work is origin from analysis and study of Ad hoc network. In this work, the simulation is done using ZRP protocol uses the Exata emulator. The purpose of this paper is to introduce various simulator parameters such as first packet received, last packet received, simulation time, throughput of ZRP, average jitter of ZRP etc. using Exata emulator.

References

- Yih-Chun Hu, Perrig Adrian, and David B. Johnson."Ariadne: ((2002) A secure On-Demand Routing Protocol for Ad hoc Networks". Mobile Communication, Atlanta, Georgia, USA.
- Manel Guerrero Zapata (2002). "Secure Adhoc On-Demand Distance Vector Routing". ACM Mobile Computing and Communications Review (MC2R), 6(3): 106--107.
- Karthik, Sadasivam,Changrani, Vishal and T. Yang Andrew. "Scenario Based Performance evaluation of Secure Routing in MANETs".
- Yuxia Lin, A. Hamed Mohsenian Rad, Vincent W.S. Wong, and Joo-Han Song. (2005) "Experimental Comparisons between SAODV and AODV Routing Protocols". In proceedings of the 1st ACM workshop on Wireless multimedia,
- Das, Samir, Perkins Charles E., Royer Elizabeth M (2009). "Performance Comparison of Two On-demand Routing Protocols for Ad Hoc Networks". Proceedings IEEE Infocom,3-12,
- David, B. Johnson David A. Maltz Josh Broch. (200)1 "DSR: The Dynamic Source Routing Protocol for Multi-Hop Wireless Ad hoc

Networks'.In Ad-hoc Networking, edited by Charles E. Perkins, 5, . 139-172,

• Kargl Frank Geiß, Alfred , Schlott, Stefan and Weber Michael(2005)."Secure Dynamic Source Routing". Proceedings of the 38th Hawaii International Conference on System Sciences .

8. Y. Hu, A. Perrig, and D. Johnson.(2003) "Packet Leashes: A Defense against Wormhole Attacks in Wireless Ad-hoc Networks". Proceedings of The 22nd Annual Joint Conference of the IEEE Computer and Communications Societies .

9. Kushwah Virendra Singh and Sharma Gaurav (2011),"Implementtation of new routing protocol for node security in a mobile Adhoc network", in proceeding of the International Journal of computer science and security(IJCSS) and published by *computer science journals* 4, 6 (2011), 550-559.

Security Architecture for Mobile Ad-hoc Networks (MANET)

Shipra Tripathi

Student, M.Tech (CSE Department), Saroj Institute of Technology and Management, Lucknow

ABSTRACT

Mobile Ad-hoc Networks are the collection of wireless computer, communicating among themselves over possible multi-hop paths, without the help of any infrastructure, such as base stations or access points. Nodes in mobile Ad-hoc network collaboratively contribute to routing functionality by forwarding packets for each other to allow nodes to communicate beyond direct wireless transmission range, hence practically all nodes may act as both hosts and routers. In other words Ad hoc networks are a new wireless networking paradigm for mobile hosts. Unlike traditional mobile wireless networks, ad hoc networks do not rely on any fixed infrastructure. Instead, hosts rely on each other to keep the network connected. One main challenge in design of these networks is their vulnerability to security attacks.

In this review paper, we discuss security issues and their current solutions in the mobile ad hoc network. One to the important nature of the mobile ad hoc network, there are numerous Security threats that create problems in the development of it. A Mobile Ad-hoc Network (MANET) is a self-organizing, infrastructure less, multi-hop network. The wireless and distributed nature of MANETs poses a great challenge to system security designers. Although security problems in MANETs have attracted much attention in the last few years, most research efforts have been focused on specific security areas, such as establishing trust infrastructure, securing routing protocols, or intrusion detection and response, none of the previous work proposes security solutions from a system architectural view. In this paper, we propose five-layer security architecture for mobile ad hoc networks. A general description of functionalities in each layer is given and we analyze the security mechanisms in military

Keywords: *Mobile Ad-hoc Network, Security, Authentication, Security Architecture, Intrusion Detection, Secure Routing*

INTRODUCTION

A Mobile Ad Hoc Network (MANET) is a network consisting of a collection of nodes capable of communicating with each other without help from a network infrastructure. A MANET has got some of the important properties like self organized and rapid deployable Capability. There are several issues in MANETS which addresses the areas such as IP addressing, radio interference, routing protocols, power Constraints, security, mobility management, bandwidth constraints, QOS, etc. The MANET security can be classified in to five layers, as Application layer, Transport layer, Network layer, Data Link layer, and Physical layer. However, the focus is on the network layer, which considers mainly the security issues to protect the ad hoc routing and forwarding protocols. When the security design perspective in MANETS is considered it has not got a clear line defense. Unlike wired networks that have dedicated routers, each mobile node in an ad hoc network may function as a router and forward packets for other peer nodes. The wireless channel is accessible to both legitimate network users and malicious attackers. There is no well defined place where traffic monitoring or access control mechanisms can be deployed. As a result, the boundary that separates the inside network from the outside world becomes blurred. On the other hand, the existing ad hoc routing protocols, such as AODV (Ad-hoc on Demand Distance vector protocol) DSR (Dynamic Source Routing), and wireless MAC protocols.

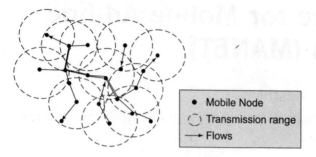

Fig. 1 Mobile ad hoc networking

Here dotted lines show the transmission range and arrow indicate flow and solid points represent the mobile hosts. Here no access point exists.

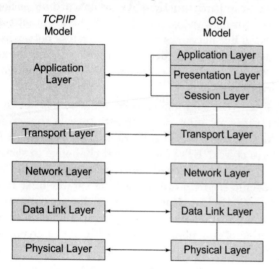

Fig. 2 MANET Security layering system.

Security goals

There are five main security services for MANETs:

- Authentication,
- Confidentiality,
- Integrity,
- Non-repudiation
- Availability.

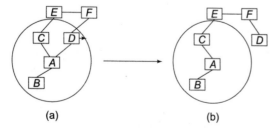

Fig. 3 Topology change in ad hoc networks

Here nodes A, B, C, D, E, and F constitute an ad hoc network. The circle represent the radio range of node A. The network initially has the topology in (a). When node D moves out of the radio range of A, the network topology changes to the one in (b).

Authentication means that correct identity is known to communicating partner. Enables a node to ensure the identity of the peer node it is communicating with. Without authentication, an adversary could masquerade a node, thus gaining unauthorized access to resource and sensitive information and interfering with the operation of other nodes.

Confidentiality means certain message information is kept secure from unauthorized party. Ensures that certain information is never disclosed to unauthorized entities. Network transmission of sensitive information, such as strategic or tactical military information, requires confidentiality. Leakage of such information to enemies could have devastating consequences. Routing information must also remain confidential in certain cases, because the information might be valuable for enemies to identify and to locate their targets in a battlefield.

Integrity means message is unaltered during the communication. Guarantees that a message being transferred is never corrupted. A message could be corrupted because of benign failures, such as radio propagation impairment, or because of malicious attacks on the network.

Non repudiation means the origin of a message cannot deny having sent the message ensures that the origin of a message cannot deny having sent the message. No repudiation is useful for detection and isolation of compromised nodes. When a node A receives an erroneous message.

From a node B, non-repudiation allows A to accuse B using this message and to convince other nodes that B is compromised.

Availability means the normal service provision in face of all kinds of attacks. Ensures the survivability of network services despite denial of service attacks. A denial of service attack could be launched at any layer of an ad hoc network. On the physical and media access control.

Layers, an adversary could employ jamming to interfere with communication on physical channels. On the network layer, an adversary could disrupt the routing protocol and disconnect the network. On the higher layers, an adversary could bring down high-level services. One such target is the key management service, an essential service for any security framework.

Among all the security services, authentication is probably the most complex and important issue in MANETs since it is the bootstrap of the whole security system. Without knowing exactly who you are talking with, it is worthless to protect your data from being read or altered. Once authentication is achieved in MANET, confidentiality is a matter of encrypting the session using whatever key material the communicating party agree on. Note that these security services may be provided singly or in combination. In this paper, we propose security architecture from a layered view, then the functionalities of each layer is described. We further analyze the application of the proposed security architecture in military applications. A Mobile Ad hoc Network (MANET) is a system of wireless mobile nodes that dynamically self-organize in arbitrary and temporary network topologies. People and vehicles can thus be internet worked in areas without a preexisting communication infrastructure or when the use of such infrastructure requires wireless extension. In the mobile ad hoc network, nodes can directly communicate with all the other nodes within their radio ranges; whereas nodes that not in the direct communication range use intermediate node(s) to communicate with each other. In these two situations, all the nodes that have participated in the communication automatically form a wireless network, therefore this kind of wireless network can be viewed as mobile ad hoc network. The mobile ad hoc network has the following typical features:

- Unreliability of wireless links between nodes. Because of the limited energy supply for the wireless nodes and the mobility of the nodes, the wireless links between mobile nodes in the ad hoc network are not consistent for the communication participants.
- Constantly changing topology. Due to the continuous motion of nodes, the topology of the mobile ad hoc network changes constantly: the nodes can continuously move into and out of the radio range of the other nodes in the ad hoc network, and the routing information will be changing all the time because of the movement of the nodes.
- Lack of incorporation of security features in statically configured wireless routing protocol not meant for ad hoc environments. Because the topology of the ad hoc networks is changing constantly, it is necessary for each pair of adjacent nodes to incorporate in the routing issue so as to prevent some kind of potential attacks that try

to make use of vulnerabilities in the statically configured routing protocol.

RELATED WORK

We classify related work to ad hoc network security into the following three categories:

1. Providing basic security infrastructure: MANET is network without any basic infrastructure hence there is no trust infrastructure like PKI for all the participating nodes in MANETs. The first step to establish a security system is to setup the basic security infrastructure and establish security associations between communicating nodes.

2. Secure routing: In MANETs, every node participates in the routing activities in MANETs. There are two concepts in secure routing here: one is exchanging routing information to keep the network connected and the other involves secure data packet forwarding.

3. Misbehavior/Intrusion detection and response: The wireless and mobility nature of ad hoc networks makes it vulnerable to intrusions and misbehaviors than in wired counterpart. Note that misbehaviors and intrusion are different both in the designing network protocols is a good example for us to follow in designing security protocols. A layered architecture can provide such advantages as modularity, simplicity, flexibility, and standardization of protocols. Follow this thought; we present here a layered secure architecture for MANETs in Figure 1. The figure depicts five-layer security architecture for MANETs, and the functionalities of each layer are illustrated as below:

SL_5	End-t-End Security
SL_4	Network Security
SL_3	Routing Security
SL_2	Communication Security
SL_1	Trust Infrastructure

Fig. 4 Security Architecture for mobile ad-hoc network

1. **Security Layer 1** Trusted Infrastructure Layer: refers to the basic trust relationship between nodes, for example, like a well deployed environment. Since in MANETs, there is no centralized authority to help establish the trust

relationship between communicating nodes, the security mechanisms in this layer are expected to be constructed in a distributed manner and are the basic building block of the whole security system. Thus, SL1 poses a great challenge to system security designers. The security association established in trust infrastructure layer must serve for the upper layer security mechanisms.

2. **Security Layer 2** Communications Security Layer: refers to the security mechanisms applied in transmitting data frames in a node-to-node manner, such as security protocol WEP working in data link layer in OSI model, or physical protection mechanisms like frequency hopping. Security Mechanisms deployed in this layer may keep data frame from eavesdropping, interception, alteration, or dropping from unauthorized party along the route from the source to the destination.

3. **Security Layer 3** Routing Security Layer: refers to security mechanisms applied to routing protocols. In MANET, nodes exchange information about their knowledge of neighborhood connectivity and construct a view of the network topology so that they can route the data packets to the correct destinations. Every node is required to participate in the routing activity and routing is an important part to keep the network connected. Hence, SL3 is of particular significance in MANETs. In fact, the routing security layer involves two aspects: secure routing and secure data forwarding. In secure routing aspect, nodes are required to cooperate to share correct routing information to keep the network connected efficiently in secure data forwarding aspect, data packets on the fly should be protected from tampering, dropping, and altering by any unauthorized party.

4. **Security Layer 4** Network Security Layer: refers to the security mechanisms used by the network protocols which perform sub-network access operations from end system to end system. For example, we can achieve the security services like peer entity authentication, confidentiality and integrity as the network layer security protocol IPSec provides, another example are the SMT mechanism from.

5. **Security Layer 5** End-to-End Security Layer: refers to end system security, such as SSL, SSH, and any application-specific security protocol.

The security protocols in this layer is independent of the underlying networking technology since the related security mechanisms are restricted to only intended parties. The provision of any security service in this layer is highly dependent upon security requirements related to specific applications. The motivation of dividing the security architecture into such five layers is rather straightforward.

Security Layer 5 defines the security mechanisms related to end application system, like SET, thus it is necessary to differentiate this layer from the underlying layers.

Security Layer 4 deals with network access control and network layer data packet protection. SL4 is in fact the security layer working at the end of network fabric. The mechanisms deployed in this layer tackle the network security problems that cannot be solved satisfactorily in the underlying routing protocols. SMT working at SL4 is a good example of security efforts done in the end systems as a remedy for the unreliable routing protocol.

Security Layer 3 in the architecture is that the inherent cooperative nature in MANETs requires every node in the network acts both as a host which needs other nodes relaying information for it and also as a router to provide routing and relaying functions to other nodes. The security mechanisms in Security Layer 3 are highly related to the network topology and are always designed with respect to specific routing protocol in use.

Security Layer 2 is a layer providing hop-to-hop communications security, i.e., it is related to the data link security and physical layer security in the wireless communications channel.

Security Layer 1 requires a trust infrastructure is to be established before communication begins to function securely; an example is the trust infrastructure established using distributed threshold cryptography in. The intrusion prevention mechanisms like encryption and signature do not eliminate the need for intrusion/misbehavior detection and response. Although the intrusion/misbehavior detection and response mechanisms are not distinctively specified in the system architecture, they are actually very important in Manet's security system and can be deployed in any layer of the system architecture according to the security requirements in each layer.

For mission-critical applications such as a military application in a hostile environment there are more stringent security requirements than in a MANET for commercial or personal uses.

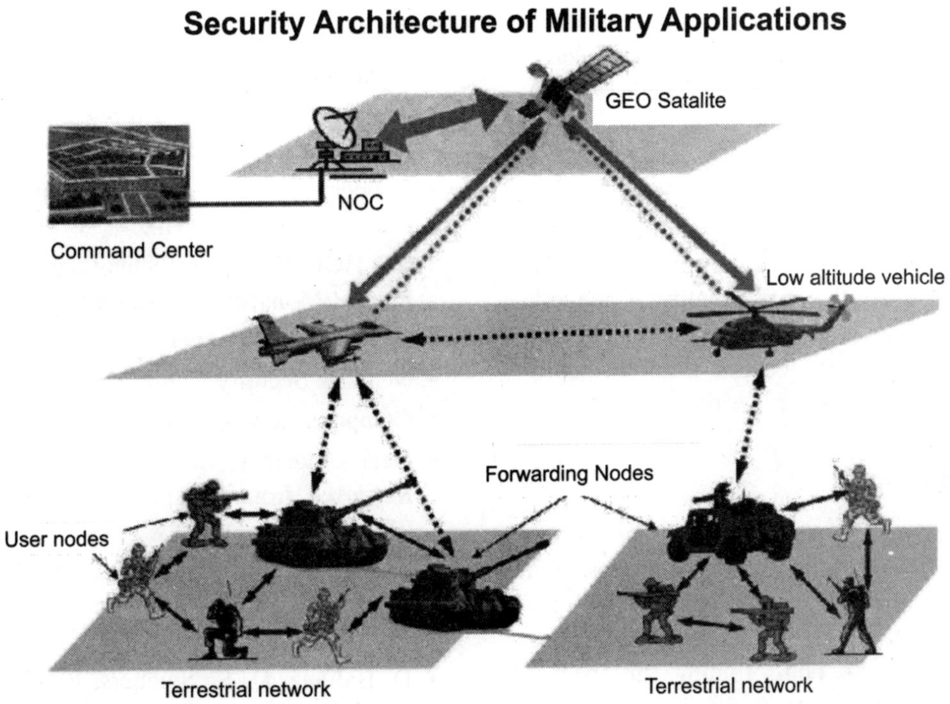

Security Architecture of Military Applications

Fig. 5 Wireless network architecture for military use

A military scenario may have higher requirements regarding both information security and routing topology security. In such a scenario, we may design the functionalities of each layer in security architecture as follows:

- Data information is protected in a most fine way in application layer so the best way to protect data information according to their different requirement is at SL5. For example, it is highly desirable to handle data confidentiality and integrity in SL5 layer, since this is the easiest way to protect data from altering, fabrication and compromise. This is especially important in a military scenario where strategic and tactical information is sent.

- Since it is impossible to deploy a centralized firewall or security gateway in an ad hoc network, there is no way for any centralized security gateway to provide network access control services for mobile nodes. Thus the task of network access control and IP data packet protection lies on the end nodes. As IPSec protocol is not applicable to a mobile scenario, we need to exploit other means to protect data packet in SL4. For example, when the underlying routing protocol supports multi- path routing, mechanisms from working at SL4 can be used to take advantage of multi-route between the communicating routes to achieve higher

reliability and increased data confidentiality when data packets are transmitted along the route from source to destination.

- Military applications require keeping network topology secret and allowing no traffic analysis in SL3. Routing protocol designers should strive to hide the network topology from unauthorized party and should be designed carefully to prevent routing level attacks, like false routing updates, DoS attacks at routing protocols, thus security services such as confidentiality and integrity are expected to be provided in SL3.

- It is desirable to conceal communications in military scenario, and this requirement is most effectively fulfilled in SL2. For example, we can take spread spectrum technologies to make the signal capture difficult or use antennas to influence signal power in space; and we can also deploy WEP or 802.1 xs to control the link access.

It seems quite natural to expect a PKI based on centralized or hierarchical offline CA to pre-establish the trust relationship for all the nodes due to the similar hierarchical relationships between soldiers and general, this is in fact infeasible due to the reasons that this cannot handle the situation of compromise since CRL is difficult to deploy in a distributed environment in a timely manner. There is one trust model particularly suited for military scenario: Resurrecting Duckling Security

Model, where a secure transient association is handled in a master slave way which is like the hierarchical relationship between soldiers and their general. The security lies in the sense that master and slaves share a common secret, while the security association is only controlled by the master. Compared with military applications, there may be relatively loose security requirements in commercial or personal scenarios, like security in routing protocol, confidentiality of network topology, and the basic trust infrastructure like PGP-like model or maybe just location-limited-channel model can be applied in these scenarios.

CONCLUSIONS

In these review paper mobile ad hoc networks, protecting the network layer from attacks is an important research topic in wireless security. This paper describes a robust scheme for network-layer security solution in ad hoc networks, which protects both, routing and packet forwarding functionalities without the context of any data forwarding protocol.

In this paper, we try to inspect the security issues in the mobile ad hoc networks, which may be a main disturbance to the operation of it. Due to the mobility and open media nature, the mobile ad hoc networks are much more prone to all kind of security risks, such as information disclosure, intrusion, or even denial of service. As a result, the security needs in the mobile ad hoc networks are much higher than those in the traditional wired networks. In this work we have dealt with security issues in mobile ad hoc networks. We have focused on designing security architecture in tackling security challenges mobile ad hoc networks are facing. We present security architecture in a layered view and analyze the reasoning for such security architecture, and apply the proposed security architecture in military scenarios. We expect this security architecture can be used as a framework when designing system security for ad hoc networks.

References

Articles Communication Networks by *Springer*:

- Security in Mobile Ad-hoc Networks: Şen, Sevil; Clark, John Andrew.
- Cooperation in mobile adhoc networks: Hu, Jiangyi; Burmester, Mike
- AD HOC Networks Technology and protocols: Prasant Mohapatra, Srikanth K.

Research and journal papers

- Network Security Comar.
- Computer networking concepts Tanenbaum.
- Data Integrity and security architecture, Retrieved from Wikipedia, http://en.wikipedia.org/wiki/Data_integrity.
- Zhang Yongguang and Lee Wenke, Security in Mobile Ad-hoc Networks, in Book Ad-hoc Networks Technologies and Protocols Springer.
- D. Balfanz, D. K. Smetters, P. Stewart and H. Chi Wong: Authentication in Ad-hoc Wireless Networks appeared in Network and Distributed System Security.
- M.S. Corson, J.P. Maker, and J.H. Cernicione, Internet-based Mobile Ad-hoc Networking, IEEE Internet Computing.
- Mishra Amitabh and Nadkarni M Nandkani, Security in Wireless Ad Hoc Networks, in Book the Handbook of Ad-hoc Wireless Networks.
- Royer, E., Toh, C. "A Review of Current Routing Protocols for Ad Hoc Mobile Wireless Networks"
- E. M. Royer, "A Review of Current Routing Protocols for Ad-hoc Mobile Wireless Networks", Elizabeth M. Royer, IEEE.
- M. Andrews, J. Cao, and J. McGowan. Measuring human satisfaction in data networks.

Study of Broadcasting and its Performance Parameter in Vanet

Yashpal Singh[1] and Anurag Sharma[2]
[1]Bundelkhand Institute of Engineering and Technology, Jhansi
[2]FET Agra College, Agra

ABSTRACT

A Vehicular Ad-hoc Network is a kind of ad-hoc network, and is a self-configuring network of vehicular routers connected by wireless links. Vehicular Ad-hoc Network is a wireless network without infrastructure. Reliable broadcasting in vehicular ad-hoc networks is one of the keys to success for services and applications on intelligent transportation system. Broadcasting in VANET is very different from routing in mobile ad hoc network (MANET) due to several reasons such as network topology, mobility patterns, demographics, traffic patterns at different time of the day, etc. In this paper we report the broadcasting in VANET, three very different regimes that a vehicular broadcasting protocol needs to work and the performance parameter of broadcasting in VANET.

Keywords: *VANET, MANET*

INTRODUCTION

According to www.di.unito.in, Broadcasting in vehicular ad hoc networks (VANET) is emerging as a critical area of research. One of the challenges posed by this problem is the confinement of the routing problem to vehicle-to-vehicle (V2V) scenarios as opposed to also utilizing the wireless infrastructure (such as cellular network). At a fundamental level, safety and transport efficiency is a mandate for current car manufacturers and this has to be provided by the cars on the road as opposed to also using the existing wireless communications infrastructure. Such applications with this real-world constraint call for a new routing protocol for vehicular broadcasting in VANET.

In this paper, we report the first comprehensive study on the subject whereby the extreme traffic situation such as dense traffic density, sparse traffic density, and low penetration of cars using DSRC technology are specifically taken into account.

The remainder of this paper is organized as follows. Section 2 presents different regimes of interest in VANET that the designed broadcast protocol should be able to handle. Section 3 discusses some performance parameters.

DIFFERENT REGIMES FOR BROADCASTING IN VANET

The three different regimes of operation in VANET are:

(a) Dense Traffic Regimes

(b) Sparse Traffic Regimes

(c) Regular Traffic Regimes

The first two of these three cases correspond to extreme scenarios. It is important to understand the characteristics of these three regimes as a good broadcast routing protocol has to be able to deal with all these three regimes. Below, we give a brief overview of these regimes.

(A) Dense Traffic Regimes

According to *ijcsia.uacee.org,* when a traffic density is above a certain value, one of the most serious problems is the choking of the shared medium by an excessive number of the same safety broadcast message by several consecutive cars. Because of the shared wireless medium, blindly broadcasting the packets may lead to frequent contention and collisions in transmission among neighboring nodes. This problem is sometimes referred to as broadcast storm problem. While multiple solutions exist to alleviate the broadcast storm problem in a usual MANET environment, only a few solutions exist for resolving this issue in the VANET context. There are three light-weight broadcast techniques; i.e., weighted p-persistence, slotted 1-persistence, and slotted p-persistence, which can provide 100%, reach ability in a well-connected network and up to approximately 70% reduction in the broadcast redundancy and packet loss ratio on a well-connected vehicular network.

Specifically, Fig. 1 shows three distance based schemes:

(i) Weighted p-Persistence Broadcasting
(ii) Slotted 1-Persistence Broadcasting
(iii) p-Persistence Broadcasting

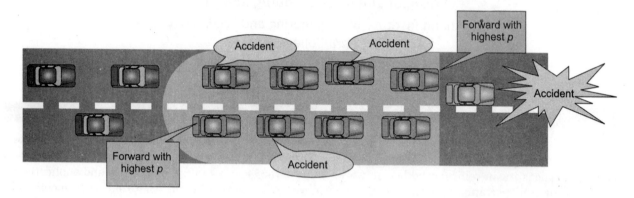

(a) Weighted *p*-persistence

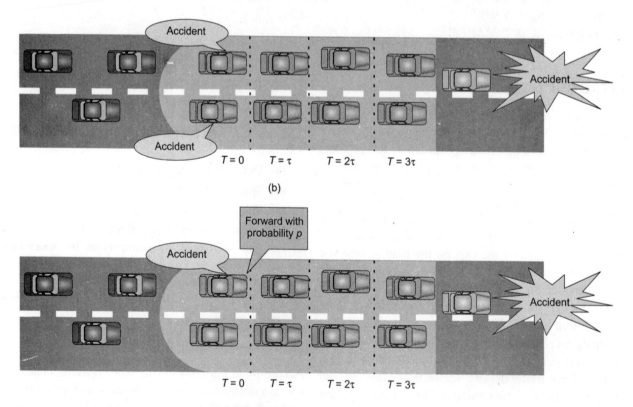

(b)

(c) Slotted *p*-persistence scheme.

Fig. 1 Broadcast suppression techniques

According to *ieeexplore.ieee.org,* The basic broadcast techniques follow either a 1-persistence or a p-persistence rule. Despite the excessive overhead, most routing protocols designed for multi-hop ad hoc wireless networks follow the brute-force 1-persistence flooding rule which requires that all nodes rebroadcast the packet with probability 1 because of the low complexity and high packet penetration rate. Gossip-based approach, on the other hand, follows the p-persistence rule which requires that each node re-forwards with a pre-determined probability p. This approach is sometimes referred to as probabilistic flooding. The slotted p-persistence scheme can substantially reduce the packet loss ratio at the expense of a slight increase in total delay and reduced penetration rate.

(B) Sparse Traffic Regimes

According to *issuu.com,* The other extreme scenario, which is very troublesome for conventional routing protocols, is the case where there are not many vehicles on the road. At certain time of the day the traffic density might be so low that multi-hoc relaying from a source to the cars coming from behind might not be plausible because the target node might be out of the transmission range of the source. To make the situation worse, there might be no car within the transmission range of the source in the opposite lane. Under such circumstances, routing and broadcasting becomes a challenging task. While there are several routing techniques which address the sparsely connected nature of the mobile wireless networks, e.g., Epidemic routing, Single-copy, Multi-copy 'Spray and Wait', there are only a few that considered a VANET topology.

(C) Regular Traffic Regime

For both sparse and dense traffic scenarios previously considered, it is likely that the local connectivity experienced by each vehicle in a network would also reflect the global connectivity, e.g., a vehicle in a dense network is likely to observe a dense local topology while vehicles in a sparse network are likely to have zero or only a few neighbors or observe a sparse local topology. More specifically, all vehicles operating in these two extreme regimes will observe the same local topology which also reflects the real global topology, i.e., some may have very few neighbors while some have many neighbors. In this case, some vehicles will have to apply the broadcast suppression algorithm while some will have to store-carry-forward the message in order to preserve the network connectivity.

PERFORMANCE PARAMETER

There are three performance parameters, which are considered for performance evaluation:

(a) Reliability

(b) Overhead

(c) Speed of Data Dissemination

Reliability: It is measured as a percentage of number of nodes that received the message at the end of simulation.

Overhead: It is measured from bandwidth consumption which is from messages transmission and beaconing transmission. Beacon size includes node's local information (e.g., identifier, position and velocity) and list of received messages identifiers as acknowledgement.

Speed of Data Dissemination: It is measured as given in below equation,

$$y(t) = \sum_{i=1}^{t} \frac{|(r_i)|}{n} * 100$$

Where represents number of node that received the message for the first time at the time I and n is the total number of vehicles in the scenario.

CONCLUSION

VANET helps ITS applications and services to be able to exchange and disseminate data easily and speedily. Most of these applications and services rely on efficient and fast reliable broadcasting protocol to provide accurate information.

There are three different regimes which we have discussed in this paper to precisely say, the names of regimes of operation in VANET are Dense Traffic Regimes, Sparse Traffic Regimes, and Regular Traffic Regimes .These have been reported in the paper to define the extreme traffic situation. The first two of these three cases correspond to extreme scenarios. It is important to understand the characteristics of these three regimes as a good broadcast routing protocol has to be able to deal with all these three regimes.

We have also described the three performance parameters, namely Reliability, Overhead, and Speed of Data Dissemination, which evaluate the performance of the protocol, working for reliable broadcasting.

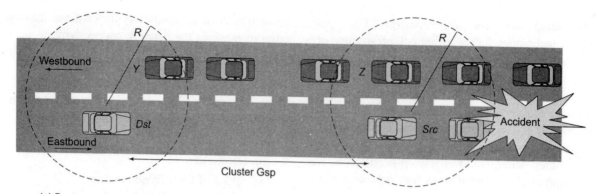

(a) Best case Scenario: packet can immediately be relayed to the target vehicles via vehicles in the opposite traffic

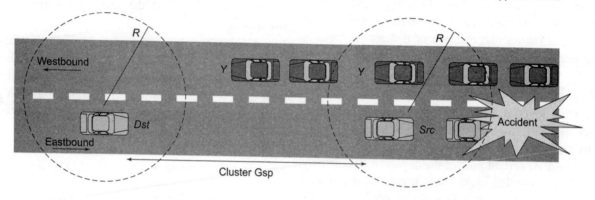

(b) Intermediate case scenario: vehicles in teh opposite direction is responsible of storecarry-forward the message back to vehicles in the message forwarding road

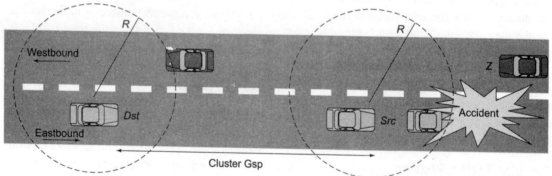

(b) Worst case Scenario: packet cannot immediately be relayed to vehicles in the opposite direction

Fig. 2   Illustration of the disconnected VANETs

References

- Retrieved from www.di.unito.it/~matteo/I09/DATA08/07MOS1P2.PDF
- *Retrieved from eshare.stut.edu.tw/EshareFile/2012_1/2012_1_e22be68f.ppt*
- *Retrieved from ijcsia.uacee.org/files/a213.pdf*
- Retrieved from books.google.co.in/books?isbn=0470661305...

The Effect of Advertisement on Consumer's Behavior

Charanjeet Kaur

Assistant Professor (Home Science), Government KRGPG Autonomous College, Gwalior

ABSTRACT

Today the whole world is under the shadow of Advertisement Empire. It proclaims itself as the voice of today. It is the curtain of the past dreams and reality of the future. Actually advertisement relate with the great depth of individual social and economic life that every aspect of purchasing influenced by advertisement. Present study is done to find out effect of advertisement on consumer behaviour.

Keywords: *Advertisement, Consumer Behaviour*

INTRODUCTION

In the field of human activities, advertisements have a great impact on human life and it occupies a unique place in consumer behavior. By advertisement and consumer research it has been observed that advertisements could be used to inspired customers to purchase.

No doubt, the object of every advertisement is to affect the human behaviour till the specific limit. Luise Harris (1962), Ralye Medkey (1970) are clarified that the consumers has shown a positive attitude hence, in the study of California Poll (1960) and marketing science institute (1961) has shown negative thoughts Professor S. Badrealam and Jiyauddern Kharuwala (1983), according to their studies, the advertisement has affected consumers psychologically. Hence, according to Boyk (1983) say that the advertisements are misguiding and the vulgarity of advertisement is also misguiding the youth.

The researcher personality like Parkar, Ralpough Naden, J. K. Golbrath Neil H. Borden etc also oppose the advertisement.

Thus, it has been cleared that effective glamorous and attractive advertisement also affect the thinking of the customers. Hence, the fake advertisement misguides the customer. The customer cannot take appropriate decision in the effect of this advertisement. This research paper had been prepared in present reference of consumerization related behavior and the study of the effect of advertisement.

OBJECTIVES

There are some objects of present research:

1. To study the effect of advertisement on the consumers behaviour.
2. To observe the effect of advertisement on different sex and age level of consumers.
3. To observe the effect of advertisement of different education level of consumers.
4. To observe the effect of advertisement on different family structures.

Development of Hypothesis

The present proposed work developed below hypothesis:

1. The advertisements have positive effect on the consumers purchasing behaviour.
2. There are the different effects of advertisement on male and female consumers.

METHODOLOGY

In proposed study 300 samples are selected through random selection method in which 150 male and 150 females are included. There are 60 words in Gwalior city from which we select 10 wards through random selection method. From each word we select 15 male and 15 female consumers for interview. Self constructed questionnaire is used for interview process. Collected data are classified, analyzed and tabulated by researcher:

Table 1 Effect of advertisement on consumers

Value	Max. effect	Min. effect	Low effect
Actual No.	84	206	10
Approx. No.	100	100	100
Per cent (%)	28.00	68.67	3.33

$\chi^2 = 111.746$, p >> 0.05 most significant

CONCLUSION

The results of the study are given below on the basis on analysis of facts:

1. The purchasing related behavior of most of the middle class consumers are affected by the advertisement.
2. The effect of advertisement is observed more in women consumers in comparison with male consumers.
3. The age group of 36-45 years is observed to be highly affected by the advertisement.
4. The effect of advertisement is observed to be decreasing with the increase in the educational level of a consumer.
5. In comparison with the consumers joint family, single family consumers are observed to be more affected by the advertisement
6. With the increase in the income of consumer, the increase of advertisement effect on them is also observed.

Table 2 Effect of advertisement and gender of consumers

Effect of advertisement	Female		Male	
	Number	%	Number	%
High	46	30.66	38	25.33
Medium	96	64.01	100	73.34
Low	8	5.33	2	1.33
Total	**150**	**100.00**	**150**	**100.00**
$\chi^2 = 5.313$	p > 0.05, Non significant		p > 0.01 significant	

Table 3 Effect of advertisement and age of consumers

Effect of advertisement	Below 25 yrs		26 to 35 yrs		36 to 45 yrs		Above 45 yrs	
	No.	%	No.	%	No.	%	No.	%
High	10	30.30	29	22.14	35	33.33	10	32.16
Medium	23	69.70	102	77.86	64	60.95	17	54.84
Low	0	0	0	0	6	5.72	4	12.00

$\chi^2 = 22.099$, p > 0.05 significant

Table 4 Effect of advertisement and education level of consumers

Effect of advertisement	High school		Intermediate		Level of education Graduation		P.G.		Professional & technical education	
	No.	%	No.	%	No.	%	No.	%	No.	%
High	3	33.33	19	29.23	15	18.29	43	33.59	4	25.00
Medium	6	66.67	46	70.77	67	81.71	78	60.94	9	56.25
Low	0	0	0	0	0	0	7	5.47	3	18.75
Total	**9**	**100.0**	**65**	**100.0**	**82**	**100.00**	**128**	**100.00**	**16**	**100.0**

$\chi^2 = 26.278$, p>0.05 significant

Table 5 Effect of advertisement and structure of family

Effect of advertisement	Female		Male	
	Number	%	Number	%
High	62	29.24	22	25.00
Medium	146	68.87	60	68.18
Low	4	1.89	6	6.82
Total	**212**	**100.00**	**88**	**100.00**

χ^2 = 4.941, p > 0.05 Non-significant

Table 6 Effect of consumers' income and advertisement

Effect of advertisement	Income/per capita/month (in Rs.)					
	150 to 299		300 to 499		500 to 999	
	No.	%	No.	%	No.	%
High	7	13.46	28	45.16	49	26.34
Medium	45	86.54	26	41.93	135	72.58
Low	0	0	8	12.91	2	1.08
Total	**52**	**100.00**	**62**	**100.00**	**186**	**100.00**

χ^2 = 41.527, p > 0.05 significant

Suggestions

Advertisement is not only a strong medium of information and communication but it is also used as a powerful medium in the field of buying and selling. This medium is used in a proper and specific way to connect the product with the consumer which leads to consumer buying the product.

The effect of advertisement is more on the behavior of consumers so, the Government banned these misguiding and vulgar advertisements. Consumer study is the key of competitive purchasing. Thus more steps should be taken to improve the educational level of the consumers. Thus it can be said that the consumer and advertisement are complementary to each other.

Brand Loyalty of Consumers: A Demographic Study

Charanjeet Kaur and Shivangi Sharma

Assistant Professor (Home Science), Government KRGPG Autonomous College, Gwalior

ABSTRACT

All the studies of science and arts focused on welfare of human beings. To achieve the goal of human welfare it's important to raise the status level of society. Consumers may look on branding as an important value added aspect of products or services as it often serves to denote a certain attractive quality of characteristics. From the perspective of brand owners branded products or services also command higher prices. The present study is carried out to find out effect of demographic factors in brand loyalty.

Keywords: *Brand Loyalty, demographic factors*

INTRODUCTION

People may often select the more expensive branded product on the basis of the quality of the brand or the reputation of the brand owner. According to en.wikipedia.org, the psychological aspect sometimes referred to as the brand image, is a symbolic construct created within the minds of people and consists of all the information and expectations associated with a product of services.

There are many different definitions of a brand, the most effective description however, is that a brand is a name or symbol that is commonly known to identify a company or its products and separate them from the competition.

According to www.bizhelp24.com, a well-known brand is generally regarded as one that people will recognize, often if they do not know about the company or its products/services. These are usually the businesses name or the name of a product, although it can also include the name of a feature or style of a product.

The overall "branding" of a company or product can also stretch to a logo, symbol or even design features that identify the company or its products/services.

American marketing Association, Chicago 1960 "A brand is a name, term, symbol or design, or a combination of them which is intended to identify the goods or services of one seller or group of seller and to differentiate them from those of competitors."

Today's competition, advertisement, unique packaging art and increased brand awareness are the main factors which raised importance of brand business to raise sell of product, reputation of firm, consumer acceptance and to know priority of customers.

According to www.consumerpsychologist.com, When a brand is created and established the product is sold more and more in numbers and develops a loyalty among the consumers as the people believe in on or more of the following: best values for money, among the best/ reliability over quality and safety and similar factors about the product. Through brand the product or entity concerned gets loyalty among consumers, command a better price or better image or respect from admirers.

Sarin and Gopalkrishnan, "Marketing in India-Text and Cases" says "Branding is important in Indian market because in retail market shopkeepers present a different range of product in front of customers to sell. In that case branding is important to raise customer's loyalty for products".

So brands have become increasingly important in today's competitive world both for competitors and for consumers of products. Brands play various roles, the most important being the role of differentiating companies and products from their competitors. However, imaging a brand has become increasingly complex and marketing efforts must be supplemented by legal protection.

Haripuram Vankatashwaral, M. Kishore Kumar and V. Rajnath 1987 studies 470 customers in Hyderabad and Sikandarabad studied influencing factors of brand selection. Results shows in 58 families shopping are done by parents. 60% customers change their brands frequently. The main factor to change the brands rapidly is quality of brands. Brand quality can bind their customers for a long time. Some customers also prefer brand packing and price also. Brand availability and price also effect selection of brand.

Raghuveer 1985 studied customers of Chandigarh and results shows that families are interested to use same brand till 5 yrs or more. Two main factors to change the brand are:

1. Quality of brand
2. Availability of brand

Shri B.M. Bhadda and Shri B.L. Porwal says brand name also affect customers. Sometimes customers purchase any products by brand names. Results shows brand name helps in 12% selling of products and 36% brand name have a worst effect or product and 56% brand name have no effect in products selling.

Dr. M. Shubramanya Sharma and Dr. N. Kusum 1995 studied 500 customers purchasing habits they analyze male and female customers and result shows that in comparison to female, male customers change their brand frequently.

OBJECTIVES OF STUDY

1. To study the brand loyalty of consumers
2. To study the effect of age on brand loyalty
3. To study the effect of education on brand loyalty
4. To study the factors that affect brand loyalty.

Hypothesis: A hypothesis is a proposed explanation for a phenomenon. It is made on the basis of limited evidence as a starting point for further investigation.

In a proposed study following hypothesis is made by researcher:

1. There is no difference in brand loyalty in different level of consumers.

METHODOLOGY

In proposed study 300 samples are selected through random selection method in which 150 male and 150 females are included. There are 60 words in Gwalior city from which we select 10 wards through random selection method. From each word we select 15 male and 15 female consumers for interview. Self constructed questionnaire is used for interview process. Collected data are classified, analyzed and tabulated b researcher:

Table details related to study are given below:

Table 1 Effect of age on brand loyalty

Use of same brand	Age group in yrs							
	Below 25		26-35		36-45		45 and above	
	No.	%	No.	%	No.	%	No.	%
Yes	24	72.73	95	72.52	46	43.81	17	54.84
No	9	27.27	36	27.48	59	56.19	14	45.16
Total	**33**	**100.00**	**131**	**100.00**	**105**	**100.00**	**31**	**100.00**

χ^2 = 22.668, p >> 0.05 significant

Table 2 Effect of education on brand loyalty

Use of same brand	Level of education									
	High school		Intermediate		Graduation		P.G.		Professional & technical education	
	No.	%	No.	%	No.	%	No.	%	No.	%
Yes	5	55.55	30	46.15	61	74.39	79	61.72	7	43.75
No	4	44.45	35	53.85	21	25.61	49	30.28	9	56.25
Total	**9**	**100.00**	**65**	**100.00**	**82**	**100.00**	**128**	**100.00**	**16**	**100.00**

χ^2 = 14.286, p > 0.05 significant

Table 3 Use of single brands by consumers

Use of same brand	Male		Female		Total consumers	
	No.	%	No.	%	No.	%
Yes	130	86.67	52	34.67	182	60.67
No	20	13.33	98	65.33	118	39.33
Total	**150**	**100.00**	**150**	**100.00**	**300**	**100.00**

χ^2 = 84.987, p >> 0.05 significant

Table 4 Reasons to change brands by consumers

Reasons to change brands	Male		Female		Total consumers	
	No.	%	No.	%	No.	%
By advertising	6	4.00	10	6.66	16	5.33
Price rise	21	14.00	12	8.00	33	11.00
To use new brand	47	31.34	52	34.67	99	33.00
By suggestions of shopkeeper	38	25.33	13	8.67	51	17.00
To just change	15	10.00	13	8.67	28	9.33
Low quality/ packaging of brands	23	15.33	50	33.33	73	24.34
Total	**150**	**100.00**	**150**	**100.00**	**300**	**100.00**

$\chi^2=26.091$, p>0.05 significant

Table 5 Effect of age to change brands

Reasons to change brands	Below 25 yrs		26 to 35 yrs		36 to 45 yrs		Above 45 yrs	
	No.	%	No.	%	No.	%	No.	%
By advertising	2	6.06	6	4.58	4	13.81	4	12.90
Price rise	0	0	13	9.93	15	14.29	5	16.13
To use new brand	21	63.64	52	39.69	18	17.14	8	25.81
By suggestions of shopkeeper	3	9.09	9	6.87	26	24.76	13	41.94
To just change	2	6.06	21	16.03	5	4.76	0	0
Low quality/ packaging of brands	5	15.15	30	22.90	37	35.24	1	3.22
Total	**33**	**100.00**	**131**	**100.00**	**105**	**100.0**	**31**	**100.0**

$\chi^2 = 77.311$, p >> 0.05 very significant

Table 6 Effect of education to change brand

Use of same brand	Level of education									
	High school		Intermediate		Graduation		P.G.		Professional & technical education	
	No.	%	No.	%	No.	%	No.	%	No.	%
By advertising	5	55.56	0	0	5	6.10	3	2.34	3	18.75
Price rise	0	0	0	0	5	6.10	21	16.41	7	43.75
To use new brand	2	22.22	25	38.46	29	35.36	40	31.25	3	18.75
By suggestions of shopkeeper/Known	0	0	14	21.54	17	20.73	18	14.06	2	12.50
To just change	0	0	7	10.77	16	19.52	5	3.91	0	0
Low quality/ packaging of brands	2	22.22	19	29.23	10	12.19	41	32.03	1	6.25
Total	**9**	**100.00**	**65**	**100.0**	**82**	**100.00**	**128**	**100.00**	**16**	**100.00**

$\chi^2 = 115.083$, p >> 0.05 very significant

RESULTS

1. Female consumers always use same brand in comparison of male consumers. Male consumers tend to change their brand frequently.
2. Age group influenced habit to change brand.
3. Education level influenced brand selection and habit to change brand.
4. Result shows that male and female customers give same reasons to change their brands just for change.

SUGGESTIONS

Above tables and statistical results shows that age, gender and education influenced brand selection and habit to change brands. Some consumers select brand due to attraction of colour, smells, price and due to impact of advertisement. Sometimes customers purchase product by brand names. So before selecting any brand consumer should be aware about brand quality.

BIBLIOGRAPHY

Andrew, A. Allentuck And Gordon, E. Binens	1977	Consumer choice, The Economics of Personal living. Harcourt Brace Jovanovich Inc New York Chicago, San Francisco Atlanta.
Badre Alam, S.	1983	Consumers and Advertising A. Socio Economic Approach. Indian Journal of Marketing Vol. XIV Nov. 83.
Converse Paul, D Crawford Merle	Nov. 1948	Family buying who does? Who influences it? Current Economics com comment - 11, page 38.
Daniela Mc Gowan	1984	Consumer Economics. Allyn and Bacon Inc. Boston, London, Sydney, Toronto.
Jacob Jacoby	1969	Personality and consumer behaviour how not to find relationship. Papers are consumer Psychology Page No. 102.
John, R- Wish Donald, G. Steely Stephen, E.Tritten		The Consumer, Prentice hall of India Private Ltd. New Delhi.
Kaurhardish	1984	Pattern of consumer preference and attitudes of the middle income groups towards expenditure on consumer equipments. Calcutta, Jadavpur Univeristy.
Kamath, Dr. Ravikala And Shobha Udipi	1994	Guide to thesis writing. Image Book Distributors Malad.
Muller Eva	1954	A study of purchases Decisions in consumer behaviour. The Dynamics of consumer Reaction P. 36-87.
Ogley Nalini	1989	Indian Journal of Home Science. Published by the Home Science Association of India June Page No. 48.
Peter, D. Bennett Harold Kassarjian	June 1993	Consumer Behaviour. Prentice hall of India Pvt. Ltd., M-97 Cannaught Circle, New Delhi.
Verghese, M.A.	1993	Indian Journal Home Science. Published by the Home Science Association of India. June Vol. 22, No. 1, P.No. 62-66.
tSu] ds-ih-	1977	vFkZ 'kkL= ds fl)kUr] lkfgR; Hkou gkWfLiVy jksM+] vkxjk] i'"B Øa- 203
eqdthZ] johUnz ukFk	1990-91	lkekftd 'kks/k ds ewyrRo] foosd izdk'ku 7] ;w-,- tokgj uxj] fnYyh 110 007] f}rh; laLdj.k
JhokLro] lq/kkjkuh	1994	miHkksDrk laj{k.k ,d v/;;u] fof/k psruk izdk'ku d`".k dqVh] xqlrk dkWykssuh] xaBk QkVd] tcyiqj
lsB] ,e-,y-	1975	vFkZ'kkL= ds fl)kUr] y{ehukjk;.k vxzoky vLirky jksM+] vkxjk&3
fla?kbZ] th-lh-	1981	vUrjkZ"Vªh; vFkZ'kkL=] fl)kUr leL;k,sa ,oa uhfr;kW] lkfgR; Hkou gkWfLiVy jksM+ vkxjkA
flag] ,l-Mh-	1988	oSKkfud lkekftd vuqla/kku ,oa losZ{k.k ds ewyrRo] dey izdk'ku 54] fizal;' koar jksM+] bUnkSj i'"B Øekad 1

The Strategy of De-Internationalization of the SMEs of the Footwear in the Area Metropolitana De Guadalajara

Pola N. Velázquez-Razo

Master's Degree in Business and Economic Studies, Economic University Sciences Center
Administrative University of Guadalajara

ABSTRACT

The aim of this paper is to analyze the exogenous and endogenous factors that determine the strategy of de-internationalization of SMEs in the sector of the footwear in the Metropolitan Zone of Guadalajara (ZMG). The proposed model explains the adoption of the strategy of de-internationalization from studies of comparative cases of SMEs in the footwear sector of the ZMG. In-depth interviews were applied to managers and staff involved during the time that the company was exporting. Analysis points out that lack of strategic planning and the instability in the foreign currency exchange rate are major factors that determine the strategy of de-internationalization in SMEs in the ZMG. Also, it is evident that the strategic imbalance during the de-internationalization strategy is not considered as a failure, but rather as an opportunity to redirect it and thus grow in the local market.

Keywords: *De-internationalization, strategy, exogenous and endogenous factors, SMEs*

INTRODUCTION

Interest in studying the strategy of internationalization of small and medium-sized enterprises (SMEs) (Andersen, 1993;)Bell, Crick, Young, 2004; Mr. de Clercq, Sapienza, Crijns, 2005; Fillis, 2006; Johanson and Vahlne 1977) and the factors that determine it, is extensive (Andersson, Gabrielsson, Ingemar, *2005;* Karedeniz and Göcer, 2007). However, there are few studies that address the strategy of de-internationalization and the withdrawal of export.

De-internationalization, in agreement with Mellahi, 2003 (quoted by Reiljan, 2005), is considered as an organisation's strategic response to reduce its participation in international and/or domestic operations in order to improve the profitability of the business as a result its external environment or its domestic context. The withdrawal of export is defined by Pauwels and Matthyssens (1999, p.10) as "an enterprise's firm decision to reduce activity in a market and a product abroad", either as a decrease in the international market share or

as a complete abandonment of the same (Crick, 2002; Pauwels and Matthyssens, 1999; Reiljan, 2005).

Research on the internationalization emphasizes incentives and obstacles/barriers that a company faces in order to internationalize (Bell and Crick, 2002; Clercq *et al.,* 2005; Cavusgil, 1984; Fillis, 2001; Johanson, Wiedersheim-Paul and Vahlne, 1977; Leonidou and Katsikeas, 1996). Among the key points considered as the dominant theories of the internationalization of enterprises there are some factors that directly influence the adoption of this strategy, such as experience, management vision, and rapid changes in the competitive environment (Andersson et al., 2004; *Baldauf, Cravens, Wagner, 2000;* Jímenez, 2007). However, research has not considered those factors that determine the output of the international markets. The adoption of the strategy of de-internationalization is a subject hardly considered and even forgotten (Benito, 2003; Pauwels, and Mathyssens, 1999; Reiljan, 2005; Turner and Gardiner, 2007).

There are contributions focused on analyzing such a strategy, particularly the importance of certain factors such as experience in the markets, the costs involved, the information one has on them, the characteristics of the entrepreneur, as well as the implementation of strategic planning to break into the international environment (Benito, 2003; Crick, 2002; Pauwels, and Mathyssens, 1999, 2002, 2004; Reiljan, 2005; Turner and Gardiner, 2007). In the long term, these factors may lead some companies to leave the markets or to redirect their strategy towards new opportunities, as a result of the external environment or the changing domestic context.

Knowing the causes that determine the behavior and the factors that determine the presence of small and medium-sized footwear enterprises (SME) in external markets is of great importance because they contribute to the generation of employment and economic development of the country. However, given their characteristics, SMEs present certain problems that shorten their stay in the market.

The Ministry of economy (2009) argues that the general problem of SMEs is associated with the following:

(a) Limited participation in trade,

(b) Limited access to sources of financing,

(c) Delinking the most dynamic sectors,

(d) Deficient training in human resources,

(e) Lack of engagement with the academic sector, and

(f) Lacking culture of innovation processes and development technology.

These constraints have an impact on the performance and permanence of the SMEs, with its consequent effect on employment and income of the nation. The majority of the footwear SME positioned in a given market, as part of their problem, do not have any expectations of growth that go beyond what they plan. Despite the importance of the number of companies contributing to the economy and job creation, only a small percentage of SMEs export.

According to a survey of the industrial situation of footwear in Jalisco, the system state of Jalisco information (SEIJAL) and the Chamber of the footwear industry of the State of Jalisco (CICEJ), there are 806 companies dedicated to this activity within the state as of 2008. Moreover, according to the same survey in 2008, which interviewed a sample size of 170 footwear companies, only 13% are engaged in export performance.

This research aims at the analysis of the strategy of de-internationalization of small and medium enterprises (SME) in the footwear sector in the Metropolitan Zone of Guadalajara (ZMG) and the factors that determine the strategy. This study is limited to the export of the production of small and medium enterprises (SMEs) in the footwear sector for several reasons.

First, the export is considered the primary means of entry to international markets for SMEs (Pauwels, Matthyssens, 1999; Crick, 2002; Leonidou, 2004). In addition, some studies show that withdrawals occur to a greater extent during export in comparison to other mechanisms of entry such as direct foreign investment (Pauwels, Matthyssens, 1999; Reiljan, 2005). Another reason is that the footwear SME that settle in a given market, do not have expectations of growth beyond the expected. Despite the contribution to the economy and employment generation, only a small percentage of SMEs export. Of these, only few manage to stay on the international markets.

During the implementation of a prior questionnaire for the selection of cases for the study, a sample of 40 manufacturers of footwear in the State found that 10 companies had ceased to export. Of the small % that manage to survive, the footwear SMEs have to face constraints that prevent their expansion of activities abroad, mainly illegal imports, informal trade in much of the country, the difficult economic environment, but above all the open trade with the Asian bloc.

For example, given the importance in exports and only to measure the problem, according to the Chamber of Footwear Industry of the State of Guanajuato and based on a study carried out by the Center for Economic Study of the Private Sector (CEESP), the damage that smuggling causes on the Mexican economy amounts to 30 billion dollars. The fiscal authorities no longer receive them, just because of the added tax value (not including the payment of duties and countervailing duties, a total of about 50 billion pesos.)

An additional problem stemmed from the periods of most recent economic crisis in the years 1995, 2001 and 2007, which have affected the economic growth of the country and the main sectors that make up the production environment. These economic crises led to a slowdown in the growth of certain sectors, particularly the manufacturing sector (Salinas, Tavera, 2007; Mendoza, 2010; Dussel, 2004 and 2009). In addition, the manufacturers of footwear, "are suffering the consequences of the opening up of trade which favored the importation of Chinese products, whose lower prices have led to the departure of many companies", says Rendón Trejo (2009, p. 2).

The existence of factors such as the lack of experience and knowledge of international markets, the increase in costs, as well as a limited production capacity that is unable to cope with the overwhelming demand abroad, has resulted in the loss of competitiveness in the industry. According to an interview of the Director of the Chamber of Footwear Industry of the State of Jalisco (CICEJ), there is no specific data of the companies that are affiliated with the chamber, how many exported and how many have ceased to do so. However, the decrease in the number of undertakings established in a formal way is clear. This has an impact on the uptake of tax revenue, not to mention the great unfair competition affecting the internal market, which harms the national productive plant, generates closing companies, and as a result, the loss of thousands of jobs. All this has been at a disadvantage to most of the footwear producers in the country including Jalisco.

With this issue, the questions of this study are: what are the factors determined by the de-internationalization strategy in the footwear industry of the ZMG? What factors determine the strategies of de-internationalization of the footwear SMEs in the ZMG?

THEORETICAL OR REFERENTIAL FRAMEWORK

Literature on internationalization, draws attention to the growing participation of small and medium-sized enterprises (SME) in international trade as a result of the intense globalization of markets, which during the first decade of the 21st century has shown dramatic and rapid changes (Leonidou, 2004).

According to the report on the world trade by the World Trade Organisation in 2008 "Trade in a globalizing world", even though there is no universal definition of *globalization*, economists use the term to refer to "the international integration of markets for primary commodities, capital and labor" (mauve *et al.,* 2003).

The internationalization strategy has been widely studied, mainly to get to know the behavior of SMEs in the international market (Wolff and Pett, 2000; Lu, Beamish, 2001; Fillis, 2001; Chetty and Campbell-Hunt, 2003; Bell *et al.*, 2003; Anderson et al, 2004; Bell, Crick, Young, 2004; Moen *et al*, 2004; Clercq, Sapienza and Crijns, 2005) and the factors that determine it (Andersson et al, 2004; Karedeniz and Göcer, 2007).

It is conceived as a way of participation and expansion in the activities of the companies in international markets. However some authors point out that some companies do not experience such growth (Penrose, 1959 cited by

Turcan, 2003) and decide to reduce the commitment in the international markets or retire altogether (Pauwels and Matthyssens, 1999; Crick, 2002).

(A) The De-Internationalization as Strategy

The de-internationalization concept was introduced by Welch and Loustarinen (1988, p. 37) who point out that "once the company moves into the process of internationalization it does not ensures its continuity" (quoted by Turcan, 2003, p. 211). Benito and Welch (1997, p. 9) define it as "those voluntary or forced actions that reduce the commitment to participation or exposure to current activities abroad". Also, they recognize the importance of differentiating between total or partial de-internationalization.

Some studies have analyzed the de-internationalization from various theoretical perspectives. From the economic field, the enterprise could consider de-internationalization in response to economic circumstances. From the perspective of strategic management, the company considers the de-internationalization in relation to the product portfolio and life cycle of the business, and from the perspective of internationalization management, it is seen as a barrier to the de-internationalization (Benito and Welch, 1997; Crick, 2002; Pauwels, and Mathyssens, 1999, 2002, 2004; Turcan, 2003 and 2011; Reiljan, 2005; Turner and Gardiner, 2007).

For his part, Turcan (2003) points out that the de-internationalization which is considered more as a process in the cross-border activity, is a consequence of the cause-effect relationship between internationalization and de-internationalization. The model proposes a conceptual framework that frames three constructs or variables:

(a) Commitment of employers influenced by psychological, social, and structural factors;

(b) Change in the dual networks that are triggered by a critical event and are dependent on the actions and intentions of both partners; and

(c) Time perceived by the entrepreneurs through the relationship of codes and memoirs (past) and the congruence and horizons (future).

Additionally, his model considers the importance of the total or partial withdrawal through the construction of a matrix where the positions of companies are located into quadrants as shown in Figure 1. In Figure 1, the location of the four quadrants is shown for the companies that are in the process de-internationalization. Quadrant 1 is formed by the companies that have fully withdrawn from international markets and instead focus on serving the local market. Quadrant IV also represents companies that withdrew completely from the market but with the difference that these companies could have ceased to operate during or before they started the process de-internationalization. Enterprises that are in quadrant II remain active on the international markets but partially de-internationalized, and finally quadrant III represents those cases not existing or known as "cells not empirical" (Non-empirical cell).

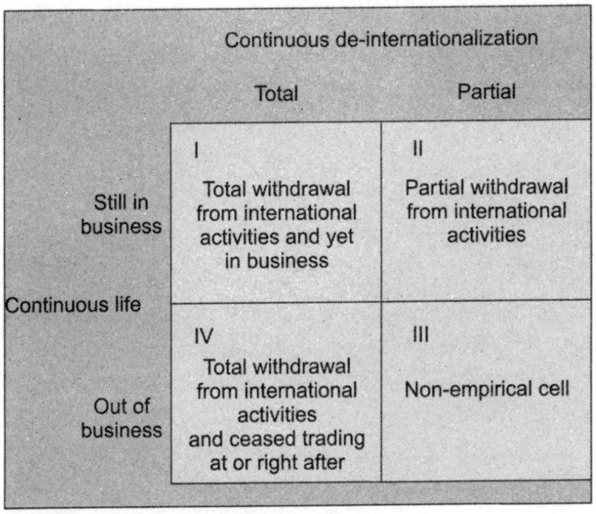

Fig. 1 Matrix showing position of companies that are in the process of de-internationalization

Source Own generation based on the model proposed by Turcan (2011)

Turcan (2003 2011) pointed out that the de-internationalization of companies can happen totally or partially (Benito and Welch, 1997; Reiljan, 2005).

The former is more likely to happen during the early stages, and it will decrease as the commitment and knowledge in foreign markets increases. This is in opposite to partial de-internationalization which tends to occur during the later stages of internationalization.

Figure 2 shows that enterprises adopt modes of entry depending on the strategies that can be considered a failure, i.e. a total withdrawal from the markets, with a shift in strategy or as a partial retreat where they opt for change in input mode, de-*franchising* or *de-exporting,* and a reduction in operations. This behavior matches the research developed by Pauwels and Mathyssens (1999, 2004). In this sense, the company may choose to retire partially or completely. In other words, they try to reorient their strategy, be it focusing on the domestic market or changing the input mode.

On the other hand Pauwels and Mathyssens (1999: 10), from the perspective of *export withdrawal,* develop a study about the process of a market

withdrawal strategy defined as "the strategic decision of a firm to rule the combination of a product/market out of its international portfolio." In other words, they are all actions taken by the company to reduce its commitments in the export market, which can be both internal (new strategic priorities) and external (dramatic changes in the competitive environment). His approach is basically based on the cognitive processes and behavior of decision-making and implementation processes. In this sense, export withdrawal is considered more as a strategy whereby an organisation carries out an adjustment between domestic resources and skills, and the opportunities and risks created by the external environment in which it unfolds (quoted by Pauwels and Mathyssens, 1999).

So the strategy for current research is understood as a process whose main characteristic lies in the decision-making process which involves processes of learning, planning, and engagement in the activities of the organisation. Six phases are identified in the process of decision-making during the retreat of export. Thus, this process is developed in the model of export withdrawal as a process:

(a) Start and accumulation of commitments on the market;

(b) Increase in stress;

(c) Two contrary reactions;

(d) Game of power;

(e) Vacuum vs. fait accompli; and

(f) Beyond the withdrawal.

Figure 3 explains the strategic process for withdrawing from the international market. The authors proposed a model of six phases conditioned by certain factors and behaviors induced by the threat of the learning environment and the dynamics of the political context.

The first phase consists of the company's gradual accumulation of both financial resources and physical and material resources (infrastructure, equipment). The second phase is when there is an increase in stress that comes with a mismatch between the objectives initially set by management and the achievement or the company's current situation. There is uncertainty among the staff, and they seek solutions to improve the situation. The third stage presents reactions in conflict that arise due to the stress of the situation.

The company seeks alternatives that enable them to make strategic decisions to resolve the conflict. Management adopts tactical measures. Two reactions arise thereby: passive and reactive. In the fourth stage there is a game of power between staff and managers.

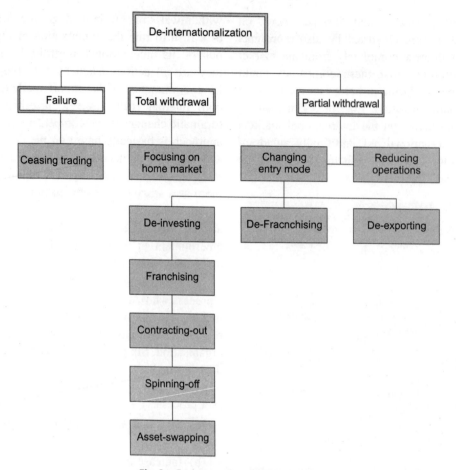

Fig. 2   De-internationalization modes
Source Own generation based on Turcan (2011).

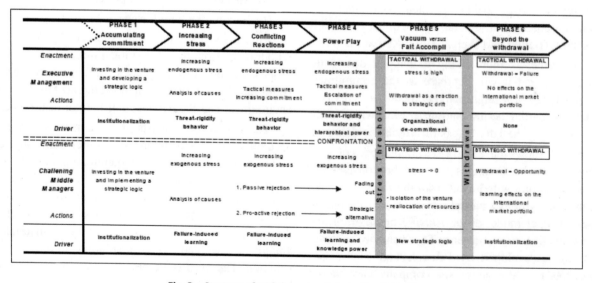

Fig. 3   Strategy of withdrawal on international markets
Source Based on Pauwels and Mathyssens model (1999, 2002).

Despite the implemented tactical measure, performance continues to decline. In the fifth stage it is formally decided to withdraw, thus decreasing strategic control.

Finally, in the last phase, two types of retirement are identified: on one hand, the tactical withdrawal which arises as a result of the threat-rigidity and management's learning of exploitation. On the other, the strategic withdrawal is characterized by being considered a "failure" that is induced by the exploratory learning of lower managers.

(B) Factors in The Strategy of De-Internationalization

Some authors note the factors involved in the strategy of de-internationalization (Reiljan, 2005; Turner and Gardiner, 2007). One of the causes for which export withdrawal could be started, as indicated by Pauwels and Mathyssens (1999), is the ambiguity of the information. The majority of managers perceive symptoms of weakness in the performance in particular markets, and they tend to make their own inferences regarding the main problems that cause the weak performance as well as probable solutions to those problems.

This process of de-internationalization coincides with Leonidou (2004) who pointed out that inefficiency in information, competitiveness in pricing, habits of consumers overseas, and political-economic obstacles, are factors that hinder exporter behavior. From another perspective, Crick (2002) considered the lack of strategic planning, including the mobilization of domestic resources as well as a large number of environmental issues arising from the weakness of the currency and the imposition of trade tariffs, as one of the reasons that might influence the decision to discontinue international activities. However, she argues that discontinuing exports can be a strategic advantage for the company if concentrating on the domestic market is more profitable.

In this sense, Reiljan (2003) also agrees in the argument that the factors intended as additional sources of knowledge tend to decrease the effect of a lack in international experience that creates changes in the strategy, with which it can increase or decrease the possibility of de-internationalization at the same time. As a result, the influence of this factor decreases as the company gradually fills its own knowledge base with the knowledge based on experience. During the time when companies think about internationalizing, they look to new markets for their product, internationalizing thus becomes one of their primary motives, and as their commitment to these markets increases, their field of activities increasingly becomes more widespread.

In a study conducted for a group of manufacturing companies in Estonia, Reiljan (2005) identifies four groups that frame the reasons for the de-internationalization, and their significance depends on the stage of globalization in which the company is located. One of the factors identified to be crucial for de-internationalization is the increase in costs, which tend to occur during a longer period of time and which also have a greater influence during the intermediate process of internationalization. This event is contrary to the change in strategy that tends to occur during the later stages of internationalization.

On the other hand, as the company increases its international experience, it looks for ways to minimize the costs arising from the partial or total dissolution of operations that are abroad. Its effect will depend on the level of commitment and experience. Nonetheless, it will have a major influence during the intermediate process of internationalization. In the study's findings, it is concluded that export withdrawals could have been caused mainly by the increase in costs and a poor performance. Moreover, the strategy of foreign owners could have played an important role in the des-investment in some of the foreign operations.

Three determining factors are proposed in this research for the adoption of the de-internationalization strategy by the footwear SMEs in the ZMG:

(a) Management's characteristics and skills,

(b) increase in costs, and

(c) economic conditions

METHOD OF RESEARCH: MULTIPLE CASE STUDIES

For this investigation the method of case studies is realized based on the approach developed by Yin (2003, p.13) which is defined as" an empirical inquiry that examines a contemporary phenomenon within its real context, when the boundaries between phenomenon and context are not evident, and which uses multiple sources of evidence". A model that shows the relationship between the strategy of de-internationalization by the footwear SMEs and the exogenous and endogenous factors is proposed.

De-internationalization strategy is conditioned by a range of factors. Based on the literature, some key variables are defined for the framework of the proposed analysis which will make it possible to consider and compare the previously mentioned scenarios. In short, the explanatory hypothetical model proposes that the strategy of de-internationalization (ED) is conditioned by the skills/characteristics of the management (HD); the increase in costs (IC); and by the economic conditions (CE).

As can be seen in Fig. 4, two types of factors are identified: endogenous and exogenous. The endogenous factors refer to all that which is associated to the resources, capabilities and difficulties of the company. The features/skills of the management and the increase in costs (for export) are primarily considered. The factors considered for a manager's capabilities/skills are the age of the entrepreneur, their experience in

the sector (years), and whether or not they made any strategic planning. The increase in costs considers the expenses incurred for exports as a proportion in the total sales during the period in which it was exported.

The exogenous factors relate to the difficulties of the economic/political context in which the company operates. In this sense, economic conditions are considered, primarily those that are conditioned by the changes in the foreign currency risk: instability in exchange rates resulting from fluctuations in the prices of export abroad, and evaluation of the currency of the

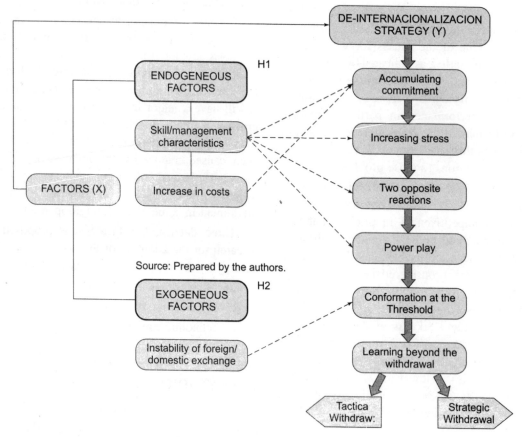

Fig. 4 Explanatory hypothetical model
Source Prepared by the authors.

exporting that causes non-competitive prices for the final buyer in the foreign country.

Both external and internal factors determine the adoption of the de-internationalization strategy, which is characterized by the transition of various stages that culminates in the reorientation of the company's strategy, whether through a tactical withdrawal seen as a failure, or a strategic seen as an opportunity for growth. The dotted lines of the figure show a relationship that will not be studied for the moment. It only describes the behavior for each company during the transition

between each stage that helps identify the withdrawal adopted by each one.

Data was collected through in-depth interviews. In case A, five key informants were interviewed. They were selected according to the experience and the level of participation during the time that the company was exporting. Selected respondents were the President of the Council (formerly CEO), the Sales Director, Sales Manager, the person in charge of the Office of Foreign Trade (whom was previously working as a direct person in charge of the Department of Imports and Exports when he was in the company). The interviews had duration of 40 minutes to an hour. An interview script was written for the interviews.

In case B, the selected key informants were the general manager (owner of the company), the person in charge of the sales area (supported for a while in the export), the person in charge of the collection area (who previously handled export operations) and the administrator (wife of the CEO). Interviews lasted approximately 40 minutes to 1 hour. For case B, some additional data for the triangulation of information was limited mainly due to the fact that the contacts were no longer available and the ones available were not able to provide the data. The characteristics of the case studies are set out in table 1 (see annex), for the analysis of the results of conducted a categorization of variables.

Table 1 Operationalization of variables

ENDOGENOUS FACTORS	
Factors	*Variables*
Skills/characteristics of the directors (CD)	Level of education
	Experience in the sector
	Knowledge of the foreign market
	Importance in the strategic planning
	Vision of long-term growth
Increase in costs (IC)	% transportation on level of export costs.
	% expenditure on export on total sales to the export.
	% costs of production on the level of the export.
EXOGENOUS FACTORS	
Economic conditions (EC)	Revaluation of the currency of the exporting
	Instability in foreign exchange rates

Source Prepared by the authors.

This facilitated the collection and analysis of the results listed below.

ANALYSIS AND FINDINGS OF THE RESULTS

Companies show a homogeneous behavior during the adoption of the de-internationalization strategy. As noted in the theory, the companies carried out an adjustment between domestic resources and the opportunities and risks caused by the environment in which these operate (Pauwels and Matthyssens, 1999).

From the first phase characterized by a gradual accumulation of resources to the last phase which culminates in the withdrawal of the international markets, there is a shift in strategy that allowed them

to take advantage of the opportunity for growth in the domestic market.

The results indicate that the answers of the respondents all agree in recognizing that the lack of strategic planning and the economic conditions prevailing in the market, prompted the decision to withdraw from international markets. In one case (case A), the importance of the costs involved in export are considered, particularly the costs of logistics which occasionally increase the final price of the product.

Some people thus also considered other factors, even when they were not decisive in the adoption of the de-internationalization strategy, if they had an influence during the export process. In general terms they consider that the knowledge of foreign markets and that having the appropriate intermediary is essential to achieve success in international markets.

CONCLUSIONS AND FINAL REFLECTIONS

The above results suggest two important conclusions for the study: The factors affecting the adoption of the de-internationalization strategy for both case A and case B, and that are considered of utmost importance by the personnel involved in the export process, are mainly the importance of strategic planning and the instability of the exchange rate caused by the economic crisis.

The de-internationalization represents a choice strategy that allows them to refocus their strategy. It also represents an opportunity to grow in other markets, particularly the domestic market.

This study presents some limitations. The first is the limited access of information in primary or direct sources. The second is the bias of the information because the results come from the perceptions of managers and staff whom are engaged on the analyzed variables.

References

- Andersen, O. (1993) *"On the Internationalization Process of Firms: A Critical Analysis"*, Journal of International Business Studies, 24 (2), 209-231.
- Anderson, NL, Polanski, M, Pieper, R, et al, 2004. *The Human Plasma Proteome: A Non-redundant List Developed by Combination of Four Separate Sources*, Mol Cell Proteomics, 3:311–26.
- Anderson, NL, Polanski, M, Pieper, R, et al, 2004. *The Human Plasma*
- Andersson, S, Gabrielsson. J & Wictor, I. 2004. International activities in small firms – examining

factors influencing the internationalization and export growth of SMEs. *Canadian Journal of Administrative Sciences. 21, 1, 22-34.*

- Arruñada, Benito (2003), "Property Enforcement as Organized Consent," *Journal of Law, Economics, and Organisation, 19(2), 401-44.*

- Baldauf Artur; "Cravens David W, Wagner U, (2000)." *Examining Determinants of Export Performance in Small Open Economies",*" *Journal of World,* 35 (1), 61-79 Database EBSCO.

- Bell, J, McNaughton, R, Young, S, & Crick, D, 2003. *Towards an Integrative Model of Small Firm Internationalization, Journal of International Entrepreneurship,* 1(3): 339-362.S

- Bell, J; Crick, D; Young, S, (2004) "*Small Firm Internationalization and Business Strategy",* *International Small Business Journal,* 22 (1), 23-56

- Benito, Welch G.R.G. 1997. "*Divestment of Foreign Production Operations*" Applied Economics, 29, 1365-1377.

- Cavusgil S, T, (1984) "*Differences among Exporting Firms Based on Their Degree of Internationalization*" *Journa! of Business Research,* 12 (2), 195-208.

- Chetty, S, and Campbell-Hunt, C, 2003. *Paths to Internationalization among Small - to Medium-Sized Firms: A Global Versus Regional Approach, European Journal of Marketing,* 37(5-6): 796-820.

- Chetty, S, & Campell-Hunt, C, 2003b. *Explosive International Growth and Problems of Success amongst Small to Medium-Sized Firms, International Small Business Journal,* 21(1): 5-27.

- Crick, D. (2002) "*The Decision to Discontinue Exporting: SMEs in Two U.K. Trade Sectors*", *Journal of Small Business Management,* 40(1), 66-77.

- Crick, D. (2002) 'The *Decision to Discontinue Exporting: SMEs in Two UK Trade Sectors',* *Journal of Small Business Management* 40(1): 66–77.

- De Clercq, Dirk Harry J Sapienza; Crijns, Hans (2005) "The internationalization of Small - Medium - Sized firms" *small business economics,* 24, 409-419.

- De Clercq, Dirk Harry J Sapienza; Crijns, Hans (2005) "*The Internationalization of*

- *Small - Medium - Sized Firms"* Small Business Economics, 24, 409-419.

- Dussel, P, E, (2009) "*The Mexican Manufacturing: Recovery Options*" Economy Advises, 357, 41-52.

- Enrique Dussel Article first published online: Deconstruction of the Concept of "Tolerance": From Intolerance Solidarity pages 326–333, September 2004. **Retrieved, http://internetaula. ning.com/profile/RodolfoRendonTrejo**

- Fillis Ian (2001) "Small firm internationalization: an investigative survey and future research directions", Management Decision, 39 (9), 767-783

- Fillis, I, 2002. *The Internationalization Process of the Craft Microenterprise,* Journal of Developmental Entrepreneurship, 7(1): 25-43.

- http://gel.ahabs.wisc.edu/mauve; the Mauve alignment system and visualization environment

- Jímenez, M. i. j. (2007) "*Determinants for the Internationalization of Mexican SMEs",* Economic Analysis, 49 (22), 111-131

- Johanson, J, & Vahlne, (1977). The Internationalization Process of the Firm: A Model of Knowledge Development and Increasing Foreign Market Commitments. *Journal of International Business Studies,* 8(1): 23–32.

- Johanson, J; Vahlne, Jan-Erik (1977) " The Uppsala Internationalization Process Model: From Liability of Foreigness to Liability of Outsidership", *Journal of International Business Studies,* 8 (1), 23-32

- Karadeniz, E; Göcer, k, (2007) "Internationalization of Small Firms, to Case Study of Turkish Small - and Medium-Sized Enterprises", European Business Review, 19 (5), 387-403.

- Leonidas C, Leonidou; Katsikeas, Constantine S, (1996) "The Export Development Process: An Integrative Review of Empirical Models", *Journal Of International Business Studies,* 27 (3); 517-551

- Leonidou, Leonidas C., (2004), "*An* Analysis of the Barriers Hindering Small Business Export", *Journal of Small Business Management,* 42(3), 279-302 ABI/INFORM Global, PROQUEST database

- Lu, J, W, & Beamish, P.L. (2001). The Internationalization and Performance of SME's, *Strategic management journal,* 22; 565-88.

- Mellahi, K. (2003) 'The De-Internationalization Process: A Case Study of Marks and Spencer', in: Wheeler, C, McDonald, F, Greaves, I. Internationalization: Firm Strategies and Management, Palgrave Macmillan, 150–162.
- Mendoza, C. j. (2010) "The Behavior of Manufacturing Industry of Mexico Before the U.S. Recession", *Journal of Economics,* 27 (75), 9-35
- Moen, T. *et al.*; (2004). A Genome Scan of a Four-Way Tilapia Cross Supports the Existence of A QTL for Cold Tolerance on UNH Linkage Group 23, Aquaculture Research, 35: 893-904.
- Moen T et al, (2004). A Linkage Map of Atlantic Salmon (Salmo Salar) Reveals an Uncommonly Large Difference in Recombination Rate Between the Sexes, Animal Genetics, 35: 81-92.
- Pauwels, P, and Matthyssens, P, (1999) "A Strategy Process Perspective on Export Withdrawal", *Journal of International Marketing* 7 (3): 10-37.
- Pauwels, P. and Matthyssens, P. (2002) 'The Dynamics Of International Market Withdrawa*l'* In S, Jain (ed.) State of the Art of Research in International Marketing, Edward Elgar Publishing: Cheltenham, UK, in Press.
- Pauwels. P; Lommelen, T; Matthyssens, p, (2004) "The Internationalization Process of the Firm: Progression through Institutionalization, Exploitative and Exploratory Learning", AIB Conference of Stockholm, 1-35
- Penrose ET, (1959). The Theory of the Growth of the Firm, Oxford University Press: New York.
- Penrose, ET, (1965). Economics and the Aspirations of Le Tiers Monde, London: University of London.
- Proteome: A Non-redundant List Developed by Combination of Four Separate Sources, Mol Cell Proteomics, 3:311–26, Moen T *et al*,; (2004). A Multi-Stage Testing Strategy for Detection of Quantitative Trait Loci Affecting Disease Resistance in Atlantic Salmon, Genetics, 167: 851-8
- Reiljan, e. (2005) "Reasons for Off-Internationalization: An Analysis of Estonian Manufacturing Companies" University of Tartu, on press, 1-28.
- Rendón, T. A; Moràl. A. a. (2009) "Guanajuato Footwear Companies," Strategies of Competition, Presentation of The Paper of the Safe Forum UAM for the Study of the Micro, Small and Medium Enterprises.
- Salinas, C, e, Tavera, C, M (2007) "The Transition of the Mexican Economy, *1982-2004, In Publication P."* 275-290.
- Turcan, R.V. (2003) 'De-Internationalization and the Small Firm', In: Wheeler, C, McDonald, F, Greaves, I, Internationalization: Firm Strategies and Management, Palgrave Macmillan, 208–222.
- Turcan, R.V. (2011) "De-Internationalization: A Conceptualization, AIB- UK & Ireland Chapter Conference on International Business: New Challenges, New Forms, New Practices" Storbritannien Edinburgh
- Turner, C; Gardiner, P. D. (2007) "Of Internationalization and Global Strategy: The Cases of British Telecommunications *(BT)" Journal of Business & Industrial Marketing,* 22 (7), 489-497.
- Wolf, J. A. & Pett, T. L. (2000), *Internationalization of Small Firms; an Examination of Export Competitive Patterns, Firms Size, and Export Performance,* Journal of small business journal, 38(2); 34-47
- Yin Robert K. (2003), *Case study research: design and methods, Applied Social Research Methods,* Sage Publications.

Online sources

World of Trade Organisation (WTO) (2008), *Trade in a Globalizing Word,* Accessed on March 3, 2010 page www.wto.org

Secretaría De Economía (N.D.) *Information Document Relating To Small And Medium-Sized Enterprises In Mexico.* Accessed on February 7, 2009, page www.cipi.com.mx

State System of Information Jalisco (Seijal) (2008), *Survey of Situation of the Footwear Industry,* Accessed on November 26, 2009 page www.seijal.gob.mx.

RECOMMENDATION AND CONCLUSION

The evidence from this study indicates that there is overall low satisfaction among Doctors working in Public and Private sector in different region. They feel the stress due to the high workload, lack of self development and growth, low support from the management and management are not paying Salary as

ANNEXURE 1

Table 2 Characteristics of the case studies

FEATURES	IF COMPANY "A" Constant exporter	IF COMPANY "B" Sporadic exporter
Foundation	1979	1944
Company size	Small	Medium
Number of workers	50 workers at the factory	150 workers
Market goal	Children's footwear and Lady of synthetic material (range justifiably)	footwear of leather woman of medium to high range, as well as leather handbags and accessories
Current markets served	20 States of the Republic (2 stores outlet own brand)	22 boutiques throughout the Republic and sale
Channel of distribution at the national level	Shoe shops, Department stores and sales catalogue (without own brand) and 2 shops	Specialty stores, Department stores and boutiques mark itself, under the schema store-in store outlet own brand
Current export markets	None	None
Time in which exported	1994-1998	Background the years 80s, store located in Houston Texas. Export to E.U. 2007-2009
Served markets	Latin America (Colombia, Chile, Costa Rica, Panama)	United States, Spain and Chile
Channel of distribution during export	Intermediary (sales agent) (promotion and direct marketing)	Broker (agent) (through trade shows and direct sales)

Source Own generation based on the data gathered during field work

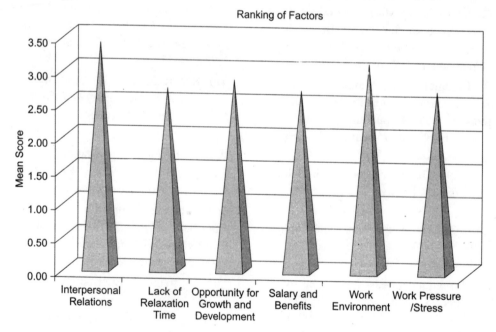

per norms especially in the Private sector. However, it was also evident that despite these findings, they are still able to carry out their professional duties.

This study reveals that less than half of the Doctors are not satisfied with their job. This study therefore recommends that focus should be given to working conditions, relations with hospital administration, salary, professional development and promotion. Since physicians are guided by their professional ethos, it is possible to conclude that their job dissatisfaction or lack of job satisfaction may indeed emanate from the failure to fulfill their professional obligations due to lack of an enabling environment. Hence there is need to pay particular attention to the physician work environment since improvements in this domain will most likely lead to job satisfaction.

References

- Alam GM, Hoque KE (2010), Who Gains From "Brain and Body Drain" Business -Developing/ Developed World or Individuals: A Comparative Study Between Skilled and Semi/Unskilled Emigrants, *African Journal of Business Management, 4*(4), 534-548

- Castillo & Cano,(2004) *Factors Explaining Job Satisfaction Journal of Agricultural Education*

- Dr Mkubwa Jack, Dissertation Submitted in Partial Fulfillment of the Requirements of the Degree of Master of Public Health in the Faculty of the Health Sciences University of Witwatersrand School of Public Health Johannesburg South Africa Job Satisfaction among Public Sector In Botswana

- Herzberg, F, Mausner, B, & Snyderman, B B (1959), The Motivation to Work, *New York: John Wiley & Sons.*

- Dasgupta Hirak,and Kumar Suresh (2009), Role Stress among Doctors Working in a Government Hospital in Shimla (India), *European Journal of Social Sciences 9*, 3

- Khan Khurram and Nemati Ali Raza (2011), Impact of Job Involvement on Employee Satisfaction: A Study Based on Medical Doctors Working at Riphah International University Teaching Hospitals in Pakistan, *African Journal of Business Management 5* (6), 2241-2246.

- Behavior: Affect in the Workplace, *Annual Review of Psychology*, 53, 279-307, 282

- Nirpuma Madaan, JK Science, Job Satisfaction Among Doctors In A Tertiary Care Teaching Hospital

- Ofili, A N; M C Asuzu, E C Isah and O Ogbeide (2004), Occupational Medicine 2004; 54:400–403 Job Satisfaction and Psychological Health of Doctors, a*t the University of Benin Teaching Hospital*

- Retrieved from Http://Www.Academicjournals. Org/AJBM ISSN 1993-8233©2011 Academic Journals ,

- Weiss, H M (2002), Deconstructing Job Satisfaction: Separating Evaluations, Beliefs and Affective Experiences, *Human Resource Management Review*, 12, 173-194

Effect of T.V. Advertisement on Purchasing Related Behavior of Different Household Equipments

Jyoti Prasad

Principal, Morar Girls College, Gwalior

ABSTRACT

In this research paper an attempt has been made to explain the importance of advertisement in our social, economic and personal life. As advertisement is directly related with social, economical and personal aspects of human life. "Any paid form of non personal communication of ideas goods or services by business firms identified in the advertising massage intended to lead to a scale immediately or eventually."

Keywords: *Advertisement, Purchase Behavior*

INTRODUCTION

American marketing association has described that advertisements are essential for success in modern business world. No business can survive without advertisement so advertisement is the must as the main purpose of every commercial organisation is to promote sale because it is the only way to commercialization the product any activity towards sales promotion may be called promotional activities, such promotional activities are advertising, with the help of T.V. The purchaser can know the money value of different articles, their types, traits and she can also purchase directly from the television.

CONCEPTUAL FRAMEWORK

The basic role of advertisement is to promote the related product and to increase the sales of related product but during this process advertisement in forms and communicate so many things to human beings.

There are so many modes of advertisement but nowadays television is playing a prominent role for advertisement. The service of television was started 1959 in India. At present more than 100 T.V. station are surviving in our country with the help of satellite.

Now television has became a centre of recreation from childhood to old age people. We all know that so many daily soaps have seen. Television also helps to give knowledge to satisfy our curiosity and thus it is became a powerful equipment for motivation.

In the present research work the researcher try to relate the relation between purchasing behaviour and advertisement through television.

The meaning of purchasing related behaviour is the consumption of consumers with the help of money is related to substaints and services.

The current paper is an attempt to evaluate whether television advertisements affect the purchasing behavior of women purchase.

OBJECTIVES

For the present study the following objectives are formulated by the researcher.

1. There should be significant difference between working and non working women in their purchasing behaviour.
2. Television affects the purchasing behaviour of women consumer.

METHODOLOGY

As the topic of present research work is to know that effect of television on purchasing related behaviour of women consumer.

Greater Gwalior is selected for sample. Selection, the sample, selection was limited only in women consumer.

The data was collected to utilize random sampling method. 300 hundred women consumer are selected from different out of 60 wards. Only ten wards selected randomly and from each ward 50 working and fifty non working women consumer are selected.

During sample selection the age of women (consumer are from 25-50 years.) Medium socioeconomic status and nuclear family were treated as controlled variables. After classification and tabulation of data following tables are created to evaluate the significance of difference between the working and non working women consumer related to their purchasing behaviour with the help of data. The importance of advertisement was also calculated. The purchasing behaviour of different household equipment like - cooking gas, pressure cooker, mixer grinder, fridge, washing machine, vacuum cleaner, television and music system are calculated.

CONCLUSION

1. The results show that the working and non working women differ significantly at 1% level of significance.
2. The advertisement effect significantly on the purchasing power of women consumer.
3. Television effects on the purchasing behavior of different household equipment.

References

- Marketing management: Varma and Agrawal.
- Financial management: Varma and R.K. Agrawal.
- Financial management : I.M. Pandey

Table 1 The level of significance of working and non working women to related with their purchasing behavior

S.No.	List of purchasing related behavior	No. of Non working women	No. of Working women	Total
1.	High level	37	79	116
2.	Middle level	92	60	152
3.	Low level	21	11	32
	Total	150	150	300

df = 2, χ2 = 25.06, p < 0.01 (significant)

Table 2 Effect of advertisement on purchasing related behavior to purchase of household equipment

S.No.	Effect of advertisement on purchase related behavior	% of Non working women	% of Working women	% of total
1.	Always	45.33	66.00	56.67
2.	Sometimes	36.00	22.00	29.00
3.	Never	18.67	12.00	15.33
	Total	100.00	100.00	100.00

Table 3 Effect of T.V. on purchasing related behavior (in percentage)

S.No.	Household equipment	% of Non Working women	% of Working women	% of total
1.	Cooking gas	0.667	04.66	05.67
2.	Pressure cooker	25.34	27.64	26.34
3.	Mixer grinder	28.00	14.00	21.00
4.	Fridge	30.00	14.67	22.34
5.	Washing machine	22.00	29.33	25.33
6.	Vaccum cleaner	27.33	25.33	26.33
7.	Television	32.00	29.33	30.67
8.	Music system	13.33	08.67	11.00
9.	Electric water heater	8.67	9.33	8.66
10.	Ceiling fan	26.00	19.33	22.67
11.	Cooler	18.00	12.67	15.33

Green Marketing: A Study of Consumer Fondness towards Green Products

Kajal Maheshwari[1] and Akansha Maheshwari[2]
[1]SB Patil Institute of Management, Pune
[2]Student, Christ University, Bangalore

ABSTRACT

The objective of this paper is to find the gap in the past research. Using the analysis the conceptual model is suggested after integrated factors product, prices, and brand image. The Conceptual framework needs to test. Research Paper attempts to examine the level of fondness towards Green Product and its conversion into buying decision. This study attempts to find the factors affecting buying decision for Green Products. Studies find that people are aware about ecological & environmental problems & most consumers perceive that Green product will reduce the same. The result of the study reveals that consumer fondness towards the Green Product may not convert it in to buying.

Keywords: *Consumer Awareness, Environmental Problems, Green Buying Behavior, Conceptual Model*

INTRODUCTION

After the industrial revolution, humans are responsible irreparable damage to the planet. They've altered ecosystem and exploited natural resources beyond their regenerative capacity. According to some studies, thirty to forty % of current environmental degradation is due to the consumption activities of private households (Grunert, 1993). Reports speak that this trend is growing (Grant, 2000: 5).

Although the level of concern and consciousness about environment is proven to be high in many countries, this doesn't translate automatically into pro-environmental behavior. A report shows that there is inconsistency between consumer environmental concern and purchase behavior. The impact of environmental consciousness on consumer purchasing behavior therefore remains unclear.

OBJECTIVES

1. The central objective of this research is to examine the models of Green Consumer Behavior define by early researchers.
2. The objective of the current study is to examine the common determinants of consumers' pro-environmental behavior through studying the models proposed in the past research.
3. The proposed conceptual model illustrates the determinants and the consequences of environmental consciousness. Through this model, the link between environmental consciousness, ecological buying behavior, and willingness to pay a higher price for a green product will be clarified. These key concepts will also be defined accordingly.

METHODOLOGY

The objective of this paper to find the research gap, Library method is used.

Literature Review

The earliest attempts to characterize the green consumer can be traced to the 1970s, when Webster (1975) published his work *Determining the Characteristics of the Socially Conscious Consumer*. Following Kilbourne and Beckman (1998), the conventional approach refers to the body of research within green marketing that is mainly concerned with the task of profiling the green consumer by the use of methods and models originated from conventional marketing theory. For several decades, social scientists have investigated the motivations of individuals who engage in pro environmental behavior (PEB). Economists, for example, tend to examine the influence of external conditions, such as income, price, and socio-economic characteristics, upon behavior. Their approach is grounded in neoclassical economic theory, which presupposes that individual decisions are based on a specific definition of rational self-interest. Other researchers have tried to find the efficiency of demographic, socio-demographic and psychographic data as a means to define green market-segments (Straughan and Roberts, 1999; Laroche *et al.*, 2001). Dimantopoulus *et al.*, (2003) presented a thorough review on the use of socio-demographics as a means to define the green consumer. Besides these studies on green market segmentation, another significant number of research papers within this mainstream marketing approach seek to apply cognitive models of decision-making in order to predict green consumer behavior by studying the relationships between knowledge, specific beliefs, attitudes and behavior in relation to the environment. In 1989, 67% of Americans stated that they were willing to pay 5-10% more for ecologically compatible products (Coddington, 1990).

By 1991, environmentally conscious individuals were willing to pay between15-20% more for green products (Suchard and Polonsky, 1991). An important challenge facing marketers is to identify which consumers are willing to pay more for environmentally friendly products. It is apparent that an enhanced knowledge of the profile of this segment of consumers would be extremely useful. The closer we move to an understanding of what causes individuals to pay more for green products, the better marketers will be able to develop strategies specifically targeted at these consumers. Following Berkowitz and Lutterman's (1968) study, Henion (1972) also thought that consumers with medium or high incomes would be more likely to act in an ecologically compatible manner due to their higher levels of education and therefore to their increased sensitivity to social problems. However, the results did not support his hypothesis: environmentally friendly behavior was consistent across income groups. Moreover, Sandahl and Robertson (1989) found that the environmentally conscious consumer is less educated and has a lower income than the average American. This brought them to conclude that income and education are not good predictors of environmental concern or purchase behavior.

Early research identified the green consumer as being younger than average (Berkowitz and Lutterman,

1968; Anderson and Cunningham, 1972; Van Liere and Dunlap, 1981). Surprisingly, this trend has been reversed in the last decade and several recent studies identified the green consumer as being older than average (Sandahl and Robertson, 1989; Vining and Ebreo, 1990; Roberts, 1996). Although most findings about the impact of consumers' demographic characteristics on their environmentally conscious behavior are contradictory (Roberts, 1996), it is clear that they exert a significant influence. However, most authors agree that demographics are less important than knowledge, values and/or attitude in explaining ecologically friendly behavior (Webster, 1975; Brooker, 1976; Banerjee and McKeage, 1994; Chan, 1999).

Model 1

This model is tested in china consumer express ecological affect & green purchase intention. There is impact of cultural values on beliefs impacting on the behavior. The cultural values are largely formed & nurtured by interpersonal relationship & social orientation.

The framework asserts that cultural values can be classified into five dimensions

> Man nature Orientations
>
> Man himself Orientation
>
> Past-time Orientation
>
> Relational Orientation

Activity Orientation

In the present study researcher try to find the relationship between cultural influences really exist for buying the green product.

A Conceptual Model

A model is tested to depict the possible interrelationship between person's Affect (Af), Knowledge (Kn) relating to ecological issues significantly influence his intention to engage in green purchase (IntP), to capture the possible impact of the "Man Nature" orientation on green purchase. In other words, though the direct impact on Af & Kn,MNO is believed to exert a positive influence on green purchase intentions. The model is formulated:

The data proved the performance of the relevant (ActP). Both Af & Kn found to similar degree of highly positive influence on Int. MNO only exhibited a significant influence on the affective component (Af) but not on the knowledge component (Kn) So there is favourable ecological affect & green purchase intentions but their level of ecological knowledege & and commitment to green purchase are still low.

The finding says both ecological affect & ecological knowledege are important determinats of consumers

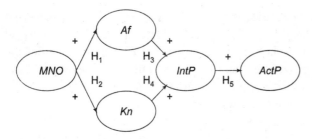

Notes Af and Kn represent ecological affect and ecological knowledge respectively.
IntP represents intention to engage in green purchase.
ActP represents actual involvement in green purchase.
MNO represents the man-nature orientation.
→ with + sign represents positive influence.
His refer to the relevant hypotheses.

green purchase intentions which in turn provides important impetus for actual green purchase.

Model 2

This model was developed by Yeonshin Kim, Daegu University Sejung Marina Choi, and University of Texas at Austin in 2000.

Applying the conceptual framework of value–attitude–behavior relationship this study key antecedents of green purchase behavior and develops a model for explaining their influence on ecological consumption. This model investigated the relationship between, the effects of collectivism, environmental concern and Perceived Consumer Effectiveness (PCE) on ecological purchase through structural equation modeling.

This model explains the potential influences of consumer value orientation and general pro-environmental concerns and beliefs on green buying behaviors.

Proposed Model

Individualism is characterized by independence, self-reliance, freedom of choice, and a high level of competition (Triandis 1989), while collectivism emphasizes interdependence, in-group harmony, family security, group-oriented goals, social hierarchies, cooperation, and a low level of competition (Triandis 1995). Perceived Consumer Effectiveness (PCE) refers to the extent to which individuals believe that their actions make a difference in solving a problem (Ellen, Weiner, and Cobb-Walgren 1991). PCE, defined as "the evaluation of the self in the context of the issue". People who have a more collectivistic orientation also rate themselves higher on collectivist traits including respectfulness, obedience, dutifulness, reciprocity, self-sacrifice, conformity, and cooperativeness than those from individualistic cultures (Grimm *et al.*; 1999). Thus, these collectivistic individuals might expect other members to perform the same behavior and thus have

greater beliefs in making differences by engaging in the behavior at the aggregate level although the behavior is performed individually.

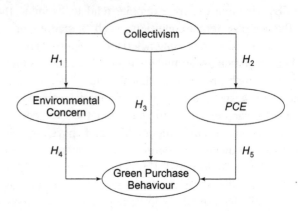

FINDINGS

Collectivism, defined as an individual-level value orientation, appeared to positively influence individuals' tendency to buy green products, but only through their positive beliefs about self-efficacy. Collectivistic individuals who value group goals and cooperation might be highly motivated to make pro-environmental choices by having stronger beliefs that their behavior would make a difference in mitigating environmental problems. Greater perceived self efficacy directly influences the likelihood that consumers actually engage in green purchase behavior. These findings seem to reflect the unique nature of pro-environmental behavior.

Environmental concerns also had a direct, positive influence on green purchase, suggesting that consumers who possess strong environmental concern may be interested in consumption of products that reflect that concern. However, environmental attitudes or concerns that reflect an individuals' orientation or belief toward the environment specifically appear to be not related to their collectivistic tendencies at a more general level.

Fundamental values that individuals hold at an abstract level can motivate and drive behavior.

Model 3

This study was done in Canada by Michel Laroche Royal Bank Distinguished Professor of Marketing, John Molson School of Business, Concordia University, Montreal, Quebec, Canada

Bergeron and Forleo tested a model to investigate the demographic, psychological and behavioral profiles of consumers who are willing to pay more for environmentally friendly products. These factors can be classified into five categories: demographics, knowledge, values, attitudes and behavior responsible to pay more.

Findings

Among the eight demographic variables studied, only "gender," "marital status" and "number of children living at home" differentiated the two segments. Consumers willing to pay more for green products reported that today's ecological problems are severe, that corporations do not act responsibly toward the environment and that behaving in an ecologically favorable manner is important

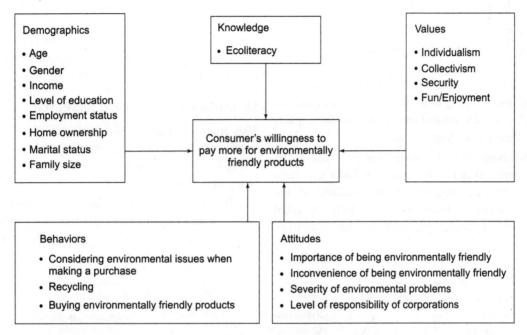

Fig. 2   Conceptual framework

and not inconvenient. They place a high importance on security and warm relationships with others, and they often consider ecological issues when making a purchase. Conversely, consumers unwilling to pay more for green products reported that companies are acting responsibly toward the environment and they admit (in average) that they do not consider ecological issues when making a purchase. These consumers attributed a lower score to the severity of ecological problems and to the importance of being ecologically friendly. These findings imply many managerial implications for green marketers, which are discussed in the next section.

Common Characteristics

After studying the above models the positive attributes that support the model of Green Consumer Behavior.

- Knowledge is recognized in consumer research as a characteristic that influences all phases in the decision process. Specifically, knowledge is a relevant and significant construct that affects how consumers gather and organize information. Knowledge about ecological issues is a significant predictor of environmentally friendly behavior even found that individuals highly knowledgeable about environmental issues were more willing to pay a premium price for green products

- Two Major Values Individualism & Collectivism implies cooperation, helpfulness, and consideration of the goals of the group relative to the individual. Behavior of collectivist people tend to be friendlier to the environment, while individualistic people tend to be more unfriendly.

- The attitudes with respect to environmentally friendly behavior are importance and inconvenience.

- Perceived level of self-involvement toward the protection of the environment. Many individuals may have high ecological concern, but feel that the preservation of the environment is the responsibility of the government and/or big corporations. We might expect this attitude to impact the willingness of consumers to spend more for environmentally friendly products.

- Among the demographic variables studied, only "gender," "marital status" and "number of children living at home" differentiated the two segments. It may be suggested that these individuals are more inclined to think of how a ruined environment may negatively impact not only on their partner, but on their children's future.

Managerial Implications

- It is of primary importance for marketers to advertise why it is convenient to purchase green products and to change consumer perceptions in a positive way.
- More and more companies educate consumers about the convenience of buying ecologically safe products.
- Information cards, window displays, and videos are used throughout the store to inform the public on the environmental and social impacts of their purchasing decisions.
- Marketers should communicate to the target audience that buying green products can have a significant impact on the welfare of the environment. Through a properly targeted advertising campaign, marketers can encourage

positive attitudes and behaviors held by ecologically friendly people.

Proposed Model

Overall, the combined results from the past research (model) portray some common variables towards green behavior. Using the analysis the conceptual model is suggested pertinent to address integrated factors product, prices, brand image. This model is need to tested.

Limitations and Future Research

This study is based on qualitative analysis which limits the knowledge of the long-term impact of the factors in above stated model. Some the characteristics contradicts many previous studies.

The proposed model needs to be tested. Proposed Model is designed only on the secondary information. Therefore, results must be used with caution. No

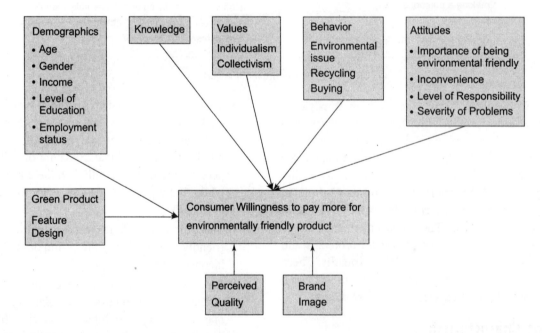

quantitative data is collected. Secondly, the research did not identify the green products; as a result the respondents' response might vary for different categories of green products. Future research should address this issue by considering focused green products.

Do the results generated in this study apply to all types of ecological products? Would we obtain the same results in India also? To answer these questions, researchers could eventually study the factors that influence consumers' willingness to spend more for ecologically compatible products, but from a completely different angle. Customers claimed they wanted to

buy ecologically compatible products, but British supermarkets were overstocked with products that the same consumers later explained were too expensive.

CONCLUSION

In conclusion, the major contributions of this study were the investigation of the major common characteristics consumers want to buy environmentally friendly products and the subsequent discussion of the implications for marketers.

This research being qualitative, the results are only taken for past research. The increase in media coverage of ecological deterioration, the recent influx of environmentally compatible products in the marketplace and the integration of ecological issues in both our educational and political systems point to the need for more research on the environmentally conscious consumer.

References

- Alba, J.W. And Hutchinson, J.W. (1987), "Dimensions of Consumer Expertise", *Journal of Consumer Research*, March, 13, 411-54

- Amyx, D.A., Dejong, P.F., Lin, Chakraborty, G. And Wiener, J.L. (1994), "Influencers of Proceedings, *American Marketing Association, Chicago, IL, New Scientist, 3, 13, 14, 151-3*.

- Anderson, T. Jr And Cunningham, W.H. (1972), "The Socially Conscious Consumer", *Journal Of Marketing, 36 7, 23-31*

- Balderjahn, I. (1988), "Personality Variables And Environmental Attitudes As Predictors Of Ecologically Responsible Consumption Patterns", *Journal Of Business Research, 17. 1, 51-6*

- Craig A. Kelley, (2001) "Marketing And Consumer Identity In Multicultural America", *Journal Of Consumer Marketing,18 , 6,534 – 542*

- Kilbourne, W.E. And Beckmann, S.C (1998), "Review and Critical Assessment of Research on Marketing and the Environment". *Journal of Marketing Management*,14 (6), 513–532

- Kilbourne, W.E. And Beckmann, S.C (1998), "Review and Critical Assessment of Research on Marketing and the Environment". Journal of Marketing Management,14 (6), 513–532

- Kilbourne, W., P. Mcdonagh, And A. Prothero. (1997), "Sustainable Consumption and the Quality of Life: A Macro-marketing Challenge to the Dominant Social Paradigm", *Journal of Macro-marketing,·*17(1), 4-24.

- Pickett, G.M., Grove, S.J. and Kangun, N. (1993), "An Analysis of the Conserving Consumer a Public Policy Perspective", *The Consumers are not so Green" in Allen, C.T. Et Al. (Eds), AMA Winter Educators' Conference*

- Purchase Intentions For Ecologically Safe Products: An Exploratory Study", AMA Winter Educators' *Conference Proceedings, American Marketing Association, Chicago, 5, 341-7*

- Reizenstein, R.C., Hills, G.E. And Philpot, J.W. (1974), "Curhan, R.C. (Ed.), 1974 Combined Proceedings, Willingness to Pay for Control of Air Pollution: A Demographic Analysis", *American Marketing Association, Chicago, IL,* 323-8.

- Roberts, J.A. (1996), "Green Consumers in the 1990s: Profile and Implications for Advertising", *Journal of Business Research*, 36(3), 217-32.

- Sutcliffe M, Hooper P, Howell R. 2008. Can Eco-Foot printing Analysis be Used Successfully to Encourage More Sustainable Behavior at the Household Level? *Sustainable Development 16: 1–16.*

- Thompson, CJ, Arsel Z. (2004). The Starbuck Brandscape and Consumers (Anticorporate) Experiences of Globalization. *Journal of Consumer Research* 31: 631-642.

- Vantomme D, Geuens M, De Houwer J, De Pelsmacker (2005). Implicit Attitudes toward Green Consumer Behavior. *Psychologica Belgica* 45 (4): 217-239.

- Wheale P, Hinton D. 2007. Ethical Consumers in Search of Markets. *Business Strategy and the Environment 16: 302–315 DOI: 10.1002/ Bse.484.*

- Williams K, Dair C. 2007. A Framework of Sustainable Behaviors That Can be Enabled through the Design of Neighborhood-Scale Developments. *Sustainable Development 15, 160–173. DOI: 10.1002/Sd.*

- Jasmin Bergeron Concordia University, Montreal, Quebec, Canada Guido Barbaro-Forleo Concordia University, Montreal, Quebec, Canada.

Tourism Industry and its Impact on Indian Economy

Urvashi Garud[1], Komal Sharma[2] and Megha Lad[3]
[1]Assistant Professor, GICTS Group of College, Gwalior
[2]Lecturer, GICTS Group of College, Gwalior
[3]MBA Scholar, Boston College, Gwalior

ABSTRACT

One or two decades before people travel only it is needed. Over the decades, tourism has experienced continued growth and deepening diversification to become one of the fastest growing economic sectors in the world. Tourism has become a thriving global industry with the power to shape developing countries in both positive and negative ways. No doubt it has become the fourth largest industry in the global economy.

Indian culture and its ten thousand year old history is a massively powerful brand on which tourism industry can grow. In developing countries like India tourism has become one of the major sectors of the economy, contributing to a large proportion of the National Income and generating huge employment opportunities. It has become the fastest growing service industry in the country with great potentials for its further expansion and diversification. However, there are pros and cons involved with the development of tourism industry in the country. The developing world has immensely contributed to the economic boost that India is currently enjoying and it's tourism sector has not been left out of the share of profits either-a major achievement for the image of brand India build up by a successful financial system in place in our country. Some economists credit this fiscal feature of success of Indian financial system to the income generated by the tourism segment, movements across the cross-section of rising business opportunities, agricultural and educational sectors opening up as well as novel and attractive packaging of brand-building for India that have in turn, benefited the travel industry as well.

Keywords: *Tourism, Global Economy*

INTRODUCTION

There are various definitions of tourism. Theobald (1994) suggested that etymologically, the word "tour" is derived from the Latin *'tornare'* and the Greek *'tornos,'* meaning *'a lathe or circle; the movement around a central point or axis.'* This meaning changed in modern English to represent 'one's turn.' The suffix -ism is defined as 'an action or process; typical behavior or quality' whereas the suffix -ist denotes one that performs a given action.

When the word tour and the suffixes -ism and -ist are combined, they suggest the action of movement around a circle. One can argue that a circle represents a starting point, which ultimately returns back to its beginning.

Therefore, like a circle, a tour represents a journey that is a round trip, i.e., the act of leaving and then returning to the original starting point, and therefore, one who takes such a journey can be called a tourist.

The OECD glossary of statistical terms defined tourism as the activities of persons travelling to and staying in places outside their usual environment for not more than one consecutive year for leisure, business and other purposes not related to the exercise of an activity remunerated from within the place visited. The Macmillan Dictionary defines tourism as the business of providing services for people who are travelling for their holiday. Holidaying is a yearly ritual in wealthy societies. Every family plans its annual holiday away from home.

DEVELOPMENT OF TOURISM IN INDIA

The developing world has immensely contributed to the economic boost that India is currently enjoying and it's tourism sector has not been left out of the share of profits either- a major achievement for the image of brand India build up by a successful financial system in place in our country. What has contributed to the economic growth of India and the tourism sector at large are factors of industrialization, education, higher number of qualified professionals, opening up of foreign markets, liberal trade policies and better advertising and strategic marketing'.

The above factors have been collectively responsible for boosting our country's economic reserves and the impact of India's economic growth on tourism.

Early Development

The first conscious and organized efforts to promote tourism in India were made in 1945 when a committee was set up by the Government under the Chairmanship of Sir John Sargent, the then Educational Adviser to the Government of India (Krishna, A.G., 1993). But it was only after the 80's that tourism activity gained momentum. The Government took several significant steps. A National Policy on tourism was announced in 1982. Later in 1988, the National Committee on Tourism formulated a comprehensive plan for achieving a sustainable growth in tourism. In 1992, a National Action Plan was prepared and in 1996 the National Strategy for Promotion of Tourism was drafted. In 1997, the *New Tourism Policy* recognizes the roles of Central and State governments, public sector undertakings and the private sector in the development of tourism were. The need for involvement of Panchayati Raj institutions, local bodies, non-governmental organisations and the local youth in the creation of tourism facilities has also been recognized.

Present Scenario

Tourists come to see things of beauty and have a good time. They also like to see interesting places, have fun, enjoy good food, good lodging, and if possible get a religious or a spiritual experience. Anybody who could provide these things attracts tourists. In short, the host country is supposed to spoil them with hospitality and give them an experience to remember.

Today tourism is the largest service industry in India, with a contribution of 6.23% to the national GDP and providing 8.78% of the total employment. India witnesses more than 5 million annual foreign tourist arrivals and 562 million domestic tourism visits. The tourism industry in India generated about US$100 billion in 2008 and that is expected to increase to US$275.5 billion by 2018 at a 9.4% annual growth rate. The Ministry of Tourism is the nodal agency for the development and promotion of tourism in India and maintains the *"Incredible India"* campaign.

According to World Travel and Tourism Council, India will be a tourism hotspot from 2009-2018, having the highest 10-year growth potential. As per the Travel and Tourism Competitiveness Report 2009 by the World Economic Forum, India is ranked 11th in the Asia Pacific region and 62nd overall, moving up three places on the list of the world's attractive destinations. It is ranked the 14th best tourist destination for its natural resources and 24th for its cultural resources, with many *World Heritage Sites*, both natural and cultural, rich fauna, and strong creative industries in the country. India also bagged 37th rank for its air transport network. The India travel and tourism industry ranked 5th in the long-term (10-year) growth and is expected to be the second largest employer in the world by 2019. The 2010 Commonwealth Games in Delhi are expected to significantly boost tourism in India further.

Moreover, India has been ranked the "best country brand for value-for-money" in the Country Brand Index (CBI) survey conducted by *Future Brand*, a leading global brand consultancy. India also claimed the second place in CBI's "best country brand for history", as well as appears among the top 5 in the best country brand for authenticity and art & culture, and the fourth best new country for business. India made it to the list of "rising stars" or the countries that are likely to become major tourist destinations in the next five years, led by the United Arab Emirates, China, and Vietnam.

Tourism worldwide is a $3,700 billion industry. This includes both internal and external tourism. Last year a total of 4.5 million tourists arrived India. It generated $4 bllion revenue. It is low figure; both in tourist arrivals and monies they spent while in India. Well it is not a priority industry for development in India. Hence its infrastructure to cater the external tourists is primitive. But consider this: - 20 million outside tourists could bring in $30 to 40 billion revenue in a year.

Tourists to India are a mix of NRIs returning home and external visitors going to exotic places. Internal tourism is not well developed although; India has a 200 million middle class with money to spend. Part of the reason is, lack of in-expensive facilities to cater to the local tourism. Still almost half of the tourism revenue of $12 billion a year in India is generated by internal tourism. With a bit of more effort this could be raised four fold.

2005 External Tourist Data

Country	External Tourists (Million)	Revenue Generated ($ Billions)	Outlook for Future
Egypt	8.5	8	Terrorism impacted negatively
China	15	20	Outlook very good; SAARS had a major impact in both 2004 and 2005
Thailand	10	9	SAARS impacted negatively
Caribbean Islands	50	40	Most Preferred US destination
UK	10	20	Second Most preferred destination for Americans
India	4.5	4	

Tourist Attractions in India

Tourists come to see things of beauty and have a good time. They also like to see interesting places, have fun, enjoy good food, good lodging, and if possible get a religious or a spiritual experience. Anybody who could provide these things attracts tourists. In short, the host country is supposed to spoil them with hospitality and give them an experience to remember.

As I said above India has to use its culture, history, exotic places, four seasons weather to its greatest advantage. Vigorous promotion of all these contents is to be a continuous affair. Places like India should be up in their mind first. India has a traditional hospitality, a continuous culture, excellent weather system, cultural diversity, two thousand year old artifacts and spiritual experience in Yoga & religion unmatched anywhere else. What more can a tourist ask for a holiday? In one package, he or she gets transported as close to the heavens as possible.

India is a country known for its lavish treatment to all visitors, no matter where they come from. Its visitor-friendly traditions, varied life styles and cultural heritage and colourful fairs and festivals held abiding attractions for the tourists. The other attractions include beautiful beaches, forests and wild life and landscapes for eco-tourism; snow, river and mountain peaks for adventure tourism; technological parks and science museums for science tourism; centres of pilgrimage for spiritual tourism; heritage, trains and hotels for heritage tourism. Yoga, ayurveda and natural health resorts and hill stations also attract tourists.

The Indian handicrafts particularly, jewellery, carpets, leather goods, ivory and brass work are the main shopping items of foreign tourists. It is estimated through survey that nearly 40 % of the tourist expenditure on shopping is spent on such items.

Despite the economic slowdown, *medical tourism* in India is the fastest growing segment of tourism industry, according to the market research report "Booming Medical Tourism in India". The report adds that India offers a great potential in the medical tourism industry. Factors such as low cost, scale and range of treatments provided in the country add to its attractiveness as a medical tourism destination.

REVIEW OF LITERATURE

Chakraborty (2008) empirically studied tourism is world's largest justifiable service industry that is generating huge revenue for tourist country. Bangladesh has lots of tourism spots but most of them unexplored by the relevant authority. Having all the minimum requirements, the tourism industry could not develop adequately in Bangladesh. The cracks of problem could not identify accurately because of paucity of sufficient Riccardo Scarpa (2004) empirically studied the relationship between tourism and economic growth for Latin American countries since 1985 until 1998. The analysis proposed is based on a panel data approach and the Arellano-Bond estimator for dynamic panels. We obtain estimates of the relationship between economic growth and growth in tourists' per capita conditional on main macroeconomic variables. We show that the **tourism** sector is adequate for the economic growth of medium or low-income countries, though not necessarily for developed countries. We then invert the causality direction of the analysis. Rather than explaining economic growth, we try to explain **tourism** arrivals conditional on GDP and other covariates such as safety, prices and education level, and investment in infrastructures. We employ a generalised least squares AR (1) panel data model. The results provide evidence that low-income countries seem to need adequate levels of infrastructures, education and development to attract tourists. Medium-income countries need high levels of social development like health services and high GDP per capita levels. Finally, the results disclose that price of the destination, in terms of exchange rate and PPP is irrelevant for **tourism** growth.

Glenn P. Jenkins(November 1989) His paper presents a project evaluation study in which the methodological tools taught in the H.I.I.D. Program in Investment Appraisal and Management are applied. It examines the feasibility of a hotel project in Cyprus covering all aspects of investment appraisal. It begins with an analysis of the market for tourism in Cyprus and a definition of the project concept. The financial appraisal analyses the project cash flow from the total investment and owners' perspectives. The economic appraisal of the project is completed after working out the economic discount rate, foreign exchange premium and a series of economic conversion factors for Cyprus. The distributive analysis identifies the project externalities and shows how these may be attributed to various economic groups. Sensitivity and risk analysis further enhances the appraisal by identifying and measuring the level of uncertainty surrounding the projected results. Finally, the study considers the impact of the project on the environment.

María Jesús Such (2007) in a recent work, Ivanov and Webster (2007) present a methodology for measuring the contribution of tourism to economic growth and apply this methodology to the cases of Cyprus, Greece and Spain. The method uses the growth of real GDP per capita as a measure of economic growth and disaggregates it into economic growth generated by tourism and economic growth generated by other industries. Our paper selects a group of Latin-Americans countries, including Argentina, Brazil, Uruguay and Mexico. This allows us to establish a first comparison based on geographical parameters (European countries vs. Latin American countries). Whilst Argentina, Brazil and Uruguay present a profile where tourism industry has a smaller weight on GDP (2,5%; 1,5%; 1,6%, respectively) in Mexico the tourism contribution to GDP is about 4,8%.

TOURISM IN INDIA AND ITS IMPACT ON INDIAN ECONOMY

1. Generating Income and Employment:

Tourism in India has emerged as an instrument of income and employment generation, poverty alleviation and sustainable human development. It contributes 6.23% to the national GDP and 8.78% of the total employment in India. Almost 20 million people are now working in the India's tourism industry.

2. Source of Foreign Exchange Earnings:

Tourism is an important source of foreign exchange earnings in India. This has favorable impact on the balance of payment of the country. The tourism industry in India generated about US$100 billion in 2008 and that is expected to increase to US$275.5 billion by 2018 at a 9.4% annual growth rate.

3. Direct Financial Contributions:

Tourism can contribute directly to the conservation of sensitive areas and habitat. Revenue from park-entrance fees and similar sources can be allocated specifically to pay for the protection and management of environmentally sensitive areas. Special fees for park operations or conservation activities can be collected from tourists or tour operators.

4. Contributions to Government Revenues:

The Indian government through the tourism department also collects money in more far-reaching and indirect ways that are not linked to specific parks or conservation areas. User fees, income taxes, taxes on sales or rental of recreation equipment, and license fees for activities such as rafting and fishing can provide governments with the funds needed to manage natural resources. Such funds can be used for overall conservation programs and activities, such as park ranger salaries and park maintenance.

Indian tourism: facts and figures
FTA: foreign tourist arrival

Foreign tourist arrivals (FTA) in India 2005-10		
year	FTA (million)	%age change
2005	3.92	13.3
2006	4.45	13.5
2007	5.08	14.3
2008	5.37	5.6
2010	6.74	12.15

Month wise foreign tourist arrival in India

month wise foreign tourist arrival in India			
month	2008	2009	2010
Jan	535631	591337	487262
Feb	501692	561393	501885
Mar	472494	541478	471627
Apr	350550	384203	370756
May	277017	300840	295124
Jun	310364	340159	340839
Jul	399866	429456	397867

Contd...

Contd...

Aug	358446	391423	365860
Sep	301892	330874	326084
Oct	444564	452566	409081
Nov	532428	521247	487873
Dec	596560	521990	513844

Top 10 sates of India in no of domestic tourist visits (08-09)

Top 10 states of India in no of domestic tourist visits (08-09)			
rank	state/UT	No	%age
1	AP	132684908	23.6
2	UP	124843250	22.4
3	TN	98265142	17.9
4	RJ	28358940	5.1
6	MH	20553401	3.8

Top 10 states of India in tourist visits

Top 10 states of India in tourist visits			
Rank	State/UT	No.	%age
1	DELHI	2339292	16.7
2	MH	2056930	15.2
3	TN	2029420	14.4
4	UP	1610092	11.3
5	RJ	1477650	10.7
6	WB	1133680	8.2

SWOT Analysis

Strength

- India's geographical location, a culmination of deserts, forests, mountains, and beaches.
- Diversity of culture i.e. a blend of various civilizations and their traditions.
- Manpower cost in the Indian hotel industry is one of the lowest in the world. This provides better margins for the industry.
- A very wide variety of hotels is present in the country that can fulfill the demand of the tourists. There are international players in the market such as Taj and Oberoi. Thus, the needs of the international tourists are fulfilled effectively.
- Rich cultural heritage and colorful festivals.

Weakness

- Lack of adequate infra.
- Transportation like road conditions are very poor specially Highways.
- A narrow minded attitude among the certain sections of the society e.g. loot and harassment of foreign tourist.

- No proper marketing of India's tourist destinations.
- India's image with poverty and diseases.
- Poor implementation of Govt. policies to promote tourism at local & regional level.

Opportunity

- More proactive roles from the govt. of India in terms of framing policies.
- Asian development bank is preparing a sub-Regional plan for development of tourism in India.
- Availability of high quality of resources.
- Allowing entry of more multinational co's, providing global perspective.
- Growth of domestic tourism. the advantage here is that domestic tourism and international tourism can be separate easily owing to the difference in the period of holidays.

Threat

- Economic conditions and political turmoil in other countries affects tourism.
- Political instability within India in J&K and Gujarat has also reduces tourist traffic.
- Terrorism is major setback for the region.
- Disorganized tourism development.
- Environmental factors also impose a threat.
- Aggressive strategies adopted by other countries like Australia, Singapore in promoting experience.

PEST Analysis

Political

- The Indian tourism industry is built on the backbone of govt. support.
- All the support services like the hotel industry, the airline industry and the tourist operators to name some are heavily dependent on the support and the co-op of the Govt.
- The hotel industry has been getting many incentives and many state Govts. are encouraging the growth of the major hotels in their state.

Economical

- The spending power of the people has been increasing in the country all over the world.
- There have been more people coming into country with more cash than ever.

- People who were previously used to come to the country on a shoestring budget and hunt aro9und for the cheapest accommodation can now afford to get in for luxury hotels. This ahs led to increase in the number of hotels in the country.
- The increase in the spending is also evident in the increase in the number of people traveling by air.

Social

- People have become careful, specially of international tourists.
- Critical condition of sanitation and recent terrorist attacks have discouraged in inflow of foreign nationals.
- More and more entrepreneurs are now adopting the fact that tourism pays and kit can be a major source of income for them.

Technology

- On-line and advance booking system throughout the country and from any international location has made it easier to access info.
- Convenient transportation facilities.
- Presence of airports at metros and sub-metros.

Key findings

- India is expected to see an influx of 10.5 million tourists by 2011, up from just 5 million in 2007.
- AP, UP, TN, KR and RJ are the leading tourism destinations in terms of tourist arrivals.
- Tremendous increase in personal domestic income (grew at CAGR of 15.32%) driving domestic as well as outbound tourism.
- The WTO (World Tourism Organisation) reports that as many as 698 million people traveled to a foreign country in 2000, spending over US$ 478 billion while on tour; if India too had a share in these results, then surely the impact of Indian economy as a contributor to rising world economy and its impact on tourism cannot be ignored.
- According to IATA (International Air Transport Association), the Asia market will have the biggest share of global international passenger traffic in the world by the year 2010 – 50% as compared with 26% in 1985.

Initiatives to Boost Tourism

Some of the recent initiatives taken by the Government to boost tourism include grant of export house status to the tourism sector and incentives for promoting private

investment in the form of Income Tax exemptions, interest subsidy and reduced import duty. The hotel and tourism-related industry has been declared a high priority industry for foreign investment which entails automatic approval of direct investment up to 51% of foreign equity and allowing 100% non-resident Indian investment and simplifying rules regarding the grant of approval to travel agents, tour operators and tourist transport operators.

The first-ever Indian Tourism Day was celebrated on January 25, 1998. The Year 1999 was celebrated as *Explore India Millennium Year* by presenting a spectacular tableau on the cultural heritage of India at the Republic Day Parade and organizing India Tourism Expo in New Delhi and Khajuraho. Moreover, the campaign *'Visit India Year 2009'* was launched at the International Tourism Exchange in Berlin, aimed to project India as an attractive destination for holidaymakers. The government joined hands with leading airlines, hoteliers, holiday resorts and tour operators, and offered them a wide range of incentives and bonuses during the period between April and December, 2009.

Future Prospects

According to the latest Tourism Satellite Accounting (TSA) research, released by the World Travel and Tourism Council (WTTC) and its strategic partner Oxford Economics in March 2009:

- The demand for travel and tourism in India is expected to grow by 8.2 % between 2010 and 2019 and will place India at the third position in the world.
- India's travel and tourism sector is expected to be the second largest employer in the world, employing 40,037,000 by 2019.
- Capital investment in India's travel and tourism sector is expected to grow at 8.8 % between 2010 and 2019.
- The report forecasts India to get capital investment worth US$ 94.5 billion in the travel and tourism sector in 2019.

India is projected to become the fifth fastest growing business travel destination from 2010-2019 with an estimated real growth rate of 7.6 %.

Suggestions

Increase of airlines seats to India

There is no open sky policy in India, hence number of commercial airline seats have not improved in last five years. If India needs external tourists, India will have to let the external airlines fly-in passengers to it.

Alternatively, India's external carrier could bring all the tourists to India. The latter requires eight fold increase in aircrafts and trained crews to handle them. A cheaper alternative will be let the other airlines fly the tourists to various India's destinations.

Hotels and Inns in Cities and at Tourist spots

There are only 103,000 hotel rooms available in India in 2005 of which only 60% can be classified suitable for tourist trade. High-end hotels in the cities are pricey and offer not much for the price. Low-end hotels & tourist bungalows are suitable for local tourism. It is the middle-end hotels, which are urgently needed to cater to the tourist trade. An additional 200,000 middle end tourist hotel rooms well distributed between cities and tourist destination will fill up the gap. There is abundance of FDI available to build the hotels. Management expertise to run these places will come with the capital monies. In order to triple or quadruple the tourist traffic from meager 5 million to about 20 million in ten years, tripling of hotels and inns capacity is essential.

Professional Expertise to Handle Tourist Traffic

Incredible India type of commercials on Western TV does not do much, if the necessary marketing effort to grab a piece of tourist trade is missing. It has to come in form of travel agent incentives, tour management expertise and marketing of a new holiday experience with slick brochures. First time tourists are to be enthralled with new experiences. Nature lovers are to be suitably guided to the game sanctuaries, beach lovers are to be guided to seaside resorts and people who came for the spiritual and Yoga experience have to reach their destination without a hitch. Visitors who come for history and culture and generally good all around time have to be suitable entertained. Greater the time spent on taking care of every need of the visitor, the better will be the free publicity obtained by word of mouth.

Medical Tourism

This is a serious money generator. A few visitors with health issues come to India for a life saving surgery for which they may have to wait months in their own country. This practice had its initiation in eighties and nineties when rich Sheiks of Middle East showed up for rest and recreation and also medical treatment at Indian medical centres. This practice continued for twenty years and has in last four years escalated to the West. It is good news for Indian medical staff. Their prowess as providers of health services at par with the West is being recognized

Tourism on Rural India

Impact of tourism on rural India will be so great that all other rural welfare scheme will be pale by comparison. Interestingly a bulk of India's cultural wealth is in the rural areas. This is what a significant percentage of visitors come to see. When they are there, they help the rural economy by staying in the local hotels, eat local food and buy local handicrafts. Every tourist whether external or internal, carries back souvenirs to show off. The latter is a cottage industry product. Each is unique and each has a local imprint on it. This will drive up the village economy. People in the villages will suddenly find themselves as entrepreneur-supplying products to a very prosperous visitor. In addition, roads, food, shops, hotels, guides will provide employment to millions. In short rural economy will get a huge boost.

CONCLUSION

Tourism industry in India is growing and it has vast potential for generating employment and earning large amount of foreign exchange besides giving a fillip to the country's overall economic and social development. But much more remains to be done. Eco-tourism needs to be promoted so that tourism in India helps in preserving and sustaining the diversity of the India's natural and cultural environments. Tourism in India should be developed in such a way that it accommodates and entertains visitors in a way that is minimally intrusive or destructive to the environment and sustains & supports the native cultures in the locations it is operating in. Moreover, since tourism is a multi-dimensional activity, and basically a service industry, it would be necessary that all wings of the Central and State governments, private sector and voluntary organisations become active partners in the Endeavour to attain sustainable growth in tourism if India is to become a world player in the tourism industry.

Tourism industry in India is growing and it has vast potential for generating employment and earning large amount of foreign exchange besides giving a fillip to the country's overall economic and social development. Eco-tourism needs to be promoted so that tourism in India helps in preserving and sustaining the diversity of the India's natural and cultural environments. As its multi-dimensional and service industry, it would be necessary that all wings of the Central and State governments, private sector and voluntary organisations become active partners in the Endeavour to attain sustainable growth in tourism.

References

- Supra, J.R., Jr., S.H. Huntsman, D.M. Theobald, and J.O. Bennett (1994), A *Modeling Approach to Quantitative Literacy,* Proceedings of the Seventh Annual International Conference on Technology in Collegiate Mathematics, Orlando, FL, November 18-21,

- Krishna, A.G., (1993) "Case study on the effects of tourism on culture and the environment: India; Jaisalmer, Khajuraho and Goa"

- Shamsuddoha Mohammad, Md. A. Hossain, Shams E. S. Shahriar, T. Chakraborty (2008) Development of Tourism Industry in Bangladesh, *Intelligent Organisation: A Roadmap to Success, February 2004*

- Martin Juan Luis Eugenio, Noelia Martín Morales, Riccardo Scarpa (February 2004) "Tourism and Economic Growth in Latin American Countries: A Panel Data Approach, FEEM Working Paper No. 26.2004

- Savvkis C. Savvides Andreas Andreou (November 1989) "Tourism, Environment and Profitability: The Case of the Paphos Holiday Co Complex, Queen's University (Canada) - Department of Economics; Eastern Mediterranean University

- Brida Juan Gabriel, María Jesús Such ,Juan Sebastián Pereyra (2007) Evaluating the Contribution of Tourism on Economic Growth, Anatolia: An International Journal of Tourism and Hospitality Research, Vol. 19, No. 2, 351-356

- Ivanov, S. and Webster, C. (2007), Measuring the impact of tourism on economic growth, Tourism Economics, 13(3), 379-388.

Critical Analysis of Change of Consumer Behavior of Students While Selecting a Professional College

Rajeev Sijariya[1] and Neel Rai[2]

[1]Principal, United Institute of Management Greater Noida
[2]Assistant Professor, Department of MBA, SR Group of Institutions, Jhansi

ABSTRACT

Fasten your seatbelts — a lot has changed in consumer behavior in all market segments during the past 24 months, especially in education sector. The new uptrend's or changes been made in the marketing concepts and also the decision making inputs of the students and guardians while choosing the right college. As previous year analysis shows that there was a huge demand of students but the supply of colleges was less, and now this scenario has been reversed. The supply of colleges is high but the demand of students is less. Due to which the north Indian institutions are making new attractive modes to attract the students so that they can take admission in there institutes. As the mode of education is changing rapidly, the conceptual consumer behavior of students are also changing rapidly. The researcher used the observation method.

Keywords: *Consumer Behaviour, Education sector*

INTRODUCTION

The issue of marketing is becoming more significant as a strategic focal point of the institutional function in education in many contexts. With the introduction of a social market India, the sense of the intermediary stage between socialism and capitalism, the need to integrate marketing within an institutional function becomes more urgent. As private Institutions of North India i.e. U.P. region- UPTU, is an emerging market in India, there is, as yet, no published research on marketing private professional education Institution with respect to the change in the consumer behavior in term of students of UP while selecting the college. The change in consumer behavior has presented marketers with the challenges as well as opportunities to reach specific target markets. The focus of this study is the marketing of professional education at private institutes and universities in North India i.e Uttar Pradesh. The aim is to investigate issues regarding students' choices and preferences of private colleges, with regards to marketing practices and strategies, and to examine their dynamic relationship.

Need for the Study

The major need of this research is to critically investigate the new uptrend's or changes been made in the marketing concepts and also the decision making ability of the students and guardians while choosing the right college according to their perception. As previous year analysis shows that there was a huge demand of students but the supply of colleges was less, and now this scenario has been reversed. The supply of colleges is high but the demand of students is less. Due to which the north Indian institutions are making new attractive modes to attract the students so that they can take admission in there institutes. This is the right time to research on the needs and try to find the solutions.

OBJECTIVE OF THE STUDY

- To study the present Marketing changes and its effect on Survival of private institutions.
- To know the phases of Institution cycle.
- To study the decision making process of the students and their guardian for selecting a college.

- To study various marketing strategies employed by privates institutions of North India.
- To know competing concepts under which organisations conduct their marketing activity.

Limitation

As the topic of the research paper is very wide and long term concept due to which the data which I collect, only covers the UP colleges and common perception of parents and students while opting or choosing the correct college to hire a good professional and technical education. So the matter no longer holds good.

LITERATURE REVIEW

Anas Al-Fattal (2010) focused to investigate issues regarding students' choices and preferences of private universities, with regards to marketing practices and strategies, and to examine their dynamic relationship. The findings show that the process of student choice of university consists of five steps, being motives, information gathering, evaluating alternatives, decision implementation, and post-choice evaluation. The findings also show the marketing mix in Syria to consist of five elements, which are teaching and learning, customer centered focus, finance, branding and environment. An association between student choice of university and marketing strategies is highlighted and a composite model, the atom marketing model, is created on the basis of evidence collected. The study reveals a two-way matrix interrelationship between the two areas; it is a "push-pull" relationship, where each is influencing and shaping the other. The study contributes to knowledge in the way it researches theories from the West in a different context. It also demonstrates a detailed description of the relationship between two different marketing models.

Shrivastava, and Rathore (2011) describes that in present era, rapid changes have been taking place in the management education and development, driven by the call for accountability, an increase in experimental techniques, the availability of educational thought, technology, innovation and recognition of the need for lifetime learning. As a lot many number of management institutions is increasing in India simultaneously, leading cut throat competition among the institutions operation. Furthermore, this increasing number of institutions developing new scene in Indian market i.e. these management institution are having a lot of challenges, issue, and opportunities to survive in long run. Opening new institution doesn't mean to sustain and compete in the market until and unless fulfilling the entire necessary

requirement as per current global changes. Moreover shortage of competent faculty members belonging to domain area and on the same corner paying the right salary to the right faculty is the biggest challenge in the present days.

Agarwal (2011) said that the purpose of education is not just making a student literate but adds rationale thinking, knowledge ability and self sufficiency to the student. Innovation in teaching pedagogy is the blood line for any management institute to deliver corporate leaders and not just MBAs. Why our academia failed in delivering effective management professionals to the corporate world? Management schools were left as machines producing the management graduates who are not able to cater to the requirements of the corporate world.

Dale and Hawes (2007) described that as colleges and universities adopt marketing orientations to an ever-increasing extent, the relative merits of mass marketing and target marketing must also be explored. Researchers identify buyer types as potential students focused on quality, value or economy. On the other axis, learner types are described as those who focus on career, socio-improvement and leisure, or those who are ambivalent learners. This conceptual model of market segments presents an innovative and useful way to examine the student market for higher educational services. As might have been expected, many academics still resist the implementation of a so-called marketing approach because they fear change and consider a marketing approach to be a challenge to intellectual integrity (e.g., Jump 2004; Sharrack 2000). Liu (1998), however, provides an important contribution to the literature, which could help overcome this reluctance. She explains the necessary (but different) role of marketing in higher education by describing how universities vary from other service enterprises. The article also identifies the social responsibilities of higher education not-for-profit organisations, explaining the unique context of higher education, and effectively arguing that short-run revenue or profit maximization should not be the primary goal.

For any university, marketing approaches create values among a university's stakeholders. These stakeholders are prospective students, current students, alumni, employers of graduates, and financial supporters. For a state-supported university, the list of stakeholders also includes taxpayers, the state legislature and perhaps the general public (Hayes 1993). Admission offices may find themselves primarily concerned with the prospective student stakeholder group. To identify market segments among prospective students, researchers build a conceptual model that goes beyond demographics. By understanding the people served by the university, it is possible to develop offerings that satisfy the needs of this target market.

According to ukessays of private university, the true growth of an economy depends on the development of a nation and its citizens as human resources and higher education plays an inevitable role in such context. Bangladesh is also not an exception to this. At present there are more than 52 private universities in the country. Therefore, now what matters in this connection is not the number but the quality. A good university must ensure quality education for its students. But to be an international standard institution of higher education it is not an easy job for a university. USTC is such a university that has already established itself as a leading private university in Bangladesh with international reputation for excellence. In a decade, it has achieved excellence in education in different disciplines through its dynamic and effective academic leadership. Due to stiff competition in the education sector in Bangladesh, private universities need to prove their quality and should develop constructive and effective marketing programs and strategies for the purpose of survival as well as expansion.

Marketing products and marketing services are different. Some principles are the same, but marketing educational services need to consider many additional factors, changing the emphasis in some areas. It is not appropriate to use a products model for services marketing, as many of the additional concepts and principles, only applicable to marketing educational services, may be ignored or forgotten. This is because a strategic marketing approach has been followed to reveal the real scenario and condition in one hand and suggest the appropriate marketing strategies on the other hand. It is important for USTC to incorporate business acumen and marketing without delay. USTC is beginning to experience the reality of the world of business and finance and, as the competition increases, the aspects such as formulating marketing planning in an appropriate and scientific manner, marketing the right educational services by the USTC, marketing of the USTC must be to the correct customers in the most appropriate places, the price of the educational packages should be right, marketing of USTC should be undertaken at the most effective time, etc., need to be ensured for timely consideration.

This research paper examines the present situation of the USTC with a realistic evaluation of SWOT analysis aiming to develop constructive and effective educational service marketing plans, programs and strategies through the careful application and evaluation of strategic models and matrixes. This paper also included key points which are based upon sound experience. There is a brief outline of the changes in the education sector within the last ten years, which have resulted in the need for realistic marketing. The models used here include Ansoff's Matrix, Boston Consulting Group's Matrix and SWOT Analysis to make the strategic marketing plans, programs and strategies suggested for the private university industry in general and the USTC in particular more pragmatic and focused.

Stripling and Masterson (2011) in their newspaper article said that in the crowded field of private colleges, only those that differentiate themselves with signature programs and unique marketing strategies can hope to thrive in a challenging economy, several panelists stressed here on Tuesday at the annual meeting of the National Association of Independent Colleges and Universities. Echoing themes espoused by many college presidents in recent years, conference presenters suggested the institutions that will emerge stronger from the recession will have done so by building upon clearly articulated identities. That means setting a finite number of realistic goals, cutting programs that don't serve those goals, and—candidly—deciding whether a college's vision can increase revenues, said Robert A. Sevier, senior vice president for strategy at Stamats Inc., a higher-education marketing company. In his session, "Six Strategic Responses in a Time of Challenge and Opportunity," Mr. Sevier argued that the economic crisis had given university leaders greater flexibility to articulate institutional visions, in part by doing away with nonviable programs. Citing Niccolò Machiavelli's The Prince, Mr. Sevier said, "This is a great time to do things you could never get away with 10 years ago." Beyond developing a coherent vision, Mr. Sevier urged college leaders to seek new revenue through grants and contracts, while taking a hard look at improving retention rates and preserving tuition dollars. In another session, "Image Is Everything," a branding consultant urged conference attendees to better define their institutions by developing more coherent and consistent messages. Too often, individual academic units create recruitment and marketing materials that fail to tie into established institution-wide themes, said Elizabeth Scarborough, chief executive officer of Simpson Scarborough.

"If an institution is going to manage its image, somebody's got to be in charge of pulling it together," she said. By way of example, Ms. Scarborough noted that different departments are prone to creating "bastardized" logos that differ in appearance from an institution's established emblem. A well-branded company like Target "would never" alter the color of its signature red trademark, but "we do that daily on our campuses," she said. At a session on leadership, Roger H. Hull, a former president of Beloit College and Union College (N.Y.), offered practical tips for college presidents on small things they could to increase their success in the job. Mr. Hull, who now runs a foundation for youth in Schenectady, N.Y., is the author of Lead or Leave: A Primer for College Presidents and Board Members.

RESEARCH STUDY

About UPTU:- Uttar Pradesh Technical University (UPTU) was established by the Government of Uttar Pradesh on 8th May 2000 vide Act No. 1248(2)XVII-V-I-I-19-2000 Uttar Pradesh Adhiniyam Sankhya 23 of 2000. Under the University Act, 'Technical Education' includes programs of education, research and training in Engineering, Technology, Architecture, Town Planning, Pharmacy, Applied Arts & Crafts and such other programs and areas that the central Government may in consultation with All India Council for Technical Education (AICTE) by notification in Gazette declare.

The University is affiliating in nature and its jurisdiction spans the entire state of U.P. in affiliating B. Tech., M.B.A., M.C.A., B.Arch., B. Pharma., B.H.M.C.T., M. Tech. and Ph.D. programs in 238 colleges/institutions imparting graduate, postgraduate and doctoral level training in all government and private institutions located all over U.P. in engineering, technology, architecture, pharmacy, hotel management and catering technology as well as M.B.A. and M.C.A. programs.

U.P. being the largest state of India with an area of around two lacs forty thousand square kilometers and population of more than 165 million people makes UPTU as one of the largest technical universities not only in India but perhaps in Asia. Because of its gigantic size and number of colleges affiliated to it and geographic dispersion, it has been sub-divided into five zones with 45-50 colleges in each zone for the ease of management and facilitating inter-zonal comparison and possible internal competition to enhance quality of teaching-learning processes.

UPTU envisions facilitating and nurturing the quality of technical education and research in its own premises as well as all affiliating institutions. The total number of affiliated colleges was 49 in the year 2000 which has now gone up to 238 and the University is still growing. The task of the UPTU at the moment includes

conducting the State level Entrance Examination U.P.-S.E.E. for admission to various programs affiliated to UPTU. Around 2,15,000 aspirants to UPTU take these entrance examination all over U.P. and in parts of Uttrakhand and Delhi. The University conducts central examinations each semester for all the affiliated colleges and institutions and declares results quickly using technology-enabled systems. At present around 150,000 students are enrolled in its various programs. More than 50,000 students are admitted every year. Medium of instructions and examinations is English.

UPTU is currently located in I.E.T. Campus at Sitapur Road in the Capital of U.P. at Lucknow but is in the process of having its own Headquarter building in its vicinity. Its NOIDA Centre and Regional office is nearing completion to facilitate closer academic and industrial interaction around that zone where a prominent cluster of private affiliated colleges exists.

Presently if we analysis the current market of education of UP, we see that now the colleges are widespread there selves geographically concentrating on the availability of the resources i.e. Students, companies etc. If the students move to the NCR or Northeast side he is very confused and in a conundrum to decide that in which college does he should move to take admission.

Now presently if we go through the some major areas or cities and the number of institutions placed over there, we can turn up ourselves to know how though the competitions is? The present total number of colleges in UPTU is 784 colleges in which the govt. colleges are 18 and the govt. universities are 10.

The tentative figures of the Professional UPTU colleges of major cite are as follows:

Therefore, while analyzing the above tentative figures of the colleges (Govt. or Pvt) area or city wise or geographical wise we can see a big cut throat completion. So as per above need of the study for the research paper stated about the Demand and Supply of the Colleges and students, the north Indian institutions are making new attractive modes to attract the students so that they can take admission in there institutes.

So according to the above paragraph, we can analysis the scenario in five (5) different stages, of higher education which are as follows:-

1. **Stage I:** 20 years back there were colleges universities like IIT's; Regional engineering Colleges, Regional Govt. Colleges and Universities.

   During the emergence of the government colleges and universities the admissions was very

Sr. No	Location	Type of Institutions	Number
1	Agra & Mathura	Pvt. Colleges Govt. College/University	48 colleges 1 University
2	Kanpur	Pvt. Colleges Govt. Colleges/University	43 colleges 3 Govt. Colleges, 1 University
3	Allahabad and Varanasi	Pvt. Colleges Govt. Colleges/University	39 colleges 1 Govt. Colleges, 1 University
4	Lucknow	Colleges/University	3 Govt. Colleges, 0 University
5	NCR (Noida, Greater Noida & Ghaziabad)	Pvt. Colleges Govt. Colleges/University	128 colleges 0 Govt. Colleges, 0 University
6	Merrut Govt. Colleges/University	Pvt. Colleges 0 Govt. Colleges, 1 University	61 colleges

difficult as the entrant has to give the entrance exams and then the final merit list was used to get listed out. Then finally admission took place.

2. **Stage II:** Emergence of Private Colleges.

By going through the above difficulties of the students while taking the admissions in the colleges to take technical educations, the private colleges thought that this is the right time to emerge their colleges to get the admission from the students for the higher education. Thus, the emergence of private colleges was opened wide in India according to region wise like Northern region, southern region, western regions, and eastern region. Which were affiliated to their local state universities and also with AICTE norms.

3. **Stage III:** Emergence of more technical universities like Uttar Pradesh Technical Universities (now GBTU), Rajasthan technical university, Uttrakhand Technical University, Jahwahar Lal Technical University Hydrabad, Rajiv Gandhi Prodyogig Vishwavidhyale, Bhopal and many more.

At this Phase when there was a huge demand of technical education and the students demands are more. Then this time the government has decided to make a technical university according to the state wise. So that every individual college have the command on their governing bodies i.e. technical universities. These technical bodies have also given the right to give the affiliation to the private technical colleges.

4. **Stage IV:** Emergence of more Private Deemed Universities like Lovely Professional university, Amity University, Galgotia University, Teerthanker University, Manav Rachna University, BBD University, Mangalyanthan University, AAI Deemed University, GLA University, Mathura, Sharda University, Central Institute of Higher Tibetan Studies, Shobhit University, Shri Venkateshwara University, Swami Vivekanand Subharti University and many more. (* these name of universities are only taken from Uttar Pradesh Region only).

In this second last phase the demand for higher education is continuing to increase with more and more students wanting a higher education today than ever before. By looking at these private colleges have decided to convert their colleges in to university by the recognition of University Grant Commission (UGC) so as to bring more wide spread courses and integrated programs which will be according to the taste and preference of the students while opting for the courses. The process of increasing private participation in higher education has already begun with a few states like Chhattisgarh and Uttaranchal having passed legislation to permit the setting up of private universities in their states. Indeed the private sector has been funding higher education in India for a long time, albeit on a very limited scale. The Birla Institute of Technology and Science at Pilani in Rajasthan, which is funded and run by the Birla Group Trust, became an officially recognized university as far back as 1964. Other institutions like the Manipal Group in Manipal in Karnataka have been running private colleges since 1953 and the Manipal Academy of Higher Education became a deemed university in 1993. Many other self-financing colleges were set up in the early 1990s and a few of them have now become deemed universities.

Apart from this the management bodies also have taken the foreign tie-ups and industrial tie up. With the main motto to attract the students so that they can choose their college

5. **Stage V:** The last phase of the phases are regarded as Transition Phase.

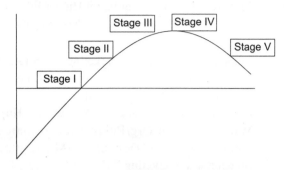

In this phase the promoter of the colleges are confused and not getting any directions to guide the guardian, students, faculty, and people related to the academic work. The main reasons for this phase are due to the more awareness to the students towards opting for the right colleges. And other factor is that the seats are now increased and the students demand is decreased.

Now the students have different perception towards the Deemed Universities. They think that deemed universities are not good affiliated universities as they are giving their own degree and it will not work in govt. sector to apply for the jobs. The major problem faced by the promoters of the colleges while promoting their colleges is that, the number of Options are increased and the parameters are more and lastly the availability of information are much available which all results to the decision making problem on college behalf.

By going to the above all factors, if we go two years back, the availability of the students use to be on quantitative bases but now the students use to chose the college on the qualitative bases. On the basis of this, there are four competing concepts under which organisations conduct their marketing activity.

They are:

1. **Product concept:** B. Tech., M. Tech., MBA, B. Pharma, B.Arch., B.H.M.C.T, MCA, B.F.A.D, etc.
2. **Production Concept:** Number of Seats.
3. **Selling Concept:** The art of selling the seats of colleges through the form of counseling i.e. direct admission or in the form of Government Counseling.
4. **Marketing Concept:** This depends on the basic targeted need of the candidates. By mentioning the features of the colleges, by show casing the infrastructure pictures, Colleges Industrial Tie-ups, placements, experience faculty ratios etc. on these parameters only the students take the decisions.

But by the above concepts the students are not finding the fair qualitative resources to take admission.

Due to which now the promoters of colleges are not finding themselves in a comfort zone or satisfactory zone. They are trying to find out the solution of the slowdown of UPTU Pvt. colleges.

FINDINGS AND SUGGESTIONS

By this study the researcher finds that-

1. Higher education in UP has expanded rapidly over the past two decades. This growth has been mainly driven by private sector initiatives.
2. For the admission point of view its very important to know the consumer perception, preference for the product, as the consumer desire is not stable, it keeps on changing.
3. It is very important to hold the pulse of a consumer.
4. Due to the change of the demand and supply of students and colleges, now the standards of the majority of the institutions are poor and declining.
5. To increase the brand awareness in the market to position its brand, it is crucial to have a dynamic brand promotion strategy.
6. The brand can also be uplifted with good position by being a best service provider in the education market.

Bibliography

- Dr. Shrivastava Sanjay, and Dr. Rathore Krishan Singh (2011), Management Education: Opportunities And Challenges In 2020-At National Conference "CONTEMPORARY ISSUES & EMERGING TRENDS" In Management And Technology. Organized By United Group Of Institutions, Greater Noida.
- Hayes, Thomas J. (1993), "Image and the University," Journal of Marketing for Higher Education, 4 (Issue 1/2), 423-425. Retrieved Http://Www.Ukessays.Com/Essays/Marketing/Private-Universities.Php
- India's Business School Faculty Crisis Article from Education Website
- Stripling Jack And Masterson Kathryn(2011), At Private Colleges' Meeting, Advice On Niche Strategies, Branding, And Leadership, The Chronicle For Higher Education, Washington

- Jump, Jim (2004), "A Prescription for Reclaiming College Admission as a Profession," Journal of College Admission, 184 (summer), 12-17.
- Liu, Sandra S. (1998), "Integrating Strategic Marketing on an Institutional Level," Journal of Marketing for Higher Education, 8 (Issue 4), 17-28.
- Marketing Management- Philip Kotler
- Mohit Agarwal (2011), Management Education: Issues, Challenges And Opportunities - At National Conference "CONTEMPORARY ISSUES & EMERGING TRENDS" in Management and Technology. Organized by United Group of Institutions, Greater Noida. ISBN 978-81-908869-3-2
- National Conference Contemporary Issues And Emerging Trends In Management And Technology By United Group Of Institutions Greater Noida ISBN 978-81-908869-3-2 Retrieved from http://etheses.whiterose.ac.uk/1115/1/ PhD_Thesis_Anas_Al-Fattal_SID200229252_Education.pdf
- Role Of Private Universities In The Higher Education Of Bangladesh: A Case Study On USTC From Strategic Marketing Perspective
- Sharrock, Geoff (2000), "Why Students Are Not (Just) Customers (And Other Reflections On Life After George), Journal Of Higher Education Policy And Management, 22 (November), 149-164.
- Student Target Marketing Strategies For Universities By Lewison, Dale M, Hawes, Jon M I SUMMER 2007Journal of College Education .Retrieved Http://Www.Nacacnet.Org/Publicationsresources/Knowledgecenter/Documents/Marketplace/Studenttargetmarketing.Pdf
- Understanding Student Choice Of University And Marketing Strategies In Syrian Private `Higher Education By Anas Al-Fattal Submitted In Accordance With The Requirements For The Degree Of Doctor Of Philosophy University Of Leeds School Of Education September 2010
- Understanding Student Choice Of University And Marketing Strategies In Syrian Private Higher Education By Anas Al-Fattal (2010)
- Retrieved from www.uptu.ac.in
- Retrieved fromwww.uptuwatch.com
- Retrieved fromwww.wekipedia.com
- Retrieved from www.youngindia.com

CRM in Banking: An Indian Perspective

Pavnesh Kumar

Associate Professor, IILM–Academy of Higher Learning, Viraj Khand, Gomti Nagar, Lucknow

ABSTRACT

For sustainable growth, the Financial Tsunami across the world and changing landscape in the financial sector has forced the banking sector to invest more in CRM technologies. Customer Relationship Management (CRM) is a process or methodology used to learn more about customer's needs and behaviors in order to develop stronger relationships with them. CRM increases customer revenues and discover new customers. CRM is now a vital part of banking organisations as after financial sector reforms in nineties new players are investing more and more in it to attract new customers and retain the older one. This paper throws light on the scope of CRM, various risks involved in its implementation and also discusses about the players in this field.

Keywords: *CRM, Banking, Marketing*

INTRODUCTION

Retail banking refers to mass-market banking where individual customers typically use banks for services such as savings and current accounts, mortgages, loans (e.g. personal, housing, auto, and educational), debit cards, credit cards, depository services, fixed deposits, investment advisory services (for high net worth individuals) etc. Before Internet era, consumers largely selected their banks based on how convenient the location of bank's branches was to their homes or offices. With the Advent of new technologies in the business of bank, such as Internet banking and ATMs, now customers can freely chose any bank for their transactions. Thus the customer base of banks has increased, and so has the choices of customers for selecting the banks. This is just the beginning of the story. Due to globalization a new generation of private sector banks and many foreign banks has also entered the market and they have brought with them several useful and innovative products. Due to forced competition, public sector banks are also becoming more technology savvy and customer oriented.

Thus, Non-traditional competition, market consolidation, new technology, and the proliferation of the Internet are changing the competitive landscape of the retail banking industry. Today, retail banking sector is characterized by following:

1. Multiple products (deposits, credit cards, insurance, investments and securities)
2. Multiple channels of distribution (call center, branch, Internet and kiosk)
3. Multiple customer groups (consumer, small business, and corporate).

The customers have many expectations from bank such as –

- Service at reduced cost
- Service "Anytime Anywhere"
- Personalized Service

With increased number of banks, products and services and practically nil switching costs, customers are easily switching banks whenever they find better services and products. Banks are finding it tough to get new customers and more importantly retain existing customers. According to a research conducted by Reichheld and Sasser in the Harvard Business Review, 5% increase in customer retention can increase profitability by 35% in banking business, 50% in insurance and brokerage, and 125% in the consumer credit card market. Therefore, banks are now stressing on retaining customers and increasing market share.

Opportunities for Banks

The banks now need to find out what to sell, whom to sell, when to sell, how to sell and how to be different to increase profitability. Banks need to differentiate themselves by adding value-added service, offerings and building long-term relationships with their customers through more customized products, enhanced value offerings, personalized services and increased accessibility. Banks also need to identify customers and products that would be most profitable and target customers with products that are most appropriate to their needs and serve the customers with greater cost efficiency.

Banks also need to find out the avenues for increased customer satisfaction, which leads to increased customer loyalty. This may be explained better from two initiatives bank took in the past –

1. Earlier what drove many bankers to invest in ATMs was the promise of reduced branch cost, since customers would use them instead of a branch to transact business. But what was discovered is that the financial impact of ATMs is a marginal increase in fee income substantially offset by the cost of significant increases in the number of customer transactions. The value proposition, however, was a significant increase in that intangible called customer satisfaction. The increase in customer satisfaction has translated to loyalty that resulted in higher customer retention and growing franchise value.

2. Bankers invested in Internet banking, believing that the Internet was a lower-cost delivery channel and a way to increase sales. Studies have now shown, however, that the primary value of offering Internet banking services lies in the increased retention of highly valued customer segments. Again customer satisfaction drives the value proposition.

Thus, banks need to retain existing customers with enhanced personalized services and products, which best suits their needs and satisfies them the most.

Customer Relationship Management (CRM)

CRM stands for Customer Relationship Management. It is a process or methodology used to learn more about customers' needs and behaviors in order to develop stronger relationships with them. There are many technological components to CRM, but thinking about CRM in primarily technological terms is a mistake. The more useful way to think about CRM is as a process that will help bring together lots of pieces of information about customers, sales, marketing effectiveness, responsiveness and market trends. CRM helps businesses use technology and human resources to gain insight into the behavior of customers and the value of those customers.

Advantages of CRM

Using CRM, a business can:

- Provide better customer service
- Increase customer revenues
- Discover new customers
- Cross sell/Up sell products more effectively
- Help sales staff close deals faster
- Make call centers more efficient
- Simplify marketing and sales process

These are the types of data CRM projects collect

(i) Responses to campaigns

(ii) Shipping and fulfillment dates

(iii) Sales and purchase data

(iv) Account information

(v) Web registration data

(vi) Service and support records

(vii) Demographic data

(viii) Web sales data

Scope of CRM

CRM primarily caters to all interactions with the customers or potential customers, across multiple touch points including the Internet, bank branch, call center, field organisation and other distribution channels.

CRM can Help Banks in Following Ways

1. **Campaign Management:** Banks need to identify customers, tailor products and services to meet their needs and sell these products to them. CRM achieves this through Campaign Management by analyzing data from banks internal applications or by importing data from external applications to evaluate customer profitability and designing comprehensive customer profiles in terms of individual lifestyle preferences, income levels and other related criteria. Based on these profiles, banks can identify the most lucrative customers and customer segments, and execute targeted, personalized multi-channel marketing campaigns to reach these customers and maximize the lifetime value of those relationships.

2. **Customer Information Consolidation:** Instead of customer information being stored in product centric silos, (for e.g. separate databases of savings account & credit card customers), with

CRM the information is stored in a customer centric manner covering all the products of the bank. CRM integrates various channels to deliver a host of services to customers, while aiding the functioning of the bank.

3. **Marketing Encyclopedia:** Central repository for products, pricing and competitive information, as well as internal training material, sales presentations, proposal templates and marketing collateral.

4. **360-degree view of company:** This means whoever the bank speaks to, irrespective of whether the communication is from sales, finance or support, the bank is aware of the interaction. Removal of inconsistencies of data makes the client interaction processes smooth and efficient, thus leading to enhanced customer satisfaction.

5. **Personalized sales home page:** CRM can provide a single view where Sales Managers and agents can get all the most up-to-date information in one place, including opportunity, account, news, and expense report information. This would make sales decision fast and consistent.

6. **Lead and Opportunity Management:** These enable organisations to effectively manage leads and opportunities and track the leads through deal closure, the required follow-up and interaction with the prospects.

7. **Activity Management:** It helps managers to assign and track the activities of various members. Thus improved transparency leads to improved efficiency.

8. **Contact Center:** It enables customer service agent to provide uniform service across multiple channels such as phone, Internet, E-mail, Fax.

9. **Operational Inefficiency Removal:** CRM can help in Strategy Formulation to eliminate current operational inefficiencies. An effective CRM solution supports all channels of customer interaction including telephone, fax, e-mail, the online portals, wireless devices, ATMs, and face-to-face contacts with bank personnel. It also links these customer touch points to an operations center and connects the operations center with the relevant internal and external business partners.

10. **Enhanced productivity:** CRM can help in enhanced productivity of customers, partners and employees.

11. **CRM with Business Intelligence:** Banks need to analyze the performance of customer relationships, uncover trends in customer behavior, and understand the true business value of their customers. CRM with business intelligence allows banks to assess customer segments, which help them calculate the net present value (NPV) of a customer segment over a given period to derive customer lifetime value. Customers can be evaluated within a scoring framework. Combining the behavior key figure and frequency to monetary acquisition analysis with a marketing revenue quota can optimize acquisition costs and cut the number of inefficient activities. With such knowledge, banks can efficiently allocate resources to the most profitable customers and re-engineer the unprofitable ones. Data warehousing solutions have been implemented in Citibank, Reserve Bank of India, State Bank of India, IDBI, ICICI, MaxTouch, ACC, National Stock Exchange and PepsiCo. And Business Intelligence players hope many more will follow suit.

Risk Involved in CRM Implementation

- **Customers may not want what they get:** A CRM system apart from improving front office operations and customer servicing also helps in coping with many services that do not need manual intervention. These are serviced by channels like IVR, Internet and ATM. Customers can get account information, information on credit balance, issue instructions for drafts or even transact through these. At the same time there may be a few customers who still prefer the traditional methods of banking. Banks need to be flexible enough to continue to extend the "personal touch" that such customers prefer.

- **Make changes internally before going for CRM:** Many banks have spent a lot of money on CRM, finding it easier to buy CRM technology than to make the major internal changes necessary to really make CRM work for them. Unfortunately for these banks, the software has often failed to deliver.

- **CRM is Business Transformation:** Too often banks have focused on the wrong areas of CRM. CRM is really about business transformation—changing the business from services-centric to customer-centric.

- **Have defined Objectives:** Many CRM implementations have been approved without examining aspects like profitability, turnover etc. CRM implementations should have well defined objectives, such as ROI, Sales etc.

- **Consider Complete Life Cycle Costs while budgeting:** Measurements of profit are often constructed to embrace only the initial cost of sale. This is of little use if the ongoing cost of servicing a customer outweigh the margin of profit that customer is generating. It is critical that banks have recognized and embraced the importance of the trend towards customer development, and that this is reflected in actual marketing budget allocation.

CRM Implementation in Banks in India - An Overview

According to NASSCOM report "Strategic Review 2004", Indian CRM market was estimated at US $ 14 million and is forecast to grow to US $ 26 million in 2005. Banking and financial services segment has a high growth potential and accounts for 22% of CRM license revenue. There are many banks such as ICICI Bank, HDFC Bank and Citibank, which are using CRM products. Disciplined work along four dimensions can significantly improve results from CRM initiatives:

Customer Segmentation - Do intensive data analysis and value-based segmentation to highlight the value of different customer segments and the underlying drivers of that value.

Design Programs - Design innovative programs focusing on customer acquisition, cross-sell, retention, loyalty, and customer service, based on customer insights, experience and industry best practices.

Design Processes - Design internal and external processes to support and sustain successful programs.

Good Decisions based on Right Information-The information from a CRM program can often guide better operational business decisions at many levels of the organisation. Gather customer information at a broader set of touch-points, perform in-depth analysis, and make critical information available to relevant stakeholders. The retail banking industry is undergoing revolutionary change. There are many players and competition is tough. Customer Relationship Management is an important weapon in this fight. The ability to mass customize the customer experience and refresh the value proposition is necessary to retain the right to do business with the customer. Consolidation and technology would become

must for sustenance and growth. The pressure will be on banks to integrate data from every channel and know what customers say so that the banks deliver what they want. As the competitions increase, banks will require the robust CRM functionalities in order to manage their most valued asset--their customers.

The Players in Indian CRM Sector

I-flex

In mid-1995 when I-flex started offering its banking product Flexcube, it was not concentrating much on the domestic market. In 1999-2000 the company started focusing on the Indian market and it has carved a niche for itself selling software solutions to private and public sector banks. Syndicate Bank is I-flex's largest customer. So far 30 branches of Syndicate Bank have gone live with Flexcube, and the bank plans to ultimately rollout the product to 200 branches. Union Bank is another customer. Deepak Ghaisas, CEO for India operations at I-flex solutions says, "The first part of our strategy is to have a direct presence in important overseas markets like the US, Netherlands and Singapore. We have our own subsidiaries in these countries. We are also planning to have two more subsidiaries in Europe and Asia-Pacific. Our second strategy is to have global alliances with partners like IBM." I-flex is also optimizing Flexcube on the Intel platform. The company also has alliances with Oracle, Microsoft (.NET) and Hewlett-Packard. The third part of I-flex's strategy is to form alliances. It has 32 such alliances with country-specific partners for pre-sales and first-level support. I-flex also has 12 support centers across India. Flexcube supports corporate, retail, investment, Internet and mobile banking as well as brokerage and derivatives. Ghaisas says, "Customers can buy these solutions independently or as a package."Internationally, its customers include Citibank, which uses Flexcube in a hundred countries, and the Developmental Bank of Singapore, which uses the software at 13 locations. Its international list of clients includes Rabo (Dutch), Shinsei Bank (Japan) and the State Bank of Mauritius. Revenue split by geographies: 32% US, 21% APAC, 21% Europe, 25% Middle East, Africa and India with the balance from Latin America and Cambodia.

Infosys Banking Business Unit

Senior Vice President Girish G Vaidya who heads the Banking Business Unit (BBU) at Infosys Technologies says, "In order to provide an end-to-end solution for banks, banking product vendors should have three products--core banking, vertical-specific CRM and risk management software." Though banks, Telcos, and software houses use traditional CRM products, the basic CRM model has problems like not satisfying the vertical requirement, which comes up in the second phase. The vertical CRM provides a 360-degree view of the customer. The Infosys Finacle CRM product is being used by the National Commercial Bank of Jamaica. The bank is using all of Infy's products, including the recently introduced CRM product. Infy has been successful in India too, bagging Unit Trust of India (UTI) as its first Indian customer for Finacle CRM. Infosys is positioning itself as the only vendor that satisfies two of the three requirements of banks, by offering core banking and four specialized products. Infosys recently bought technology from Trivium and created Finacle CRM, a banking-specific CRM product. Vaidya says, "Infy does not have a product for risk management for treasuries but we have alliances to fill up the gap. However, there is a big opportunity in services such as assets liability management and trading risk management."Vaidya believes that retail banking is undergoing a major change in core banking areas. Instead of customers going to banks, it is the bank that is coming closer, offering delivery channels such as, Tele banking, Internet and phone banking, with a range of products. Speaking on the company's business strategy Vaidya says, "Our strategy is two-fold. On the one hand we will offer an end-to-end range of products--core banking, Internet banking and CRM, which will address the need for emerging technologies. Secondly we will form strategic alliances-BBU has alliances with Sun Microsystems, IBM and HP."For the overseas market, Vaidya says, "We work with business alliance partners. Currently we have business alliance partners in 18 countries."

For the Indian market Infy has a direct sales model. In recent months, Info has bagged projects from Punjab National Bank and UBI. Its clients in the banking space include ICICI Bank, Global Trust Bank, UTI, and ABN AMRO--these banks are using at least three of BBU's products in India. The division has 66 customers in 19 countries. National Commercial Bank of Jamaica and First Bank of Nigeria is its overseas customers. 54 % of revenues come from India. Infosys offers Finacle--a core-banking product, CRM, Treasury for foreign exchange and money market. Finacle eChannels is the Internet banking solution for retail customers while Finacle e-Corporate is the Internet banking solution for corporate customers. Infosys has a global alliance with Sun Microsystems to jointly market a technology platform that aims to address enterprise banking and transaction-intensive network computing requirements.

Vaidya says, "About 60 to 70% of our banking customers are using Sun hardware." Sun's platforms and technologies will power the Finacle suite of banking products. ICICI Bank has been using Infosys's banking solutions on Sun for a long time now. Vaidya adds, "We provide solutions both on. NET and J2EE. We also have alliances with other hardware vendors--IBM and Hewlett-Packard (originally Digital). These alliances help us to increase our market reach and opportunity. Sharing technology know-how with the rest of Infosys helps enhance product efficiency so that it works better on diverse hardware platforms."

Sanchez Capital Services

The customer list of Sanchez Capital Services includes Vysya Bank, which has implemented Sanchez Profile, a core banking application, in 150 branches. Karungthai in Thailand is using Sanchez's core banking software at 600 branches. Other customers using the company's banking products are MetLife and Bank of Nova Scotia. Jerxis Vandervala, Senior Vice President at Sanchez Capital Services, says, "Our parent company, Sanchez Data Systems, that has operations in the US and India, is planning to offer banking solutions based on an ASP model for smaller banks such as cooperative banks. Currently there are 200 banks in the US using our ASP-based solution. We are planning to launch these services in India soon. Prices are still being worked upon. Smaller banks will be in a position to save on capital investments by availing of this offering."Sanchez's strategy for India is that it works with system integrators such as Tata InfoTech and IBM. Overseas, Sanchez works with PwC, IBM, Compaq, Datawell, Oracle and Sun. Sanchez Express provides CRM and Business Intelligence functions. For Internet banking Sanchez has an alliance with ING Worldwide. Sanchez CRM is a real-time Java-based CRM. Its product line includes Wealth Management, Ledger, Sanchez FMS and Web CSR (Customer Service Application) for call centres and back offices.

Zenith InfoTech

Zenith InfoTech is a banking product solution provider catering to nationalized and cooperative banks. Project value is lower in this sector, but Zenith InfoTech is eyeing the huge number of potential customers-there are thousands of cooperative banks in India. Zenith InfoTech's CEO Akash Saraf says, "The needs of nationalized and cooperative banks are different from that of private banks. However, they need the same level of customer service as private banks, though their budgets are limited in comparison. Our strategy is to offer an equivalent solution at a lower price with faster implementation." Typically, private banks such as ICICI spend ₹25 to 40 lakh per branch for computerization. In comparison, smaller banks can offer the same level of customer service for an IT spend of ₹4-6 lakh per branch. "Our flagship product, Banc724, can be easily implemented within 2-3 months while other banking solutions can take 6-12 months for a roll out. Typically, smaller banks will see a return on investment (RoI) in just 8-9 months," adds Saraf. There are several sub-brands under the Banc724 umbrella--core, retail, Internet and mobile banking and a Point of Sale (debit and credit) solution. Zenith Infotech's clients include Central Bank of India, Allahabad Bank, Oriental Bank of Commerce and UCO Bank. Abroad it has customers in Bangladesh and Sri Lanka. The company offers banking services to Citigroup, ABN AMRO and Developmental Bank of Singapore.

Polaris

For more than a decade, Polaris has been providing software services in the banking, financial services and insurance segment. The company provides customized solutions to leading banks and financial services institutions-Citigroup and American Insurance Group from the US; Commerz bank and UBS Warburg in Europe; and NEC, Hitachi and Shinsei in Japan. On the domestic front, Polaris has designed several applications for Citibank and it has implemented a product framework for Himachal Pradesh Cooperative Bank. Recently, Polaris merged with OrbiTech Solutions, a technology subsidiary of Citigroup, and has further strengthened its position in the global BFSI solutions space. "The 'know-how' of Polaris banking solutions delivery combined with the 'know-why' of OrbiTech will provide the new merged entity a superior delivery platform for future customer acquisitions," says Govind Singhal, Executive Director of Polaris Software Lab. "The OrbiPack framework is capable of processing over 10-million customer transactions, giving us the space to leverage the large relationship mining expertise of Polaris. Asia and India are the major markets we work in," adds Singhal. Polaris now plans to accelerate its growth and capitalize on new opportunities by acquiring new customers and enhancing existing relationships. OrbiTech has products in the trade/cash management, treasury, cards, private banking, and corporate banking segments. Post merger with OrbiTech Solutions, Polaris has acquired 57 product/solution Intellectual Property Rights (IPR) and a package of 17 products within the OrbiPack suite of products developed and used within Citigroup during the last 10 years.

Logica

The company has operations across the world. In India & SAARC its clients include both local and international banks. Logica plays at the very high end of the banking software space. The company is implementing a RTGS (real-time gross settlement) solution for the Reserve Bank of India and for Sri Lanka. The Indian implementation started last year and is expected to be completed by the end of 2003 or in early 2004. Sri Lanka just kicked off last month. The company is working with SI partners, particularly for mainframe work. Over 40 people at Logica India are working on the RBI RTGS project. "We have global partnerships," says Louwke van der Steen, Country Manager at Logica for India and SAARC. "However, we can deviate from that when it is required to do so in the local market."While Logica's core competency lies in providing software and services to central banks, it has other offerings. "We use our work with central banks as a jumping board to offer a portfolio of offerings by following up on project implementations with participating banks," adds van der Steen. Logica has done ATM switching work for Centurion Bank and Indus Ind Bank in the country. It has a branch banking product--Questor. Vander Steen believes that India needs to adopt technology more rapidly, especially on the mobile front. Customer education is required to create this market but he believes firmly that "it will pick up."

HMA STAR Ware

HMA STAR ware's Chairman Harish K Murthi says, "In the last five years banks were bogged down with union issues. Today they are looking at technology as a way to be competitive." Murthi cites the figure of ATMs in India that is expected to explode from the present 7 000 to 37,000 in the next five years. Another market expected to set a scorching pace is the POS (Point of Sale terminal) market. Murthi compares Korea to India-Korea has over 2,00,000 POS terminals versus a mere 50,000 in our country. "In technology, we have a lot of catching up to do," adds Murthi. HMA was the first company in India to sell ATMs, especially to public sector banks. That, incidentally, is HMAS's first line of business.

HMAS is the distributor and implementation partner for Oasis products, from OTG Canada, in the SAARC region. The IST switch from Oasis has been well received in India with over 33% of the market (amongst all live switches in India) in a short span of 18 months. Then there's middleware. HMAS has been selling banking middleware not only in India but also in Cambodia and Maldives. A recent development has been the growing interest in using Triple DES encryption and HMAS expects many banks to adopt this standard. HMAS has just started putting payment gateways in place. "Banks are talking to us for payment gateways and implementations are in progress." A payment gateway could cost anything between ₹20-30 lakh to ₹3-4 crore depending upon the features, throughout required in terms of number of transactions, etc.HMA STAR ware's customers include Vysya Bank and Syndicate Bank. HMAS has sold its card management system (ATM cards) to 51 Indian banks. This system was created in-house and it runs on Windows NT. 60 developers work on this solution. The company works with Infy and I-flex. It recently tied-up with Thales e Transactions, the French card payment systems and POS terminal company. Murthi would like to have 50:50 revenue split between products and implementation, but the mix varies from year to year.

Nucleus Software

Nucleus Software focuses on BFSI and it has a strong presence in South-East Asia with offices in Tokyo, Hong Kong and Singapore. It also has offices in London, Australia and the US. A sales office in Dubai caters to Middle East markets. Recently the company bagged an order that is expected to be in excess of half a million dollars from the Arab National Bank in Saudi Arabia. In the coming year, Nucleus plans to focus on emerging markets in the Middle East, Japan, Singapore and Australia. 65% of Nucleus Software's revenues derive from overseas markets, mainly from Japan (staff strength: 130 people) and Singapore (80 people), 5% from the US, 1.5% from the rest of the world and 20% from India.

Nucleus works with channel partners where it doesn't have a direct presence. "We have about ten channel partners in Italy, Mauritius, Malawi, Philippines, Korea, Thailand, Oman and Emirates. Our customers include ICICI, IDBI, HDFC, PNB Paribas, Scotia Bank, GE-Capital, GE-Countrywide, Orix, American Express, Bank of America and CitiFinancial," says Niraj Vedwa, Nucleus Software's Vice President of sales & marketing.

There's no doubt that it's big business. A report by the Tower Group states that banks will "allocate over one-fourth of their technology budgets, approximately $ 37.5 billion on a global basis, on core banking software, hardware and services. A recent NASSCOM-McKinsey study on the global software business revealed that the Banking, Financial Services and Insurance (BFSI) segment would continue to be the largest vertical and drive software revenues. According to this study, the BFSI segment contributed $ 68.3 billion out of a total market size of $ 326.8 billion in the year 1997, a 21% contribution. By the year 2008, the BFSI segment contribution is expected to grow to $ 261.7 billion out of a total market size of $ 1010.4 billion, a 26% contribution. These figures highlight the importance of BFSI to the software industry. A Gartner report says that banking software will grow at a CAGR of 13.5% from 2000 to 2005. The total revenue from packaged software was $ 22 billion in 2002 and is expected to grow at 8% to reach $ 38 billion in 2005. Industry pundits estimate that Indian banks spend ₹150 crore and above on software and hardware for core and Internet banking on an average.

CONCLUSION

The Indian banking sector is growing leaps and bounds and with the changing world economic order the Indian banking industry is carving its own way to reach the unbanked population. India as a nation at present is going through a transparency revolution, so it has become mandatory on the part of the banking sector as well to be cost effective and transparent. The CRM tools and techniques can give the solution to the above problem.

References

- Banking Services Chronicle Editorials November 2004 & subsequent issues
- Books and Reports
- Business magazines
- Business Today January 2005 and subsequent issues
- Customer Relationship Management: Getting It Right by Judith W. Kincaid Published by HP Books and Prentice Hall PTR
- Fourier Susan, Susan Dolsacha & David glen Mick, (1998) "Preventing the premature death of relationship marketing", Harvard Business Review, Retrieved from http://ssaravanakumar.articlesbase.com/banking-articles/crm-in-banking-1302680.html
- Retrieved from http://www.expresscomputer.com
- Retrieved from http://www.indiainfoline.com
- Retrieved from http://www.mbrit.com
- Retrieved from http://www.sas.com
- *Internet Sources*

- *Janal Daniel. S. "Online Marketing hand book", Van Nostrand Reinhold, New York, USA.*
- *Mittal, R. K. (2000), "Net-banking is the way to go", Indian Management, 39, 6.*
- *Padwal, S.M. (2000), "Need for redesigning information Technology (IT)/Information system (IS) Architecture in Indian Banks, Prajnan.*
- *Philip Kotler, (1999) "Marketing Management: Analysis, Planning, Implementation and control, "Englewood cliffs, Prentice Hall, New Jersey.*
- *Report of the committee on technology up-gradation in banking sector" Reserve Bank of India.*
- *Semih Onut Ibrahim Erdem Bora Hosver Customer Relationship Management in Banking Sector and A Model Design for Banking.*

A Study of Rural Marketing in India

Preeti Sharma[1] and Rubina Pathan[2]

[1]Reader, Department of Management Studies Indore Institute of Computer Application, Indore,
Madhya Pradesh
[2]Assistant Professor, Department of Management Studies, Malwa Institute of Technology, Indore,
Madhya Pradesh

ABSTRACT

In recent years, rural markets have acquired significance, as the overall growth of the economy has resulted into substantial increase in the purchasing power of the rural communities. On account of green revolution, the rural areas are consuming a large quantity of industrial and urban manufactured products. In this context, a special marketing strategy, namely, rural marketing has emerged. But often, rural marketing is confused with agricultural marketing the latter denotes marketing of produce of the rural areas to the urban consumers or industrial consumers, whereas rural marketing involves delivering manufactured or processed inputs or services to rural producers or consumers. This research paper also explains the present scenario of Indian Rural Market, Evolution of Rural Marketing, Growth of Rural Marketing and reasons for improvement in Rural Markets.

Keywords: *Agriculture, Consumer, Indian Rural Market and Rural Marketing*

INTRODUCTION

In recent years, rural markets have acquired significance, as the overall growth of the economy has resulted into substantial increase in the purchasing power of the rural communities. On account of green revolution, the rural areas are consuming a large quantity of industrial and urban manufactured products. In this context, a special marketing strategy, namely, rural marketing has emerged. But often, rural marketing is confused with agricultural marketing the latter denotes marketing of produce of the rural areas to the urban consumers or industrial consumers, whereas rural marketing involves delivering manufactured or processed inputs or services to rural producers or consumers. With the increase in purchasing power and the demand for wide variety of products by the farmers, the rural market offers new and greater opportun8ities to manufactures of several consumer and industrial products in India. But to tap this vast expanding market, companies need to develop effective marketing and advertising strategies based on their study and understanding of rural consumer behaviour.

There could be several approaches in defining the Indian rural market. It will not be an exaggeration if the whole of India, excluding the metropolitan's cities, the various districts headquarter and large Industrial Township is considered as the rural market. Alternately all villages with a population of less than say, 40,000 or 50,000 can be considered as forming the rural market.

The concept of Rural Marketing in India Economy has always played an influential role in the lives of people. In India, leaving out a few metropolitan cities, all the districts and industrial townships are connected with rural markets. The rural market in India is not a separate entity in itself and it is highly influenced by the sociological and behavioral factors operating in the country. The rural population in India accounts for around 627 million, which is exactly 74.3% of the total population. The rural market in India brings in bigger revenues in the country, as the rural regions comprise of the maximum consumers in this country. The rural market in Indian economy generates almost more than half of the country's income.

Table 1 Growth in Rural Markets by Product Categories

Product Category	Growth (%)
After Shave Lotions	51.9
James/Jellies	37.8
Butter/Margarine	36.4
Napkins	32.3
Acne Preparations	28.3
Sanitary Napkins	24.6
Air fresheners	24.5
Phenyls	20.8
Packaged Atta	17.3
Perfume/Deodorant/Cologne	16.3
Shampoo	14.2
Hair Dyes	14.1
Hair Remover	11.0

Source Dobhal, 2005

The vast untapped potential, increasing income and purchasing power, improved accessibility and the increasing competition in urban markets make rural markets an attractive destination for jaded marketers of products and services. Entry into rural markets reduces the risk of depending only on the urban market. In the case of all fast moving consumer goods (FMCGs) taken together, sales in rural markets contribute to 30% of the overall sales. The sale from various segments is shown in Table 2.

Table 2 Rural Market Share

Market	Population (In Millions)	Contribution To FMCG Sales (%)
Metro	11	28.7
Class-I	90	18.7
Small Towns	90	22.4
Rural	750	30.1

Source Shukla and Shrivastava, 2006

While for all FMCGs the percentage contribution to sales is more than 30%, there are at least five products where the rural market has a larger share than the urban market.

Table 3

Non-Durable Product	Share of Rural Market (%)
Washing Cakes/Bars	65
Batteries	64
Blues	57
Iodized Salt	54
Safety Razor Blades	53
Washing Powders	47

Contd...

Contd...

Toilet Soaps	44
Tea	43
Biscuit	39
Shampoo	38
Toothpaste	31

Source Dobhal, 2005

LITERATURE REVIEW

According to "G. Srinivas Rao" in his book "Rural marketing in India", Rural Population in India accounts for more than 70% of its overall population. The Rural markets are coming up in a huge way due to its untapped immense potential. The consumers in these rural areas are different from their urban counterparts in their buying behavior; the reasons for this differentiation are many like Age and life cycle stage, Occupation, Economic condition, Lifestyle, Personality and self beliefs etc.

Basu Purba (2004), suggested that the lifestyle of rural consumers is changing. Rural Indian market and the marketing strategy have become the latest marketing buzzword for most of the FMCG majors. She added the strategies of different FMCG companies for capturing rural market like Titan's Sonata watches, Coco Cola's 200ml bottle, different strategies of HUL and Marico etc. She takes into consideration the study of National Council for Applied Economic Research (NCAER).According to the NCAER projections, the number of middle and high-income households in rural area is expected to grow from 140 million to 190 million by 2007. In urban India, the same is expected to grow from 65 million to 79 million. Thus, the absolute size of rural India is expected to be double that of urban India.

The economic growth in India's agricultural sector in last year was over 10%, compared with 8.5% in the industrial sector. This implies a huge market potentiality for the marketer to meet up increasing demand. Factors such as village psyche, strong distribution network and market awareness are few prerequisites for making a dent in the rural markets. The model is of the stolid Anglo-Dutch conglomerate Unilever Group, which has enjoyed a century-long presence in India through its subsidiary Hindustan Lever Ltd. It was Hindustan Lever that several years ago popularized the idea of selling its products in tiny packages. Its sachets of detergent and shampoo are in great demand in Indian villages. Britannia with its low priced Tiger brand biscuits has become some of the success story in rural marketing.

OBJECTIVES OF THE STUDY

The main objectives of the study are;

- To study the Rural Marketing Perspective.
- To study the profile of Indian Rural Market.

CHARACTERISTICS OF RURAL MARKET

The rural market of India consists of about 80% of the population of the country. Apparently therefore, in term of the number of people, the Indian rural market is almost twice as larger as the entire market of U.S.A. or U.S.S.R. the market is not only large, but very much scattered geographically. It is also as diverged as it is scattered it exhibited linguistic, religion and cultural diversities and economic disparities, and hence it can easily be considered as more complex than the market of a continent as a whole. The market is generally undeveloped as the people who constitute the market are so. Poor standard of living, low per capital income and economic, social and cultural backwardness are the characteristics of the market. The literacy level is generally law even though this varies from one art of the country to the other. Another important feature of the rural market is that, at least in the present contest, it is largely agricultural oriented. Here again the much

heard of "green revolution" and the resultant prosperity is confined to a few select areas in the country. As a consequence, the effective demand based for a large variety of consumer items as well as the wealth generating inputs is confined to selected pockets and not spread over the rural markets.

INDIAN RURAL MARKET

Rural marketing in India is not much developed there are many hindrances in the area of market, product design and positioning, pricing, distribution and promotion. Companies need to understand rural marketing in a broader manner not only to survive and grow in their business, but also a means to the development of the rural economy. One has to have a strategic view of the rural markets so as to know and understand the markets well. In the context of rural marketing one has to understand the manipulation of marketing mix has to be properly understood in terms of product usage. Product usage is central to price, distribution, promotion, branding, company image and more important farmer economics, thus any strategy in rural marketing should be given due attention and importance by understanding the product usage, all elements of marketing mix can be better organized and manage.

Table 4 Evolution of Rural Marketing

Phase	Origin	Function	Major Products	Source Market	Destination Market
1	Before Mid-1960 (from Independence to green revolution)	Agricultural Marketing	Agricultural Product	Rural	Urban
2	Mid-Sixties (Green revolution to Pre-liberalization Period)	Marketing of Agricultural Inputs	Agricultural Inputs	Urban	Rural
3	Mid-Nineties (Post-liberalization period on 20th century)	Rural Marketing	Consumables and Durables for Consumption and Production	Urban and Rural	Rural
4	21st century	Developmental Marketing	All Products and services	Urban and Rural	Urban and Rural

While there is a general tendency to equate rural India to Balance of Payment market, here are some of the consumption numbers that will blow your mind

- 46% of the soft drinks sales happen in the rural areas.
- Rural India accounts for 49% of motorcycle sales.
- Rural India accounts for 59% of Cigarettes sales.
- 53% of FMCG sales happen at Rural India.

- Talcum powder is used by more than 25% of rural India.
- Lipsticks are used by more than 11% of the rural women and less than 22% of the urban women.
- Close to 10% of Maruti Suzuki's sales come from the rural market.
- Hero Honda, on its part, had 50% of its sales coming from rural market in FY'09.
- Rural India has a large consuming class with 41% of India's middle-class and 58% of the total disposable income accounting for consumption.

- By 2010 rural India will consume 60% of the goods produced in the country.
- In 20 years, rural Indian Market will be larger than the total consumer markets in countries such as South Korea or Canada today, & almost 4 times the size of today's urban Indian market.

GROWTH OF RURAL MARKETING

Infrastructure is improving rapidly. In 50 years only 40% villages connected by road, in next 10 years another 30%. More than 90% villages electrified, though only 44% rural homes have electric connections. Rural telephone density has gone up by 300% in the last 10 years; every 1000+ pop is connected by STD

Social Indicators have improved a lot between 1981 and 2001. Number of "pucca" houses doubled from 22% to 41% and "kuccha" houses halved (41% to 23%). Percentage of BPL (Below Poverty Line) families declined from 46% to 27%. Rural Literacy level improved from 36% to 59%. Low penetration rates in rural so there are many marketing opportunities.

Table 5   Market Share (Urban and Rural) for white goods and FMCG products

Durables	Urban	Rural	Total (% of Rural HH)
CTV	30.4	4.8	12.1
Refrigerator	33.5	3.5	12.0
FMCGs	Urban	Rural	Total (% of Rural HH)
Shampoo	66.3	35.2	44.2
Toothpaste	82.2	44.9	55.6

Marketers can make effective use of the large available infrastructure like Post offices 1,38,000, Haats (periodic markets) 42,000, Melas (exhibitions) 25,000, Mandis (agri markets) 7,000, Public distribution shops 3,80,000, Bank branches 32,000. Proliferation of large format rural retail stores which have been successful also. DSCL Haryali stores, M & M Shubh Labh stores, TATA/Rallis Kisan Kendras, Escorts rural stores, Warnabazaar, Maharashtra (annual sale Rs 40 crore).

REASONS FOR IMPROVEMENT IN RURAL MARKETS

Socio-economic changes (lifestyle, habits and tastes, economic status) Literacy level (25% before independence more than 65% in 2001) Infrastructure facilities (roads, electricity, media) Increase in income, Increase in expectations. MART, the specialist rural marketing and rural development consultancy has found that 53%

of FMCG sales lie in the rural areas, as do 59% of consumer durable sales, said its head Pradeep Kashyap at the seminar. Of two million BSNL mobile connections, 50% went to small towns and villages, of 20 million Rediffmail subscriptions, 60% came from small towns, so did half the transactions on Rediffmail shopping site.

In this scenario the job of the Marketer becomes even more difficult in the sense that he has not to fight other competitors but also the imitated products. The advantages that these products enjoy in the rural markets are that the Imitators who are in the villages are making these and they are offering More Margins & Better credit Facilities. To solve this problem the Marketer has to educate the consumer about his product and show him the benefits of his products over the imitated ones.

Table 6   Need-Product Relationships and the changes happening in Rural India

Needs	Old Products	New Products
Brushing Teeth	Neem sticks, Charcoal, Rocksalt, Husk	Toothpaste, Tooth powder
Washing Vessels	Coconut fibemr, Earthy materials, Brick Powder, Ash	Washing Powder, Soaps and Liquids
Transport	Bullock Cart, Horses, Donkeys	Tractors, LCVs, Mopeds, Scooters, Motor cycles
Irrigation	Wells, Canals, water lifters, Wind Mills	Bore-wells, Motors, Power Generators, Pump Sets
Hair Wash	Shikakai powder, Retha, Besan	Shampoos and hair care soaps

Some Live and Practical Examples of Rural Marketing

- One very fine example can be quoted of Escorts where they focused on deeper penetration. They did not rely on T.V or press advertisements rather concentrated on focused approach depending on geographical and market parameters like fares, melas etc. Looking at the 'kuchha' roads of village they positioned their bike as tough vehicle. Their advertisements showed Dharmendra riding Escort with the punch line 'Jandar Sawari, Shandar Sawari'. Thus, they achieved whopping sales of 95000 vehicles annually.
- HLL started 'Operation Bharat' to tap the rural markets. Under this operation it passed out low–priced sample packets of its toothpaste, fairness cream, Clinic plus shampoo, and Ponds cream to twenty million households.

- ITC is setting up E-Choupals which offers the farmers all the information, products and services they need to enhance farm productivity, improve farm-gate price realization and cut transaction costs. Farmers can access latest local and global information on weather, scientific farming practices as well as market prices at the village itself through this web portal - all in Hindi. It also facilitates supply of high quality farm inputs as well as purchase of commodities at their doorstep.
- BPCL Introduced Rural Marketing Vehicle (RMV) as their strategy for rural marketing. It moves from village to village and fills cylinders on the spot for the rural customers. BPCL considered low-income of rural population and therefore introduced a smaller size cylinder to reduce both the initial deposit cost as well as the recurring refill cost.

CONCLUSION

Thus looking at the challenges and the opportunities which rural markets offer to the marketers it can be said that the future is very promising for those who can understand the dynamics of rural markets and exploit them to their best advantage. A radical change in attitudes of marketers towards the vibrant and burgeoning rural markets is called for, so they can successfully impress on the 230 million rural consumers spread over approximately six hundred thousand villages in rural India.

Bibliofraphy

- Dobhal, S. (2005a), Good, bad or downright ugly? Business Today, 14(1), 10-11. ·
- Dobhal, S. (2005b), Land ho! Business Today, 14(1), 20.
- Srivastava, Deepa and Shukla. K. (2006) Conversion of Anthocyanin pigment to chlorophyll in Catheranthus roseus flower due to viral infection. 131-132.
- Bhalla, G. S, and Singh Gurmail (2001), Indian Agriculture-Four Decades of Development, New Delhi: Sage.
- Basu, Purba (2004), Research on Living Style of Rural Consumers, 5-8.

A Study on Customer Satisfaction-Private Vs Public Banks

Rajesh S. Pyngavil[1] and Monika Mittal[2]

[1]Associate Professor, Gitarattan International Business School, Rohini, Delhi
[2]Assistant Professor, Prestige Institute of Management, Gwalior

ABSTRACT

Banking operations are becoming increasingly customer dictated. The demand for 'banking super malls' offering one-stop integrated financial services is well on the rise. The ability of banks to offer clients access to several markets for different classes of financial instruments has become a valuable competitive edge.

Convergence in the industry to cater to the changing demographic expectations is now more than evident. Bancassurance and other forms of cross selling and strategic alliances will soon alter the business dynamics of banks and fuel the process of consolidation for increased scope of business and revenue. The thrust on farm sector, health sector and services offers several investment linkages.

We can recognize where we need to make changes to create improvements and determine if these changes, after implemented, have led to increased customer satisfaction. **"If you cannot measure it, you cannot improve it."**

Core heart of the Indian banking Industry lies in the hands of the two sectors that is private sector banks and public sector banks and a comparison on the customer satisfaction is a must to come out with the true picture of the services provided by the two to the customers.

Keywords: *Customer Satisfaction, Banking Sector, Private Bank, Public Bank, Customer Satisfaction Model*

INTRODUCTION

According to www.linkedin.com, Banking in India originated in the last decades of the 18th century. The oldest bank in existence in India is the State Bank of India, a government-owned bank that traces its origins back to June 1806 and that is the largest commercial bank in the country. Central banking is the responsibility of the Reserve Bank of India, which in 1935 formally took over these responsibilities from the then Imperial Bank of India, relegating it to commercial banking functions. After India's independence in 1947, the Reserve Bank was nationalized and given broader powers. In 1969 the government nationalized the 14 largest commercial banks; the government nationalized the six next largest in 1980.

Currently, India has 88 scheduled commercial banks (SCBs) - 27 public sector banks (that is with the Government of India holding a stake), 29 private banks (these do not have government stake; they may be publicly listed and traded on stock exchanges) and 31 foreign banks. According to www.bankbazaar.com, They have a combined network of over 53,000 branches and 17,000 ATMs. According to a report by ICRA Limited, a rating agency, the public sector banks hold over 75% of total assets of the banking industry, with the private and foreign banks holding 18.2% and 6.5% respectively.

The working of the customer's mind is a mystery which is difficult to solve and understanding the nuances of what customer satisfaction is, a challenging task. This exercise in the context of the banking industry will give us an insight into the parameters of customer satisfaction and their measurement. This vital information will help us to build satisfaction amongst the customers and customer loyalty in the long run which is an integral part of any business. The customer's requirements must be translated and quantified into measurable targets. This provides an easy way to monitor improvements, and deciding upon the attributes that need to be concentrated on in order to improve customer satisfaction.

EARLY HISTORY OF BANKING IN INDIA

According to en.wikipedia.org, Banking in India originated in the last decades of the 18th century. The first banks were The General Bank of India, which started in 1786, and the Bank of Hindustan, both of which are now defunct. The oldest bank in existence in India is the State Bank of India, which originated in the Bank of Calcutta in June 1806, which almost immediately became the Bank of Bengal. This was one of the three presidency banks, the other two being the Bank of Bombay and the Bank of Madras, all three of which were established under charters from the British East India Company. For many years the Presidency banks acted as quasi-central banks, as did their successors. The three banks merged in 1925 to form the Imperial Bank of India, which, upon India's independence, became the State Bank of India.

Indian merchants in Calcutta established the Union Bank in 1839, but it failed in 1848 as a consequence of the economic crisis of 1848-49. The Allahabad Bank, established in 1865 and still functioning today, is the oldest Joint Stock bank in India. When the American Civil War stopped the supply of cotton to Lancashire from the Confederate States, promoters opened banks to finance trading in Indian cotton. With large exposure to speculative ventures, most of the banks opened in India during that period failed. The depositors lost money and lost interest in keeping deposits with banks. Subsequently, banking in India remained the exclusive domain of Europeans for next several decades until the beginning of the 20th century.

According to en.wikipedia.org, foreign banks too started to arrive, particularly in Calcutta, in the 1860s. The Comptoire d'Escompte de Paris opened a branch in Calcutta in 1860, and another in Bombay in 1862; branches in Madras and Pondichery, then a French colony, followed. Calcutta was the most active trading port in India, mainly due to the trade of the British Empire, and so became a banking centre.

Around the turn of the 20th Century, the Indian economy was passing through a relative period of stability. Around five decades had elapsed since the Indian Mutiny, and the social, industrial and other infrastructure had improved. Indians had established small banks, most of which served particular ethnic and religious communities.

The presidency banks dominated banking in India but there were also some exchange banks and a number of Indian joint stock banks. All these banks operated in different segments of the economy. The exchange banks, mostly owned by Europeans, concentrated on financing foreign trade. Indian joint stock banks were generally undercapitalized and lacked the experience and maturity to compete with the presidency and exchange banks. This segmentation let Lord Curzon to observe, "In respect of banking it seems we are behind the times. We are like some old fashioned sailing ship, divided by solid wooden bulkheads into separate and cumbersome compartments."

By the 1900s, the market expanded with the establishment of banks such as Punjab National Bank, in 1895 in Lahore and Bank of India, in 1906, in Mumbai - both of which were founded under private ownership. Punjab National Bank is the first Swadeshi Bank founded by the leaders like Lala Lajpat Rai, Sardar Dyal Singh Majithia. The Swadeshi movement in particular inspired local businessmen and political figures to found banks of and for the Indian community. A number of banks established then have survived to the present such as Bank of India, Corporation Bank, Indian Bank, Bank of Baroda, Canara Bank and Central Bank of India.The fervour of Swadeshi movement lead to establishing of many private banks in Dakshina Kannada and Udupi district which were unified earlier and known by the name **South Canara** (South Kanara) district. Four nationalised banks started in this district and also a leading private sector bank. Hence undivided Dakshina Kannada district is known as "Cradle of Indian Banking".

Nationalization

According to finance.**india**bizclub.com, By the 1960s, the Indian banking industry has become an important tool to facilitate the development of the Indian economy. At the same time, it has emerged as a large employer, and a debate has ensued about the possibility to nationalise the banking industry. Indira Gandhi, the-then Prime Minister of India expressed the intention of the GOI in the annual conference of the All India Congress Meeting in a paper entitled *"Stray thoughts on Bank Nationalisation."* The paper was received with positive enthusiasm. Thereafter, her move was swift and sudden, and the GOI issued an ordinance and nationalised the 14 largest commercial banks with effect from the midnight of July 19, 1969. Jayaprakash Narayan, a national leader of India, described the step as a *"masterstroke of political sagacity."* Within two weeks of the issue of the ordinance, the Parliament passed the Banking Companies (Acquisition and Transfer of Undertaking) Bill, and it received the presidential approval on August 9, 1969.

According to en.wikipedia.org, A second dose of nationalization of 6 more commercial banks followed in 1980. The stated reason for the nationalization was to give the government more control of credit delivery. With the second dose of nationalization, the GOI controlled around 91% of the banking business of India. Later on, in the year 1993, the government merged New Bank of India with Punjab National Bank. It was the only merger between nationalized banks and resulted in the reduction of the number of nationalized banks from 20 to 19. After this, until the 1990s, the nationalized banks grew at a pace of around 4%, closer to the average growth rate of the Indian economy.

Liberalization

According to en.wikipedia.org, In the early 1990s, the then Narsimha Rao government embarked on a policy of liberalization, licensing a small number of private banks. These came to be known as New Generation tech-savvy banks, and included Global Trust Bank (the first of such new generation banks to be set up), which later amalgamated with Oriental Bank of Commerce, UTI Bank(now re-named as Axis Bank), ICICI Bank and HDFC Bank. This move, along with the rapid growth in the economy of India, revitalized the banking sector in India, which has seen rapid growth with strong contribution from all the three sectors of banks, namely, government banks, private banks and foreign banks.

The next stage for the Indian banking has been setup with the proposed relaxation in the norms for Foreign Direct Investment, where all Foreign Investors in banks may be given voting rights which could exceed the present cap of 10%, at present it has gone up to 49% with some restrictions.

The new policy shook the Banking sector in India completely. Bankers, till this time, were used to the 4-6-4 method (Borrow at 4%; Lend at 6%; Go home at 4) of functioning. The new wave ushered in a modern outlook and tech-savvy methods of working for traditional banks. All this led to the retail boom in India. People not just demanded more from their banks but also received more.

According to www.vbeyond.com, currently, banking in India is generally fairly mature in terms of supply, product range and reach-even though reach in rural India still remains a challenge for the private sector and foreign banks. In terms of quality of assets and capital adequacy, Indian banks are considered to have clean, strong and transparent balance sheets relative to other banks in comparable economies in its region. The Reserve Bank of India is an autonomous body, with minimal pressure from the government. The stated policy of the Bank on the Indian Rupee is to manage volatility but without any fixed exchange rate-and this has mostly been true.

In March 2006, the Reserve Bank of India allowed Warburg Pincus to increase its stake in Kotak Mahindra Bank (a private sector bank) to 10%. This is the first time an investor has been allowed to hold more than 5% in a private sector bank since the RBI announced norms in 2005 that any stake exceeding 5% in the private sector banks would need to be vetted by them.

In recent years critics have charged that the non-government owned banks are too aggressive in their loan recovery efforts in connection with housing, vehicle and personal loans. There are press reports that the banks' loan recovery efforts have driven defaulting borrowers to suicide.

Trends in Indian Banking Industry

According to www.financialexpress.com, The current year has seen some very positive influences on the financial industry. A host of initiatives have been taken in the recent past to ramp up the regulations for the private banking sector and along with that a new dimension in outlook toward customers, technology and banking as a sector on the whole has been adopted.

Looking ahead, the banks need to identify their key focus area for the coming year and work towards building a comprehensive and focused growth strategy for themselves enabling them to draw out their respective plans. Given the cut-throat nature of bank competition, targeted technology investments with measurable ROI can provide solid opportunities for them.

Banks are also succeeding at reallocating IT resources away from maintenance to new projects, though maintenance costs still weigh heavily. This reallocation is crucial given that the strategic IT investments of today are the competitive differentiators of tomorrow. Highlighted are some of the relevant issues that banks face today:

Banking Business Areas

Bank offers a wide range of services to the society. The products are backed by extensive delivery channels such as extensive branch network, ATM's, phone banking, net banking and mobile banking.

Key business areas are

- **Wholesale banking**: for the corporate, the bank provides a wide range of banking services, including working capital finance, trade service, transactional services, cash management, online service tax payments etc. Both the funds as well as non fund based exposures to middle market based customer segments have been pegged on overall basis to around 25% to retain the quality of overall wholesale banking portfolio.
- **Retail Banking**: The bank provides a full range of financial products and services like savings, fixed deposits, current and Demat account, loans, bills payments etc. Revenues of the retail banking segment are derived from interest on retail loans, net of commission (net of subvention received) paid to sales agent, and interest earned from other segments for surplus funds placed with those segments. Expenses of this segment primarily comprise interest expense on deposits, costs, other direct overheads and allocated expenses.
- **Treasury operations:** Bank has three main product areas Foreign exchange and derivatives, local currency money market and debt securities and equities. On the forex front the bank performs well in foreign and local currency debt securities. Most of the revenues were generated from plain vanilla and spot forward contracts as well as certain derivatives products.

Classification of Banks

Private Banks are banks that are not incorporated. A non-incorporated bank is owned by either an individual or a general partner(s) with limited partner(s). In any such case, the creditors can look to both the "entirety of the bank's assets" as well as the entirety of the sole-proprietor's/general-partners' assets.

"Private banks" and "private banking" can also refer to non-government owned banks in general, in contrast to government-owned (or nationalized) banks, which were prevalent in communist, socialist and some social democratic ("liberal") states in the 20th century. Private banks as a form of organisation should also not be confused with "Private Banks" that offer financial services to high net worth individuals and others.

Public Banks are the banks which are owned by the government in general and are also called nationalized banks.

These banks are not required to add the word limited at the end of their names. The bank is permitted to carry on banking business with members of the general public.

INDIAN BANKING SCENARIO

According to bmsproject.weebly.com, The Indian Banking industry, which is governed by the Banking Regulation Act of India, 1949 can be broadly classified into two major categories, non-scheduled banks and scheduled banks. Scheduled banks comprise commercial banks and the co-operative banks. In terms of ownership, commercial banks can be further grouped into nationalized banks, the State Bank of India and its group banks, regional rural banks and private sector banks (the old/ new domestic and foreign). These banks have over 67,000 branches spread across the country.

The first phase of financial reforms resulted in the nationalization of 14 major banks in 1969 and resulted in a shift from Class banking to Mass banking. This in turn resulted in a significant growth in the geographical coverage of banks. Every bank had to earmark a minimum %age of their loan portfolio to sectors identified as "priority sectors". According to www.researchandmarkets.com, The manufacturing sector also grew during the 1970s in protected environs and the banking sector was a critical source. The next wave of reforms saw the nationalization of 6 more commercial banks in 1980. Since then the number of scheduled commercial banks increased four-fold and the number of bank branches increased eight-fold.

After the second phase of financial sector reforms and liberalization of the sector in the early nineties, the Public Sector Banks (PSB) s found it extremely difficult to compete with the new private sector banks and the foreign banks. The new private sector banks first made their appearance after the guidelines permitting them were issued in January 1993. Eight new private sector banks are presently in operation. These banks due to their late start have access to state-of-the-art technology, which in turn helps them to save on manpower costs and provide better services.

During the year 2000, the State Bank of India (SBI) and its 7 associates accounted for a 25% share in deposits and 28.1% share in credit. The 20 nationalized banks accounted for 53.2% of the deposits and 47.5% of credit during the same period. The share of foreign banks (numbering 42), regional rural banks and other scheduled commercial banks accounted for 5.7%, 3.9% and 12.2% respectively in deposits and 8.41%, 3.14% and 12.85% respectively in credit during the year 2000.

CURRENT SCENARIO

The industry is currently in a transition phase. On the one hand, the PSBs, which are the mainstay of the Indian Banking system, are in the process of shedding their flab in terms of excessive manpower, excessive non Performing Assets (Npas) and excessive governmental equity, while on the other hand the private sector banks are consolidating themselves through mergers and acquisitions.

According to www.researchandmarkets.com, The private players however cannot match the PSB's great reach, great size and access to low cost deposits. Therefore one of the means for them to combat the PSBs has been through the merger and acquisition (M& A) route. Over the last two years, the industry has witnessed several such instances. For instance, HDFC Bank's merger with Times Bank ICICI Bank's acquisition of ITC Classic, Anagram Finance and Bank of Madura, Centurion Bank, Indusind Bank, Bank of Punjab, Vysya Bank are said to be on the lookout. The UTI bank- Global Trust Bank merger however opened a pandora's box and brought about the realization that all was not well in the functioning of many of the private sector banks.

Private sector Banks have pioneered internet banking, phone banking, anywhere banking, and mobile banking, debit cards, Automatic Teller Machines (ATMs) and combined various other services and integrated them into the mainstream banking arena, while the PSBs are still grappling with disgruntled employees in the aftermath of successful VRS schemes. Also, following India's commitment to the W To agreement in respect of the services sector, foreign banks, including both new and the existing ones, have been permitted to open up to 12 branches a year with effect from 1998-99 as against the earlier stipulation of 8 branches.

AGGREGATE PERFORMANCE OF THE BANKING INDUSTRY

According to www.docstoc.com, Aggregate deposits of scheduled commercial banks increased at a compounded annual average growth rate (Cagr) of 17.8% during 1969-99, while bank credit expanded at a Cagr of 16.3% per annum. Banks' investments in government and other approved securities recorded a Cagr of 18.8% per annum during the same period.

In FY01 the economic slowdown resulted in a Gross Domestic Product (GDP) growth of only 6.0% as against the previous year's 6.4%. The WPI Index (a measure of inflation) increased by 7.1% as against

3.3% in FY00. Similarly, money supply (M3) grew by around 16.2% as against 14.6% a year ago.

The growth in aggregate deposits of the scheduled commercial banks at 15.4% in FY01% was lower than that of 19.3% in the previous year, while the growth in credit by SCBs slowed down to 15.6% in FY01 against 23% a year ago.

The industrial slowdown also affected the earnings of listed banks. The net profits of 20 listed banks dropped by 34.43% in the quarter ended March 2001. Net profits grew by 40.75% in the first quarter of 2000-2001, but dropped to 4.56% in the fourth quarter of 2000-2001.

Consequently, banks have been forced to explore other avenues to shore up their capital base. While some are wooing foreign partners to add to the capital others are employing the M& A route. Many are also going in for right issues at prices considerably lower than the market prices to woo the investors.

CUSTOMER SATISFACTION

Customer satisfaction, a business term, is a measure of how products and services supplied by a company meet or surpass customer expectation. It is seen as a key performance indicator within business and is part of the four perspectives of a Balanced Scorecard.

In a competitive marketplace where businesses compete for customers, customer satisfaction is seen as a key differentiator and increasingly has become a key element of business strategy.

Measuring Customer Satisfaction

Organisations are increasingly interested in retaining existing customers while targeting non-customers; measuring customer satisfaction provides an indication of how successful the organisation is at providing products and/or services to the marketplace.

Customer satisfaction is an ambiguous and abstract concept and the actual manifestation of the state of satisfaction will vary from person to person and product/service to product/service. The state of satisfaction depends on a number of both psychological and physical variables which correlate with satisfaction behaviors such as return and recommend rate. The level of satisfaction can also vary depending on other options the customer may have and other products against which the customer can compare the organisation's products.

According to www.wbiconpro.com, because satisfaction is basically a psychological state, care should be taken in the effort of quantitative measurement, although a large quantity of research in this area has recently been developed. Work done by Berry (Bart Allen) and Brodeur between 1990 and 1998 defined ten 'Quality Values' which influence satisfaction behaviour, further expanded by Berry in 2002 and known as the ten domains of satisfaction. These ten domains of satisfaction include: Quality, Value, Timeliness, Efficiency, Ease of Access, Environment, Inter-departmental Teamwork, Front line Service Behaviors, Commitment to the Customer and Innovation. These factors are emphasized for continuous improvement and organisational change measurement and are most often utilized to develop the architecture for satisfaction measurement as an integrated model. Work done by Parasuraman, Zeithaml and Berry (Leonard L) between 1985 and 1988 provides the basis for the measurement of customer satisfaction with a service by using the gap between the customer's expectation of performance and their perceived experience of performance. This provides the measurer with a satisfaction "gap" which is objective and quantitative in nature. Work done by Cronin and Taylor propose the "confirmation/disconfirmation" theory of combining the "gap" described by Parasuraman, Zeithaml and Berry as two different measures (perception and expectation of performance) into a single measurement of performance according to expectation. According to Garbrand, customer satisfaction equals perception of performance divided by expectation of performance.

The usual measures of customer satisfaction involve a survey with a set of statements using a Likert Technique or scale. The customer is asked to evaluate each statement and in term of their perception and expectation of performance of the organisation being measure.

Customer Satisfaction Model

The Customer Satisfaction Model is a macro level framework the links the 2 extended Ps (people and performance), and reflects the impact of the traditional Ps (product, price, place, promotion).

(Source http://faculty.msb.edu/homak/homahelpsite/webhelp/Customer_Satisfaction_Model.htm)

While conceptually simple, the framework captures the essence of marketing:

The CSM links together several fundamental business and marketing concepts:

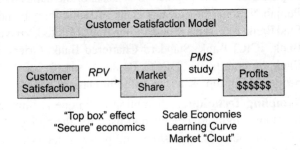

(Source:http://faculty.msb.edu/homak/homahelpsite/webhelp/Customer_Satisfaction_Model.htm)

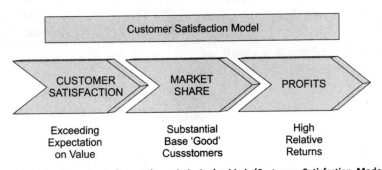

(Source http://faculty.msb.edu/homak/homahelpsite/webhelp/Customer_Satisfaction_Model.htm)

RESEARCH METHODOLOGY & DESIGN

Statement of the Problem - With the phenomenal increase in the country's population and the increased demand for banking services; speed, service quality and customer satisfaction are going to be key differentiators for each bank's future success. Thus it is imperative for banks to get useful feedback on their actual response time and customer service quality aspects of banking, which in turn will help them take positive step to maintain a competitive edge.

Objective of the Research

- To identify the variables used by individuals for selecting a bank.

- Identify the variables to determine the marketing strategies of the bank.
- Conduct a comparative analysis of service of private banks and public banks and its impact on customer satisfaction.

Scope of the Study

Scope of the study is very wide as Indian Banking sector is growing at a very fast rate. The research is significant in the following manner:

- Helpful in tracing out the variables of utmost importance to the customer with respect of their expectation from the banking sector.
- Helps in finding out the lacking in the sector in which customers are not fully satisfied.
- The data base attached to the report can be used by the banks in order to tap potential customers.
- The study will be of a great help to the banks in developing a favorable marketing strategy.

Population: The population consists of the banks like Punjab National Bank, State Bank of India, Punjab and Sind Bank, Axis Bank, South Indian Bank Limited, Vijaya Bank, ICICI Bank, Standard Chartered Bank, Oriental Bank of commerce, HDFC Bank. A sample of 150 people which represent the different class of people.

Sampling Technique: Sampling technique is Simple Random sampling. The method used for the collection of data is observational study and personal interview.

Hypothesis

Ho (null hypothesis): "There is no significant difference between the services provided by the private and the public banks".

H1 (Alternate Hypothesis): "There is a significant difference between the service provided by the private and the public banks."

Tool of Data Collection: Questionnaire prepared by the researcher was used for the collection of Data. Few examples of the questions asked in the questionnaire are:

- Bank handles your account efficiently, without mistakes?
  - (a) Very Satisfied
  - (b) Satisfied
  - (c) Dissatisfied
  - (d) Very Dissatisfied
  - (e) No Experience
- The level of privacy bank offers?
  - (a) Very Satisfied
  - (b) Satisfied
  - (c) Dissatisfied
  - (d) Very Dissatisfied
  - (e) No Experience

Research Duration: Duration of the research was 3 months.

Data Sources: Data for the purpose of research is collected from two major sources these are Primary sources and Secondary sources.

DATA ANALYSIS AND INTERPRETATION

Table 1   Age Group of Respondents

Age group	No of Respondents	%age
18-28	49	32.67
28-40	36	24
40-60	46	30.66
60 and above	19	12.67
Total	**150**	**100**

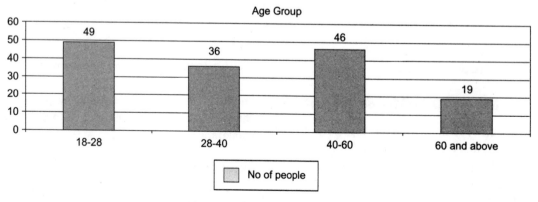

Fig. 1   Age group of respondents

The above table and figure depict the details of age group of respondents for the study. It is clear from the table that majority of respondents belongs to the age group 18- 28 (32.67%) and 40-60 (30.66%).

Table 2 Educational Qualification of Respondents

Particulars	Number of Respondents	%age
UnderGraduate	30	20%
Graduate	87	58%
Professional	27	18%
Doctorate and others	06	4%
Total	**150**	**100%**

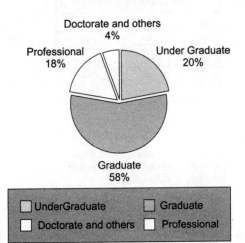

Education Qualification

Fig. 2 Educational Qualifications of Respondents

It is very clear from the above table and figure, the major share of the respondents been the part of the study are graduates. The percentage is above 50% (58%). 20% of respondents were undergraduates, 18% were professionally qualified such as law, medicine etc. Only 4% of the samples taken for the study posses other qualification like M.Phil, PhD. etc.

Table 3 Occupation of Respondents

Particulars	No of Respondents	%age
Student	24	16%
Service	75	50%
Business	36	24%
Others	15	10%
Total	**150**	**100%**

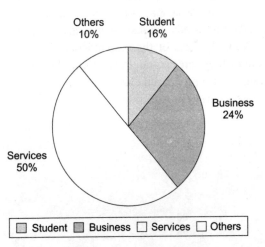

Occupation

Fig. 3 Occupation of respondents

It is evident from the table no 4 and figure no 4 that the majority of the respondents who were being the part of the study belongs to service class. It comprises of 50% of the total sample taken for the study. It can be inferred that service class people are very much concerned about bank account. Business class people hold 24% of the total sample. It very well noted that a good number of students (18%) also posses bank account.

Table 4 Type of Account Hold by Respondents

Particulars	%age	No of Accounts
Savings Account	78%	117
Current Account	22%	33
Total	**100%**	**150**

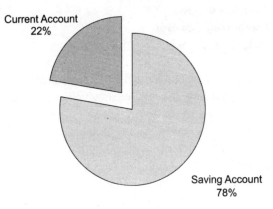

Type of Account

Fig. 4 Type of Account Hold by Respondents

It is very clear and evident from the above table and pie chart that a lion share of the respondents who were the part of the study possess savings account. The share is 78%. Only 22% of the respondents possess current account, they are particularly doing business. They belong to entrepreneurial class. The service class people who are salaried in nature have savings account.

Table 8 Parameter Rating by the Customers: Private Banks

Parameter	No of people	Rank
Ease in Operations	71	1
Speedy service	70	2
ATM Facility	63	4
Courteous staff	66	3
Fixed deposit service	56	5
User Friendly E Banking	52	6
Locker facility	44	7

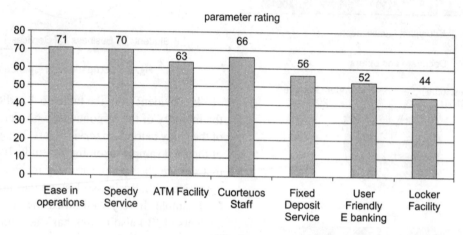

Fig. 5

(b) Public Bank

Parameters	No of People	Rank
Ease in Operations	78	1
Speedy service	73	2
ATM Facility	62	4
Courteous staff	68	3
Fixed deposit service	59	5
User Friendly E Banking	42	7
Locker facility	43	6

The above two tables and two figures provide a deep insight regarding the facilities which are considered for satisfaction by customers. It is very much evident from the ranks based on the number of respondents opted for the different facilities, both in case of private and public sector bank the factor ease to operation has emerged as the most influencing one followed by speedy service and delivery. Courteous staff is the third rank factor for both private and public sector banks. E banking is not considered as a prime one for both the customers of private and public sector banks. It can be revealed from the above analysis that, the present time customers are very concerned about the soft facilities such as courteous staff, speedy service etc rather than hard facilities such as ATM facility or locker facility.

Objective - impact of services provided by public banks and private banks on customers

The main objective was to test the impact of services provided by public banks and private banks on customers for the purpose **Z-Test was applied and the calculated figure at 5% significance level derived as 3.47 against the table value 0.4997.** It is inferred that calculated value is higher than table value so, Ho (null hypothesis) "There I no significant difference between the services provided by the private and the public banks got rejected and H1 (Alternate Hypothesis)" There is a significant difference between the services provided by private and the public banks" got accepted.

FINDINGS

1. There is clearly seen a rise in the level of the market share of the private banks and they are reaching close to the public banks in terms of the market share which is an indicator of the customer satisfaction with the services offered and delivered by the private banks.

2. The banks in both the sectors have been rated good by the customers in handling their accounts

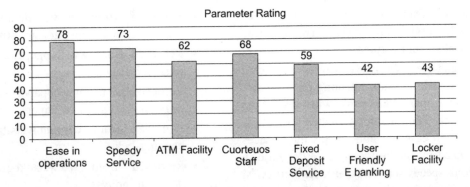

Fig. 6

Table 6 Application of Z test

Particulars	Mean	Standard Deviation	(Standard Deviation)²	Table Value
Private Bank	54.18	4.94	24.43	
Public Bank	50.98	6.29	39.62	0.4997

without making mistakes that is making customer account correctly and adequately.

3. Customers of private banks however seemed to be dissatisfied by the extra charges which they are levied on the credit cards, debit cards, cheque dishonour, charges for getting a DD made etc. which is not in the case of the public banks.

4. With respect of the calls answered by the bank the private banks clearly hold an edge with their young and well trained workforce and public banks are somewhat lacking in this aspect.

5. In case of both the banks the customer can easily reach out the desired person in order to cater to the customers need.

6. Both the banks whether private or public are maintaining the level of privacy of the account information of their customers and are not disclosing the information to any other person.

7. Queues are a major problem seen in case of public banks which the banks are not managing properly which is to a great extend managed efficiently and effectively by the private sector banks.

8. Staff of both the banks is adequately knowledgeable regarding the services offered by the banks and are able to provide good advice to the customers.

9. The staffs of private bank are more active and are providing 100% attention to the customer which is a bit missing in case of public banks.

10. Because of mostly young and professionally well dressed employees the staffs in private banks is

smarter and look more profession than the staff in the public bank.

11. It has also been seen that few public sector banks such as Punjab and Sind bank, kangra cooperative bank etc are even not providing it customers with debit card and ATM facilities which has become one of the necessities of today's banking services.

12. Many of the public sector banks are still not having fully centralised and inter linked computerised branches till today which is leading to inconvenience to the consumers and leading to dissatisfaction.

13. Public sector banks are also not marketing their services and product offerings as good as the private sector banks are doing.

14. Private sector banks are requiring a higher minimum balance to be maintained in the account by the customers other wise they are deducting charges from the account of the customer which is not in the case of public banks where the initial or minimum account balance to be maintained is much lower.

15. The research's main objective was to test the impact of services provided by public banks and private banks on customers for the purpose Z-Test was applied and the calculated figure at 5% significance level derived as 3.47 against the table value 0.4997. It is inferred that calculated value is higher than table value so, Ho (null hypothesis) "There I no significant difference between the services provided by the private and the public banks got rejected and H1 (Alternate

Hypothesis)" There is a significant difference between the services provided by private and the public banks" got accepted.

16. Positive and Negative analysis were conducted to identify various factor affecting the customer to choose a particular bank with respect to their service. The data got tabulated and it was found that in case of public banks the services were ranked by the customers in order Ease in operations, speedy services, courteous staff, ATM facility, Fixed deposit service, Locker facility, User friendly E banking and in of Private banks the services were ranked as Ease in operation, Speedy services, courteous staff, ATM facility, Fixed deposit service, user friendly E banking and locker facility.

RECOMMENDATIONS AND SUGGESTIONS

1. The marketing strategy should highlight ease of operations, speedy services, and better support for the call and on site visit.

2. Aggressive advertising should be undertaken to increase awareness, hence using a pull strategy.

3. Public banks which are not yet providing services like ATM, Credit cards should take some concrete steps in this respect.

4. Private Banks should also focus and should not levy unnecessary charges on the customers which dissatisfy the customers of these banks.

5. Few banks were found not be providing E banking facility to the customers the banks should implement the E banking services in order to compete with other competitor banks providing the e banking service to its customers.

References

- Retrieved from www.linkedin.com/skills/skill/Banking_Domain.
- Retrieved from www.gomamu.com/subjects/finance/text/banking_industry.html.
- Retrieved from www.oppapers.com › History Research Papers.
- Retrieved from www.oppapers.com › Business & Economy Research Papers.
- Retrieved from www.universityparadise.com/banking-india/
- Retrieved from www.bankbazaar.com/guide/banks-in-india/
- Retrieved from info.indiafascinates.com/**banking/banks**-in-india/
- Retrieved from www.goldentwine.com/ind/inv/invbnk.htm.
- Retrieved from en.wikipedia.org/wiki/**Banking in India.**
- Retrieved from www.gomamu.com/subjects/finance/text/banking_industry.html.
- Retrieved from dc406.4shared.com/doc/wgEg4LqC/preview.html.
- Retrieved from finance.**india**bizclub.com/info/**Indian banking industry.**
- Retrieved from http://www.experts123.com/q/how-many-nationalized-banks-are-there-in-india.html.
- Retrieved from *en.wikipedia.org/wiki/**Banking in India.***
- Retrieved from http://books.google.co.in/books?id.
- Retrieved from http://www.scribd.com/doc/55171700/8/Growth-and-Present-Status-of-Banks.
- Retrieved from http://files.embedit.in/embeditin/files/NQS86Rxful/1/page_4.swf
- Retrieved from www.vbeyond.com/industry_verticals.html.

Brand Salience of the Private Label Brands in Retail

S.V. Dongardive[1] and Anil Pande[2]

[1]HOD, Department of Commerce, Elphiston College, Fort, Mumbai
[2]Assistant Professor, University of Mumbai, Jamanalal Bajaj Institute of Management Studies

ABSTRACT

Today, in retail, and in every product category, retail outlets are aggressively stocking private label brands/products next to national brands. Retailers often use private labels in their stores to attract the customers. From packaging down to performance, private labels are giving the national brands a run for their money.

The important question is how private label brand can ever hope to compete with big brands in the market? Probably the answer can be related with the delivery of the brand. The unique advantage of private label brand is that they provide the end delivery or fulfillment to consumer within the preview of the store brand. A consistent delivery mechanism and careful attention to detail may lead consumers to prefer the in-store brand to competing offerings. Brand is on the top of the mind is also a salient – that is top of the mind awareness.

The current study on brand salience focuses on understanding and creating salience level to some private brands among the customers across various demographic segments. This will also focus on the narrow range attributes which can be used effectively to create the private label brand. The study concludes that in view of the stiff competition in the global business arena where business have to survive and grow on the basis of volume instead of margins, careful study of salience attributes will constitute the essential plank of private label brands marketing. This implies that retailers will have to focus on the inclusion essential variables while creating and developing the private label brands.

To this end, the retailers need to continuously assess and reassess how customer perceive their overall store brand and services to implement appropriate corrective action for successfully placing the in-house brand in the store.

Keywords: *private label brands, In house brand, brand salience, narrow range attributes, national brands, store brands, delivery mechanism*

INTRODUCTION

There is always a clutter at the point of purchase due to some reasons like SKU proliferation, brand extension by the manufactures, me – to- products, private labels and copy cats. This clutter causes the customers to accidently pick up wrong products. Hence retailers and manufacturers try to differentiate their brands and SKUs by using visual salience methods. Some try to give visual appearance to entire category.

It is seen that 80% of the success is just 'showing up'. But unfortunately at the time of purchase many of the brands do not show up. So getting the consumer to think about your brand at the time of purchase is most important challenge that brands face today.

Brand Salience

Salience is conceptualised as the probalbility that a customer will think of the brand at some point of time. This is a broader interpretation than the usual frame of reference for the term 'salience', which is conceptualised as the prominence of the brand , is commanly used intercheably with, and measured via, top of mind awareness with the product category cue.

Brand that is at the top of the mind is also salient- top of the mind awareness is not the only way in which this salience can be expressed. This salience level was converted from the number of times the brand could be mentioned.

Brand Salience Defined

Brand Salience is an extent to which the brand visually stands out from the competition.

Brand salience is the degree to which your brand is thought about or noticed when a customer is in a buying situation. It is seen that strong brand have high brand salience than the weak brands. As we say, Brand salience is the top of the mind awareness, so it is awareness of the consumers when asked to recall the brand within the category. Brand salience is also what comes to consumers mind at the purchase situation. So it is the memory of your brand and its linkages to other important memory structures.

Drivers of Brand salience

According to various researches Brand salience is the function of Quantity and Quality of the consumer's memory structures. Brand salience is the step before consideration of brand or a 'thought of' before consumer considers a brand for final purchase. Thus it is mentally screened out.

(a) Quantity of memory structure

At the time of purchase (buying situation) consumers are often driven by mental cues- that trigger thought around brand consideration set.

E.g. If, think to have some homemade food, quickly, at home, less than ₹20. I am likely to consider Maggie noodles, which costs ₹20, which is projected and promoted as healthy and nutritious food.

Here my memory structure is linked to the brand. Hence Maggie noodles are more salient to my mind structure. So at a buying situation Maggie noodle is more thought of.

With the above example, we can infer, what buyers remember about brand is not which is always the same across buying decisions. So quantity of memory structure makes decisions.

(b) Quality of memory structure

Qualities of brand salience are nothing but the strength of association and attribute relevance. E.g. With the earlier example, I have other food stuff available worth ₹20. But I have strong value for cleanliness, nutritiousness and relevance of my budget that increases the brand salience. So Brand Salience is a function of:

(a) The quantity of memory structures a customer is linked to.

(b) The quality of these structures as defined by the strength of association and relevance of the structure.

Thus by building quality and quantity of the memory structures one can maximize the number of consumers who will think of your brand and number of times they think of your brand in various buying situations. So it is 'shows up'.

Two approaches to build salience:

1. Focus on building and communicating different cues against a common equity: Focus on important equity for your brand. Do consumer research to understand the most important relevant cues which link to your benefit. Use these cues to maximize memory structure associations. e.g. Maggie noodles, healthy and nutritious can be executed like "good for my kids", for people on diet, good to eat any time. Thus these can lead to nutritious healthy offering.

2. Create distinctive executional memory structures: To increase quantity and quality of executional memory structures, the focus should be given on the following aspect. e.g. Maggie noodles, logo, color, picture on wrapper, ₹20, song, jingle, etc are examples of creating executional memory structures. This creates platform which enables customer to easily remember your brand in buying situation. So salience is very important step in ensuring your brand gets considered for purchase.

Private Label Brand:

In every cotegory, retail outlets are aggressively stocking private label products next to national brands, and often sing private labels to attract customers into their stores. From packaging down to performance, private labes are giving stiff competition to the national brands.

To find out salience level of some of the private label brands among the customers across various demographic segments and to focus on creating brand salience by focussing on some narrow range of attributes is one of the objective of this research.

A private label brand, often referred to as an in-house brand or store brand, is that which is owned by the retailers themselves.

Examples: Shopper Stop: STOP, Kashish, Life, Vettorio Fratini, Elliza Donatein, and Acropolis

Indian Scenario of Private Label Brands

The store brand is different from the brand in the store. In fact most people do not remember the private label brand in the stores and have great difficulty in articulating the value of these brands. Since the in-store brands are never going to be sold anywhere else except in the stores, the fortunes of these brands are indelibly linked to the fortunes of the stores and store brands. This view is applicable to almost all the leading brands and stores across the world. What drives the consumers is the store brand rather than Private label brand in the store.

Currently some private labels generate approximately 60% to 80% of the revenue for the stores. Some of these brands have taken a natural level of growth in certain areas. For instance, one of the oldest men's wear brand John Miller, has achieved critical mass to exist as standalone brand. Unisex brands such as Bare (denim and leisurewear), Ajile (sportswear) and Rig (utility week end wear) have also been registering volumes to serve as individual store brands.

Shoppers Stop is one of the leading retail stores in India. It began by operating the chain of department stores under the name Shoppers stop in India. Shoppers stop has also operating a number of specialty stores like Crossword Bookstores, Mothercare, Brio, Desi café`, Arcelia. Shoppers Stop has seen the increase in the margin share of private label brands by approx 18%. It has brands such as Life, Kashish and Vittorio Fratini in its portfolio. The private labels at the store are growing at the rate of 40-45%.

As retailing continues to change, the improved use of private label brands has come to forefront as a key business asset in developing the differential advantage to the retailers. In fact private labels can set the retailers apart from the competition, and they can attract customers into the stores. Today retailers are shifting their emphasis on development of private label brands into high gear by using variety of strategies to build the image of their brands, expand their brand recognition, and raise their brand image in the market place.

India's largest retailer by sales, Pantaloon Retail, too is looking at an increase of about 10-15% for its private label apparel brands like John Miller, Scullers, Indigo Nation besides others.

The Growth of Private Labels

Due to current wave of consumption, a prominent growth of the private label brand is realized from past few years. Some private brands have brand exclusivity and name but lack big advertisement budgets, big price tags and consumer awareness. The entry of big businesses in the retail foray and consumer readiness to shop and spend ensures the availability of private label brands and further growth of the private label brands.

Researches confirmed nearly 40% of the products we shop from the retailers are private labels in various categories. Shoppers like Westside, Shoppers Stop, Reliance Fresh, Big Bazaar, Globus, pantaloon and so on heavily rely on in house brands for revenue growth.

In nutshell, private label brands are revenue spinners, generate revenue at lesser capital input, they are accepted by the consumers and they are steadily evolving too. But then question arises

(a) What makes customers buy them, knowingly or unknowingly?

(b) What makes the retailers go all the way to launch and maintain these brands?

(c) What makes these brands successful despite no advertising?

(d) What is a rational behind stocking these brands?

(e) What should be ideal composition on the shelf space of the retail store?

Retail sector in India have shown remarkable growth. This can be depicted from the research study done by E&Y in year 2009-10.

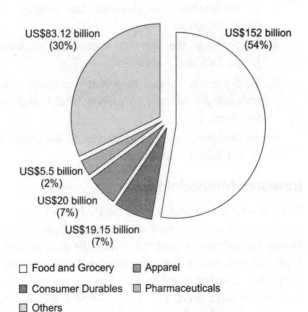

Retail Sector in India

- □ Food and Grocery
- ■ Apparel
- ▨ Consumer Durables
- ▨ Pharmaceuticals
- □ Others

Private Labels and their potential:

According to a FICCI-Ernst & Young 2007 report, as quoted in The Marketing White book 2009-10, the retail sector in India was worth $280 billion, of which organized retail comprised 5% at $14 billion. In an ASSOCHAM-KPMG joint study, the size of the retail industry was pegged at $353 billion in 2008. It was estimated to grow to $410 billion by 2010, of which organized retail would value approximately $51 billion.

According to Images Retail Report 2009, as quoted in "Indian Retail: Time to Change Lanes" by KPMG; private label brands constitute 10-12% of organized retail in India. Of this, the highest penetration of private label brands is by Trent at 90%, followed by Reliance at 80% and Pantaloons at 75%. Big retailers such as Shoppers Stop and Spencer's have a penetration of 20% and 10% respectively. Globally, store brands constitute nearly 17% of retail sales. In fact, international retailers such as Wal-Mart and Tesco have 40% and 50% of in-house brands in their stores.

Private labels are becoming more innovative, are adding more value to the consumers and are able to offer innovation that is similar to an established brand. Customer in this case is getting a similar quality at a much lower price. This is especially true in the apparel brand because there it is not just the price advantage that works, but also the design sensibility. The designs are both done in-house and are outsourced as well.

Objectives of the Study

1. To understand and elaborate the concept of Brand Salience.
2. To find out the ways to create and enhance Brand Salience.
3. To focus on various important parameters, to enhance the salience of private label brands in the store.
4. To evaluate the factors responsible for creating Brand Salience for the product.

Research Methodology

The given topic and objectives of the study need in-depth survey of primary as well as secondary data source. Hence the attempt is made to collect the data actually form the consumers through structured questionnaire form the suburban locality of Mumbai region. Data is also collected from the online sources and online questionnaire method too.

Further in order to confirm the parameters and clear the concepts of various terms, secondary data search is done through various websites, magazines and the reference books from the libraries. The survey data so collected was analyzed by using Microsoft Office Excel.

Data Analysis and Inference

66 respondents gave feedback to the questionnaire hoisted on the internet and 47 responses to the same questionnaire were collected actually.

61 numbers were females and 52 were males.

Value for money was the major attribute responded by 57% respondents followed by quality of the product 41%.

In private label brand 74% of the respondents responded that quality of the product is most important aspect.

49% responded that they usually buy that brand of product which they are aware of and used earlier.

Price was important factor for 445 of the respondents.

52% try new brand, store image and product display was more important for them.

58% feel that private label brands would be successful in categories like apparels and 56% responded for food and beverages.

More number of men was aware of private label brands and more men purchase from supermarkets and malls. They focus on durability and availability of the range of the product.

Data analysis revealed some important facts about the behavior of the consumers while at buying situation. It revealed that the parameters of quality, range of product line, store image and visual display are important parameters for the brand salience at a broader sense. Along with the earlier factors advertisement, advertisement message, emotional connect, product placement, promotions and mental connect of the consumers at a buying situation play very important role for the creation of brand salience.

CONCLUSION

It is important for the retaiers to create salience for their store as well as fro private labels by focusing more on low price and value related attributes. Low price, better offers and value attributes can draw in more customers to the store as they associate private label brands with those attributes. That will create brand awareness among the customers. Once brand awareness is created it in turn will increase brand recall and hence high degree of brand salience.

Recommendations and Suggestions

In order to create brand salience by the retailers, for their private label brands, retailers must focus on above the line and below the line activities. Brand building exercise should be cautious activity which must focus on the quality, availability, utility of the product. For retailers building store image would be the best way to create the salience for their private labels.

References

- Nag, A., (2009), Strategic Marketing, *Macmillan India Ltd., New Delhi.*
- Hooley, Grahm, Nigel, F. Piercy, Brigittee, Nicoulaud, (2009), Marketing Strategy and Competitive Positioning, 4th Edition, *Porling Kindersley (India) Pvt. Ltd.*
- Patrick, M. Dunne, Robert F. Lusch, David, A. Griffith, (2005), 2nd Edition, *Thomson Asia Pte. Ltd. Singapore.*
- Kotler, Philip, Armstrong, Gary, Y. Prafulla, Agnihotri, Ehas Ul Haave, (2010), Principles of Marketing, 13th Edition, *Porling Kindersley (India) Pvt. Ltd.*
- Retrieved http://www.britannica.com/ebchecked /topic/365730/marketing/27254/retailers
- Retrieved from http://www.google.com/
- Retrieved from http://www.scribd.com/doc/ 19615001/non-store-retailing

- Swapna Pradhan, (2007), Retailing Management, Tata McGraw-Hill, New Delhi, Some of the Private Label Branding Strategies Used By Retailers:
- Developing the partnership with well known celebrities, noted experts and institutional authorities.
- This allows the retailer to align with individual whose personal reputation creates immediate brand recognition, image, or credibility. Like future bazaar uses Mahendra Singh Dhoni, a Cricketer and Globus and Provogue uses Karina Kapoor, a film celebrity.
- Developing a partnership with traditionally higher end supplier to bring an exclusive variation on their highly regarded brand name market.
- Wal-Mart recently signed an exclusive trademark licensing agreement to use the General Electric name on small appliances. This partnership offers a win-win situation to both the parties. Retailer get the exclusive private label with great image and the opportunity to expand customer base, customer appeal, ratchet up price points, and raise margins. Manufacturer builds volume and gains access to broad new market spectrum.
- Reintroducing product with strong name recognition that have fallen from the retail scene. Old brand names do not die. They get recycled.
- Branding an entire department or a business, not just a product line. Target has taken up its private label branding strategy to one step ahead by branding its entire supermarket section.

Effect of Advertising on children and their Role

Sujit Kumar Dubey[1] and Pradeep Agrawal[2]

[1]Associate Professor, [2]Faculty of Management Studies, Banaras Hindu University, Varanasi

ABSTRACT

Success of a product mainly depends on awareness and persuasive communication between the buyer and maker. Now days the marketers are targeting children for the role of sheet anchor to sail their products. Children's' behavior over past few years have become more independent and contradictory as well. They enjoy freedom in almost everything they do, with more sovereignty in decision making than before.

Compared to earlier generations, now family purchase decisions have been more children specific or kid centric. They are seen as major influencer in family decisions, being unreasonably vocal about their needs and wants which are otherwise known as pester power. Marketing for children is all about creating such pester power because advertisers now know what powerful medium children can become.

Keywords: *Pester Power, Buying Behavior, Product Advertisement*

INTRODUCTION

In this competitive world the tug of war between the consumer goods is getting tougher day by day. Marketing organisations are making all possible efforts to capture the market by creating greater awareness and long-run acceptability of their products and brands. Making the target audience aware mainly depends on the persuasiveness of the communication and here comes the role of Advertising. Advertisements have that persuasive power that motivates the King Pin of the market – "Consumers". The effectiveness of the advertisement depends on the extent up to which the message is received and accepted by the target audience.

Advertising may be in the form of printed material such as magazine, newspaper advertisements, pamphlets, posters etc. or it may also involve radio, television and now this channel of advertisement is getting wider through the web advertising.

Children – The Pester Power

Pester Power refers to children's ability to nag their parents into purchasing items they may otherwise not buy. Marketing to children is all about creating pester power because advertisers know how much power they have in influencing the purchase decisions. Children, who are presumed to be soft-hearted, are the target of marketers due to their over-vulnerability. Marketers initially lure the children by showing them glamorous and eye-catching advertisements and later dominate their mind by repeating them again and again. In other words, children get addicted to watching these advertisements and get restless. Their restlessness is same as a drug addict without getting regular doses of drugs.

Gone are the days when children were over- indulged in outdoor games. Today, children are more of 'Techno-kids'. They prefer watching TV, surfing net, playing computer games as a better option over playing outdoor games. Out of all the substitutes, Television has become the most favorite substitute for the outdoor games and is now considered as the Best Full Time Friend. On an average a child between the ages of 2 years to 15 years spend 3-4 hours a day and about 20 hours a week watching television. Marketers use television as a medium since it affords access to children at a much early age than any other media can accomplish. This may be because of lack of understanding of textual literacy up to a certain age.

However, the considerably new channel of advertising emerging these days is World Wide Web. Now, children have started using the internet and browse through hundreds of websites of their own interest. Marketers have observed both children's increasing use of internet and ability of net to provide a unique environment. Advertisements targeted towards children are designed in such a way so as to have maximum impact. Effective advertising thus involves the ability to cater right product at right time through right medium for a right audience.

Literature Review

Many earlier researches have concluded that children participation in family purchase decision is increasing and television advertisements are playing important role in defining their product choice and buying behavior pattern.

Bansal (2004) elaborated on three stages of middle-class Indian youth – early Youth, Middle Youth and Late Youth. She pointed that the early youth are basically dependent on their parents' funds and therefore try to influence them in buying products of their choice. On the other hand the Late Youth are working youths who give equal priority to career advancement and children. They take suggestions from their family and children for purchase in the area of household, kid products, personal clothing, food and entertainment.

A vast number of children have been found to watch television in India and prefer it to reading *(George, 2003)*. *Singh (1998)* opined that purchase requests by children are strongly simulated by commercials or by a friend who has recently purchased a product.

Wilson and Wood (2004), Hansen et al. (2005) found television ads targeted at children persuade them to nag their parents by arousing a desire in them to acquire the desired product, thereby influencing the family buying decisions.

Hastings et al., (2003) asserted that children receive advertising messages which have more to do with fantasy and fun than health and nutrition.

Galst and White (1976) and Stoneman & Brody (1982) made an attempt to measure the effect of television advertising in shaping purchase- related behavior of children. They exposed children to advertisements of food products in an experimental situation and then observed the effectiveness of these ads on the selection of products and brands.

Solomon (1982) in his study revealed that Children are targeted directly with messages of what food products to buy, which would influence them to pester their parents when shopping.

Keane and Willetts (1994) stated that parents often find it difficult to deny their children food that features their favorite cartoon characters or celebrities that they have seen on television.

Kunkel et al. *(2004)* reported that television advertisements are effective in influencing children who lack the relevant knowledge, but still want their parents to get them endless array of products which they have seen in advertisements. Television commercials are also changing children's eating habits. Unhealthy and junk food commercials have resulted in their increasing demand among the children.

Even in the *March, 2004 issue of India Today*, it was mentioned that Aggressive marketing of food products via children has led to a nation of obese young generation.

The above thoughts and opinions clearly depicts that with the augmenting rates of watching TV hours of children, the marketers are capturing more and more section of children's innovative brain. These advertisements have such a serious impact on the immature minds of children that they get tuned to buy the products as shown in the lucrative advertisements. The biggest evidence of the over indulgence of children in advertisement is that they are so well-versed with the taglines of products. How can we forget the ad of Complan with the jingle- 'I am a Complan boy…I am a Complan Girl', ad by the Rasna Girl saying "I love you Rasna". Few of the latest ads in the lot include ad campaign of Mc Donalds depicting the two kids pretending to be Boyfriend and Girl Friend, Maruti Esteem's "My daddy's big car" slogan, Pepsodent- "Pappu and Papa", Surf Excel's "Daag Achchey Hain" and many more…..

The Indian Context

Indian culture is collectivistic which means that Indians emphasize their self as relational and interdependent with in-group members such as family and relatives. Traditionally, the joint family system was dominant form of family with multi-generations living together. However, with modernization, the joint family is giving way to nuclear family structures. Another development which has taken place in the recent years is that the proportion of women in the workforce has increased to a great extent. This has caused a shift in the role of purchase agent for the family from women to children. Children are increasingly becoming the buyers for the entire family. In most of the Indian families children are consulted not only for buying the products which are intended to be consumed by them but also for the products not meant for them.

Joint Survey of Cartoon Network & Synovate Indian reveals that kids have major influence both as direct and indirect consumers in India and spend nearly 291 crores as pocket money. The survey done in 14 Indian cities covering 4,043 children found that 84% of parents took their children while going for shopping and accept that kids influence major purchases such as television sets, cars, mobile phones.

Objective of the Study

1. To study the attitude of children towards ads.
2. To know the most preferred media by children.
3. To determine the category of product advertisement, that children like to watch most.
4. To know the role played by the children in purchase decisions of the family.

Scope of the Study

The study has been carried out in some selected schools of Varanasi.

Sample Design

A total of 200 respondents from different schools of Varanasi were chosen for the study using Convenience sampling method.

Data Collection

The primary data was collected through questionnaire and partially through direct interviews. A multiple choice questionnaire was designed for the purpose.

Data Analysis and Interpretation

The study focusing on Children of age group 08 to 17 years studying in class 5th to 9th the fact that 82% of the children like watching TV while only 18% showed no interest for TV (Table 1).

Table 1 Do you like watching TV

		Frequency	%	Valid %	Cumulative %
Valid	Yes	164	82.0	82.0	82.0
	No	36	18.0	18.0	100.0
	Total	200	100.0	100.0	

Table 2 Which Media Source attracts most for gaining information

		Frequency	%	Valid %	Cumulative %
Valid	Television	148	74.0	74.0	74.0
	Newspapers/Magazine	4	2.0	2.0	76.0
	Radio/FM	16	8.0	8.0	84.0
	Hoardings on road	20	10.0	10.0	94.0
	Internet	12	6.0	6.0	100.0
	Total	200	100.0	100.0	

In this technological advanced world there are various media sources that provide various information to a child. Out of the present media sources Table 2 clearly shows that 74% children get their information through television while 10% come across the ads from hoardings on roads and displays at shops. As an audio-visual medium television provides more information to children and leave a very long lasting impact.

A comparative analysis of Table 3, 4, 5 and 6 shows that 84% children watch TV programs regularly while only 8% are regular newspaper/magazine readers. It points out the fact that spread of TV audience is wider than newspaper readers among children. TV being an audio-visual medium is enjoyed by them.

While 14% of the children admitted that they enjoy listening radio on a regular basis, the percentage was 20 for those who regularly surf on internet.

Most of the children are habitual of those programs that they see or listen regularly. Few of them also show interest in reading particular magazines or columns in newspapers and time to time wait for them. However, it's the electronic media that enjoys a wider audience altogether when compared to print media.

Table 3 Frequency of viewership

		Frequency	%	Valid %	Cumulative %
Valid	Regular	168	84.0	84.0	84.0
	Sometimes	28	14.0	14.0	98.0
	Never	4	2.0	2.0	100.0
	Total	200	100.0	100.0	

Table 4 Frequency of Reading Newspapers/Magazine

		Frequency	%	Valid %	Cumulative %
Valid	Regular	16	8.0	18.0	18.0
	Sometimes	128	64.0	64.0	82.0
	Never	56	28.0	18.0	100.0
	Total	200	100.0	100.0	

Table 5 Frequency of listening radio/FM

		Frequency	%	Valid %	Cumulative %
Valid	Regular	28	14.0	14.0	14.0
	Sometimes	152	76.0	76.0	90.0
	Never	20	10.0	10.0	100.0
	Total	200	100.	100.0	

Table 6 Frequency of Surfing Net

	Frequency	%	Valid %	Cumulative %
Regular	40	20.0	20.0	20.0
Sometimes	108	54.0	54.0	74.0
Never	52	26.0	26.0	100.0
Total	200	100.0	100.0	

Product Advertisements

Children like various advertisements according to their mood, taste, habit, choice etc. They really enjoy the contents of the advertisement if they find it worth watching. Children remember many products due to their advertisements and most of the time they are able to recall those advertisements immediately after seeing the product in the market. The study shows that a majority of children like advertisements which relate to food products and soft drinks. They find fun in watching such ads and feel that the product is really enjoyable to eat or drink.

Referring to data from Table 7 it can be clearly concluded that 44% of the children like the advertisements relating to food products. And around 22% love watching advertisements of soft drinks. They even reprise the jingles while eating or drinking the advertised products.

Table 7 Most desirable product

		Frequency	%	Valid %	Cumulative %
Valid	Food Products	88	44.0	44.0	44.0
	Soft Drinks	44	22.0	22.0	66.0
	Toys	12	6.0	6.0	72.0
	Stationary	16	8.0	8.0	80.0
	Clothes	12	6.0	6.0	86.0
	Mobile and Electronic gadgets	20	10.0	10.0	96.0
	Other things	8	4.0	4.0	100.0
	Total	200	100.0	100.0	

Role of children in buying decisions of their parents

Children not only help their parents in household activities but also in their buying decisions. Parents seek for the opinion of children regarding their choice and preference about various products. They purchase some products of their choice but on the whole get influenced by others especially family members in numerous household purchase decisions. Due to influential impact of children in families, some purchase decisions are highly dominated by children

From Table 8, it can be assumed that almost all (nearly 94%) of the children believe that they help their parents in buying decisions for the products that are used by the family. At times children end up buying a particular product on behalf of their parents because of an urgent need or even lack of time to buy a product. Most often such need comes from the most elderly member of the family and they ask the child to make the actual purchase.

However sometimes this pester power can be dangerous as the children without rational thinking,

Table 8   Do you help your parents in buying decisions

		Frequency	%	Valid %	Cumulative %
Valid	Yes	188	94.0	94.0	94.0
	No	12	6.0	6.0	100.0
	Total	200	100.0	100.0	

go for emotional and impulsive buying. Not only this they become stubborn and forcefully ask their parents to buy that particular product of their choice rather than looking at its household utility. Therefore it is

very important for the parents to keep a control on the purchase requests of their children. Table 9 shows the opinion of children regarding the reaction of parents on the suggestions made by the children to purchase any product.

Table 9   How do parents react to suggestions for buying any product

		Frequency	%	Valid %	Cumulative %
Valid	Agree	12	6.0	6.0	6.0
	Mostly Agree but sometimes Disagree	124	62.0	62.0	68.0
	Ignore	24	12.0	12.0	80.0
	Mostly Disagree, but sometimes Agree	20	10.0	8.0	90.0
	Disagree	20	10.0	10.0	100.0
	Total	200	100.0	100.0	

A sum total of 68% (62 + 6) respondents agreed that their parents accept the suggestion given by them for purchasing any product. According to these respondents, the preference and suggestions given by them are welcomed by the family and their parents keep them in mind while making the purchase decision. 62% of the children were of the opinion that their parents generally accept the suggestion made by them while only 20% (10 + 10) accepted that their parents mostly do not take their suggestion into consideration while 10% feel that their parents ignore their suggestion while making purchase.

Advertisements Vis-à-vis Buying behavior of children

Advertisements have major impact on the buying behavior of children. They bait children in trying the advertised brands. Some advertisements target various desires or wants of children and influence them in purchasing that product. Advertisements also influence their attitude and purchase behavior. Table 10 gives us the idea of the extent up to which advertisements affect the buying behavior of children.

Table 10 Do you get influenced with the ads

		Frequency	%	Valid %	Cumulative %
Valid	Always	24	12.0	12.0	12.0
	Often	116	58.0	58.0	70.0
	Sometimes	36	18.0	18.0	88.0
	Rarely	16	8.0	8.0	96.0
	Never	8	4.0	4.0	100.0
	Total	200	100.0	100.0	

Around 58% of the total respondents believe that ads often evoke their desires in buying a product. While 12% believed that they use to buy the product only after watching the ad of that product, another 12% (8 + 4) respondents believed that their purchase decisions were rarely or never driven by the advertisements on various medium.

FINDINGS

On the basis of the study conducted in Varanasi, the under mentioned facts were found-

- The study helped to conclude that although there are various media present in present scenario but most of the children like to watch TV over any other media channel. Hence TV can be considered as the best source for advertising any product to children. However children are also influenced by displays and hoardings on the roadside. Radio also occupies a significant place whereas Newspapers and Magazines have least approach to this age group.
- When asked to recall the advertisements, most of the respondents recalled advertisements of food products and soft drinks immediately. They also showed keen interests in gadgets like mobile phones.
- The study revealed that children play a vital role in their parent's buying decisions. A large number of parents seek the opinion of their children before purchasing the products especially for the household purposes. Moreover most of the parents positively react to the suggestions made by their child and consider them while making purchase decisions. They prefer to purchase such products, which are not only liked by them, but also by their children.
- It is also observed from the study that children get interested to purchase the product or demand the product after viewing its advertisements. Nearly 82% of the children accepted that their

buying decisions are largely governed by the advertisement of concerned products.

CONCLUSION

Children constitute an important target market segment from marketing perspective. The role that a child plays in making decisions concerning the family has also promoted researches to draw attention towards this subject. The amount of influence exerted by children varies by product category and stage of the decision making process. For some of the products they are good initiators, for some they are information seekers and then buyers whereas for some categories they influence the purchases made by their parents.

Children are effectively fitting into the consumer role majorly for the nuclear families where both the parents are working. Moreover, exposure to mass media and open discussions with parents ensure that children are not only aware of the new brands available, but also know how to evaluate them on various parameters.

An analysis of children as consumers help in the formulation of marketing strategies by identifying the interests, attitudes and motivational points for children who show interest and great involvement in making purchases. It is also clear that they act as purchasing agents for the family and are delegated the task of purchasing products which they themselves do not consume. Such products should also be identified and the marketers should understand the attributes and features that are preferred by these purchasers.

References

- Bansal, et al., (2004), *What Risks Should Investors Care About?* Working Paper, Duke University
- Belch, George E. Michael A. Belch (2003), "*Advertising and Promotion: An Integrated Marketing Communication Perspective.*
- Brody, G.H., Stoneman, Z. & Burke, M. (1987), Child Temperaments, Maternal Differential

Behavior and Sibling Relations, *Developmental Psychology, 23, 354-362.*

- George Wilson, Katie Wood (2004), The Influence of Children on Parental Purchases During Supermarket Shopping, *International Journal of Consumer Studies 28, 4 329-336, September 2004. Wiley Online Library*

- Glast, J.P. and White, M.A. (1976), The Unhealthy Persuader: The Reinforcing Value of Television and Children's Purchase Influencing Attempts at the Supermarket, *Child Development, 47,1089-96*

- Hansen, J., et al., (2005), Efficacy of Climate Forcing, J. Geophys. Res., 110, D18104, Doi:10.1029/2005JD005776

- Hastings, Gerard (2003), "Social Marketers of the World Unite, You Have Nothing to Lose But Your Shame," *SMQ, 9(4 Winter), 14-21*

- India Today, March 2004. *Trans Asian Media New Delhi*

- Keane, A., A. Willetts (1994), "Factors That Affect Food Choice," *Journal of Nutrition & Food Science*, 94(4), 15-17.

- Kunkel, B.L. Wilcox, J. Cantor, E. Palmer, S. Linn, And P. Dowrick (2004), "*Psychological Issues in the Increasing Commercialization of Childhood,*" Report of the APA Task Force on Advertising and Children.

- Solomon, H. et al., (1982), *Content and Effect of Children's Commercials.* Paper Presented At The Annual Meeting Of The Eastern Psychological Association, Baltimore, April 1982, Available From The Educational Resources Information Center, Institute Of Education Sciences, US Department Of Education; Clearinghouse Number: IR010579,

Customer Satisfaction between Public and Private Insurance Sectors

Silky Vigg[1], Garima Mathur[2] and Satyam Dubey[3]
[1]Senior Assistant Professor, Jagannath International Management School, New Delhi
[2]Associate Professor, Prestige Institute of Management, Gwalior
[3]Alumni, Prestige Institute of Management, Gwalior

ABSTRACT

Perceived benefits rather than actual benefits are the backbone of marketing of goods and services, and marketing of life Insurance is no exception. The insurance business has been changing across the globe and the ripple effects of the same can be observed in the domestic market as well. Liberalization of insurance industry has witnessed an accelerated growth in life insurance business. In this growing competition, the customer is truly the king. Products are being designed, redesigned and customized to suit the changing preferences of customers, taking into account different factors like age, gender, family, status and employment and income levels. The importance of customer satisfaction cannot be underestimated. After all, customer satisfaction can impact every aspect of your business from earnings to stock profits. This paper is an attempt to know the customer satisfaction insurance companies and to compare the satisfaction between public insurance companies and private insurance companies.

Keywords: *Customer Satisfaction, Insurance Sector*

INTRODUCTION

Customer Satisfaction

Perceived benefits rather than actual benefits are the backbone of marketing of goods and services and marketing of life Insurance is no exception. So, insurance sector found a new dimension to increase its business. Insurance products packaged savings features with risk management feature.

Insurance sells promise to pay on future date for a redefined contingency. Insurance is an arrangement to deal with the unpleasant contingencies. The essence of insurance is sharing of losses and substitution of certainty for uncertainty. The insurance business has been changing across the globe and the ripple effects of the same can be observed in the domestic market as well. The rising per capital income increased the demand for insurance to cover risk of old age and death. Insurance Sector is a major contributor to the financial savings of the household sector in country which are further channelized into various investment avenues.

Liberalization of insurance industry has witnessed an accelerated growth in life insurance business. The size of the life insurance market increased on the strength of the growth in the economy and concomitant increase in per capita income. This resulted in a favorable growth for the LIC and to the new insurers. In this growing competition the customer is truly the king. Products are being designed, redesigned and customized to suit the changing preferences of customers taking into account different factors like age, gender, family, status and employment and income levels. The importance of customer satisfaction cannot be underestimated. After all, customer satisfaction can impact every aspect of your business from earnings to stock profits. That is why customer satisfaction surveys are so important. Customer satisfaction surveys measure and evaluate the attitudes, opinions and satisfaction levels of your customers and clients. The objective of this study is to know the customer satisfaction from the insurance companies and to compare the customer satisfaction between the public & private insurance sectors.

REVIEW OF LITERATURE

Today, it would be difficult to find a company that doesn't proudly claim to be a customer-oriented, customer-focused, or even-customer driven enterprise. But look closer at how these companies put their assertions into practice, and often you discover an array of notions and assumptions that range from superficial and incomplete to misguided There is nothing wrong with the notion of customer satisfaction per se. "The problem comes with its pursuit, which if fraught with peril. Most plans to improve customer satisfaction stand on two shaky – and dangerous – assumptions". What they create is an illusion – the customer satisfaction trap. Too often, measurement of customer satisfaction is misleading – they tell you very little about where you are, and they can't show you where to go. But the importance of customer satisfaction cannot be underestimated. After all, customer satisfaction can impact every aspect of your business from earnings to stock profits. That is why customer satisfaction surveys are so important.

Customer satisfaction surveys measure and evaluate the attitudes, opinions and satisfaction levels of your customers and clients. Clara Xiaoling Chen (2006) examined that "what determines the relevance of customer satisfaction measures?" He measured relevance in the context as the strength of the relation between different customer satisfaction measures and future revenues. Using structural equation modeling on the 51 markets of the research site over a 20-quarter period, he found that future revenues are positively associated with client satisfaction and doctor satisfaction but negatively associated with patient satisfaction. The result was driven by conflicting interests between clients and patients. He also found that the extent to which a customer group influences the purchasing decision affects the relevance of customer satisfaction measures. Finally, he found that customer bargaining power enhances the relevance of customer satisfaction measures. Peter C. Verhoef (2003) in the ERIM Report Series, examined the effect of relational constructs, such as satisfaction, trust and commitment on relationship performance (that is, positive word-of-mouth communication and the margin provided by each customer) of customers of an insurance company. A central issue concerned the effect of duration on the associations between relational constructs and relationship performance.

The empirical results provided strong evidence of duration dependent effects of satisfaction and trust. He also researched that for effective Customer Relationship Management (CRM), it is essential to have information on the potential value of customers. Based on the interplay between potential value and realized value, managers can devise customer specific strategies. In his article he introduces a model for predicting the potential value of a current customer. Furthermore, he discussed and applied different modeling strategies for predicting this potential value.

The study by Byeongyong Paul (2005) also examined the relationships among market structure and performance in property-liability insurers over the period 1992-1998 using data at the company and group levels. Three specific hypotheses are tested: traditional structure-conduct-performance, relative market power, and efficient structure (ES). The results provided support for the ES hypothesis. The ES hypothesis posited that more efficient firms can charge lower prices than competitors, enabling them to capture larger market shares and economic rents, leading to increased concentration. Both revenue and cost efficiency were used in the analysis, and that was the first study to use revenue efficiency in this type of analysis. The results for the sample period as a whole and by year were consistent. The overall results suggest that cost-efficient firms charge lower prices and earn higher profits, in conformance with the ES hypothesis. On the other hand, prices and profits were found to be higher for revenue-efficient firms. Revenue X-efficiency was derived from activities such as cross-selling and may rely heavily on the use of detailed information from customer databases to identify potential customers. The implications of the research was that regulators should be more concerned with efficiency (both cost and revenue) rather than the market power that arises from the consolidation activity taking place in insurance. Jagdish Pathak (2003) developed a fuzzy logic based expert system that can evaluate and identify the elements of fraud involved in insurance claims settlement. It helped to decide if the claims settled are genuine or there exists an element of fraud which needs substantive testing by an auditor. . The main contributions of this paper were the 'index of ambiguity' and the fuzzy-logic based methodology which detected an element of fraud in the previously settled insurance claims.

Rao (2006) attempted to understand the customer awareness, usage and perception towards the internet as a channel for insurance distribution. The results indicate that though the awareness is high, the usage is notably low. Customers perceive trust/credibility, support, information, communication and prospecting as significant factors affecting their decision of choosing Internet for insurance products. Shannon W. Anderson (2005) also proposed a framework that synthesizes research on customer satisfaction in air line industry. Mayuram S. Krishnan (1998) studied the drivers of customer satisfaction for financial services. The paper discusses a full Bayesian analysis based on data collected from customers of a leading financial services company. The findings show that satisfaction with product offerings is a primary driver of overall customer satisfaction. The quality of customer service with respect to financial statements and services provided through different channels of delivery such as new information technology enabled automated call centers, and traditional branch offices, are also important in determining overall satisfaction. Gerald R. Faulhaber (1995), developed a structural model which incorporated bank decisions on productivity, risk taking and customer satisfaction into an equilibrium model of banking markets. This structural model estimated directly for 219 large U.S. banks, 1984-1992. The results are: (i) banks differ widely in their ability to manage risk; (ii) there are substantial inefficiencies due to demand/capacity mismatches; (iii) greater customer satisfaction correlates with greater profitability, principally due to higher levels of demand; (iv) very large bank-specific effects that previous research discovered appears to have been largely captured in the structural model.

Peter C. Verhoef (2003) formulated a theoretical model in which he postulated that if a customers` behavior is perceived as not optimal, customers will adjust this behavior based on their current satisfaction and payment equity. Furthermore, customers will also include new experiences. In our empirical study we particularly investigate customer referrals and the amount of services purchased. Our results show positive effects of current satisfaction and payment equity on referrals, while also changes in satisfaction and payment equity affect customer referrals. With respect to the amount of services purchased, our estimation results reveal a positive significant effect of only changes in satisfaction.

Research Design and Methods

The design chosen for this study is exploratory in nature. The population of the study consists of customers using insurance services. The Sampling frame of the study is the customer using insurance services in Delhi and NCR region convenience sampling technique (non

probability technique) has been used and the sample size is 250 customers. Data has been collected through a self made questionnaire and face-to-face interview has been conducted. To check the consistency of the questionnaire, item to total correlation has been used. Z-test is used to compare the significance difference in customer satisfaction between the public sector and private sector insurance companies.

H_0: **There is significant difference in customer satisfaction in insurance between private and public respondents.**

RESULTS AND DISCUSSION

Consistency Measure

Firstly consistency of all items in the questionnaire is checked through item to total correlation. Under this correlation of every item with total is measured and the computed value is compared with standard value i.e. (0.2722).if the compared value found less than standard value then the whole item is statement dropped and has been termed as inconsistent.

Z-test

Z- Test has been applied here to see whether there is a significant difference between insurers of public and private companies. The value of z-test is 0.808 which is less than standard value, 1.96 at 5% level of significance, the null hypothesis is accepted. There is no significant difference between public and private sector insurance respondents.

The results were also supported through the interviews taken while getting data filled. The unstructured interview with some of the respondents indicated that the services offered by both type of organisations were more or less same so is the customer satisfaction. Customers viewed most of the services as good especially at the time of buying policies. Though in few services such as response over phone, corporate image, environment were perceived better according to their interviews in the private insurance companies. However, overall customer satisfaction was same for both.

Though study also reveals that for it is becoming mandatory for the organisations to improve their quality. As competition increases quality will become only the true differentiator. Successful companies will be those that are on quality. We must realize that competing on price means we are dependent on what the competition is doing for success. Company that wish to surge ahead successfully into the new millennium would need to ingrain a quality culture. Every aspect of the company functioning would have to been governed by the quality principle.

CONCLUSION

The study reveals that there was no difference in the customer satisfaction but a company should continually assess and reassess how customer perceive company services so as to know whether the company meets or exceeds or is below the expectations of their customer such an appraisal. However it is a tedious task because customer services are complex in nature and dynamic in action. Company may pay attention to potential failure points and service recovery procedure which become integral to employees training. In other words it amount to empowering to employee to exercise responsibility, judgment and creativity in responding customers' problem.

References

- Clara Xiaoling Chen (July 2006), *Relevance of Customer Satisfaction Measures in a Setting with Multiple Customer Groups: Evidence from a Health Insurance Company*, Management Accounting Section (Mas) Meeting

- Yasuyuki Fuchita, Autumn (2005), Customer Satisfaction Surveys as a Means of Improving Disclosure, *Capital Markets Research Nomura Capital Market* Rev Iew, Vol. 8, No.3, Pp. 14-20,

- Peter C. Verhoef, (May 2000), *The Effect of Relational Constructs on Relationship Performance*, Erim Report Series Reference No. Ers-2000-08-Mkt

- Peter C. Verhoe & B. Donker (March 11, 2003), *Predicting Customer Potential Value: An Application in the Insurance Industry*, Erasmus Research Institute of Management (Erim)

- Vicente Cuñat Martinez & Pompeu Fabra (September 4, 2002), *Trade Credit: Suppliers as Debt Collectors and Insurance Providers.* London School of Economics & Political Science (Lse) - Financial Markets Group

- Martin Englund, Jim Gustafsson, Jens Perch Nielsen & Fredrik Thuring, (August 2006) Claim Prediction Using a Multidimensional Bühlmann-Straub Credibility Estimator with an Extension to Incorporate Evolutionary Effects - Applied to an Insurance Portfolio of Commercial Policie Festina Lente and University of Copenhagen

- Byeongyong Paul Choi & Mary A. Weiss, (December 2005), Empirical Investigation of Market Structure, Efficiency, and Performance in Property-Liability Insurance. *Journal of Risk and Insurance, Vol. 72*, No. 4, Pp. 635-673,

- Sangkil Moon & Gary Russell, (September, 2005). *Predicting Product Purchase from Inferred Customer Similarity: An Autologistic Model Approach* Henry B. Tippie College of Business

- Jagdish Pathak, Navneet Vidyarthi, (2003), *A Fuzzy-Based Algorithm for Auditors to Detect Element of Fraud in Settled Insurance Claims Odette School of Business Administration,* Working Paper No. 03-9

- D. Venkoba Rao, (December 2006), Internet Impact of Insurance Distribution, *Journal of Services Marketing, Vol. Iv*, No. 4, Pp. 35-42,

- Knut K. Aase (February 13, 2007), *Wealth Effects on Demand for Insurance,* Nhh Dept. of Finance & Management Science Discussion Paper No. 2007/6

- Peter C. Verhoef, Philip Hans Franses & Janny C. Hoekstra, (2008), *The Effect of Relational Constructs on Relationship Performance,* Erim Report Series Reference No. Ers-2000-08-Mkt

- Antje Brigitte Mahayni & Erik Schlogl, June 5, 2003. *The Risk Management of Minimum Return Guarantees,* University of Technology, Sydney - School.

- Mayuram S. Krishnan & Venkatram Ramaswamy, (June 1999), Customer Satisfaction for Financial Services: The Role of Products, Services, and Information Technology, Ross School of Business Paper No. 99-004.

- Gerald R. Faulhaber, (May 1995), *Banking Markets: Productivity, Risk and Customer Satisfaction,* University of Pennsylvania - Management Department.

- Peter C. Verhoef, Philip Hans Franses & B. Donkers (March 11, 2003), *Changing Perceptions and Changing Behavior in Customer Relationships* Erim Report Series Reference No. Ers-2001-31-Mkt

- Dilip Mookherjee & Charles M. Kahn (November 1996), *Competition and Incentives with Non-Exclusive Contracts,* University of Illinois at Urbana-Champaign - Department of Finance

ANNEXURE

Item	Corr. Value	Consistency	Accepted/Dropped
Working hours of the insurance co	0.451802	consistent	accepted
Prompt services of the co' employees	0.505224	consistent	accepted
Knowledge of the agents	0.329648	consistent	accepted
Credit facility against policies	0.329646	consistent	accepted
Features of policies	− 0.20617	inconsistent	dropped
Smooth transaction	− 0.134152	inconsistent	dropped
Response on phone	0.480029	consistent	accepted
Corporate image	0.665791	consistent	accepted
Documentation required	0.784234	consistent	accepted
Friendly atmosphere	0.746708	consistent	accepted
Behavior of company employees	0.50440	consistent	accepted
Physical setting of the company	0.5247	Consistent	accepted
Network of branches	0.7043	consistent	accepted
Redressal of complaints	0.39963	consistent	accepted
Min. Premium amount	0.56114	consistent	accepted
Max. risk covered	0.98938	consistent	accepted
Easy premium payment process	0.220912	consistent	accepted
Safe investment of premium funds	0.3875	consistent	accepted
Good returns on invested money	− 0.2403	inconsistent	dropped
Administrative charges	− 0.0906	inconsistent	dropped
Other charges	0.3202	consistent	accepted
Advice given by agents/advisors	0.5414	consistent	accepted
Innovative schemes	0.3021	consistent	accepted
Timely reminder of premium	0.4595	consistent	accepted

Consumers' Preference for the Survival of FMCG Companies in Rural India (A Case Study of Hindustan Unilever Limited)

Vijay Kumar Gangal[1] and Nitika Gautam[2]
[1]Director, Ashoka Centre for Business and Computer Studies, Nashik
[2]Research Scholar, Dayalbagh Educational Institute, Dayalbagh, Agra

ABSTRACT

From last few years, the growth of Indian economy registered substantial increase in purchasing power of rural India which attracts the Indian Inc. & MNCs. Simultaneously in reference to FMCG products, the saturated urban market forced to companies to tap the virgin Indian rural market. The prologue of currency, transport, and communication has increased the reach of rural market.

This paper highlights factors responsible for the boom in rural marketing, consumers' preference for FMCG products based on 4 'A's (i.e. Awareness, Affordability, Adoptability and Availability). The study is an analytical in nature. Convenient sampling method has been adopted for administering the questionnaires Likert Scale. Questionnaire/schedule have been administered to total 200 in Respondents of rural areas of Agra district. Secondary data have been collected from reputed journals, websites and magazines. The study has been carried out from Jan. 2011 to June,.2011.

Indian rural market has a huge size and demand base. The rural market has changed significantly in the past one decade. In today's scenario, Consumer is the king because he has got various choices around him. If you are not able of providing him the desired result he will definitely switch over to the other provider. Therefore to survive in this competitive competition, you need to be the best. Consumer is no more loyal in today's scenario, so you need to be always on your toes. Hence the consumers are Fish Where Fish Are "Reaching villages that offer better potential".

Keywords: *Consumers Preference, FMCG Products, Rural India*

INTRODUCTION

"India lives in her villages," as described by Adi Godrej, Chairman, Godrej Group, "the rural consumers are discerning and the rural market is vibrant". At the current of growth, it will soon outstrip the urban market. The rural market is no longer sleeping but we are."

India`s fast moving consumer goods (FMCG) is on a roll. Riding on the back of increasing demand and changing consumer preferences- thanks to higher disposal incomes and the retail revolution- the sector has been posting double-digit growth over the past couple of years. The sector has seen the emergence of new product categories and products that seek to fulfill the increasing aspirations of a new generation of Indians, who are turning out to be very demanding consumers.

All marketing starts with the consumer. So consumer is a very important person to a marketer. Consumer decides what to purchase, for whom to purchase, why to purchase, from where to purchase, and how much to purchase. In order to become a successful marketer, he must know the liking or disliking of the customers. He must also know the time and the quantity of goods and services, a consumer may purchase, so that he may store the goods or provide the services according to the likings of the consumers. Gone are the days when the concept of market was let the buyer's beware or when the market was mainly the seller's market. Now the whole concept of consumer's sovereignty prevails. The manufacturers produce and the sellers sell whatever the consumer likes. In this sense, "consumer is the supreme in the market".

As consumers, we play a very vital role in the health of the economy local, national or international. The decision we make concerning our consumption behavior affect the demand for the basic raw materials, for the transportation, for the banking, for the production; they effect the employment of workers and deployment of resources and success of some industries and failures of others. Thus marketer must understand this.

Preference (or "taste") is a concept, used in the social sciences, particularly economics. It assumes a real or imagined "choice" between alternatives and the possibility of rank ordering of these alternatives, based on happiness, satisfaction, gratification, enjoyment, utility they provide. More generally, it can be seen as a source of motivation. In cognitive sciences, individual preferences enable choice of objectives/goals. The study of the consumer preference not only focuses on how and why consumers make buying decision, but also focuses on how and why consumers make choice of the goods they buy and their evaluation of these goods after use. So for success of any company or product promotion it is very necessary to depart its concentration towards consumer preference.

Fast moving consumer goods (FMCG) are popularly named as consumer packaged goods. Items in this category include all consumables (other than groceries/pulses) people buy at regular intervals. The most common in the list are toilet soaps, detergents, shampoos, tooth paste, shaving products, shoe polish, packaged food stuff, household accessories, extends to certain electronic goods. These items are meant for daily or frequent consumption & have a high return.

A major portion of the monthly budget of each household is reserved for FMCG products. The volume of products circulated in the economy against FMCG products is very high, as the number of products the consumer uses, is comparatively very high. Competition in FMCG sector is very high resulting in high pressure on margins.

FMCG companies maintain intense distribution network. Companies spend a large portion of their budget on maintaining distribution networks. New entrants who wish to bring their products in the national level need to invest huge sums of money on promoting brands. Manufacturing can be outsourced. A recent phenomenon in the sector was entry of multinationals and cheaper imports. Also the market is more pressurized with presence of local players in rural areas and state brands.

- **Changing lifestyles**

  Rising per capita income, increased literacy and rapid urbanization have caused rapid growth and change in demand patterns. The rising aspiration levels, increase in spending power has led to a change in the consumption pattern.

- **Low penetration and low per capita consumption**

  Due to the large size of the market, penetration level in most product categories like jams, toothpaste, skin care, hair wash etc. in India is low. This is more visible when comparison is done between the rural and the urban areas. The average consumption by rural households is much lower than their urban counterparts. Existence of unsaturated markets provides an excellent opportunity for the industry players in the form of a vastly untapped market as the income rise.

COMPANY PROFILE

Type	Public Limited Public company
Industry	Fast Moving Consumer Goods (FMCG)
Founded	1933
Headquarters	Mumbai, India
Key people	Harish Manwani (Chairman) Nitin Paranjpe (CEO & Managing Director)
Products	Home & Personal Care, Foods, Water Purifier
Revenue	₹20,869.57 crore & 4064.3 (USD in Millions)
Employees	Over 65,000 direct & indirect employees
Parent	Unilever Plc

(**Source** www.hul.co.in)

REVIEW OF LITERATURE

Rural market is one of the best opportunities for the FMCG sector. In some sense we can say that rural market is future of FMCG. As per research of Purba Basu, (faculty of ICFAI business school), the lifestyle of rural consumers is changing. Rural Indian market and the marketing strategy have become the latest marketing buzzword for most of the FMCG majors. She added the strategies of different FMCG companies for capturing rural market like Titan's Sonata watches, Coco Cola's 200ml bottle, different strategies of HUL and Marico etc. She takes into consideration the study of National Council for Applied Economic Research

(NCAER). According to the NCAER projections, the number of middle and high-income households in rural area is expected to grow from 80 million to 111 million by 2007. In urban India, this is expected to grow from 46 million to 59 million. Thus, the absolute size of rural India is expected to be double that of urban India.

According to Pradeep Tognatta, (former vice president of ˙LG) The economic growth in India's agricultural sector in last year was over 7%, compared with 3% in the industrial sector. This implies a huge market potentiality for the marketer to meet up increasing demand. Factors such as village psyche, strong distribution network and market awareness are few prerequisites for making a dent in the rural markets. The model is of the stolid Anglo-Dutch conglomerate Unilever Group, which has enjoyed a century-long presence in India through its subsidiary Hindustan Lever Ltd. It was Hindustan Lever that several years ago popularized the idea of selling its products in tiny packages. Its sachets of detergent and shampoo are in great demand in Indian villages. Britannia with its low priced Tiger brand biscuits has become some of the success story in rural marketing.

Rajesh K Aithal of IIM(L) had done his research on rural telecom in India. He explain that Rural markets are an important and growing market for most products and services including telecom. The characteristics of the market in terms of low and spread out population and limited purchasing power make it a difficult market to capture. The Bottom of the pyramid marketing strategies and the 4 A's model of Availability, Affordability, Acceptability and Awareness provide us with a means of developing appropriate strategies to tackle the marketing issues for marketing telecom services in rural areas. Successful cases like the Grameen Phone in Bangladesh and Smart Communications Inc in Philippines also provide us with some guidelines to tackling the issue.

The Economic Times (2003), "The rural market likes it strong" the strength of rural markets for Indian companies. Financial express, June 19, 2000 has published the strategy about FMCG majors, HLL, Marico Industries, Colgate Palmolive have formula had for rural markets.

Dr. Vijay Pithadia stated that "Promotion of brands in rural markets requires the special measures. Due to the social and backward condition the personal selling efforts have a challenging role to play in this regard. The word of mouth is an important message carrier in rural areas. Infect the opinion leaders are the most influencing part of promotion strategy of rural promotion efforts.

T. Mamatha (2008) says that consumer behavior is a very complex phenomenon, which needs more efforts to understand, explain and predict. In order to get a clear understanding of the same, every marketer should realize that consumer behavior is, in fact, an assumption every marketing manager must make, if he plans to market on any basis other than hit-or-miss. Although some individuals find it difficult to make this assumption, one must agree that behavior is not so erratic or mysterious that it defies explanation.

Dr. Sanjeev Kumar and Dr Singh M R P (2008) "Brand aspirations and brand switching behavior of rural consumers – a case study of Haryana" Changing socio- economic environment was greatly affecting the ruralities and marketer's influence was clearly observable in terms of changing consumption pattern, which was reflecting in products and brand choices of rural ties. Income is the biggest influence on the purchase decisions and consumption pattern.

Study of rural marketing in the present scenario in India (2009) "While we all accept that the heart of India lives in its villages and the Indian rural market with its vast size and demand base offers great opportunities to marketers, we tend to conclude that the purse does not stay with them. Nothing can be far from truth. Rural marketing involves addressing around 700 million potential consumers, over 40 per cent of the Indian middle-class, and about half the country's disposable income.

As per concern of my research, it is a detail study of different FMCG products used by rural consumers. It will provide detail information about consumers' preferences towards a good number of FMCG products which is too unique and different from those above researches.

NEED OF THE STUDY

India's rural market is gaining importance day by day. As the income level is increasing the demand for FMCG products also increasing. As the income level of consumers increases the demand of FMCG products is increasing continuously. The study of consumer preference in FMCG helps for marketer to understand consumer preference to survive and successes in the competitive market of FMCG. The potentiality of rural markets is seen by MNC's as a 'woken up sleeping giant'. In those days, Most Fast Moving Consumer Goods (FMCG) companies in India are introducing customized products especially for rural population. The various need of the study is given as follows:-

- To know the determinates that contributing to the rural market boom, 4 A's of rural marketing mix (Affordability, Awareness, Availability and Acceptability) for the Survival of FMCG Companies.
- Know about the choices of rural consumers.

OBJECTIVES OF THE STUDY

- The main objectives of this study are:
- To study consumer preference in reference to fast moving consumer goods companies in rural India.
- To find out the motives of the purchase and the factors affecting purchase decision based on 4 'A's (i.e. Awareness, Affordability, Adoptability and Availability) for the Survival of FMCG Companies in rural India.

Hypothesis

- Ho: There is no significant difference in consumers' expectations and observations Regarding the FMCG products.

- Ha: There is significant difference in consumers' expectations and observations Regarding the FMCG products.

RESEARCH METHODOLOGY

The study is an analytical in nature and Likert Scale has been adopted. Convenient sampling method has been adopted for administering the questionnaires.

Primary data have been collected with the help of a structured Questionnaire, information schedule administered to total in Respondents rural areas of Agra district. Secondary data have been collected from reputed journals, websites and magazines. The study has been carried out from Jan. 2011 to June. 2011.

ANALYSIS AND FINDINGS

The Table No. 1 is presenting the profile of respondents.

Table No. 3 is showing the mean, SD and calculated Z-value (which has been compared to 1.96) of the factors affecting purchase decision based on **4 'A's (i.e. Awareness, Affordability, Adoptability and**

Table 1 Profile of Respondents

Basis	Category of Respondent	Number	Percentage
Age (Years)	20-30	60	30
	30-40	70	35
	40-50	50	25
	50-60	20	10
	Total	**200**	**100**
Monthly Income	Less than 2000	25	12.5
	2000-5000	75	37.5
	5000-10,000	50	25
	Above 10,000	50	25
	Total	**200**	**100**
Occupation	BUSINESS	100	50
	FARMER	25	12.5
	PRIVATE SERVICE	25	12.5
	GOVT. SERVICE	50	25
	Total	**200**	**100**
Education	Illiterate	50	25
	Below SSC	25	12.5
	SSC	50	25
	Graduate/PG	25	12.5
	Others	50	25
	Total	**200**	**100**
Expected Monthly Expenditure	Less than 4500	60	30
	4500-9500	70	35
	9500-14500	50	25
	A Above 14500	20	10
	Total	**200**	**100**

(**Source** Survey Analysis)

Availability) and **Parameters (40)** wise in rural India. This table shows the results of test of hypothesis of 4 A`s with their different Parameters wise. **Here "A" indicates that 'Ho is accepted' and "R" indicates that 'Ho is rejected'.**

Table No. 4 Position of HUL company at different Parameters on the basis of weighted mean of HUL and which has been used for calculating the Spearman`s rank correlation i.e. + 0.10.

Survey reveals that Weighted mean and standard deviation was used to find that consumer preference towards FMCG products of company like HUL in rural areas of Agra district based on 4 'A's Awareness, Affordability, Adoptability and Availability.

The product factors that affect the purchase of consumers like Design, Quality, Packaging, Durability etc. Similarly the factors like Small size products, Low priced sample packets, Price scheme in case of price of any product.

While in case of **Promotion,** consumer prefer some promotional offers like Buy 1 get 1 free, Prize contests etc. are variables under 4 A's which affect the consumer preference in FMCG in rural areas is showing in the Table No. 3.

FINDINGS

On the basis of survey analysis the following findings have been observed:

It gauges that the skincare & fragrance have been found as the prime reasons for using bathing soaps (personal wash). However meager numbers of respondents have mentioned that they use it for medicinal purpose and enhance beauty (Table No. 2).

It can be traced from Table No. 2 that the utilitarian aspect of detergent (laundry) i.e., removal strains has been found the most dominating reasons for its purpose. The few respondents bought it for its fragrance value. The consumers buy detergent due to its primary function for cleanliness & few respondents buy it for its fragrance.

Table No. 2 highlights that the cleanliness followed by freshness have been as the primary motives for the purpose of toothpaste (oral care). Some of the respondents also purchase it's for the purpose of protection of germs and whiteness value.

Table No. 2 gauges into the reason for buying hair oil &it is found that the respondents have been buying it for hair care and good looks.

Table 2 The Motives of the Purchase for FMCG Products

MOTIVES Personal Wash	Frequency	Percentage	MOTIVES D. Oral Care	Frequency	Percentage
1. Fragrance	40	20	1. Taste	30	15
2. Skincare	30	15	2. Bad Breath	40	20
3. Medicinal	15	7.5	3. Whiteness	30	15
4. Enhance beauty	25	12.5	4. Check germs	40	20
5. Brand	30	15	5. Fragrance	20	10
6. Price	20	10	6. Freshness	40	20
7. Packaging	10	5	TOTAL	200	100
8. Small size	30	15	**E. Hair Care**		
TOTAL	200	100	1. Brand	40	20
Laundry			2. Price	20	10
1. Fragrance	25	12.5	3. Fragrance	40	20
2. Remove strains	75	37.5	4. Small size	30	15
3. Cleanliness	50	25	5. Hair care	40	20
4. Skin friendly	50	25	6. Good look	30	15
TOTAL	200	100	TOTAL	200	100
C. Skin Care			**H. Deodorants**		
1. Brand	30	15	1. Brand	75	37.5
2. Price	25	12.5	2. Price	25	12.5
3. Packaging	40	20	3. Packaging	70	35
4. Small size	30	15	4. Small size	15	7.5
5. Fragrance	15	7.5	5. Fragrance	15	7.5
6. Enhance beauty	30	15	TOTAL	200	100
7. Skincare	30	15			
TOTAL	200	100			

(**Source** Survey Analysis)

Table No. 3 discusses the factors influencing the purchase decision of the respondents consumers buying is influence the most by the product factor due to design, quality, durability but few respondents are not satisfied with the product range, packaging, image and size of the product.

Table 3 showing the Mean values, SD and calculated Z-value

FACTORS	Expectations		Observations		Z-value	Ho
	Mean	SD	Mean	SD		
PRODUCT	4.41	0.87	3.98	1.18	2.93	R
Brand Name	4.09	1.24	3.55	1.44	2.84	R
Design	4.13	1.15	4.3	0.9	− 1.16	A
Quality	4.08	1.25	4.08	1.25	0	A
Packaging	4.37	0.98	3.78	1.26	3.70	R
Durability	4.36	0.78	4.21	0.79	1.35	A
Made from safe environment material	4.49	0.82	3.94	1.25	3.68	R
Image	4.85	0.36	3.88	1.27	7.35	R
Shape/size	4.34	1.02	3.96	1.21	2.37	R
product range	4.95	0.22	4.09	1.29	6.57	R
PRICE	4.39	0.92	3.68	1.22	4.64	R
Cheapest price	4.51	0.87	3.33	1.49	6.84	R
Price scheme	4.46	0.88	3.7	1.27	4.92	R
Pricing policy	4.64	0.95	3.71	1.39	5.54	R
Cash discount	4.56	0.67	3.68	1.21	6.36	R
Competitive price	4.05	1.12	4.11	0.94	− 0.41	A
Value for price paid	4.35	0.86	3.68	1.11	4.77	R
Low priced sample packets	4.43	0.85	3.8	1.16	4.38	R
Small size products	4.15	1.13	3.43	1.15	4.47	R
PLACE	4.24	0.91	3.92	0.92	2.48	R
Appealing shop atmosphere & decor	4.01	1.05	3.72	1.07	1.93	A
Shop has the lowest price in the area.	4.3	0.9	4.11	0.88	1.51	A
Malls and super markets.	4.34	0.79	3.92	0.73	3.90	R
Greater mobility	4.2	0.97	3.24	1.36	5.75	R
Shop is conveniently located.	4.27	0.95	3.74	1.12	3.56	R
Product display is attractive	4.45	0.68	4.33	0.72	1.21	A
Well-known shops	4	1.17	3.81	1.06	1.20	A
Use of transport like autos, camel carts.	4.49	0.62	4.39	0.61	1.15	A
Haats and mandis	4.16	1.09	4.04	1.10	0.77	A
Government shops	4.07	1.22	3.52	1.49	2.86	R
Supply chain	4.31	0.73	4.15	0.75	1.53	A
Distribution system	4.22	0.79	4.07	0.72	1.40	A
PROMOTION	4.22	0.86	4.02	0.95	1.56	A
Celebrity endorsement	4.04	1.06	3.95	0.79	0.68	A
Sales agent	4.22	0.96	4.03	0.98	1.35	A
Buy 1 get 1 free	4.41	0.5	4.33	0.57	1.06	A
Free gifts/lucky draws	4.45	0.51	4.15	0.79	3.19	R
Message/languages/presentation of ad.	4.12	0.45	3.98	0.84	1.47	A
Emotional value system	4.19	0.7	4	0.81	1.77	A
Visual merchandising	4.29	0.64	4.12	0.77	1.77	A
Samples/coupons	4.09	1.24	3.55	1.44	2.84	R
Premium/bonus offer	4.13	1.15	4.3	0.9	− 1.16	A
Prize contests	4.08	1.25	4.08	1.25	0	A
Demonstration at fairs and Exhibitions.	4.37	0.98	3.78	1.26	3.70	R

(**Source** Survey Analysis)

Table 4 showing the Position of HUL Company at different parameters

Factors	Expectations Rank	Observations Rank
PRODUCT		
Brand Name	32	35
Design	29	4
Quality	34	13
Packaging	13	27
Durability	15	6
Made from safe environment material	7	22
Image	2	24
Shape/size 17	20	
product range	1	12
PRICE		
Cheapest price	5	39
Price scheme	8	32
Pricing policy	3	31
Cash discount	4	33
Competitive price	37	10
Value for price paid	16	34
Low priced sample packets	11	26
Small size products	28	38
PLACE		
Appealing shop atmosphere & decor	39	30
Shop has the lowest price in the area.	20	11
Malls and super markets.	18	23
Greater mobility	25	40
Shop is conveniently located.	22	29
Product display is attractive	9	2
Well-known shops	40	25
Use of transport like autos, camel carts.	6	1
Haats and mandis	27	16
Government shops	36	37
Supply chain	19	7
Distribution system	23	15
PROMOTION		
Celebrity endorsement	38	21
Sales agent	24	17
Buy 1 get 1 free	12	3
Free gifts/lucky draws	10	8
Message/languages/presentation of ad.	31	19
Emotional value system	26	18
Visual merchandising	21	9
Samples/coupons	33	36
Premium/bonus offer	30	5
Prize contests	35	14
Demonstration at fairs and Exhibitions.	14	28

(**Source** Analysis Work)

Malls and super markets, Greater mobility, Shop is conveniently located, Product display is attractive, Value for price paid, Cash discount, and pricing policy, the consumers are showing their dissatisfaction.

Appealing shop atmosphere & décor, Shop has the lowest price in the area, Product display is attractive, Well-known shops, Use of transport like autos, camel carts and Haats and mandis are some factors are good and satisfying to consumers.

SUGGESTIONS

- The study reveals that soaps and detergent brands of HUL and are more popular in urban markets. Since real India lives in rural areas and it is potential market for all types of soaps and detergents. In the study it is advised to the company develop a tailor made marketing mix with more emphasis on product mix should be designed by the companies. Rural sales promotional activities should be strengthened especially HUL to take the advantage of rural market potential.

- Rural consumer environment must be understood before the creation of add.

- HUL should be introduced low priced sample packs of products. & initiate low units packs of products.

- Rural mindset accepts the brands easily, which are close to their culture. This point must be reflected in ad for rural markets.

- Sponsorships to the Melas and Hats must be considered in a significant manner.

- Selection of brand ambassadors, lyrics must not be ignored in this regard.

- Companies should be introduced the special rural products, like Chic Shampoo sachets @ ₹1, Parle G Tikki Packs @ ₹2, customized TVs by LG, Shanti Amla oil by Marico. All these brought positive results for them.

- If a product is for kids, anganwadis and schools are a good place to tap them and their mothers. Similarly, mandis and village influencers act as a catalyst in pushing a brand/product.

- The Language and content must be according to the suitability of rural environment. Background figures are also a deterministic factor. Admissibility of brand ambassadors plays an important role in this regard. Special promotion measures are the strong applicable factors in this regard.

- To think local we have to act local.

CONCLUSION

Indian rural market has a huge size and demand base. The rural market has changed significantly in the past one decade. In today's scenario, Consumer is the king because he has got various choices around him. If you are not able of providing him the desired result he will definitely switch over to the other provider. Therefore to survive in this competitive competition, you need to be the best. Consumer is no more loyal in today's scenario, so you need to be always on your toes. Hence the consumers are Fish Where Fish Are "Reaching villages that offer better potential".

References

- Kumar, Binay. BBA (M&S) Amity School of Business, Amity University, Noida Project Title: *Rural Marketing*.

- European Association for Comparative Economics Studies (EACES) 9th Bi-Annual Conference: Development Strategies - A Comparative View. *SCMS Journal of Indian Management*, January - March, 2008.

- Marketing to Rural Consumers- Understanding and tapping the rural market potential International Journal of Business and Management September, 2008. *Marketing Mastermind, September*, 2010.

- Jha, Neeraj, (2000) *"Gung-ho on rural marketing", The Financial Express, Rural Marketing*, Ravindranath V. Badi and Naranyansa V. Badi, Himalaya Publishing,

- Retrieved from www. ncaer.com

- Retrieved from www.mgmtparadise.com

- Retrieved from www.indiamba.com/faculty columns/Articles.

- Retrieved from www.ruralmart.com

- Retrieved from www.businessmapsofindia.com

Customer Satisfaction at Domino's: An Empirical Study in Gwalior Region

Vinod K. Bhatnagar[1] and Dharmendra Kushwah[2]

[1]Assistant Professor, Prestige Institute of Management, Gwalior
[2]Assistant Professor, BVM College of Education, Gwalior

ABSTRACT

Customer satisfaction, a term frequently used in marketing, is a measure of how products and services supplied by a company meet or surpass customer expectation. As far as satisfaction of customers is concerned, firms generally ask customers whether their product or service has met or exceeded expectations. Therefore we can say, expectations are a key factor behind satisfaction. Brand loyalty also played an important role in customer satisfaction, when consumers become committed to your brand and make repeat purchases over time. Brand loyalty is a result of consumer behavior and is affected by a person's preferences. Loyal customers will consistently purchase products from their preferred brands, regardless of convenience or price. Some of the factors which influence to brand loyalty of customers are Customers' perceived value, brand trust; customers' satisfaction, repeat purchase behavior, and commitment are found to be the key influencing factors of brand loyalty. The purpose of this study is to examine the factors influencing the liking and satisfaction of customers towards Dominos' Pizza. A questionnaire survey was prepared and distributed to various age groups of customers who visit and have Pizza at Gwalior's Domino's Pizza. Twenty nine questions were prepared out of which 8 are related with demographic information and 21 were related with the main objectives of the study. Likert scale based questions were asked in second section of questionnaire. The data collected through questionnaire were analyzed and interpreted by using SPSS software. Chi-square test and factor analysis were used to interpret the data. We found that all the five factors showed liking and satisfaction level in favour of Domino's Pizza.

Keywords: *Customer Satisfaction, Liking, Brand Loyalty and Dominos Pizza*

INTRODUCTION

Customer satisfaction, a term frequently used in marketing, is a measure of how products and services supplied by a company meet or surpass customer expectation. Customer satisfaction is defined as "the number of customers, or percentage of total customers, whose reported experience with a firm, its products, or its services (ratings) exceeds specified satisfaction goals. In a survey of nearly 200 senior marketing managers, 71% responded that they found a customer satisfaction metric very useful in managing and monitoring their businesses.

It is seen as a key performance indicator within business and is often part of a Balanced Scorecard. In a competitive marketplace where businesses compete for customers, customer satisfaction is seen as a key differentiator and increasingly has become a key element of business strategy.

As a result of customer satisfaction, consumers become committed to your brand and make repeat purchases over time. Brand loyalty is a result of consumer behavior and is affected by a person's preferences. Loyal customers will consistently purchase products from their preferred brands, regardless of convenience or price. Companies will often use different marketing strategies to cultivate loyal customers, be it is through loyalty programs (i.e. rewards programs) or trials and incentives (ex. samples and free gifts).

The American Marketing Association defines brand loyalty as: The situation in which a consumer generally buys the same manufacturer-originated product or service repeatedly over time rather than buying from multiple suppliers within the category (sales promotion definition).

The degree to which a consumer consistently purchases the same brand within a product class (consumer behavior definition). Brand loyalty, in marketing, consists of a consumer's commitment to repurchase or otherwise continue using the brand and can be demonstrated by repeated buying of a product or service, or other positive behaviors such as word of mouth advocacy. There are so many factors which have suggested that loyalty includes some degree of pre-dispositional commitment toward a brand. Brand loyalty is viewed as multidimensional construct. It is determined by several distinct psychological processes and it entails multivariate measurements. Customers' perceived value, brand trust, customers' satisfaction, repeat purchase behavior, and commitment are found to be the key influencing factors of brand loyalty. Commitment and repeated purchase behavior are considered as necessary conditions for brand loyalty followed by perceived value, satisfaction, and brand trust. One of the most influential writers on brand loyalty claimed that enhancing customer loyalty could have dramatic effects on profitability. Among the benefits from brand loyalty — specifically, longer tenure or staying as a customer for longer — was said to be lower sensitivity to price while recent research found evidence that longer-term customers were indeed less sensitive to price increases. We have attempted to find out that what the factors which influence the customer satisfaction are. For this purpose we have researched on one of the Domino's outlet in Gwalior.

REVIEW OF LITERATURE

Surprenant (1977), explained that Satisfaction Leads to Desirable consequences such as repeat purchase, acceptance of other products in the line, brand loyalty, store patronage and ultimately higher profits and increased profit share.

Tse and Wilton (1988), examined that satisfaction is the consumer's response to the evaluation of the perceived discrepancy between prior expectation and actual performance of the product as perceived after its consumption.

Sepannen, et al., (2004), examined that consumers always expect for a product or service of better quality, which is easy to use or consume and of lower costs than ever before. By improving operations, a business or an organisation can improve internal efficiency, effectiveness, adaptability and customer service.

Evellyne, Elisante & Reuben (2009), found that the speed of service delivery, responsiveness and curtsy of company's staff are most responsible factors for customer satisfaction.

Singhi & Jain (2009), focused on Metro Trains and Customer Satisfaction in Delhi. They noticed that the organisation should aim not only at satisfying the customer but also focus on delighting him. The objective of their study was to propose a framework of the major dimensions that have an impact on the perceived quality of services provided by Delhi Metro Trains and their overall satisfaction, they found that all aspects need to be given attention to, depending on the importance attach to them by customers and customers were satisfied with the services provided by the Delhi Metro Trains.

Kaushik and Gupta (2009), found that new entrants can deliver the best quality at competitive price to have market share in herbal, simultaneously Campaigns and event management in colleges by cosmetic companies help them to increase sale, because consumers are 15-20 and 20-25 age group belongs to school and colleges. Consumers are ready to move towards herbal products. So any company can easily get them by having perfect marketing mix, balance price and quality.

Yesodha Devi N &, Kanchana V.S. (2009), examined that Quality & Taste are the two major factors to select a restaurant. Customers are more discerning and demanding and they always wants to experiment with the money they spend, they also found that the Indian restaurant industry has come of age by diversifying its services and is trying to cater to the Indian taste buds and is staying in competitive arena amongst international giants and is able to provide better services to the customers.

OBJECTIVES

Following are the objectives of the study:
1. To check the reliability of standardized measure.
2. To identifying the underlying factors affecting the liking and satisfaction towards Domino's Pizza level among different age group of customers.

RESEARCH METHODOLOGY

The study was exploratory in nature and a self-designed questionnaire was used to collect the data. For taking the responses of the respondents Likert-type scale of 1-5 was used. The total population was 50 customers of Gwalior region. The sample size was 50 respondents.

The tools used for the data analysis were the reliability, through Cronbach's alpha method. Factor analysis was applied using SPSS 16.0 software to identifying the underlying factors.

RESULTS AND DISCUSSION

Item to Total Correlation

Item to total correlation of scale was computed on SPSS-16 software and corresponding improvement in reliability was also considered. The reported item to total statistics is given in annexure I. It was found that by dropping item 21 the reliability will be improved and hence item 21 was dropped for the further analysis.

Reliability

Reliability of the questionnaire was evaluated using SPSS-16 software and the reliability test values were as given below:

The reliability value from the above table indicates that the reliability coefficient Cronbach's Alpha value was .925 which is more than 0.7; indicating that the reliability is high and it could be used for the study.

Factor Analysis

In this research work KMO (Kaiser-Meyer-Olkin Measure of Sampling Adequacy) and Barlett's Test of Sphericity was used to ascertain that the data is appropriate for factor analysis.

Factor analysis was done by using SPSS-16 software and the principal component factor analysis with Varimax Rotation and Kaiser Normalization was applied. The outcome was the emergence of five factors. The Kaiser-Meyer-Olkin Measure of Sampling Adequacy should be more than .5 for a satisfactory factor analysis to proceed and in present research work the Kaiser-Meyer-Olkin Measure of Sampling Adequacy came out .779. The above facts indicate that the data collected on customer liking and satisfaction was suitable for factor analysis.

DESCRIPTION OF FACTORS

1. **Predilection (liking):**   The first factor emerged to be the Predilection (liking). This factor has emerged as the most important determinant with a total variance of 41.616. There were ten elements in this factor and it include packaging is attractive (.923), it is fresh (.917), it is good

Table 1   Item to total correlation

S. No.	Items	Item-Total Correlation	Consistency	Accepted/ Dropped
1	I like Domino's Pizza rather than others.	.843	Consistent	Accepted
2	I like Domino's Pizza because it is fresh.	.882	Consistent	Accepted
3	I like Domino's Pizza because its packaging is hygienic.	.837	Consistent	Accepted
4	I like Domino's Pizza because packaging is attractive.	.906	Consistent	Accepted
5	I like Domino's Pizza because of its taste.	.882	Consistent	Accepted
6	I like Domino's Pizza because it offers discount coupons.	.708	Consistent	Accepted
7	I visit Domino's Pizza because its location suits me.	.777	Consistent	Accepted
8	I visit Domino's because it is according to my status.	.808	Consistent	Accepted
9	I visit Domino's because of its brand image	.345	Consistent	Accepted
10	I visit Domino's Pizza because of the variety of Pizza's are offered by it.	.414	Consistent	Accepted
11	I visit Domino's because I am influenced by my parents.	.065	Consistent	Accepted
12	I am satisfied with the order delivery system.	.420	Consistent	Accepted
13	My appetite & relish decline due to delay in order delivery.	.230	Consistent	Accepted
14	I am satisfied with the home delivery system of Domino's.	.528	Consistent	Accepted
15	I am satisfied with the services provided by the staff of Domino's.	.626	Consistent	Accepted
16	I am influenced to come again & again by the behavior of the staff of Domino's.	.498	Consistent	Accepted
17	I wish that there must be more Domino's outlets in the city.	.504	Consistent	Accepted
18	I would like to recommend Domino's to others.	.563	Consistent	Accepted
19	Here order is served perfectly and on time.	.827	Consistent	Accepted
20	I visit Domino's very frequently.	.773	Consistent	Accepted
21	I visit Domino's occasionally.	.004	Inconsistent	Dropped

Table 2 Reliability Statistics

Cronbach's Alpha	Cronbach's Alpha Based on Standardized Items	No of Items
0.930	0.925	21

Table 3 KMO and Bartlett's Test

Kaiser-Meyer-Olkin Measure of Sampling Adequacy.		.779
Bartlett's Test of Sphericity	Approx. Chi-Square	970.034
	df	210
	Sig.	.000

Table 4 Factor Analysis for items of Customer Predilection (Liking) and Satisfaction

Factor Name	Eigen Value Total	% Var.	Items Converged	Loading
Predilection	9.156	41.616	04. I like Domino's Pizza because packaging is attractive.	.923
			02. I like Domino's Pizza because it is fresh.	.917
			I like Domino's Pizza rather than others.	.901
			08. I visit Domino's because it is according to my status.	.885
			03. I like Domino's Pizza because its packaging is hygienic.	.863
			07. I like Domino's Pizza because it offers discount coupons.	.861
			20. I visit Domino's very frequently.	.846
			19. Here order is served perfectly and on time.	.829
			16. I am satisfied with the services provided by the staff of Domino's.	.542
Satisfaction	3.303	15.016	17. I wish that there must be more Domino's Outlets in the city.	.824
			18. I would like to recommend Domino's to others.	.804
			14. I am satisfied with the home delivery system of Domino's.	.679
			15. I am satisfied with the services provided by the staff of Domino's.	.546
			10. I visit Domino's Pizza because of the variety of Pizza's are offered by it.	.450
Services	1.745	7.930	12. I am satisfied with the order delivery system.	.668
			10. I visit Domino's Pizza because of the variety of Pizza's are offered by it.	.661
Excitement	1.556	7.075	16. I am influenced to come again & again by the behavior of the staff of Domino's.	.523
			13. My appetite & relish decline due to delay in order delivery.	.811
Influenced	1.527	6.939	11. I visit Domino's because I am influenced by my parents.	.890

rather than others (.901), it is suitable to status (.885), its packaging is hygienic (.863), it offers discount coupons (.861), I visit very frequently (.846), order is served perfectly and on time (.829), satisfaction with the services provided by the staff of Dominos (.542).

2. **Satisfaction:** The second factor appeared to be the satisfaction. This factor has a total variance 15.016. Major element of this factor include requiring more Domino's outlet in the city (.824), recommend Domino's to others (.804), satisfaction with the home delivery system (.679), satisfaction with the services provided by the staff of Domino's (.546), satisfaction with the variety of Pizza's are offered by it (.450).

3. **Services:** The second factor emerged to be the services. This factor has a total variance 7.930. Major element of this factor includes delivery system (.668) and variety of Pizza (.661).

4. **Excitement:** The forth factor emerged as the excitement. This factor has a total variance 7.075. Major element of this factor includes behavior of the staff (.523) and appetite & relish decline due to delay in order delivery.

5. **Influence:** The fifth factor emerged as the influence. This factor has a total variance 6.939. Major element of this factor includes customer are influenced by my parents (.890).

CONCLUSION

The Domino name carries the company's main brand as market leader in its field of operation. Since inception Domino's has been very understanding while identifying customers' needs and publicizing the Domino's brand with developing new products and use of technology (information technology and E-commerce). The present study was conducted on the basis of 50 respondents focusing on the liking and satisfaction of Domino's Pizza. A scale 1 to 5 designed to collect the data and five factors namely Predilection (liking), Satisfaction, Services, Excitement, and Influence. All the five factors showed liking and satisfaction level is in favour of Domino's Pizza.

References

- Kaushik, N. & Gupta D. (2009). A study of consumer buying pattern of cosmetic products in south Haryana. *Indian Journal of Marketing, 39* (9)

- Mwanakinbula, E., Ole Gabriel, E., & Mwanakimbullah R., (2009), Managing the Operations of A Utility Company for Customer Satisfaction: An Application of Quality Function Deployment Function (QFDF). *Journal of IMS Group,* 6 (2), 1 – 20.

- Seppanen, M.S., Kumar, S. and Chandra. C. (2004). *Process Analysis and Improvement, Tools and Techniques.* McGraw-Hill Irwin, Boston, Burr Ridge, IL, USA. P. 366.

- Singhi, R. & Jain M., (2009). Metro Trains and Customer Satisfaction – An empirical Study in Delhi. *Journal of IMS Group,* 6 (2), 85-95.

- Suprenant, C. (1977). *Product Satisfaction as a Function of Expectation and Performance.* Consumer Satisfaction, Dissatisfaction and Complaining Behavior. Papers from a marketing research symposium, day, Ralph L. Editor, Indiana, University, Bloomington, Indiana Polis. P. 36-37.

- Tse D. K. & Wilton P.C. (1988). Models of Consumer Satisfaction Formation: An Extension. *Journal of Marketing Research.* 25. 204-212.

- Yesodha Devi N. & Kanchana V.S. (2009). A study on Customer Preference & Satisfaction towards Restaurants in Coimbatore City. *Indian Journal of Marketing. 39* (10).

ANNEXURE

Table 5 Descriptive Statistics

	Mean	Std. Deviation[a]	Analysis N[a]	Missing N
VAR00001	1.7800	1.21706	50	0
VAR00002	1.8200	1.32002	50	0
VAR00003	1.8600	1.17820	50	0
VAR00004	1.8200	1.33539	50	0
VAR00005	1.7200	1.29426	50	0
VAR00006	2.1200	1.34983	50	0
VAR00007	2.1000	1.34392	50	0
VAR00008	2.0400	1.27711	50	0
VAR00009	2.6600	1.31878	50	0
VAR00010	2.1800	1.04374	50	0
VAR00011	3.0600	.84298	50	0
VAR00012	1.9800	1.02000	50	0
VAR00013	2.8800	.87225	50	0
VAR00014	2.5400	1.16426	50	0
VAR00015	2.5600	1.03332	50	0
VAR00016	2.1400	1.06924	50	0
VAR00017	2.6600	1.39401	50	0
VAR00018	2.4600	1.40277	50	0
VAR00019	1.9600	1.21151	50	0
VAR00020	1.9800	1.18649	50	0
VAR00021	2.1200	1.27199	50	0
BART factor score 1 for analysis 1	$-6.6613381E-18$	1.00000000	50	0

a. For each variable, missing values are replaced with the variable mean.

Table 6 Total Variance Explained

Compo-nent	Initial Eigenvalues			Extraction Sums of Squared Loadings			Rotation Sums of Squared Loadings		
	Total	% of Variance	Cumulative %	Total	% of Variance	Cumulative %	Total	% of Variance	Cumulative %
1	10.797	49.078	49.078	10.797	49.078	49.078	9.156	41.616	41.616
2	2.678	12.173	61.251	2.678	12.173	61.251	3.303	15.016	56.632
3	1.540	6.998	68.249	1.540	6.998	68.249	1.745	7.930	64.562
4	1.222	5.555	73.804	1.222	5.555	73.804	1.556	7.075	71.637
5	1.050	4.772	78.576	1.050	4.772	78.576	1.527	6.939	78.576
6	.899	4.087	82.663						
7	.743	3.376	86.039						
8	.669	3.042	89.080						
9	.468	2.128	91.208						
10	.441	2.003	93.212						
11	.281	1.279	94.491						
12	.249	1.131	95.622						
13	.232	1.056	96.678						
14	.193	.876	97.554						
15	.159	.721	98.275						
16	.109	.496	98.771						
17	.095	.433	99.204						
18	.070	.320	99.524						
19	.050	.226	99.750						
20	.037	.166	99.916						
21	.018	.084	100.000						
22	2.352E-16	1.069E-15	100.000						

Extraction Method: Principal Component Analysis.

Table 7 Component Matrix[a]

	Component				
	1	2	3	4	5
BART factor score 1 for analysis 1	1.000				
VAR00004	.938				
VAR00002	.924				
VAR00005	.916				
VAR00001	.887				
VAR00003	.881				
VAR00019	.862				
VAR00008	.853				
VAR00007	.826				
VAR00020	.803				
VAR00006	.741				
VAR00015	.655				
VAR00018	.596	.426		-.422	
VAR00014	.558	.413			
VAR00016	.551		-.439	.406	
VAR00021		-.744			
VAR00017	.540	.670			
VAR00010	.457	.640			
VAR00012	.454	.505			
VAR00009			.563		.410
VAR00011			.595	.603	
VAR00013				.436	.538

Extraction Method: Principal Component Analysis.

a. 5 components extracted.

Table 8 Rotated Component Matrix[a]

	Component				
	1	2	3	4	5
VAR00004	.923				
VAR00002	.917				
VAR00001	.901				
VAR00008	.885				
VAR00003	.863				
VAR00007	.861				
VAR00005	.859				
VAR00020	.846				
VAR00019	.829				
VAR00006	.675				
VAR00016	.542			.523	
VAR00017		.824			
VAR00018		.804			
VAR00014		.679			
VAR00015	.400	.546		.409	
VAR00012			.668		
VAR00010		.450	.661		
VAR00009			-.617		
VAR00013				.811	
VAR00011					.890
VAR00021		-.404	-.441		-.509

E04xtraction Method: Principal Component Analysis.

Rotation Method: Varimax with Kaiser Normalization.

a. Rotation converged in 9 iterations.

Table 9   Component Score Coefficient Matrix

	Component				
	1	2	3	4	5
VAR00001	.128	−.045	.040	−.095	−.028
VAR00002	.123	−.002	.017	−.130	−.033
VAR00003	.112	.050	−.016	−.178	−.054
VAR00004	.122	−.057	.037	−.041	.057
VAR00005	.107	.012	.115	−.115	−.099
VAR00006	.073	−.030	−.036	.020	.254
VAR00007	.130	−.085	−.023	−.080	.154
VAR00008	.120	−.015	−.064	−.078	−.033
VAR00009	−.011	.186	−.476	.070	.159
VAR00010	−.039	.049	.336	.131	.009
VAR00011	.011	−.134	−.002	.060	.628
VAR00012	.024	−.043	.402	−.044	.068
VAR00013	−.124	.062	−.106	.644	.013
VAR00014	−.062	.280	−.180	.076	.084
VAR00015	−.054	.185	−.108	.260	.016
VAR00016	.063	−.224	.195	.324	.004
VAR00017	−.065	.321	.062	−.082	−.081
VAR00018	−.063	.374	−.111	−.035	−.218
VAR00019	.082	−.023	.013	.118	−.143
VAR00020	.109	−.137	−.018	.160	.018
VAR00021	.045	−.092	−.246	.234	−.295
BART factor score 1 for analysis 1	.083	.035	.009	.017	.005

Extraction Method: Principal Component Analysis.
Rotation Method: Varimax with Kaiser Normalization.
Component Scores.

Table 10   Scale Statistics

Mean	Variance	Std. Deviation	N of Items
46.4400	267.231	16.34720	21

Table 11   Questionnaire

S. No.	Statements/Questions	Options				
1	I like Domino's Pizza rather than others.	1	2	3	4	5
2	I like Domino's Pizza because it is fresh.	1	2	3	4	5
3	I like Domino's Pizza because its packaging is hygienic.	1	2	3	4	5
4	I like Domino's Pizza because packaging is attractive.	1	2	3	4	5
5	I like Domino's Pizza because of its taste.	1	2	3	4	5
6	I like Domino's Pizza because it offers discount coupons.	1	2	3	4	5
7	I visit Domino's Pizza because its location suits me.	1	2	3	4	5
8	I visit Domino's because it is according to my status.	1	2	3	4	5
9	I visit Domino's because of its brand image.	1	2	3	4	5
10	I visit Domino's Pizza because of the variety of Pizza's are offered by it.	1	2	3	4	5
11	I visit Domino's because I am influenced by my parents.	1	2	3	4	5
12	I am satisfied with the order delivery system.	1	2	3	4	5
13	My appetite & relish decline due to delay in order delivery.	1	2	3	4	5
14	I am satisfied with the home delivery system of Domino's.	1	2	3	4	5
15	I am satisfied with the services provided by the staff of Domino's.	1	2	3	4	5
16	I am influenced to come again & again by the behavior of the staff of Domino's.	1	2	3	4	5
17	I wish that there must be more Domino's Outlets in the city.	1	2	3	4	5
18	I would like to recommend Domino's to others.	1	2	3	4	5
19	Here order is served perfectly and on time.	1	2	3	4	5
20	I visit Domino's very frequently.	1	2	3	4	5
21	I visit Domino's occasionally.	1	2	3	4	5

List of Contributors

Akansha Maheshwari

Student Christ University, Bangalore

Amitabh Joshi

Faculty, Prestige Institute of Management, Dewas

Anamika Jain

Department of Food Technology, Jiwaji University, Gwalior

Anant Deshmukh

Associate Professor, Department of Business Management, RTM Nagpur University

Anant Deshmukh

Associate Professor, Department of Business Management, RTM Nagpur University

Anil Pande

Assistant Professor, University of Mumbai, Jamanalal Bajaj Institute of Management Studies

Ankur Pareek

Associate Professor, Department of Mechanical Engineering, Government Engineering College, Ajmer, Rajasthan

Anshika Vasandani

Lecturer (MBA) at SR Group of Institutions, Jhansi

Anurag Sharma

FET Agra College, Agra

Arun Kumar Singh

Research Scholar, Department of Accountancy and Law, Dayalbagh, Agra

Ashish Saxena

SRITM College, Jabalpur

Bimal Jaiswal

Director, IMS, Lucknow University, New Campus, Lucknow

Charanjeet Kaur

Assistant Professor Home Science Government KRG PG Autonomous College, Gwalior

Charanjeet Kaur

Assistant Professor, Home Science, Government KRG PG Autonomous College, Gwalior

Deepti Bhargava

Head, Department of Management Studies, Shrinathji Institute of Technology and Engineering, Nathdwara, Rajsamand, Rajasthan

Dharmendra Badal

Faculty and Incharge (Computer Division), Bundelkhand University, Jhansi

Dharmendra Kushwah

Assistant Professor, B.V.M. College of Education, Gwalior

G.P. Dinesh

Dean Management Studies, Ballari Institute of Technology and Management

Garima Mathur

Associate Professor, Prestige Institute of Management, Gwalior

Garima Mathur

Associate Professor, Prestige Institute of Management, Gwalior

Gaurav Jaiswal

Assistant Professor, Prestige Institute of Management, Gwalior

Geetika Puri

Assistant Professor, School of Business Administration Lovely Professional University

Hina Agrawal

Research Scholar, Department of Accountancy and Law, Faculty of Commerce, Agra

Jitka Odehnalová

Faculty of International Relations, University of Economics, PragueWinston Churchill Sq. 4, 130 67 Prague, Czech Republic

José G. Vargas-Hernández

Master's degree in business and economic Studies Economic University Sciences Center administrative University of Guadalajara

Joshua O. Miluwi

Department, Commerce and Management, Career College and Barkatullah University Bhopal

Jyoti Prasad

Principal of Morar Girls College, Gwalior

Kajal Maheshwari

S.B. Patil Institute of Management, Pune

Komal Sharma

Lecturer, GICTS Group of College, Gwalior

Krishan Kant Yadav

Student (M.E.-IV Sem.), Shri Ram Institute of Technology, Jabalpur

L. N. Koli

Associate Professor, Department of Accountancy and Law, Faculty of Commerce, Dayalbagh Educational Institute (Deemed University), Dayalbagh, Agra

Manoj Kumar Gupta

Research Scholar, Bundelkhand Universicty, Jhansi

Megha Lad

MBA Scholar, Boston College, Gwalior

Mohammed Naveed U

Faculty HKBK College of Engineering, Department of Management Studies

Monika Mittal

Assistant Professor, Prestige Institute of Management, Gwalior

Naela Kamil

Faculty Member, IILM Academy of Higher Learning, Viraj Khand, Gomtinagar, Lucknow.

Navin Shrivastava

Assistant Professor, BIMTECH, Greater Noida

Navita Nathani

HOD, Management, Prestige Institute of Management, Gwalior

Neel Rai

Assistant Professor MBA Department, SR Group of Institutions, Jhansi

Neel Rai

Sr Group of Institutions, Jhansi

Neeraj Dubey

Senior Lecturer, Department of Management Studies, ShriRam Institute of Information Technology, Banmore, Near Gwalior

Neha Sharma

MBA Scholar, Prestige Institute of Management Gwalior

Nikhil Atale

Faculty Datta Meghe Institute of Management

Nitika Gautam

Research Scholar, Dayalbagh Educational Institute, Dayalbagh, Agra

P. D. Saini

Associate Professor Department of Accountancy and Law, Faculty of Commerce, Dayalbagh Educational Institute (Deemed University)

Pavnesh Kumar

Associate professor, IILM–Academy of Higher Learning. Viraj Khand, Gomti Nagar, Lucknow

Poonam Yadav

Research Scholar, Govt. K.R.G. Autonomous P.G. College, Gwalior

Pradeep Agrawal

Research Scholar in Faculty of Management Studies, Banaras Hindu University, Varanasi

Prakash Vir Khatri

Senior faculty member of the University of Delhi.

Pramod Kumar

Head, Department of Accountancy and Law, Faculty of Commerce, Dayalbagh Educational Institute (Deemed University), Dayalbagh, Agra

Preeti Sharma

Reader, Department of Management Studies Indore Institute of Computer Application Indore, Madhya Pradesh

Rajeev Sijariya

Principal, United Institute of Management, Greater Noida

Rajesh S Pyngavil

Associate Professor, Gitarattan International Business School, Rohini, Delhi

Rajesh Shrivastava

Faculty, Shri Ram Institute of Technology, Jabalpur

Rajnish Ratna

Ph.D. Scholar (IIT Kharagpur) and Assistant Professor (HR&OB) Amity Business School, Amity University Sector 125, Noida

Rakesh Kumar Arora

Research Scholar, Bundelkhand Universicty, Jhansi

Renusharma

Agra

Rubina Pathan

Assistant Professor, Department of Management Studies, Malwa Institute of Technology Indore, Madhya Pradesh

S. N Ghosal

Retd. Banker and faculty member of reputed Management Institute, Kolkata

S. V. Dongardive

H.O.D. Department of Commerce, Elphiston College, Fort, Mumbai

Sakshi Bagga

Lecturer, GAD Government College, Tarn Taran

Sandeep Shrivastava

Lecturer, Management Department, Aditya College, Gwalior

Satyam Dubey

Alumni, Prestige Institute of Management, Gwalior

Saurabh Goyal

Assistant Professor and Head, Department of Management Studies, ShriRam Institute of Information Technology, Banmore, Near Gwalior

Shailja Jain

Department of Home Science (Food and Nutrition), Government KRG PGAutonomous College, Gwalior

Shanul Gawshinde

Student, Prestige Institute of Management, Dewas

Shipra Tripathi

Student M.TECH (CSE Department) Saroj Institute of Technology and management Lucknow

Silky Vigg

Senior Assistant Professor Jagannath International Management School, New Delhi

Sneha Alan

Assistant Professor, S.B. Patil Institute of Management, Pune

Sonam Bhadauriya

Department of Applied Business Economics, Dayalbagh Educational Institute (Deemed University), Dayalbagh, Agra

Sujit Kumar Dubey

Associate Professor Faculty of Management Studies, Banaras Hindu University, Varanasi

Suman Yadav

Assistant Professor in Swami Shraddhanand College, University of Delhi

Supriya Nagvani

Career Counselor at SR Group of Institutions, Jhansi

Swami P. Saxena

Associate Professor (Finance) Dayalbagh, Educational Institute (Deemed University)

Syed Yaseen

Aakash Institute of Management Studies Bangalore Karnataka

Tarun K. Tayal

Agra

Uma Yadav

Officer, Bank of Baroda

Urvashi Garud

Assistant Professor, GICTS Group of College, Gwalior

Vartika Verma

Research Scholar, Dayalbagh, Agra

Vijay Kulkarni

Director, Aditya Institute of Management, Pune

Vijay Kumar Gangal

Director Ashoka Centre for Business and Computer Studies, Nashik

Vijay Kumar Gangal

Director, Ashoka Centre for Business and Computer Studies, Nashik

Vinod Gavande

Principal, RBT College, Mauda, District Nagpur

Vinod K. Bhatnagar

Assistant Professor, Prestige Institute of Management, Gwalior

Vishnu Mishra

SRITM College, Jabalpur

Yashpal Singh

Bundelkhand Institute of Engineering and Technology, Jhansi

About the Editors

Dr. Sher Singh Bhakar joined PIMG as Director on 3rd November, 2003. Dr. Bhakar has been extensively involved in various research activities including supervising summer projects and postgraduate dissertations of MBA final semester students (have guided 100 post graduate dissertations till date). He is presently working on research papers in the area of Supply Chain Management, Forecasting, Quality Control, MRP Productivity and Value Addition in Retailing. He has published 65 research papers, book reviews and case studies in refereed journals and books and as a member of editorial team published a book titled Organisational Challenges: Insights and solutions published by Excel Books, New Delhi. Under his guidance 2 scholars have already submitted final Ph.D. thesis and 6 are under process of submission of their Ph.D. thesis.

Dr. Bhakar has attended and presented papers in about fifty conferences and seminars across the country. He has conducted inhouse training programs for some of the most reputed organisations in the country such as Essar Steel, Eicher Motors, Syncom formulations etc. and has organized and conducted Executive Development Programs on ISTD platform. He has conducted sessions in the area of Supply Chain Management in Faculty Development Programs organised by DAW and Vikram University, Ujjain. He is visiting faculty to ITM Nagpur and IITTM Gwalior.

Dr. Tarika Singh is presently Associate Professor in Finance in Prestige Institute of Management. She is awarded her Ph.D. in the area of Corporate Finance on the Topic, "Comparison of Traditional Versus Economic Value Added as a Performance Measure: A Case Study of Selected NSE Companies" in 2010 from Jiwaji University, Gwalior. She is a management post graduate with Dual Specialization in Finance and Marketing from Banasthali Vidyapeeth. She has been in the profession with Prestige Gwalior for the last six years. Earlier she was employed with GE money India in operations department. She was organising secretary for 3rd International Conference organised in the month of December 2011. She has coordinated and organised a research methodology workshop and co-organised one international conference. She has headed and guided different groups in different case writing workshops, all the cases developed during these cases writing workshops have been published by European Case Clearing House. She has authored/co-authored more than 50 publications in various known International and National Journals She has also presented her articles in various academic and professional conferences. She has been on the Panel of Reviewers of a number of journals being published from India and abroad. She is also a member of Indian Accounting Association. In addition she is also an AMFI certified mutual fund advisor.

Prof. Krishan Kant Yadav is working with PIMG from July 2005. He obtained M.Phil. (C.S.) from Vinaka Mission deemed university in 2007 and Master of Computer Application Degree from Bundelkhand University, Jhansi (UP). He has more than six years of teaching experience. His area of interest is software engineering. He has twelve publication to his credit.

Aashish Mehra obtained MBA degree from Institute of Commerce Management Jiwaji University Gwalior. He has 9 years of industrial/corporate experience and 6 years of teaching experience. His area of interest is Branding, Advertising, Brand Positioning, Services and Strategic Marketing. He has 12 publications to his credit.